W9-CKS-253

Language Acquisition

Studies in first language development

Stewart Robertson

Language Acquisition

Studies in first language development

Edited by

PAUL FLETCHER *and* MICHAEL GARMAN

CAMBRIDGE UNIVERSITY PRESS

Cambridge
London   New York   New Rochelle
Melbourne   Sydney

Published by the Press Syndicate of the University of Cambridge
The Pitt Building, Trumpington Street, Cambridge CB2 1RP
32 East 57th Street, New York, NY 10022, USA
296 Beaconsfield Parade, Middle Park, Melbourne 3206, Australia

© Cambridge University Press 1979

First published 1979

Phototypeset in V.I.P. Times by
Western Printing Services Ltd, Bristol
Printed in Great Britain at
The Pitman Press, Bath

Library of Congress Cataloguing in Publication Data
Main entry under title:
Language acquisition.
Bibliography: p.
Includes index.
1. Children – Language. I. Fletcher, Paul J.
II. Garman, Michael.
LB1139.L3L323   155.4′13   78–67305
ISBN 0 521 22521 3 hard covers
ISBN 0 521 29536 X paperback

For our parents

Contents

vii

Preface

The collection of papers presented here is the outcome of a long period of discussion and preparation. To begin with, we had planned to collect already published papers into a volume which would be a suitable text for a lecture course on language development, for undergraduate and postgraduate students of linguistics. For various reasons none of the collections we could envisage seemed entirely appropriate: in particular, they were unable to achieve one of our major aims, namely that the papers build up a coherent picture of changes in the developing language of children as they mature. In the end we decided that the only solution to the problem was to plan what we saw as the ideal set of chapters for our purpose, and then to commission original essays on these topics by asking among the people best qualified, in our opinion, to write them. The outcome of this decision is a range of chapters from researchers in Europe, the USA, Canada and Australia, providing, at the end of the second decade of intensive research into language development, a contemporary view of the subject area, with special reference to English. There is of course no guarantee that we are currently at a stage in the development of the subject which will prove to be historically significant: nevertheless, there are reasons for concluding that this is an appropriate time to assess the state of the art, and to do it in the way we have here.

First, recent intensive research in two areas, that of so-called prelinguistic behaviour on the one hand, and linguistic behaviour after the age of 3 on the other, now allows us to trace development through from birth to the early school years. Second, the organization we have imposed on this collection is an attempt to provide a coherent perspective for the student of the subject. In reaction against the excessively 'grammatical' approach of child language research of the 1960s, the scope of research in this decade has broadened to include the analysis of conversations, the functions of children's utterances, the development of pragmatics, and a host of other, more circumscribed topics. The energy and enterprise of researchers is not in doubt, and much that is valuable has emerged from their efforts. Nevertheless the inevitable

ix

fragmentation that has resulted makes an overall perspective difficult to achieve, particularly for the student, and we have consequently adhered to relatively traditional subheadings – we have used the linguistic levels of phonetics/phonology, grammar (intrasentential) and semantics (lexical) – within which chapters 1–16, in the first two Parts of the book, provide as far as possible a chronological account of development. In this way we hope that the student approaching language development, from whatever discipline (psychology, linguistics, education, language pathology, anthropology, etc.) will gain an appreciation not only of the course of language development (as studied mainly in English-speaking children), but also of the application of analytical linguistic techniques to the data provided by these children (and those of other language communities). The third Part of the book (chapters 17–22) deals with the contexts and determinants of acquisition – the biological bases and the relevance of cognition, the analysis and relevance of conversation, and other variables affecting acquisition.

The book has assumed its final shape with more than a little help from family, friends and colleagues. In particular we wish to thank for their formative advice and encouragement David Crystal, Jeremy Mynott and Roger Wales. Whether or not they would agree with our final decisions, for which we are accountable, only they can say. We are grateful also to Clare Davies-Jones, who in seeing the book through has suffered with admirable patience the delays that have beset it, and to Penny Carter for her careful and effective subediting.

PAUL FLETCHER

MICHAEL GARMAN

January 1979
University of Reading

Contributors

WILLIAM J. BAKER	University of Alberta
MELISSA BOWERMAN	University of Kansas
ROBIN N. CAMPBELL	University of Stirling
ANNE LINDSAY CARTER	University of California, Berkeley
EVE V. CLARK	Stanford University
DAVID CRYSTAL	University of Reading
BRUCE L. DERWING	University of Alberta
JOHN DORE	The Rockefeller University
PAUL FLETCHER	University of Reading
MICHAEL GARMAN	University of Reading
ROBERT GRIEVE	University of Western Australia
PATRICK GRIFFITHS	University of York
ROBERT HOOGENRAAD	University of Lancaster
DAVID INGRAM	University of British Columbia
ANNETTE KARMILOFF-SMITH	University of Geneva
MADELEINE LÉVEILLÉ	Stanford University
ALISON MACRAE	University of Edinburgh
MICHAEL P. MARATSOS	University of Minnesota
JOHN C. MARSHALL	University of Nijmegen
LISE MENN	Massachusetts Institute of Technology
PAULA MENYUK	Boston University
ROBERT SMITH	Stanford University
CATHERINE E. SNOW	Harvard Graduate School of Education
RACHEL E. STARK	The Johns Hopkins Hospital, Baltimore
PATRICK SUPPES	Stanford University
ROGER WALES	University of Melbourne
GORDON WELLS	University of Bristol

Part I

THE TRANSITION INTO LANGUAGE

Introduction

1.0. In recent years, the earliest stages of language development, and their relevant prelinguistic antecedents, have received increasingly detailed attention from a number of researchers (Bloom, 1973; Bruner, 1975; Carter, 1975b; Dore *et al.*, 1976; Ferguson, 1976; Huttenlocher, 1974; Nelson, 1973b; Rodgon, 1976; Snow, 1977a, Stark *et al.*, 1975; and others). Among the more important research areas in these earliest stages we may note the following:

1. *Prelinguistic vocalizations of infancy.* What, if anything, anticipates subsequent phonological development in these vocalizations? Do they show a discernible developmental progression?
2. *Vocabulary.* What does the earliest vocabulary look like, in comprehension and production? How does vocabulary develop during the period of single-word utterances?
3. *The single-word stage.* What is the nature of single-word utterances in the period before the first word combinations are produced? Do they foreshadow syntax? When can we reliably identify 'parts of speech'?

The first Part of this volume consists of six chapters which review the state of knowledge in the areas just outlined. The first two chapters, by Stark and Crystal, address the first issue, looking at the development of segmental and prosodic aspects of early vocalizations, and taking us up to the transition into a truly linguistic system. In this transitional area, Menyuk and Menn, Carter, and Griffiths are all concerned with the nature of transitional elements insofar as they reveal particular lines of subsequent development: thus, Menyuk and Menn show how phonological elements and processes emerge out of what they call *proto-words,* Carter traces the beginnings of lexical items in *sensorimotor morphemes,* and Griffiths examines the development of propositions and reference during the single-word stage. The chapter by Grieve and Hoogenraad looks at first words in the linguistic system, thus following on from Menyuk and Menn, and Carter in particular, and looking towards the chapters by Ingram, Clark and Macrae in Part II: Griffiths' chapter similarly makes contact with both Macrae and Garman in that Part.

2.0. So much for the organization of Part I. The main purpose of this introduction is to indicate in a little more detail the main paths of research for those encountering it for the first time. Thereafter, the chapters speak for themselves.

2.1. Stark's chapter concentrates exclusively on the nature of the vocalizations of the prelinguistic child, and the extent to which we may interpret their order of emergence as a developmental progression towards a linguistic system. As such, it is not concerned with the relationship that may exist between perception and production prior to the emergence of the first word. On this issue, Ferguson (1976) suggests that, initially, the production and perception systems are largely independent of each other, and that they only gradually become integrated. He further suggests that, towards the end of the first year of life, the child is controlling two qualitatively different production systems, (a) a *babbling* system, which is continuous with certain features of early vocalizations, but is not in direct contact with subsequent phonological development, and (b) a (proto-) *phonological* system. The earliest vocabulary is composed of *prewords* of the babbling system, alongside true *first words* of the phonological system. Further, Ferguson states a developmental priority of prewords (PWs) over first words (FWs), suggesting that a typical balance would have a dozen PWs to one FW. Babbling, while ultimately a 'dead-end' system, will continue to provide stable forms in early vocabulary for another few months beyond the appearance of FWs. Putting together the principal elements of Ferguson's account, we have the picture in figure 1. To begin with, the child has certain perceptual skills, starting with the perception of speech vs. nonspeech, and subsequent recognition of particular phonetic forms (Ferguson cites the child's turning to a clock in response to an adult saying *tick-tock*), as early as 5 months. Crystal in his chapter notes that awareness of prosodic contrasts is found as early as 2 to 3 months. While the earliest productions are most usefully described in their own terms (i.e. as purely production-system phenomena), the child rapidly develops structural constraints which process what he perceives, and which also therefore increasingly affect the nature of his vocalizations. It is in this way that the production and perception systems start to merge and what the child utters has increasingly to be described in terms of input as well as of output. However, as late as Ferguson's stage (iv), Babbling, we are still very far from adult forms, on account of immature vocal tract development and incomplete control of articulators.

For Stark, 'babbling' is a more restricted notion, distinct from 'vocal play'. It emerges first as a series of reduplicated forms, around 6 months, and subsequently develops into 'nonreduplicated babbling' and 'expressive jar-

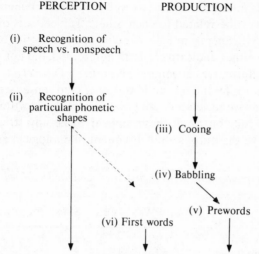

PERCEPTION   PRODUCTION

(i)   Recognition of
speech vs. nonspeech

(ii)   Recognition of
particular phonetic
shapes

(iii) Cooing

(iv) Babbling

(v) Prewords

(vi) First words

Figure 1. Six stages towards the development of early vocabulary (after Ferguson, 1976)

gon' around 9 months or later. It is at this point that Stark makes contact with Ferguson's PW and FW forms, of course. But, in addition to PWs and FWs, it is important to take note of a further concept, the *phonetically consistent form* (PCF) of Dore *et al.* (1976): not only do PCFs fail to approximate to adult forms but also, unlike PWs, they do not show consistent application to objects or situations, and yet are stable in production and are clearly potential precursors of vocabulary items in the full sense. In this context too we have to take account of Carter's description of a further transitional element, the *sensorimotor morpheme* (SM): this is a communicative unit which seems to be, at least initially, only partially stable in form. But its forms are bound to gesture and context in a consistent way. Moreover, it also seems to show 'A definite control exerted by the sound of an adult word', more particularly in respect of word-initial elements. Finally, the chapter by Menyuk and Menn, approaching from the point of view of the child's phonological development, also identifies a transitional element, the *proto-word*: Menyuk and Menn argue that the first year child stably processes speech, both in perception and production, beyond the domain of the segment (consonant or vowel), and beyond even the syllable. For a slightly later stage of development, we would want to call this processing unit the word, but prior to this we recognize the proto-word. Out of such processing domains, it is argued, the child gradually extracts the elements of his phonological system.

So among the transitional phenomena at the end of the first year we have

PWs, PCFs, SMs and proto-words, as well as the slow beginnings of FWs. How far may these be related to each other? Table 1 sets out a probable answer. PWs are distinct from FWs in being apparently not based on adult forms; PCFs are either 'indicative' (partly referential, but not reflecting 'the partitioning of alternatives in genuine reference'; Dore *et al.*, 1976: p. 20), or 'grouping' (not referential even in this restricted sense; see also chapter 6 below). SMs, as we have seen, are phonetically stable within limits. And proto-words, in relation to all these, appear to be any strictly prelexical forms which serve the purpose of subsequent phonological analysis by the child.

TABLE 1. *The relationship between first words and transitional elements*

	FWs	PWs	PCFs	SMs	Proto-words
Phonetically stable	+	+	+	±	±
Referentially stable	+	+	±	+	±
Adult-based	+	−	−	+	±

2.2. A number of studies have looked at early language comprehension and/or production for evidence of early vocabulary (Benedict, 1979; Blank, 1974; Bloom, 1973, 1974; Carter, 1975b; Gleitman *et al.*, 1972; Huttenlocher, 1974; Nelson, 1973b; Piaget, 1962). The findings of Benedict (1979) basically extend those of Goldin-Meadow *et al.* (1976) for 2 year olds to the earliest phase of vocabulary growth. Drawing just one representative child from Benedict's study, we have the picture set out in figure 2. The quantitative findings for the group of eight children that Benedict studied may be summarized as follows:

(i) comprehension vocabulary (C) exceeded production vocabulary (P) roughly fivefold

(ii) at the 50-word level, C was around five months in advance of P

(iii) C items were acquired at a rate of about 22 new words per month, and P items at a rate of about 9 new words per month, between the 10-word and 50-word levels

Valuable as it is in answering certain basic questions regarding early vocabulary, this gross quantitative picture really tells us very little about what the child is doing. For one thing, not all early vocabulary items are acquired on a once-for-all basis (Bloom, 1973); and for another, the individual history of particular words can only be documented with careful reference to the contexts of their use (Carter, 1975b, chapter 4 below). Perhaps most important of all, we need to know the nature of early vocabulary items. Benedict used a modified version of Nelson's (1973b) system of classifica-

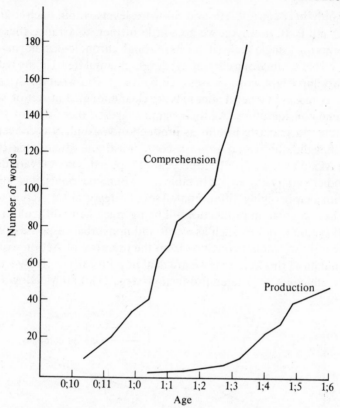

Figure 2. Number of words in comprehension and production by age in one subject (Elizabeth) (from Benedict, 1979)

tion, comprising four major classes, Nominals (General and Specific), Action words (also sub-classified – see further below), Modifiers, and Personal–Social words. She found that all four categories were present from the earliest phase (as Nelson (1973b) claimed; cf. also Bowerman, 1976b: p. 118). Furthermore, the dominant classes, up to the 50-word level, were General nominals and Action words, accounting for 75 per cent of C items and nearly 70 per cent of P items. This apparent similarity between C and P, however, masks certain important developmental differences: in P, General nominals predominate over Action words, with their relative share of vocabulary increasing between the 10-word and 50-word levels. In C, on the other hand, Action words are initially dominant, at the 10-word level, but their relative share of total vocabulary declines while that of General nominals increases, so that the two classes are comparable with each other at the 50-word level. Thus, looking at C and P separately, we find striking differences not only between the 10- and 50-word levels within each, but also between C and P. If, however, we go a little further, to arrange these two developments on a single scale (in terms of rough chronological norms), it is perhaps possible to discern a continuing developmental trend in the balance of these two important word classes (see figure 3). But what do these two categories represent? General nominals are clear enough, but Action words require some consideration. As their name suggests, these do not simply refer to verbs, particularly insofar as production vocabulary is concerned: indeed, if they did, this would seriously conflict with the situation described by Goldin-Meadow *et al.* (1976) for 2 year old speech. The relevant details from Benedict's study are set out in table 2. As Benedict notes, it is possible to work with a more highly differentiated set of categories for Action words in comprehension than in production – it being much more difficult to elicit verbs than symbolic noises such as *woof!* and nonverbal responses. Whatever the reason, we cannot conclude from the presence of Action words in production data of this kind that we are dealing with early verbs. Verbs are apparently elements of a later production stage (Goldin-Meadow *et al.,* 1976).

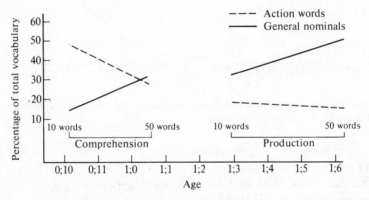

Figure 3. General nominals and Action words between the 10-word and 50-word levels in comprehension and production (after Benedict, 1979)

Concerning the sorts of meanings that are encoded in earliest vocabularies, Clark (chapter 8 below) justly emphasizes the high degree of commonality that is found among children of the same cultural background. It seems reasonable to recognize three basic stages.

(i) The earliest stage, where the child has no productive vocabulary, but will turn to gaze at a familiar object in his environment when that object is suitably named (e.g. the *tick-tock* example in Ferguson, 1976). Such

Table 2. *Categories of Action words, in comprehension and production (after Benedict, 1979)*

Action words	Comprehension No.	%	Production No.	%
	144*	36	75*	18
Social action games (Peek-a-boo; What does doggie say?)	61	15	44	11
Events (*eat* – nonverbal response)	3	1	not possible	
Locatives (*Where's X? Put X in*)	21	5	5	1
General action/Inhibitors (*Dance, jump, get X/No. Don't touch*)	59	15	26	6

* Distribution significantly skewed, $\chi^2 = 53\cdot21$, df = 4, p. $< 0\cdot01$

behaviour requires a mental representation of both the phonetic form and the referent – though in each case the percept is probably highly particularized, resulting in fluctuating recognition of the form, and underextension of its 'meaning'.

(ii) The foundations for productive vocabulary are laid with increasing control of vocalizations and the development of conceptual object–action schemas (in the sense of Huttenlocher, 1974) and also of concepts such as 'off', 'more', 'my/mine', etc. (Benedict, 1979; Bowerman, 1976b). However, the range of available vocalizations may become differentiated and stabilized before the concepts encoded by them become precise (Carter, 1975b, chapter 4 below). On the other hand, 'it certainly appears that children may possess a considerable capacity for mental representation of object properties in the period before they name many objects' (Huttenlocher, 1974: p. 366). This is a phase of great plasticity, and considerable interaction between the two aspects of development presumably takes place. The emphasis is on the here and now, and gestural support is common in production. The number of words comprehended increases quite rapidly, especially towards the end of this stage, although underextension (Anglin, 1975; Reich, 1976) may still be found. Also, at this stage, the form that a child will respond to for an object/event may not be related phonetically to the form that the child will produce for the same object/event (though, naturally, adults are quick to incorporate the child's production form into their own speech to the child). As further evidence of the plasticity of this stage, the child may employ certain naming forms so widely as to defeat all the analyst's most ingenious attempts to isolate meanings for them.

(iii) Further development consists mainly of building up an intermediate level of representation (the semantic level) between the level of the sound schema and that of the related object/event schema: cf. the 'consensus' considerations put forward in Bowerman (1976b: p. 101; cited in support are Bloom, 1973; E. V. Clark, 1974a; Nelson, 1974; Schlesinger, 1971b; Slobin, 1973; Wells, 1974). This progressive detachment of the 'meaning' of a word from its conceptual schema allows for an extension of word use: *Mummy* comes to have a meaning which is not tied to certain perceptual attributes of the child's own mother. Overextensions are also found, of course, and these have excited much interest: cf. Part II, Introduction and chapter 8 below. Here it is enough to note that Huttenlocher (1974) reports children around the age of 1 year overextending the meanings of words in production but not in comprehension. Huttenlocher's own explanation for this is couched in terms of the relative difficulty of processes of retrieval (involved in production) over recognition (involved in comprehension). However, the determination of retrieval and recognition in language use is a complex issue, and we ought to consider other, perhaps co-existent, possibilities. Thus, Clark (chapter 8 below) suggests that the child may overextend productively on account of a simple scarcity of items in his productive vocabulary, from which the 'nearest' fit has to be made. And we ought not to rule out the operation of early 'metaphoric' use of language, in certain instances.

This account, of course, does not provide a definite answer to the question 'which comes first, cognition or language?' As Bowerman (1976b) suggests, the 'cognition first' viewpoint is probably to be seen as a reaction against earlier Whorfianism, and more recent attitudes tend to be more interactionist. Thus, while there undoubtedly is some conceptual prestructuring, the emergence of language has an effect on concurrent and subsequent cognitive development, and vice-versa.

2.3. Many of the studies referred to so far pay attention to the child's earliest words not just as items in a developing vocabulary but also as communicative acts in particular situations. A basic problem has been to decide whether single-word utterances are *holophrases* (i.e. 'really' single-element instantiations of sentences, much reduced as a result of essentially extralinguistic developmental factors), or whether they are radically different from the two- and three-word combinations that emerge later.

Much support has gathered for the holophrase view (Stern and Stern, 1928; de Laguna, 1927; Leopold, 1949a; McCarthy, 1954; Werner and Kaplan, 1963; Greenfield, 1968; McNeill, 1970; Antinucci & Parisi, 1973). But it raises problems, and Bloom (1973) argues that there is no evidence for the existence of linguistic relations in single-word utterances prior to the emergence of word combinations. Dore (1975), reviews the issues; cf. also chapter 6 below.

Rodgon (1976) reports a recent attempt to reach a conclusion on the matter. Her approach was to hypothesize that *some* single-word utterances prior to word combinations might be analysable holophrastically, in terms of eight types: (i) S-V-O, (ii) Locative, (iii) Possessive, (iv) *I want to* —, (v) Negative, (vi) *Where*, (vii) Attributive, (viii) *Hi/Bye*. The nonholophrastic types recognized were (i) Naming and (ii) Repetition. Rodgon first observed which relations each of the ten subjects was expressing holophrastically. She also tested sensorimotor correlates of linguistic development in these terms, and observed the effect of training a subject to express in two-word combinations certain relations which that subject was already expressing holophrastically.

From this study, Rodgon draws a number of specific conclusions, tending towards the following general observations: 'there not only appears to be no simple relationship between holophrastic and combinatorial expression of the same relation, there also appears to be no simple relationship between a child's total proportion of holophrastic speech and the proportion of combinatorial and sequential speech which he produces' (1976: p. 103). The clear negative implications here relate not just to the pre- and postcombinatorial levels of language development, but also to the connection between linguistic and other abilities (tested in 'sensorimotor correlates'). In this connection, we ought to take note of the warning voiced by Corrigan (1978) that in such investigations we have to be precise about which cognitive tasks are involved. This is because a child may be simultaneously at one sensorimotor stage on one task and at others for other tasks. In her own study, Corrigan took the Piagetian concept of 'object permanence' and observed how it was attained, in relation to linguistic development, in three subjects (aged 0;9, 0;10 and 0;11 at the outset) as part of an eighteen-month longitudinal study. She concludes that, while there is no general correlation between object permanence ranking and length/complexity indices of language development, there is a general correlation between the onset of search for an invisibly displaced object and the start of single-word utterances, and between the attainment of object permanence and a spurt in vocabulary growth.

3.0. Beyond this, it seems unwise to place too much trust in accounts of so-called early nonlinguistic 'prerequisites' to linguistic development. But we may conclude this introduction with a review of the major early achievements that relate to skills that are implicated in subsequent linguistic behaviour. Bruner (1975) and Snow (1977a) provide reliable guidance here. Thus, there is the development of differential responding to people versus other entities in the earliest perceptual world of the infant (Trevarthen, 1974b); the ability to maintain eye–eye contact (Jaffe *et al.*, 1973; Robson, 1967; Stern, 1974); responding with a smile to an adult's smile (Brackbill, 1967); imitation of facial and manual gestures (O. Maratos, 1973); and following an adult's line of regard (Scaife and Bruner, 1975). Bruner (1975) presents compelling evidence that much of what we think of as natural linguistic behaviour involves such actions and awarenesses as these: joint attention, the ability to take turns in a joint enterprise, imitation, etc. From a somewhat different area of investigation, Snow (1977a) reports that important developments take place before the end of the first year of life in the way that adults (typically mothers) address their children. Clearly, eye–eye contact binds subsequent joint enterprise of many kinds, whether these are structurally imitative or not, and whether linguistic or not. Further, around the time that ability to follow an adult's line of regard is reported, Snow notes that mothers tend to respond to a variety of heterogeneous child vocalizations, as if they represented the child's contributions to a hypothetical discourse (e.g. 'Yes, what a nice little wind that was!' following a burp). This pattern continues, as a form of adult-dominated 'language' game, until the child is around 6 months. At this point, Snow reports a shift by mothers away from the sort of comment that 'builds in' the child's contribution and towards comments on objects and actions in the child's vicinity. It is as if mothers first habituate their child to a to-and-fro 'language' situation, and then switch to a routine that will encourage the introduction of elements of the child's world into this conversational orbit. There is a considerable interval, therefore, between the emergence of eye–eye contact and the beginning of the mother–child dialogue routine that presumably relies heavily on this skill.

By this stage, the child has started to enter into the turn-taking routine in an active way, and is becoming increasingly dominant in it. Further, Bruner (1975) notes that around this time a child will 'give' an object to an adult, but will not spontaneously release the object into the adult's hand: which may be the result of the child's not seeing the adult as a recipient in a potential to-and-fro 'object game'. However, it is possible for the adult at this stage to initiate an object-change routine (paralleling the quasi-conversational routine described by Snow) by removing the object from the child's grip and treating the child's subsequent reaching gesture as a response in a to-and-fro routine. It is also at this stage that Carter (1975b, chapter 4 below) reports the preliminary establishment of a link between stable vocalizations and gestures. A little later on, around the beginning of regular speech, the child himself may initiate a joint action enterprise, and Bruner points out that this involves the child looking upon the adult as a potential recipient–agent. The child's responses subsequently grow more stable (Snow, 1977a) in relation to adult utterances, at around the time that Carter observes the emergence of sensorimotor morphemes. Further development from this point consists in (a) an increasing reliance on the vocalization component over the gestural in the child's overall communication system, and (b) an ability to specify objects by *name*. Each of these developments apparently occurs along with the ability to search for invisibly displaced objects (Corrigan, 1978). Finally, towards the end of the single-word stage, Bruner reports that the child will frequently initiate an object-game by linguistic means. The developing linguistic system, which for Bruner is itself an outgrowth of action, becomes an initiating component of an action routine.

1. Prespeech segmental feature development*

Rachel E. Stark

1. Introduction

In the first part of the twentieth century, investigators who studied infant vocal output had two quite different aims in mind. One group wished to trace the development of the adult spoken language system, usually German or English; the other group was concerned with scales for measuring psychological development in infants. Both groups lacked the tools for adequate description of infant vocal behaviour. Their findings consequently yielded little understanding of the developmental processes which might be involved.

In the 1930s and 1940s, phonetic transcription began to be used for the purposes of description of infant sounds (Fisichelli, 1950; Irwin and Chen, 1946, 1947; Leopold, 1947; Lewis, 1951). Irwin and his colleagues used a limited transcription system in which few vowel or consonant items other than those of American English were represented. They studied a large number of infants, some on a longitudinal basis, and were able as a result to draw up an inventory of vowel and consonant types present at each age level. This inventory, which was based upon group means, indicated that vowels predominated in the infant's output in the early months of life both in terms of overall frequency of occurrence and of the ratio of vowel to consonant types produced. Consonants showed more rapid growth than vowels in both respects throughout the first two years of life. These data also indicated that consonant types produced at the back of the mouth were acquired first and those produced more anteriorly were acquired later. Vowels appeared in the reverse direction, that is, from front to back. A later study in which tape recordings were employed confirmed these findings in general (Fisichelli, 1950). Lewis (1951) studied only one infant's vocal output but made extensive longitudinal phonetic analyses. He was one of the first to try to account for the developmental sequence in acquisition of consonants and vowels, which he found to be similar to that reported by Irwin. He noted that the

* This work was supported in part by a grant no. NS 09628 from the National Institute of Neurologic Diseases, Communication Disorders and Stroke.

early appearing back consonants (/ç/, /ɣ/, /g/, /x/ and /k/) were produced in comfort; the later appearing /m/ and /n/ phonemes were first associated with discomfort but, as the infant accumulated experience of relief from discomfort, the sounds became associated with that relief and were produced in comfortable states also. Lewis further believed that other front consonants, e.g. /p/ and /b/, produced in the later period were associated with the experience of feeding.

In subsequent studies, problems with the use of phonetic transcription quickly became apparent. Some sounds eluded all attempts to transcribe them by this means. Acoustic analyses revealed differences between infant and adult productions which were not accounted for by the phonetic transcription system (Lynip, 1951); and the problems of establishing interjudge reliability, which became more apparent after tape recordings began to be used, seemed insurmountable. Because of these problems, few advances were made in the next decade. Although it was contrary to the evidence already accumulated, the view was frequently expressed that prespeech vocal behaviour was a completely random activity, subject to no developmental laws. In this activity, the infant was said to produce 'all possible sounds'. Jakobson (1968) is most widely quoted in support of this view but others have espoused it also (Lenneberg, 1962; Osgood, 1953; Rees, 1972). This view also implies that there is a sharp discontinuity between the period of random articulatory activity and the production of first words which *is* subject to developmental laws having certain universal aspects (Jakobson, 1968).

From the 1960s onward interest in the developmental processes reflected in prespeech vocal behaviour began to be manifested. Bever (1961) reanalysed Irwin's data in terms of magnitude and rate of change in production of phonemes throughout infancy. Bever identified three distinct developmental periods: 0 to 3 months, 4 to 11 months, and 12 to 18 months. He showed that there was a cyclic pattern of segmental feature development in each of these periods, with a peak of activity in the mid portion of each cycle. Patterns of vowel and consonant acquisition were found to differ from one another in a number of ways, thus suggesting that 'vocalic activity does not emerge by the same process as consonantal'. The developmental periods, and the cycles of activity within each, correlated well with other aspects of neurological development and in Bever's view reflected central nervous system maturation.

Menyuk (1968) reviewed data obtained by Nakazima *et al.* (1962) and concluded that the rank ordering of mastery of distinctive features in the babbling of these infants was similar to that shown by a somewhat older group of American children in their word productions (Templin and Darley,

1960). The data suggested a 'hierarchy of feature distinction which might be a linguistic universal, probably dependent on the developing and productive capacities of the child'.

Other studies conducted at this time were based upon the Jakobsonian view that the sounds of all languages are present in the infant's output. These studies were concerned with the factors which governed the infant's selection from his repertoire of those phonemes which are appropriate for the language he is to learn. Some were concerned with hypotheses about the role of imitation (Webster, 1969). In others a shaping process was hypothesized in which the phonemes of the language spoken by the child were selectively reinforced by the adults in his environment (Siegel, 1971).

Studies of vocal conditioning have indeed shown that rate of vocal output may be brought under control by appropriate contingent rewards (Rheingold *et al.*, 1959; Sheppard, 1969; Weisberg, 1963); and that, over the short term, the relative frequency of occurrence of particular utterance types may be influenced in the same manner (Routh, 1969; Wahler, 1969). In the most exhaustive study of its kind, however, Wahler identified vocal behaviours appearing in the output of an individual infant throughout the first year of life. He found that, by selective reinforcement, the frequency of occurrence of new vocal behaviours could be increased at the expense of old and vice versa. However, the form of each new vocal behaviour was not under experimental control and was not predicted by the experimenters. Wahler concluded that a shaping process was not responsible for the changes in vocal behaviour which were documented.

2. Auditory and acoustic analyses

More recently, investigators have returned to naturalistic observation methods, that is, to the study of infant vocal output recorded in a variety of naturally occurring situations over time. In all of these studies both listener judgments and techniques of acoustic analysis were employed. In some, the relationship between infant vocalization and the later development of meaningful speech received emphasis (Carter, 1975b; Dore *et al.*, 1976; Nakazima, 1962, 1966, 1970; Oller *et al.*, 1976; Kewley-Port and Preston, 1974; Preston *et al.*, 1969). In such studies the international phonetic alphabet (IPA) was used to trace successive approximations in the infant's output to the phonetic values in the spoken language of adults and to examine the contexts in which these approximations were used. The transcriptions of one listener might be relied upon or the transcriptions of a number of listeners might be examined in order to abstract information about phonetic features upon which they were able to agree. Spectrographic analyses were used to study features, such as time of onset of voicing in stop consonants, in segments upon which a satisfactory level of agreement was reached.

In other studies, the development of the infant's vocal behaviour as a means of expression in its own right was emphasized (Rose *et al.*, 1975; Stark and Nathanson, 1974; Stark *et al.*, 1975; Vuorenkoski *et al.*, 1971; Wasz-Höckert *et al.*, 1968; Zlatin, 1975). In these studies context is also considered to be highly important. However the investigators have found it more useful and appropriate to analyse infant vocal behaviour in terms of auditory and/or spectral features rather than phonetic transcription.

2.1. Descriptive feature systems

Auditory and spectrographic features have been identified and studied primarily by investigators who have had to deal with the output of very young infants. Phonetic transcription is least appropriate and useful in this case. The feature systems developed for this purpose are shown in table 1. It should be noted that the features are considered to be descriptive and not in any sense distinctive. Wasz-Höckert *et al.*, (1968), Vuorenkoski *et al.* (1971) and Truby and Lind (1965) employed spectrographic features to describe vocalizations produced in quite rigidly defined circumstances. Zlatin (1975) and Stark *et al.* (1975) employed auditory and spectrographic features to describe utterances produced in certain broadly defined states (e.g. cry, noncry, laugh). Zlatin (1975) used a segmental transcription system and then examined spectrographic data in order to find out how well the listeners' judgments correlated with acoustic features which she had previously identified as indicating the presence of an articulatory event, such as glottal stop or glottal aspirate. However, this procedure does not establish the validity of the system. The articulatory gestures implied cannot be observed directly, and it can only be assumed that they were made.[1]

Stark *et al.* (1975) chose instead to allow listeners to examine the spectrographic representation of an utterance and to listen to it at the same time. The procedure has the advantage of increasing interjudge reliability considerably. The units for which judgments are to be made may be defined clearly in terms of interval and segment duration, and the system improves the judges' ability to detect features in both modes. It will be noted that certain features, namely, place of articulation for consonants, tongue height and position for vowels, and nasality of vowels have been omitted from this system. These features could not be judged reliably in either mode.

[1] This objection does not apply to the Truby and Lind features. These investigators present cineradiographic data which do yield direct evidence of vocal tract gestures.

Until it becomes possible to use invasive procedures such as fibre optics, electrodes for electromyographic recording, or ultra sound, without hazard to the infant, an auditory judgment–spectral feature system may offer the best approach to certain questions. The results obtained must be interpreted cautiously and with the aid of information about vocal tract structure in the infant. However, in spite of their different approaches to the analysis of infant vocalization, there is considerable agreement among investigators. This agreement makes it possible to trace segmental feature development through the first year of life at least in a preliminary way; and to relate that development to the acquisition of early forms of spoken language acquired in the second year of life.

3. Stages of vocal development

The stages of development of vocal behaviour like those of other skills are now thought to be hierarchical in nature. Each new stage of development incorporates the one before and builds upon it. In each stage, features of vocal output which were present in the previous one enter into new combinations with one another. Apparent discontinuity from one stage to the next reflects a quantal jump in development rather than a lack of relationship between the adjacent stages.

3.1. Stage I: Reflexive crying and vegetative sounds (0 to 8 weeks)

In stage I only reflexive sounds (e.g. crying, fussing) and vegetative sounds (e.g. burping, swallowing, spitting up) are produced. Crying and fussing have certain features in common. Their segments, i.e. vocal units separated from one another by at least 50 msec. of silence, are:
(i)   predominantly voiced – breathy voicing may be present but completely voiceless portions, which seem always to be associated with forceful expulsion of air, are brief and relatively infrequent
(ii) predominantly egressive in breath direction – expiration is prolonged and voiced inspiratory (ingressive) segments, which sometimes occur immediately after a cry, are always brief
(iii) predominantly vowel-like – the vowels are judged to be mid or low front vowels (Lieberman *et al.*, 1971); nasal and liquid consonant-like elements are found in low level crying and fussing, and glottal stops are often observed to initiate or terminate a cry segment; however, the major portion of each cry–discomfort segment is a long vowel
On the average, cry segments are about one second in duration (Ringel and Kluppel, 1964; Stark and Nathanson, 1974; Truby and Lind, 1965).

Table 1. *Acoustic, auditory, and phonetic features or attributes of infant sounds employed by different investigators*

Stark et al. (1975)	Truby and Lind (1965)		Wasz-Höckert et al. (1968)
Descriptive features of vocalization	*Spectrographic features of pain-elicited cry*	(Notation)	*Attributes of groups of cries (birth, pain, hunger, and pleasure)*
Features of breath direction voicing, pitch, and loudness	Phonation (basic voiced cry)	⌒	* Length in seconds General (average) pitch in Hz
Egressive vs. ingressive	Dysphonation (Turbulence)	⋀⋀	* Maximum pitch
Silence (of less than 50 msec.)	Hyperphonation (pitch shift)	◁○	* Minimum pitch Pitch shift
Voicing: voiced, voiceless, breathy	Voiceless		
Voicing change	Inspiratory cry		* Amount of pitch shift in Hz Voice quality Voiceless signals Half-voiced signals Voiced signals Subharmonic break
Forceful expulsion of air			
Pitch: absent, normal, high			
Pitch shift			
Pitch contour: flat, rise, fall, or combination thereof			* Melody form Rising–Falling Falling Rising Flat Falling–Rising No form Nasal signals Glottal plosives
Rapid pitch glide			
Loudness: normal-to-loud, faint			
Degree of constriction of vocal tract above glottis	Zlatin (1975)		
Open (vowel-like)			
Closed (consonant-like)			

Features of vowel-like sounds

Phonetic feature	(Notation)	
Nonsyllabic	NS	No glottal plosives
Vocalic	V	Glottal plosives
Glottal stop	ʔ	Only glottal plosives
Glottal aspirate	h	Vocal fry
Supraglottal constrictive	C	Tense
Supraglottal glide	G	
Nasal	N	Vuorenkoski et al. (1971)
Syllabic nasal	N	

Glide
Glottal stop
Voice quality features
Harsh
Vocal fry
Pharyngeal friction
Subharmonic break

Features of consonant-like sounds

Friction noise
Trill
Nasal
Liquid
Stop
Click
Fricative

Phonetic feature	(Notation)	
Additive nasal resonance	~	(pain-elicited cries only)
Dysphonation	⌇	* Bi-phonation
Glottal fry or harsh quality	w	* Furcation
		* Stuttering
Hyperphonation	◁	* Latency
Saliva constrictive; diacritic placed above segmental variant (s)	○	* Change of pitch/100 msec. Hz
Brief duration	◂	* Vibrato
Prolonged	⋈	

* Attributes of pain-elicited cries rated and included in 'abnormal cry score'

They occur in long series which may occupy as much as five minutes with only brief pauses. Discomfort (fussing) sounds are a little over one half second in duration, and they occur in short series only (Stark *et al.*, 1975). Extremely high pitches and sudden shifts in pitch are more common in pain than in hunger cry; a reflexive hiccoughing motion of the diaphragm, which is associated with forceful expulsion of the air, is more characteristic of hunger or other spontaneous cries. The expulsion of air gives rise to rapid alternation of voicing with voiceless breath noise in these types of cry. Wasz-Hockert *et al.* (1968) refer to the phenomena as 'glottal pulses'. Other voice quality features, such as vocal fry (creaky voice), harshness, and subharmonic break, are very common in both types of cry.

The class of vegetative sound may be subdivided into grunts and sighs associated with activity, and clicks, stops and other noises associated with the management of nutrients (air and liquids). They are:

(i)   equally likely to be voiced or voiceless – about 25 to 30 per cent of all vegetative sounds are voiceless *throughout* and thus barely audible

(ii) equally likely to be produced on an outgoing or ingoing breath – ingressive portions are not more prominent in terms of frequency of occurrence than egressive

(iii) equally likely to be vowel-like or consonant-like – the consonant elements are clicks, stops, friction noises and trills

(iv) very brief (330 msec. on average for egressive vegetative sounds (mostly grunts and sighs), and 140 msec. for those which are ingressive)

These feature sets reflect both the configuration of the infant vocal tract (see figures 1 and 2) and the physiologic manifestations of cry and vegetative activity (Bosma *et al.*, 1965; Bosma, 1972, 1975). The young infant is a compulsive nasal breather except during cry. The mouth is filled by the tongue which rests against the lower lip and maintains apposition with the soft palate. During cry this apposition is given up. The soft palate and pharyngeal wall move backward (dorsalward). The jaw is lowered and with it the tongue which shows median grooving. The opening of the mouth gives rise to the vowel-like character of most distress sounds. However, the tongue tends to resume apposition with the soft palate in low level crying and discomfort sounds and when it does a nasal or liquid consonant-like sound results (Stark and Nathanson, 1974).

In addition, active crying alters the respiratory pattern observed at rest. The expiratory phase of respiration is greatly increased in duration; cineradiographic data indicate a generalized constriction of the pharyngeal area and the opening to the larynx. The pharynx and larynx are elevated above the rest position. During the very brief inspiratory phase, the pharynx is expanded by outward movement of the pharyngeal walls and sometimes

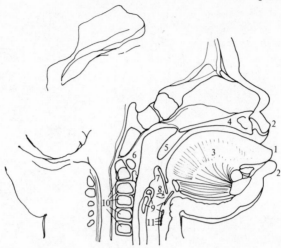

Figure 1. Sagittal section through the head of the newborn infant in midline (after Bosma, 1972; original figure drawn by H. Bartner). Notice that the larynx is high, at about the level of the first to the third cervical vertebrae. It is very closely suspended from the hyoid cartilage. The tongue is large, filling the oral cavity and resting upon the lower lip. The oropharyngeal area is the only portion of the vocal tract in which the tongue may change its position, except when the mouth is opened. Adjustments in vocal tract configuration take place in this area in response to cry, sucking and swallowing, and possibly also to changes in the head position. These adjustments are necessary to maintain patency of the airway and to ensure adequate ventilation. *Key.* 1 tongue blade, 2 lips, 3 body of tongue, 4 hard palate, 5 soft palate, 6 posterior pharyngeal wall, 7 epiglottis, 8 vocal and ventricular folds, 9 cartilages of larynx, 10 cervical vertebrae, 11 trachea

also by extension of the head and neck. The soft palate moves towards the tongue so that breathing is at least partly through the nose during inspiration.

The class of vegetative sounds is associated primarily with maintaining patency of the airway for respiration and defending it against penetration by substances which might choke the infant; and with intake and output of fluids. Vegetative sounds include coughing, belching, and sneezing which persist into adult life. In the very young infant, however, the positioning of structures in the pharyngeal area of the vocal tract is highly unstable. Sensory receptors in the pharyngeal region are of great importance for maintaining airway patency. Thus, respiratory movements are exaggerated and are constantly forced to adapt to reflexes such as rooting reflexes, swallowing and stimulation to the nostrils. Many of these adjustments give rise to brief stops, clicks and other noises which occur without voice and may be expiratory or inspiratory. They can only be recorded with the aid of a sensitive air microphone or a throat microphone.

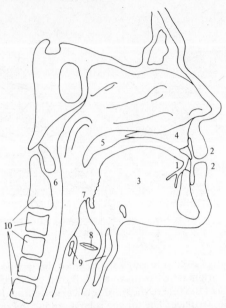

Figure 2. Sagittal section through the head of the adult in midline (from Zemlin, 1968). The larynx has descended to the level of the third to the fifth cervical vertebrae. Downward and forward growth of the face has increased the size of the oral cavity in relation to the tongue. The tongue is now capable of assuming positions at different heights in front, mid and back of the mouth, and also of a considerable range of motion within the mouth (for Key see figure 1)

Thus, cry–discomfort sounds have some of the characteristics of speech, namely prolonged vowel sounds, nasal and liquid consonant-like sounds, predominance of expiration, and temporal organization of output over a prolonged vocal episode, which are not present in vegetative sounds; and vegetative sounds have other characteristics of speech, namely voiced and voiceless nonsonorant consonant-like elements, which are not present in cry. Some of the characteristics of these two different sound types are combined with one another in cooing (see also Wolff, 1969).

3.2. Stage II: Cooing and laughter (8 to 20 weeks)

Cooing (comfort) sounds are produced in comfortable states usually in response to smiling and talking on the part of the mother. These sounds are sometimes referred to as vowel-like, but in fact they do contain brief consonantal elements (Lewis, 1936; Nakazima, 1962; Oller et al., 1976; Stark et al., 1976). They usually appear between 6 and 8 weeks of age. According to Oller (1976), Nakazima (1962) and Murai (1960) comfort sounds have a quasi-resonant nucleus, that is, they take the form of a syllabic nasal consonant or a nasalized vowel. The lack of resonance reflects the fact that the mouth is less widely open than during cry. The consonantal elements, usually transcribed as /ç/, /g/, /x/ and /k/, are all produced at the back of the mouth where the tongue and palate are most likely to resume contact with one another. Thus a new combination of features is formed in cooing sounds, of the voicing and egressive breath direction typical of cry and the stops, trills, and friction noises previously present in vegetative sounds only (see figures 3 and 4). Careful listening suggests that this new combination emerges primarily because, as the infant gains control over voicing, he becomes able to express pleasure as well as discomfort vocally (Stark, 1978). He is, however, unable at this time to inhibit vegetative activity of the vocal tract. This activity, which leads to constriction in the oral pharyngeal region, is frequently superimposed upon pleasure voicing, thus giving rise to the brief nonsonorant consonantal elements which are present in many cooing sounds. The nasal consonants are similar to those found in cry.

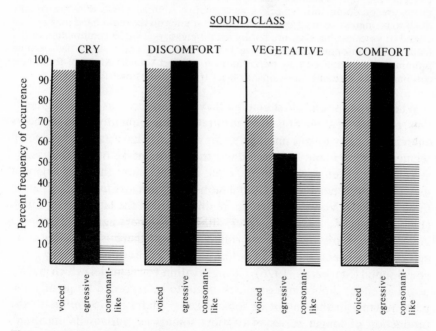

Figure 3. Percent frequency of occurrence of the features voiced (in whole or in part), egressive (in whole or in part) and consonant-like, in cry, discomfort (fussing), vegetative and comfort (cooing) sounds. Notice that the comfort sounds resemble cry and discomfort sounds with respect to voicing and breath direction; but resemble vegetative sounds with respect to frequency of consonant-like elements

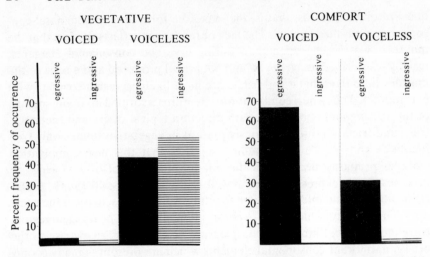

Figure 4. Percent frequency of occurrence of the features of breath direction (egressive vs. ingressive) and voicing (voiced vs. voiceless) in the consonant-like elements found in vegetative and comfort (cooing) sounds. Notice that these elements are predominantly voiceless in vegetative sounds, where they are equally likely to be ingressive or egressive. In comfort sounds on the other hand they may be voiced or voiceless but they are hardly ever ingressive. Thus, a combination of the features of consonant-like, egressive breath direction, and voicing has become prominent and acquired new importance in comfort sounds. Many of these new consonant-like elements are stops, or brief friction noises or trills

When cooing sounds first emerge they are produced as single segments only, each one of about 500 msec. in duration. Subsequently these segments enter into series with one another, series which may have as many as 3 to 10 segments within them. In some infants there is an intake of breath (usually voiceless) between each segment, while in others more than one segment may be present per breath. Glottal stops and voiceless intervals separate these segments. Vowels become more diversified in the later cooing sound (Lieberman *et al.*, 1976); however, although listeners agree in hearing a greater variety of vowels in the infant's output, there is even less good agreement between them than before in their transcriptions of any *given* vowel sound (Stark *et al.*, 1976). Changes within vowel nuclei, which may be heard as either diphthongs or glides, begin to be recorded frequently and more reliably in the output of some infants. Zlatin (1975) refers to the production of longer series of comfort sounds as 'early syllabification', although the segments produced are not like the syllables of adult speech in their timing or their feature content.

From 12 weeks of age, the frequency of crying drops markedly and in most infants primitive vegetative sounds begin to disappear. At 16 weeks of age sustained laughter emerges (Gesell and Thompson, 1934). In the earliest laugh sounds a rapid alternation of voiced and voiceless portions initiates laughter. This alternation, which might be transcribed as /hahaha/, resembles the glottal pulses of spontaneous crying (see p. 22 above). The series usually terminates with a segment which resembles the infant's cooing.

3.3 Stage III: Vocal play (16 to 30 weeks)

There may be some overlap of the end of stage II with the beginning of stage III. The essential character of stage III, however, is that longer series of comfort sounds disappear and the infant reverts to production of single segments in which he prolongs vowel- or consonant-like steady states and also slows down the rate of any change occurring within the segment, for example, in pitch, voicing, or degree of constriction of the vocal tract. As a result the segments are of greater duration (700 to 1500 msec. on the average) than comfort sounds. Also, consonantal elements are now produced more anteriorly in the mouth.

During this period the infant begins to adopt oral tidal respiration. Downward and forward growth of the facial skeleton increases the size of the oral cavity and thus gives the tongue more room to manoeuvre within it. Also, specialization and changes in concentration of mucosal sensory receptors are taking place in the pharyngeal region as a result of enlargement of surface areas and also possibly actual reduction in the number of receptors present. The capacity for discrimination of touch, pressure and movement at the apical portion of the tongue and at the lip margins may assume greater importance than before (Bosma, 1975).

In stage III the infant produces over and over again primitive segment types characterized by:

(i)   high pitch and extreme pitch glides
(ii) low pitched growling, pharyngeal friction, or, less frequently, vocal fry
(iii) voiced and voiceless egressive friction noises and trills – the friction noises and trills are produced by approximating tongue and pharyngeal palate, tongue and both the alveolar ridge of the palate and the lips, or the lips with one another, and by blowing air, saliva, or food through the constriction formed by these structures
(iv) syllabic nasal consonant sounds (/m̩/ and /n̩/)
(v)   exaggerated voiceless clicks, e.g. lip smacking and friction noises
(vi) vowels in which tongue height and position are more varied than in stage II

All of the features of these segment types except (vi) were present in stages I and II. Now, however, they are divorced from their previous cry, vegetative or comfort sound contexts, and are used in a great variety of situations. Notice that many of these segment types (e.g. lip smacking and voiced inspiratory sounds) although found in adult spoken languages are not phonological universals.

The above segment types make their appearance in different orders in the output of different infants, except that segment types (v) and (vi) may always appear towards the end of stage III and continue into stage IV. One infant may use the first two types of segments (high pitch and/or extreme pitch glides and low pitched segments) alternately for many weeks and then abruptly switch to the third type (voiced and voiceless friction noises and trills) engaging in the practice of the latter sound types for a brief time only, perhaps as little as a portion of one day. Another infant may show these behaviours in completely the reverse order. The order of appearance of the above segment types in vocal play may be determined in part by the role of maturation of nuclei within the central nervous system by which the vocal tract is controlled. The development proceeds upward (cephalward) and downward (caudalward) from the oral pharynx, but may do so at different rates in different infants.

It has been suggested that, in this play, the infant explores and maps the vocal tract at a time when its spatial co-ordinates are changing rapidly (Mattingly, 1973). Thus, the infant updates sensory information about oral and pharyngeal spaces by touch, pressure, and activity within these spaces. The activity has also been viewed as a secondary circular reaction according to Piaget's (1952) description of stage III of sensory motor development.

Towards the end of this period some of the above features begin to be combined with one another in still longer segments. For example, a vocal play sound may be initiated with a high pitch vowel and/or pitch glide, and terminate with a voiced trill. Longer series of vocal play segments are also produced and in these series imprecisely articulated stop-vowel syllables may appear. In these syllables, a brief trill or friction noise may occur as the stop is released into the vowel. The vowel formant transition is irregular and may be highly variable in rate, sometimes extremely slow. Oller (1976) refers to these series as 'marginal babbling'.

3.4. Stage IV: Reduplicated babbling (25 to 50 weeks)

Reduplicated babbling may be defined as the production of series of consonant–vowel syllables in which the consonant is the same in every syllable. Examples are /ənənə/ or /ædædə/. Quite often, as indicated, a very brief vowel initiates the series. Thus, the series of syllables in reduplicated bab bling are stereotyped and lack the richness of output which is present in the vocal play series produced at the end of stage III. Labial and alveolar stops and nasals, and /y/ glides are the most frequently used consonants in this babbling. Listeners still have difficulty in deciding upon the place of articulation. Inspection of videotapes indicates that, in the case of stops and nasals, because the tongue is still relatively large in relation to the oral cavity, the tongue blade may close against the alveolar ridge but also be resting against the lips which are partially closed around it. Thus, some of the acoustic cues are likely to be intermediate between those of bilabial and of alveolar consonants of adult speech. The vowel nuclei are all fully resonant at this time.

The total syllable duration and the duration of consonant–vowel transitions are now close to those of adult speech. The tongue no longer separates from the palate as though the constrictions so formed were forced open by the air pressure building up behind it, with an abrupt tap as in earlier nasals, or with a trill or friction noise as in earlier stop-vowel syllables. The opening of the constriction now appears to be well controlled. Fine control of timing, e.g. of the onset of voicing in the stop-vowel syllables, may be different from that found in adult speech. There is some evidence that all possible values of this timing are equally likely when stop-vowel syllables first appear. However, by 11 months of age, infants of different language communities strongly favour a simultaneous release of the stop and onset of voicing, or values which are very close to synchrony of these two gestures (Enstrom and Stoll, 1976; Kewley-Port and Preston, 1974; Preston *et al.*, 1969). Adult languages are likely to show more than one modal value of voice onset time. These values correspond to the categories of phoneme sometimes referred to as voiced, voiceless unaspirated, and voiceless aspirated. In addition, Oller and Smith (1977) have found that the final syllable of a babbled series shows significantly less lengthening as compared to nonfinal syllables than in the case of adult speech or adult imitations of babbling.

Reduplicated babbling is not used in communicating with adults except perhaps towards the end of this stage in ritual imitation games. During stage IV, infants begin to communicate by means of gestures of reaching, pointing, grasping and rejection. The utterances which accompany these gestures are described by Carter (1975b) in previous work and in chapter 4 below.

3.5. Stage V: Non-reduplicated babbling and expressive jargon (9 to 18 months)

In stage V, reduplicated babbling is replaced by babbling in which vowel, consonant–vowel and even consonant–vowel–consonant syllables appear and the consonants as well as the vowels may be *different* from one syllable to another. The consonants already found in reduplicated babbling are present in this variegated babbling (Oller's term, 1976). To these are added new elements, and in particular the fricatives (/s/, /x/, /ʁ/ and /ç/) which are practised at the beginning of this stage, and high front and mid and high back vowels, both rounded and unrounded. Fricatives require that the infant create and *maintain* a narrow constriction within the mouth as air is directed through it. Thus, fricative production requires a higher level of control and skill than any of the consonants produced thus far. High back and high front vowels, both rounded and unrounded, require adequate space within the oral cavity; this space may simply not be available in the infant until the second six months of life.

Towards the end of stage v, a variety of stress and intonation patterns are imposed upon nonreduplicated babbling so that, according to parents, the babbling 'sounds like a foreign language', hence the term 'expressive jargon' (Gesell and Thompson, 1934). Some infants spend several months in this activity; others proceed more rapidly to stage vi, the production of first words, which will not be described here. Dore (1973) refers to the former group as 'intonation babies' and suggests that they are more socially adept, better able to express their attitudes and perhaps to manipulate adults than the latter group whom he refers to as 'word babies'; 'word babies' are more interested in naming objects. Nelson (1973b) finds that children who are developing meaningful speech may also be classed as 'referential' or 'expressive' according to the strategies they use in learning how to put words together. It is not at present known whether the same infants are likely to be 'expressive' or 'referential' in both developmental stages.

Dore *et al.* (1976) identify a transitional period between babbling and first words in which certain phonetic forms are used consistently to express primitive groupings of experience and in play rituals. Also, Oller *et al.* (1976) have shown that there are certain commonalities of phonetic structure from the babbled utterances of stages iv and v to the child's first attempts to produce meaningful speech. They predicted correctly that babbling would, in continuity with meaningful speech, show the following characteristics:

(i)   reduction of consonant clusters
(ii) deletion of final consonants
(iii) devoicing of final consonants where these were present
(iv) a greater number of initial stops than initial fricatives and affricates
(v)   a greater number of /w/ and /y/ glides than of liquids in the prevocalic position
(vi) a greater number of apical than of velar consonants

These findings also implied a relationship between babbling and phonological universals. It would appear that those sounds which the infant is capable of producing at the end of the prespeech period *and* upon which patterns of rapid alternation between consonant and vowel may readily be imposed are the sounds most likely to find their way into adult phonological systems (see also Cruttenden, 1970).

4. Summary

As the above descriptions indicate, there is a lawful developmental sequence in segmental feature production from reflexive sound making to first word production. In spite of individual differences, the progression may have certain aspects which are universal.

It has been suggested that the earliest productions provide a matrix of primitive metaphonological features from which babbling, jargon and speech ultimately derive (Oller, 1976). But in fact most, if not all, of the articulatory features of speech are present in the earliest sounds of infants in a remarkably well-organized form. For example, the feature stop, produced at the glottis, initiates many cry segments and the feature bilabial place of articulation is present in the brief clicks of sucking. The appearance of these gestures under given circumstances is highly reliable; they are executed with great rapidity and are co-ordinated with one another in the sense that crying reactions will pre-empt some vegetative behaviours (e.g. sucking) and other vegetative behaviours (e.g. coughing) will pre-empt crying.

These gestures, and the pattern of auditory–spectral features resulting from them, are not organized in a manner that resembles speech. The features do not form compact bundles but simple and quite limited associations with one another in primitive segment types. Certain feature combinations are not present at all, e.g. there are no bilabial stops. Also, there are few transitions from one articulatory gesture to another involving different structures or different parts of the vocal tract in a continuous pattern of movement. Thus, it may be the set of features within the segment which strikes the listener as 'primitive', not the features themselves.

At the beginning of each stage of development, new segmental feature combinations are brought under control. Nasals, friction noises and stops are produced at a more anterior place of articulation; supraglottal stops and fricatives develop from friction noises and trills. As this control is acquired, the ability to move rapidly from open (vowel-like) to closed (consonant-like) positions of the vocal tract within a segment may be temporarily lost. Regression to a simpler overall organization of series of segments may also be observed and is present in the transition periods between all of the stages described above except IV (reduplicated babbling) and V (expressive jargon). Even here a period of transition may be marked by the 'practice' of true fricatives and/or of the high front and back vowels referred to above as taking place within stage IV, and concomitant regression to simpler prosodic forms.

Thus, the development of more complex and more compact bundles of features is cyclical in nature. Once new segment types are mastered, they are incorporated into more complex overall patterns of segment series; the prosodic patterns may also be elaborated within each developmental cycle.

Vocal behaviour must also be related to the development of speech perception skills which is only now beginning to be studied (Eilers, 1976; Kuhl, 1976) and to cognitive and social development. As knowledge of the stages of segmental feature production in infants increases, it will become possible to ask still more interesting questions about the ways in which these stages are influenced by other aspects of infant development.

2. Prosodic development

David Crystal

1. The nature of prosody

Unlike the well-established fields of grammar and segmental phonology, the field of prosody requires a certain amount of exposition, before one can talk about its development in children. What range of data is to be subsumed under this heading? For present purposes, it will be useful to select three main themes from the prosodic literature, reviewed, for example, in Crystal (1969, 1975): (a) What is excluded from the domain of a prosodic theory? (b) What variations in prosodic form may be identified? (c) What range of prosodic functions may be established?

The first question may be answered briefly, as its purpose is solely to relate prosody to other areas with which it is often confused. Given a specification of semiotic behaviour as 'patterned human communication in all its modes' (Sebeok *et al.*, 1964), then prosodic features can be identified as one component of the auditory–vocal dimension of communication, i.e. excluding the visual ('kinesic'), tactile ('proxemic') and other communicative modes referred to globally under the general heading of 'nonverbal communication' (see Argyle, 1975). Within the auditory–vocal area, a distinction is conventionally made between *segmental* and *nonsegmental* phonology, the latter usually being defined as the 'residue' of the former – what is left *after* one has studied the vowel/consonant/syllabic system of sounds. More positively, one can define nonsegmental phonology as any linguistically contrastive sound effect which cannot be described by reference to a single segment (phoneme), but which either (i) continues over a stretch of utterance (minimally, a syllable), e.g. extra loudness; or (ii) requires reference to several segments in different parts of the utterance, e.g. the use of breathy voice on vowels. Within this field, prosody is a term which traditionally has referred only to certain aspects of this variability, namely linguistic variation in pitch, loudness, speed and rhythm (including pause) of speaking. Other aspects were either ignored, or grouped loosely together under the heading of 'paralanguage' (e.g. nasal, husky, or whispered vocal effects). In the language acquisition field, the term 'prosody' has tended to

33

follow this orientation, though one sometimes sees it used where it plainly has a more general meaning, namely, all aspects of nonsegmental variability. Certainly, with few exceptions, the attitude adopted to prosody is very much that of the 'residue' referred to above. It is regularly assumed that segmental phonology, grammar and lexicon can be analysed without reference to prosodic features, which may, if at all, be mentioned only in passing. The methodological fallacy here is particularly worrying with reference to grammar, at the early stages of development, but its implications cover all aspects of language structure and function. There are signs, particularly in the recent literature on the interactional analysis of early language, that the importance of prosody is becoming increasingly realized; but this literature also illustrates the difficulty of working precisely within this domain, as will be discussed below.

Turning now to the second question raised above: what prosodic variability to recognize? A traditional misconception here is to talk of a child's 'prosody', implying that this is in some sense a single, homogeneous phenomenon. The linguistic literature shows very plainly, however, that several different kinds of patterning are involved in prosodic analysis, and it is important to distinguish these, in order to specify precisely what it is that is being acquired. The present chapter will be restricted to those aspects of prosodic patterning the importance of which is generally agreed among the various approaches (the terminology and particular theoretical emphasis used is that of Crystal (1975)).

(i) The primary focus must be on the way in which the several prosodic characteristics of the speech signal are integrated to produce a totality, which expounds meaning. The linguistic use of pitch, or *intonation,* ultimately develops into the most complex of all the prosodic systems, and for the adult it can to a considerable extent be studied formally as an autonomous system. But from a semantic point of view, intonation is merely one factor in communicating a meaning – as is clear when we consider what range of vocal characteristics enter into the definition of such tones of voice as sarcastic, angry, parenthetic, etc. Particularly for the first two years of life, nonintonational features (such as variations in loudness, duration, rhythmicality) are of considerable importance in the expression of meaning. This is so, not only for attitudes, but also for grammatical patterning. For example, when one tries to decide whether a sequence of two lexical items constitutes one sentence or two, one must listen out for far more than pitch contour and pause (the two features usually referred to): they may be linked by extra loudness, longer duration, marked rhythm, or with some shared paralinguistic feature (e.g. marked tension, or nasality) – all of which requires one to place intonation in its proper perspective. Intonation nonetheless has attracted most attention in the developmental literature, and the following discussion reflects this emphasis.

(ii) A basic distinction is postulated between pitch *direction* and pitch *range*. A pitch may fall, rise, stay level, or do some combination of these things within a given phonological unit, e.g. fall–rise on a syllable; and these directional *tones* are usually isolated as one system of intonational contrastivity. But any of these tones may be varied in terms of range, seen as a separate system of contrasts, e.g. a falling pitch used relatively high, mid or low, or being widened or narrowed in some way.

(iii) Features of pitch direction and range, along with features of rhythm and pause, are organized into prosodic configurations, or *tone-units* (or 'primary contours', 'sense groups', etc.), which expound meanings over and above the accompanying 'verbal' meanings. Tone-units provide the most general level of organization that can be imposed upon prosodic data, equivalent in status to the notion of 'sentence' in grammatical analysis.[1] For example, the normal tone-unit segmentation of the utterance

When he comes/ tell him I'm out/

is as indicated by the slant lines. In general, the assignment of tone-unit boundaries seems motivated by syntactic reasons, e.g. to mark the boundary between clauses (see further, Crystal, 1975: ch. 1). We might accordingly expect such a fundamental notion to be an early characteristic of prosodic development (see below).

(iv) The prosodic feature which seems to carry the next most important linguistic contrastivity is the placement of maximum prominence on a given syllable (or, occasionally, on more than one syllable). This is primarily a matter of pitch movement, but extra loudness is involved, and duration and pause may be used to heighten the contrast between what precedes and follows. The prominent, or *tonic* syllable may be seen capitalized in the utterance

Because we stayed until MIDNIGHT/ we got in TERRIBLY late/

This is the focus of most of the discussion on intonation in the context of generative grammar (e.g. Bresnan, 1971), where the aim was to demonstrate that tonicity (i.e. tonic syllable placement) had a syntactic function, being used to disambiguate sentences or signal a distinction between grammatical and ungrammatical. While this sometimes happens, the alternative view (which I share) is that of Bolinger (1972), who argues that the factors

---

[1] One awaits the demonstration that tone-unit sequences operate generally and systematically (cf. paragraphs), though some interesting suggestions along these lines have already been made (e.g. Fox, 1973).

governing tonic placement are primarily semantic, e.g. the signalling of new information in context.

(v) The next most noticeable prosodic characteristic is the specific direction-range of the tonic syllable, e.g. whether the *tone* of the syllable is high–falling–wide, low–rising–narrow, etc. These tones seem to signal primarily attitudinal information, though certain tonal contrasts can expound grammatical meaning, e.g. the 'asking' versus 'telling' distinction in tag-questions:

> You're CÒMING/ÁREN'T you/
> You're CÒMING/ÀREN'T you/

The third question raised at the beginning of this chapter concerned the range of functions which these prosodic patterns might be said to perform. Here five roles need to be distinguished.

(i) In a *grammatical* function of prosody, the prosodic feature(s) signal a contrast, the terms of which would be conventionally recognized as morphological or syntactic in a grammar, e.g. positive/negative, singular/plural, statement/question. These contrasts are common in tone languages, such as Twi, but some of these may also be found in English, where tone-units, tonic syllables and tones can all perform grammatical roles (cf. the tag-question contrast above). In a related sense, prosody may be used obligatorily to mark a grammatical distinction already overt in word order or morphology, as in co-ordinated utterances such as

> I'll ask the FÍRST question/ and you ask the SÈCOND one/

(ii) The *semantic* function of prosody subsumes a speaker's organization of meaning in a discourse, whereby he signals which parts of what he is saying are most important, which parenthetic, etc. This includes the emphasizing of a relatively unexpected lexical item in an utterance, as Bolinger argues (1972), as well as reflecting the presuppositions about subject matter or context when focusing on a specific item, as when, for example *There was a* BUS *in the road* implies a context where someone had queried whether this was in fact the case.

(iii) The *attitudinal* function of prosody is usually distinguished from (ii), on similar grounds to the classical distinction between denotation and connotation. Personal emotions are signalled concerning the subject matter or context of an utterance, e.g. anger, puzzlement, surprise. It is unclear how far such emotions use prosodic features specific to a language, and how far they rely on universal characteristics of emotional expression (cf. Bolinger, 1964).

(iv) The *psychological* function of prosody is evident from the several experiments which have shown that performance in short-term memory, recall, perception and other variables is affected by the prosodic character of the utterance, e.g. words containing tonic syllables are more readily recalled (cf. Leonard, 1973).

(v) The *social* function of prosody signals information about the sociolinguistic characteristics of the speaker, such as his sex, class, professional status, etc. (Crystal, 1975: ch. 5). The importance of this function in facilitating social interaction in dialogue is being increasingly recognized, e.g. when the intonation of a stimulus sentence prompts someone to respond, or implies that no further comment is needed. The role of prosody in expressing the illocutionary force of a speech act, such as persuading or commanding, is also now seen to be significant – though whether one might refer to this as primarily a social, attitudinal, semantic or grammatical role is very much an open question!

This last point raises a principle of fundamental importance, which needs to be emphasized, in view of the extent to which it is neglected in child language studies – namely that there is no one-to-one correspondence between the above categories of prosodic form and prosodic function, nor between any of the individual features subsumed within these categories. A rising tone, for example, signals far more than a questioning meaning, and a grammatical question may be uttered using other tones than rising ones (for discussion and references, see Crystal, 1969: ch. 1). It is accordingly fallacious to assume that a child who uses rising tones is thereby 'asking a question', 'making a questioning speech act', or the like: everything depends on the careful analysis of the accompanying behaviour and situation before one can be justified in ascribing such an interpretation to the utterance.

2. Prosodic acquisition

Given the limited empirical study which has taken place (almost entirely within the first two years of life), talk in terms of clear stages of development in this area may well be premature. On the other hand, the evidence which is available does agree so far on several points, hence the following progression. Five stages can be distinguished, of which the last two are particularly important.

Stage I. There have been many studies of the prelinguistic antecedents of prosodic features, usually under the heading of 'infant vocalization'. On the whole, these studies recognize a period of biologically determined vocalizations (e.g. the 'basic cry' pattern, underlying hunger, pain. etc. states described in Wolff (1969: p. 82)), and a period of differentiated vocalizations which permit general attitudinal interpretation only (e.g. 'pleasure', 'recognition'). Systematic variation in these vocalizations can be ascribed to such factors as the baby's sex or environment. There seems to be little difference in their physical characteristics and attitudinal function across languages. This stage, from birth until around 6 months, is reviewed in detail in Crystal (1975: ch. 8).

Stage II. The first sign of anything linguistic emerging is the awareness of prosodic contrasts in adult utterances directed to the child. This has long been known to be present in children from around 2 to 3 months, as the reports in Lewis (1951) testify. But this literature is rather anecdotal, and experimental studies are lacking which attempt to separate prosody from other semiotic features of the stimuli, and to identify the roles individual prosodic features might play within the adult utterance, e.g. whether pitch or loudness are discriminated first. Kaplan (1970), for example, demonstrated that a contrast between falling and rising tones could be discriminated from around 4 months, but it is difficult to be sure of the relative roles pitch and loudness had to play.

Stage III. The increasingly varied vocalizations of children around 6 months have begun to be studied in detail, using a combination of acoustic, articulatory and auditory criteria, and it is possible to isolate a wide range of nonsegmental parameters in terms of which the patterns of crying, babbling, etc., can be classified. Stark *et al.* (1975), for example, cite breath direction, pitch, loudness, and several kinds of glottal and supraglottal constriction; within pitch, they distinguish contrasts of range, direction and continuity.

Gradually, these nonsegmental features come to resemble prosodic patterns of the mother tongue – from as early as 6 months, according to most scholars (see the review in Crystal, 1975: p. 136). Initially, the resemblance is only hinted at, by the occasional use of a language-specific prosodic characteristic within a relatively long stretch of nonlinguistic vocalization. Such instances are very striking when they occur on a tape, as they stand out as something much more familiar, discrete and transcribable than the general background of utterance. Increasingly, at this time, babbling patterns become shorter and phonetically more stable: accordingly, when a babbled utterance of only one or two syllables is used in conjunction with a language-specific prosodic feature, the result is going to be very much like an attempt at a meaningful utterance. Such combinations are quickly focused on by parents, who will comment on what they think the baby is 'saying', often providing lexical glosses. It is, however, very difficult to be precise about the nature of the development at this stage. To say that a language-specific feature has been detected is to say very little: recognition of language-specificity involves both phonetic notions (e.g. the 'community voice quality' or characteristic 'twang' of a language) and phonological notions (e.g. the selection of contrasts which produce an identifiable accent), and it is by no means clear how to distinguish these in the child's vocalization at this stage. The boundary area between the phonetic use of pitch, loudness, etc., during the first 6 months of life, and the phonological use of pitch that has emerged by around a year, is totally uncharted territory (cf. Olney and Scholnick, 1976).

Stage IV. However the transition to phonology takes place, it is evident that learned patterns of prosodic behaviour are characteristic of the output of the child during the second half of the first year. These patterns can be studied both formally and functionally. From the formal viewpoint, the increasingly determinate and systematic character of these patterns is readily statable: a configuration of features is involved, using primarily pitch, rhythm and pause. This configuration has been variously labelled: a prosodic 'envelope' or 'matrix' (Bruner, 1975: p. 10) or 'frame' (Dore, 1975). Weir (1962) had previously talked about the splitting up of utterances into 'sentence-like chunks', at this stage. Lenneberg (1967: p. 279) describes the process thus:

> 'The first feature of natural language to be discernible in a child's babbling is contour of intonation. Short sound sequences are produced that may have neither any determinable meaning nor definable phoneme structure, but they can be proffered with recognizable intonation such as occurs in questions, exclamations or affirmations. The linguistic development of utterance does not seem to begin with a composition of individual, independently movable items *but as a whole tonal pattern.* With further development, this whole becomes differentiated into component parts . . .' (my emphasis)

The important point is that these primitive units have both a segmental and a prosodic dimension, but it is the latter which is the more stable, and the more readily elicited. In one child studied at Reading, aged 1;2, the phrase *all-gone,* regularly said by the parent after each meal, was actually rehearsed by using the prosodic component only: the child hummed the in-

tonation of the phrase first, viz. , only then attempting the whole,

producing an accurate intonation but only approximate segments ([ʌʔdʌ]). The phrase could be easily elicited after any meal, but it was not until a month had gone by that the child's segmental output became as stable as his prosodic. Menn's Jacob (1976a: pp. 195ff.) also produced 'proto-words' with a distinctive prosodic shape – the ones reported being used at 1;4 for a peekaboo game, an item with demonstrative function (êsɑ), and, later, a name-elicitor (zɨ). Dore (1975) refers to the formally isolable, repeated, and situationally specific patterns observed at this stage as 'phonetically consistent forms', whose 'protophonemic' segmental character is complemented by a distinctive prosody, which is the more stable.

From a functional point of view, these prosodically delimited units can be interpreted in several ways – semantic, syntactic and social 'explanations' have all been mooted. The latter view is perhaps the most widely held: here, prosody is seen as a means of signalling joint participation in an action sequence shared by parent and child. This view, emphasized particularly by Bruner (1975), is part of a developmental theory wherein vocalization is seen as one component in a communication activity alongside such non-vocal behaviour as reaching and eye-contact. In a peekaboo game, for instance, both the utterance and the activity of hiding-and-reappearing are obligatory, interdependent components (as the absurdity of attempting to play the game without either indicates). And when adults play these games, the lexical character of the utterance regularly varies ('Peep-bo', 'See you', etc.) whereas the prosodic features display much less variation. Another example is in action sequences such as nuzzling the child or jumping him up and down, where there are parallel prosodic patterns. The development of 'turn-taking', either between parent and child (Snow, 1977a) or between children (Keenan, 1974) also involves prosodic delimitation and inter-dependence. One Keenan twin, for example, would regularly take the prosodic character of the other's utterance and 'play' with it. Another child, studied at Reading, marked the end of a jargon sequence with a distinctive two-syllable pitch movement (˙ .), which was openly described by his parents as 'their cue to speak'.

Several attempts have been made to describe the social or 'pragmatic' functions of such utterances, especially using the metalanguage of speech act analysis. Dore, for example (1975: pp. 31ff.), argues that prosodic features provide crucial evidence for the development of speech acts. Primitive speech acts are said to contain a 'rudimentary referring expression' (lexical items) and a 'primitive force indicating device' ('typically an intonation pattern', p. 31), as in labelling, requesting and calling. The distinction between referent and intention is pivotal: 'whereas the child's one word communicates the notion he has in mind, his prosodic pattern indicates his intention with regard to that notion' (p. 32). Likewise, Menn says about Jacob (1976a: pp. 26–7), 'he . . . consistently used certain intonation patterns in conjunction with actions that communicated particular intentions, so we can ascribe meaning to his use of those contours'. The difficulty with all such approaches, of course, is empirical verification of the notion of 'intention'. As has been argued in other areas of child language, the fact that parents interpret their children's prosody systematically is no evidence for ascribing their belief patterns to the child's intuition. At best, one can argue, as does Menn (1976a: p. 192) that 'consideration of adult interpretation of intonation contour on vocalizations does give us information about what the child *conveys,* if not what he/she *intends'.* It is difficult to go beyond this, and know that a child at this stage intends a distinction between, say, 'calling' and 'greeting' (two of Dore's categories). Searching for one-to-one correlations between prosody and other aspects of the child's behaviour is unlikely to be successful, because the situations in which the language is used are often indeterminate, and the gestures and other kinesic features accompanying are usually ambiguous. There are also fewer pitch patterns available in a language than there are situations to be differentiated. It is possible that more detailed behavioural analyses will give grounds for optimism, but these ought to begin with the most concrete, determinate and replicable of situations (e.g. the daily, ritualized settings referred to in Bruner (1975) and R. Clark (1977)). Attempting to establish developmental speech act theories using as sole data a sample of unstructured, spontaneous play interaction is liable to produce a set of unfalsifiable interpretations about what went on. The intuitive plausibility of interactional approach to the study of utterances at this stage is thereby much reduced.

As an alternative to a social approach, it is possible to see these prosodic frames – or primitive tone-units, to use the terminology above – primarily as having a formal or grammatical role. Bruner, for instance (1975), at one point describes the function of these frames as 'place-holders': a mode of communication (such as a demand, or a question) is established using prosody, and primitive lexical items are then added. In a stretch of jargon, from around 12 months, it is often the case that one will recognize a word within the otherwise unintelligible utterance (cf. also several of the utterances in Keenan (1974)). And the transitional stage between one- and two-element sentences also contains uninterpretable phonetic forms which may perhaps be interpreted as remnants of a primitive prosodic frame (cf. Dore *et al.,* 1976; Bloom, 1973). Dore *et al.* (1976: p. 26) in fact suggest seven transitional stages at this point:

(i)   prosodically un-isolable, nonphonemic units ('prelinguistic babbling')
(ii) prosodically isolable, nonphonemic patterns ('prelinguistic jargon')
(iii) prosodically isolable, nonphonemic units ('phonetically consistent forms')
(iv) conventional phonemic units ('words')
(v)   word plus 'empty' phonetic forms in single prosodic pattern ('presyntactic devices')
(vi) chained conventional phonemic units forming separate intonation patterns ('successive single-word utterances')
(vii) prosodically complex patterns ('patterned speech')

The phonological and phonetic details of the development of these frames into determinate tone-units with a definable internal structure are, however, not at all clear, so little empirical work having been done. In particular, it is unclear whether tonicity or tonal contrastivity develops first, or whether they emerge simultaneously. The suggestion that the development is simultaneous is based on the observation that tonicity contrasts are early evidenced in jargon sequences (in which sequences of rhythms are built up which resemble the intonational norms of connected speech), whereas tone contrasts are early heard in the use of lexical items as single-word sentences. Menn, for instance, finds her child's semantic control of certain tones on 'babble carriers' and their contrastive use on words to be almost simultaneous (1976a: p. 186). If one ignores jargon, however, as being both less central to communicative development and less systematic in its patterning, then it would seem that tone develops before tonicity. Polysyllabic lexical items at this stage tend to have fixed tonic placement (Atkinson-King, 1973), though they may vary in terms of pitch direction and range, e.g. *dàda* (said as daddy enters the room), *dáda* (said when a noise was heard outside at the time when daddy was expected). Of the two, range seems to become contrastive before direction, especially high versus low, but also wide versus narrow. Most of the contrasts noted by Halliday (1975), for example, involve range rather than direction – mid versus low first, later high – e.g. the distinction between seeking and finding a person, signalled in his child by high versus mid–low range, from around 1;3. Eight pitch range variations are in fact used by Halliday in his transcription (very high, high, mid high, mid, mid low, low, wide, narrow), as well as four directions (level, fall, rise, rise–fall). The notion of high versus low register is discussed further in Konopczynski (1975), and a great deal of early child data can be interpreted in this way, e.g. in Keenan (1974) and Menn (1976a).

Based on Menn (1976a), Halliday (1975), and my own study, a tentative analysis of early tonal development – the contrasts involving both direction and range – emerged as follows:

(i) Initially, the child uses only *falling* patterns. Menn states that – except for imitations of adult rises – her child used rises on words only after these words were first used with falls (1976a: p. 195). Halliday's range contrasts are all on falling tones (1975: p. 148).

(ii) The first contrast is *falling* versus *level* tones (high level in Halliday (1975: pp. 150–1)), the level tone often being accompanied by other prosodic features, e.g. falsetto, length, loudness variations.

(iii) This is followed by *falling* versus *high rising* tones, the latter being used in a variety of contexts. Menn's special study of rising tones brought to light a large number of contexts between 1;1 and 1;4, including offering, requesting, attention-getting, and several 'curiosity' noises (e.g. when peering). Several of these notions, moreover, are complex – e.g. 'request' includes requests for help, recognition, permission, to obtain an object, etc., all of which are distinguishable in the situation (1976a: pp. 186ff., 198–9). The 'natural' distinction between fall and rise is characterized as 'demanding' versus 'requesting/offering' (p. 193). Halliday's high rises are first used in association with falls, as compound tones (1975: p. 151).

(iv) The next contrast is between *falling* and *high falling* tones, the latter especially in contexts of surprise, recognition, insistence, greetings. Halliday reports a high falling contrast between 1;1 and 1;3, and further distinguishes a mid fall.

(v) A contrast between *rising* and *high rising* tones follows: the Reading study suggested a particular incidence of high rises especially in playful, anticipatory contexts. Menn notes the latter mainly in 'intensification' contexts: the child gets no response to an utterance with a low rise, and repeats the utterance with a wider contour – the extra height, according to Menn, is the 'essential information-carrying feature' (1976a: pp. 193–4). Halliday's mid versus high rise emerges at 1;3 to 1;4.

(vi) The next contrast is between *falling* and *high rising–falling* tones, the latter being used in emphatic contexts, e.g. of achievement (e.g. *thêre,* as an extra brick is placed on a pile) or impressiveness (e.g. *bùs* vs. *bûs,* the former being used by one child studied to refer to 'any' vehicle, the latter to a *real* bus). Menn reports a mid–high–low contour at 1;4; Halliday has a similar contrast from as early as 1;1, but regularly from 1;3.

(vii) Next appears a contrast between *rising* and *falling–rising* tones, the latter especially in warning contexts, presumably reflecting the *be čareful* pattern common in adults; cf. Halliday (1975: p. 154), between 1;4 and 1;6.

(viii) Among later contrasts to appear is that between high and low rising–falling tones, especially in play contexts.

These features appear on isolated lexical items to begin with, and for a while cannot be distinguished from a prosodic idiom (i.e. an invariant prosodic pattern accompanying a fixed lexicogrammatical utterance, as in a nursery-rhyme line). Only later, when the same lexical item is used with different prosodic characteristics, can we talk with confidence about the patterns being systemic and productive. At this point, too, the tones come to be used in juxtaposition, producing the 'contrastive syntagmas' and prosodic 'substitution games' reported by Weir (1962), Carlson and Anisfeld (1969: p. 118), Keenan (1974: pp. 172, 178) and others.

We may compare, at this point, the conclusions of some recent work on the acquisition of tone languages: Hyman and Schuh (1974), Li and Thompson (1977) on Mandarin, and Tse (1978) on Cantonese. These studies agree that the tone system is learned in advance of the segmental, and that the period between 1;0 and 1;6 is especially important. There is also agreement that the earliest tonal contrast is one of range: high level versus low in the case of the Cantonese child, high level versus falling in the case of Mandarin. After this, rising and compound tones appear, with low rises appearing to be more difficult than high. Finally, at a much later stage, tone sandhi rules are acquired. In short, despite the very different linguistic status of lexical tone and intonation, there is a close parallel in the acquisition process. Some theoretical explanation for this, in terms of perceptual and production constraints, is provided in the above references.

Particularly with the intonational studies, one must remember that the situational interpretations used cannot be taken at face value. In much the same way as has been argued for syntax and segmental phonology (Howe, 1976; Lenneberg, 1976), it is necessary to free the mind from the constraints of adult language analyses, where situational notions such as 'question', 'request', 'permission', etc., are normal. As already agreed, it is insufficient to show that adults can differentiate these patterns and give them consistent interpretations, as several studies have succeeded in doing (e.g. Menyuk and Bernholtz, 1969): as Bloom points out (1973: p. 19), this is no evidence of contrastivity for the children. Detailed analysis of both the phonetic form and the accompanying context of utterance, moreover, readily brings to light instances of contrastivity which have no counterpart in the adult language. Halliday's child, for example, for a while used rising tones for all 'pragmatic' utterances (those requiring a response, in his terms), and falling tones for all 'mathetic' utterances (those not requiring a response (1975: pp. 29, 52)). Menn's child between 1;0 and 1;8 used a class of nonadult rising tones, e.g. between 1;1 and 1;3 he used a low rising tone (peak 450 Hz) to 'institute or maintain social interaction' (the 'adult-as-social-partner' function) and a high rising tone (peak 550 Hz) for 'instrumental use of the adult' ('obtaining an object or service') (1976a: p. 184). In the case of a child studied at Reading, the falling–rising tone was initially used only in smiling-face contexts, with a generally 'playful' meaning, and never to express doubt or opposition, as it frequently does, with frowning or neutral face, in adults.

These are all examples of a relatively familiar form conveying an unfamiliar function. The converse also applies. Throughout this stage of development, the range of phonetic exponents of the prosodic frame increases markedly, to include contrasts in loudness, duration, muscular tension and rhythmicality, not all of which are used in the adult language. At around 1 year, contrasts have been noted between loud and soft, drawled and short, tense and lax, and rhythmic and arhythmic utterances. Halliday (1975) noted, in addition to the pitch direction and range contrasts already described, several other prosodic and paralinguistic features: slow, long, short, loud; sung, squeak, frictional and glottalized. Contrastivity involving two or more prosodic parameters emerges, e.g. the use of a low, tense, soft, husky, spasmodic voice (a 'dirty snigger'). Carlson and Anisfeld (1969) distinguish loud and soft, and staccato and drawled articulations, amongst others. Other examples are the use of marked labialization, falsetto voice for whole utterances, and spasmodic articulations (lip trills, 'raspberries', etc.). It is regrettable that a more comprehensive phonetic description of this stage of development does not exist.

Stage V. Tonic contrastivity (or 'contrastive stress', as this area is often, misleadingly called) appears as sentences get more complex syntagmatically, with the appearance of two-word utterances at around 1;6 (Bloom, 1973; Clark *et al.,* 1974: p. 49).[2] The general developmental process seems clear. Lexical items which have appeared independently as single-element utterances, marked thus by pitch and pause, are brought into relationship (whether syntactic, semantic or collocational need not concern this chapter). At first, the lexical items retain their prosodic autonomy, with the pause between them becoming reduced, e.g. *daddy/ . garden/*. Often, long sequences of these items appear, especially repetitively, e.g. *dàddy/gàrden/ sèe/dáddy/dáddy/gàrden/dàddy/gàrden/sèe/*. (Such sequences of course defy analysis in terms of the usually cited grammatical–semantic relations.) The next step is the prosodic integration of sequences of items, usually two, into a single tone-unit. How general a process this is, is unclear, but in several English combinations studied, it was the case that one item became more prominent than the other; it was louder, and had an identifiable pitch movement. There was a rhythmic relationship between the items (anticipating isochrony), and intervening pauses became less likely in repeated versions of lexical sequences. This step is considered to be of central theoretical importance, because it is claimed to be the main means employed by the child for formally expressing grammatical–semantic relations within a sentence – 'the simple concatenation under one utterance contour of the words which interact to create a compositional meaning that is different from the meanings of the two words in sequence' (Brown, 1973: p. 182). Unfortunately, the process of concatenation is not so 'simple' as Brown suggests. All the following sequences have been observed (. = short pause, – and — = pauses of increasing length).

DÀDDY/ — ÈAT/	DÁDDY/ — ÈAT/
DÀDDY/ – ÈAT/	DÁDDY/ – ÈAT/
DÀDDY/ . ÈAT/	DÁDDY/ . ÈAT/

[2] A single-word polysyllable in principle allows for a contrast, e.g. DÀ*ddy* versus *dad*DÝ. There is no evidence of such forms at this stage (Atkinson-King, 1973).

DÀDDY/ÈAT/   DÁDDY/ÈAT/
daddy ÈAT   DÁDDY eat/
DÀDDY eat   DÁDDY EÀT/[3]

It is accordingly often difficult to decide whether we are dealing with one sentence or two – especially if the context is unclear, e.g. the child is looking at a picture. In the above example, the subject–verb relation, so 'obvious' to the adult observer, may motivate one set of decisions. However, in the following examples (each of which may be found with any of the above twelve patterns), the 'compositional meanings' are by no means so clear:

DÁDDY/CÀR/ (child is looking at daddy in a car)
DÁDDY/MÙMMY/ (child is looking at a photograph of both)
DÁDDY/NÒ/ (daddy has left the room)
DÁDDY/DÀDDY (said while being held by daddy)

Prosody, it seems, cannot be used by the analyst as a primitive discovery procedure for semantics or grammar – just as it cannot be in the adult language. It is one factor, and only one, in the simultaneity of language, behaviour, situation and adult interpretation which constitutes our analytic datum. In certain settings, prosody will be a primary determinant of meaning; in other settings, it will be discounted. The way in which these factors operate upon each other in these various settings is however by no means clear (see further, Eilers, 1975).

However it is arrived at, it is plain that around 1;6 in most children, two-element sentences within single prosodic contours are used, and tonic prominence is not random. In the adult language, the prominence in a sentence consisting of one tone-unit is in 90 per cent of cases on the last lexical item (Chomsky and Halle, 1968: pp. 17ff.; Crystal, 1969, 1975: ch. 1). Bringing the prominence forward within the tone-unit is possible, for both grammatical and semantic reasons. In the former case, one may be constrained by rules of cross-reference within the sentence (e.g. *Jack saw* JÍM/ *and* HÈ *said* . . ./); in the latter case, one may be making a (referential or personal) contrast between lexical items (e.g. *the* RÈD *dress/ not the* GRÉEN *dress/*). The presuppositions and attitudes of the speaker also promote marked tonicity (e.g. *I* WÀNT *a red dress/*, *he* ÌSN'T *coming/*). At the two- to three-word stage in children, there will obviously be little to note in relation to the prosodic marking of grammatical or lexical relations – such contrasts are likely to be more apparent when clause sequences appear. The most fruitful way of analysing variations in tonicity at the two-element stage, as a result, is therefore to establish a relationship between the changes in the

[3] A compound-tone unit, such as this, is in fact singled out by Du Preez (1974) as an important transitional stage.

child's environment and his prosody. Wieman (1976), for example, attempts to show that new information in a sentence affects tonic placement, whereas old information does not (cf. also Gruber, 1967). If a child is given a marble, he might say /got MÀRBLE/, but thereafter he is likely to say /sÈE marble/, because *marble* is old information the second time. It is not difficult to hear examples which do not confirm this hypothesis, however; and plainly, there are difficulties in working with notions of 'information', 'presupposition' and the like with young children. How does one know that what is 'new' to the observer, interpreting the situation in terms of adult expectancies, is also going to be new to the child? How does one establish the emergence of personal, attitudinal contrastivity, equivalent to the emphasis an adult might give, quite out of the blue, to the following sentence: *I* LÌKE *Bartok* (I've decided!) (Where it is not necessarily the case that this had previously been in doubt – 'I didn't know you DÌDN'T like him', one might respond).

3. Future research

Once grammatical patterns and lexical sets develop, then the tracing of prosodic patterns becomes a much more straightforward task. What is important here is for researchers to remember the important role prosody has in the adult language in relation to the delimitation and integration of such structures as relative clauses, co-ordination, adverbial positioning, direct/indirect-object marking, etc. (cf. Quirk *et al.,* 1972). Very little research seems to have been done on the later development of such patterns, but it is probable that this kind of learning continues until puberty (and, in terms of the development of one's stylistic control over prosody, e.g. in dramatic speaking, into adult life). Four research tasks suggest themselves:

(i) We need to follow the development of specific prosodic features in given grammatical lexical structures; questions have been quite well studied, but little else (cf. Menyuk, 1969; Wode, 1975).

(ii) Analogous studies are needed of the comprehension of these features. See, for example, Cruttenden's (1974) study of certain aspects of intonation in a restricted class of co-ordinated utterances (football results), which showed that awareness of the rules involved was in the process of development between 7 and 10 years; also the developing awareness of co-referential pronouns in certain co-ordination contexts, as in Chomsky (1969), Maratsos (1973).

(iii) Several sociolinguistic studies have now been made which show the importance of prosody in the variety of language adults use in talking to children (e.g. Blount and Padgug, 1977; Ferguson, 1977); there has however been much less discovered about whether children's prosody shows comparable 'exaggerated' characteristics, though this is a common impression. This is certainly the case, according to Weeks (1971), who reports the emergence of a wide range of nonsegmental characteristics with a variety of functions, in children between 1 and 5 years: exaggerated intonation, loudness, high pitch and 'clarification' (slower, carefully enunciated speech) characteristics were of particular importance. Likewise Sachs and Devin (1976) report the use of higher pitch and wider intonation patterns when 3 to 5 year old children talk to a baby or doll, or role-play a baby, but the relevant information here is introduced informally. In general, it is unclear how widespread a phenomenon this is.

(iv) Lastly, it is particularly important to focus on the specific role prosodic variables (especially tonicity) play in psycholinguistic experimentation, e.g. in experiments involving recall, paraphrase, comprehension, and imitation. Varying the prosodic input does influence response patterns, as has been shown both for normal children (e.g. Du Preez, 1974) and adults (e.g. Cutler, 1976), and in the context of disability, for example by Goodglass et al. (1967) and Stark et al.(1967). Du Preez, for instance, shows very plainly that children have a predilection to imitate tonic syllables: words occurring finally in a tone-unit are imitated first, and those earlier in the tone-unit are imitated only when they are given marked tonicity, the tonic apparently 'act [ing] as a signal to notice what to follow' (1974: p. 71). On the other hand, the common strategy of 'leaving the prosody out', by presenting a series of stimuli in identical tones of voice, involves assumptions which themselves require investigation (such homogeneous sequences are abnormal in parent–child interaction; how far might such unfamiliar stimuli affect responses?). Here, as in the other research areas listed, the problems are urgently in need of systematic investigation.

3. Early strategies for the perception and production of words and sounds

Paula Menyuk and Lise Menn

1. Introduction

Not until this past decade has the notion of the development of perceptual and productive phonemic contrasts during the so-called 'prelinguistic' period been taken seriously by linguists. Previously it was held that during this period infants engaged in playful sound-making. The sounds produced were held to be largely a product of the random exercise of the human infant's vocal mechanism for sound-making, and, therefore, the sounds produced were universal. Further, Jakobson (1968) suggested that there was a silent period between the production of babbled utterances and the production of first words. This silent period indicated the discontinuity between the two periods. Some behaviourist researchers, in contrast to this, suggested that this 'prelinguistic' period was one during which the child's perception and production of sound contrasts was 'shaped' by parental input to take on gradually the characteristics of the adult's perception and production of sounds in the native language. This shaping occurred through the principles of conditioning (i.e. observing stimulus–response–reward relations). These sound generalizations were then chunked into words and the words into sentences. The most perceptually salient sounds were those mastered earliest. Therefore, no discontinuity could be said to exist between so-called 'prelinguistic' and linguistic behaviour (Olmsted, 1966; Staats, 1967).

Recent data on the discrimination and production of speech sound contrasts by infants and studies of the behaviour of their caretakers over this period indicate that both these positions are questionable (Ferguson, 1976). That is, contrary to the Jakobsonian position, the child is actively engaging in linguistically important behaviour during the first year of life, not merely producing random vocalizations (Menyuk, 1971), and no silent period exists between babbling and first words. Contrary to the behaviourist position, there is no indication in the data that caretakers systematically isolate and contrast speech sound categories for their children or reward in some systematic way approximations to the contrasts presented. What does occur

49

is a reduction in the number of utterances that are long babbled strings, and an increase in the number of utterances that appear to be transitional between babble and words in various respects or that appear to have the characteristics of words. In this chapter we will review current data on the phonological linguistic abilities of children (not their morphological or syntactic abilities) during this reduction in babbling to beginning of word acquisition period. We will suggest some of the ways in which earlier developments are a prerequisite to development during this period and in what important ways developments during this period are markedly different from previous and later periods. We will discuss some differences in language processing strategies, perceptual and productive, used during this period as compared to others to account for the language behaviour observed. Finally, we will suggest some much needed research in order adequately to describe the development of phonemic contrasts during this period.

2. Perception of phonemic contrasts

It should be stated that although there are a number of studies of speech sound discrimination by the infant and by children approximately 3 or more years of age, there are comparatively fewer studies of this behaviour during the latter months of the first year of life until the beginning of the third year of life. This age period is the most pertinent one for our discussion. Therefore, any conclusions reached concerning the development of perception of phonemic contrasts during this period must be highly tentative. We shall review those studies which have direct bearing on the issue of developmental changes in speech processing before and during this period.

2.1. Development of speech processing

Before this period the infant gives evidence of a capacity to discriminate between speech sound syllabic segments that contrast the features of initial consonants (±voice as in /pa/ versus /ba/; ±coronal as in /ba/ versus /da/) or those that contrast the fundamental frequency pattern (steady versus rising or falling) (Morse, 1974). It has been suggested that the human infant is neurologically preprogrammed, in terms of feature detectors, to be sensitive to those acoustic features which mark speech sound differences (Eimas, 1974). Two studies have been carried out during the age period of 10 to 21 months (Shvachkin, 1973) and 17 to 22 months (Garnica, 1973) which test children's ability to learn to associate nonsense syllabic sequences, that differ only in one feature of initial consonants or of vowel and consonants,

with objects. These studies, unlike those of infant speech sound discrimination, indicate that there is a developmental progression in the child's ability
to make these distinctions. That is, some distinctions or feature contrasts are
learned before others by all children, and, therefore, presumably, some
distinctions are easier to detect than others in these association experiments.
In the infant discrimination studies no such developmental progression in
feature distinctions between consonants has been observed. Further, the
±voice discrimination found with infants as young as 1 month is the latest
distinction observed by children in the association studies. In addition, in the
Garnica study, unlike the Shvachkin study, it was found that although all
children learned some feature distinctions before others (i.e. a developmental progression was observed with all children) and that some feature distinctions were more likely to be acquired before others by the population as a
whole, there was considerable variation among the children in the exact
sequence of acquisition of differentiations.

In addition to the above experimental studies there have been some
detailed observational studies of the child's comprehension of words during
the latter part of the first year of life and the begininning of the second
(Lewis, 1963; Nakazima, 1970). These data indicate that the child understands a set of words in relation to certain contexts and expectations. That is,
the environment in terms of the communicative behaviour of the addressor
(gesture, facial expression and prosody of the utterance) plus the objects and
actions in the situation appear to cue the child to the content of the utterance
heard and to produce appropriate behaviour. Barton (1976) found that
children between the ages of 27 and 35 months were able to discriminate
between minimal pair words that contrasted most of the English late-
acquired speech sounds, including the ±voice contrast of stops in final
position (*log/lock*) and the two liquids in consonant clusters (*clown/crown*).
He noted, however, a strong response bias among these children in favour of
familiar words. Error rates were highest when both the words in a pair were
unfamiliar. These findings, Barton argues, indicate that studies of phonemic
contrast acquisition using nonsense syllable stimuli probably underestimate
children's actual ability to discriminate between minimal pair words.

Finally, it has been suggested, although not tested, that by the time the
child is well into the word production period her perceptual categorizations
are those of adult surface phonemic forms (Smith, 1973). Another suggestion is that the child has perceptually categorized the phonological segments
in the word as a sequence of identified segments (equal to those of the adult)
and unidentified noises (Ingram, 1974a), or as Wilbur (in press) suggests,
partially identified noises. Both these suggestions concerning perceptual
categorizations are based on what the child produces en route to adult-like

production of words and on the child's ability to distinguish similar sounding words in discourse. Menn (1976a) argues for the same position as Wilbur on the ground that avoidance and exploitation strategies (see section 3.4 on the origin of phonological rules) could not be used by children under 24 months of age unless they were able to differentiate between the favoured and disfavoured sounds. It seems entirely reasonable to suppose that perceptual representations underlie productive realizations. The problems are the differing interpretations of perceptual representations that experimenters give based upon productive data, and the lack of data on the relation between perception and production.

It should be clear by now that not only have the studies of the development of perception of phonemic contrasts during this period been few in number but, also, that the data base on which conclusions are drawn are quite varied in nature; observation versus experiment, nonsense versus real words, perception versus production. The above pieces of evidence indicate the following: the human infant at age 1 month is capable of discriminating between some acoustic parameters that mark speech sound differences; by age 9 to 13 months the infant appears to be able to comprehend the meaning of phonological sequences in certain contexts, that is, gestalt comprehension of phonological sequence plus context rather than phonological differentiation of sequences; the child is able to learn to associate objects and nonsense syllables that contrast many of the initial consonant features during the period of 10 to 22 months; the child can distinguish between minimal pair words that contain most English singleton phonological contrasts by 35 months. Added to these findings are those which indicate that there are individual differences among children in the sequence in which they observe phonemic contrasts in the abstract domain of nonsense syllables. Infants discriminate between a feature that the child has difficulty in discriminating between (±voice). Familiarity of lexical items plays a role in the ability to observe phonemic contrasts. If this is the case one might assume there are individual differences in the sequence of development of contrasts observed in words since different children might be exposed to different sets of lexical items with varying frequency.

Although the data are sparse and also confusing, if we try to outline what the child does developmentally in order to recognize words and begin to talk in a manner similar to an adult the following seems to occur. First, shortly after birth, the child distinguishes between sound patterns that come from different sources: human versus other animate and inanimate objects, or, in other words, displays the ability to differentiate between speech and non-speech. The child at this time is also capable of discriminating between speech sound categories and of producing phonated sounds. Second, the child observes recurring patterns in human sound sequences and recurring patterns in nonlinguistic events. Third, the child recognizes that recurring patterns in human sound sequences occur in conjunction with recurring events, and learns to re-produce aspects of these sound patterns in certain specific situations. During this period acoustic patterns of human sound sequences may be stored as wholes or gestalts just as visual or motor patterns may be stored as gestalts. No further analysis of the dimensions of the acoustic, visual or motor image occurs. Fourth, the child begins to analyse the contents of these speech sound patterns and the situations in which they are produced. The analyses of the speech sound sequence are translated into articulatory gestures. Each of these developmental changes on the way to listening and speaking like an adult reflects developmental changes in the competences available to the child for analysing and translating the phonology of the language, analysing and translating recurring nonlinguistic events and, finally, relating the two.

Much of what occurs phonologically during the first year of life appears to be based on the biological readiness of the human infant to acquire language. Thus, at a very early period of development the infant behaves differentially to signals that are human speech or speech-like as compared to those that are not. Also at a very early age the infant displays sensitivity to and can discriminate between speech signals on the basis of acoustic parameters that the adult also uses to discriminate between speech signals. We do not have a complete picture of what these parameters are but they appear to include voicing onset time, locus of second formant transition and changes in fundamental frequency pattern. Differences in vocalization patterns occur during this early period which indicate that there is a sequence in the production of phonological segments which may, in part, be accounted for by increasing control of the output of the vocal mechanism. It is also during this period that the infant indicates discrimination between different prosodic patterns, produces babbled strings that have different prosodic patterns, and appears to categorize these patterns at least in terms of affective communicative intent. In summary, the child during this period can discriminate between sounds, produce syllabic strings that are marked prosodically and use prosodic patterns in communication. All of these abilities seem necessary prerequisites to listening and speaking like an adult. However, it does not seem to be the case that the capacity to discriminate between segments *on the basis of feature distinctions* or to produce the phonological segments in the language on this basis is used in the beginning to recognize and reproduce recurrent phonological sequences.

Given the evidence of the studies we have reviewed on the development of perception of phonemic contrasts, some basis other than the distinctive feature appears to be used initially. Although the distinctive feature has long been held to be the basis of speech sound discrimination in both children (Menyuk, 1971) and adults (Miller and Nicely, 1955; Wickelgren, 1966), the role of the distinctive feature in speech perception (storage and retrieval of phonological information) has been questioned. Data on response time in a recognition task indicate that the syllable is much more accessible to the adult perceiver than the segment and feature. The latter are focused upon with greater delay. This also appears to be the case developmentally.

At the end of the first year of life or the beginning of the second children more frequently select to listen to word length utterances than to connected speech and more frequently produce word length utterances or so-called 'jargon' phrases than babbled strings (Menyuk, 1972). During the transition from babbled utterances to word approximations or compressed sentences (Branigan, 1977) the child appears to recognize most recurring patterns in sound sequences only in conjunction with specific events. Some exceptions to this are the child's own name or the word *no* which are repeated very frequently in varying contexts. Only later does the child indicate recognition of sound patterns in a variety of situations. Thus, the word, or phrase, or sentence, depending on the chunking strategy of the child, appears to be initially stored as phonological sequence plus situation. Later the child may recognize the word in a variety of situations and still later when it is presented in isolation. It is suggested that phonological contrasts are first observed between words, then syllables and finally in terms of distinctive feature contrasts between segments.

Evidence for syllabic decoding as preliminary to feature analysis has been suggested by several researchers and is reviewed in Menyuk (1972, 1976). The role of the syllable in generative phonology has recently been explored (Kahn, 1976) and substantial evidence is given that the syllable is a necessary element in phonological descriptions that claim psychological reality. Further, there is now evidence of distinct acoustic patterns of formant transitions from stop Cs to V (rising transitions, or falling transitions, or both rising and falling) and these may form the basis of perceptual categorizations (Stevens, 1972). Thus, resolution of a category requires information that exceeds the segment or features of a segment. (See also Fujimura and Lovins, 1978.)

However, analysis in terms of the contrastive features of syllables probably does not occur at the initial stages of this period of development. We would suggest, rather, with Ferguson and Farwell (1975), that words are contrasted and identified as wholes, and, indeed, are identified not only in terms of a phonological event but, also, in terms of the context in which they occur. Thus, *cup* in the child's lexicon may at the beginning stages of its identification represent only the cup that he drinks milk from and not any cup in the environment. Is it feasible to suggest storage of phonological contrasts in terms of whole words plus meaning at this initial period? Certainly the productive lexicon of the child is small at the beginning of the word production period. Children in one sample population achieved a lexicon of fifty spoken words at a mean age of 19·6 months (Nelson, 1973b). How far the recognition vocabulary of children exceeds their spoken vocabulary when it consists of one to ten words is not clear, but one would assume by not too great an amount for storage of words as wholes. However, it is also clearly the case that this strategy will not carry the child too far as the lexicon increases.

At this point, it is suggested, the word is analysed in terms of syllabic features. Since a great many of the words presented to the child are composed of one syllable (*shoe, boat*) or reduplication of syllables (*papa, momma*) or syllable plus diminutive (*doggie, kittie*), use of the syllable as a data base for determining contrasts does not stretch the child's ability to break up words (and phrases) – or the imagination – too far. Does this mean that the distinctive features of sound segments cannot be employed by the child? The evidence of minimal pair studies indicates that these contrastive elements can be used in test circumstances by the child, but with effort and training. That is, the distinction is not available to the child. The following is an outline of the developmental changes in speech processing proposed.

1. Readiness in processing speech
   A. Distinction between speech and nonspeech
   B. Discrimination between speech sound categories and prosodic patterns
   C. Production of CV sequences marked prosodically
2. Analysis of meaningful unit(s)
   A. Phonological sequence and situation
   B. Phonological analysis and situational analysis
   C. Analysis of syllabic features of phonological sequences
   D. Analysis of distinctive feature content of sequences

2.2 Processing strategies

The above conclusions are highly tentative and are based on the slim data of studies of perception during this period, the early production of phonological sequences, some notions about the course of development in all aspects of the language which seems to proceed from generalization to differentiation to abstract generalization, and the speech perception strategies of adults. The data indicate that the hierarchy in speech perception by adults is that represented by steps 2B, C and D above. The distinction between young children and adults is that the adult unlike the child (a) has easy access to all steps, and (b) has the ability to keep all aspects simultaneously in mind during processing (Menyuk, 1977).

Two models of processing, among others, have been discussed in the literature on adult perception of speech. One is analysis by synthesis and the other is synthesis by analysis (Fodor *et al.*, 1974). If the synthesis by analysis strategy is employed by the child then it might be the case that phonemic contrasts are categorized first in terms of feature contrasts or bundles of features of segments and then that bundles of features are chunked together for recognition of words. An analysis by synthesis strategy would lead to determination of the largest meaningful unit and then further analysis of this unit in terms of its content and context of occurrence. This latter strategy seems to account for the data much more adequately than the former. We further suggest that the first subanalysis in terms of acquisition of phonemic contrasts is the syllable. As we have stated this is just a suggestion. There are some data, however, which bear on the question of whether or not early analysis is in terms of features. Barton (1976) investigated the ability of children age 20 to 24 months correctly to discriminate between words which contrasted initial stop voicing (*pear/bear, coat/goat*). He found that although most of the children were able to do it, many of them first required considerable pre-training. Thus, even though infants are capable of discriminating between minimal pairs of syllables on the basis of voicing onset time, this strategy is not spontaneously used by young children when the domain of analysis is the word. Under these conditions children seem initially to use some lexical look-up procedure to determine similarity or difference (i.e. the meaning) *before* they attempt a phonological analysis. Adults apparently do the same (see Brown and Hildum, 1956). The fact that some children preserve the initial voicing distinction in their *production* of words with initial stops (Hildegard Leopold, for example), long before children can be shown to observe this distinction in nonsense syllables or words, need not imply that the perceived distinction is on the basis of the ±voice distinction of segments but, rather, that these lexical items might be stored and retrieved as unsegmented wholes.

Can one speak of *the* development of the perception of phonemic contrasts or a universal sequence of development? Although an analysis by synthesis strategy might be universally employed by all children there are several factors which might lead to individual differences in the sequence of development. A factor that was touched upon previously is the chunking strategy of the child. Some children appear to chunk together larger units than words (compressed sentences) and work on those for further analysis, whereas others work on words (Branigan, 1977). These two different strategies would obviously lead to differences in sequence of acquisition of phonemic contrasts. A second factor is lexical repertoire. If it is the case that a lexical look-up procedure is used in minimal pair discrimination tasks before further analysis, as it is by adults, then those pairs that contain familiar lexical items would be distinguished before those that do not. Since children will vary to some exent in their lexical repertoires individual differences will be observed.

We are still left with trying to account for *both* universals and individual differences in studies of discrimination of minimal pair words and nonsense syllables. We will make the following, again tentative, suggestion. First, perceptual saliency of phonemic contrasts of the syllable may account for whatever universality exists in the order of phonemic distinctions observed. Thus, for example, the distinction between /la/ versus /wa/ might be less perceptually salient than /ga/ versus /da/ because of the nature of the acoustic differences between the pairs. However, this may only be the case with nonsense syllables. In attempting to determine perceptual saliency of contrastive syllables one would need to take into account different vowel contexts (i.e. co-articulation effects on acoustic outputs) and this has not systematically been done. Individual differences in minimal pair nonsense syllable tasks might be accounted for by the child attempting to use a strategy of analogy for recall. That is, when attempting to determine the difference between and to recall nonsense syllables reference might be made to lexical items that are similar. No attempt has been made to probe for the strategies used by children in these experiments by, for example, asking them what they have done or providing known word analogies and examining rate of acquisition of distinctions under the latter circumstances.

Still another factor which may lead to individual differences in sequence of development of phonemic contrasts is the state of knowledge of the child at the time of sampling. Just as production of a phonemic distinction in a particular case might not imply an awareness of the phonemic status of the contrast involved but only of the difference between the particular words, so some phonemic contrasts that are collapsed by the child in production might co-exist with an awareness of distinctions (Eilers and Oller, 1976). Since different children may be working on different problems at different times in the acquisition of phonemic contrasts they may be *attending* to different aspects of the phonological system and, therefore, be more or less aware of certain contrasts at given times. Experiments systematically examining the relation between perception and production of phonemic contrasts in the same children in the domain of words over this developmental period need to be carried out.

These comments are being made to suggest that choice of stimuli in any study of the perception of phonemic contrasts (nonsense versus real sequences, consonantal plus vowel composition of sequences) and the state of knowledge of the child (lexical repertoire, productive strategies) may all affect the child's perceptual processing of 'phonemic' contrasts, and, thus, the competence the child displays at any given time.

3. Production of phonemic contrasts

A traditional question in the study of child language has been: 'when does the average child acquire each of the phonemes of English?' Years of data-gathering and advances in linguistic theory have shown that while this question can be given rough normative answers, it is simply the wrong question to ask if we want to understand the way in which an individual develops the ability to pronounce the words of his/her language. We do not have the space to expose all the false assumptions that make this a bad question, but we will begin this section by discussing two of the important ones.

The first is that normal children resemble one another sufficiently in acquisition of phonology that information about the 'average' child will predict the development of the individual. This is not the case. Normal children can vary widely in the age at which they become able to produce the various sounds of English, and in the order in which they acquire the ability to produce each of those sounds. A second false assumption is that a 'phoneme' is a well-defined object for the purpose of study of acquisition of phonology. Leaving aside the lively and highly relevant controversy about the nature of the phoneme within linguistic theory, it is still clear that the phoneme is not a 'unit' for acquisition. There are two important groups of facts which contradict this false assumption. The phoneme does not generally correspond to a single phonetic target, or to targets which are grouped in similar ways for all phonemes. In English, some phonemes are represented by single, narrowly defined phonetic targets (/f/ seems to be an example) while others have allophones which vary greatly in sound. Furthermore, these allophones may be in free variation (usually subject to positional restriction: e.g. 'optional' use of released or unreleased final stops), stylistic variation, or variation conditioned by neighbouring sounds (palatal pronunciation of /t, d/ before /r/). What degree of mastery of allophonic variation should then be counted as 'acquisition'?

Besides the variation in the number and diversity of the target phones that 'belong' to a phoneme, there is considerable variation in the difficulty that each phone presents to the child depending on the neighbouring sounds in the word in which it occurs and on its position in the word. Even if it is the case that there is a single target phone /f/, for example, which is essentially invariant across context in the adult language, children will still have differing degrees of difficulty in producing it depending on such factors as whether it occurs initially, medially or finally, whether it is part of a cluster, and what other consonants occur in the word. While some of these factors have been known and taken account of in the literature for a long time (Olmsted, 1971; Templin, 1966), others have been brought out only in recent work. For example, it seems that position in a word affects the difficulty of different sounds differently; fricatives are sometimes acquired first in final position, while stops fare best in initial position for most children. It should however be remembered that individual variation across children may affect these general tendencies in any particular case.

It is now known, furthermore, that if there are two consonants within the same word which are formed with different positions of articulation, the combination presents problems which neither consonant alone would present. (See Vihman (1978) for a recent review of the literature on this topic.) A child who can say *do* and *egg* correctly may still say [gɔg], [dɔ], [dɔd], or possibly even [ɔg] for *dog* in the earlier stages of the acquisition of phonology. Other contextual effects are also found in individual children's speech; many of them are idiosyncratic phonotactic rules, but even these fall into general groups from which we can make generalizations about how the context of a phone affects its difficulty. Many such rules are exemplified in chapter 7 below. Altogether, it has become clear that the Jakobson picture of successive splitting-off of contrasts and the structuralist model of the acquisition of phonemes are inadequate as theories of the acquisition of the ability to produce the phonemes of one's language. At this point there is no mature theory to replace them, so we will attempt, instead, to show something of the depth and richness of the phenomena which such a theory will be called on to explain.

It is useful to begin with a task analysis of what is involved in the acquisition of phonology, for in that way our thinking about it is less apt to be constrained by existing theory. To even begin to talk, a child must be able to say a recognizable word at an appropriate time. Furthermore he or she must produce it, not as a solo game or in sociable imitation, but spontaneously, when it is socially and/or pragmatically opportune: *bye-bye* at parting, *cookie* when a cookie is really desired and when there is someone around who might be able to produce a cookie. To do this requires the ability to recall both sound and meaning, and the ability to produce some approximation of the sound, all within a few seconds' time.

If instead of looking at the skilled language-user we focus on the develop-

ment of language production in children, we can construct the following rough sequential task analysis:
Production tasks:
(i)   to learn to produce a variety of vocal sounds
(ii) to learn to produce vocal sound patterns so that they more or less match sounds which are heard (imitation)
(iii) to learn to remember certain sound patterns well enough to produce them without just having heard them (delayed imitation)
(iv) to learn to produce specific sound patterns in situations where they have been produced by others or by oneself in the past (situation-bound word use, to be discussed below as 'signalling' use of words)
(v)   to become able to produce a word in a novel setting as a means to an end (beginning of 'symbolic' use of words – see below)

Each of these tasks is first accomplished by a child for just a few sounds or sound patterns. Furthermore, wherever we have evidence of what the child is going through, we find that it is carried out laboriously and clumsily. Then, for each task level, greater degrees of skill develop. Instead of being able to handle only one or two special cases, the child develops routines which become both more general and more automatic. For example, on task level (iv) a child at a certain age may be able to imitate one or two well-known sound patterns, but at a later time he/she may be able to imitate a large variety of unfamiliar words: some general routines for transducing 'what one hears' to 'what one says' have been developed during the elapsed time. It should be noted that the existence of such routines on level (ii) (imitation) carries no implication that any general routines have been developed on the next level (delayed imitation). That is, a child who can imitate new words with a particular degree of skill may be unable to produce them as well after a time lapse.

In this section we will survey the following issues concerning the beginning of children's language use:
1. What is the relationship between babbling and speech?
2. What type of linguistic analysis is appropriate for early speech?
3. What is the origin and the nature of rules of child phonology?

3.1. Transition from babbling to speech

During this period, the child continues to learn to produce vocal sound (task i), improves his/her ability to imitate and to imitate with delay (tasks ii and iii), begins and becomes adept at learning to 'signal' with particular words (task iv), and, finally, starts to use a few words in a symbolic way (task vi), thus making the major cognitive breakthrough required of the early period of language. Detailed longitudinal studies show that the boundary between late babble and speech is in general a fuzzy one. It is not merely that there is normally a temporal overlap between what were once thought to be disjoint stages of 'prespeech' and 'speech'. The fuzziness is much more serious than that. There are also individual recurrent entities in a child's production that cannot be classified unequivocally as either 'babble' or 'speech', and in some children these forms are quite prominent. They seem to occupy a pivotal position in language development in such children, and careful consideration of their form and function illuminates the nature of the transition from babble to speech in the general case.

Some of these transitional items, which we shall refer to as proto-words (see Menn, 1976a) are well-defined meaningful sound patterns that are apparently not modelled on any adult word; as their functioning becomes more word-like, in ways which we shall discuss below, they can be regarded as words invented by the child (see especially Halliday, 1975). Other proto-words are in origin adult words which have become subjects for the child's sound play. Menn's subject Jacob (1976a) was fond of wandering about producing vocal variations on two themes, his name and the word *okay*. Other transitional items, not counted as proto-words because they lack identifiable articulated sounds that recur across instances, are the jargon stretches which are uttered with communicative intent and with eye contact, gesture and intonation patterns appropriate to that intent (Menn and Haselkorn, 1977). However, in some children, these jargon stretches have 'real' words embedded in them (Branigan, 1977; Jones, 1967). Thus, proto-words, words and jargon stretches containing real words can all be produced during the same period of development.

We can find, among proto-words, phonologically interesting kinds of variability across instances (tokens) which would be anomalies from the adult point of view. These anomalous variations are very important for constructing a model for the acquisition of phonology, because they help us see more clearly what it is the child needs to learn and to look at it in a way less coloured by our knowledge of mature linguistic behaviour. Menn's Jacob had two prominent proto-words, one modelled on the adult word *thank-you* and the other apparently his own creation, which showed very striking variation across tokens. Within his lexicon, these were among the most variable items, but he had less variable items and items that were produced without much variation present during the same period. [ioio], as we referred to it, appeared randomly in a great variety of phonetic shapes which can be unified by saying that Jacob was varying the timing of front–back articulations against the timing of lowering and raising the tongue. Depending on the way in which he co-ordinated these orthogonal gestures, his output was variously heard as [ioio], [wiʌwio], [wejaweja], [iʌiʌiʌ], [ajaj], [ajʌajʌ], etc. Division of these sequences into 'phones' obscures the simple unity of the underlying pattern which we describe in words and which also can be captured within the recently developed formalism of autosegmental phonology (Clements, 1976; Goldsmith, 1976; Menn, 1978).

Thank you also exhibited wild variations on an underlying pattern. Unlike [ioio] it can be segmented into a CVCV sequence without violence, but there was evidence that the two consonants formed a prosodic unit of a peculiar kind: each could appear as virtually any nonlabial stop, from dental to velar (including palatal); the medial one usually but not always voiced, the initial one voiced. The vowels were also variable; the first one was usually less back than the second. Examples include [geika], [dɛjdʌ], [gigu], [gaita], [dɛgʌ], and a few with vocalic [m] in place of the second vowel.

These variations are explained in terms of the problems posed by the adult model word, which has neither vowel nor consonant harmony and was Jacob's first word; the point of the example is not that the reason for Jacob's treatment of it is hard to find, but that the notation and conceptualization of a traditional theory are inadequate to the description. One does much better in this case to work with prosodic units and underspecified (archiphonemic) elements. Here we have been focusing on phonological rather than semantic–functional aspects of the transition from babbling to speech. The two, however, are richly connected (again, see Halliday, 1975) and therefore, even in a chapter on the acquisition of phonology there are aspects of semantic–pragmatic development which it is not possible to leave out.

The major thread in semantic–pragmatic development during the transition from babbling to speech is the gradual freeing-up of proto-words from the narrow pragmatic circumstances in which they almost always first appear. Halliday (1975) and Clumeck (1977), among others, concur with Menn and Haselkorn (1977) in finding that the first word-like objects, whether self-created or derived from an adult model, are tightly bound to specific functions – some accompany particular actions, some are greetings or farewells, some accompany pointing, some are used as labels, others as demands. They are, at this early stage, essentially vocal signals, and may be compared to adult words which have very limited pragmatic range, like greetings and cries of *ouch*. The meanings of such items, for both adult and child, are best characterized as 'what you say when you do X'.

Proto-words do not remain restricted in this fashion, however, for more than a few months. They develop what is called 'symbolic autonomy' – the potential for being used for a variety of ends. Even the most impoverished of the adult language (e.g. *ouch*) has some degree of symbolic autonomy, for an adult can use it in reporting what he/she or another said as well as when actually communicating present pain. A child's vocable has developed symbolic autonomy if he/she can use it for a variety of pragmatic ends. For example, children may start by using *hello* only as 'what you say when you pick up a telephone', and then develop the ability to use it (along with gesture) as a request to get an adult to talk on a toy telephone. Or, a word like *down* or *boom* may begin as action accompaniment to dropping, throwing, or pushing objects over, and then later be used to describe the fall of an object or to request permission to cause an object to fall. As a proto-word develops the full degree of symbolic autonomy possessed by a word of the adult language, it must become able to be used with a variety of intonations – rising, falling, and more complex contours as well. In this way, the semantic–pragmatic development is interwoven with the suprasegmental aspect of phonological development.

3.2 Determining appropriate modes of analysis for early speech

We are compelled to realize that near the onset of speech production there is some word-by-word learning to pronounce (probably different amounts for different children) in which the whole word is an indivisible target. To such words, our familiar notions of 'phone' and 'phoneme' do not apply, for these are entities that are *comparable across words*. Note that even in adult language, lexical (word-by-word) specification of sounds is occasionally necessary, although it is a marginal phenomenon. For example, the phonetic variability of the vowel in *no* is much greater than the variability of the vowel in the word *know* (as a main verb) and quite distinct from the great range of the 'same' vowel in the phrase *you know*. In such a state of affairs, a feature bundle (phonemic) specification of a vowel is inadequate; lexical (word-particular) specification is necessary.

Near the onset of speech, we may find many forms which similarly do not decompose into entities which are comparable across words. A particular child may say one adult /t/-initial word with a [t] and vary between a [t] and a [d] for others. He may produce the vowel of one word rather stably and the vowel of a similar word with a great deal of variation. Some proto-words, like [ioio] and *thank you* of the previous section may be very poorly controlled. Phonological idioms occur. Moskowitz (1970) introduced this term to describe occasional words which are atypical of a particular child's output in being very close approximations of an adult model word which contains sounds or sound patterns that the child in question cannot usually produce. If we take the position that the child's first pass at phonological analysis takes the word or the syllable as an atomic unit, then at some point a subdivision of these atomic long units must begin. (This is not to imply either that it is necessarily carried to a full segmentation or that long hierarchical units have no role to play in adult language.) Given what we know of other unevennesses in language development, the analysis underlying production probably proceeds by slow steps and leaves some items unanalysed. The problem with trying to explore this hypothesis, of course, is that since analysis is a matter of internal organization and reorganization of information, it may show few external symptoms while it is in progress.

3.3 Distinguishing between phonetics and phonemics in production

At some point, we have inferred, phonetic and phonemic analysis across words begins, quite possibly via an intermediate stage where the atomic units are syllable-length or consist of syllable-onset units and syllable-nucleus-plus-coda units. It is still impossible with present techniques to assess the course of development of the child's ability to subdivide and compare words in perception. We can, however, work out some of the aspects of this transition for speech production, the beginning of the acquisition of target phones and the acquisition of phonemic contrast in production. The process of bringing articulation of segments under control in the production of a variety of words, and the intertwined but distinct process of constructing the set of phonological oppositions of a language, both take place gradually. The two developments are not always in step with one another. For example, a child who cannot yet produce the consonant clusters /sn/, /sm/ may represent them by [hn], [hm] or by the voiceless nasals N,M. The *contrast* between the singleton nasals and the /s/+nasal clusters is preserved, but the articulation is incorrect, and the child's apparent target has only some of the features of the adult cluster. Assuming the child's production of these incorrect clusters is stable, then both contrast and control are good, but the target is wrong.

Another kind of developmental pattern occurs when the child had difficulty in controlling his production of similar sounds, perhaps to the extent that two phones which are distinct in the adult language seem to be confused, and yet an analysis of the child's error patterns reveals that he is indeed aiming at distinct and appropriate targets. Menn's Jacob, for example, for several weeks (1;7:29 to 1;8:22) had great difficulty with /ɔ/. In the speech around him, this phoneme had two allophones, a higher and more rounded one before /r/ and a lower, more centralized one in other environments. Even though Jacob seldom hit either of these targets correctly, producing [o], [u], [a], [ɔ] and [æ] during the weeks in question, a plot of his attempts at *door, more, horsie* as compared with *on, off* shows that the two allophones were distinct targets (see figure 1), more or less accurately located in the vowel space, and also distinct from the other vowels with which they overlapped in production. Contrast with other phonemes was correct, and so was location of phonetic target, but control, also a phonetic matter, lagged behind.

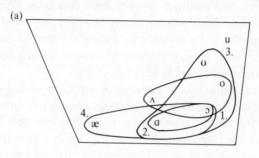

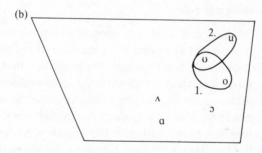

Figure 1. Distribution of attempts by subject to produce [ɔʷ] and [ɔ] during 21st month

(a)   ɔ
1. *on,* 8 tokens
2. *off,* 4 tokens
3. *ball,* 16 tokens
4. *walk,* 3 tokens

(b)   ɔʷ
1. *more,* 2 tokens
2. *door,* 6 tokens

On the other hand, a child may control a sound nicely, and yet fail to preserve the contrast between that sound and similar sounds. This is the commonly reported case, as for example when a well-articulated [ts] is used to represent /c/ and /ts/, or /f/ and /p/ are rendered by a clear [p]. It should be added that recent instrumental results, such as those of Chaney (1978) and Macken and Barton (1980) are likely to force re-examination of all conclusions when those conclusions are of the form 'child X does not make the distinction between phones *a* and *b*' or 'child X has a target identical with adult target *c'*. These instrumental studies indicated that some children make reliable productive distinctions which adults cannot hear. Macken and Barton, for example, have shown in four children followed over a number of months that the first stage of acquisition of initial voicing contrast in English is the maintenance of a contrast imperceptible to adults. During this stage the voicing onset time distribution for initial C+voice targets and C−voice targets were distinct, but the voice onset time means for the +voice and for the −voice targets lay quite close together and both within the range perceived by English-speaking adults as voiced (short lag).

It should be noted that this result alone is sufficient to make an external-reward theory of the acquisition of phonology completely untenable. Adults cannot 'shape' the child's pronunciations to produce this imperceptible differentiation of, say, *big* from *pig*, since they cannot hear the differences. The child himself must be somehow making the differentiation in the attempt to match the adult model.

3.4 Origin of phonological rules

David Ingram (1976a) suggests that at or around a certain point in a child's speaking-life, he gets control of a system for learning to say most one- and two-syllable adult words on a few hearings. We might say that at this point the child has developed a method for transducing some auditory patterns to sequences of articulatory gestures. Some of these transductions result in the production of relatively faithful renditions of the model word, while others result in considerable distortion. Although the notion needs some elaboration (see Ingram, 1974a, chapter 7 below; Kiparsky and Menn, 1977; Menn, 1978), a child's transduction system for getting from model to production is essentially his set of child-phonology rules. Notice that this formulation treats /a/→ [a] as a rule, just as much as /f/→ [p]; ways-of-saying-sounds which are accurate and ways-of-saying-sounds which are inaccurate, we hold, are the same sort of thing for the child. Both the accurate rules and the inaccurate ones may change as the child develops.

Ingram has noted that in several cases, children's rate of acquisition has taken a rapid upswing at the point where about fifty words have been acquired; before that time, 'the child does not seem to have a productive sound system' (1976a: p. 22) – or, in our terms, a transduction system. He therefore refers to it as the 'period of the first 50 words'. However, the '50' is only an approximation (Nelson (1973b), for example, observed such an upswing in many of her sixteen cases, but usually somewhat before fifty words were attested), so we prefer to call this early period the 'exploratory period'. The upswing which Ingram describes is in some cases a very well-defined occurrence, appearing in one such case (Menn, 1971) to be the consequence of the invention of a single powerful simplifying rule. On the other hand, the transition from the exploratory period to the following period (Ingram's 'period of simple morphemes') may happen much more diffusely. Jacob, who used few simplifying rules, still showed a modest rate of output vocabulary growth at eighty words, and could not have been said to have passed from a rule-inventing 'stage' to a rapid-acquisition 'stage'.

This brings us to the necessity of dealing with individual strategies during the exploratory period. There are two groups of strategies which have been described in the literature. The first group may be characterized as *selection* strategies. These have been identified as *avoidance* and *exploitation.*

Normal children must have some kind of knowledge of the phonetic quality of their own productions, or they would never learn to talk. Without auditory feedback they would, of course, be in the same situation as deaf children, who have to rely on signals from others as to whether they have got a word right. However, this knowledge derived from auditory feedback need not be conscious. Indeed, one way to account for children's receptive behaviour when adults imitate their mismatches ('I didn't say *fiss,* I said *fisss*!) has been to assume that children's conscious ability to monitor their own productions is faulty, and that a child who says [gʌk] for *truck* or [beit] for *plate* is unaware of doing so. In general, this did seem to be the case. It seemed far-fetched to credit any under 2 year old with enough metalinguistic awareness to choose to attempt or not to attempt words of the adult language on the ground of the sounds they contained. However, it has recently been shown that some beginning speakers do in fact behave in just this fashion; they select which words to try on phonetic grounds. In cases of avoidance, the child avoids attempting to say words containing certain sounds; in cases of exploitation, the child shows a great bias towards words with a particular sound or natural class of sounds and produces that set of sounds rather well. These phenomena may indeed be common, but simply hard to document, because in order to prove that a child is behaving in such a fashion, one needs a corpus large enough to be sure that the observed biases of distribution are not random. The case for avoidance is strengthened if it can be shown that the child understands a fair number of words containing the sound which she fails to say (Farwell, 1976; Ferguson and Farwell, 1975; Menn, 1976b).

Avoidance is the antithesis of rule formation, of course, while exploitation is an example of the use of nondistorting rules (/a/→[a]-type). Much more familiar, since they are more obvious in operation, are rules which yield mismatches between the model word and the child word. These rules are the result of the other group of strategies, the *modification* strategies.

Either some children are not very aware of which sounds they can match, or they want to talk so badly that mismatches are not important to them. During the exploratory period, many children, perhaps most, have created a fairly large set of child-phonology rules, which may be regarded as highly systematic routines for reducing the complexity of adult words to a pronounceable level. In chapter 7 below Ingram will discuss such rule systems in detail; here we will discuss the available evidence on how such rule systems arise in the first place.

The child's earliest attempts at adult words usually do not show such rules operating. Instead, rules gradually come into play after the first few adult-modelled words are established, either by a process of the assimilation of a new adult word to forms which the child has already learned to say or by the collapse of two similar-sounding words towards one another. An excellent example of the first type of rule formation is given by Vihman (1976) for a child learning Estonian as her first language. This child initially showed a great deal of selectivity in her production, and among the constraints which her words obeyed was the following: if the word contained two vowels of differing heights, the first one must be more open (lower). Now it happens that the Estonian words for *father* /isa/ and *mother* /ema/ both violate this constraint. For a short time the child tried just [sa] for *father*, and used no word for *mother*. Then, for almost four months, she used no word for either, despite the fact that 'both father and mother made earnest attempts to elicit the words /ema/ and /isa/'. Finally at 15½ months, the child invented a metathesis rule to solve the problem: '/ema/ emerged as [ami] or [ani]. . . at which time /isa/ also reappeared, now pronounced [asi], and the word /liha/ "meat" was reproduced, following the same rule, as [ati]'.

Less spectacular rules also originate in the same way. New words are modified so that they comply with sound patterns already existing in the child's speech. We shall say that when a sound pattern found in some words of a child's speech is extended to a word in the adult language which does not comply with that pattern, the new rules, which are formed thereby, have been created by the *carryover* of the old sound pattern to the new word.

The other process of rule formation which has been distinguished, *consolidation,* is one in which two or more words of similar sound patterns, both of which the child can initially articulate, co-exist as distinct in the child's speech for some time (although one or both may be unstable in form). Then the patterns collapse together in production – one of the patterns is used for both words. At this point, then, at least one of the adult patterns has been modified by the child, and we express this fact by saying that the child has created one or more rules that relate (his percept of) the adult form to his output form. Jacob, for example, had a period of time in which [tei] from *table* and [ti] from *tea* were both produced for both words; then *tea* stabilized to [ti], and shortly (but *not* immediately) afterwards [ti] became the form also used for *table*. At this point, an /ei/→[i] rule had been created, and it later generalized to some other words, for example, giving [kiːk] for *cake*. Such cases again show that child-phonology rules are neither of purely articulatory origin nor are they automatically available to the child as he begins to speak.

4. Some conclusions

The data on the development of phonemic contrasts during the period when lexical morphemes are not being stably and consistently produced (from babbling to word(s)) are quite limited. We will, nevertheless, attempt to come to some tentative conclusions. First, one of the most important developments during this period is acquisition of knowledge that phonological sequences convey distinct meanings apart from the contextual situations in which they are initially perceived and produced and can be used generatively in unique situations. This development is obviously dependent on the ability to observe consistencies in phonological sequences (i.e. to categorize in some way morphological units) and, therefore, is dependent on earlier discrimination abilities. However, the development during this period is remarkably different from the previous period in that it is not simply sounds that are being discriminated and perhaps categorized but sequences of sound and meaning are being simultaneously categorized.

Second, the initial categorization of phonological sequences appears to be based on the auditory images formed by word gestalts. Initial analysis of these gestalts may be based on the syllabic patterns of these units rather than segments or features. Third, and very importantly, both individual differences in the sequence of development of phonological contrasts and in the utilization of strategies for the acquisition of these contrasts can be observed. Contrary to previously held notions, children apparently achieve the ability to discriminate between particular phonemes in somewhat different orders and to reproduce differences using different strategies. Some children organize their output on the basis of a word, others on the basis of phrase plus word (compressed sentences) and still others on a combination of both. Different children use the different strategies of avoidance, exploitation, and at least two sorts of modification strategies (rule formation).

Finally, the previously held notion that the order of development of productive contrasts faithfully follows the order of development of perceptual contrasts is not supported by the data even in studies which are limited to examination of discrimination of minimal pair words or reproduction of these words. This seems reasonable, given that not only are the task requirements different but also that strategies employed by individual children in the perceptual task may vary from those employed in the productive task. Pure application of logic tells us that the child cannot reliably match specific targets in his language without being able to hear what they are (except for the trivial case of accidental coincidence between a favourite syllable and a real word of the language). In this sense production cannot precede perception. On the other hand, if the child cannot handle a task involving deciphering a syllable without semantic support and yet can produce that same syllable as the name of an object, then for the tasks involved, production, trivially, certainly will be 'better'.

At this point, what we can do is suggest that the great task-dependency of perception and production in itself is evidence for the active nature of the processing of speech. Therefore, it involves many kinds of knowledge. The psychoacoustic substrate of perception and the facility of articulator movement which are *likely* to be determined by maturation, are so far from determining what is 'perceived' and 'produced' that great individual differences are to be expected.

The orderly and universal development of phonemic contrast that previous researchers have suggested does not seem to be supported by the data of the more detailed studies that have been carried out recently. This is a challenge rather than a confounding. The task for future researchers in this aspect of linguistic development appears to be two-fold. Since the product of these developments is similar (i.e all children achieve the ability to distinguish between and reproduce all the patterns of phonemic contrasts in the language and appear to do so by approximately age 6 or 7) one task is to determine the limits on the *range* of strategies that may be employed by children to achieve this product. A second task might be a determination of which aspects of the range of strategies employed are indeed universal and when these occur developmentally. It seems unreasonable to suppose that perception and production of phonological units are unrelated to each other and it also seems unreasonable to suppose that the strategies employed are infinitely variable. However, it is also unreasonable, given the findings of recent studies, to approach the task by asking children to distinguish minimal pair words or nonsense syllables and asking still other children to reproduce these differences during this period of development. These recent data indicate that this is not what the children conceive of as their task when acquiring phonemic contrasts.

4. Prespeech meaning relations: an outline of one infant's sensorimotor morpheme development*

Anne Lindsay Carter

It is already known that important events in the linguistic ontogeny occur before as well as after the onset of syntax. The periods of babbling and of first words, for example, have received considerable attention in the recent literature. However, overshadowed by the greater salience and recognized linguistic importance of these two behaviours, the span of development which connects them chronologically – and, it will be argued, developmentally – has been less thoroughly investigated. This is the period during which, according to Ferguson (1976), it is typical for a child to produce sounds with fairly stable significance that are not based on adult language. With the understanding that the term 'meaning' may require extensive qualification in a nonlinguistic application, this interval may be called the period of prespeech meaning relations.

To a degree, the prelinguistic tendency to produce stably significant but idiosyncratic sounds is already recognized. Together with the nineteenth- and early twentieth-century baby diarists, Werner and Kaplan (1963), von Raffler Engel (1964) and a few very recent investigators have drawn attention to the phenomenon, and investigators looking for the very beginnings of adult language almost always report several such utterances. Yet the child's own unique but recognizably significant vocalizations that show up in first word protocols are usually either not treated at all or not accorded a fully separate status from more clearly word-like utterances. There are several reasons for the general de-emphasis of this phenomenon. For many investigative purposes, for example studies of language-based semantic development previously undertaken by Clark (chapter 8 below), prelinguistic utterances like these are clearly irrelevant. For other purposes the fact that borderline linguistic utterances vary in conventionality is most appropriately handled by explicitly expanding the concept 'word' (or other linguistic term) to include them; considerations of utterance force for example, such as those presented by Griffiths (chapter 6 below), represent one type of analysis in

* Support for this study was received from Fellowship No. 1–F32–MH05743 from the National Institute of Health.

which the degree of conventionality in early utterances is of little importance. Finally, among the structurally minimal, intrinsically variable (i.e. as classes), articulatory error-prone and often homonymic utterances of this primordial level, it is sometimes difficult to distinguish the conventional – i.e. those which represent the infant's version of an adult word – from the idiosyncratic; they are often similar in both phonetics and usage.

Nevertheless, recent studies show the latter, when recognizable as such, also to be worthy of treatment in their own right: First of all, they are being reported increasingly frequently; Ferguson (1976) claims that the typical active lexicon around the end of the first year consists of roughly a dozen or so such vocalizations, along with only one or two representing an adult word. Secondly, they frequently demonstrate a number of interesting properties unrelated to words. Further, several investigators attribute to them a language development role linking the child's earliest phonological and earliest semantic acquisitions. This chapter therefore concerns several reports of these prelinguistic productions and, most centrally, a case study of their continuing later development. Most of the chapter will in fact be taken up with this single longitudinal study of prelinguistic utterances which, demonstrating their slow accrual of linguistic attributes, suggests (for the case in question at least) that the overall conception of linguistic development should be expanded to include such utterances from their outset.

Although as yet only marginally studied, this kind of idiosyncratic utterance has acquired a plethora of designations. For present purposes it is most convenient to use the type/token designation 'vocable' (Werner and Kaplan, 1963) as a general-purpose indicator of the significant prelinguistic vocalization, and 'sensorimotor morpheme' when a gestural context, gestural significance, or in general nonsemantic significance, is involved as well. Although gestures do not accompany all vocables, their co-occurrence – often critically important in disambiguating what is usually an exasperatingly primitive sound – is apparently extremely frequent in general. Moreover the presence of a stably associated gesture helps to demonstrate that not only as token (instance) but also as type (class), the significance of the sound is basically pragmatic, a fact, as will be shown, of considerable importance in tracing vocable development. Gestures will accordingly play a fundamental descriptive role in the vocable development to be traced in this chapter. In its use here the Piagetian term 'sensorimotor' indicates however not only a frequently co-occurring gesture for a particular vocable type (and the likelihood of this co-occurrence for a representative token), but also, in all applications of the phrase 'sensorimotor morpheme', the active, pragmatic nature of infant intelligence in the vocable period. The associated term 'morpheme' indicates merely that sound class having the smallest unit of significance in the infant's unconventionalized system of communication (Bloomfield, 1926).[1]

Before turning to the several studies of prelinguistic utterances, note should be taken of one or two of the closely related infant studies that, although differing in their approach, also deal with the pragmatic foundations of language. Giving less attention to specific utterances and their pragmatic–communicative categories, these studies focus directly upon developing patterns of attention, action, social interaction and the interrelationship of the three phenomena as they apply to language development, and necessarily, though indirectly, to any contemporaneous language-antecedent vocables. Space limitations preclude dealing with these investigations in any detail; however glimpsing even a fragment of this important ongoing activity may help provide the perspective necessary for a valid and somewhat longer look at the vocables themselves.

1. Studies of prelinguistic communicative processes

Exemplifying the type of study which is based upon a broad spectrum of communicative processes, Bates *et al.* (1975) undertook a longitudinal examination of 'performatives prior to speech'. Based upon videotapes of visits to the homes of three subjects and the administering of various Piagetian-type tasks, they concluded that there exist three stages in the development of prelinguistic communication, which they labelled, using Austin's (1962) linguistic–philosophical terminology, perlocutionary, illocutionary and locutionary. In the perlocutionary stage, from birth to about 10 months, the infant's signals are not intentionally communicative. In the illocutionary stage, the following two new phenomena appear: (a) a 'proto-imperative', the intentional use of an adult to obtain a desired object, and (b) a 'proto-declarative', defined as the intentional use of an object as a means to obtain adult attention – as in showing, giving, pointing, etc. In this stage gestures represent the dominant mode of communication. Although Bates *et al.* (1975) do not explicitly say so, it is presumably the second period during which sensorimotor morphemes will first appear. In the third or locutionary stage, beginning in their subjects somewhere between 12 and 16 months, words with referential value are first used.

Also illustrating the process-oriented study of prelinguistic development, Bruner (1977) and his collaborators are currently investigating three children over an age range of 3 to 24 months, recording the infants' interactions

[1] When describing the morphological units of adult language the term 'morpheme' has numerous technical ramifications to which its use here does not necessarily pertain.

with their mothers on videotape. Their primary interest is in the development of social 'formats', clearly specifiable types of mother–child interaction whose evolutions can be studied independently and in which the mother's as well as the infant's behaviour is of critical significance. The 'object attend' format, for example, is described in a single case report by Ninio and Bruner (1978) treating the sociolinguistics of reference and labelling. This report demonstrates among other things the breadth of their interest, which includes any behaviour or behavioural context which is felt to influence the development of those social functions out of which labelling evolves; for example, turn-taking, attention-sharing, motor skills, dialogue structure, mother's utterance types, mother's predisposition to respond – all underlining their social process orientation. Despite a differing emphasis however, this particular social–motivational analysis dovetails exceptionally well with a report by Carter (1978b) demonstrating the evolution of vocables associated with pointing and showing into a variety of linguistic determinatives, including the open class of object names. The ability of these two studies to combine harmoniously illustrates not only the complementarity and mutual dependence of sociolinguistic and vocable studies in the larger perspective, but also their initial feasibility as separate lines of investigation.[2]

2. Studies of prelinguistic vocalizations

Balancing the prelinguistic social and cognitive process emphasis in the last several years are several category-oriented studies focusing (like the above-mentioned) more specifically upon the fact and nature of prelinguistic vocables, including studies by Halliday (1970, 1973, 1975), Dore (1973), Dore et al. (1976) and Carter (1974). Using handwritten notes of his son's 8 to 16 month utterances, many or most 'unrelated to adult language', Halliday (1975) derived an evolving vocable meaning system, characterized in terms of seven categories, which he labelled instrumental, regulatory, interactional, personal, heuristic, imaginative and representational. At six week intervals, he compiled utterance taxonomies based upon these seven

[2] For a sampling of other recent contributions to the area of action, attention and social interaction in prelinguistic communication, Trevarthen's (1974a, 1974b) and Bower's (1974a) work on early levels may be noted, also reports by Escalona (1973), Newson (1974), Lock (1975) and Collis and Schaffer (1975), among others, and the volumes edited by Richards (1974) and Lock (1978). The latter constitutes an explicit and thorough treatment of the topic. An honors thesis by Sugarman (1973) treats early development of communicative intentions within an action–attention framework narrowly matching that of Bates et al. (1975). For a fascinating look at the attentional-comprehension side of prelinguistic development, see Huttenlocher (1974).

categories, with developments in successive taxonomies consisting mostly in the proliferation of utterances within category lines. Halliday's fundamental purpose in the taxonomies was to demonstrate the gradual expansion of these functions. Of particular value for the present study however is his generous inclusion of specific vocables and glosses, which are useful for comparative purposes; for example (from 1;1½ to 1;3) [mnŋ] – 'Give me that'; [ˌaːˌda] – 'Look a picture'; [ã ã] – 'No let's don't do that'; and [ˌaː] – 'Yes I want what you just offered.' (Comparable vocables for another subject are indicated in table 1, items 1, 2, 7 and 8 respectively.)

Dore *et al.* (1976) videotaped four children for one hour per month for an eight month period, with ages at onset ranging from 0;11 to 1;4. In the first months of his investigation many infant vocalizations (designated 'phonetically consistent forms') were intermediate between prelinguistic babbling and words in the sense that, like words but unlike babbling, the forms (a) were readily isolable units bounded by pauses, (b) recurred frequently, (c) could be correlated to a degree with situational context and (d) exhibited a proto-phonemic structure insofar as their elements were more stable than babbling sounds. At the same time, phonetic variability for a given phonetically consistent form was much more extensive than that of an imitated word. These vocables were alternatively characterized as affective, instrumental, indicating and 'grouping' expressions, signifying respectively feelings, object want, object indicating, and the combination of a subjective state and an indication.

As in Halliday's (1975) study, Dore's inclusion of specific utterances and their interpretations is helpful for comparative purposes. Briefly illustrating the types of sounds observed, around one year of age, affect expressions were often simply vowels, such as [æːː], to indicate pleasure; [iːː], protest; and [eːːː], success (and presumably satisfaction). The use of vowels as affect designators is commonly reported for the latter half of the first year, although reports show no pronounced overall tendency towards a particular vowel–affect correspondence. Halliday's son produced at 9 to 10½ months [a], glossed as 'That's nice' and [ø], glossed as 'That's interesting.' Von Raffler Engel (1964, 1972) described the use at 8 months of [i] to indicate a desired object, [u] as a sign of disapproval, and [ʊ] as an expression of inquiring marvel at a new object. In the case of a second year child, David, studied by the author (Carter, 1974), [ə] (or [ɜ]) was used to express dissatisfaction and the wish for almost anything, including adult attention (and labelled accordingly the General Want Expresser). In this case, even though the vocable occurred in the second year, its global application, minimal and neutral articulation, and conditions of occurrence – frequently stressful situations when regression could be expected – marked it as a probable first year residuum.

3. Sensorimotor morpheme development: a case study by the author

The General Want Expresser notwithstanding, the author's case study findings centre upon an essentially *consonant*-based system of vocables, whose inception and development in the second year, serving as an illustration of sensorimotor morpheme development, is the primary concern of this chapter. In the study of David, the ten one-hour play sessions that yielded the behavioural observations were videotaped at fairly regular intervals covering the second year of this healthy, intelligent, only child of middle-class college-educated parents. The unconstrained sessions were recorded at a nursery school and involved the presence of David, his mother and two or three other mother–infant pairs. Except for the other participants, the play environment, location, set-up, toys, refreshments, etc., remained constant for all ten sessions. The taping occurred behind a one-way window.[3]

Attuned, like the studies of Dore *et al.* (1976) and Halliday (1975), more to the 'what' of prelinguistic development (though, as indicated, certainly not unrelated to those social interactive studies more explicitly directed to the 'how'), this study likewise delineates an infant's prelinguistic vocalizations occurring prior to and leading into the acquisition of words. The present analysis is somewhat contrastive with other vocable studies however, in that the major goal is to demonstrate that the subject's vocables were strong antecedents of lexical development, in the sense that they themselves each transformed in orderly fashion into one or more words, and to briefly sketch this second year development. As it is incumbent upon one sustaining such a position to show that what eventually evolved into words were not words in the first place, a significant portion of the discussion below is aimed at demonstrating the alinguistic nature of his early second year vocalizations following, in the next section, a brief presentation of their basic production parameters.

3.1 Description of David's vocables

The significance of the utterances in question, most of which were not yet stable or contrastive in the thirteenth month but fully developed by the fourteenth (Carter, 1974), was originally inferred from the pronounced tendency for certain segmental categories to be uniformly produced with

---

[3] The ten tapes were originally recorded by Wanda Bronson, to whom the author is indebted.

certain gestures. For example, when reaching indicatively towards an object, David usually uttered an [m] (voiced bilabial nasal) sound; when pointing, an [l] or [d] (voiced alveolar lateral or stop); when slapping at an object to request its removal, a [b] (voiced bilabial stop); when shaking his head negatively, an [n] (palato-alveolar nasal); and when reaching to the receiver to give or take an object he produced an [h] or (reduced) glottal fricative (cf. table 1). Although some variability was observed in the sound classes, the single consonant in each case, usually initial in an open syllable, was highly predictable. Reaching sounds, for example, included [mm], [ma], [may], [mə]; pointing sounds, the alveolars [la], [lae], [da], [dæ], [də];[4] ridding sounds, [ba], [bæ], [bə]; give–take sounds, [hɪ], [hɪy], [he], [hə], [hm]; and disapproval indicators, [nə], [na], [næ], [now], often reduplicated, and also noninitial nasals such as [əən]. Most observed instances of all classes were produced with a slightly falling or 'declarative' intonation, and repeated many times. As both types and tokens, these gesture-accompanying sounds will henceforward be referred to as sensorimotor morphemes, or simply morphemes. In the analysis of the 12 to 16 month range, the virtual exclusiveness of association and extremely high frequency of co-occurrence (on the average, over 80 per cent) of a particular gesture with each monosyllabic morpheme gave reason to believe that its significance was approximately that of the gesture. Their frequent co-production and invariant goal at that time led also to the postulation of a unitary cognitive action pattern, or *communicative sensorimotor schema,* that contained the structural bond linking each gesture–vocalization pair. The parameters of these goal-defined schemata, documented in Carter (1974), are displayed in table 1.

In David's gesture–morpheme co-productions the significance of his indicative gestures was fundamentally pragmatic, with no question of truth value or even for the most part accuracy of representation. These communicative movements – whose still visible origins were usually their noncommunicative counterparts (reaching, pushing, turning away to avoid, etc.) – were, in keeping with the orientation towards success of the sensorimotor period, more effect- than meaning-oriented. In any given instance, once the gesturally expressed goal was achieved – by whatever means, whether through accident, his own actions or as the result of communication – his attempt to communicate always immediately ceased or changed direction, and by the same token, until its achievement was complete, even when the receiver (usually his mother) clearly showed that she understood him but was unable

---

[4] The term alveolar is used to indicate articulation made at or in the general area of the alveolar ridge, and is intended to be sufficiently loose to include sounds which would correspond to well-defined alveolar and dental articulations in the adult language.

Table 1. *Simplified description of David's eight communicative schemata in the period 12 to 16 months**

Schema	Gesture	Sound	Goal	No. of instances† (1st 4 play sessions)
1. Request Object	reach to object	[m]-initial	Get receiver's help to obtaining object	342
2. Attention to Object	point, hold out	alveolar-dental ([1] or [d])-initial ([y]-initial–a few instances only)	Draw receiver's attention to object	334
3. Attention to Self	sound of vocalization	Phonetic variants of *David, Mommy*	Draw receiver's attention to self	142
4. Request Transfer	reach to person	[h]-initial (constricted & minimally aspirated)	Obtain object from, or give to, receiver	135
5. Dislike	prolonged, falling intonation	nasalized, especially [n]-initial	Get receiver's help in changing situation	82
6. Disappearance	waving hands, slapping	[b]-initial	Get receiver's help in removing object	32
7. Rejection	negative headshake	[ʔəʔə]	Same as for Dislike (above)	20
8. Pleasure–Surprise–Recognition	(smile)	flowing or breathy [h] sounds, especially *hi, ha, oh, ah*	Express pleasure	20

* Reproduced with permission from N. Waterson and C. Snow (eds.), *Development of Communication*. Copyright © 1978, by John Wiley & Sons Limited.

In the initial report of David's communication (Carter, 1974), a ninth schema was included. This, the Request Transfer of Self schema, has often been excluded by the author from subsequent reports, as it demonstrates a number of properties reducing its construct validity significantly below the level of the other eight schemata: (a) it appeared rather late in the protocol, several months after the other schemata were first seen; (b) it was manifested via two entirely disparate vocalization–gesture combinations, failing to demonstrate the phonetic and motor unity that, in addition to functional unity, bolstered the construct validity of other schemata; and (c) one of its representative vocalizations was undeniably an adult to help, the gestural expression of his wish and corresponding sensorimotor morpheme inevitably continued unabated until he was forcefully distracted, and sometimes even to the point of tears. The inferential (and later demonstrable) significance of the accompanying sensorimotor morpheme, presumably as indicated closely matching that of the gesture, was accordingly also pragmatic. Because the usual pragmatic goal of the overall gesture–vocalization act was to obtain the assistance of others in altering his environment, beginning around the fourteenth month most morpheme productions were amenable to treatment in their own right as requests but, it must be stressed, upon these grounds only. In keeping with the claim that they were fully prelinguistic, the existence of syntactic or semantic parameters usually associated with the concept 'request' is not implied.

3.2. Evidence of a development prior to language

Vocal language in at least one well-established tradition (e.g. Werner and Kaplan, 1963) begins with the onset of symbolism, requiring therefore a semantic component, not only in the general sense of Peirce (1932) and Morris (1946) of a connection between sign and referent (which is demonstrated in the *index*), or even of a sign having the power to characterize more than a single instance of the referent (as demonstrated in the *icon*). In this tradition, the semantics of linguistics requires a sign which is connected with the referent only through convention or some other arbitrary assignment (i.e. a *symbol*). Arguments against the linguistic nature of David's 12 to 16 month morphemes will focus upon their lack of what linguists holding this position commonly intend in the term 'semantics'.

It should first be acknowledged that in a more general semiotic sense a semantic component inhered in even the accompanying gestures, at least to the extent that they included in their signification the object with respect to which action was sought. However the sort of object indication contained in

---

word from the outset. Its tentative schema status notwithstanding, it represented an occasionally recurring behaviour whose parameters are included here for the record.
(i) Gesture: raising hands or leg in order to be lifted by parent. Vocalization: [ə] or [əp]
(ii) Gesture: leaning down when sitting in parent's lap. Vocalization: *down*

† Frequencies representing total (both simultaneous and nonsimultaneous) instances of each gesture–vocalization pair were derived from four videotapes of play behaviour, recorded at approximately one month intervals. The total length of videotaped data from which these frequencies were obtained came to less than four hours.

directional aspects of acts such as pointing, reaching and indicatively waving is merely indexical, while the configurational representation of the desired action itself is at most iconic. Further, in functionally indicative gestures the diffuse interrelation of act, object and force indication automatically precludes the specification of a pure sign–object or sign–action relation that is intrinsically separable from pragmatic information. David's gestures thus lacked symbolic representation and therefore definitely failed, as might be expected, to meet the structural requirements of linguistic signification. At the same time there is no reason to believe that the early sensorimotor morphemes were other than essentially redundant vocal gestures having no more underlying structure than, and serving in each case simply to intensify and gain attention for, the motorically conveyed message. It was in fact only by virtue of a given gesture's predictable co-occurrence (and the resultant inference of related significance for the vocalization) that the initially primitive sounds were interpretable at all. Moreover the purely pragmatic interpretations thus obtained were in each case supported by subsequent vocal developments throughout the year.

Logically, the possible existence of a strict semantic, or symbolic, component in even the earliest morphemes of his second year cannot be positively eliminated; on the other hand there is as indicated no evidence for any such component and several pieces of evidence against it. First, although the indicative use of gestures demonstrates that David was capable of communicating pragmatic intentions, there is little to suggest that even those few 12 to 16 month *non*schema vocalizations that (in contrast to sensorimotor morphemes) did resemble adult words were truly representational or strictly semantic (cf. Carter, 1978b, section on object naming). At the same time the Piagetian stages (4 and 5) inferred for the first months of analysis argue against a mature representational ability during this, the period of morpheme establishment (Piaget, 1952).

Secondly, detailed analyses of the gradual development of words have demonstrated that many of those adult words that did eventually evolve (in a manner to be described) out of each sound class were, from the perspective of adult language, interconnected only ontogenetically, through their common pragmatic roots in a single morpheme; by the twenty-fifth month, the semantic domains of a given morpheme's word-approximating products (cf. figures 1,2,3) were always different, usually mutually exclusive, and often so widely separated in adult usage as to make the claim of a common developmental origin of any sort seem unlikely (cf. three of the Attention to Object schema products, *there, look* and *the*). That the putative products of each schema did share a common origin in an early sensorimotor morpheme was in fact independently documented in previous analyses. As indicated, however, for some time after it first became intentionally communicative at around 13 months, the demonstrably pragmatic parent morpheme generally produced no evidence of semanticity. Coupled with its own salient lack of semantic evidence extensive semantic heterogeneity among its year-end evolutionary products reduces the likelihood that the 12 to 16 month parent morpheme could have represented a semantic as well as pragmatic proto-class.

The third argument against linguistic semanticity in the original mor-phemes, in turning upon the probability that most of them were not word imitations, points also to a significant degree of phonetic independence from the adult language. Among a variety of evidence, it was phonetic evidence which indicated most vividly that these early vocalizations were not word imitations, in particular the pattern of morpheme development over the year, which is to be touched upon here and illustrated more fully in the following sections. In the first several months, the common phonetic ele-ment in the sound class predictably associated with a given gesture was usually, as previously indicated, the initial consonant, with a variable trailing vowel seemingly produced only as an unintended but inevitable concomit-ant of consonant production (cf. the Request Object schema's [ma], [mə], [mɔ], . . . accompanying an object reach). Later phonetic developments in each schema support this interpretation, showing David's subsequent atten-tion focusing on shaping the trailing vowel, gradually producing from the original morpheme one or more C+V forms with recognizably distinct and stable vowels around mid-year (e.g. [mow], [moy]), and then upon the acquisition of a final consonant for each of these, producing recognizably distinct and stable C+V+C forms around year end (e.g. *more, mine*). In each stage of segment increase, the potential for acquisition of diverse stable endings often resulted (through the schema's gradual assimilation of one or more rudimentary adult words; cf. section 3.5) in an increase in the number of significant morpheme variants, all bearing the same initial consonant as the original morpheme and rooted in the same pragmatic category, and simultaneously in a heightened sound and usage similarity of each pre-existent variant to an adult word (cf. figures 1,2,3; Carter, in press).

Given its demonstrably organic role in the gradual phonetic and semantic evolutions, and the resultant multiplicity of products (as outlined for three schemata of figures 1,2 and 3), it seems generally unlikely that the original morpheme itself was a word imitation, especially in view of the extreme variability of all segments but its initial consonant. When clear imitations, usually object names, did show up in the protocol either temporarily or permanently, their initial appearance was by contrast in the form of fixed C+V, C+V+C, or even more complex structures; e.g. the 12 to 16 month

productions, [ba] for *bottle*, [mɪyr] for *mirror*, and the rote *what* [əm] *doin'*
(Carter, 1974). Such considerations do not argue against any adult phonetic
influence at all on the formation of the original consonantal monosyllables.
It is conceivable, for example, that if in the first year [m] sounds had tended
to predominate in parental speech at feeding time, perhaps in words such as
milk, mama and *more*, the [m] could have acquired for David a significance
vaguely associated with the desire for food and (later) other objects, eventually producing the stable Request Object [m]. However, from the foregoing
considerations, a single specific verbal target for the early Request Object
[m]s or most other morphemes seems unlikely.

It is assumed then, that the original set of sensorimotor morphemes in the
12 to 16 month period represented a system of pragmatic categories whose
sounds, significances, and therefore the connections thereof, were mostly
determined by forces other than the influence of conventional language
structures *per se*. Though the possibility of peripheral language input in the
form of phonetic contagion from ambient speech sounds cannot be eliminated, this influence would seem to have been little more than that exerted on
first year babbling, upon which speech influences can also often be observed.
Further, other possible bases for the formation of his eight sound classes may
be hypothesized, pointing to conceivably cross-linguistic origins (cf. section
4). Working from these and the above considerations, the 12 to 16 month
consonantal monosyllables will be treated as legitimately prelinguistic in all
three respects.

3.3. Establishing the bases for linguistic antecedence

For present purposes the main interest of these sounds lies not with their
being prelinguistic vocalizations however, but in the fact that they generated
by degrees adult words, thus serving as structural antecedents to conventional lexical development. In this structural relationship they represented
forms essential to any description of David's development, meeting the
criterion for what are henceforward labelled *strong linguistic antecedents*.
Two operational factors in the descriptive analyses support this characterization: (a) the ability of the schema system exhaustively to delineate
David's observed utterances in the early months of the second year, and (b)
the susceptibility of each category of this fairly complete system to longitudinal tracing, leading gradually into the acquisition of linguistic elements
by year end.

3.4. Completeness of the descriptive system

The eight sensorimotor morpheme categories in table 1 accounted for 91 per cent of David's observed communications in the 12 to 16 month interval. However the presumed descriptive ability of this schema system was based not only upon the large proportion of the observed utterances which it could account for, but also upon the nature of the remaining 9 per cent, comprising mostly items which for various reasons appeared less important to later linguistic development, such as mumbling, babbling, stimulus reactions (e.g. *uh-oh*, produced automatically upon the fall of an object anywhere in the room) and a few rote phrases and word-like utterances which later often disappeared from the lexicon.

The exhaustiveness of this simple taxonomy might have theoretical import. It is conceivable that, for any number of reasons, the eight categories represented what amounts to a rude outline of the expressible aspects of this infant's cognitive–phenomenological world. However any formal hypotheses to this effect would presuppose the ability to demonstrate that the observed utterances actually exhausted the utterance types for this age span. Unfortunately no formal basis was found for assessing the representativeness of play session samples. There does seem, on the other hand, little in the way of *a priori* reasons for a year-long systematic discrepancy between communicative formats of home and play session, except in a possibly increased inhibition in the play sessions, and David's spontaneity and talkativeness in all sessions argue against this likelihood. All considered, including its year-long phonetic and functional consistency, ability to describe most utterances in even later play sessions, and possession of a compelling cognitive symmetry (which for space reasons will be treated elsewhere; cf. Carter, 1974), the strongest implication is that the set of eight schemata represented a nearly complete picture of David's overall production tendencies in the period 12 to 16 months, and to that extent therefore a prototype communication system in the technical sense.

3.5. Demonstrability of schemata evolutions into words

Considerations of exhaustiveness and systematicity in the 12 to 16 month utterance classes, although contributing to the descriptive bedrock for the construction of subsequent longitudinal analyses, themselves relate directly only to the issue of chronological antecedence. The major factor in the claim of strong, or descriptively necessary, antecedence for David's morphemes is the fact that they were capable of being traced longitudinally. Because the eight types of utterance were, methodologically speaking, solidly established in the 12 to 16 month interval, having as they did operational criteria, negligible or no overlap, high frequencies, high interjudge reliability,[5] and collectively representing a comparatively exhaustive taxonomy of utterance types, they could for the most part be treated as facts rather than hypotheses in attempts to trace their subsequent evolutions. Because they were well grounded, later minute changes in each were noted in the confidence that the resultant utterance represented a modified prior form rather than an independent emergence. It was especially important that most observed changes throughout the entire year were both incremental and very slow, since in the fairly widely spaced play session samples large or sudden changes could not be distinguished from emergent phenomena. In the case of every or practically every schema, the shape of its sensorimotor morpheme development was an element-by-element transformation of sound as well as of meaning, until by year end both sound and use approximated that of an adult word, by which time the communicative importance of the gesture had diminished considerably. Through the process of phonetically based assimilation briefly mentioned in section 3.2, the morpheme usually generated more than one word, however. (The Attention to Object schema alveolars for example produced *look, these, this, the, that* and *there*; Carter, 1978b.)

The detailed specification of elements and relationships in the separate schema evolutions which was provided in previous reports cannot be duplicated here. Even without this documentation however it may be of interest to take a somewhat closer look at the kinds of changes observed by noting a few developmental aspects held in common by all schemata. Although the evolution of each differed to some extent, certain broad facts have resulted from the analyses – to date those of the Request Transfer (Carter, 1975a), Request Object (Carter, 1975b), Attention to Object (1978b) and Disappearance schemata (1979).

First, as the initial prelinguistic categories themselves suggest, in the second year the sounds of utterances often predetermined to a large extent their significance for David. In so doing, they also structured the evolution and outcome of each schema, illustrated in the diachronic profiles of figures 1, 2 and 3. Like its original sensorimotor morpheme, the linguistic products of the Request Object schema were [m]-initial; of the Attention to Object

[5] Interjudge reliability obtained for characterization of schemata in the first four play sessions has been assessed at 93 per cent. This and all related obtained reliability measures for the coding categories of utterance transcription, gesture, gesture–vocalization time relationship, gesture contour (essentially the number of morphemes produced while it was sustained), object of regard, receiver, location of sender and gestural object are presented and discussed in Carter (1974).

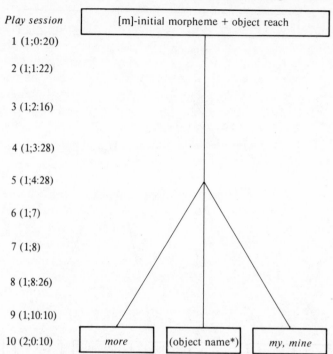

Figure 1. Verbal developments in the Request Object schema. Reproduced with permission from *Journal of Child Language 2*

* The origin of object names in the strictest sense was the Attention to Object schema (Carter, 1978b, figure 2 below), which showed a gradual evolution of referential skills not seen in the Request Object schema. Once object naming had fully evolved, however, names were immediately utilized to request objects as well as to point them out

schema, alveolar-initial; and of the Request Transfer schema, [h]-initial (and later [hw]-initial, as a result apparently of confusion between the two sounds; Carter, 1975a). In each schema, phonetic similarity of origin and outcome was due ultimately to the basic process of schema augmentation: its phonetic–functional assimilation of a rudimentary adult word.

The nature of this word incorporation process (diagrammatically represented in the figures by a schema branching) was partially revealed in the fact that for several months almost all newly acquired utterances manifested, via an accompanying gesture, the precise function of one of the eight pre-existent schemata. As it turned out, most of these new acquisitions were primitive imitations of certain words which could themselves legitimately be used either in isolation or in salient short phrases by adults – and were in fact

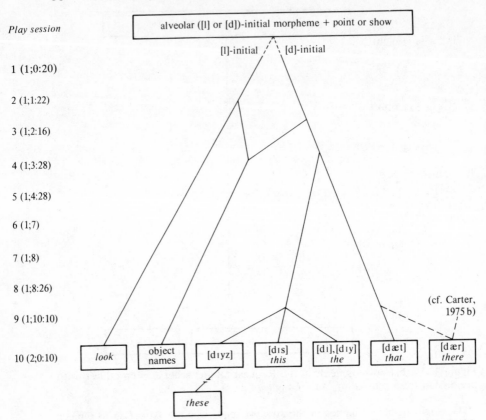

Figure 2. Verbal developments in the Attention to Object schema. Reproduced with permission from A. Lock (ed.) *Action, Gesture and Symbol*. Copyright by Academic Press Inc. (London) Ltd

frequently so used by his mother – specifically for the eight functional purposes to which David put them; e.g. *more* and *mine*, used to request and retain objects; *look* and *there*, to point out objects; and *have one* (often produced as a rote unit by David) and *here*, to request to give or take objects. From the usual close functional correspondence between a new acquisition and one of David's pre-existent schemata, it was gleaned that an observable functional, and most likely gestural, similarity in its adult usage to that of one of the eight prelinguistic schemata was initially necessary for a particular adult word to be potentially incorporable into his permanent lexicon. Additionally and equally surprisingly, a systematic compilation of his later developing utterances gesturally manifesting one of the eight schema functions revealed that virtually all new forms of that schema function bore the same initial consonant that characterized the original sensorimotor morpheme

(cf. previous examples). It is inferred therefore that the extent of its phonetic, as much as or more than functional, similarity to a schema morpheme
initially determined whether a word modelled in parental speech could be
incorporated into David's early production vocabulary, and furthermore to
which of the pragmatic schemata it would be assimilated if incorporated. If
this inference is correct, a definitive control was thus exerted by the sound of
an adult word over its initial functional correspondence (upon incorporation
of an imitative fragment of this word) that marked for David the origin of an
evolving lexeme–meaning relationship. Phonetic control of this sort might
be viewed as limiting or distorting, since it apparently restricted the set of
potentially incorporable words and biased their initial significance. However it would probably be more realistic to view it as the condition which
permitted many words to develop at all, in providing the phonetic and
functional guidelines necessary for coping with a potentially unlimited
domain of sound–significance correspondences, at a time when the recognition of not only the usefulness but even the possibility *in principle* of a fixed,
one-to-one, relationship between sounds and significances had probably

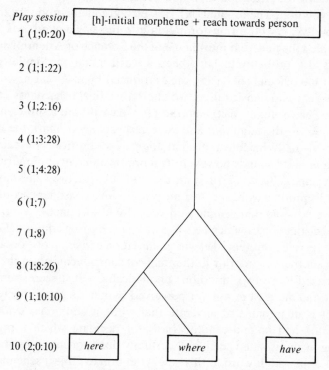

Figure 3. Verbal developments in the Request Transfer schema

only recently dawned and the elaborate prerequisites and entailments of conventional correspondences were not yet comprehensible. The importance of the guiding aspects of this incorporation process is perhaps underscored in the recognized difficulty at the borderline linguistic level of developing a meaningful use of adult nonsubstantive forms: the verbs, adverbs, adjectives, articles, etc., which, although demonstrably problematic acquisitions, dominated (as types) the year-end schema products (e.g. *more, mine, these, the, this, there, that, look, here, where, have*).

That an incorporated form did, as claimed, represent a word imitation was usually revealed in its later phonetic and functional evolutions rather than in the parameters of its initial appearance in the protocol. The [ma], [mə], etc., of the Request Object schema generated around mid-year only two forms, the stable [mow] and [moy], whose functions, manifested in the object reach, initially looked no different from that of the original morpheme class. However the subsequent phonetic augmentation of these two forms, creating respectively *more* and *mine* around year-end, revealed that the mid-year [mow] and [moy] may at some point also have been imitations of these two adult words. Attention to Object schema morphemes demonstrated a similar evolution. The original [la], [lə], etc., gradually produced the single [lʊ] by mid-year, whose transformation into the single word *look* by year-end revealed the mid-year morpheme of the *l*-branch of Attention to Object alveolars also probably to have been a word imitation. Similarly, in the *d*-branch the original [da], [də], etc., produced by mid-year a stable [dæ], which by year-end had acquired two alternative final consonants, [t] and [r] (or [ər]). The resultant [dæt] and [dær] (or [dæər]) bore a sufficiently close resemblance to the adult *that* and *there* respectively to mark the two later forms as virtually incontestable imitations. By contrast with each of the mid-year *m* and *l* sounds however, its more than one evolutionary product makes it impossible to certify that the mid-year [dæ] was an imitation of either of its product words at any time prior to final consonant acquisition. It is perhaps possible that around mid-year David was unable to articulate a phonetic distinction of which he was aware; i.e. barring additional evidence it cannot be ruled out that [dæ] was an imitation of *that* on one occasion and *there* on another, even prior to the final consonant acquisition that overtly distinguished these two imitations phonetically. Yet it seems more likely that *that* and *there* were not yet perceived by him as phonetically distinct forms. It is unarguable at any rate that without additional evidence the investigator had at mid-year no basis for deciding which form he was imitating in the isolated [dæ], and certainly none for imputing the significance of either adult word to this new Attention to Object schema expression. The best generalization regarding the necessarily somewhat variable procedures for determining word incorporation is that not until a form appeared which demonstrated stronger phonetic similarity to one particular word than to any other (together with an appropriate use) was David judged to be unequivocally intending the production of that word. This conclusion usually required at least a three-segment structure. However, as illustrated above, the phonetic and functional continuity of development up till that point in the protocol often suggested that a more primitive antecedent (if composed of more than one fixed segment and producing no more than the one verbal product) might also have represented an imitation of that word. It was virtually never possible in the transformation from sensorimotor morpheme to word to specify a single moment of acquisition.

Generally, after the play session debut of some form which was determined on diachronic grounds to be a phonetic predecessor of an adult word, not only its phonetic shape but also its use changed gradually – and seemingly independently. While on the phonetic side was demonstrated a gradual and orderly front-to-back increase in its stable segments, resulting in successively more accurate pronunciations, on the meaning side was revealed an equally gradual shift in emphasis from pragmatic (effect-oriented) to semantic (meaning-oriented) significance, and finally to what might be termed an incipient awareness of the word's syntactic potential. (Empirical bases for distinctions in meaning are provided in Carter, 1978b.) Both types of development resulted presumably from the gradually increasing familiarity and salience of the form in question, permitting the infant in both production and comprehension to devote increasing attention to details of its sound and usage. At year-end, the result of these developments in most schemata was the establishment of one or more active vocalizations, the particulars of each closely matching a single adult word, and for each of which the stable conjunction of a new (semantic) meaning and fixed, fairly complex sound structure distinguished it thoroughly from its primitive gestural roots.

4. The potential for generality

These observations represent a preliminary synopsis of David's sensorimotor morpheme development, hopefully giving an accurate impression of the language developmental role played by an initially alinguistic behaviour. If it should appear from this outline (although bare and incomplete) that the sensorimotor morpheme construct is valid and necessary in his case, it is not yet certain what sort of generality can be expected. However Ferguson and others imply that the generality of the prespeech sound–significance relation is undoubted. Further, although a comparison with other vocable studies suggests that individual differences may play a significant role in the inclusion or exclusion of certain categories in the infant's vocable scheme, evidence supports some degree of generality for David's sensorimotor morpheme classes in particular, and at a level of description requiring no additional inferences beyond that simply of relatedness in gesture and vocalization significance. At this minimal inference level in fact, the particular sound–significance categories inferred for David appear remarkably frequently in the infant literature. To illustrate briefly, the [m]-initial vocalization-plus-object reach (or other indication of object desire) has been reported by Gregoire (1939), Leopold (1949a), Jespersen (1922), Halliday (1973), Bates (1976), Dore *et al.* (1976), Greenfield and Smith (1976) and additionally by parent friends of the author. In these reports the subjects' languages included French, Danish, Italian, English and English–German, suggesting interlinguistic applicability. An equally large number of instances and range of languages exist for babies who were reported to produce alveolars with pointing, nasals with dislike gestures, and *oh* and *ah* with manifestations of pleasure. However perhaps the most succinct indicator of possible generalizability is to be found in a set of opinions expressed by nineteenth- and early twentieth-century language scholars to the effect that the particular phonetic correspondences listed in table 1 are widespread among infants the world over, and furthermore that their basis for generality in each class is a physiological or psychological origin predetermining the significance of the vocalization.

In addition to producing often a remarkable consensus in the literature concerning the cross-linguistic applicability of David's sound–significance categories, these investigators presented the generally shared beliefs that the origin of the Request Object [m] and the Attention to Self *mama* and variants was the use of labial muscles in sucking; of the Attention to Object alveolars, their outwardly directed character, making them the articulatory counterparts of pointing; of the Dislike and Rejection nasals, the fact that they represented the vocal equivalent of 'turning up one's nose'; and of the Pleasure–Surprise–Recognition *oh* and *ah,* a reflexive response to surprise or pleasure observable also in nonhuman primates. (For specific citations, see Carter, 1978a.) Although no opinions were found concerning the origin of the Disappearance [b], its obstructive and/or expulsive character suggests, along the same lines, that it might have originated in the rejection of food, representing in origin as well as outcome the 'negative' of the Request Object [m] (a relationship paralleled in the segmental designations themselves, bilabial stop versus continuant.) It may also be speculated that the Request Transfer [h], for which again no opinions were vouchsafed, originated in the infant's gasp, whimper or panting sound immediately prior to taking the breast or bottle. Jacqueline Sachs (personal communication) indirectly supports this possibility (and its generalizability) with a lovely observation concerning the use of this type of sound in her daughter's first year.

'The panting (several sharp breaths) started with the sound she made when being placed at the breast – a sharp intake of breath. We noticed when she first got solid food that there was this same breath just before a bite, and it soon turned into a little panting noise (3 or so in and out breaths) when the food was being offered too slowly. At about 11 months she started to use the panting sound when she was interested in getting something other than a bite of food.'

This example illustrates the sort of evidence for association and generalization which might verify the developmental connection between the early production contexts and later communicative significance of a sound class whose proposed origin is physiological.

Although language independence of any sound–significance relation has always been treated as an interesting possibility, it is currently considered a generally untenable one for conventional language. Therefore, to be able to draw the implication from a wide variety of independent and highly respected sources – Wundt, Darwin, Stern, Bühler, Leopold, etc. – that most of David's language antecedent vocables are interlinguistic is startling indeed. However these opinions need further researching to reach the status of precisely articulated scientific hypotheses. The putative developmental connections have not yet been carefully documented in even a single case. Some of the languages cited are interrelated historically and phonetically, making language-*dependent* influences an often equally plausible cause of interlinguistic similarity. Further, the literature provides examples also of sound–significance relations diverging from David's pattern, demonstrating that any generality which might ultimately be ascribed to the eight sound classes would represent no more than a somewhat predictable tendency. Even so, in view of the need to explain their genesis (in David's case at least) in other than linguistic terms, the possibility of a fairly general physiological or psychological origin, like the alternative possibilities of an origin in ambient speech contagion or in a combination of these naturalistic and environmental influences, seems worthy of exploration.

5. Summary

The existence of strong linguistic antecedents in the sensorimotor period was not given much thought in the recent two decades, in which, due to a prevailing interest in formal aspects, investigations were mostly limited to later acquisitions. The last several years, however, have witnessed a rising interest in linguistic antecedents in the prelinguistic period, with Bruner and others turning towards the examination of the structure of mother–infant interactions that engender early utterances, and Bates *et al.* (1975) and others examining the relationship between linguistic and Piagetian developmental stages. The new interest is reflected in investigations not only of prelinguistic communication but also of possible noncommunicative linguistic antecedents, such as the studies by Sinclair (1972) and Greenfield *et al.* (1972).

Out of the sizable group of available prelinguistic studies, it was the current work on prelinguistic sound–significance relations that defined the major topic area of this chapter. Because fundamental emphasis lay upon the demonstration of strong or descriptively necessary antecedence, in order, among other things, to establish continuity with the remainder of this collection, primary attention within this investigative area was given to the author's case study of sensorimotor morpheme development.

In this study, the development of David's alinguistic sensorimotor morphemes met the requirement of strong linguistic antecedence in demonstrating a documentable continuity of developmental change in both sound and usage as they gradually transformed into words. The eight sensorimotor morphemes themselves, overtly prelinguistic consonantal monosyllables co-occurring with indicative gestures, were felt to be best characterized as pragmatic entities. Their basic purpose like that of the co-occurring gestures was effects, not meanings, and evidence suggests that they were initially devoid of symbolic content. While the developmental continuity of utterance function was demonstrated in the sustained but gradually diminishing accompaniment of particular gestures, long-term continuity of form was demonstrated in a synchronic and diachronic consistency in the phonetics of utterances sharing the same gestural function. The importance of sound both in determining the significance of these early vocables and as a vehicle for their continuous transformation into words was thus demonstrated. Finally, possible evidence of phonetic generality in David's sensorimotor morphemes was found in a disproportionate number of instances reported by other infant investigators of the same sound–significance correspondences, potentially supporting, for various reasons, the inference of their alinguisticity and their separate derivations from even earlier oral behaviours.

5. First words

Robert Grieve and Robert Hoogenraad

Until recently, the study of the child's first words might have been described as a limited pursuit of the child's limitations.

The child's limitations, when he first begins to produce words, are well known. By definition his linguistic resources are limited, as is his experience of using language. And while he will have experience of the physical environment – he will be crawling, if not walking, by the time first words are held to appear and actively exploring his surroundings – this experience will not be extensive, for at this time the child is still in the care and control of others. Further, his caretakers will typically be few in number, a fact which serves to remind us of the limited extent of the social world in which the young child participates. Thus certain limitations, on his early linguistic resources, and on his experience of the use of language with respect to his constrained social and physical environment, are readily apparent.

However, students of early language development have typically gone further and attributed additional limitations to the child and his early attempts at language. For example, it is held that the child's first words consist of names or requests, confined to the 'here and now'. That is, their status is limited, being confined to expression of the child's current needs and wants, or to the naming of objects or aspects of immediately present environment. And although it is usually recognized that the child understands language before he begins to produce it – the phenomenon of comprehension preceding production (but see Bloom, 1974 vs. Ingram, 1974b) – when he does begin to produce his early words these again are held to be limited. Thus when the child begins to produce language he does so 'one word at a time', where each utterance is confined to but a single word. Further, these one-word utterances may frequently exhibit the phenomenon of overextension, where the child is held to apply a term over a wider range of application than would an older child or adult – e.g. *dog* is used to refer to dogs, but also to cats, pigs, sheep, etc. This phenomenon, frequently described in the work of the diarists, is one of the most commonly reported characteristics of early speech (E. V. Clark, 1973a), and

93

it again suggests a limitation – the child uses one word in place of several.

Thus various limitations are held to persist in the child's first use of words – he has a limited vocabulary, he produces words one at a time, these words are of limited status and they exhibit limitations in their use. The further conclusion about these limitations on early words – that the child who produces them is himself limited: in his conceptual resources and intentional abilities – has been found inexorable, and has rarely been resisted.

1. The nature of first words

There has recently been concern, however, about the data base in the study of early language, and it may be that the sources of information required for adequate understanding of what the child is trying to do with his early utterances need to be much more extensive than had previously been supposed. Hence our suggestion that study of the child's first words might be described as a limited pursuit of the child's limitations. Previous approaches to study of the child's first words themselves exhibit limitations, in conceptual background and methodological procedure, and this might well account for why so many limitations were attributed to the child and his early attempts to produce language. It is with these considerations in mind that we now examine how the study of the child's first words should proceed. We begin by recalling some observations and experiments on the child's early utterances.

A recurrent debate concerns the time at which the child's first words appear. In a classic review of earlier work (McCarthy, 1954), two widely different answers can be discerned. One view suggests that words first appear around 9 months, before the child is walking; another view suggests that words do not appear until around 1½ years. Of course such differences might well result from the manifestly different rates at which children develop. However, we will suggest that the solution does not lie in individual differences so much as in different views of what constitutes language. This problem is well illustrated by the following comments of a young mother on her child's first words (in a letter to the second author):

> 'Jacqueline actually started by making noises "P", Ah Ah, Bah, Mm – very definite and then attempted to make words like Mummum, Daddad (9 months). At 11 months was using some words but not necessarily understanding. Bow-wow always for a dog but often for other objects too. "Bird", Mumum, Dadad – knew all these and would use them at appropriate time but also at others . . . At 14 months was saying her first words. Mum, Daddad, Gone. "There-it-is" (all in one word).'

The sequence is thus like this: at 9 months Jacqueline 'attempted to make words', at 11 months she 'was using some words but not necessarily understanding' and at 14 months she 'was saying her first words'. Her commonsense tells this mother that her child is using her first words when she uses them as an adult might, properly with the right meaning; nonetheless she describes the child's earlier attempts as words too.

These observations are useful in two ways. First, they emphasize that the child's first words do not spring from nowhere – in fact the child has been communicating and interacting with others, especially the mother, virtually from birth, as recent work on precursors to language makes clear (e.g. Bruner, 1974; Trevarthen, 1974a). Thus the child's first words do not represent the onset of communication, but rather a point on the continuum of the child's developing ability to communicate effectively. Second, the observations illustrate the important problem of how to decide when the child's early utterances are properly described as words (cf. Campbell and Grieve (in press) for an historical perspective on this issue). For example, most recent studies of the child's first words begin when the child is producing words in a recognizably adult-like way (e.g. Bloom, 1973; Greenfield and Smith, 1976; Nelson, 1973b). An exception is the study of Halliday (1975) who adopts a quite different perspective. For reasons that will become apparent, we find Halliday's approach congenial, and we therefore turn to its description.

Halliday's theory of language function and language structure (see Halliday, 1970; Kress, 1976) provides a characterization of what the child must learn during his development of language. In essence, he claims that languages have grammar so that meanings, having their origin in disparate functions of language, can find simultaneous expression in the same utterance. Grammar is thus a means of expressing simultaneous strands of meaning. Halliday cites such functions as the *textual,* which allows utterances to be related to each other and to the context; the *ideational* and *logical,* aspects of language structure that are most commonly studied and give 'content' to utterances; and the *interpersonal,* which serves to structure and regulate the use of language in its social role.

The important point is that for the adult his language allows, indeed forces, him to do all these things simultaneously in each utterance. But the child, when he begins to learn to speak, does not have the structural means to accomplish this: he does not combine words, or inflect them, and it is claimed that each of his early words has a constant prosodic modulation, so that he does not use intonation as a variable on words, for example. These claims relate to the child's earliest use of words, between the ages of 9 and 15 months or so, a phase which Halliday (1975) has termed 'proto-language'.

Halliday's study of the development of speech in his son Nigel during the proto-language phase, when he observed the child's utterances and gestures, deducing their communicative force on intent across the wide range of everyday activity, led him to conclude that during this phase Nigel used words *only* to regulate social interactions. The child's earliest use of words, and for some 6 months after their first appearance, was thus solely a manifestation of the interpersonal functions of language. In English these would be largely realized by aspects of syntax and prosody, for instance by the systems of mood and voice, first position in the clause ('subject' in the traditional sense), direction and range of intonation, etc.

There are several reasons why it is plausible to suppose that the proto-language phase, as characterized above, though so far observed and described in detail for only one child, will prove to be a regular feature of language development. First, the child does not seem to make use of the ideational (or the logical) content function in his proto-language, neither imparting information to, nor extracting information from, his interlocutors. And though use may be made of the textual function (for example in deixis – in pointing or using words to draw attention to objects, for instance), the child's early proto-language utterances seem primarily concerned with the interpersonal function, as Halliday suggests, where social interaction is initiated, reciprocated and maintained.

Second, it is consistent with ideas about the child's social and communicative development from birth through his first year of life, recently developed by Bruner (1974) and Trevarthen (1974a), that his earliest use of words should have this interpersonal nature. It emerges from these studies that the child is predisposed to interact with others from birth or soon after, and that the form of this interaction goes through an orderly genesis of differentiation and elaboration. Even the child's actions on objects, it is stressed, derive from, and are used as part of, social interaction. Trevarthen speaks of the growth of 'intersubjectivity': the child slowly elaborates the means to break his subjective isolation by manipulating and regulating the responses and behaviour of others. It is natural to expect that the child's first use of words will be to elaborate further this process of regulation and structuring of interaction with his mother and others.

The third reason why we might expect the proto-language phase to be characteristic of the earliest use of words derives from considerations about the environment in which the child finds himself. The child's world is a social world: this is to some extent obvious, but nonetheless worth stressing, for its significance for language development is frequently overlooked. In western society, the child's mother is usually his most constant companion; and in the extended family of other cultures, while the child may be in contact with a greater number of adults and children, we would still expect him to form relationships that are close and significant with a limited group of adults and other children. (Only in institutions, we would argue, is the child likely to be frustrated in this search for constancy and stability, and it is a commonplace that his linguistic development is accordingly slower than that of his peers who are not in institutions.) Thus the number of people with whom the child interacts in meaningful and regular ways is constrained, and this of course may be further constrained by the shyness, and even fear, of strangers that begins to manifest itself at 9 months or so, and which does not begin to abate until about $1\frac{1}{2}$ years of age (Morgan and Ricciuti, 1969).

Within this constrained social world the child has a well-defined role, and others have well-defined roles vis-à-vis the child. He is frequently involved in regular ritualized routines; he is totally dependent on other people for his sustenance, comfort and well-being; and it is the actions and reactions of those others towards him and his environment that make some things salient and of interest, and imbues them with meaning. It is from this constrained world that the child derives his early meanings, and it is here that he learns how to mean. Consider an example. A mother shows her child a bird mobile, says *Look at the birdie* and in prolonging the first vowel of *birdie* and giving it tonic stress, she makes the word salient and part of the ritual. When the child later uses the word *birdie*, or some variant of it, it seems reasonable to suppose that his intention is not referential – 'There is the birdie' – or informative – 'That's a birdie' – or whatever: he may simply intend to draw his mother into the ritual and to share again the common interest. Thus for the child his earliest words may be a means of sharing experience rather than a means for talking about experience, and if this is so the textual function is not primarily represented in the child's earliest words (cf. chapter 6 below).

Such an interpretation may not readily appeal, for it suggests that the force of the child's early words is to be sought in the significance they have for him, and clearly such significances may be idiosyncratic, and highly variable across children. This point is well illustrated, though with reference to an older child, in the following episode drawn from Richard Hughes' novel, *A High Wind in Jamaica*. Hughes describes how a child reacts to the experience of an earthquake and a hurricane. When a mild earth tremor occurs, Emily suspects that it is an earthquake she is experiencing, but she is not sure. When this is later confirmed, it has a great effect on her, and she is able to make plans for the future. 'If ever she went back to England, she could now say to people, *I have been in an Earthquake.*' However, Emily's subsequent experience of a very destructive hurricane did not have a similar effect, for she merely considered it to be a bad storm. As Hughes points out:

'If Emily had known this was a *Hurricane,* she would doubtless have been far more impressed, for the word was full of romantic terrors. But it never entered her head: and a thunderstorm, however severe, is after all a commonplace affair. The mere fact that it had done incalculable damage, while the earthquake had done none at all, gave it no right whatever to rival the latter in the hierarchy of cataclysms: an Earthquake is a thing apart.'

Although Emily is well beyond the stage of the child who is producing his first words, this example is nonetheless interesting, for it serves to remind us that words may have certain significance for their user, a significance that is not readily apparent to an outside observer. Although the very young child is typically unable to serve as an informant on his language, it should nevertheless be borne in mind that a word may have a significance for him quite different from that which the adult may assume it to have.

2. Methodological problems

Fairly obvious conceptual and methodological problems now arise. In Halliday (1975: pp. 148–57), for instance, we are required to accept both his glosses of Nigel's proto-language words, and his functional categorization of Nigel's vocabulary. This becomes particularly problematic when we become aware of the number of word forms that appear more than once, with different glosses, in different subsystems. Is this a case of early homophony? Or should a single, more general, gloss have been provided? In order to overcome such problems – essentially the problem of how to allow other students of the phenomenon to check their interpretations against one's own – it will be necessary to have very fine-grained analysis of typical interactions in which the word is used. Film or videotape provides the technical means of doing this, but it is not clear that adequate descriptive means are available. While the objects and events in the context are not difficult to describe, and while attentional factors can be noted, the child's affective and motivational state, clearly of prime importance to the hypothesis, is less well understood and hence less easy to describe objectively. Adults constantly interpret the child's motivational and affective state, but the signs they use are difficult to specify and hence the factors which direct our interpretation are difficult to make objective. Further study of the processes of interaction between adult and child are clearly required.

Two factors which particularly conspire to make the task of describing and interpreting the child's first words a difficult one concern the form of these words, and the nature of their meaning. By way of illustration, here are three words used by a young child, observed in a recent study.[1] Rebecca was recorded in five videotaped play sessions with one of us. The words occurred only in the last few sessions, when she was beginning to get used to the comparative stranger and when she began to interact with him more easily.

/dɛ/: accompanies and punctuates actions: 'There, that's done'

/odi/: after any untoward happening: 'That wasn't the way it should have been, was it!'

/hija/: presenting object, or about to: 'Come and join in this game', 'Do something with this'

Consider first the form of these words: the fact that they are presented here in a solid phonemic form should not blind us to the fact that, for many children at least, these early utterances are extremely variable in their realization. This is a consequence of the child's lack of skill in articulation and, more importantly, his difficulty in co-ordinating the various articulatory gestures involved. (Children vary enormously in this regard: some have all but mastered the skill at 9 months, but we have observed an otherwise competent child who was almost inarticulate in this sense at $1\frac{1}{2}$ years, and who did not begin to master articulation properly until he was about $2\frac{1}{2}$ years of age. It is not necessary to spell out in detail the consequences for the child in terms of how well he is understood, and the effect this may have on the course of his linguistic development.) It is in fact not clear that the phonemic principle applies at all to the child's first words: we would not expect it to until the child's vocabulary begins to expand dramatically, usually between $1\frac{1}{2}$ and 2 years. For the child in the proto-language phase the problem is not primarily keeping many different words apart in pronunciation, but rather to produce, or rather to reproduce, a given form: this is more likely to be for him the problem of producing a given vocal gesture, a synergy of articulatory gestures. Indeed, many of the child's earliest words may be unword-like in any conventional sense: the investigator, looking for the precursors of language as he knows it, may be likely to dismiss the child's *mmm*s and *eee*s as mere affective noises. The child may even, as Halliday points out, use ritualized gestures, and Carter (1978a) has described a child who used a combination, a constant dyad, of word and gesture in the early phase of his language use (at 12–16 months). Now if we allow that the child may make use of such unconventional means of expression we have a problem, for we do not have a ready notation for representing such forms phonemically, let alone phonetically. This no doubt goes some way towards explaining why

---

[1] 'Studies of semantic development in young children': SSRC Grant HR 2516 to Robert Grieve and Robin Campbell, assisted by Robert Hoogenraad and Theresa Bowe.

such forms have been so rarely noted as precursors to language use, and why the proto-language phase has not been generally recognized.

Having considered the form of the child's early utterances, now let us consider problems associated with their meaning. If a proto-language word is recognized by the investigator as a word of the mother tongue, then he is likely to feel that it does, or should, mean what he knows it to mean. If it does not suggest a recognizable word, the investigator is likely to ignore it, for it will be used with a meaning qualitatively different from the meaning an adult word would have. Recall that it is being suggested that the child's early words have meanings derived primarily from the interpersonal function of language, and that in the adult language such meanings are carried by aspects of prosody, syntax, lexical choice, etc. Such meanings are notoriously difficult to describe in the adult language – what is the meaning of rising intonation, of subject, of passive voice, etc.? The glosses given above for Rebecca's three words are intended as no more than tentative, and only suggest the sort of things children might mean with their proto-language words. We cannot pretend to have captured her intended meaning at all precisely – we observed her for too short a time, across too narrow a range of situations, and in insufficient depth, to have assessed it at all confidently. She was also with a comparative stranger when she used the words, though she did try hard to incorporate him into her social world. Methodologically this implies that an adequate study of the child's earliest use of words needs to be embedded in a global study of the child's social world. Careful diary studies can fulfil this requirement, and indeed recent insightful comments on early language development arise in studies by parents of their own children (R. Clark, 1974; Ferrier, 1975; Halliday, 1975).

The source of the child's early words should also be considered. Clothed in their phonemic representation, the three words of Rebecca cited above have an obvious source: *there, oh dear, here y'are.* In form (and also, more globally, in their general meaning) they are recognizable as familiar words and phrases, and that was no doubt why we spotted them, and understood them. But, as we have already implied, there is a problem about the source of the child's proto-language words (and we include in this gestures and noises used in a consistent and meaningful way). With words and phrases such as Rebecca's, the child has heard them used by adults in situations that he can understand. However his experience of the situation in which a word is used, and from which he probably infers its meaning, is different from that of adults. Consequently it would be strange if he did not often get the meaning, and the form, wrong. Whether we should call the child's meaning in such instances an invented meaning, as Halliday (1975) suggests, is a moot point. It might be better not to, for the child, at least in many instances, may really believe that words have the meanings he employs when he first uses them. More generally, if we recognize that not only the meaning of the word but also its form may undergo considerable transformation, both in the course of the child's developing apperception and in his word reproduction, and that the child may find the source of these 'words' not just in speech but in all of the adult's meaningful actions, then the origins of the child's words will be difficult to identify. Not only are the potential sources immense, but we will need a thorough understanding of the child, his perceptions, his experience, his motoric abilities (e.g. the processes involved in articulation), etc. Another potential source for the child's proto-language words consists of his own actions and noises. As suggested above, the proto-language phase is preceded by an extended period during which the infant has been using an array of gestures and noises that others have treated as meaningful, whatever their intentional basis on the part of the infant (Trevarthen and Murray, 1975). The child may well import these into his proto-language, but until investigations have linked these two phases in a single longitudinal study, it will not be clear to what extent this takes place.

Whatever the source of the child's earliest words, the nature of the relationship between adult and infant will ensure that the adult usually does his best to try to interpret the child's utterances. We should mention in passing that the adult's *mis*understanding almost certainly has a vital function to play in language learning – it would be a mistake to suppose, because it is imperative for the investigator to understand the child, that therefore any adult interacting with the child must learn his proto-language. Here it is surely relevant to note that the older siblings of second and subsequent born children can often interpret the young child's utterances more readily than adults – presumably because they are cognitively closer to the infant and share more of his experience. As a general consequence, second and subsequent born children begin to speak, in a recognizably adult way, later than first born children.

3. Procedural difficulties

Turning now from problems with the form, meaning and source of the child's early words, we must now consider certain procedural difficulties. Recall that we are operating with the view that language has grammar in order that meanings which originate in disparate functions of language can find their simultaneous expression in each utterance. The proto-language has no grammar in the required sense, though Halliday does claim that it has a systemic organization. If we have ignored this aspect of Halliday, it is because the systemic organization appears to have no visible effect on the form of the proto-language words. It is of course reflected in their use, but we suspect that another investigator, using the *same* classificatory scheme and the *same* words and glosses might have classified them in a different way. That is, Halliday's classification appears to be to an extent arbitrary. This may arise because the classification system is not fully adequate. It is a feature of the adult's lexical system that words can be classified in many ways – each word falls into a number of different semantic fields, or alternatively, most words are a complex of meaning elements (e.g. 'semantic features', 'prototypes', 'family resemblances' or whatever). We should allow the possibility that the child's proto-language words combine a number of meanings simultaneously, and may therefore require some form of multiple classification. While some words in Halliday's classification of Nigel's words do occur in more than one functional subsystem, many more appear as if they should also do so. Halliday's systemic classification does not readily lend itself to such multiple classification.

Further, to substantiate the claim that the proto-language has no grammar, it must be shown that the child has no productive means of combining meaning. Potential sources for the combination of meaning include the systematic use of prosody (e.g. tone or intonation) as a separate meaning system; the construction of words out of meaningful parts (e.g. nasal sounds in all words with negative connotation); the combination of word and gesture; etc. Although such combinations have been noted – Nigel's words all have a constant prosodic modulation; and recall Carter's (1975a) description of a child who used dyads of word and gesture – there is so far no evidence that these are used as separate meaning systems. However, Halliday has noted that, towards the end of his proto-language phase, Nigel did begin to combine meaning, using intonation as a second meaning system, although only with some words at first. This introduces a potential incongruity, for now the child's words may carry, as part of their constant form, a tone that is used elsewhere as a variable. This might be expected to lead to a degree of instability in the child's language system and may explain why the full differentiation into two separate systems of meaning, one lexical and the other prosodic, appears to reach completion in a very short time. The child has now learned that there can be a structural means of combining functions, and he has control of the rudiments of a grammar.

For some time after entering this new phase the child will continue to use one word at a time, although now single words will be used, potentially at least, with different intonations. The fact that investigators have disagreed over whether the young child uses intonation productively or not (cf. Brown, 1973) may well derive from failure to recognize these separate phases in the child's linguistic development (but see Crystal, 1975). It should also be noted that the common practice of describing the syntax and semantics of the child's utterances in terms of the adult language is not ratified by the view of language adopted here, since it attempts to maintain a distinction between the functions of language and the structural means of expressing them. It remains true throughout the child's linguistic development that he has to discover what language can do – the functions of language; *and* he has to discover how to realize these functions – the grammar of the language he is learning.

4. Comprehension

But what of the child's comprehension of language at this stage? In one of the few studies so far reported, Huttenlocher (1974) suggests that the child does have some understanding of language during the proto-language phase. She claims that the child tends first to understand proper names and words for things and animals, then action words. However, it is possible that this is an artefact of her quasi-experimental method and conceptual framework. Though far from simple, it is easier to test for comprehension of words for objects and actions than of words such as *don't, pretty, hot, bad, dirty*, etc., which the child might well be expected to understand, given the functions of language in his life. As a result of the conceptual framework she brings to her study, Huttenlocher tests for comprehension of the adult meaning of words; but, as we have suggested, the child may understand words to have meaning that differs from the adult meaning. For example, he may suppose *hot* to be a prohibition, and to mean something like 'don't touch that thing' (Edwards, 1978b). Thus it is perfectly reasonable, when language is viewed from a functional perspective, that the child may understand certain words in a consistent way, but in a way different from their accepted adult meaning.

Viewing language functionally has another methodological consequence for study of the child's early comprehension. This can be discussed with respect to one of Huttenlocher's examples. A girl of 10 months is said, by her mother, to understand *no* since she stops eating paper when her mother says *no*. However she also stops when her mother says *yes* in a similar tone of voice; and this is taken to indicate that the child does not in fact understand *no*. We must demur. It may indicate this, but it need not, for the child presumably still knows she is doing something she ought not to be doing – after all, the mother said *no* only a moment earlier. In such a situation there are strong prior constraints on the meaning of the mother's utterance, and part of this meaning is carried by 'tone of voice'. For instance, *no?* with a rising intonation does not mean the same thing as *no!* with a strongly falling intonation. This is as much part of the structural resources of language as are syntax, lexis (word meaning), etc. The child attempts to understand what is going on, and he uses language, to the extent that he is able, to further this process of understanding. But what he decides to do on the basis of this understanding is a separate issue: for instance he might understand what is said to him, but decide to ignore it, or even do something to the contrary.

5. Conclusions

Our discussion of the general nature of the child's use of words in the very early phase of language learning, from about 9 months until 16 months or so, preceding the child's first excursion into the adult language, suggests that the proto-language phase constitutes a bridge between language precursors and the child's subsequent language development. The discussion has been intended to illustrate that the debate in the literature over when the child's early words first appear in fact concerns fundamental differences of opinion about what language is and what it is for with respect to the child. Our attention to one view, which owes a great deal to the work of Halliday, has been deliberate, for this view seems to us to possess several advantages. It emphasizes the social aspects of language development (see Ryan, 1974) – that language is learned in a constrained social context, and that early utterances are frequently employed to initiate and maintain the sort of social interaction the child has long been used to. In turn, this emphasizes that the child's first words are continuous with what has been happening before words first appear. It is also clear that this view raises points of theoretical interest, involved with considering how language structure is related to language function; and that it raises interesting problems in relation to methodological procedures.

This brings us to our final point. Some years ago, Chomsky reminded students of early language development that their empirical enterprise would need to be 'carried out in devious and clever ways' (Chomsky, 1964b). Although being devious is straightforward enough, so to speak, being clever is harder. The problems of observation and their relation to theory are still not resolved, far less the yet more difficult problems associated with experimentation in very young children. We believe Chomsky's admonition should remain at the front of our minds, for questions about the conceptual apparatus that is brought to study of language development – our view of language, our view of the child – and how this interacts with methodological procedures – whether concerned with observational or experimental study – lie at the heart of language development research. With reference to the child's first words, it is this that the present chapter has been trying to illustrate.

6. Speech acts and early sentences

Patrick Griffiths

1. Introduction

In the course of normal child development, the earliest syntactic constructions are to be observed at the age of about 18 months. For some children the
age may be much nearer 1 year; for others, in excess of 2 years. These first
sentences are just two words long. The characteristic which seems to make
observers feel that the words are united into a sentence is that a single
intonation contour spans both words. The two-word sentences of the 18
month old child may be regarded as genuinely containing two words because
the component words occur independently and in other combinations. They
are thus different from certain fixed expressions, which may appear earlier
and which, from an adult point of view, seem to contain several words, but
which are unanalysed wholes in terms of the child's system.

The advent of two-word sentences is a momentous advance: it marks the
beginning of duality of pattern in a child's linguistic productions (Halliday,
1975). Before this time each meaningful utterance is composed immediately
of sounds. From this point onwards, each utterance is a sequence of words
and the words are made up of sequences of sounds. Of course, some
utterances will still be only one word long, but in principle there is now an
intervening level of patterning between sound and meaning. Some hold that
language begins with this big step, because the mediating level, *syntax*, is
often regarded as an important defining characteristic of human language.
As far as linguistic *form* is concerned this is correct, but there are other ways
of looking at language and 'From the functional point of view, as soon as
there are meaningful expressions there is language . . .' (Halliday, 1975: p.
6).

Children start to use expressions with some phonetic stability and a
reasonably consistent relationship to the situations in which they are uttered
at the age of approximately 9 months. Again, this must be qualified by
admitting that there is wide individual variation. In this chapter, I aim to
show that the transition from these early asyntactic utterances to the first
syntactic constructions is bridged by functional continuity. An account

which avoids a sharp break at the onset of syntax accords well with the feeling, often expressed by child language investigators (e.g. Brown, 1973: p. 245; Wells, 1974: p. 258), that successful linguistic communication takes place, from the earliest stages, between children and adults familiar to them. There certainly are differences between adult language and early child language, but the adult's sense of partaking in meaningful linguistic interaction with another language user does not suddenly dawn or become markedly more insistent when the child first makes sentences; it is already there when this step is taken.

2. Speech acts

Searle (1969), in his elaboration of some of J. L. Austin's ideas, points out that speakers perform a variety of acts in and through speaking. The 'basic units of linguistic communication' are *illocutionary acts*, e.g. asking a question, making a statement, request, promise or prediction, issuing a threat or a command. In performing illocutionary acts speakers may also have to perform acts of *referring* and *predicating*. In addition, but of much less concern to me here, they move their vocal organs and arouse feelings such as boredom, inspiration, alarm and determination in their addressees.

In performing illocutionary acts speakers generally also convey messages with some *content* to their addressees. That is, they may express a proposition about something (or some things). In different illocutionary acts any given content is presented differently: in a command, as a proposition which the addressee must cause to be true; in a question, as an incomplete proposition for which the speaker wants a true completion or a complete proposition which the speaker wants verified; in a promise, as a proposition which the speaker undertakes to make true; etc. In other words, the same content may be put to the addressee with any one of a variety of different *illocutionary forces* (henceforth abbreviated to *force*). It is in transmitting content that speakers refer and predicate. Referring is the process of using a linguistic expression to pick out for one's addressee an individual entity – a particular person, thing, place, event, etc. – or a particular set of entities. Having picked out some entity or entities to talk about, one completes the content of an illocutionary act by predicating. An illustration: on particular occasion, in the right sort of context, the interrogative sentence *May I borrow those books?* may be used to perform an illocutionary act of requesting; that is, the utterance may have the force of a request. The expressions *I* and *those books* will then have been used to refer (to the speaker and 'those books') and *borrow* to predicate a relationship between the speaker and the books (and a lender who is not overtly referred to in this example).

Illocutionary acts, like acts of referring, are strongly context bound: in a different context *May I borrow those books?* could be used to ask a simple factual question. The import of this is that if we wish to investigate force we need to know the contexts in which the utterances occurred and not only which linguistic forms were used. There are no straightforward syntactic indicators uniquely paired with each of the kinds of force. There are strong correlations between command, question and statement force and, respectively, the imperative, interrogative and declarative forms of sentence. However, interrogative sentences may also be used in making offers and requests, etc.; imperative sentences may be used to ask questions or with the force of warning or advice, etc.; and declarative sentences may be used to perform illocutionary acts with any force whatever (e.g. *I order you to stop* is a declarative sentence which may be used with the force of a command; *It will rain tomorrow* could, in appropriate contexts, be a bet, a promise or a prediction, etc.).

In seeking to demonstrate functional continuity across the onset of syntax, I shall be examining contextualized utterances of children with a view to determining what forces they manifest and, secondly, for those utterances which have content, whether reference and predication are overtly signalled and distinguishable. The enterprise is saved from being an endless catalogue only to the extent that generalizations can be made. Some readers will notice similarities between this programme and Dore's (1974, 1975) description of 'the single-word utterances of one-year-old children' as performing 'primitive speech acts'. The affinity is recognized, but I trust that a number of differences will become apparent in the course of my discussion. One difference is worth remarking upon immediately. In his two articles, Dore does not distinguish between utterances which are *communicative*, in the sense of representing an intention on the part of the child to say something to an addressee, and those which are merely *informative* to a perspicacious adult listener (see Lyons (1977a: vol. I, p. 33) for an account of this distinction). I shall be treating only those utterances which seem to be communicatively intended. Thus, I shall not take account of two of the 'primitive speech acts' which Dore admits, 'labelling' and 'practising', since he says that the child does not address them to anyone and does not wait for a response. Furthermore, we are told that 'practising' utterances are apropos of nothing in the environment.

3. Force in the holophrase period

I shall use the time-honoured term *holophrase* to characterize children's presyntactic utterances. As indicated above, the holophrase period spans the age range of roughly 9 to 18 months. In this period, each 'sentence' is only one 'word' long. Calling these utterances *sentences* would suggest, incorrectly, that they exhibited syntactic structure. *Word* would be inappropriate too because they do not have the property of combining with other words to make phrases and sentences. Most holophrases, however, have *uses* which are comparable to those of sentences: they are used in the performance of illocutionary acts. In what is surely one of the best recent studies of the holophrastic period, Bloom (1973) rejects the term *holophrase* as unwarrantedly imputing knowledge of syntactic structure to the child. I accept the point, but I believe that she gives insufficient weight to the patent fact that her 'conceptual notions underlying single-word utterances' have more in common with the meanings of sentences than of words, especially if *meaning* is stretched to include consideration of force. It seems to me that a fair measure of agreement exists on the types of force attested, despite the welter of technical terms which have been employed to describe them.

3.1. Requests

Carter (1974) reports a study of the communicative behaviour in monthly videotape recordings made of one child, David, in a play-group setting. Her report is concerned mainly with the period 12½ to 16 months. She postulates nine 'communicative schemata' into which David's communicative acts are categorized and claims that 91 per cent of his recorded vocalizations could be accommodated in the system. Eight of the nine schemata served as 'requests for minor or major transformations of his environment . . .' (Carter, 1974: p. 82). She hypothesizes that all eight stem from neonatal expressions of discomfort (for which see Bühler, 1930).

One of the categories which Carter judges to have the highest construct validity is the 'Request Object Schema'. David would make an open-handed reaching gesture towards an object while uttering an [m]-initial monosyllable. One of her transcribed examples is: 'David turns around and sees his mother eating a cookie. He says, [me. b miy.] and reaches for the cookie. Mother gives him the cookie, and he eats quietly' (1974: p. 117). In the phonetic transcription, *b* marks a pause and the full stops represent falling intonation. Carter's study is notable for the care taken over attempting to justify the classification. She found that the gestures could be more reliably classified than the associated vocalizations: 97 per cent versus 69 per cent interjudge agreement. Furthermore, 'gestures are usually very clear in their communicative intent . . . *they indicate their goals by attempting to accomplish their goals*' (1974: p. 8). Correlation of gestures and vocalizations provided a basis for sorting vocalizations into categories. Thus, because they occurred with the same open-handed reach, the monosyllables of the 'Request Object Schema' could be treated as equivalent despite variations in vowels and intonation. And the perspicuity of the gestures allowed the forces of the schemata to be assessed with some confidence.

An essential condition for an illocutionary act to be a request is that it should count as an attempt to get an addressee to do something (Searle, 1969: p. 66). For this there must be an addressee. Carter suggests that the vocal parts of the schemata were often deployed specifically to gain the attention, usually in the form of eye contact, of an addressee, usually David's mother (1974: pp. 38n, 130–2; see Huttenlocher (1974) for more on the role of eye contact). Did David want the cookie or was he merely pointing it out? That is, were his requests attempts to get something done? 'The primary criterion for assessing various types of intentionality in each instance was the goal which, once achieved, resulted in the child's quieting or adopting a new mode or direction of behavior . . .' (Carter, 1974: pp. 60–1), and, in other examples, David persisted for longer when his requests met with initial indifference or refusal. Halliday (1975) locates the emergence of a linguistic system in his son Nigel's development in the period 9 to 10½ months. One of the four uses to which Nigel could put an utterance at this stage was the 'instrumental function' whose most general exponent was [nā], which Halliday (1975: p. 148) glosses as 'Give me that'. The gloss is an imperative sentence – the form correlated with the force of commanding. However, I know of no evidence that shows that children of this age understand the authority relationships which distinguish the otherwise identical forces of command and request.

Elsewhere in his book (e.g. 1975: p. 33), Halliday glosses the same item as 'I want that' and Carter alludes to a 'General Want Expresser' (1974: p. 86), which David used to express 'a general state of dissatisfaction'. Are these to be taken, not as requests, but as statements about the children's desires? Shall we say that it is the shrewd adult who calculates the 'implicature' (see Grice, 1975 and also Gordon and Lakoff, 1971) that if the child is venting his desires something should be done about them? No. Remember that these utterances were generally addressed to parents who usually could and would meet the child's needs. Parents treat them as requests and that is the only basis young children have for discovering the force of what they are able to utter. Incidentally, this claim does not extend to cries of displeasure emanating from the cradle. These are neither requests nor statements because they are not communicative; they occur independently of the presence of an addressee (Bühler, 1930). Because adult responses, in part, determine the force of children's utterances – stemming from the simple fact that language is minimally a two-person game – there is little harm in researchers taking into account parental interpretations of children's communicative intentions. These interpretations are an essential component of the data (cf. Halliday, 1975: p. 24). Children's requests may initially be less generalized across situations than the Carter and Halliday examples discussed above. For instance, when Allison Bloom first used *more*, at 16 months, it was a request for more food (Bloom, 1973; see also Leopold, 1939: pp. 97–8; Sully, 1896: p. 141).

Another type of request commonly reported in early child language calls for the performance of an action. Dore (1974, 1975) provides the following example: 'J tries to push a peg through a hole and when he cannot succeed he looks up at his mother, keeping his finger on the peg, and utters /ʌʔʌʔʌʔ/ . . . ; his mother then helps him push the peg, saying *Okay*.' Gopnik (1977) reports that the three children whom she observed all used *more* to request repetition of an activity. Halliday (1975) calls Nigel's requests of this type 'regulatory'. An observation of Bloom's suggests that children might not at first realize that language can be used to specify whether one wants an object or an action (I do not doubt that 1 year olds know which they want). The observation concerns Bloom's daughter at the age of 16 months: 'Two days after she had first used "more" to request the recurrence of food, she used the word to request her baby sitter to tickle her again, after having been tickled just previously' (Bloom, 1973: p. 69). Also, Carter notes that David's 'General Want Expresser' could be used for 'any schema request' (1974: p. 86).

It might appear reasonable to argue that, in early requests, the vocalized holophrase indicates request force and that the child's gestures transmit the propositional content. Their nonvocal and their iconic (see Lyons (1977a: vol I, p. 102) for definition) nature makes gestures doubtful candidates for linguistic status. Rather, I think, early holophrases are 'paraphrases' of items in an original system of gestural communication. This view is supported by the observations of both Carter (1974) and Halliday (1975) to the effect that systematic gestures, which at first co-occurred with holophrases (and had preceded them ontogenetically), gradually lost their dominant role, *before the end of the holophrase period.* I suggest that the earliest requests have force without content. The child, then, is in much the same position as I would be in if the only entry in my phrase book to survive my shipwreck on a foreign shore – a fragment from a single soggy page – were an undivided phonetic sequence translating 'I request of you'. I could probably secure assistance by uttering it while I mimed and pointed, but my utterance, like the child's, would be a holophrase without internal structure and my gestures would not count as knowledge of the foreign language.

However, in some requests children impart a little content with the force. Leopold's daughter used *up* from the beginning of her seventeenth month as a request to be lifted (1939: p. 35) and it was then in contrast with at least one other request, *da* (1949a: p. 8). In these may be seen the first signs of predication, insofar as the child's utterance communicates something of the nature of the required action (lifting versus giving). Similar contrasts are on record elsewhere (e.g. Carter, 1974). However, the predication is not clearly distinguished from the indication of force, because these holophrases were initially used only to make requests (this is likewise true of *up* and *away* in the usage of Bloom's daughter (1973: pp. 88, 90)). But even when these forms come to be uttered, as they soon do, as an accompaniment to the child's own actions (Gopnik (1977) mentions this as the first use for *up* in the three children whose language she observed), it is still hard to decide when *up,* etc., cease to be ritualistically parts of the actions and become comments on those actions, i.e. primitive *statements.*

Content also begins to accompany request force when the child 'names' objects in asking for them. Carter (1974: pp. 175–6) reports that in the session recorded when David was almost 17 months old, he made all his requests for objects by naming them, whereas a month earlier only 40 per cent of object requests were made in this way and there were hardly any in earlier sessions. I take cases of this sort, which are reported elsewhere, to be examples of illocutionary acts which include acts of referring (using linguistic expressions to single out particular objects or sets of objects for one's addressee).

A further species of request is the 'negative request' or interdiction. Examples are: Bloom (1973), *no* as an expression of 'rejection'; three of Carter's (1974) schemata, those she calls 'dislike', 'disappearance' and 'rejection'; Dore's (1974, 1975) 'protesting'; and *no*, for 'refusal', in the speech of the three children reported by Gopnik (1977). These differ in predicational flavour from the requests discussed above but they are not, at least initially, 'positive requests' to which a marker of negation has been added. They may be negative in adult terms, but there is no significance to the difference for the child: either way, the surroundings are unsatisfactory and he or she requests someone to alter things.

Finally, the names of familiar people are frequently reported to be used to summon the attention of those people; that is, as *vocatives* (see, e.g., Dore 1974, 1975 – 'calling'). Carter's (1974) 'Attention to Self' schema is akin but more primitive: David used arbitrary sounds to call his mother. Vocatives are requests of a special kind, because no communication can take place until one has the attention of an addressee. Nigel first segregated an intonation pattern out of holophrastic unities in a use which I would call vocative

(Halliday, 1975: pp. 67, 154). Starting in the period 15 to 16½ months, he would utter *Mama, Anna* or *Dada* with rising intonation to mean 'Where are you?' (Halliday's gloss) but with a falling contour for greeting one of them.

3.2. Statements

Halliday (1975: p. 21) asserts that Nigel did not use language in the 'I've got something to tell you function' until 1;10 (cf. Atkinson, 1974). This is the function in which language is 'used as a means of communicating information to someone who does not already possess that information . . .'. The definition is a little too wide to fit the force of stating, but it is concerned with the same matter. Three things are important about statements: the specific purpose of a statement is the communication of information (the propositional content); the content is presented as being true; and there should be a reasonable supposition on the part of the speaker that the content will be news to the addressee (a question from the addressee may be the basis for such a supposition; which admits as statements speech acts in which the addressee already knows the content, e.g. answers in a quiz).

Why should stating not be possible from the beginning? I surmise that all holophrases, not just requests as I suggested above, have only got force and not content, at some early stage. Now, whereas one may easily use non-linguistic means to elaborate 'I request of you' into a worthwhile communication, the same is not true in respect of statements. Read out accurately the phonetic sequence which corresponds to 'I state to you' in some land whose tongue you do not know and your audience will wait for linguistic goods you cannot deliver. The child is probably in the same predicament at the beginning of his speaking career. Griffiths and Atkinson (1978) noted, in the usage of seven children, that the forms *door, on, off* and *open* were in each case first used as requests and only later with statement force. Perhaps it is easier for a child to assess the meaning of a form when it is used to make a request, because the effect is then acted out visibly by an obliging addressee.

The possible types of holophrastic statement would be predications on entities already at the focus of addressee's attention and references supplied for other people's predicates. An example of the latter is *I*, in response to *Who killed Cock Robin?*; it is as good a statement here as *I killed Cock Robin*. In my experience, holophrastic children do not answer questions of this complexity, but Bloom provides a case which might represent the former possibility (1973: p. 92): 'Allison used "stop" from 13 months in situations where some ongoing event ceased, for example, when music ended on her phonograph, when the car stopped, when the food blender was turned off, etc. "Stop" always occurred as a COMMENT on CESSATION; there was no record of Allison's using the word as a request or direction.' These are potentially statements because they are not requests, but there are problems. Were they communicatively intended (i.e. did an addressee have to be present for her to say *stop*)? Are they perhaps closer to reference (i.e. was Allison pointing out a particular event, the termination of something, each time)? The second doubt appears to be settled by Bloom's account of an evening stroll when Allison was 14 months old (1973: p. 97). Allison noticed the moon and said *moon* as she was being wheeled along in a 'stroller'. When her mother stopped at an intersection Allison looked at the moon and said *stop*. Bloom is of the opinion that Allison was speaking of the moon, which had seemed to her to be moving while she was moving. If this is so, then the utterance might have constituted a statement in which *stop* was predicated of a public object, to which she might be said to have referred earlier by means of its name. Comments on 'disappearance' (e.g. Bloom, 1973 – later development of *away*), 'emptiness' where something is expected (e.g. Bloom, 1973 –*no*; Gopnik, 1977 –*gone*) and nonrequest uses of *up*, *down*, *off*, etc., similarly, provide cases of which one might maintain that 'the utterance was a predicate to a subject implied in the situation' (Leopold, 1949a: p. 27: cf. de Laguna, 1927). All of these are more characteristic of the end than the beginning of the holophrastic period, which is as it should be because, if this interpretation can be sustained, the utterances are performing a role like that of a part of a sentence rather than a whole sentence.

The following was recorded from G, a child whom I studied. He was $21\frac{1}{3}$ months old at the time but still essentially a holophrastic speaker (see Griffiths *et al.* (1974) for data collection details).

I hand G a toy train.

     G: *mummy, choo choo mummy*

G holds the train up to his mother, saying: *mummy*

     Mother: *What's that?*

     G: *choo choo mummy*

In each case *choo choo* had the higher pitch of its tone group and, certainly the first time, *choo choo* had the higher stress in its tone group. I take these utterances of G's to be communicative, because he repeated himself when his mother failed to respond at first. Similar examples could have been culled from many other studies of language acquisition. The puzzle is what to make of the 'naming' of the train; I regard *mummy* as having been used vocatively to secure and maintain his mother's attention. Is G making a statement in which he predicates of the object in his hand that it is a member of the class of trains: *(a) choo choo*? Or, is he stating an equational relationship between the object in his hand and whatever *(the) choo choo* is used to refer to (an entity in memory, I would assume)? Huttenlocher (1974) provides some evidence which points to young children being able, in comprehension tasks, to treat adult nominals as either definite or indefinite; so the issue cannot be settled by making a general claim about how young children use their 'nominals'. Lyons (1977b), discussing this sort of case, calls it *proto-reference* and says that, because of the indeterminacy, it might equally well be called *proto-predication*.

However, no matter which of my two suggested interpretations of G's *choo choo* utterances is taken, he would in either case appear to be using them to make statements. This would gain support from the fact that, in the final utterance quoted, G was apparently answering a *What's that?* question. 'Answering' *What's that/this?* questions in a manner satisfactory to adults was at this time a newly acquired skill too. Unfortunately, all of this is also compatible with a proposal of Atkinson's (1974) that G had misinterpreted the adult questions as mere attention directing devices, to which uttering the 'name' of the object was an appropriate way of confirming that one had indeed allowed one's attention to be directed to the object.

My conclusion here is that if children can be said to make any statements at all in the holophrase period they do so near the end of this period. Bearing in mind that considerations of truth are involved in making statements – the content is presented as being true – it is interesting that Carter reports that, at the age of about 16 months, David began to mock and misuse his primitive communication system 'deliberately breaking the rules, then laughing heartily after each incongruous utterance' (1974: p. 90). Truth only has significance against a background in which 'fibs' are possible (cf. the 'imaginative function' in Halliday (1975)).

3.3 Other forces

My comments on G's comprehension of *What's that?* obviously raise the issue of whether children themselves ask questions in the holophrase period. Leopold's daughter began to use an interrogative intonation pattern on some of her forms at the age of 15 months but, throughout the holophrastic stage, it was used to call attention to things and to make requests, not to ask for information (1949a: pp. 13–14). The only exception he mentions is *there*, a form which when it was used with rising intonation, in his daughter's eighteenth month, was taken to mean 'What is that?'; but this might have been an adult misunderstanding of one of the child's attention directing strategies. And it is equally possible to view Dore's (1974, 1975) example of 'Requesting (answer)' as merely an attempt by the child to draw attention to something. Halliday glosses one of Nigel's forms, in the period 15 to $16\frac{1}{2}$

months as 'What is that?' (1975: p. 31), but he classifies its function as 'interactional' because it was used to initiate dialogue through shared attention to something. I have already suggested that Nigel's utterances which Halliday glosses as 'Where are you?' were vocative rather than questions about location (young children understand the *where*-questions of others as writs of *habeas corpus*, that is, as requests). Thus it seems that children say hardly anything with the force of a question in the holophrase period. Shortly before the advent of syntax, however, adults begin to interpret some of their utterances as meaning 'What is that?' and, then, the child may almost be said to have acquired one particular type of question. Notice that I am talking about the illocutionary act of questioning, not the interrogative form of intonation. Since questions and statements are both rather special through being centrally concerned with the transmission of content, it is not surprising that where the one type of force is absent the other is missing too.

I have now covered the major types of force to be found in the holophrase period: requests and vocatives, with statements and questions as very marginal latecomers. *Greetings* (and ritualized farewells: *bye bye*) are attested from an early age (Bloom, 1973: p. 98; Dore 1974, 1975 – 'greeting'; Halliday, 1975 – 'interactional function'). *Assent* to someone else's request or command is usually indicated simply by compliance, but see Leopold on later uses of *ja* (1939: pp. 92–4). As far as I can determine there are no other well-substantiated forces carried by holophrases. Various expressions of disgust and pleasure catalogued in the literature are not obviously intentionally communicative, although they are certainly often informative to an observant adult. I treat 'giving and receiving words', expressions of triumph (*there!*) and the child's directing attention to something noticed as precursors of reference (in section 4 below).

4. Reference

Atkinson (1974) points out that communicating a proposition involves getting one's addressee to attend to some entity (or entities) and then saying something about it/them. Unless the addressee can identify the entities on which to hang the predication the whole act will fall flat. He also notes that the business of bringing something to one's addressee's attention can be decoupled from the process of predicating. For example, *Look!, Do you see that?, Remember the plane that skimmed the top off our apple tree?* are ways of bringing something to the focus of an addressee's attention and then an utterance such as *It belongs to a child language research group* can be used to say something about it. Of course, *it* in the follow-up is a referring expression, but it does very light duty here, serving merely as a place holder for something salient in the addressee's attention. Atkinson notes that in certain circumstances it is even reasonable to perform only the first half of this two-part routine, as when one directs the attention of other people in a queue by pointing to a speck in the distance and saying *Bus!* He maintains that young children do just this in a large proportion of their linguistic interchanges.

The phenomenon is certainly widely attested. Leopold's daughter used *there* and [əʔ] from before her first birthday and *da* from immediately after it to direct people's attention to things in her surroundings (1949a). She usually pointed as she uttered one of these holophrases. Bloom's daughter used [ə] with rising intonation a great deal in her fourteenth month, in combination with a pointing gesture, to draw attention to things (1973). At 15 months *there* replaced [ə] in this role. Some of the items which Halliday (1975) enters under 'personal function', from the earliest period (9 to 10½ months) onwards, appear to be attention directors too. G (the child whom I mentioned in section 3.2 above) used *see* for this purpose. The form was first noticed when he was 15½ months old. An incident which occurred when G was 21 months old gave good grounds for believing that he used it with communicative intent. He held up a toy horse to one of my colleagues and said *see*. She was engrossed in making a phonetic transcription and did not respond. G then said *see* again. When she still paid no heed he got up and walked to her, holding out the horse and saying *see* a third time. She then acknowledged his effort by looking at the horse and asking *What's this?*, whereupon G, apparently satisfied, lost interest in the matter. G also used *see* to direct attention to events, particularly if they consisted in his succeeding in a difficult action. When he began to use *there* at 21¾ months it was as an alternative to *see*, both for pointing out objects and drawing attention to his motor successes. One of the children in Gopnik's report (1977) used *there* in both of these ways too.

I have already illustrated G's use of an 'object name', *choo choo,* to direct attention to something. He did the same with the 'names' of many other objects as well, and similar examples are extremely common in the literature. A connection between the 'demonstrative' routines illustrated immediately above and directing attention with the aid of an object's 'name' is documented by Carter (1974). The schema which she regards as best attested and justified by her data is the 'Attention to Object' schema. Initially the vocal part of this schema was represented by approximations to *look* and *that.* These were increasingly replaced by object names and *replace* is a term justified here because the carefully recorded gestural components of the schema (pointing or holding up) remained constant across the transition.

It seems to me that in using language to direct people's attention to things in the environment, children are learning to refer to those things; in directing attention with the aid of 'object names' they are acquiring a device which will later allow them to refer to absent entities, things which cannot be pointed to at the time of utterance. Why do children indulge in referring without going on to say something about the objects thus brought to the addressee's attention? I reject the teleological explanation that they know (or Nature knows) that eventually they will have to be able to perform the speech act of referring and that this is what sets them practising. The answer seems to lie, rather, in the comfortable way in which attention directing finds a place in conversational interaction between children and parents: *dialogue* (see Snow (1977a) for an account of the origins of dialogue, at age 3 months, and Shugar (1978) for later developments). Halliday, I believe, pinpoints the relationship I am striving to convey when he talks of 'meanings of an interactional kind involving the focussing of attention on particular objects in the environment, some favourite objects of the child which are used as channels for interacting with those around him' (1975: pp. 19–20). Against the possible objection that drawing attention to things for no other reason than to have the pleasure of dialogue seems too frivolous to be credible, let me remind the reader of the pure nonsense 'sound play' conversations reported by Keenan (1974). An excellent example of the same type, but from an earlier age than Keenan's twins, is recorded by Carter (1974: p. 170). I take most instances of imitation – Dore's 'repeating' (1974, 1975) – to be conversational but not communicative.

Finally, I have observed 'giving and receiving' forms in holophrase speech: *here, ta, 'kyou,* etc. (cf. Carter, 1974 – 'Request Transfer Schema'). The fact that the same forms are used both in taking something from and thrusting something upon an addressee suggests that they too are merely being used to direct attention. Handing over or taking the object concerned may just be a rather forceful and concrete way of drawing attention to it.

5. Putting things together

According to the case presented in sections 3 and 4 above, the presyntactic child can use speech to make requests, give greetings, call for the attention of an addressee (vocatives) and, perhaps, is beginning to make statements and ask questions of a rudimentary kind. In the routines for directing attention the child has the ability to refer to entities in the immediate environment. To be credited with syntax the child has to start putting these separate speech acts together. Bloom (1973), more than anyone else, has brought to general notice the fact that the holophrase period is not a single rung on the ladder of linguistic development. Numerous changes take place during this time. I shall now summarize some of those which herald the start of syntax.

The two earliest ways in which *separately significant* components enter into single communicative acts are the combination of intonation patterns with sequences of sounds and the combination of a gesture and an utterance. In her sixteenth month, Leopold's daughter distinguished two uses of *da* by means of intonation: with one prosody it was a request for whatever she was pointing to, but with a different one it was used merely to draw attention to objects (1939: p. 62). In the former use intonation carries the request force and the sound sequence, *da,* is used (with a pointing gesture) to refer to the desired object. I have already mentioned Halliday's (1975) report of Nigel's use of intonation to signal vocative force with the referring expressions *Mama, Anna* and *Dada.* Carter (1974: p. 119) noticed in the play sessions recorded at 14½ months and at 16 months that David frequently used a headshake simultaneously with an utterance to 'negate' the utterance. Halliday (1975: p. 45) reports similar instances from a slightly later age. The interesting difference between these and the earlier gesture + utterance combinations is that, rather than being paraphrases of each other, gesture and utterance are now each being used for a different part of an illocutionary act.

In the first half (or longer) of the holophrase period each communicational transaction usually involves only one holophrase, which may be repeated. A switch to a different holophrase closes the book on the previous transaction and shows that the child's interests have departed on a radically different tack. In the later part of the holophrase period, however, unifying threads begin to be discernible in successions of holophrases. They are still holophrases, in that each is set apart from its neighbours, intonationally and usually by pause and, sometimes, by adult interventions, but they have a thematic unity. This phenomenon has received careful treatment in the work of Bloom (1973) and Scollon (1974), but it has also been observed by others (e.g. Carter, 1974: p. 110; Halliday, 1975; Leopold, 1949a; Menn, 1973). Bloom (1973) noticed a sharp increase in such successions of related holophrases near the end of Allison's seventeenth month. At first, each holophrase would be related to an event in a sequence of actions in which the child was engaged: what happens first gets talked about first and the next holophrase relates to what comes next in the temporal sequence of events. The number of holophrases thus 'chained' might be as large as six. However, these soon gave way to 'HOLISTIC successive utterances, in which the entire situation appeared to be defined to begin with, and utterances were not tied to particular movements or shifts in context' (Bloom, 1973: p. 47). That these successions are not mere accidental juxtapositions of holophrases is strongly suggested by Scollon's finding that, apparently owing to concentration being diverted to putting things together, the individual holophrases often suffered phonetic regression to earlier forms (1974). For instance, when Brenda, the child he studied, pretended to step on his tape recorder she said [tʰei] and then [tɛʔ] (*tape, step*: drawing attention to the tape recorder – referring to it – and then predicating) but on the same day she was able to pronounce these forms as [tʰeip] and [tɛpʰ] when they occurred as isolated holophrases. In passing, it may be noted that Brenda's pretence could perhaps be used to argue that she was making a special kind of statement here: a threat.

Soon the first sentences are made, in the sense that two words – generally no more than two – are united into one tone group by a single intonation contour. Leopold (1949a: p. 28) notes that some of these earliest sentences betray their origins in holophrase successions by having the same level stress on each item. Their connection with the holophrase period is illustrated even more strikingly by functional continuity. Most people would be willing to credit the child with language at this point, but utterances are still put to the same range of uses as before. Admittedly, it now becomes easier to decide that some utterances are being used to make statements, but a large proportion of utterances can be characterized as 'a word to indicate the wish and a word to specify its domain' (Leopold, 1949a: p. 22). For 'wish' read 'request force' and remember that vocatives are a species of request. For substantiation of this claim, see Wells (1974: p. 262), Campbell (1976) and Smoczyńska (1978). At first the order of words evinces some variability but it soon shows signs of settling into the adult mould.

With regard to statements, most of them consist in the child drawing attention to something and then saying something about it, that is, predicating. Alternatively, when the protagonist is either the child or a salient entity in the situation, he or she may combine a vocative and a predicate. Are we to say, of the first type of statement, that the name, 'noun', or demonstrative (*this* or *that*) used in drawing attention to the person or object is the *subject* of the sentence? No, it is simply a reference to a protagonist somehow involved in the proposition being conveyed. Bowerman (1973a) presents a convincing set of arguments against the use of the grammatical term *subject* in the description of early sentences. Statements containing two referring expressions are also now within the child's capacity, when the relationship between the two entities referred to is a locative one. The predicate is not expressed overtly by anything other than word order (Bloom, 1970; Bowerman, 1973a; Brown, 1973; Schaerlaekens, 1973).

Referring without predicating – simply drawing attention to things – continues apace. Some of the utterances used are now two words in length: a demonstrative word and a name or 'noun', a vocative with one of these, or a 'possessive' construction. For examples of possessives see Bloom (1970), Bowerman (1973a), Brown (1973) and Schaerlaekens (1973). As with locative statements, word order is again the only indicator of syntactic construction. Schaerlaekens' study is of particular interest for showing that locatives and possessives are clearly distinct structures. The entities located and the possessors are almost coincident sets in the child's world but, thanks to the word order of the dominant form of the genitive construction in Dutch, the former were usually found in first position in two-word constructions and the latter in final position, in the speech of Schaerlaekens' subjects (1973); whereas in the speech of children learning English both types of item appear in initial position.

The child now has a foundation in syntax, but it is one which has gradually welled up under a superstructure which first took shape when the child was less than 1 year old.

Part II

THE DEVELOPING LINGUISTIC SYSTEM

Introduction

0.0. The aim of the chapters in Part II is to shed light on what we have characterized elsewhere as 'still the central problem: the child's constant development of more complex forms' (Fletcher and Garman, 1978: p. 133). With the exception of chapter 16 by Karmiloff-Smith, who looks at development after 5 years of age, they concentrate on children's language from the first word combinations to the time of entry to school. While it is no longer accepted that the child has established the major part of his linguistic competence by the fifth birthday, the period between 1;6 and 5;0 is one of great change and considerable achievement. This period is chronicled in the following chapters, which consider the child's language at each linguistic level, and are thus designed to provide a developmental perspective – a sense of how the language system changes. Chapter 7 (Ingram) describes the development of the phonological system from 1;6 on, and chapter 8 (Clark) considers the development of lexical structure. Apart from chapter 16, the remaining chapters concern grammar. Chapter 11 (Derwing and Baker) is devoted to morphology, and the general development of syntax is dealt with in chapters 10, 15 and 9: Garman deals with early syntax (essentially the structure of simple sentences) and Bowerman gives an account of complex sentence acquisition; Macrae provides a complementary view on early syntactic forms and their description. The remaining chapters concern the development of important syntactico-semantic systems: chapter 14 (Fletcher) looks at the verb phrase, chapter 12 (Maratsos) at pronouns and determiners and chapter 13 (Wales) at deixis.

1.0. Linguistics and language acquisition

Since the Dedham conference (see Bellugi and Brown, 1964) research into child language development has been greatly influenced by linguistic theories and descriptive frameworks, and particularly by transformational-generative theory.[1] To set the chapters presented here in context, it would be

[1] Other syntactic frameworks are however widely used. See Crystal *et al.* (1976) for a detailed application of the description used by Quirk *et al.* (1972), and Dever (1978) for a thorough-going tagmemic approach.

useful to review this relationship, and to consider its advantages and disadvantages for studies of language development.

1.1. Phonology

Explanations for the child's errors in pronunciation, and their gradual eradication, have been linked with phonological theory since Jakobson's pioneering contribution (1968). The direct descendants of Jakobson are those linguists who have dealt with phonological development within a generative framework, accounting by rule for the relationship between the child's phonetic form and a presumed 'underlying' representation. The relationship between the child's form and the form he is attempting to pronounce changes over time, and this has also been considered within the generative framework (in most detail by Smith (1973)). The interpretation of the child's forms within a framework designed for adult language can be distorting in a number of ways. Here we will briefly mention three topics which are relevant: perception, homonymy and rule learning.

1.1.1. Perception. Phonological theory for adults has no place for perception as a variable, but with young children the possibility that perceptual difficulties are a factor in immature pronunciation has at least to be considered. The evidence concerning early perception is assessed in detail by Menyuk and Menn in chapter 3 above. For the period Ingram considers, the relevance of perceptual factors is a matter of dispute. Smith, for example, (1973: p. 134) hypothesizes that the child 'does not begin to speak until he has learned to perceive at least the majority of the contrasts present in the adult language'. The evidence presented for this 'full perception' view is convincing, and the conclusion that perception was in advance of production seems reasonable at least for the child who was the subject of his study. Smith's position is provided with experimental support by Barton (1976). Others disagree, both on the evidence of spontaneous speech and from experimental work. Ingram himself, in an earlier paper (1974c) puts forward a partial perception hypothesis, and M. L. Edwards (1974) reports experimental data which indicate that even up to the age of 3;0 certain contrasts are not perceived – in particular fricative contrasts. The partial perception hypothesis is also maintained by Braine (1976b). There are clearly considerable difficulties in constructing reliable experimental techniques to tap the child's perceptual abilities, and while the balance of the evidence (see particularly Barton (1976)) would suggest that children can discriminate adult contrasts by the age of 3, there are still gaps in our knowledge, and perception problems cannot yet be ruled out as a factor in the errors children make in pronunciation.

1.1.2. Homonymy. The judgment by a linguist or a parent that the child's pronunciations of two different adult words are the same may be a function of his own linguistic system. Kornfeld and Goehl (1974) and Macken and Barton (1980) argue that children make consistent phonetic distinctions which are not perceived as distinctions by adults because they fall within the range of variation for a set of phones belonging to a *single* adult phoneme. Macken and Barton isolate three stages in the development of initial stop contrasts, using voice onset time (VOT) as a dependent variable. First, their subjects make no consistent distinction between, say, /p/- and /b/-initial words; at the second stage, they make a consistent contrast, but since it is *within* the VOT range for *one* of the adult phonemic categories, /b/, the contrast is not perceived by adults. Finally, the adult voice onset times are controlled, and the voicing distinction is acquired, productively. The research illustrates again how adult frameworks can be misleading, in this case because the phonetic facts can be distorted by the imposition of an adult transcriptional system; the necessity for instrumental analysis before any decisions are made about certain aspects of the child's phonological system is also demonstrated.

1.1.3. Rule learning. One of the predictions of a rule-based approach to the child's phonological system is that any change in the system will be 'across-the-board': the pronunciation change will immediately apply to all the lexical items to which it is relevant (Smith, 1973: pp. 138ff.). The alternative view is one of lexical diffusion (Hsieh, 1972) – pronunciations spread gradually through the lexicon, and there is a period of time during which there will be considerable variability until the pronunciation stabilizes. It is crucial here to know what is meant by 'immediately' and 'gradually': indeed, Smith (1973: p. 140) acknowledges that 'usually any change was spread over a period of several days, or rarely, weeks, with free variation between old and new forms occurring first in a few words, then in a majority'. This would seem on the face of it to be compatible with the diffusion hypothesis and to fit with the large-sample study of Olmsted (1971). He found in a sample of 100 children from 1;3 to 4;6 that there was a high degree of variability in the phonetic realization of adult phonemes for spontaneous speech. The children in the sample did not learn phones across the board, nor substitute one and only one phone for the adult target. It seems that the across-the-board and diffusion hypotheses may not be totally incompatible. A change in pronunciation may begin gradually in a few frequent, new or otherwise salient words, and only then spread, more or less rapidly, through the rest of the relevant vocabulary. The process of learning how to pronounce could quite easily involve both item learning and rule learning at different substages. Again, more information is needed.

The problems created by using adult-like realization rules are avoided by Stampe (1969), whose term *phonological process* is used and developed by Ingram. The development of phonology is seen not as the acquisition of a set of rules, but as the gradual elimination of a set of simplifying procedures by the child over the period until he acquires adult forms. This approach maintains the universalist perspective introduced to child phonology by Jakobson, while at the same time allowing for individual variations in the ways in which children operate within the processes and the ages at which they leave them behind. As more evidence becomes available it is clear that in phonology as in other areas we are confronted by considerable individual variations in acquisition strategy, and it is as important to be able to explain this as to account for general tendencies.

2.0. Grammar

2.1. Morphology

The inflectional morphology of English has been examined in detail by, among others, Brown (1973), Berko (1958), Menyuk (1969) and de Villiers and de Villiers (1973a). Some of these studies have relied on spontaneous speech and others, since the pioneering work of Berko, have used elicitation techniques. English is not inflectionally rich, and hence the scope of the studies is restricted. Brown numbers among his fourteen grammatical morphemes three (*in*, *on* and the articles – grouped as one morpheme) which are not in fact inflectional. Others (regular plural, present tense, possessive, third person, contractible copula and third person contractible auxiliary *be*) have the same phonemic shape.[2] The chapter by Derwing and Baker greatly extends Berko's original experimental study, and also adds a new dimension to our knowledge of morphology by considering its derivational aspect. Little systematic work exists on English derivational morphology. This partly reflects a relative lack of interest in what are primarily lexical processes on the part of transformationalists, who with some exceptions (e.g. Chapin, 1967) have not concerned themselves so much with this area until

---

[2] For many English speakers it is probably the case in fast speech that contracted *has* is also pronounced as [s] or [z] in the appropriate environments, making six distinct grammatical forms with the same phonemic realization – a remarkable homonymity.

recently (see Halle, 1973), and partly the concentration by child language researchers on the earliest stages of grammatical development, where there is little evidence of derivation. In addition this area is one of semi-productive processes, whereas for the most part inflectional morphemes are fully productive. Derwing and Baker take an experimental approach, which enables them to make reliable claims about morpheme recognition using the commonest derivational morphemes: *-er,* which can be agentive or instrumental; the adverbial marker *-ly*; the adjective marker *-y*; the diminutive *-ie*; and compounds like *bird-house*. Their results suggest that none of these 'rules' (e.g. 'add *-y* to *dirt* to form an adjective') is productive for children under 5 years. This might at first sight seem surprising, since the spontaneous speech of children under 5 will certainly contain words like *dirty, smelly, rainy*. It is however not possible to tell from such data that children using the forms have devised a rule for production or analysis. As always, the crucial data will be mistakes or elicitation techniques of the kind Derwing and Baker provide.

2.2 Syntax

Under the impetus of the Chomskyan revolution this is the area of acquisition research that flourished most extensively in the 1960s. Much of the work has been influenced by that of Brown, his associates and students. Particularly influential has been the hypothesis that the acquisition of syntactic structures 'develops in an approximately invariant form in all children' (1973: p. 58). This research depended heavily on the construction of grammars for child language data, and reaches its apogee, fittingly, in Brown's summation of a decade's work in *A First Language*. The grammar writing tradition presents problems, however, partly because of difficulties in the transformational framework itself, partly again because of the potential distortion of looking at child language in terms of an adult framework, and the limited explanatory power of grammars. To enumerate some of the reasons for a gradual disenchantment with grammar construction as an end in itself:

(i) The data-base for grammars consists of utterances of the language and native-speaker intuitions – the intuitions concern grammaticality, ambiguity and sentence-relatedness. A grammar, in Chomsky's terms, is observationally adequate if it generates the set of grammatical sentences of the language, and descriptively adequate if its structural descriptions match native-speaker intuitions. Achieving observational adequacy is difficult for a number of reasons, one of which is the variation inherent in children's language, at any point in time and as it changes over time. The variation can range from the intermittent use of grammatical morphemes such as past tense in obligatory contexts (Brown, 1973: pp. 54ff.), to restrictions on the use of particular kinds of embedding: Limber (1976) reports considerable restrictions on relative clauses attached to subject NPs. It has been suggested that it may be possible to handle the first kind of variation by variable rules (see Labov and Labov (1978) for an application of such rules to child language data), but there does not seem to be a suitable mechanism for restricting the application of recursive phrase structure rules for the second kind. A much more serious methodological shortcoming, which ensures that grammars for child language cannot have the status of adult grammars (of being at once theories of the language and representing the native speaker's knowledge of it, so far as structural descriptions are concerned) is our general inability to check with the child whether a sentence, which a grammar written for his 'language' generates, is or is not 'grammatical'. Grammars written for adults generate an infinite set of sentences, and it is this projection which can be evaluated. A grammar is successful (in one respect) if it does not predict sentences which the native speaker would reject as ungrammatical. It is not possible to match this method with the child under 5, much less go further and ask if the grammar captures 'linguistically significant generalizations'. (For a criticism of grammar construction for the early stages of children's word combination, see Matthews (1975).)

(ii) Quite apart from the methodological difficulties inherent in trying to fit adult grammar to child data, the diversification of transformational theory at the end of the 1960s outstripped the capacity and willingness of language researchers to continue to apply adult frameworks consistently (particularly as the different theories were less obviously concerned with formalism).

(iii) Another set of reasons arises from the recognition (fluently articulated in Campbell and Wales (1970)) that children (like everyone else) speak sentences in contexts, and that linguistic competence involves not only the learning of sentence forms but the understanding of the relation of these forms to larger units, and to the context in which they are spoken (the child has to learn to say sentences which are *appropriate* in both these senses). It is not of course a necessary consequence of this recognition of what language learning entails that sentence-grammars are eliminable, but the opening of these new horizons has stimulated much effort in investigation of the structure of conversations, for example, and has tended to reduce the importance of sentence-grammars. The interest in matters beyond the sentence has to an extent accompanied developments in linguistic theory, particularly in discourse analysis and pragmatics.

(iv) A further factor in the removal from their central place of sentence-grammars has been scepticism concerning the explanatory value of Chomsky's language acquisition device, and a movement since the beginning of this decade at least to attempt to explain linguistic development in terms of cognition (see Levelt (1975) for a detailed account). The views adopted vary from cognitive–deterministic to cognitive–linguistic–interactionist (as explained in the Introduction to Part III), but the net result is the same – the stripping from grammars of their association with the language acquisition device, and hence a reduction in status to convenient descriptive frameworks.

(v) A similar dissatisfaction with the limited explanatory value of grammars has expressed itself in studies concerned with *process* – the ways in which syntactic structures are used and understood. Grammatical descriptions of the language product are used for identification purposes – to isolate, say, relative clauses. Hypotheses concerning the processing of these entities (e.g. the parallel function strategy – Sheldon, 1974) are then experimentally tested. Bowerman's chapter considers a number of examples along these lines. For the majority of researchers then, the writing of a transformational rule for some child language data no longer has potential epistemological significance, though there are exceptions (see Fay, 1978; Hurford, 1975; Mayer, Erreich and Valian, 1978). How then are syntactic descriptions regarded? It would clearly be a mistake to overreact against the early distortion of the importance of syntax by neglecting it altogether. What seems to happen is that adult syntactic descriptions are used as heuristics. While it would be generally accepted that it is not appropriate to characterize the task of language learning for the child as one of acquiring syntax, nevertheless syntax is still a central part of the learning process, and also an area that we can successfully describe. In several chapters here syntax is more functionally orientated than it was in the mainstream of the grammatical approach to child language. This is particularly true of the chapters by Maratsos, Fletcher and Wales.[3] These all involve the paradigmatic axis of syntax, and so are of necessity more closely concerned with function than the chapters by Garman and Bowerman, which are mainly concerned with the syntagmatic dimension. Macrae provides a functional approach to syntagmatic description. Together, the papers contribute a developmental perspective on syntactic development and present, more diffusely, an account of current thinking on methodology and theory in this area.

---

[3] Wales' chapter is in fact about a heterogeneous set of syntactic features, united under a functional label.

3.0. Lexis

Lexis is the area of language development which has traditionally been the domain of the psychologist, and which has been extensively studied in the last half-century particularly in terms of its growth (see McCarthy (1954) for a review). From a linguistic point of view however there are more interesting questions that can be asked about the vocabulary, or lexicon, that depend on the extension of the notion of *structure* into this area of semantics. There are two aspects of lexical structure which have been investigated more or less extensively in young children: sense-relations like antonymy and hyponymy (defined in Lyons (1963)), and semantic features (included as part of the semantic representation for a generative grammar in Katz and Fodor (1963)). Once again research begins as an application of categories from adult frameworks to children, and once again child language studies have gone beyond the first formulations.

The original theoretical contribution was Clark's *semantic feature hypothesis* (SFH) (see for example E. V. Clark, 1973a). The Katz–Fodor theory suggested that words be represented semantically as bundles of atomic components or features. Each language had a number of features sufficient to characterize the sense (but not the reference) of each word sufficiently to differentiate it from every other word. Thus *man*, *bull*, *ram* would share the feature +*male*, but would have other features in their lexical entries to differentiate them. In this way relationships among words could be made explicit, as well as their differences. The SFH suggests that when the child begins to learn words he has only partial entries in his lexicon, where these entries nevertheless correspond to adult lexical entries by containing a subset of the adult features. The child begins his lexical inventory with words which only have one or two features in them, and lexical learning consists of adding features to entries until the adult set is achieved. The major evidence cited in favour of this hypothesis was the phenomenon of overextension of reference of words by children between 1;0 and 2;6: the extension of early learned words like *dog* to entities like *cow* which might in some respects (four-leggedness) resemble them. The suggestion is that the child's lexical entry for *dog* and *cow* will be specified in the same way, by general features like 'four-legged' and/or 'fur/hair-covered'. Only when he acquires more specific features will the appropriate labelling behaviour ensue. In addition to the early overextensions in spontaneous speech, E. V. Clark reported experimental work (e.g. by Donaldson and Balfour, 1968) which appeared to support the hypothesis.

The relationship between linguistic theory and developmental research can be seen to have become less close in semantics than in other areas, and for much the same reasons. The semantic theory itself has been attacked, particularly concerning the identification and labelling of semantic components (Bolinger, 1965; Lyons, 1977a: pp. 317ff.). Researchers have extended their interests to take in the cognitive underpinning of lexis and reference (e.g. Nelson, 1974; Rosch *et al.*, 1976), and to consider strategies for learning and using lexical items (E. V. Clark, 1973b; Huttenlocher, 1974). In chapter 8, E. V. Clark represents the current state of knowledge concerning the building of a vocabulary, concentrating on the early stages, and considering the various factors which may affect this process, including the semantic complexity of the lexical items, the child's conceptual framework and the strategies children may use to interpret new words.

4.0. Development after five

Chapter 16, by Karmiloff-Smith, brings together a variety of studies on various aspects of syntactic–semantic development which have in common the fact that they supply information on children over 5 years. One of the assumptions of early research was that most language learning took place before the child went to school. The first influential counter-evidence was provided by Carol Chomsky (1969), and a wide range of studies since have substantiated her demonstration that in specific areas of comprehension or production there are still gaps well into the early school years. Karmiloff-Smith reviews the studies by Chomsky and others, and considers the interacting factors involved in their findings – the child's cognitive abilities, the linguistic complexity of the structures he is dealing with, the methodology of the investigation. Her own research indicates that developmental progressions in certain areas can be discerned in children after 5 years, and that even as late as 9 years an important change takes place in their metalinguistic awareness – their ability to reflect on language-as-an-object, and to make judgments (as adults can) which rely on intralinguistic factors.

7. Phonological patterns in the speech of young children

David Ingram

1. Introduction

Between the ages of 1;6 and 4;0, the young child undergoes considerable development in phonological ability. Starting with a small vocabulary of approximately fifty words, the child proceeds from single-word utterances, of very simple phonological form (cf. chapter 3 above), to multi-word utterances that are relatively high in intelligibility. Phonological ability improves through an increase in the ability to produce adult sounds and combine them into more complex phonological structures. Elsewhere (Ingram, 1976a), I have referred to this stage as one in which children acquire 'the phonology of simple morphemes'.

Years ago Jespersen (1922) noted the distinctness of this stage of phonological acquisition from the one that precedes it. In characterizing it, he emphasized the regularities that occur in the child's words (pp. 106–7):

> 'As the child gets away from the peculiarities of his individual "little language", his speech becomes more regular, and a linguist can in many cases see reasons for his distortions of normal words. When he replaces one sound by another there is always some common element in the formation of the two sounds . . . There is generally a certain system in the sound substitutions of children, and in many instances we are justified in speaking of "strictly observed sound-laws".'

For example, Jespersen mentioned the observation that children in different linguistic communities show a tendency to replace velar stops with alveolar ones. The child who says [tæt] for *cat,* will also say [do] for *go.* This general pattern would then qualify as a sound law for this stage of development. Approached in this way, a child's words at any point could be described by specifying the sound laws operating in his speech.

In recent years, sound laws as described by Jespersen have been referred to as *phonological processes,* a term used by Stampe (1969). Stampe sees these processes as consisting of a universal set of hierarchically ordered procedures used by children to simplify speech. They are universal to the

133

extent that every child is born with the facility to simplify speech in a consistent fashion. They are hierarchical in that certain processes are more basic than others. Phonological development is understood by Stampe as a gradual loss of these simplifying processes until the child's words finally match their adult models.

The establishment of the various phonological processes in the speech of young children has been the goal of much recent research (cf. Ingram, 1976a and the references cited there). This research basically consists of attempts to propose generalized statements describing common substitutions in the speech of young children. This chapter will attempt to describe the phonological patterns found in the words used by children between 1;6 and 4;0 through the establishment of phonological processes. It will begin with a description of the more common processes found thus far, with evidence provided from children learning diverse languages. Once the utility of process analysis has been shown, the chapter will then briefly discuss the limitations of this approach. Specifically, the process approach does not explain the striking fact that there is also tremendous individual variation from one child to another. The discussion will conclude with evidence showing that development during this stage also needs to take into account phonological preferences that vary from child to child.

2. Phonological processes

2.1. Substitution processes

A common characteristic of the phonological analysis of the speech of young children is the determination of *substitutions* in the child's words. This is done by comparing the child's word to the adult model and noting the correspondences between the two. Take, for example, the child who says [bɑt] for *book*. The correspondences between the first two segments in the child's form and those in the adult model are a match so that no substitution has taken place. For the final segment, however, adult [k] has been replaced by [t]. The postulation of processes not only describes substitutions, but attempts to explain them. In this case, the difference between the two segments is one of place. The process involved can be described as one which tends to replace velar stops with alveolar ones.

By examining samples of children's words from several children both within and across languages, it is possible to isolate the more common substitutions that occur and subsequently postulate general processes. The first major type of processes are those that result in the replacement of one segment by another. Below are five of the more common *substitution pro-*

cesses, with examples from a variety of children. (For data taken from published works, references follow the first mention of the child's name. Otherwise, data are taken from the author's own files. Also, phonetic transcriptions have been altered to conform to those used throughout this book.)

Stopping. Fricatives, and occasionally other sounds, are replaced with a stop consonant.

English
A (Smith, 1973) 2;9 *sea* [tiː]; *sing* [tiŋ]; *say* [tʰei].

French
Suzanne (Deville, 1890–1) 1;9 *fleur* 'flower' [pø]; *chaud* 'hot' [tɔ]; *seau* 'bucket' [tɔ]; *sel* 'salt' [te].

Hungarian
(examples from Kerek, 1975) /viraːg/ 'flower' [bijaːg]; /faːzik/ 'he is cold' [paːzik]; /saija/ 'his mouth' [taːja].

Fronting. Velar and palatal consonants tend to be replaced with alveolar ones.

English
Joan (Velten, 1943) 2;0 *shoe* [zu·]; *shop* [za·p]; *call* [ta·]; *coat* [dut]; *goat* [dut]; *goose* [du·s].

French
Suzanne 1;11 *chaise* 'chair' [sɛ]; *chat* 'cat' [sa]; *cassé* 'broken' [tase]; *cou* 'neck' [tu]; *gâteau* 'cake' [tatɔ].

Polish
Hania (Zarębina, 1965) 1;11 /dz'eŋkuje/ 'thank you' [dz'ekuje]; /tʃasu/ 'time' [ts'as'u]; /dzembi/ 'If I were' [z'embi]. (But note: /koniki/ 'pony' [kaniki].)

Gliding. A glide [w] or [j] is substituted for a liquid sound, i.e. [l] or [r].

English
Jennika 2;1 *lap* [jæp]; *leg* [jek]; *ready* [wedi].

Estonian
Linda (Vihman, 1971) 1;9 *raha* 'money' [jaha·]; *Rosbi* 'Robert' [jo·bi]; *ruttu* 'fast' [jut·u].

BUT *French*
Elie-Paul (Vinson, 1915) 1;9 *lampe* 'lampe' [ãp]; *la* 'the' [a]; *lapin* 'rabbit' [apɛ̃].
Suzanne 1;10 *lapin* [apɛ̃]; *laver* 'wash' [ave]; *lire* 'read' [i]; *lune* 'moon' [um].

Vocalization. A vowel replaces a syllabic consonant, a process particularly characteristic of English.

Philip (Adams, 1972) 1;9 *apple* [apo]; *bottle* [babu]; *bottom* [bada]; *button* [bʌtʌ]; *dinner* [dindʌ]; *hammer* [mænu].

Vowel neutralization. Vowels tend to be changed into oral and often centralized vowels, i.e. [a] or [ʌ].

Joan 2;0 *back* [bat]; *hat* [hat]; *yard* [zaːd]; *hug* [had].

The stopping process is widespread and is one of the more established patterns in children's speech. Fricatives are the most commonly affected group of sounds, although resonants will also occasionally be affected. While stopping is common, the actual patterns of its application by individual children are not. Children typically will not necessarily change all of their fricatives into stops, and it is not possible to predict which ones individual children will select (cf. Ingram (1977) for a more detailed discussion of this).

Fronting is also quite common across children, although some children reveal preference for it more than others. It is important to realize that there are actually two processes involved here, fronting of palatals, and fronting of velars; and children may show one and not the other. Also, the process interacts with stopping so that it is not unusual to find an English or French child replacing [ʃ] with [t].

We know less about the process of gliding, although it is well-documented in English. An examination of data from seven French children did not reveal any cases of it. Interestingly, French does not use word initial [j] and has also restricted use of [w], suggesting that English children may be substituting glides since they are available in other words in the child's language. This may indicate that the substitutions used in phonological processes are significantly influenced by the child's phonological system, not just by universal tendencies.

Vocalization is common in English where syllabic consonants often occur. For the velarized [ɫ], the most frequent substitution is a back rounded vowel, either [o] or [u]. In other cases, an [a]-like vowel occurs, although the substitution may also be affected by the tendency to assimilate unstressed vowels to stressed ones.

The last process, vowel neutralization, is an especially early one and is normally not characteristic of this rapid period of development. Joan (Velten, 1943) appears to be highly atypical in this regard. Also, nasal vowels appears to be acquired quite early by French children. Other processes do affect vowels, however, such as the tendency to unround front rounded vowels, and the occasional tensing of lax vowels. Since vowels develop quite rapidly, the processes which affect them seem to be lost earlier than those for consonants.

2.2. Assimilatory processes

Another general group of processes that will result in mismatches between the child's form and the adult model is the one that is composed of tendencies to assimilate one segment in a word to another. Even if the child has acquired a particular adult sound in some words, there may be certain contexts where his production may be altered. While detailed research is necessary on this topic, the following processes are relatively common:

Voicing. Consonants tend to be voiced when preceding a vowel, and devoiced at the end of a syllable.

> *English*
> A *paper* 2;3 [beːbə]; 2;7 [beibə]; 2;7 [peːpə]; 2;8 [pʰeipə]; *tiny* 2;4 [daini]; 2;7 [taini]; 2;8 [tʰaini].
> Kristen 1;5 *pig* [bik]; *paper* [bɛpi]; *toes* [doʂ].
> Jennika 1;6 *bed* [bɛt]; *bib* [bip]; *bird* [bit]; *egg* [ek].
>
> *French*
> Jacqueline (Bloch, 1913) 1;7 *popo* 'chamber pot' [bobo]; *pelle* 'shovel' [beː]; *poule* 'hen' [bu] [buː] [bubu].

Consonant harmony. In C_1VC_2 (X) contexts, consonants tend to assimilate to each other in certain predictable ways. Three frequent patterns are:

> (i) Velar assimilation: apical consonants tend to assimilate to a neighbouring velar consonant:
> Jennika 1;7 *duck* [gʌk]; *sock* [gʌk]; *tongue* [gʌŋ].
> A 2;2 *tickle* [gigu]; *truck* [gʌk]; *taxi* [gɛgi].
> (ii) Labial assimilation: apical consonants tend to assimilate to a neighbouring labial consonant:
> Daniel (Menn, 1975) *tub* [bʌb]; *table* [bʌbu]; *steps* [bɛps]; *tape* [bejp].
> (iii) Denasalization: a nasal consonant will denasalize in the neighbourhood of a nonnasal consonant:
> *French*
> Elie-Paul 2;1 *mouton* 'sheep' [potɔ̃]; 2;2 *morceau* 'piece' [baʃo]; *mouchez* 'blow nose' [bøʃe]; *monsieur* [poʃø].
> Fernande (Roussey, 1899–1900) 2;1 *malade* 'sick' [balaːd]; *mange* 'eat' [baʃ]; *menton* 'chin' [baːtoː]; *marcher* 'walk' [base].

Progressive vowel assimilation. An unstressed vowel will assimilate to a preceding (or following) stressed vowel.

English
Joan 2;0 *bacon* [búːdu]; *birdie* [búːdu]; *flower* [fáːwa]; *hammer* [haːma]; *table* [duːbu].

French
Fernande 1;7 *oiseau* 'bird' [pogʸo]; *pomme de terre* 'potato' [tɛtɛt].

Voicing as described actually refers to two separate but related processes. One of these, the devoicing of final consonants, is well documented as a characteristic of languages. The other, the voicing of prevocalic consonants, requires some discussion. To date, this process has been predominantly observed for English. There is the possibility, as mentioned in Ingram (1974a: p. 60), that what transcribers have recorded as voiced consonants are actually voiceless unaspirated ones, since English speakers hear voiceless unaspirated consonants as voiced ones. While it may be true that transcribers have made some errors in hearing voiceless unaspirated segments as voiced ones, there is evidence to suggest that voicing does take place. Firstly, Smith (1973) made this distinction in his data, and they show a gradual shift from a voiced substitution to a voiceless unaspirated to the correct voiceless aspirated. Second, there is evidence in Bloch (1913) that his French-learning daughter voiced prevocalic consonants at the beginning of her phonological development. Since French [p] is voiceless unaspirated, it is highly unlikely that Bloch was in error. Lastly, recent evidence (e.g. Gilbert, 1977) shows that voice onset time for voiceless stops is less stable and takes longer to develop than for voiced ones.

Young children show various kinds of consonant harmony or assimilation (see above for three frequent patterns). This is an area that is not particularly well documented and one that requires more research. One problem is that some children appear to assimilate more than others, and that the various possibilities for assimilation are quite numerous. It may be that phonological preferences (discussed in section 3.3 below) determine a great many of the variations that occur. Menn (1975) has proposed that there is a strength hierarchy that determines the direction of assimilation, where weaker consonants become homorganic to stronger ones. The hierarchy, from strongest position to weakest, is velar, labial, dental. This means, for example, that dentals will assimilate to both labials and velars, with the latter being a stronger tendency. She uses this hierarchy to explain patterns in her son Daniel's speech, which fell into four types.

(1) b – d   e.g. *bed* [bɛd]; *boots* [buts]
(2) k – p, d   e.g. *cup* [kʌp]; *cuddle* [kʌdu]
(3) t – b ⟶ b – b   e.g. *tub* [bʌb]; *table* [bʌbu]
(4) b – g ⟶ g – g   e.g. *big* [gɨg]; *back* [gæk]

She states (p. 295): 'The rule is that C_1 assimilates to C_2 if C_1 is weaker than C_2 on the strength hierarchy.' Further analyses of this kind are required to establish more general observations on consonant harmony.

The denasalization process is characteristic of French and shows how the phonology of a specific language may result in particular processes being emphasized. The process is not as operative in English, presumably because of the tendency to have initial stress. I have observed one English child, Daniel, who at 2;10 said [bən'ík] for *Monique*, his babysitter, and [bˡʃέl] for *Michelle*, a neighbourhood acquaintance.

Since vowels develop rapidly, progressive vowel assimilation is a process that is usually lost early. Children differentiate vowels within a word early in development, although isolated cases of assimilation occur for several months.

2.3. Syllable structure processes

Although it has not been explicitly mentioned, the notion of syllable is clearly of importance in understanding all the processes so far discussed. Substitution processes will vary according to the place of the sound in the syllable. For instance, stopping of fricatives is usually lost for final fricatives before it is for syllable initial ones. Stated differently, fricatives are easier to produce postvocalically than prevocalically. The notion of syllable is also important in assimilatory processes. The voicing of consonants differs according to the place in the syllable. For consonant harmony, it is known that children often have an early restriction that the consonants in CVC structures must be homorganic. With vowel assimilation and denasalization, the important factor is that a segment in an unstressed syllable is likely to 'weaken' or assimilate to a segment in the stressed syllable.

Besides these syllabic influences, there are specific phonological processes which are directly motivated by the tendency of young children to simplify syllable structure. For most children, the direction is towards a basic CV syllable. Some of the more basic *syllable structure processes* include the following:

Cluster reduction. A consonant cluster is reduced to a single consonant.

English
Philip 1;11 *clown* [kaon]; *play* [pe]; *train* [ten]; *dress* [dɛs].
French
Elie-Paul 2;1 *bleu* 'blue' [bø]; *clef* 'key' [ke]; *grand* 'big' [gã]; *prends* 'take' [pã].

Estonian
Linda 1;9 *klaun* 'clown' [kaum]; *kleit* 'dress' [kit·]; 1;8 *prillid* 'eye-glasses' [pil'·a]; 1;9 *kruvi* 'screw' [kup·].

German
Dorothy 2;2 *fliegen* 'fly' [fiːkən]; *trinken* 'drink' [tikən]; *grosse* 'big' [gosə]; *schreiben* 'write' [saibən].

Deletion of final consonants. A CVC syllable is reduced to CV by deleting the final consonant.

English
Jennika 1;5 *bib* [bi]; *bike* [bai]; *more* [mʌ]; out [aɒ].

French
Suzanne 2;0 *air* 'air' [ɛ]; *allumette* 'match' [me]; *assiette* 'plate' [asɛ]; *autruche* 'ostrich' [ɔsu].

Deletion of unstressed syllables. An unstressed syllable is deleted, especially if it precedes a stressed syllable.

English
Jennika 1;9 *banana* [nǽnʌ]; *bicycle* [báikɒɫ]; 2;3 *Granola* [ówʌ] ; 1;11 *Jennika* [géŋkʌ]; *potato* [dédo].

Romanian
Eileen (Vogel, 1975) 2;0 *maşina* 'the car' [ʃína]; *prosopol* 'the towel' [sépɒ]; *lumina* 'light' [ninːə]; *papuşă* 'doll' [puʃa].

Reduplication. In a multi-syllabic word, the initial CV syllable is repeated.

English
Philip 1;9 *Anne-Marie* [mimi]; *cookie*, [gege]; *Rogers* [dada]; *TV* [didi]; *water* [wawa].

French
Jacqueline 1;11 *asseoir* 'sit' [sisi]; *bravette* 'bib' [ʌɛʌːɛ]; *bouche* 'mouth' [bubu]; *poupée* 'doll' [pepːe]; *serviette* 'napkin' [üɛüɛ]; *vache* 'cow' [vava].

The reduction of clusters is one of the most widespread processes observed. The direction of the deletion is also predictable in many instances. One of the most regular patterns is the deletion of sonorants when they occur in combinations with stop consonants. The deletion of [s] is also common, although there are cases where [s] has been retained instead of the stop. This situation may result if the child has an [s] preference (see section 3.3 below). In nasal and stop clusters, stops are usually retained, although the nasal will often be kept if the stop is voiced.

Both the deletion of final consonants and unstressed syllables are also frequent, although the latter seems to persist longer than the former. When final consonants do begin to appear, they develop gradually, with certain sounds appearing before others. Although conclusive data still need to be collected, there does appear to be a tendency for the appearance of final nasals to occur early. Also, fricatives tend to be easier in final position than initially, although there is individual variation. Some suggestions for the order of appearance of final consonants are presented in Renfrew (1966).

The last process mentioned above, reduplication, occurs quite early in children's speech and is often lost by the time the stage under discussion begins. Some reduplications persist, however, and other partial reduplications continue to occur, e.g. [babi] for *blanket,* when the consonant is reduplicated. Of some interest is the fact that children vary greatly in their tendencies to reduplicate. Some seem to like to do it a lot, whereas others rarely do it. There is also a relation between this process and the deletion of final consonants. Some children acquire their final postvocalic consonants through the use of reduplication, e.g. *bag* [baga], based on Ross (1937).

3. Other aspects of phonological development

The establishment of phonological processes in the speech of young children is in itself an advance in the description of phonological development between 1;6 and 4;0. Given just the small number of processes mentioned in section 2, one could say a great deal about any random phonological sample of a child. To do this, however, would impose certain limitations, some superficial but others more substantive, which should be pointed out. This section will briefly discuss some other aspects of phonological development that are also important in understanding this stage of acquisition.

3.1. Dynamic considerations

In studying a young child's speech, one is constantly confronted by the fact that the system being observed is under constant change, i.e. it is not static but dynamic, at any time showing both older and newer developments. This is highly important in the study of phonological development, and is manifested in a variety of ways.

One of the most striking consequences is the *phonetic variability* that children show in their pronunciation of words. The examples from a variety of children given in section 2 may have conveyed the impression that these were the only ways they said these words. In reality, children will often show a variety of productions for the same words. Jennika, for example, produced the following forms for *blanket* on the same day, 1;6:24: [bwati], [bati], [baki], [batit]. Works in English have often avoided the mention of phonetic variability (e.g. Velten, 1943), although the French diarists (e.g. Roussey, 1899–1900) were usually very careful to record alternative forms. Bloch (1913: p. 39), for example, found this very characteristic of the period of development discussed in this chapter:

> 'This mobility is much less noticeable during the early months than in the later ones . . . it seems that during the months preceding 1;9, when the vocabulary was limited to around 40 words and language was used less frequently, pronunciation was more fixed than after this time, when the vocabulary grew every day and the linguistic work of the child became more active.'

Whether or not this stage has more mobility than the previous one needs to be studied, but the fact that it exists is well established (if often ignored).

One reason for phonetic mobility is presumably the fact that children are gradually moving from one pronunciation of a word to another; put differently, phonological processes are not lost suddenly but gradually. Thus, the analyst must not only isolate and describe the phonological processes children use, but also state the percentages of their occurrence both within and across words. Stating this percentage with the forms for a single word is important because it appears that some words are more phonetically variable than others. The reasons for this are not well understood, although they probably include phonetic complexity, and novelty of the word. That is, the more complex a word is, and the more recent has been its acquisition, both appear to contribute to higher variability in pronunciation.

Another highly important factor in the description of phonological development is the notion of *word* (cf. Ferguson and Farwell, 1975). At any point, children will usually have *frozen forms* in their speech, which are pronunciations that occur early in development and persist when better pronunciation might be expected. Philip, for example, at 1;9, was still saying [gege] for *cookie* even though his production from other words suggested that he should have been able to say *cookie*. Also, children will produce occasional *advanced forms*, productions that are better than what might be expected, given the child's phonological abilities. Jennika, for example, used [bwati] for *blanket* at 1;5, although her form settled into [bati] at 1;6 and [badæ] at 1;8. The advanced use of a cluster was not representative of her system.

The simultaneous occurrence of advanced and frozen forms with more typical forms of production shows the dynamic nature of the child's system. Phenomena like this indicate that it is not always possible to generalize about phonological processes since the words must also be considered which they affect. A particular process may not occur in all instances because of certain peculiarities of individual words, not because the process is necessarily being lost.

The inclusion of the words themselves as a significant factor in how the child's phonological system is used, leads me to claim that the description of that system based on process analyses (as described in section 2 above), i.e.

adult form + phonological processes = child's form

is inadequate. As I have argued elsewhere (Ingram, 1974a, 1975b, 1976b), it is necessary to consider the possibility that children actively operate on adult forms to establish their own phonological representations of these words. That is, there is (a) the adult form; (b) the child's representation of the word; (c) the child's spoken form. For example, Philip's form of [gege] for *cookie* persists because he has established this form as the representation of this word, and this representation becomes resistant to phonological processes. With new words that show advanced form, we can say that that child has not yet established a representation, so that the form has not yet conformed to the child's system. The claim that the child has a system of his or her own is controversial (cf. discussion in Ingram, 1976c), yet it appears to account for some otherwise inexplicable aspects of young children's phonological patterns.

The existence of phonetic variability and lexical influences shows that phonological processes cannot be stated simply. Even if a complete list of possible processes could be compiled, problems concerning their degree of operation and effects in certain words must be considered. The inclusion of these factors into process analyses, however, provides a broader description of early phonological development.

3.2. Nonisomorphic processes

Thus far, phonological processes have been assumed to be isomorphic in relating adult form to the child's production. That is, there is a one-to-one correspondence between each element in the adult form and each one in the child's. The child who says [gɔg] for *dog* has an isomorphic relation between the initial segment of the output and the adult model's initial segment [d]. In this case, the substitution is [g] for [d] with the process involved being that of velar assimilation. These individual isomorphic processes, then, are grouped under more general titles such as cluster reduction, voicing, etc.

While these processes help to explain most of the substitutions children make, there are cases where nonisomorphic processes are involved, i.e.

where the relevant process cannot be explained by referring to one-to-one correspondences between the adult and child forms. To explain these, a broader view of the notion of process needs to be developed.

One example of this kind comes from a young German child, Dorothy. At 2;2:26, she was recorded several times producing the word *Flugzeug* /fluktsɔik/ 'airplane' as [suktɔix]. Within a typical process analysis, we could propose that initial f→s and the final k→x by substitution processes. Although none of the processes mentioned earlier covers these, we could propose that these are possible but not necessarily widespread processes. However, a more direct explanation is possible. Notice that both syllables of her word have similar place relations of alveolar, then velar. We could say that the f→s change is triggered by the t–k sequence in the second syllable. (There are no other cases of f→s in the data.) The change of k→x looks unusual at first, but can be accounted for by proposing that she is balancing the syllables by having one fricative in each. The juxtaposed elements of the two syllables are both stops ([k, t]), and the outermost are both fricatives. There is a combination of factors causing the pattern and they are far from isomorphic.

The data above could possibly be incorporated into syllable structure processes, but this becomes even more difficult for the case described by Priestly (1977). Around 1;10 to 1;11, his son Christopher showed a number of words that all had the following shape:

(a)	*banana*	[bajan]	1;10	(c)	*carrot*	[kajat]	1;11
	chocolate	[kajak]	1;10		*peanut*	[pijat]	1;10
(b)	*Brenda*	[bɛjan]	1;10	(d)	*steamer*	[mijat]	1;10
	panda	[pajan]	1;10				

Group (a) was by far the predominant pattern. The processes the child seemed to follow were these:
(i)   change all multi-syllabic words into the structure C_1VjVC_2
(ii) after cluster reduction, place the initial consonant of the adult word into the C_1 position
(iii) if the second consonant of the adult word is an obstruent, place it into the C_2 position (group a)
(iv) if the second consonant of the adult word is a sonorant, skip it and place the next consonant into the C_2 position (group c)
(v)   if the second consonant is a sonorant, but there is not a third consonant, place the sonorant into C_2 (group b: the [d] in these is presumably deleted previously by cluster reduction)
There are no obvious explanantions for some cases, such as *streamer*, which, by the above rules, should have been [tijam], instead of [mijat]. There is yet

another peculiarity in Christopher's pattern. The only final consonants in his words are [m, t, s, n, l, ŋ, k]. Of these, [s, n, l] never occur word initially, and thus this may exemplify another of Christopher's principles.

Regardless of how one would like to analyse these data, it is clear that analyses by processes alone would fail. Instead, one will need to resort to the notion, mentioned above, that the child constructs a system of his own. In many cases, this system may not be obvious. With Christopher, however, the child has organized the adult forms in a very specific way, and this varies a great deal from the adult models. Children in this stage of development will use both phonological processes of the sort discussed as well as others that result from his active organization of the representation of words.

3.3 Phonological preferences

Much of this chapter has shown very general processes children use to simplify the words of the adult language. In sections 3.1 and 3.2 observations have been made which show ways that children may differ from each other, despite choosing from a similar (perhaps universal) set of processes. There is another striking way in which children construct a phonological system that results in marked differences between children. This is the result of individual *phonological preferences* from child to child.

A phonological preference is used here to refer to a preference by a child for a specific articulatory pattern. This preference may be for a particular class of sounds, such as fricatives or nasals, or for a particular kind of syllable structure. The result is that the child will produce an unusual number of words that show the preferred sounds or syllable structure. The data from Christopher are an example of a phonological preference for a particular syllable structure.

It is not particularly unusual to find children who have a preference for a particular sound or group of sounds. Philip, a child mentioned in several examples so far, had for several months a phonological preference for nasal consonants. This preference showed itself in a variety of ways, such as using many words with nasals and showing a tendency to assimilate non-nasal consonants to nasal ones. Here are some examples from his sample which show this:

candle	[naɲu]	1;7	[naɲu]	1;9
candy	[ɲaɲi]	1;7	[naɲi]	1;9
cream	[mim]	and	[miŋ]	1;9
down	[naɵ]	1;7	[naɵn]	1;9
hammer	[mænaɵ]	1;7	[mænu]	1;9

meow	[memaɒ]	1;7		
plane	[me]	1;7		
sandwich	[nanu]	1;7	[nænu]	1;9

Notice that nasal assimilation does not account for the medial [m] in *meow*. When a child has a preference such as this, several processes will usually be involved.

The fact that preferences like these can lead to individual variation between children can be shown by looking at data from three French children in the production of fricatives. French has the following word initial fricatives: [f, v, s, z, ʃ, ʒ]. These can be divided into three distinct places of articulation – labial, dental, and alveo-palatal. Table 1 presents the substitution patterns for these fricatives for three French children as reported by their fathers (a dash indicates no words used with the sound). Elie-Paul has a marked alveo-palatal preference, shown by his use of [ʃ] for several of the fricatives. Some examples are: *casser* /kase/ 'break' [ʃe]; *chaud* /ʃo/ 'hot' [ʃo]; *jus* /ʒu/ 'juice' [ʃü]. Fernande, on the other hand, has a dental preference, using [s] throughout her language, e.g. *baiser* /bɛsɛ/ 'kiss' [bɛse]; *bonjour* /bɔ̃ʒür/ 'good morning' [busu]; *bravo* /bravo/ 'bravo!' [baso:]; *café* /kafe/ 'coffee' [kase]; *fil* /fil/ 'thread' [sil]; *manger* /mãʒe/ 'eat' [base]. Both Elie-Paul and Fernande had a difficult time with [f], and neither acquired it before age 3. Suzanne, on the other hand, found the labials quite easy and acquired both by 1;11, even though both adult [s] and [ʃ] still were not acquired. Even though labials did not occur for other fricatives, we could still describe Suzanne as having a labial preference of sorts. The more striking differences between these three children can be described as the result of different preferences for particular places of articulation.

While the above preferences show preferred sounds, there may also be differences dependent on the place of sound in a word. Concerning conson-

Table 1. *Substitution patterns for French fricatives by three French-learning children*

Adult sound	Elie-Paul 1;11	Substitutions Fernande 2;4	Suzanne 1;11
/f/	–	s	f
/v/	–	s	v
/s/	ʃ	s	s (t)
/z/	ʃ	–	z
/ʃ/	ʃ	s	s
/ʒ/	ʃ	s	ʒ

ants, one can speak of three basic positions: initial, medial, and final. Children may vary concerning their preferences for each of these positions. Christopher (Priestly, 1977) had definite preferences for initial and final consonants, using only [j] in medial position, with a preferred structure C_1VjVC_2. However, Padmint (based on Ross, 1937) preferred initial and medial consonants. To avoid final consonants, he would reduplicate vowels: e.g. 1;8 *bag* [baga]; *book* [buku]; *brick* [biki]; *dog* [dɔgɔ]; *pot* [pɔtɔ]. Lastly, Stern and Stern (1928) report that their son Günter from 1;11 to 2;4 had a preference for medial and final consonants. Initial consonants were either omitted or replaced by [h] and occasionally the palatal fricative [ç]. As with the French fricatives, there are children who show preferences for each possible alternative.

Data like these show that the use of a highly common set of phonological preferences does not mean that the phonologies of individual children will necessarily look very similar. The distinct preferences of each child may result in the outputs of individual children being quite different. Even though children have similar possibilities to choose from, they appear to choose in very different ways.

There is one further observation that needs to be made about individual children. The unusual or interesting changes exemplified above are not seen in all children, i.e. some keep very close to the adult models and use only the most familiar phonological processes. This in itself results in individual variations between children, and yet this topic has been rarely discussed in the literature. It may even be that these children constitute a majority, and that the cases most often cited in the literature are atypical in their phonological development.

4. Summary

At the beginning of this chapter it was suggested that much of the rapid phonological development taking place between the ages of 1;6 and 4;0 can be described by looking for general phonological processes. These are essentially statements about how children simplify adult words. After a brief description of some of the more general processes in children's speech, it was suggested that this form of analysis had two main limitations. One concerned the problem of the child's language being dynamic in nature, so that any analysis needs to take into account both old and new developments, as well as the gradualness of phonological change. The second limitation was that the child's active organization of his own system was not taken into account. The processes which a child may evolve in these cases look very different from those more commonly found in the literature, and they show a willingness on the child's part to break down the more frequent isomorphic relation that is maintained between adult forms and the child's production. The use of different organizational principles can account for some of the individual variation between children. It was specifically suggested that the phonological preferences of individual children will also contribute to marked differences. Phonological development in this stage can be shown to consist of both the general phonological processes and also the unique phonological preferences that children show in various productions of speech forms for the language they are acquiring.

8. Building a vocabulary: words for objects, actions and relations*

Eve V. Clark

When children start to talk, they talk mainly about the 'here and now'. But to do so, they have to work out which words can be used for talking about objects, actions and relations in different conceptual domains. This chapter focuses on which words children seem to acquire first, how they go about working out new word meanings, and how they build up their vocabularies.

1. First words

Children clearly learn a good deal about different objects, actions and relations before they ever begin to talk. They learn to identify objects that can move on their own and make other things move – a primitive class of 'movers' that probably includes people, particularly adult caretakers familiar to the child, and vehicles like cars and trains. They also identify objects that can easily be moved by themselves or by other people, 'moveables' such as items of clothing (shoes, socks, gloves) or toys (balls, rattles, teddy bears). They identify possible recipients, usually people they can give objects to or leave objects with. They know the places where objects are usually kept, e.g. the toy box. And they are also familiar with instruments for eating (a spoon or fork) or for playing certain games, e.g. a stick used to knock down blocks (see Clark, 1977a; Clark and Clark, 1977). In fact, one can plausibly argue that children have already organized much of their knowledge about particular categories of objects, actions and relations before they start on language at all. While it is important to keep such conceptual development distinct from language development, it clearly provides a critical foundation for language to be built on.

The 'here and now' provides the major topic for children's one- and two-word utterances, a topic reflected in their early vocabulary (see, e.g.,

* The preparation of this chapter was supported in part by the National Science Foundation Grant no. BNS 75–17126. I am particularly grateful to Elaine S. Andersen, Mary Louise Edwards, Catherine Sortor and Lyris Wiedermann for bringing some of the data discussed here to my attention.

Bohn, 1914; Boyd, 1914; Grant, 1915; Guillaume, 1927; Nice, 1915, 1917; Nelson, 1973b). Young children talk about food: *juice, milk, cookie, bread* and *drink*, to list the commonest terms used. They talk about body-parts, starting with terms like *eye, nose, mouth* and *ear*, and later going beyond the face to the upper and lower limbs, and details of those limbs (see Andersen, 1978). They talk about clothing: *hat, shoe, diaper* or *nappy*, and *coat*. They talk about animals; *dog, cat* or *kitty, bird, duck* or *hen, cow, horse* and *sheep* appear by 1;6 or 2 years (see especially Nice, 1915). They talk about vehicles, the commonest being *car, truck, boat* and *train*. They talk about toys, with *ball, block, book* and *doll* being the ones mentioned earliest. They talk about various household items, often those that seem to be involved in their daily routines: *cup, spoon, bottle, brush, key, clock* and *light*. And finally, they talk about people: *dada* or *papa, mama* or *mummy*, and *baby* (the latter usually in self-reference). In summary, the first fifty or so words that children acquire today fall into the same categories as the first words of half a century ago, and the actual words occurring most frequently in each category are essentially the same too.

Where do children get their first words from? While the answer has to be, from their caretakers, it turns out that their caretakers seem to anticipate the young child's world in their own choice of words (Brown, 1958). This anticipation is directly reflected in the baby talk words available in many different languages. Baby talk words, which are often substituted for the adult equivalents, include conventional onomatopoeic words for the sounds made by animals, e.g. *meow* or *woof-woof* in lieu of *cat* and *dog*; words for certain games and for toys, e.g. *patty-cake, peekaboo, choo-choo* (train); words for routines and bodily functions, e.g. *wee-wee, night-night, upsy-daisy* (said while lifting or righting the child); and words for certain kin terms such as *mummy* and *daddy* (Ferguson, 1964, 1977). In fact, an examination of the domains covered by baby talk words across different languages shows a very close correspondence with just those domains children seem to talk about first, the domains that make up the child's 'here and now'.

Although the words children use for members of particular categories are very similar, a list of the objects these first words refer to does not necessarily reveal what children talk about. For example, when a child says *truck*, he might be picking out the truck because it's a mover, a moveable, or a place – one of the roles the object could play in the event in question. Recently, Greenfield and Smith (1976) have argued that one-word utterances (just like longer, more complex utterances) name particular roles, not just the objects themselves. For example, children name movers (usually the instigators of an action) as in *mummy* said as the mother puts on the child's shoe, or *dada* said as he gets into the car. They also name moveables affected by an action, as in *spoon* said as the child drops his spoon, and they name recipients, usually people, and places too. They also talk about actions, or states that result from actions, as in *down* said after sitting down, or *off* after turning off a light (see Farwell, 1977).

Greenfield and Smith argued that children typically come to talk about the roles that different objects have in much the order just presented. The earliest roles talked about – movers and moveables – may be more salient to young children. Both, potentially, involve movement. This could be why words for potential movers (people, animals and vehicles) and for potential moveables (clothing, toys and food) make up the bulk of children's early vocabulary.

1.1. First meanings

When children begin to understand and produce their first words, do they use them in the same way as adults? Have they attached the same meanings to them as adults? The answer to this question is probably no. Children clearly cannot start out with ready-made adult-like meanings for each new word they hear. There is no way for them to divine automatically the full adult meanings. Rather, they have to work out the meanings of new words, relying on the context of use, nonverbal clues, general knowledge, use by other speakers and knowledge of other related but contrasting meanings. The process of working out the full adult meaning may take children a long time.

On hearing a new word, children make a preliminary hypothesis about its meaning and then, if necessary, gradually modify their original hypothesis until their meaning eventually coincides with the adult one. The first hypotheses children come up with may result in a mismatch with adult usage in several ways: (a) *overextension* – the child's meaning may overlap with the adult's but extend beyond the adult category named by the word in one or more directions; (b) *underextension* – the child's meaning may cover only part of the adult category named and nothing else; or (c) *no overlap* – the child may make a false start, picking a meaning that has no overlap with the adult's (see Clark and Clark, 1977). In the case of (c), the child will simply fail to communicate. In the case of (b), detectable from refusals to use a word, the child's actual usage will often be indistinguishable from the adult's. In the case of (a), the child may use a word in many contexts judged inappropriate by an adult.

Overextensions are fairly common in the speech of children under $2\frac{1}{2}$ years, and diary studies since the last century recorded them in considerable detail for many different languages (e.g. Kenyeres, 1926; Leopold, 1939,

1949b; Palovitch, 1920; Preyer, 1889; Sully, 1896; Taine, 1877). Children's overextensions appear to rely heavily on similarity of shape, but they are also based on similarities of movement, texture, size, sound and taste, as well as on more global judgments of similarity between situations (E. V. Clark, 1973a). To give a couple of examples, one child used the word *mooi* (moon) first for the moon and then for a cake, round marks made by blowing on a cold windowpane, writing on windows and in books, round shapes in books, tooling on leather book covers, round postmarks on letters, and the letter O (Chamberlain and Chamberlain, 1904). Another child, acquiring French, used *nénin* (breast) first for breast or food and then for a button on a garment, the point of someone's bare elbow, an eye in a portrait and the face of someone in a photograph (Guillaume, 1927). In each instance, the children seemed to have seized on some similarity of shape (roundish), and maybe size as well, in their overextensions of the original words (see further Bowerman, 1976b; E. V. Clark, 1973a, 1975).

The relatively incomplete meanings revealed by such overextensions are gradually narrowed down as children find out more about how each word is used and as they acquire other words that are related in meaning to those that are overextended (E. V. Clark, 1973a; Leopold, 1939, 1949b; Moore, 1896; Pavlovitch, 1920). For example, a child might begin by using the word *dog* to pick out a variety of different animals (usually four-legged, mammal-shaped entities), but upon acquiring *moo* or *cow* restricts his overextended use of *dog* which now shares the animal domain with the word *cow*. The acquisition of other animal terms helps the child progressively narrow down the application of *dog* until it coincides with adult usage. In the case of underextensions, of course, the child would have to expand the range of application for a word so that, again, his usage would come to coincide with the adult's. Working out adult meanings, therefore, goes hand-in-hand with acquiring a larger vocabulary.

1.2. Communicating with few words

Another important factor in considering children's early words and word meanings is the extent to which they have to make do with the limited resources they have for communicating what they want, what interests them and what is happening. In the absence of the 'right' word, children presumably stretch whatever words they have to fit a particular situation. And the word that seemed the closest in meaning, that most nearly fitted, would be the best. A general communicative strategy of this type should be particularly useful to children who are still working out the full adult meanings (Clark, 1977c).

Some evidence that children do stretch their resources in just this way comes from the asymmetry that has been observed between children's early production of words and their comprehension of them. Thomson and Chapman (1975), for instance, looked at how young children understood some of the words they had overextended in production. They would show a child who had previously used the word *doggie* for cows and horses as well as dogs, two pictures (e.g. a dog and a horse) and say 'Show me the doggie.' Four of the five children they studied showed a distinct preference for choosing the appropriate adult referent for at least half the words overextended in production. For instance, one child aged 1;11 overextended *apple* to numerous other spherical and round objects (balls, cherries, tomatoes, biscuits, etc.) in production, yet in comprehension stuck to the appropriate adult referent, an apple. In other words, children may continue to overextend certain words in production *after* they have worked out the adult meaning just because they do not yet have enough words to talk about all the things they want to. This stretching of resources may result in asymmetries between production and comprehension in early word use (see Huttenlocher, 1974; Moore, 1896).

2. Mapping words onto conceptual domains

Although children start off by talking about a rather limited number of conceptual domains, they quickly begin to expand their horizons – and their vocabularies. From two or so on, they rapidly add to their repertoire of labels for objects, actions and relations. However, the actual words they use are not always a good guide to precisely what they are talking about. For example, children's early vocabularies tend to contain a preponderance of terms that, for adults, are nouns – names of object categories. Sometimes these terms seem to pick out only the object involved in some event, but at other times the object and the action affecting it are inseparable. For instance, some children use the word *door,* for adults a noun picking the object of an action, where others use *open,* a verb picking out the action alone (see Griffiths and Atkinson, 1978; Guillaume, 1927). In each case, the terms are applied, as single-word utterances, in similar contexts – the opening or closing of doors, lids, corks and other objects that may impede access. Word class, then, is not necessarily a good guide to the categories young children talk about (Stern and Stern, 1928).

Children's early words also include terms like *up, down* and *off* – particles with the apparent role of proto-verbs – usually used for talking about the state of something or the outcome of an action such as turning the light on or off, dropping something, or sitting down (Farwell, 1977; Greenfield and

Smith, 1976). And from 1;6 or 2 years onwards, they begin to use certain verbs like *go* (for motion and in set expressions like *go home,* and also for the usual noises made by different animals and objects), *do* or *make* (general purpose action verbs), *see* or *look* (used as deictic words for calling attention to something, on a par with *here* or *that*), and a growing number of more precise words for talking about everyday actions, e.g. *drink, eat, push, sit* and *throw* (Clark, 1978c).

In addition to looking at children's early words, investigators have also studied the build-up of vocabulary for specific conceptual domains such as space, time, dimensionality, kinship, plant names and animal names. In some domains, the set of terms making up the semantic field are hierarchically related to each other in various ways such that the meaning of one term includes part or all of the meanings of others. For example, among dimensional terms, *tall* and *wide* both include the meaning of *big,* and among kinship terms, *grandmother* includes the meaning of *mother.* In other domains, the majority of the terms in the semantic field form a taxonomy – a set of terms that are mutually exclusive. For example, in the domain of colour, terms like *red, blue, green* and *yellow* all contrast with each other at the same level of specificity and are mutually exclusive. The same is true of animal terms like *dog, cat, cow* and *horse.* Both types of semantic field, though, have engendered the same questions. First, in what order do children acquire the different terms? And second, what determines their order of acquisition?

Attempts to answer these questions have shown that several different factors play a role in children's acquisition of semantic fields. The main ones identified up to now are parental selection of words, semantic complexity, and the strategies children bring to the acquisition of word meanings.

2.1. Parental selection of words

Adults, Brown (1958) argued, select the words they use to their children. Although they could name most objects in many different ways (*a dog, an animal, the landlord's brute, the bull-terrier, Rex*), they select the name they feel will be most useful to young children. This leads them to use *dog* rather than *animal* (which is too general to be useful) or *bull-terrier* (which is too specific). In selecting their words, then, adults try to anticipate what will be most useful to young children trying to talk about their world. But this is only the first step. Adults also supply sets of words in such a way that it is clear they are related in meaning and belong to the same semantic fields. For example, they frequently elaborate on what small children say, and in the process, they offer other words for the same domain. Rogers (1978), for example, observed that if 2 year olds mentioned size in any way, their parents would promptly offer a variety of alternative descriptions, all containing other words for dimensionality. If a child said he had a little block, for instance, the parent might elaborate as follows: 'Yes, that's a little one, isn't it? It's not as big as this one. It's not as tall, is it? Here's another one, a bigger one. See, it's taller', and so on (see also Nice (1915) for rather similar data on animal terms). Adults, then, indicate to young children which words belong in the same semantic fields (i.e. apply to the same conceptual domains) and in this way presumably help them to work out some preliminary meanings. One result of this is that very young children could know that certain words were related in meaning without being at all sure what their precise meanings were (Clark, 1972).

Parental selection of vocabulary may also play a role in the degree of specificity with which children learn to break up different domains through naming. Adults typically supply labels at the generic or basic level of categorization (see Berlin *et al.*, 1973). This accounts for why adults will name a picture for 2 year olds with a basic level term like *dog* while using a more specific term like *spaniel* when naming the same picture for another adult (Anglin, 1975). Avoidance of more general terms like *animal* as well as of more specific ones like *spaniel* should affect how children build up taxonomies for domains like those of animals, toys, or vehicles. However, two things remain unclear: the status of basic level terms for children, and the actual pattern of vocabulary acquisition for taxonomies.

First, are adult basic level terms also basic level terms for children? The common overextension of animal terms like *dog* to all sorts of other animals would suggest that this is not the case. An adult basic level term might function as a superordinate for a child at one stage, and only later, after the acquisition of other contrasting and mutually exclusive animal terms, drop down to assume the role of a basic level term. Moreover, some of the vocabulary studies suggest that terms from different adult levels may be at the same level of contrast for young children. For example, the terms *bird* (for adults, in contrast with *mammal, fish* and *reptile*) and *duck* and *chicken* (for the adult, basic level terms subordinate to *bird*) are among the earlier animal terms children acquire, and are usually acquired at the same time. And rather than constituting a superordinate and two basic level terms, they seem to express the following contrasts: winged things that fly (*birds*), that go in the water (*ducks*) and that don't fly (*chickens*). To put this more elegantly, children are probably picking out the medium for each category – namely, air, water and earth – and the three terms are in effect all at the same level of categorization. Whether this constitutes a basic level for children or not is unclear. Basic level terms for adults, then, may not be basic level terms for children.

Second, at what point do children start to add terms like *animal,* on the one hand, and *spaniel* or *terrier,* on the other, to terms like *dog*? One assumption implicit in the view that adults start out by selecting basic level terms as most useful to children is that children will first build up domains at that level of categorization and only later branch out to other higher and lower levels. While young children do have a number of adult basic level terms in their vocabulary (Rosch *et al.* 1976), they appear to start adding both superordinates and subordinates very early on. Take, for example, those children who know and name many different species of animals (e.g. *bird; robin, sparrow, hawk, kingfisher*), or many different types of vehicle (e.g. *car, truck, plane; Volvo, Ford, Plymouth,* etc.), as well as certain superordinates, as young as 2½ years (Nice, 1915). Data like these suggest that children very quickly start to build their taxonomies at several different levels at once. There is no clear line that marks the introduction of terms superordinate and subordinate to adult basic level ones. Some children start to acquire more specific level terms after only two or three basic level ones, others after nine or ten. Moreover, this varies with the domain being talked about. At this point, then, we must conclude that adults do not stick exclusively to basic level terms. They must provide both more general and more specific terms for certain domains very early, perhaps for those domains their children show a special interest in, or that they themselves are expert in. And the actual environment of language acquisition presumably affects this too; for example, children growing up on a farm are more likely to learn a more elaborate animal taxonomy early on than children growing up in the middle of a town.

2.2. Semantic complexity

Another factor in the acquisition of vocabulary is the relative semantic complexity of the terms within a particular semantic field. The simpler the meaning of a term, the earlier it seems to be acquired by the child. Semantic complexity, therefore, plays an important role in some domains in answering the question, 'What determines order of acquisition?' The notion of semantic complexity, of course, can only be applied to domains where the terms are hierachically structured in such a way that the meaning of one term partly or wholly includes the meanings of other terms in the same semantic field. Since production of a word in itself is not enough to tell us whether a child really knows what it means, studies of relative complexity of meaning have relied more on comprehension to identify children's patterns of acquisition.

Among the domains where semantic complexity appears to be a major determinant of order of acquisition are the following:

(i) *Dimensional terms.* With adjectives for describing dimensionality (e.g. *big, tall, wide*), children first work out the meanings of terms that are relatively simple semantically, such as *big,* and then go on to work out progressively more complex meanings such as *tall,* then *wide,* then *deep.* Each of the latter includes the meaning of *big,* applicable to any object with dimensionality, plus some further conditions on where the word can apply. *Tall,* for instance, applies only to objects with primary extension in the vertical plane (see Bierwisch, 1967). The relative complexity of dimensional terms is reflected both in children's comprehension and in their production – at first they use only the simpler terms (e.g. Brewer and Stone, 1975; Clark, 1972; Donaldson and Wales, 1970).

(ii) *Kinship terms.* When children are asked to give definitions of different kinship terms such as *mother, brother, grandfather* and *uncle,* the simpler the term is semantically, the more sophisticated their definitions are. Simple kinship terms like *mother* are easier to define than more complex ones like *grandfather* or *uncle* (Haviland and Clark, 1974). In addition, Deutsch (1977) found that children's production of the appropriate kinship terms upon demand and their ability to use a small artificial kinship system depended heavily on relative semantic complexity, with children doing best on the simpler terms.

(iii) *Possession verbs.* Some possession verbs, like *give* and *take,* are produced and understood very early. Verbs with more complex meanings, like *buy, sell,* or *trade,* however, may cause difficulty to 7 and 8 year olds. *buy,* for instance, includes the meaning of *take,* plus some other conditions, and children need quite a long time to work out what those other conditions are (Gentner, 1975).

(iv) *Spatial terms.* Some terms for spatial relations, such as *in, on* and *under,* are understood and produced very early, but others, with more complex meanings, such as *in front of, between,* or *below,* take a bit longer for children to work out (E. V. Clark, 1973b, 1977a; Johnston and Slobin, 1977).

(v) *Deictic terms.* Deictic terms, like *I, there, this* and *come,* are yet another domain where the relative complexity of different terms affects the order of acquisition. Children first acquire the relatively simple contrast between *I* (the speaker) and *you* (the addressee), and only later work out those between *here* (the place where I am) and *there* (the place where I am not) or between the even more complex *come* and *go,* or *bring* and *take* (Clark, 1978a; Clark and Garnica, 1974).

Semantic complexity appears to be a good predictor of order of acquisition in semantic fields like these. In each case, the simplest terms are acquired first, followed by progressively more complex ones. Note, however, that the same criteria ought presumably to apply to taxonomies: there, the simplest terms are the superordinates, but they are not acquired first. What might account for this difference? Semantic complexity characteristically applies to fields that consist of relational terms – adjectives for describing relative extent or lack of extent along different dimensions, nouns expressing kinship relations, verbs expressing possessive relations, or prepositions expressing spatial relations. Taxonomies, on the other hand, consist of category names and are not relational in meaning. While the necessary research has yet to be done, this difference may prove to be a critical one.

2.3. Knowledge, context, and strategy

A third factor affecting the acquisition of vocabulary is children's prior knowledge about objects and their possible relations to each other. By the age of 1 or 1½ years, they know, for instance, that cups usually stand upright (i.e. with their openings upwards), that they hold liquid, and that people drink from them; they know that chairs have a flat, supporting surface and that people sit on them; they know that cars move and that they go along roads, and so on. They have already amassed a great deal of general knowledge about the world around them.

When children try to work out new word meanings, this general knowledge is combined with any contextual clues available. For example, adults will indicate what they are talking about not only through the actual words they use but also by turning around, looking, or even pointing. They will sometimes even demonstrate or indicate by gestures what they expect the child to do in response to what they say. In asking a small child to put away his toys, for instance, an adult may glance first at the toys and then at the box where they are usually kept, or else hold out the box towards the child (Garnica, 1978). Contextual clues like these, together with what children know about the objects involved, provide the basis for their initial hypotheses about what words and utterances mean. Although these hypotheses may not be correct from an adult point of view, they provide children with strategies for both producing and understanding new words.

These strategies also play a role in determining order of acquisition. This is because the *a priori* conceptual organization built up by children maps more directly onto some adult meanings than onto others (see Slobin, 1973). Where their strategies coincide with or fit the adult meanings, children will have little or nothing to acquire, but where their strategies either fail to coincide or coincide only in part, children will have to learn precisely which knowledge is relevant to adult meanings, and which is not. And this may involve relinquishing some strategies, changing others and even constructing entirely new ones.

To take an example, consider how children appear to use their knowledge of spatial relations in the acquisition of spatial prepositions. Let us start with what young children appear to know. Imagine a 1½ year old being shown a box and a small toy mouse. If allowed to play with them, the child will put the mouse *in* the box, regardless of whether the box is lying on its side or has its opening facing up. If a toy table is substituted for the box, the child will put the mouse *on* the table, rather than under or beside it. In effect, children of this age appear to base their selections on two *rules* for dealing with objects, containers and surfaces (E. V. Clark, 1973b):

Rule 1: If B is a container, A belongs inside it

Rule 2: If B has a supporting surface, A belongs on it

These two rules are ordered, with the first taking precedence over the second since children always treat containers as containers even if they also present a supporting surface.

These *a priori* rules affect the order in which children work out the meanings of prepositions like *in, on* and *under*. Notice that the meaning of *in* coincides with rule 1, and the meaning of *on* with rule 2. Given instructions like 'Put the A in/on/under the B', even 1½ year olds appear to understand *in* every time (by rule 1), *on* only with surfaces (by rule 2), and *under* never (by rules 1 and 2). But by the age of 3, most children have mastered all three meanings. With more complicated spatial prepositions, however, 3 and 4 year olds *revert* to their earlier reliance on the strategies captured by rules 1 and 2. For example, when asked to 'Put the A below the B' on a staircase, many 4 year olds place A on top of B or on the topmost stair (Clark, 1977a; Clark and Clark, 1977).

In placing one object in relation to another, E. V. Clark (1973b) observed that children always made them touch. For example, when copying an array that consisted of a glass and a mouse about an inch apart, children as old as 3 would put the two right next to each other so that they touched. Is contact between objects also basic to children's *a priori* ideas about spatial relations? If so, it should show up in other settings as well. For instance, children should find it easier to move one object *towards* another than to move it away. Macrae (1976a) found this was the case: children acted out instructions with *to, into* and *onto* apparently correctly while getting those with *from, out of* and *off* wrong (see also Garman *et al.*, 1970). This *a priori* preference might be represented by a third rule, applied in conjunction with rules 1 and 2:

Rule 3: If A and B are related to each other in space, they should be touching.

Like rules 1 and 2, rule 3 will in many cases have to be relinquished. It does not apply, for instance, to spatial prepositions like *near, beside,* or *above,* quite apart from terms like *from* or *out of.*

A priori knowledge, then, and the strategies children derive from it are yet another factor to be taken into account in considering which meanings are easy or hard to acquire. Strategies, semantic complexity and parental word selection all contribute to how children fill in the semantic fields for each conceptual domain. But each, so far, provides only a glimpse of what is involved in the process of acquiring a vocabulary.

3. Conclusion

Building up a vocabulary is a complicated process, and one that takes a long time. By 1½ years or so, children may have around fifty words, and a couple of years later, many have several hundred. But the process does not stop there, at the age of 4 or 5. Children as old as 8 or 9 are still working out complicated word meanings, e.g. the meanings of terms like *promise, cousin* and *although.* And adults go on acquiring vocabulary over many years. Words like *inconcinnous* or *widdershins* send many of us to the dictionary.

The present chapter has focused mainly on the early stages of acquiring a vocabulary. At first, children talk about the 'here and now' and they show considerable agreement, across time, across children and across languages, in the first words they pick up for talking abut people, animals, vehicles, toys, clothing, food and body-parts. This is probably because adults select the words they use to young children, choosing those most likely to be useful given the nature of the young child's world. Later, as children begin to build up larger sets of terms for different conceptual domains – semantic fields of words related in meaning – it is necessary to take into account more than parental word selection. The relative complexity of word meanings and the nature of the child's *a priori* general knowledge also play important roles in the process of acquiring more and more new words – and their meanings.

9. Combining meanings in early language

Alison Macrae

It is an important day in a child's life when he begins to combine meanings in his speech according to different semantic relations, identifying the same person on separate occasions as agent of an event, possessor of an object or location of an action. His expressive power increases substantially and foundations are laid for the syntactic development of later stages. The search for the origins, nature and development of this ability has inspired many in recent years and they have encountered many successes and difficulties. This chapter begins with analyses of children's earliest two-word utterances which suggest that children at that point are expressing semantic relations in their speech. Other investigators have suggested that the germs of this ability can be demonstrated earlier in the child's communication and we follow them back to the prelinguistic period. In reviewing the resulting development, the status of the analyses produced by these authors is questioned and suggestions are made for a more detailed outline of research objectives and a more varied approach to data collection, so that the extent of the child's control over the expression of semantic relations can be identified more clearly.

1. Two-word utterances

On the face of it, the obvious place to start looking for the earliest expression of semantic relations is in the speech produced by children who are just beginning to utter two-word strings. Many children spend a few weeks producing utterances restricted to one or two words in length, with an occasional more ambitious effort, before launching into the multi-word utterance, so there is a reasonably stable period from which a sample can be obtained which is large enough for an interesting analysis. This is the seam worked by the recent pioneers in this area, Bloom (1970), Bowerman (1973a), Brown (1973), Schaerlaekens (1973) and Schlesinger (1971b, 1974), and we shall discuss these studies in this section. They all subscribe to what is called the method of rich interpretation in that they attempt to go

161

beyond the surface form of the child's utterance and, with the aid of what-ever contextual cues might be available, attribute a semantic interpretation to it. They then aim to develop an appropriate model of the semantic relations apparent in their children's speech, establish how selective the spread of relations was that manifested itself and compare the analyses across children. The studies differ principally in the type of model selected and the type of comparison made but all are concerned with the way children appear to combine meanings at this stage.

Schlesinger (1971b) was concerned to distinguish between cognitive and linguistic structures in his model of speech production and proposed an intermediate level of analysis. This was the level of semantic intentions and represented the concepts (unspecified as to grammatical category) and relations between them which the child had selected and intended to com-bine verbally. Thus, underlying each utterance was an I-marker indicating just those concepts and their relations which would be expressed in the utterance. Realization rules were then applied to these markers, which assigned order to the constituent parts of the utterance, and category rules classified the concepts according to their part of speech in the resulting utterance. For example, underlying *pretty boat* would be an I-marker indi-cating that PRETTY is an attribute of BOAT. This marker would then be input to the realization rule

R Att (a, b) →N (Adj a + N b)

Indicating that, since the attributive relation was to be expressed between the two elements, the adjective, a, should be ordered before the noun, b, and the resulting expression would function as a noun in a more complex utterance, such as *see pretty boat*. The details of Schlesinger's model were not fully worked out but its theoretical contribution is important, in its recommendation of a model which largely avoids a separate syntactic level in the early stages of development and acknowledges the nonisomorphism between cognitive and linguistic analyses.

Schlesinger had acquired his data from colleagues, reworking some of the speech collected by Brown, Braine and Ervin-Tripp and so he derived the children's semantic intentions from a consideration of the surface form of their utterances. Bloom also studied American English-speaking children but in collecting her data she took careful note of the context of utterance, describing the activity in which the child was engaged and features of the situation she considered relevant to the interpretation of the utterance. Her major emphasis was on one aspect of the nonisomorphism between utterance and meaning. She carried out an extensive analysis of the use of negative expressions by her three children, demonstrating that, while the three functions of negatives – rejection, indication of nonexistence and denial – developed separately in the children's speech, they were not initially granted separate linguistic expression. Kathryn used *no* for all three functions and Eric went through a phase of using *no more* indiscriminately although previously he had restricted this form to expressing nonexistence. This indicates that a catalogue of the separate linguistic forms which a child produces may underestimate the attention to semantic detail and distinctions of which he is capable. Bloom extended this argument as well to cover the 'grammatical relations' (as distinct from the 'functional relations' expressed in utterances containing fixed forms such as *no, more, gone*) exemplified principally by Noun + Noun combinations such as the famous *Mommy sock*. Just because a child utters *Mommy sock* on two separate occasions while engaged in clearly distinct activities, this does not mean that he cannot appreciate that the relation between Mommy and the sock is different in the two cases. Bloom then constructed a grammar, based on Chomsky's model, which assigned distinct deep structures to these utterances in accordance with the semantic differences which the contextual information suggested. The grammar actually generated three-word strings from which the earliest utterances were derived by means of reduction transformations. Thus, for Bloom, the semantic analysis was important but preparatory to a generative syntactic model.

The spirit of Bloom's argument was extended further at her own expense by Melissa Bowerman. Just as Bloom had pointed out that earlier analyses had underestimated the distinctions of which the young child was capable, Bowerman questioned whether Bloom was justified in using syntactic categories, such as subject, in her analysis. Bowerman emphasized how her children appeared to be sensitive to the category of agency. Initially they used only verbs which took agentive subjects, later graduating to verbs like 'fall over' whose subjects are patients rather than agents. She assembled other distributional arguments against a generative syntactic model and advocated the adoption of a case grammatical approach to these early utterances. She did so rather grudgingly, noting that not even this (Fillmore, 1968) would be adequate since again the children proved to be more selective in their use of the category 'objective' than the adult formulation would indicate.

Schaerlaekens adopted a more exploratory line than Bloom and Bowerman in her work, advocating the use of a 'semantic relations model' to analyse child language which was not tied to a specific model of adult language. Her data consisted of 200 two-word utterances from each of six Dutch-speaking children who formed two sets of triplets. She based her analysis on adult interpretations of the children's speech and, having categorized the child's utterances on the basis of these interpretations, checked whether there was regularity in the surface structure of the utterances which would indicate that the child had productive control over the relation. For example, when Maria described an action and the object affected by it, the utterance always contained a noun followed by a verb, and when she produced what adults interpreted as a possessive relation, the object always came first, followed by the possessor. She was credited with control over these two relations. However, when she used an intransitive verb in conjunction with a noun which indicated location, the word order was variable and so the relation did not appear in the grammar written for her data. On the basis of these strong criteria, Schaerlaekens concluded that the possessive and locative relations between two nouns (called relations of fixed allocation and coincidence in her study) were productive in all six subjects but the children varied in how advanced they were in the differentiation of predicate constructions into the relations of subject–verb, object–verb, indirect object–verb, undifferentiated qualification, deixis, negation/affirmation and place.

In the face of these contrasting analyses, Brown assumed the role of co-ordinator and set himself the task of comparing and summarizing the results from various studies, including his own. He took twelve samples, covering five languages (English, Finnish, Mexican Spanish, Samoan and Swedish), for which he could assign a semantic interpretation to each utterance. Like Schaerlaekens, he adopted an eclectic classification system, borrowing heavily from the case grammarians, but, unlike her, did not treat word order as an important feature. For each sample, he calculated the percentage of utterances classified by a particular semantic relation and claimed that eight were particularly prevalent across the data as a whole. In his data, they accounted for 70 per cent of the children's utterances at the earliest stage, although other investigators report a much lower figure (Arlman-Rupp et al., 1976). He admitted that the cut-off point between prevalent and infrequent constructions was arbitrary. The 'major meanings' determined in this way were agent and action, action and object, agent and object, action and locative, entity and locative, possessor and possession, entity and attributive, demonstrative and entity.

Brown's comparison could be extended further. For example, if we consider the relations that Schaerlaekens isolated as being productive in her children's speech we find that, allowing for loose translation between the different classification systems, all Brown's relations appear in Schaerlaekens' list, except for agent and object, which he acknowledges as the most marginal of the relations he chooses, and which fails to appear at all in some of his samples. On the other hand, Schlesinger (1971b: p. 74) notes how frequent the 'agent + direct object' construction was in the speech of a Hebrew-speaking girl he studied. Other discrepancies are apparent. Only 8 per cent of the two-word utterances which Bowerman (1973b) summarizes have the form Noun + Noun while these surface structures are very frequent in Schaerlaekens' data. Schaerlaekens notes that the early command of the possessive relation in her children may be a consequence of their being triplets since this result does not appear in the data of other Dutch investigators. Brown comments on the high frequency of naming utterances in Sarah's data, which he attributes to her mother's attempt to elicit as much speech from her as possible while the investigators were around and resorting to the strategy of getting her to name objects for them. It is to be expected that the semantic features of children's speech will be highly susceptible to the individual's experience and features of the testing situation. This is evident from the details of Brown's comparison where the frequency ranking of the eight basic relations is radically different between his subjects.

2. Extension to younger children

The work we have been considering relies very heavily on the view that communication between 2 year old children and adults is remarkably successful, so that the child's semantic intentions are in principle accessible to the adult through his interpretation of the child's utterances. The same claim of communicative sophistication is also made about younger children in the so-called holophrastic period. Several authors have therefore sought to extend the method of rich interpretation back into the one-word period and challenge the assumption that use of semantic relations develops only when two-word strings appear. After all, if a child can be said to express the possessive relation by uttering *Mommy sock* in an appropriate context he should also be credited with a very similar skill if he can pick up the same sock, saying *Mommy,* and so convey the information to others that the sock belongs to Mommy.

Rodgon (1976) has analysed the one-word utterances of her ten subjects in this way, using contextual information to determine the role played by the item in the child's utterance. She claimed that around 50 per cent of the children's single-word utterances could be given a holophrastic interpretation in this way. The two largest categories of utterances were those in the 'I want' group where the child indicated what he was assumed to want to acquire or to do (e.g. *doll, read*) and the 'subject–verb–object' group where the word the child produced was assigned one of these grammatical categories in the adult's expansion of his utterance. Locatives, attributives and possessives rarely occurred in her sample by comparison, together accounting for about 5 per cent of the total number of holophrastic utterances.

Greenfield and Smith (1976) carried out a more intensive longitudinal study of the spontaneous one-word speech of two boys and identified the gradual appearance in their samples of different semantic functions. Both boys started by using language performatively, as an accompaniment to action. This was followed by a period characterized by the relation between an entity and action, producing such functions as agent, object, action or state of agent or object and dative. Later came relations between two entities such as location or 'animate being (or object) associated with an object or location' as when Matthew said *fishy* pointing to an empty fish tank. Finally, the children indicated the modification of an event, e.g. saying *again* to ask for the repetition of an event. Once these functions had all become established in the children's speech, they did not start combining them in two-word utterances but spent some time still using the separate functions. Greenfield and Smith claim that at this stage it was possible to predict which function would be encoded by a consideration of which item would be more informative in the context of utterance. For example, if a child wanted an object, he was more likely to name the object rather than indicate his desire for it, but if he wanted to reject an object being forced on him, he was more likely to say *no* than name the object.

Indeed, why insist on any verbal component at all? The child who cries long enough to catch his mother's attention then points to the desired cup also succeeds in communicating to the mother his realization that she can act as agent to bring the object to him (Lock, 1977). Bruner (1975) has pointed out how ideal are many of the games played by mothers and infants for helping the child to structure his experience according to the categories which will later be useful to him in learning the language around him. Perhaps we should attribute a rudimentary understanding of the roles of donor and recipient to a 1 year old infant who can play games of give and take with his mother and see in his play a rudimentary expression of the semantic relations of agent and dative. It would be quite consistent with most of the work reported here to make such a claim. By his actions, whether verbal or not, the child manages to engage the adult's attention and co-operation in some activity in such a way as to enable both parties to agree on a particular structuring of the event which can be interpreted in categories akin to case roles. The child can then be seen to appreciate, draw attention to, manipulate, or express the relations between these roles.

The picture which emerges from these studies is that of a pre-verbal child preparing a matrix of relations which he can communicate nonverbally. The development of the following eighteen months consists largely in substituting words for gestures, first singly and then in combination, shadowing at the lexical level the pattern of development evident earlier in the transition from action to gesture. The viability of this argument largely depends on there being an 'isomorphism between grammatical structure and the structure of action' (Bruner, 1975: p. 5). Once the child has mastered certain roles and actions in his play, the transition to linguistic expression is not seen as very problematic.

This is part of the story. Very shortly, the child starts to talk about 'segments of action' which he has come to differentiate in his play but he also achieves much more. He gets to grips with the choice between alternative codings of an event or situation which language forces on a speaker, distinguishing between the locative expressions *X on top of Y* and *Y underneath X* applied to a situation which is ambiguous insofar as it allows for either description. He states future intentions and refers to past events, neither of which can be directly observable in his action. He also makes an onslaught on the possessive relation, understandably finding difficulty in distinguishing it from related concepts. In other words, while much of his language reflects part of his ongoing activity, he is already learning to use language to free himself from immediate action.

So far, we have assumed that the data for analyses using the method of rich interpretation consist of the child's utterances plus a description of the activity in which the child is engaged and an account of selected aspects of his physical environment. As such, it seems to be a reasonable way of accounting for the development of the ability to code action linguistically. On the other hand it is not clear how it handles the developments which take place over this period which are less directly related to ongoing activity. It is likely that much interesting information is lost by this method as we have described it, so it is worthwhile to look more closely at the method of rich interpretation to determine exactly how it does operate and how it might be supplemented to capture other aspects of the child's semantic development.

3. The method of rich interpretation

The grammars written for the language of 2 year old children are quite different theoretical constructs from those written for adult language. The latter aim to characterize the linguistic intuitions of the native speaker on grammaticality and synonymy and as such represent how certain speakers perceive the regularity of their language, however poorly defined that notion may be. How this model is related to mechanisms of speech production and perception is still no more than a challenge to psycholinguistics; and how either is related to the regularity perceived by investigators in spontaneous speech samples is a question rarely asked.

The analyses we have been reviewing fall into none of the categories outlined above. Ever since Adam produced his famous *pop go weasel* reply to Brown's attempts to elicit linguistic intuitions from him, investigators have been reluctant to attempt to produce competence models for their data, sometimes claiming that such a venture is in principle impossible. In practice it is very difficult, especially as long as the basis for the adult models remains shrouded in mystery. The work cited in this chapter also rejects the approach which looks for regularity in the speech samples *per se*. In emphasizing the importance of semantic relations for an adequate understanding of the children's speech, they deny the validity of a purely distributional analysis of surface forms which makes no contact with the child's cognitive system. Nor do they set out to produce an explicit processing model, although Schlesinger's work can be seen as preparatory to such a model. Bowerman sets her work a similar aim, claiming that her grammars represent 'neither competence . . . nor merely performance, but, rather, that knowledge of linguistic structure which lay beneath their ability to produce utterances' (1973a: p. 13).

The method of rich interpretation is seen as a way to bridge the gap between the surface forms which the child produces and the understanding which gave rise to these forms. It relies on the semantic interpretation of the child's utterance by an adult who is usually present at the time of this utterance. It assumes that children of this age are reasonably successful communicators so, while the analysis so produced may not be the particular one which the children understood by their utterance (Bowerman, 1973a: p. 187), it is near enough to enable the investigators to produce grammars 'which approximate as closely as possible the functional concepts, categories and rules for word combination of children's linguistic competence' (p. 195).

Perhaps it is useful to make a distinction here between expression and communication, and observe (with Howe, 1976) that what this work documents is a valuable account of how adults interpret children's utterances. It is still an empirical question what the relation is between what the child tries to express and what he succeeds in communicating to others and one which should be approached directly and with as much ingenuity as possible. Only half the story has been told so far. As it deals with utterances which adults can classify within their own constructs, it concentrates on the fruits of a developmental process which should be seen from the angle of the child and the confusions he experiences in uncovering the relations of the adult system.

These adult interpretations are interesting in their own right. To start with, there appears to be a large gulf between those directly using the method and their colleagues whom they try to convince about the reliability of their interpretations (Matthews, 1975). Schaerlaekens (1973: p. 50) claims 'No two-word sentences recorded during the pursuance of this study were uttered which were not understood by the investigator.' On the other hand, sceptics find little difficulty in producing alternative interpretations on the basis of reported data. For example, Bloom (1970) reports the utterance *girl fish* made by Gia while looking at a picture of a girl in a bath-tub with a toy fish. This utterance could presumably be casting the girl in the role of agent while acting on the object fish, or indicating the locative relation between girl and fish, or specifying the togetherness of both entities with a comitative relation, or ascribing possession of the fish to the girl. Bloom is in fact obscure on the precise relation holding between girl and fish in this particular example, but nonetheless comments on 'the consistency with which the surface word order corresponds to the inherent grammatical relation within the utterance' (1970: p. 11). The readiness with which the adult involved in the event settles on one interpretation is remarkable. It suggests that far more information is being used for semantic interpretation than is captured by a description of the activity in which the child is engaged, and invites further investigation of the cues being used.

One defence of the method of rich interpretation which is commonly made is that under normal circumstances adults constantly interpret children's utterances in just these ways. Indeed the most significant part of the linguistic input to the child is probably these adult interpretations, whether expanded or extended, of the child's own utterance. Cross (1978) has shown that the mothers of linguistically accelerated 2 year olds are more likely to produce semantic continuations of their children's utterances than mothers of a control group. Nelson (1973b) found that an extremely important factor in the smoothness and speed of language development was the extent to which a mother took the 'language proposals' of her child seriously and tried to make as much sense out of them as possible. It appears to be crucial that adults should convey to the child the interpretation they are placing on his utterances, by taking up the child's initiative and developing it further in the interaction. Paradoxically, however, the fact that such feedback is so important to the child raises doubts as to the assumption that the child at this stage is expressing a relation in his speech. Rather than Gia drawing attention to, say, the possessive relation between girl and fish in the example quoted, it may be that she was inviting the adult to specify for her the relation holding between the referents of her words and the appropriate linguistic means of expressing this relation. Only when adults follow through this invitation can the child learn the ways in which the language chooses to organize the coding of events and states experienced nonlinguistically.

A second feature of these studies based on this method is that the utterances are predominantly described in the categories important for adult models of competence although, as we indicated earlier, they do not purport to be competence models even for the children. The crucial question is whether these categories are ones which are available to the child at all.

There are a few studies which take this problem as their concern and propose a mismatch between adult and child categories. For example, Howe (1976) has challenged the need for separate categories of location, attribution and possession in describing the child data, supporting her criticisms in addition with an appeal to linguistic arguments about the close kinship of these relations. Similarly, Griffiths (1974a) suggests that Bowerman could have simplified considerably a grammar written for one of her children if she had given recognition to these common roots of location and possession.

Edwards (1978a) has produced a sensitive analysis of his children's use of possessive and negative constructions. Despite Bloom's work on the different functions of the negative and the tendency of authors to avoid 'possession' as a category, replacing it by composites like 'fixed allocation' in deference to the child's obvious shortcomings in appreciating the true implications of ownership, we would expect these categories to be distinct. However, Edwards argues that both largely stem from experience of social prohibition where the child is thwarted in his actions by someone, and that his understanding of terms such as *busy* and *sharp* may well have a similar basis. From this we could argue that social prohibition is a strong force in the child's experience and one which helps him to structure his actions and to make him receptive to a variety of linguistic categories. As such it should receive prominence in a characterization of his language. It requires considerable patience to uncover such features of the child's experience since no formula for discovery is available, but attempts of this kind should be encouraged before it is concluded that it is impossible to gain access to the child's linguistic competence.

Some authors have proposed that their interpretations must be supported by some other feature of the child's speech pattern, in particular the word order of the utterance and the restriction on the relations produced. Schaerlaekens insisted that the children's utterances should show a regular word order before she attributed to them control of the relation. Such a criterion is conservative: children may try to express a relation without imposing a fixed order on the words, as indeed the adult language allows, for example, in the two expressions *The book is Mary's* and *Mary's book*. Also, consistent word order may be artefactual, arising not from an attempt at syntactic control but from extralinguistic factors. For example, a child for whom all the utterances described as 'entity + locative' have the entity ordered before the location, may either be giving evidence of an effort at control of this particular relation, or may be naming items in the order in which they are perceived and consequently first names the more salient object. Since word order becomes so important later on, it is valuable to trace its beginnings and investigate its proper role at this stage.

It is common for authors to emphasize not just the relations which appear in the children's speech but also what does not appear, so as to demonstrate that the expressive power is still restricted and thus argue that the interpretations placed on the utterances by the adults are indeed the product of the child's maturing linguistic system and not the product of the adult's imagination. Brown emphasizes that the eight prevalent semantic relations produced by the children he sampled represent only a small selection of the relations possible, and he uses this as a justification of rich interpretation as a method of investigating the development of the child's expressive control of his language. However, we have already seen how sensitive this tally is to factors in the testing situation. What may be changing is not the child's control of relations in his language but rather the type of interaction in which adult and child engage, so producing a change in the interpretation the adult gives the child's utterance. Brown points out the parallel between these particular semantic relations and the achievements of sensorimotor intelligence. This suggests that the restrictions in semantic relations attributed to the child are a reflection of the restricted activities in which the child engages. How these constraints are related to the child's developing mastery of his language is difficult to determine without a more explicit account of the task facing the child, of the kind to be developed in the next section.

4. Towards the control of semantic relations

Imagine a kitchen cupboard. On the top shelf are kept the pots. On the second shelf are kept the pans. This arrangement can be described in at least two ways: *The pots are kept above the pans* and *The pans are kept below the pots*. Language can either cause the pans to be seen as the reference point for the location of the pots or the pots as the reference point for the location of the pans. A cat and dog are fighting. We can comment equally easily that *That dog is attacking the cat* or *The cat is fending off the dog*, perceiving the contest from the point of view now of the dog, now of the cat. In this case we can also comment impartially 'They are just playing.' At the end of long negotiations, the Browns are likely to tell their friends 'We've finally sold our house to that nice couple', the Smiths, who see the occasion as one of celebrating that they've just bought their first home from the Browns. From these examples we can see that a single event or state, conceived objectively in some way, as, for example, in the eye of a camera with known limitations, gives rise to alternative descriptions in language. Language imposes a perspective on the situation casting either the Smiths or Browns in the role of agent, cat or dog as patient, pots or pans as location, depending on the choice of predicate in the description.

Not without reason. The two descriptions of the contents of the kitchen cupboard can be called into service as answers to inquiries about the whereabouts of the pots and pans respectively and would be inappropriate if used on the reverse occasions. Our perception of an event is seldom 'objective' in the sense of being receptive to all possible interpretations but rather selective as a function of the wider task in which we are engaged and our interests within it. Semantic relations are not given directly in a situation but are related to the speaker's perception of it. Thus to discover the basic semantic relations of a language is to discover the way in which native speakers of the language most readily structure their understanding of events. We assume that both discoveries have to be made by the child learning his language. Indeed, Nelson (1973b) comments on the disruption of the acquisition process caused by a mismatch between the child's cognitive structuring of his environment and the categories relevant to the language being learned.

Again we notice the inadequacy of the method of rich interpretation as a means of investigating the child's efforts at expression. To add an adult's description of the context to an account of the child's utterance is simply to reinforce the adult-centred nature of the exercise, since it is a description of the adult's view of the event, not the child's view, and it is the latter which would be the source of the utterance, not the former.

One can argue that in the majority of cases, the two perspectives will coincide. Adult and child are intent on pulling a doll to bits and the child exclaims *arm off* after triumphantly detaching the said limb from the body. It would require considerable ingenuity to argue that both participants here perceived the event differently with respect to the aspects which are relevant to the interpretation of the utterance. However, precisely because these examples are overdetermined, they are relatively uninformative about the nature of the developmental process and obscure the achievements of the period by confounding the child's understanding of the components of action, the combinatory potential of language and the correct means of expression of relational information.

How can we determine the child's achievements over the period of two-word utterances? Firstly, we need some detailed account of the task undertaken and the goal towards which he is aiming. Ultimately he will be able to express semantic relations in his speech, embellishing them with appropriate inflections and selecting the correct word order for the sentence structure chosen. For example, he will be able to separate the syntactic category of subject from the case role of agent and so begin to gain control over passive constructions. This we could call the period of syntactic control. The child will then be able to express a variety of semantic relations according to the custom of his linguistic community.

Prior to this, it may be that, although the child does not have control over the standard means of expression of semantic relations, he exercises his own control over his speech and expresses the relations in a way which is consistent, although idiosyncratic. For example, Schaerlaekens' children lacked the full inflectional system of Dutch but consistently expressed utterances which were assumed to be possessive constructions by placing the object possessed first and the animate possessor second. Similarly young children's difficulties with tests of passive constructions are generally attributed to their assumption that the first-named nominal is the instigator of the action described by the sentence. At this point we assume that the children have a fair understanding of the various semantic relations as linguistic objects: they realize that language has a means of identifying not just objects and events but also of identifying relations which can hold between these constructs, but their attempts at the means of expression appropriate to their language community are still inadequate. We could call this the period of primitive syntactic organization.

Children may well bypass that period, contenting themselves with a period of semantic expression in which they share adults' understanding of the basic semantic relations and realize that they can be expressed directly in the language but are variable in the way in which they express the relations themselves, e.g. ordering the attribute equally before or after the entity, as in Brown's example. In this period, there may well be regularity in the child's utterance with respect to the context and ongoing activity, as Weisenburger (1976) points out.

More interesting for the cognitive psychologist, however, is the period which presumably leads up to this point, that of semantic development, where the child is attempting to combine meanings and discover the semantic relations which are important to his language but is still confusing categories which the language would distinguish. We have already noted the child's difficulty in distinguishing categories of social prohibition as an example of this period of development.

Even earlier is the period of structured action, where the child experiences and acts appropriately in several roles and towards object categories which later will be chosen to play a part in the semantic structure of the language.

Thus the action roles of donor and recipient map onto the semantic cases of agent and dative in an appropriate linguistic context, and so the child's understanding of those roles is properly some part of his preparation for language acquisition. On the other hand, a preoccupation with attending to disappearance or placing objects in containers may well mislead the child into overgeneralization at a later stage, where the language does not accord the same importance to some categories as does the prelinguistic child.

Such are some of the developments which probably have to take place before children acquire full expressive control over semantic relations in their language. Different relations probably develop at different rates and create problems of their own. For example, a child may well have a stabilized word order for agent–action relations before he begins to express locative relations, and yet acquire appropriate control over locative expressions relatively quickly and labour long over the distinction between subject category and agentive case. There is also likely to be interaction between different relations during their development, so this is not an attempt to propose a 'stage model' for the development.

The advantage of outlining a hypothetical course of development is to help clarify, first, the different levels at which children can be said to understand semantic relations, and so see more clearly the problems they may have in moving between levels. Rather than ask the highly ambiguous question 'What are the semantic relations which appear in the speech of 2 year old children?' it would be more profitable to carry out detailed studies into the characteristics of one of these periods for particular semantic relations. For example, one could ask, 'When the child expresses an utterance interpretable as a locative relation, is there any regularity apparent in his word order?' which would be answerable at a first level by inspection of his spontaneous utterances. Any observed regularity of this kind should be supplemented by tests of the limitations of the structure, e.g. offering the child two descriptions of a locative relation with words in opposite orders to check that he does discriminate between them. One could ask, 'At what point does the child distinguish between categories of location and possession?' testing this by careful use of 'Whose?' and 'Where?' questions. A question such as 'What are the origins of the dative relation in the child's structuring of his action?' does not have ready research tools at its disposal and requires of the investigator an open mind and quick ear and eye, probably aided by clues from the child's early nonlinguistic characteristics and habits. One way of investigating the relations attended to by a child in the period of semantic expression would be to misinterpret some utterances and see how much 'misinterpretation' the child would tolerate and of what kind. Bushnell and Aslin (1977) point out the pitfalls and advantages of this method.

Few of the questions will be answered simply and most will require a variety of approaches before we even know what cannot be answered. In time, however, a picture can be built up of how children develop control over the expression of the basic semantic relations of their language.

10. Early grammatical development

Michael Garman

1. Introduction

We are concerned here particularly with the nature of children's early word combinations, and to a lesser extent with the way in which children progress towards the increasingly adult-like grammatical system that subsequently develops during the preschool period. The earliest period of word combinations has traditionally been taken to represent a distinct phase of linguistic development (e.g. Nice, 1925; Stern and Stern, 1928); and so it is not surprising that, more recently, it has been intensively studied, especially since Braine's (1963) description, where it is referred to as 'the first phase' of grammatical structure, extending for 5 to 6 months from 'the month in which the first word combination (i.e. utterance containing two or more words) was uttered'. In the three children Braine looked at, the first word combinations occurred around 1;7 to 1;8. At first, the number of different word combinations increased slowly, but they 'showed a sudden upsurge' around 2;0 to 2;2, and this was associated with 'a marked increase in the structural complexity of utterances' (Braine, 1963: p. 2). We have *prima facie* evidence, then, that the earliest attempts at word combination are distinguishable, both quantitatively and qualitatively, from what comes later. It has proved a difficult task, however, to make much headway in understanding the nature of this early linguistic system (witness the fact that, thirteen years later, Braine (1976a) is concerned with essentially the same problems).

But there has been progress: more and better data have been gathered in the meantime, and we have also learned something about preparing ourselves to approach the data adequately. As a result, we are now surely closer to a satisfactory understanding of early grammatical development. But, of course, there are still a number of highly controversial issues, of which two in particular need to be identified in an introductory survey such as this: (a) Are children's earliest word combinations evidence for a truly *syntactic* ability, or can they be accounted for purely on a semantic level? (b) Is there really a distinct 'early phase', as Braine (1963) suggested, discontinuous

177

with what precedes and follows, or should we see instead a continuity in grammatical development? We shall be making contact with these issues, and some others, in what follows; but we shall try primarily to build up a coherent and comprehensive developmental picture of the present state of knowledge. Clearly, this picture will be patchy in some places, and tentative, since it relies a good deal on research that has been carried out relatively recently, and which is often therefore neither comprehensive nor conclusive. But by the same token, it is worth attempting, if only because it would not have been a realistic enterprise even a few years ago.

2. Preliminary considerations

Where then ought we to start? The picture must begin with developments just prior to the onset of word combinations, since (a) early constructions prove to have interesting antecedents in what is generally referred to as the single-word period, and (b) for some time after the emergence of early constructions a good deal of the communicative burden continues to be borne by single-word utterances. (The focus of this survey will be exclusively on *productions* throughout: *comprehension* of grammatical structures, which may be considerably in advance of production, is very difficult to test in the earliest period, and its relation to production thereafter is not entirely clear – see Clark *et al*., 1974.) As to the further end of the picture, developments reported for age 4;6 provide a convenient terminus: of course, this involves a slice across a continuum, but some such reference point is required for depicting certain aspects of the developing system. Furthermore, it will become clear that the picture succeeds less and less in capturing the qualitative aspects of grammatical development beyond the early period: chapters 13 to 17 provide more detailed treatment of a number of areas, and it is enough for this chapter to make contact with them.

We shall naturally be primarily concerned with the description of constructional types, and their order of emergence: but much information will be missed unless other factors are taken into account as well. Grammatical development does not take place in a vacuum, or along one dimension, and we shall accordingly gather evidence not just on mean length of utterance (MLU) and constructional types but also on the quantitative and qualitative aspects of vocabulary development. We shall argue that these four aspects, when taken together, help to throw light on the course of early grammatical development, and possibly even on the nature of the system that emerges. We must first briefly consider what evidence is available to us.

Vocabulary size. The literature on vocabulary size goes back to Smith (1926) and related studies (for a useful discussion, see McCarthy, 1954), in what we may call the older tradition. More recently, studies have been carried out which yield more precise information on the growth of vocabulary in the early period (up to around 2;0); Benedict (1979), Corrigan (1978), Goldin-Meadow *et al.* (1976) and Nelson (1973b) are representative of this modern approach. We shall have to be cautious in using Smith's (1926) data for reasons that are clearly recognized in McCarthy's (1954) review: in particular, 'the score on [Smith's test] was made up of a composite of items, on some of which credit was allowed for recalling and speaking the word in the test situation, and on others of which credit was allowed for mere indirect evidence that [the child] "understood" the word' (p. 532). The more recent tradition has been much more careful in separating production from comprehension. But Smith is valuable in providing quantitative data from the first word up to 6;0, for quite large groups.

Word classes. Again, there is a split between the older and more recent approaches. The findings for the 3;0 to 4;6 period in Templin's (1957) study are probably reliable, in spite of the fact that they depend on adult parts-of-speech categories: it appears that the methodological difficulties involved in such an analysis are not so apparent beyond 3;0 as they are in the earlier stages. Corrigan (1978) and Benedict (1979) provide valuable information for the earliest period, and Goldin-Meadow *et al.* (1976) for the period around 2;0; but there is a regrettable gap to be bridged from here to age 3;0 on.

MLU. This has been the subject of some discussion, both regarding its inherent reliability or usefulness as an index of grammatical development and also concerning whether it is morphemes (MLUm), syllables (MLUs) or words (MLUw) that should be measured. Brown (1973) shows an ambivalent approach: he recognizes that the usefulness of MLU declines at later stages of development, and that it is a language-specific index, but his stages of grammatical development, i–v, are nevertheless strictly defined in terms of MLU. One reason for this is because his approach to the study of grammatical development has been to write grammars for his child subjects at different developmental points, and this requires that some convenient measure be established in order to equate the samples being studied. We may question whether MLU is a *linguistic* measure at all, of course: and the 'grammar writing' approach is itself open to criticism (cf. Matthews, 1975). But Brown's contribution to the field has been such that his stages are frequently the natural ones for other researchers to refer to. Accordingly, it is necessary to emphasize that in this discussion we shall *not* be referring to Brown's stages, but rather attempting to work in terms of stages that are defined *qualitatively* (i.e. in accordance with their characteristic organizing principles), since, if such can be found, they will clearly tell us more about the nature of the emerging system.[1] We shall therefore be using MLU in a noncriterial way.

As with vocabulary studies, MLU has an older tradition to look at, along with more recent work. Nice (1925) started the older tradition, noting that 'when a child first begins to put words together, a large part of his talking is still done in single words. For instance, during the all-day conversation of my fourth daughter, H at two years (her first sentence had appeared four months earlier) 7 sentences of three words were used, 352 of two words, while 683 words were employed singly. This gave an average sentence length of 1·35 words' (pp. 370–1). McCarthy (1954) reviews several studies (Davis, 1937; Day, 1932; Fisher, 1934; McCarthy, 1930; Shirley, 1933; Smith, 1926; Smith, 1935; Young, 1941; and others), from which it is possible to build up a reasonably consistent pattern. When this pattern is compared with that of Templin (1957) for the 3;0 to 8;0 period, it appears to be somewhat conservative, but there is generally a very good match with modern MLU estimates in the younger age range (e.g. Eric, Gia and Peter in Bloom *et al.* (1975) are very close to the pattern, with Kathryn noticeably advanced over the others). This may seem surprising, in view of the difference involved in counting words (the older tradition) and counting morphemes (as in Brown's approach): but Arlman-Rupp *et al.* (1976) have found that, for Dutch at least, 'either the MLUw or the MLUs could be used in place of the MLUm with little or no loss of information, at least for children of this age (2;0–2;6)' (p. 269). Part of the reason for this may simply be that MLU is a relatively insensitive measure (Griffiths, 1974a: p. 113); or certain languages may have interestingly high correlations between syllables/words/morphemes; or it may be that characteristically such high correlations are found in early versus later grammatical development. However this may be, we shall make use of the older tradition of MLU studies, since this provides sufficiently reliable information from 1;2 up to (and beyond) 4;6.

Constructional types. This is the central issue, of course, and the one that presents the greatest difficulty. The older tradition, found in McCarthy (1930), Davis (1937) and Templin (1957), yields a classification of utterances into six principal types:

1. (Functionally complete but) structurally incomplete
2. Simple without phrase
3. Simple with phrase

---

[1] The existence of qualitatively different stages of development does not necessarily imply a discontinuity of development between these stages: a discontinuity exists only in the case where the transition is so sharp that elements of the old system are not to be identified with those of the new system. Where transitional phenomena exist, continuity may be preserved between two very different states of affairs.

4. Compound and complex
5. Elaborated
6. Incomplete

(with fourteen subtypes of the Incomplete category). Templin (1957) gives information concerning the relative proportions of these constructional patterns ranging from 3;0 to 8;0, and McCarthy (1930) covers the period from 1;6 to 4;6. We shall refer to this information insofar as it is helpful in building up the developmental picture, but it has to be used circumspectly. To begin with, there is the problem that it relies on the application of adult-like grammatical classifications at the earlier stages. It might be argued that, inasmuch as type 1, 'Structurally incomplete', is the dominant constructional pattern early on, this problem is correspondingly reduced, since it is the least adult-centred category of the six. Unfortunately, it is so defined as to include a number of subtypes, ranging from 'expletives' (which are inherently nonstructural and hence cannot appropriately be called 'structurally incomplete') to 'naming' (which may cover immature or mature language use, depending on the situation) and also ellipsis ('answers in which omitted words are implied because they are expressed in the question'), as well as other phenomena. For remarks on the importance of ellipsis (and on the traditional reluctance to recognize the mature grammatical control that it demands) see Crystal *et al.* (1976: pp. 13, 50, 81, etc.); see also the reference there to Quirk *et al.* (1972). Type 2, 'Simple without phrase', is by contrast quite readily identifiable; but it becomes developmentally significant only around 2;6, and conveys very little information about the nature of the grammatical system up to that point. The next largest category for the earlier period is 6, 'Incomplete'; but this again tells us very little, since it includes such heterogeneous factors as 'Omissions from both main and subordinate clause' (i.e. something has gone wrong with an attempt at a relatively mature construction) alongside '. . . Definite, . . . indefinite article omitted'. The catalogue of errors continues as follows: 'Essential words present, but sentence loosely constructed because of . . . omission of conjunction, . . . insertion of parenthetical clause, . . . changes in form halfway in sentence. Example: "We have – my brother has a motor-cycle".' Clearly, developmental changes in the relative proportion of such a mixed category will tell us very little; and even a breakdown of 6 into its subtypes (as provided in Templin (1957) for the period from 3;0 to 8;0) yields only a thinly interpretable picture.

Types 3 and 4 are fairly straightforwardly distinguishable, as involving phrasal versus clausal expansions respectively. Type 4 is actually a conflation of Davis' (1937) 'Complex sentence (one main clause, one subordinate clause)' and 'Compound sentence (two independent clauses)', and the pattern of development shows a small beginning at 2;6, somewhat later than the emergence of type 3. This is basically the pattern of emergence recognized, on different grounds, in Crystal *et al.* (1976), where phrasal co-ordination is set one stage earlier than clausal co-ordination (see further below). Finally, type 5, 'Elaborated', covers '(1) simple sentence with two or more phrases, or compound subject, or predicate and phrase; (2) complex sentence with more than one subordinate clause, or with a phrase or phrases; (3) compound sentence with more than two independent clauses, or with a subordinate clause or phrases'. To a large extent, this category is identifiable with more complicated structures recognized at Crystal *et al.*'s (1976) Stage V, through to Stage VII (their age range for these is from 3;6 to 4;6, which ties in well with the data from McCarthy (1930)). There is, therefore, a fair amount of useful information in the older tradition on qualitative construction-analysis, particularly from 2;6 to 3;0 on: but its usefulness for the earlier period is extremely limited.

Fortunately, as we have seen, more recent studies are available which have looked particularly closely at this early period. It will become apparent that the most important gap in the developmental picture occurs in the qualitative analysis of constructional types around 2;0 to 3;0; here recent studies (from the 1960s on) have tended to be piecemeal (i.e. concentrating on the development of particular constructions) rather than comprehensive, and they have often looked at the data from such different theoretical viewpoints that comparison and interrelation of findings is extremely difficult. The older tradition hardly helps (for the reasons suggested above). The picture remains incomplete – all the more tantalizingly because this is the period in which particularly important developments seem to be taking place. We shall have to wait for detailed research in the modern tradition to advance into this area from the earliest period; and an obviously important future development here will be the publication of Roger Brown's analysis of data relating to his Stages III–V.

A final point: as mentioned above, we shall be trying to work in terms of qualitative stages in the developmental picture here, and we shall adopt Stages I and II from Crystal *et al.* (1976) as providing a convenient framework for discussion. The purpose is purely expository: Stage I extends up to the onset of word combinations, and Stage II covers the earliest (generally two- to three-word) constructions. We shall pay particular attention to the transitions leading into and out of Stage II, and shall not prejudge the issue of whether these transitions are abrupt or gradual.

3. Stage I

Vocabulary size. The evidence from Smith (1926), for the period 0;8 to 1;6, shows a slow beginning, with a fivefold increase at 1;3 to around the twenty-word level. Rather surprisingly, however, the next gain, at 1;6, was found to be very small (there was found to be a further rapid increase at 1;9). More recent work does not corroborate this fluctuation in gain, and if we consider Benedict's (1979) findings together with those of Corrigan (1978), we get a more reliable picture wherein there is *either* a fairly rapid steady increase with the fifty-word level being attained relatively early (i.e. around 1;2 to 1;3), or a slow start with a later increase, to attain the fifty-word level around 1;10 (with many children falling somewhere between these two patterns).[2] If we think of fifty words at 1;6 we shall be comfortably within these limits (see figure 1). Perhaps rather surprisingly, this earliest vocabulary gain period is not vigorous in comparison with what follows in Stage II. To illustrate, we may use Smith's estimate of vocabulary at 4;6, which, if it were built up from scratch at a constant pace, would require around 275 items at 1;6. The actual rate, if maintained, would yield only around 20 per cent of the 4;6 total.

MLU. The figure of 1·2 words at 1;5, in for example McCarthy (1930) and Smith (1935), reflects the fact that word combinations frequently have just started to appear at this age (see figure 1). There are individual differences of course: although Bloom's Eric and Gia, and Lightbown and Hood's Peter are marginally below this level (Bloom *et al.,* 1975), Brown's Eve is already at 1·5 MLUm at 1;6 (Brown, 1973).

Word-classes. Using a word classification system based on Nelson (1973b), Benedict (1979) estimates around 61 per cent of the fifty-word level vocabulary to consist of 'Nominals' (50 per cent general, 11 per cent specific), 19 per cent of 'Action' words, and around 10 per cent each for 'Modifiers' and 'Personal-social' words. 'Nominals' can be straightforwardly mapped into an 'N' category for syntactic description (see further below, pp. 188–9). However, 'Actions' are *not* to be so directly mapped into a syntactic 'V' category, since they include responses to social-action games such as 'What does the doggie say?' and 'locative action words' such as *in* accompanying action.

Constructional types. It may seem premature to enter anything under this heading for Stage I, but there are two important issues to be discussed. For the first, Branigan (1976) cites Bühler (1922), Jespersen (1922), and Stern

---

[2] We should note here the suggestion in Bloom (1973) that the early period of vocabulary development may be characterized by a fairly unstable population, some items dropping out of use for a considerable period of time.

(1924) in the older tradition as having observed the phenomenon of what we may call 'word successions' (WSs), i.e. successions of single-word utterances, comprising usually not more than two words (but see Clark et al., 1974) which seem to have some linear coherence without actually constituting what one would recognize as an intended word combination. More recently, Bloom (1973) (who calls them 'successive single word utterances'), McNeill (1974), Scollon (1974) (who calls them 'vertical constructions'), Greenfield and Smith (1976), Rodgon (1976) and Branigan (1976) have tried to interpret them in the light of current theories of single-word and early combinatorial utterances. It is not immediately clear that WSs are exactly precursors of word combinations, since they are reported to occur alongside early combinatorial speech (though WSs may well prove to have earlier roots in Stage I). On the other hand, for researchers who regard earliest word combinations as essentially semantic (e.g. Bowerman, 1973a, 1973b; Brown, 1973; Greenfield and Smith, 1976, and now Braine, 1976a), WSs may have more significance.

How are such successions of single-element utterances to be recognized? Typically, the constituent words are said to occur within a unitary context, and to be interpretable as converging on a single topic in that context; they are, however, separated by a pause which helps to distinguish them from true word combinations; and each has utterance-type prosodic features of stress and a distinctively terminal intonation contour. There are a number of problematic issues in this account, however (see chapter 2 above). Attending to some of these issues, Branigan (1976) reports that there are some intonational (pitch and duration) features which relate WSs to combinatorial speech, and he claims further that 'semantic relations are first coded in sequential, single word form and later as two word utterances' (p. 61). In this view, WSs exist alongside combinatorial speech as a result of the child's attempts to encode particular semantic relations, certain of which emerge prior to others; those that have emerged earlier will have passed through WSs into combinatorial speech, while later semantic relations will still be encoded as WSs (see figure 1). The thrust of this account is towards a continuum of development between Stage I and what follows, and in this connection we ought to take note of Rodgon (1976). She reports that McNeill (1974) found 'observably different patterns in intonation contours' between WSs and combinatorial speech and interprets this, together with her own evidence of word order variability, as placing WSs apart from combinatorial speech (1976: p. 107).

The second of the Stage I phenomena referred to above, which is also reported in Bloom (1973), is the 'placeholder' (the most famous example being Allison's wídə). Dore et al. (1976) call such elements 'empty forms',

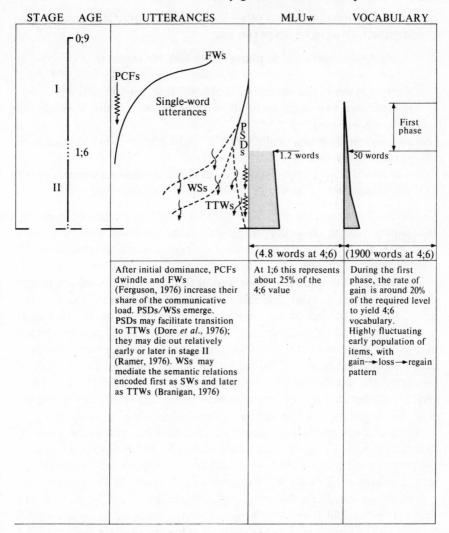

STAGE	AGE	UTTERANCES	MLUw	VOCABULARY
			(4.8 words at 4;6)	(1900 words at 4;6)
		After initial dominance, PCFs dwindle and FWs (Ferguson, 1976) increase their share of the communicative load. PSDs/WSs emerge. PSDs may facilitate transition to TTWs (Dore *et al.,* 1976); they may die out relatively early or later in stage II (Ramer, 1976). WSs may mediate the semantic relations encoded first as SWs and later as TTWs (Branigan, 1976)	At 1;6 this represents about 25% of the 4;6 value	During the first phase, the rate of gain is around 20% of the required level to yield 4;6 vocabulary. Highly fluctuating early population of items, with gain→loss→regain pattern

Figure 1. Stage I roots of grammatical development
PCF   =phonetically consistent form
FW   =first word
WS   =word succession
PSD   =presyntactic device
TTW   =early two/three-word utterance
SW   =early single-word utterance
-ww→   =dwindling developmental feature
⌒   =possible developmental continuity

and recognize in addition four other kinds of 'pre-syntactic device' (PSD), yielding the following five types in all:

> *dummy elements* (a single phonetically variable segment, e.g. [ə] in [ə] *more*)
>
> *dummy forms* (a phonetically variable syllable, e.g. [dæ]in [dæ] *bottle*)
>
> *reduplications* (a single word uttered usually twice in one intonational unit, e.g. *car car*)
>
> *empty forms* (a phonetically stable unit which appears in sequence with various conventional words, e.g. *wídə*)
>
> *rote productions* (a fixed sequence of two conventional words; i.e. the constituent words do not enter into other combinations)

Dore *et al.* (1976) remark of these forms that 'they ease the task of acquiring relational syntactic constructions by providing the child with "linguistic placeholders" so that he can deal with one aspect of linguistic structure apart from others' (p. 24; see figure 1).

But what are the relative proportions of PSDs to single-word utterances during later Stage I? And how relatively numerous are WSs? Data on the distribution of PSDs and word combinations in the speech of two children at ages 1;0 to 1;7 and 1;4 to 2;0 are set out in Dore *et al.* (1976), and are related also to the distributional pattern for single-word utterances and 'phonetically consistent forms' (PCFs) which are interpreted by Dore *et al.* as 'intermediate between prelinguistic babbling and words'. In spite of a 4 to 5 months' discrepancy in their linguistic development, the two children show a fairly consistent picture over the 5 to 6 month time-scale, as set out in figure 2. Single-element productions dominate until the latter part of the observation period, which suggests that, qualitatively, Stage I is not invalidated by the presence of PSDs and a few very early true combinations; the child is still largely reliant upon single-word utterances (SWs) and PCFs. Towards the end of the period, PCFs die away, and both children have progressed into Stage II, with Child B already showing the rapid increase in combinatorial speech which Braine (1963) characterizes as terminating 'the first phase' of grammatical development. For both children, combinatorial speech increases at the expense of PSDs as well as of single-word utterances.

Turning back for a moment now to WSs, we may represent their distribution relative to single-word utterances and combinatorial speech in a similar fashion, using Branigan's (1976) data from David. This child was studied from 1;7 to just over 1;10, during which period he shifted from a reliance on single-word utterances to WSs and two-word combinations. The data apparently consist of 320 utterances in all, with 167 of these being single-word types (the existence of PCFs is not referred to), 90 being word successions,

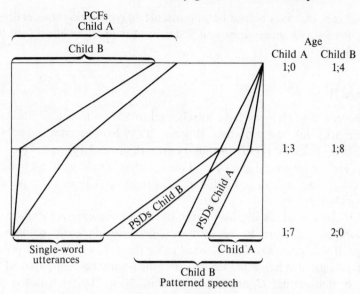

Figure 2. The relative proportions of single-word utterances, PCFs, PSDs and patterned speech (word combinations) in two children (after Dore *et al.*, 1976)

and 63 being two-word combinations. The relative proportions of these categories shift developmentally (cf. Branigan, 1976: p. 63, table 1) in the way set out in figure 3. The pattern here shows a shift away from single-word speech, which is consistent with Dore *et al.*'s (1976) findings. However, word successions do not appear to have dwindled in David's total output as his two-word utterances increased. This is, of course, consistent with Branigan's view that children are concurrently encoding later semantic relations as word successions and earlier ones as true word combinations.

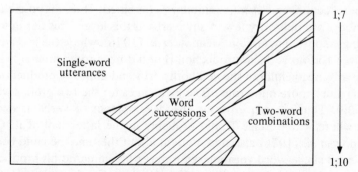

Figure 3. The relative proportions of single-word utterances, word successions and two-word combinations in one child (after Branigan, 1976)

Further research is required here, particularly concerning the relative proportions of word successions and PSDs in individual children (see below, pp. 189–91).

4. Stage II

Vocabulary size. Here we have to rely exclusively on the older tradition, so our remarks must be tentative. But Smith (1926) has unmistakeable evidence of a period of rapid vocabulary growth around 1;6 to 2;0 (see figure 4). At 1;9 the observed gain rate, if maintained, would yield 50 per cent of total vocabulary at 4;6, while that at 2;0 would yield almost 100 per cent of 4;6 vocabulary.

MLU. By contrast with this picture of rapidly growing vocabulary, MLU development appears to be fairly sluggish during early combinatorial speech. If we again take the reported value for 4;6 as a reference point, the observed rate of increase for 1;6 to 2;0 would account for only around 60 per cent of that value. Consistent with this, Nice (1925), quoted above, described her child H. at 2;0 as relying on single-word utterances for about 65 per cent of a corpus of more than 1000 utterances, and on two-word combinations for a further 34 per cent. This is very close to Dore *et al.*'s (1976) Child A at 1;7 (figure 2), and relates to what is still a fairly low MLU of around 1·3. The figure of 1·7 at 2;0 (e.g. Shirley, 1933) probably represents a distributional pattern that is closer to Dore *et al.*'s (1976) Child B at 2;0 (also figure 2).

Word classes. There is very little information available. We noted above that Benedict's 'Nominals' category could be related to an 'N' category at a syntactic level, but that it was not possible to read off her 'Action' words as instances of 'V'. Her data show 19 per cent Action words at the fifty-word level, and a breakdown of this yields only 6 per cent for the subtypes 'General action' and 'Action inhibitors' combined. Thus it is possible to say that there are only very few, if any, verbs at this level. This ties in with the findings reported in Goldin-Meadow *et al.* (1976), where the less advanced children had no verbs in production (but did have some nouns), while the more advanced children showed both verbs and nouns in production (with nouns much more numerous). The mean ages for the two groups were 1;9 and 2;0. Thus we can envisage the development of verbs as occurring somewhere within Stage II and probably in the latter half of it. Goldin-Meadow *et al.* (1976) also note that 'at about the time the child became a proficient single-word vocabulary producer he increased his production of multi-word utterances as well' (p. 199), which fits the chronology for the end of Braine's (1963) first phase, with its rapid quantitative and qualitative increase in structures (end of Stage II). At first it seems strange that such syntactically central elements as verbs may be infrequently found in early word combinations: but if it is the case, it will serve to underline the distinctiveness of the early system, and we shall be looking at this in more detail below (p. 204).

Constructional types. We make contact here with the task addressed in Braine (1963), which was essentially to try to improve our understanding of the nature of early word combinations. As we have seen, the older tradition is particularly unhelpful at this point. One encouraging feature should be mentioned in this connection, however; the proportion of type 1 'Structurally incomplete' (presumably largely composed at this stage of single-element utterances) is set at just over 50 per cent of total output at 2;0 (cf. McCarthy, 1930), and this seems to be consistent with the picture emerging from Dore *et al.* (1976) and Branigan (1976). The real problem, however, is that the older studies fail to elucidate the nature of the considerable remainder of the child's utterances. Thus, the data from Branigan's (1976) study of David suggest a shift at Stage I/Stage II from a pattern where single-word utterances are statistically dominant to one where two-word, single-word and word succession utterances all have roughly comparable frequencies: and Ramer (1976) discusses data that show PSDs at up to 40 per cent of combinatorial speech in some children aged 2;0.

Some suggestions put forward in Braine (1976a) may help us to draw things together here. He recognizes three basic patterns of early construction: (i) the 'groping' pattern (GP), as in *allgone car ~ car allgone,* with no positional consistency of elements; (ii) the 'positional associative' pattern (PA), as in *all gone,* with positional consistency of elements but no productivity; and (iii) 'positional productive' patterns (PP), such as *no down, go there,* where there is positional consistency and productivity. Only the last pattern lies at the heart of the developing grammatical system, and it is tempting to speculate on the role of the other two. In this connection, we might suggest that there are two alternative modes of grammatical development, which we may call 'fluent' and 'nonfluent'. In the fluent mode, the developmental path starts from PSDs: Dore *et al.* (1976) say of these that 'what the child acquires are *syntagmas* . . . McNeill (1974) claims that, unlike one-word productions, the child's earliest multiple-word utterances are organized as syntagmas which represent conceptual schemas in terms of phonetic strings' (p. 25). Such multi-syllabic syntagmas are intonationally well integrated; and we may suspect that they function as early routines and in this sense are developmentally related to positional associative patterns. In this connection also it is probably relevant to quote R. Clark (1977) who sees imitation as providing routines which may be an aid to the discovery of rules: a child

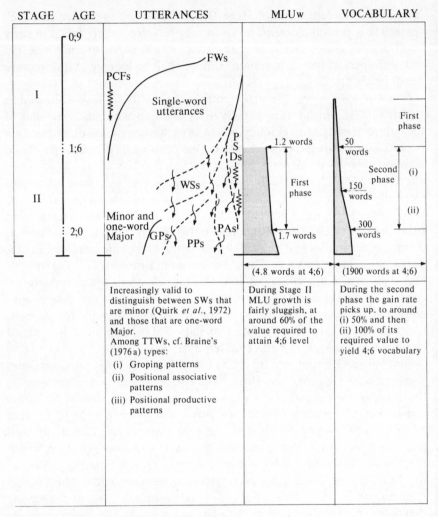

Figure 4. Stage II grammatical development

PCF   = phonetically consistent form
FW   = first word
WS   = word succession
PSD   = presyntactic device
GP   = groping pattern
PA   = positional associative pattern
PP   = positional productive pattern
SW   = early single-word utterance
TTW   = early two-/three-word utterance
-vwwv► = dwindling developmental feature
⌒   = possible developmental continuity

'gradually extracts grammatical information from the repertoire of imitated sequences at his disposal' (p. 341). Thus, this developmental path leads, by way of *analysis,* into the core grammatical system (from PAs into PPs, in figure 4).

The alternative, nonfluent mode may be seen as starting from word successions. Their relatively discontinuous structure seems to relate them to groping patterns, whch may 'often be produced with evidence of uncertainty and effort, that is, haltingly, with repetitions or with hesitation pauses between constituents . . .' (Braine, 1976a: p. 11). This developmental path leads, by way of *synthesis* (and some inconsistency of word order), into the core grammatical system (from WSs and GPs, in figure 4).

However this may be, it does not of itself represent a structural analysis. Is it possible to make useful statements concerning the syntax of early constructions? Crystal *et al.* (1976) have tried to do so; although their attempt is in a remedial context, it is based on normal developmental patterns, and so it is relevant to our concern here. Working in the system of grammar used in Quirk *et al.* (1972), they classify utterances (simultaneously) at three levels, of *clause* (and sentence), *phrase* and *word.* We shall adopt this approach to illustrate certain structural properties of early word combinations (below): but we must first briefly touch on the notion of a syntactic *profile,* which is crucial to this approach. The profile has been developed primarily in view of the unsatisfactory nature of grammatical *scoring* (i.e length/complexity indices, of various types) as a way of comprehensively assessing the nature of abnormal and normal speech samples at the level of morphology/syntax. As such, it is discussed and exemplified extensively, in a remedial context, in Crystal *et al.* (1976) and Crystal and Fletcher (1979): but analogues can be discerned in earlier work, e.g. Dever and Bauman (1971) in the tagmemic tradition (although the emphasis there is very much on the associated quantitative index), and Lee (1974), more in the TG tradition (who refers explicitly to 'profiles' even though her main emphasis continues to be placed on the quantitative scoring of selected grammatical features).[3]

By way of illustration, we shall now profile the salient features of the published samples for Andrew, Kendall 1 and 2, Jonathan 1 and 2 and David 1 and 2, from Braine (1976a). We are concerned to supplement Braine's own careful semantic analysis of these samples with an account at the level of syntax. It is, of course, notoriously difficult to be clear about the distinction between these levels (cf., e.g., Bloom *et al.,* 1975; Bowerman, 1975, 1976a, 1976b; Braine, 1976a). However, it seems to be possible in practice to work with distributional patterns that are usefully stated in terms

---

[3] Lee (1974) is also noteworthy for her use of a developmental measure of grammatical ability, and this is particularly evident too in the work of Crystal *et al.* (1976).

of such gross categories as N and V: these are clearly syntactic. Much finer statements, in terms of the meanings of particular words, are semantic. Between these two extremes, there is a continuum, and we should not expect to find a clear-cut boundary. We shall accordingly be prepared to 'follow the data' in the direction of a finer analysis, insofar as this allows us to identify typical and stable patterns of early combinations. As a result, we shall be more meaning orientated than the very 'lean' approach of Braine (1963), but much more sensitive to considerations of syntactic form than the 'rich' approach of Braine (1976a). Some examples may help to make this point clear. As a number of researchers, from Bloom (1970) on, have pointed out, it is necessary to consider the possibility that very early utterances such as *Daddy car* and *Daddy teeth* are grammatically distinct ('Daddy is in the car'; 'Daddy is brushing his teeth'). Braine's (1963) 'pivot grammar' (see also McNeill, 1966a) being unpromising in this regard, the emphasis shifted subsequently towards descriptions which could *derive* superficially similar utterances from schemata that were distinct in *underlying* form. Such 'rich' approaches (see Bowerman (1973a) for an exploration in the method) fell prey to problems associated with adapting models of grammatical *competence* to *performance* data (Matthews, 1975); and many researchers, despairing of being able to justify particular grammatical formalizations for corpora of early constructions, fled from syntactic descriptions almost entirely, in the direction of semantically based ones. We thus have a continuum of studies, ranging from lean distributional analyses, through mixed formal–functional classifications, to rich semantic interpretations, all trying to shed light on early utterances. Bloom *et al.* (1975) argue for the validity of grammatical as well as semantic levels of analysis for such utterances: but even they find it convenient to classify such syntactically different forms as *red car* and *light hot* under the same heading of 'Attribution' (Eric III), and *more toy* and *do again* under 'Recurrence' (Gia III). Likewise Braine (1976a) classifies *this Nina* 'This is Nina's', alongside *Andrew book* 'Andrew's book' (Jonathan II); places *here light, here this* and *this light* in the category of 'Indicating or Identifying forms' (David 1 and 2); *want milk, want my hat, want come in* and *gimme ball, I-can't get it, Can-I-have ball* in 'Requesting Expression + What is Requested' (David 2); *Kimmy swim* alongside *Kimmy ride bike* in 'Actor/Action' (Kendall 2), etc. Such semantically orientated analyses lead to their own conclusions, which may be both consistent and interpretable: but they say very little about the child's emerging syntactic ability, and may actually obscure certain syntactic differences between earlier and later expressions of one and the same functional category.

For our particular purpose here, we shall use somewhat different notation and categorization from that found in Crystal *et al.* (1976): in particular, we shall not assume in advance the validity for Stage II of S (subject), O (direct object) and C (complement) elements. Such adaptation is within the spirit of the profiling approach, since the optimal profile has to be determined in the light of the task required of it: what we primarily require is consistent and appropriate profiling across the samples to be compared.[4]

We shall recognize the following N and V patterns:

> NV (*Kendall walk* 'Kendall's walking/will walk', etc.)
> VN (*carry it* 'I'm carrying it', 'I'll carry it', etc.)
> NN (*Daddy teeth* 'Daddy's brushing his teeth')

In addition, we have to provide categories for words like *up, down, in, on, out, away, here, there*, etc. which occur frequently with Ns and Vs. Braine (1976a), like Crystal *et al.* (1976), regards *here* and *there* as rather a special category, and we shall follow this more fine-grained approach here, distinguishing

> NH/T (*doggie here/there* 'There's a doggie here', etc.)
> VH/T (*sit here/there* 'I'll sit here', etc.)

from the others which we shall represent as

> NA (*ant away* 'The ant's crawling away', etc.)
> VA (*go away* 'The car's going away now', etc.)

There is a distinct type of NN pattern to be commonly found also, where (usually) the N in the second position encodes a spatially extensive object (something which can be crawled into, or looked into, etc.) which locates the first N: such an element may also locate a V, thus yielding the twin patterns

> NN$_{loc}$ (*Kendall pool* 'Kendall's in the pool', etc.)
> VN$_{loc}$ (*ride car* 'I'm riding in the car', etc.)

Further, both V and N may pattern with some descriptive term, which we shall label X, as in *shirt wet* 'My shirt's wet', *Kimmy girl* 'Kimmy's a girl', *be hot* 'This is hot', etc.: accordingly, we set up the types NX and VX. Finally, we also have to locate here instances of two Vs in sequence, as in *wanna go, want blow, go ride*, etc., which we shall enter under VV.

All these patterns are at what Quirk *et al.* (1972) would call clause level; but a number of constructions are not of this general type, since they involve

---

[4] The level of description used in the profiles here is similar to that found in appendix c of Bowerman (1973a), except that we shall systematically distinguish between such constructions as *That Kimmy* 'That is Kimmy's' and *That Kimmy ball* 'That is Kimmy's ball', as well as marking the points of similarity.

typically one main stress rather than two, and constitute what Quirk *et al.* would call *phrase structures.* The importance of prosodic information is quite clear here (even though problems of interpretation remain – see chapter 2 above), where the phrase structure NN (generally 'possession', as in *Daddy car* 'Daddy's car') is to be distinguished from the clause structure NN illustrated above. Unfortunately, it seems to be traditional to publish samples of word combinations without including prosodic information, and Braine (1976a) is no exception. As a result, what we are able to profile from this source is open to reinterpretation at a number of points, but we shall in any case need to recognize the following categories:

TN (*the box, this car*)
PronN (*my box*)
NN (*doggie tail* 'doggie's tail')
AdjN (*big stick*)
NumN (*two car* 'two cars')
PrN (*in box* 'in a box')
PrH/T (*in here/there*)

In addition, we may usefully include the lexically specified (very frequently occurring) types *more* N and *other* N; and *all gone,* which frequently seems to occur as a (single-stress) unit at clause level, may be represented as IntX, which will also cover similar patterns such as *all done* and *all wet.* In many cases, too, a verb and adverbial element seem to function as a unit, which we may represent as VPart (versus VA at clause level).

At word level, we shall set up just *-ing, -ed* (regular past tense) and *-s* (regular plural).[5]

Further, an important developmental pattern is described in Crystal *et al.* (1976) as 'the blending of the patterns of Clause and Phrase structure, which were separate from each other at Stage II . . .' (p. 70). Blends are expressible as formulae such as X + N: NP, etc., which may be verbalized as 'Some element of clause structure (X) occurs in construction with a clause element N (in whatever order), and the N is expanded at phrase level.' Thus, *my Daddy gone* and *like my Daddy* would each satisfy this formula (with *my Daddy,* PronN at phrase level representing the expansion of the N element at clause level).

One final point: it is crucial for a syntactic profile to cover a representative cross-section of data. The profiles presented here will necessarily be fairly restricted, since in many cases the lack of intonation marking makes it

[5] It is worth emphasizing that the incorporation or exclusion of particular structural types is largely an empirical matter: we start with a plausible classification, but modify it in response to the data. The test is, does the analytic framework allow us to identify developmentally relevant data?

difficult to know just how to classify an utterance. For this reason, we shall concentrate on only the clear instances of affirmative declarative constructions, since these constitute the bulk of the data, and will provide a sufficient basis for illustration. The omission of single-word utterances from the samples we shall use is even more serious: profiles do not give clear results on excerpted data, and an important quantitative and qualitative part of the data is going to be missing from what appears below. An important point arises here: the nature of early word combinations cannot be adequately described just by looking at the word combinations alone, as these published samples would imply. Word combinations form part of a system which ought to be studied (as in Bowerman, 1976b) in its entirety.

The profiles are presented in tables 1–4. Figures entered for structure features indicate the number of instances of those features in the sample; parentheses enclose instances that are of questionable status in the grammatical system. Looking at these data samples, even with such simplified profile charts as those used here, we can discern a number of developmental trends at Stages II–III:

1. *Clause-structure strength, both in numbers and in spread across types.*
   Kendall 1, Kendall 2 and David 1 fit this pattern. Kendall 1 and 2 show very even development, gradually pushing down into structures at Stage III (see below). Steven, in Braine (1963), also belongs here, but represents (as far as the data go) a less mature version of the pattern: i.e. the clause dominance in that sample is the result of an apparent extreme weakness at phrase level.

2. *Clause-structure strength in numbers, with balanced spread at both levels.*
   David 2 fits this pattern, thus representing (if we may exclude the possibility of sampling accidents) a developmental shift from David 1 in the direction of extending the range of phrase structure types to bring them more into line with the spread at clause level. Braine's (1963) Gregory also belongs here, but represents (like his Steven) a less mature version of the pattern, having little spread at either clause or phrase level.

3. *Phrase-structure strength, both in numbers, and in spread across types.*
   Only Jonathan 1 belongs here, of all the samples studied (but there is no reason to suppose that this pattern is in any sense unusual).

4. *Phrase-structure strength in numbers, with balanced spread at both levels.*
   Andrew and Jonathan 2 represent this pattern; in Jonathan 2 this represents a shift in the direction of greater clause spread (i.e. the converse of the shift in David 1 and 2).

Table 1. *Profile of Andrew (Stage II)*

Clause				Phrase		Word
NN	NA 18	NX	TN	PrN	more N 6	-*ing*
	NH/T		PronN 2	PrH/T 13	more X[†] 6	
	NN$_{loc}$		NN	VPart 1	other N 11	-ed (2)
NV 6* 3	VA 3	VX	AdjN		IntX 21	
VN 3	VH/T	OTHER	NumN		OTHER	-*s*
VV	VN$_{loc}$		*it*			
X + N: NP 2			X + V: VP 10		X + A: AP 9	

* Order of elements reversed.
† X in *more* X covers Adj and V.

Having briefly illustrated the characteristics of this approach, we obviously should not ignore the evidence from such thorough-going investigations as Bloom (1970), Bloom *et al.* (1975), Bowerman (1973a), Braine (1976a), Schlesinger (1971b, 1974), Wells (1974) and others. Unfortunately, as we have suggested above, it is not very easy to synthesize the findings of such studies as these, because they not only use different analytical categories, but establish these categories more or less at semantic/cognitive levels which frequently (and intentionally) do not reflect distinctions of formal patterning at the grosser syntactic level.

In conclusion, then, we have suggested that the nature of very early grammatical (i.e. morphosyntactic) ability is within reach of the profiling approach illustrated here. It seems fair to say that a good deal of work remains to be done, in profiling common developmental patterns as well as the more idiosyncratic paths, before we can conclude that early structures are purely a function of semantic relations.

5. Stage III

Important developments seem to take place beyond Stage II, making our relative lack of knowledge all the more tantalizing.

Vocabulary size. Smith's (1926) data show a noticeable slackening in gain between 2;0 and 2;6, such that if later growth were maintained at this rate only around 60 per cent of 4;6 vocabulary would be attained. Total vocabulary is just less than 500 items at 2;6.

Table 2. *Profiles of Kendall (Stage II and III)*

Kendall 1	Clause				Phrase	Word
NN 5	**NA 7**	**NX 5**	TN	PrN	**more N 1**	*-ing*
	NH/T 2		**PronN 2**	PrH/T 1	*more* X	
	NN_{loc} 3		**NN 11**	VPart	*other* N	*-ed*
NV 18	VA	VX	AdjN		IntX	
VN 7	VH/T	OTHER	NumN		OTHER	**-s 1**
VV	VN_{loc} 2		**it 4**			
X + N: NP 1	**X + V: VP**				**X + A: AP 1**	
NVN 1	NVA		TAdjN		Pron	
	NVH/T		PronAdjN			
	NVN_{loc}	OTHER	AdjAdjN		OTHER	
	VNH/T		NumAdjN			
XY + N: NP	XY + V: VP				XY+ A: AP	

Kendall 2	Clause				Phrase	Word
NN 4	**NA 7**	**NX 14**	TN	PrN	**more N 1**	**-ing 4**
	NH/T 5		PronN	**PrH/T 1**	*more* X	
	NN_{loc} 4,* 1		**NN 17,* 2**	VPart 4	*other* N	*-ed*
NV 29,* 3	VA	VX	**AdjN 5**		IntX	
VN 5	VH/T 1	OTHER	NumN		OTHER	**-s 1**
VV	VN_{loc} 2		**it 3**			
X + N: NP 1	**X + V: VP 2**				**X + A: AP 1**	
NVN 9,* 1	NVA		TAdjN		Pron	
	NVH/T 1		PronAdjN			
	NVN_{loc} 3	OTHER	AdjAdjN		OTHER	
	VNH/T* 2		NumAdjN			
XY + N: NP	XY + V: VP 1				XY + A: AP	

* Order of elements reversed.

Table 3. *Profiles of David (Stages II and III)*

David 1			Clause			Phrase	Word
NN	NA	NX	**TN 3**	PrN	**more N 3**	*-ing*
	NH/T 7		PronN	PrH/T	*more X*	
	NN loc		NN	**VPart 2**	*other* N	*-ed*
NV 1	VA	VX	AdjN		IntX	
VN 21	VH/T 2	OTHER	NumN		OTHER	*-s*
VV 2	VN loc		it 4			
X + N: NP 3			X + V: VP		X + A: AP	
NVN	NVA		TAdjN		Pron	
	NVH/T		PronAdjN			
	NVN loc	OTHER	AdjAdjN		OTHER	
	VNH/T		NumAdjN			
XY + N: NP			XY+ V: VP		XY + A: AP	

David 2			Clause			Phrase	Word
NN	NA	NX 5	**TN 5**	PrN	**more N 11**	*-ing*
	NH/T 18		**PronN 4**	PrH/T	*more X*	
	NN loc		NN 3	**VPart 10**	*other* N	**-ed (1)**
NV 3	VA	VX	AdjN 3		IntX 3	
VN 51	VH/T 3	OTHER	NumN 1		OTHER	-s 1
VV 8	VN loc		it 9			
X + N: NP 8			X + V: VP 10		X + A: AP	
NVN 4	NVA		TAdjN		**Pron†6**	
	NVH/T		PronAdjN			
	NVN loc	OTHER	AdjAdjN		OTHER	
	VNH/T		NumAdjN			
XY + N: NP			XY + V: VP		XY + A: AP	

† Pron covers pronoun forms other than *it* at Stage II.

Table 4. *Profiles of Jonathan (Stages II and III)*

Jonathan 1	Clause			Phrase		Word
NN	**NA 1**	NX	TN	**PrN 1**	**more N 14**	*-ing*
	NH/T 2		PronN	**PrH/T 1**	*more* X	
	NN_{loc}		**NN 7**	VPart	*other* N	-ed
NV 2	VA	VX	**AdjN 34**		**IntX 4**	
VN 5	VH/T	OTHER	NumN		OTHER	-s 1
VV	VN_{loc}		*it*			
X + N: NP		X + V: VP			X + A: AP	
NVN	NVA		TAdjN	Pron		
	NVH/T		PronAdjN			
	NVN_{loc}	OTHER	AdjAdjN		OTHER	
	VNH/T		NumAdjN			
XY + N: NP		XY + V: VP			XY + A: AP	

Jonathan 2	Clause			Phrase		Word
NN	**NA 8**	NX 7,* 2	TN	PrN	**more N 5**	*-ing*
	NH/T		PronN	**PrH/T 4**	*more* X	
	NN_{loc} 15		**NN 24**	VPart 2	other N 4	*-ed*
NV 15	VA	VX	**AdjN 47**		**IntX 7**	
VN 12	VH/T	OTHER	**NumN 18**		OTHER	-s 5
VV	**VN_{loc} 2**		*it*			
X + N: NP 3		**X + V: VP 4**			**X + A: AP 4**	
NVN	NVA		TAdjN	Pron		
	NVH/T		PronAdjN			
	NVN_{loc}	OTHER	AdjAdjN		OTHER	
	VNH/T		NumAdjN		**NumNN 1**	
XY + N: NP		XY + V: VP			XY + A: AP	

* Order of elements reversed.

MLU. By contrast with vocabulary development, MLU shows a considerable jump between 2;0 and 2;6, going from 1·7 to 2·7 words (the children in Bloom *et al.* (1975) show the increase soon after 2;0). This indication that considerable grammatical development is taking place around this time is reinforced by consideration of the fact that Brown's Stages I and II both fall within these MLU limits, and his Stage III practically coincides with the upper limit. However, in order to interpret this rapid increase in utterance length, we have to inquire into the nature of the grammatical system, which we shall now consider.

Word classes. Again, we have frustratingly little evidence to work with. Nelson (1976) has documented a progression in the use of adjectives between 2;0 and 2;6: this appears to shift from a basically predicative pattern (encoding transitory states of objects, as in *light hot* 'The light is hot') to a dominant attributive pattern (encoding basic physical characteristics, as in *red ball*). We may also cite here Goldin-Meadow *et al.*'s (1976) findings, mentioned above, which seem to document a developmental shift just before the beginning of Stage III. However, if we look at the profiles discussed above, we find that at both clause and phrase levels, there is a good deal of evidence for the syntactic category V, and this is also true of the apparently less mature samples for Gregory and Steven (Braine, 1963).

Constructional types. Apart from an increase in the proportion of type 2, 'Simple without phrase', and a corresponding decrease in type 1, 'Structurally incomplete', the older tradition has little enough to say. But what it does say is important: what is happening between 2;0 and 2;6, in these terms, is that type 2 takes over from type 1 as the dominant constructional type (a dominance that remains throughout our period of study). It is also noteworthy that type 6, 'Incomplete', starts to decline (this trend also continues), and that type 3, 'Simple with phrase' starts to increase.

Figure 5. Stages III–IV grammatical development

PCF	=phonetically consistent form
FW	=first word
WS	=word succession
PSD	=presyntactic device
GP	=groping pattern
PA	=positional associative pattern
PP	=positional productive pattern
SW	=early single-word utterance
TTW	=early two-/three-word utterance
˷ⱳⱳⱳ˲	=dwindling
⌣	=possible development continuity

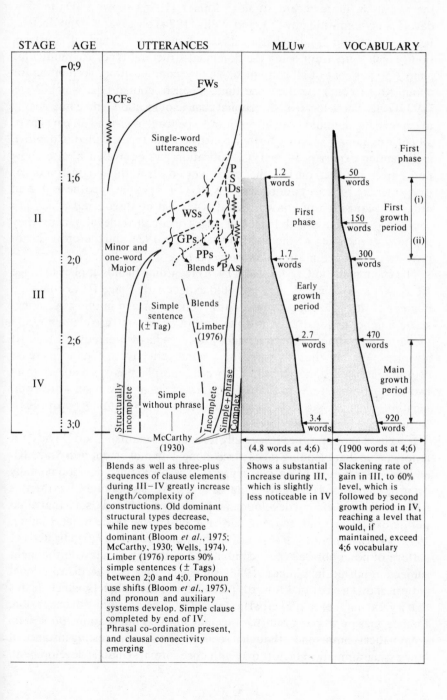

STAGE	AGE	UTTERANCES	MLUw	VOCABULARY

(Figure labels, reading within the chart:)

0;9

I

FWs

PCFs

Single-word utterances

1;6

II

P S Ds

WSs

GPs

Minor and one-word   PPs

Major   Blends   PAs

2;0

III

Simple sentence (± Tag)   Blends

Limber (1976)

2;6

IV

Structurally incomplete

Simple without phrase

Incomplete

Simple + phrase   Complex

3;0

McCarthy (1930)

MLUw column:
1.2 words
First phase
1.7 words
Early growth period
2.7 words
3.4 words

VOCABULARY column:
First phase
50 words
First growth period
(i)
(ii)
150 words
300 words
470 words
Main growth period
920 words

(4.8 words at 4;6)   (1900 words at 4;6)

Blends as well as three-plus sequences of clause elements during III–IV greatly increase length/complexity of constructions. Old dominant structural types decrease, while new types become dominant (Bloom *et al.*, 1975; McCarthy, 1930; Wells, 1974). Limber (1976) reports 90% simple sentences (± Tags) between 2;0 and 4;0. Pronoun use shifts (Bloom *et al.*, 1975), and pronoun and auxiliary systems develop. Simple clause completed by end of IV. Phrasal co-ordination present, and clausal connectivity emerging	Shows a substantial increase during III, which is slightly less noticeable in IV	Slackening rate of gain in III, to 60% level, which is followed by second growth period in IV, reaching a level that would, if maintained, exceed 4;6 vocabulary

In what ways do these signs of significant grammatical development show themselves in more recent studies? Ramer (1976) shows PSDs in slow developers diminishing by 2;3, and Wells (1974) observes a steep decline, between 1;10 and 2;3, in what is called an 'Operator + Nominal' construction (which shifts from being the dominant structural type, accounting for almost 50 per cent of all constructions, to second position, accounting for about 20 per cent). At the same time, a constructional type which Wells (1974) calls 'Static locative, directional change of location', increases steeply to become the dominant category (from 14 per cent to around 30 per cent of all constructions), and two further constructional types, called 'Cognitive and wanting experiences' and 'Classification and equivalence' also show noticeable increase during the same period. But these constructional categories are primarily addressed in Wells (1974) to the hypothesis that an order of acquisition of constructional types can be discovered which has some correspondence with Piagetian stages of cognitive development: they are hardly syntactic (see the discussion above, p. 192), and therefore do not provide us with the information we need here.

The claim made in Crystal et al. (1976) regarding blends applies to Stage III as well as to Stage II. So we should expect early Stage III to contain a number of three- to four-element constructions formed in this way, alongside a number of constructions which consist of three clause elements, and the latter type should show a tendency towards its own blends as Stage III advances. We are thus allowing for a rather effective means to increase overall sentence length (measured in words, morphemes or syllables), from two-word combinations in Stage II to four-, five- and even six-word combinations by later Stage III. Such a mechanism would certainly boost MLU. But what evidence do we have for it?

If we look at our profiles (especially Kendall 2, Jonathan 2 and David 2), it is noticeable that blending takes place along with movement into Stage III, and the distribution of entries suggests that blends are developmentally prior to increase of elements at clause level. We should note that there is some evidence also for a developmental order within blends, such that noun phrase expansion tends to occur earlier in postverbal position (cf. Limber, 1973, 1976). Limber's (1976) study of children aged 2;0 to 4;0 indicated the pattern of noun phrase types (combining his nursery group with the eight subjects reported in Limber, 1973) shown in table 5. The distributional pattern shows a clear bias towards personal pronoun subjects, which means that a great number of preverbal nouns will have no possibility of expansion. Limber goes on to point out that this may have no implications for strictly grammatical competence, though it seems to show an interesting instance of how extragrammatical factors may influence formal syntactic development.

Table 5. *Percentage distribution of four NP types in subject and object position, 2; 0–4; 0* (From Limber, 1976)

	Type of NP			
Position of NP	Impersonal	Personal	Inanimate	Animate
Subject	18	65	4	11
Object	28	4	51	12

In Crystal *et al.* (1976) the distinction is represented by distinct formulae, X(Y) + S: NP versus X(Y) + C/O: NP, at Stages II–III; and it has been found within that approach that both normal and delayed language samples regularly show the development of C/O: NP earlier than S: NP.

Not all Stage III developments contribute to increasing MLU, however, since not all grammatical development is concerned purely with extending the length of possible utterances. There is qualitative development to take account of, in the way that word classes are restructured. Take pronouns, for instance: although high numbers of these commonly occur in Stage II samples, the development of the pronoun *system* belongs basically within Stage III. Pronouns, at this stage, are pro-NPs, i.e. single words in parallel distribution with phrases of more than one word. Furthermore, as soon as the distribution of, for example, the first person pronoun forms *I* and *me* is established in Stage III speech, these forms become morphemically complex. Limber (1973) says of early pronoun use that it 'avoids the problem of selecting names altogether and is quite satisfactory when objects are immediately present and in some sense perceptually salient' (p. 173). The development of the pronoun system does not occur until considerably after 1;6, and may be argued to be one of the qualitative shifts that helps to set Stage III off from Stage II. For example, the Bloom *et al.* (1975) data on pronoun use for 'agent'/'actor' and for 'affected object' show different developmental paths converging after 2;0: Eric and Peter started off with many more instances of pronouns (in proportion to the number of utterance types) than Gia and Kathryn, but to begin with their pronouns are systemically quite restricted (high frequencies for *I* and *it*). Gia and Kathryn started off with much lower proportions of pronouns, and showed a sudden upsurge in their use for 'agent'/'actor' around 2;0. The pattern of pronoun use for 'affected object' shows Peter and Eric shifting from pronominal to nominal encoding (cf. what was noted above regarding phrasal expansion of postverbal noun elements), while Gia and Kathryn shift in the other direction. By the end of Stage III, we may interpret the Bloom *et al.* data as suggesting a ratio of preverbal to postverbal pronoun use of the order of 2:1 (around 75 per cent and 40 per cent of preverbal and postverbal noun elements, respectively). Conflating Limber's (1976) impersonal and personal pronoun categories, the same pattern seems to emerge (table 5 above).

Other areas of grammatical development in Stage III include copula and auxiliary verbs, and these of course do operate in line with increasing MLU. But the really important point is, again, the *systemic* character of the development of these forms, especially the auxiliary. The Stage III development of the verbal system is all the more striking in that, as we have seen, the acquisition of basic verb forms seems to take place relatively late in Stage II; possibly the syntactic centrality/complexity of the verb is reflected in its late acquisition. Certainly, its development in Stage III has important grammatical consequences: the marking of tense, mood and aspect are language-specific features which emerge in Stage III verb development, and negation is brought within the verb system too during this period.

Chapters 12 and 14, by Maratsos and Fletcher, provide more detailed treatment of these topics, as does chapter 13, by Wales, for deictic elements. We shall simply note that these developments in Stage III represent a qualitative shift away from Stage II; if a boundary between early and later grammatical development is sought, it is to be found here, in the way that particular grammatical *forms* are increasingly bound up in, and restructured by, systems of (language-specific) grammatical *contrasts*.

6. Beyond Stage III

The first point to make is that developments within Crystal *et al.*'s (1976) Stage IV may not represent a distinct stage at all (at least as far as purely grammatical development is concerned). Let us review the evidence.

Vocabulary size. There is apparently something distinctive about the growth of vocabulary between 2;6 and 3;0: Smith (1926) finds a big jump, representing the fastest gain period of the whole developmental curve. The gain is such that, if it were maintained, total 4;6 vocabulary would be substantially exceeded: Smith found almost 1000 items by 3;0.

MLU. There is a steady increase in MLU between 2;6 and 3;0 in the older literature, attaining around 3·4 words at the end of the period. It is worth noting in this connection that Brown's Stage III (2·75 morphemes) and Stage IV (3·5 morphemes) are set more widely apart than other consecutive stages in his approach.

Word classes. There is very little to say under this heading for this period. The validity of such 'adult' categories as adjective and pronoun seems beyond dispute, given our considerations above, and accordingly the Templin (1957) data on the relative proportions of the parts of speech at the close of Stage IV are potentially interpretable. Having said this, however, we are not much further on: all the more so since the Templin (1957) data show very little shift in proportions of word classes throughout the preschool period.

Constructional types. By the end of Stage IV, we find much to agree with in Leopold's (1949b) observation concerning his daughter (at 2;11), that 'with the mastery of complex sentences, the linguistic development has reached the last stage. In the future only refinements can be expected. In general, it is astonishing how little her language differs from recognised usage' (p. 37).

Concerning more recent studies, it is the plan of succeeding chapters in this volume to describe the nature of various aspects of grammatical development in some detail for roughly the Stage III–IV (and later) period. We shall accordingly restrict our observations to two issues that are rather central, especially to verb phrase development, and which would otherwise go relatively untouched.

(i) *The development of questions.* Brown (1973) observes that 'the development of the simple sentence modalities of interrogation, negation and the imperative is the subject of Stage III [NB Brown's Stage III], and so I will say here only enough to indicate that the semantic beginnings are in Stage I' (p. 180). There are two broad categories to be distinguished; the *yes/no*-type and the *wh*-type. It is important to note that, in terms of the gross distributional patterns of our profiles above, the *yes/no*-type cannot be recognized until verb–subject inversion takes place: it is *not* possible to find a *syntactic* precursor for this, since rising intonation is not in itself a grammatical feature. The child who signals *yes/no*-questions by intonation alone is doing so because the appropriate syntactic control has not yet emerged.

Syntactically, *wh*-questions are found earlier, by virtue of their word class distinctiveness: they involve what we may enter on a profile chart as a 'Q' element (see Crystal *et al.,* 1976), and the data presented in Braine (1976a) show a number of *wh*-questions at Stage II and early Stage III. Brown (1973) observes that 'in Stage III English, one finds the full flowering of *wh*-questions in their many different forms and I shall argue that the precursors that appear in Stage I must be generated by some simpler mechanism' (p. 181): this view would argue for a qualitative shift during our Stage III. Tyack and Ingram (1977), observing twenty-two children from 2;0 to 3;11, have found a rough order of development among *wh*-types in production as follows: *what, where, why, how, when*, with a high frequency of *yes/no-, what-* and *where*-questions by 2;0. *Why-* and *how*-questions increased with age, while *who-* and *when*-questions remained rare types throughout the period of investigation.

Following Hurford's (1975) claim that a particular rule drawn from a particular model of grammatical competence seemed to provide the correct framework to account for Eve Hurford's development of both *yes/no*- and *wh*-questions around 1;10 to 2;6, Prideaux (1976), Kuczaj (1976) and Maratsos and Kuczaj (1978) have argued strongly, from different positions, that this is not the case. Prideaux (1976) provides an explanation in terms of processing strategies, which are claimed to account for the data in Klima and Bellugi (1966) as well as in Hurford (1975). Whatever the validity of his particular strategies, Prideaux's approach is a valuable reminder to child language researchers that it is not necessary to rely on 'untestable and empirically suspect formal notions of deep structures and movement rules' (1976: p. 421).

Finally, Savic (1975) presents valuable longitudinal data from Jasmina and Danko, Serbo-Croatian-speaking twins. They were studied from 1;1 to 3;0, as was the adult speech addressed to them during this period. Both children showed closely similar patterns of development, with *what*-questions emerging first (1;2 to 1;5), followed by *yes/no*- and *where*-types (1;5 to 1;9), then *who*- and *how*-types (1;9 to 2;1), followed by others. The early similarity with the English data reported by Tyack and Ingram (1977) is striking. What is also provided in the Savic study, however, is a measure of the effect of adult–child interaction in this progression: adults tended to use *what*- and *where*-questions to begin with (when the children were producing *what*-questions), then started to include *yes/no*-, *how*- and *who*-types, and subsequently others which included *why*- and *when*-questions. Apart from the early coincidence of the *what*-type in both adult and child speech, a common pattern seems to show around a 6 month time-lag between frequent adult use of a question type and the emergence of that type in the children's speech. Gradually, the adult–child frequencies converge, over the following 10 to 12 months. The picture, of course, is more complicated than this simplified version, and Savic points out that there is not a simple relationship between (a) the order of emergence of question types in the children's speech and the order of address of question types by adults to the children, or (b) the frequency of child and adult question types. Nevertheless, such work provides important cues to the nature of the developing system, and, valuably, plots changes in the system against shifts in adult speech as the child's system develops (see also chapter 18 below).

(ii) *The development of negatives.* Concerning negatives, Brown (1973) finds 'evidence of negative intentions ordinarily expressed with some single negative word and never in the well-formed adult way' (p. 181) in the early stages. Bloom (1970) presents an account which looks at the relationship of syntactic form to semantic function in the developing linguistic system. Bloom points out that early negative constructions, with the Neg placed outside the sentence, 'were among the least syntactically complex' (p. 171) in their internal structure (leading to the conclusion that the presence of a negative element constrains the length and complexity of the whole utterance). Part of this difficulty may result from the semantic complexity of negation, and Bloom distinguishes the semantic categories of 'nonexistence' (which is the dominant early function), 'rejection' and 'denial'. For our immediate purposes, we need to take note of the important changes that occur around Stages II–III, whereby the Neg element is progressively differentiated according to semantic function, is incorporated within sentence structure, and whereby the overall complexity and frequency of negative structures increases. Wode (1977) attempts to provide a theory of the acquisition of negative constructions which will allow for predictions to be made, and which will be relevant for languages other than English (his own data are German). His four-stage system is criticized in Park (1979), however, for failing to account even for German data: Park's conclusions suggest that, contrary to Wode (1977), nonanaphoric *nein* emerges prior to anaphoric *nein* (for this distinction, see Bloom, 1970: p. 151); that incorporation of *nein* within sentence structure is not tied to its replacement by the form *nicht*; and that there is no difference between the syntactic complexity of utterances involving anaphoric and nonanaphoric negative elements.

7. Concluding remarks

This survey of the emerging grammatical system is, of course, in large measure tentative. It will be clear that in many places optimistically straight lines have been drawn across gaps in our understanding, and a number of controversial issues have been glossed over. But, taking the picture as it has emerged, what can we conclude? (a) We badly need more information on word class development, especially concerning the way the earliest categories relate to those that develop towards the end of Stage II and into Stage III.[6] (b) There appears to be a trading relationship between the development of syntax and vocabulary. The first, leisurely period of vocabulary growth (Stage I) leads into the first constructions (early Stage II), and vocabulary then develops rather rapidly. By contrast, early constructions develop only slowly until near the end of Stage II when there seems to be rapid development (coinciding with the appearance of verb forms), which

[6] Braine (1976a) concludes that it is 'a major virtue' of his analysis that 'it makes an issue of the acquisition of part-of-speech categories' (p. 89). The work of Benedict (1979), Corrigan (1978), Goldin-Meadow *et al.* (1976) and Nelson (1973b, 1976) reinforces the point. For a suggestive theoretical framework, see Lyons (1966), in terms of which the primitive nature of noun elements and the derived nature of predicators accords with the developmental pattern reported here.

is maintained throughout Stage III. Vocabulary growth is again relaxed during this stage, and enters its second (and major) growth period only after the syntactic achievements of Stage III have been accomplished. (c) There may be (at least) two distinct modes of development into early word combinations, the analytic and the synthetic, whose ramifications may persist to later stages. (d) Grammatically, Stage III appears to be qualitatively different from Stage II, but we are not yet able to conclude whether this shift involves a true discontinuity.

Finally, this survey has left untouched the development of complex sentences. This is obviously a major issue: for Crystal *et al.* (1976), phrasal co-ordination (at Stage IV) and clausal connectivity (at Stage V) are defining characteristics of further Stages of grammatical development. On the other hand, Limber (1973) has evidence that attempts at complex sentence formation are to be found much earlier. Bowerman (chapter 15 below) provides a detailed discussion of the field. Here, as elsewhere in the study of grammatical development, we need to bear in mind that precursor elements may be functionally present in the system for a considerable period before they bring about a systemic change.

11. Recent research on the acquisition of English morphology

Bruce L. Derwing and William J. Baker

1. Introduction

Traditionally, morphology or 'word-structure analysis' is divided into two broad areas: inflectional and derivational. A morphological construction presumably arises by the addition of some 'meaning modifying element' (such as a prefix, suffix, infix, or even a separate root or stem) to some 'basic' root or stem element which carries the 'core' meaning of the resulting combination. The construction type is called inflectional if the resulting word is construed to be a mere 'paradigmatic variant' of its base (as when the suffix *-s* is added to the English noun, *cat*, to yields its inflected form, *cats*) but derivational if it is construed to represent an entirely 'different word' (as when the suffix *-er* is added to the English verb *teach* to yield the derived noun, *teacher*).[1] The research described here was concerned with the acquisition of a variety of English morphological construction types, and associated rules, in each of these two major categories. -

Our research was motivated initially as part of the general quest for the 'psychological reality' of various formal linguistic analyses and associated concepts. This concern arose with the realization that language forms (such as words) could be analysed in a variety of ways, none of which bore any necessary relation to the psychological states or activities of the speakers of the language involved. If linguistics was to become anything more than a discipline of arbitrary formal taxonomies (a concern no less relevant to the 'new' linguistics of the generative grammarians as to their various 'structuralist' precursors[2]), it would be necessary to show that at least some of its formulations matched the knowledge, intuitions, or other testable capacities of a responsible number of ordinary or 'typical' native language users. For

---

[1] See Nida (1949) and Matthews (1974) for readable discussions of the kinds of linguistic criteria which enter into such lexicographical decisions.

[2] Indeed, as Hymes & Fought (1975) observe, the generative grammarians in fact represent but one (rather extreme) phase of a much longer 'structuralist' (or 'autonomous') linguistic tradition which goes back at least as far as Saussure (see also Derwing, in press).

reasons which are discussed in detail elsewhere (Derwing, 1974; Derwing and Baker, 1977), the careful investigation of the acquisition of some of these morphological constructions in English promised to shed much valuable light on quite a range of fundamental theoretical questions of this kind.

2. The learning of morphological rules

One of the more intriguing ideas suggested for formal descriptive linguistic accounts is that of the linguistic rule. Since normal language use is at least to some extent 'motivated' (French *motivé*, Saussure, 1916), 'free' (Jespersen, 1924), 'regular' (Bloomfield, 1933), or 'creative' (Chomsky, 1964a), it is obvious that language acquisition must not be limited to the mere imitation or rote learning of forms and their associated meanings, but must also involve the extraction or abstraction of a certain quantity of general principles or rules. But how extensive is the extraction, or how abstract the abstraction? The linguist may identify in or impose upon his description any number or manner of regularities or generalizations, but the extent to which the ordinary language learner follows suit is an open question (see Derwing, 1977).[3]

But just as linguistic creativity in general is our clue that at least some rule learning of some kind must take place in language acquisition, the same phenomenon (perhaps better called 'psychological productivity') also provides a suitable test for the evaluation of knowledge of specific rules by particular speakers. Bloomfield put the matter this way:

> '[W]e may say that any form which a speaker can utter without ever having heard it, is regular in its immediate constitution and embodies regular functions of its constituents, and any form which a speaker can utter only after he has heard it from other speakers, is irregular . . . A regular analogy [i.e. rule] permits a speaker to utter speech-forms which he has not heard . . .' (1933: pp. 274–5)

The best-known early attempt to exploit this kind of a test for rule knowledge is that of Berko (1958). Her approach to guarantee 'novelty' was to make use of nonsense material for her stimulus stems. She reasoned that if a native speaker (such as a young child) could, for example, 'pluralize' such

---

[3] This is especially obvious in the area of morphology. Clearly, words like *cat* and *cats, teach* and *teacher,* could be – and at some early stage undoubtedly all are – learned as isolated wholes, quite without the learning of any general principles of either 'pluralization' or 'nominalization'. It is clearly an empirical question whether such rule learning ever takes place – and the extent to which it takes place – for the typical learner and user of English.

unfamiliar stems in the same ready, consistent way he did real, familiar ones, this would demonstrate that the child had mastered some general principle(s) of pluralization which went beyond the knowledge of those specific plural forms to which he had been previously exposed. By extending this logic and method to a variety of inflectional and derivational constructions, Berko thus showed that quite a number of such general morphological rules had been acquired by at least one sample of English-speaking children – and by the very early age of 5 years and even less. Subsequent research has since served to confirm this finding for other populations of children, as well (see especially Koziol, 1970; Natalicio, 1969; and, for another language, Dingwall and Tuniks, 1973).

These important initial experimental efforts left at least two key questions unanswered, however. First, although this research demonstrated rather conclusively that *some kind* of morphological rule learning had taken place (an important discovery in itself, since this is not *a priori* known to be true), it was nevertheless too restricted in conception and scope to broach the question of what *particular* rules might have been learned (see Derwing, 1974). Furthermore, this research also failed to provide much information at all on how such rule-knowledge developed over time, that is, from its incipient stages through to its full, mature realization in the adult. Since the first of these questions has already been treated in some detail elsewhere (Derwing and Baker, 1977), we shall concentrate only on the second here.

A particularly notable recent study of the 'progress of development' of a linguistic rule is that of Innes (1974). Innes replicated that part of Berko's experiment which involved the production of novel plural forms, but increased the number of nonsense stimuli employed from 9 to 24 (by adding representatives for each of the single stem final consonantal phonemes) and also extended the size and age range of the subject sample from Berko's random 80, aged 4 to 7, to a balanced sample of 120 boys and girls, aged 2 to 8. Innes' results not only showed remarkable agreement with Berko's, which were gathered on the other side of the continent from an entirely different generation of children ($r = 0.96$ for comparable items and subject ages), but also added to them a developmental perspective. Due to vast individual differences within age categories, this developmental picture was extremely obscure in Innes' age-based analysis, but when she reanalysed her results in terms of internally generated 'performance groups' (based on overall scores for the full set of 24 nonsense stems), the group modal responses on each item yielded a developmental sequence which conformed very closely to the following pattern: (a) no knowledge of a productive pluralization rule (as indicated by a general failure to master any of the novel stimuli); (b) mastery of all but the fricative stems (including affricates); (c) mastery of all but the sibilant fricative stems (i.e. stems ending in a phoneme from the set {s, z, š, ž, č, ǰ}; this was the sole stage uncovered by Berko, which she described as characteristic of 'children'); (d) mastery of all stems except the /z/-stem (the only stem-type in the stimulus set which 'already sounds like a plural'); and finally (e) mastery of all stems. These results strongly suggest a fine-tuning 'feature' approach to the acquisition of a morphological rule which is analogous to E. V. Clark's (1973a) hypothesis of word meaning development. In particular, the correct distribution of the /ɨz/ allomorph of the regular English plural is apparently arrived at very systematically in the typical case, by the gradual identification of added phonetic features which more closely delineate the appropriate stem class. Efforts are now under way to quantify this notion of 'stage of rule development' and to extend its application to much larger and more varied samples of experimental data.

From another recent and much more extensive study (Derwing and Baker, 1976), we now also have much new controlled experimental data on the question of the relative *ease of acquisition* of a number of productive inflectional processes in English. Based on the Berko-type responses of 112 children, aged 3 to 9, to some 67 distinct nonsense stems in each of five different inflectional categories, the following overall 'percent correct' scores were achieved: (a) progressive morpheme (83·3); (b) plural morpheme (78·0); past tense morpheme (76·6); (d) possessive morpheme (75·2); and (e) present tense (or 'third person singular') morpheme (71·5). These differences, all statistically significant (p < 0·001 for all but one comparison), establish a hierarchy of difficulty which conforms perfectly with the mean acquisition order established by Brown and confirmed by several other studies of children's spontaneous speech (Brown, 1973: pp. 274ff.). This adds considerable strength to the conclusion that these five morphological categories are indeed characteristically acquired in the order indicated, a situation which now begs earnestly for a satisfactory explanation.

Despite Brown's own very pessimistic assessment (p. 368), readily adopted by Clark and Clark (1977: p. 346), considerations of frequency may still have a very important role to play in determining the course of language acquisition. True enough, the performance of subjects on most aspects of our inflections test could not be well predicted from the stem class frequency data garnered from either the Rinsland (1945) or Carroll, Davies and Richman (1971) word counts. In other words, the total frequency of real exemplars of a particular stem class in English could not in general account for the greater part of the variance in our subjects' performance in inflecting novel, unfamiliar stems of that same class. One apparent reason for this, however, is that rule learning simply does not take place on an individual stem class basis. As already indicated, there is considerable support in Innes (1974), and now also in our own study, for this view. In particular, the developmental schedule for the main English inflections, at least, indicates strongly that the various stem types are not mastered individually, on a one-by-one basis, but rather that entire classes of stem types are mastered almost simultaneously, as though on the basis of shared phonetic features. It is clear that all of the vowel-final nonsense stems in our study, for example, represented approximately the same level of difficulty throughout, despite the fact that some of the stem types concerned occur with very high frequency in ordinary usage (such as stems in final /i/ or /ɽ/), while others are much less frequent and even very rare (such as stems in final /u/ or /ɔ/). In this situation, then, it is not the frequency of a particular stem type which should figure importantly in the ease of learning a particular inflection, but rather the overall frequency of the major *classes* of stem types which are critically involved. Thus, if we consider the total frequencies of those stem type classes which correspond with the three regular allomorphs of the plural, possessive, present tense and past tense morphemes in English, we find that our frequency and performance data relate in a generally consistent, monotonic way, provided that allowance is also made for the special, purely articulatory difficulties associated with those stem types which end in consonant clusters. It is therefore likely that frequency considerations do indeed play an important role in the acquisition of the English inflections, but that other factors, such as perceptual saliency, semantic and/or grammatical complexity and the like, interact with frequency to present a picture which is far too complicated to be resolved in terms of simple linear relationships for isolated variables.

Another confounding factor which seems to have been ignored in previous studies of the relationship between frequency and acquisition order is the role of what might be called the 'competition' among alternative or conflicting formal patterns, leading to a multivariate notion of 'rule strength'. This phenomenon can be illustrated by reference to some of the real, irregular nouns which we also included in our inflections test. As expected, we found that performance and token frequency were very closely related for most of the irregular plural forms tested. This simple relationship broke down on a few of the items, however, in that performance on some relatively high frequency forms (such as *men*) was on a par with that on certain other, much less frequent forms (such as *teeth*). The main clue to the source of the problem lay in the kind of errors which subjects typically made to such items: almost always these were 'overgeneralized' responses, in which the stems in question were treated as regular forms (such as *mans* for *men* and *tooths* for *teeth,* etc.). Our data also indicate clearly that this regular pattern for a resonant-stem word (such as one that ends in /n/, e.g. *pans, beans, guns,* etc.) is both much more frequent and performatively much stronger than is the regular pattern for a fricative-stem word (such as one which ends in /θ/, e.g. *deaths, myths, faiths,* etc.). Thus while frequency considerations indicate that the particular irregular form *men* ought to be much easier to learn than the other irregular form *teeth,* these same considerations also suggest that the competing 'overgeneralized' pattern in **mans* ought also to be stronger than the corresponding competing pattern in **tooths.* (Moreover, this regular pattern for /θ/-stems is even further weakened by the competition it itself faces from plurals which involve a stem change to /ð/, such as *mouths, baths, youths,* etc., not to mention uncertainties or 'double forms' involving either a /θ/ or a /ð/.) The end result of this conflict is thus a virtual tie in overall performance on these two items.

One other aspect of our recent research has been the investigation of the acquisition of various productive rules of English derivational morphology. The following five patterns were selected for initial study, on the basis of their relatively high frequency in available samples of spontaneous child speech: (a) *-er* nominalizations, both 'agentive' (AGT), e.g. *teach* + *-er* = *teacher,* and 'instrumental' (INST), e.g. *erase* + *-er* = *eraser,* in function; (b) the *-ly* adverb (ADV), e.g. *slow* + *-ly* = *slowly*; (c) the *-y* adjective (ADJ), e.g. *dirt* + *-y* = *dirty*; (d) the *-ie* or *-y* affectionate-diminutive (DIM), e.g. *dog* + *-ie* = *doggie, pig* + *-y* = *piggy,* etc.; and (e) the noun compound (CMPD), e.g. *bird* + *house* = *birdhouse.* Presentation frames were constructed to elicit each of these constructions (e.g. 'A man who *teaches* is called a (*teacher*)', etc.) and these frames were presented to subjects using a variety of real and nonsense stimuli. (For full details of method and analysis, see Derwing, 1976.) The 'per cent correct' results for the six nonsense stems employed are summarized in table 1 for a total sample of 150 subjects.[4]

These results indicate that the AGT, ADJ and ADV constructions each exhibit a consistent developmental trend from lower to higher performance and retain their relative rankings throughout the childhood period: the AGT rule is productive for the majority of subjects by the early school years, ADJ by the middle years, and ADV by the late (junior and senior high school) period. All are productive for the majority of adults.

The results for the INST construction are notably different, however. Though this construction ostensibly represents the same formal pattern as the AGT rule, performance on the former lags consistently behind that on the latter, and the INST rule is not mastered by the majority of subjects until

---

[4] The original study consisted of only 95 subjects, aged 8 and over. The data for the younger subjects were provided by Marckworth (1977).

Table 1. *Total correct of n nonsense stems (per cent)*

Construction	Preschool (n=15)	Early (n=40)	Middle (n=40)	Late (n=28)	Adult (n=27)	All (n=150)
AGT	7	63	80	86	96	72
CMPD	47	50	65	79	70	63
ADJ	0	30	55	86	100	57
INST	7	35	45	64	59	45
ADV	0	13	20	79	81	38
DIM	7	5	10	14	33	13

the late school period (versus the early period for AGT). This statistically significant effect ($p < 0.001$) may, however, also be explained by evoking the notion of 'competing' rule patterns as just discussed above. For while both the INST and AGT constructions involve the nominalization of a verb stem by the addition of the -*er* suffix, only the former 'instrumental' variant is faced with a strong competing pattern, namely, the use of no suffix at all (cf. the verb *bat,* the instrumental *bat* and the agentive *batter;* other verbs which conform to this pattern are *ski, skate, lift, hammer,* etc.). Support for this hypothesis comes from the fact that the error responses to the INST presentation frame ('He *erases* with a(n) (*eraser*)') almost always involved the repetition of the bare, nonsuffixed stem (i.e. in accord with the competing 'null' pattern), whereas the AGT presentation frame yielded very few such responses. Furthermore, the response pattern for the real verb *cook* in the AGT frame revealed a strong tendency even in middle and late subjects to provide the 'overgeneralized' response in **cooker,* indicative of a very potent regular pattern in -*er* and consistent with the view that the agentive noun *cook* represents a rather isolated exception to this pattern and so is learned relatively late in the course of language development.

This same phenomenon may also be responsible for what is perhaps the most striking feature of table 1, namely, the response pattern for the CMPD construction. This is the only rule which even approaches productivity for a majority of the preschool subjects tested, yet performance on it scarcely rises above a two-thirds level at any stage thereafter, even for the adults. But this pattern, too, is faced with a strong competitor, specifically, the possessive construction (e.g. *bird's house*), which is not only quite appropriate for the particular elicitation frame employed in our test ('A house for *birds* is called a (*birdhouse*)'), but is also consistent with the most common type of 'erroneous' response elicited from our subjects. (Notice that the *-ly* adverb is also faced with a strong dialectal and stylistic competitor, viz. a form with no suffix, and this fact may help account for the relatively late acquisition of a productive ADV rule by most subjects.)

The DIM construction, finally, though it seems to exhibit a certain measure of consistent development, did not achieve productivity for a majority of subjects in any of our groups, including the adults. The fact, however, that this finding was also true for both of the real stems we employed (namely, *horse* and *cat*) suggests that in this case, at least, it may have been the elicitation frame itself that was at fault, rather than a lack of knowledge of the rule on the part of our subjects.

In any event, the research described has certainly broadened our understanding of the acquisition of morphological rules to a considerable extent, though many gaps still remain and much work must still be done. This is especially true insofar as the discovery of underlying *explanations* is concerned. We are at last beginning to acquire a fairly substantial body of hard data concerning the course of language development in this area, but we are still a long way from being able to predict the results of our experiments with any confidence.

3. Morpheme recognition in the child and adult

Alongside the morphological rule, another fundamental concept which derives from the descriptive linguistic literature is that of the morpheme itself. Loosely speaking, a morpheme is a minimal, meaningful unit of speech, or, in the general case, a class of such units which are non-contrastive yet 'semantically similar' (see Nida, 1949). Though this conception has proved useful as a practical guide for the formal, morphological analysis of language samples, the vagueness of the term 'semantically similar' has given rise to a host of analytical problems which have long been recognized in linguistics but never satisfactorily dealt with. One such difficulty is that of trying to demarcate between a strictly descriptive (or synchronic) analysis of a language and an etymological (or diachronic) one. Does the *tail* of *tailor* represent the same morpheme as the *tail* of *tails* or *tailcoat*, for example (cf. the Middle English meaning 'cut' and such parallel 'clear' relationships as those between *teacher* and *teach, actor* and *act,* etc.). Or does the word *tidy* share a common morpheme with the word *tide* (cf. Middle English *tyde,* meaning 'time'), on the same pattern as *dirty* and *dirt?* Or, to take an even more extreme case, should the assonance and rhyme of sets of 'semantically related' terms such as *flitter, flow, flare* and *glitter, glow, glare* also be construed in morphological terms (that is, as in Bolinger's analysis (1950: p. 119), should *fl-* be treated as a morpheme meaning 'phenomenon of movement', *gl-* as 'phenomenon of light', and the remaining elements *-itter*, *-ow* and *-are* as morphemes meaning 'intermittent', 'steady' and 'intense', respectively)? Clearly, as Bolinger points out, 'the lower the specification of meaning, the larger is the number of forms which may be subsumed under one morpheme' (1950: p. 122). So where should the linguist draw the line (cf. Matthews, 1974: p. 57)?

For the 'straight' or 'autonomous' linguist, of course, there is no nonarbitrary way to make this (or virtually any other) decision. The problem can, however, be reasonably reformulated in *psychological* terms, as follows: what are the practical, operational limits of 'morpheme recognition' for the typical (i.e. normal, but linguistically untrained), monolingual, adult native speaker of a language – and how does this skill develop i.1 the child? We have begun some extensive research on both of these questions, but can only summarize our main findings here.

If typical speakers have the ability to recognize anything resembling the linguist's notion of the morpheme at all, there are presumably two variables, at least, which ought to play a crucial role in this recognition process. One of these, of course, is semantic similarity, as introduced in the examples above. The second critical factor is similarity in sound, or phonetic similarity. Thus, though a baby *pig* is called a *piglet,* a baby *cat* a *kitten,* and a baby *dog* a *puppy*, the phonetic discrepancies in the second case make its morphological analysis less clear (does *kitten* contain the morpheme *cat*?) than the first (*piglet* from *pig*?), while the third (*puppy* from *dog*?) is the most dubious of all. The main focus of the research described below was thus to attempt to assess the role of both phonetic and semantic similarity in whatever ability native speakers of English might have to recognize or identify common 'morphemes' among pairs of common words in their language.

The first stage of this research involved the establishment of similarity scales for selected word pairs along both of these axes, using large (n>100) samples of adult speakers as subjects (see Derwing, 1976 for details). As the result of these rating experiments, 50 word pairs were next selected from the original set which best represented the full range of variation along both dimensions, and these pairs were then used in a series of attempts to tap the psychological skill of 'morpheme recognition'. Altogether, three different elicitation techniques were tried in this phase of the study, the first of which (following Berko, 1958) failed to produce much in the way of coherent results. The other two approaches did, however, yield results which were not only very consistent and highly in accord with the pre-experimental hypothesis (namely, that both phonetic and semantic similarity ought to play a crucial role in the ease of morpheme recognition, though the second, meaning criterion ought to predominate), but also correlated very highly with one another (r = 0·90). The two tasks were (a) to state whether one word of each pair (the generally longer or 'derived' form) 'came from' the other (using a five-point rating scale which ranged from 'No doubt' to 'No way') and (b) to state whether the thought of such a relational possibility had ever come to mind prior to the test ('Yes', 'Not sure', or 'No'). Generally speaking, both of these procedures yielded 'certain' responses (i.e. 'No doubt' or 'Yes') for the majority of adult subjects (n = 65) only if the semantic similarity of the word pair had been rated as about 2·00 or above (on a scale of 0 to 4) *and* if the phonetic similarity rating was at least about 1·75 (on a scale from 0 to 6). As expected, there was a good deal of individual variation involved in this study, and a few subjects even claimed to identify clear 'comes from' relationships among word pairs as dissimilar in sound and/or meaning as *eerie – ear* (9%), *ladder – lean* (8%), *Friday – fry* (5%) and *feather – fly* (3%). But to elicit such responses from even as much as a quarter of the sample, the similarity range had to reach about 2·0 and 1·6 on the semantic and phonetic dimensions, respectively, excluding such potentially 'tempting' pairs as *precious – price* (21%), *fabulous – fable* (20%), *kitty – cat* (20%), *necklace – lace* (20%), *sweater – sweat* (15%), *timid – tame* (14%) and *spider – spin* (9%). By way of contrast, many other pairs were given 'certain' ratings by over 90 per cent of the subjects on the 'comes from' test (e.g. *quietly – quiet, teacher – teach, dirty – dirt, eraser – erase, lawyer – law, wonderful – wonder,* and *doggie – dog*), while others received virtually no such ratings at all (e.g. *weather – wind, puppy – dog, cranberry – crane, bashful – bash* and *carpenter – wagon,* all of which were rated 'No doubt' by 1% of the subjects or less). Few of these results are in any way surprising, though they do provide evidence (if there ever was any substantive reason to suppose otherwise) that the very abstract kind of generative phonological analysis espoused by such books as Chomsky and Halle (1968) is of very doubtful psychological validity, at least for the kind of native speakers which we tested. This is so because the analysis in question presumes certain etymological relationships which seem often to fall well beyond the psychologically viable 'similarity limits' suggested by our study.

In a recently completed and not previously reported follow-up study, we now have some indications of the developmental sequence involved in the area of morpheme recognition, as well. The natural expectation in this phase of the research, of course, was that those morphological relationships which were the most obvious to the most adults ought also to be the ones most easily recognized by children, and hence the earlier they ought to be identified.

In general, this expectation was borne out. Figure 1 is a scattergram for

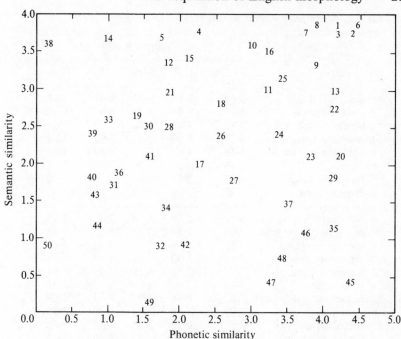

Figure 1. Mean semantic and phonetic similarity for the 50 word pairs (the pairs are numbered as in table 2 below)

the 50 word pairs employed in this study, plotted as a function of the experimentally derived measures of semantic (vertical axis) and phonetic similarity (horizontal axis), and numbered roughly in order of the overall means on the 'comes from' test. The subject sample consisted of 120 children (6 boys and 6 girls per grade), representing grades 3–6 and aged 8 to 12 (ELEM), grades 7–9, aged 12 to 15 (JHS), and grades 10–12, aged 15 to 18 (HS); plus the original sample of 65 adults, all university (UNIV) students ranging in age from 18 to 50, with a mean age of about 22. Table 2 shows the mean ratings for each item and subject category on the 'comes from' test, and the rules separate the five groups of items which achieved overall ratings of 'No doubt' (means above 3·50), 'Probably' (between 2·50 and 3·50), 'Can't decide' (1·50–2·50), 'Probably not' (0·50–1·50) and 'No way' (below 0·50).

There is a noteworthy stability among these data, in that those items which receive a given rating by the children tend to receive a comparable or higher rating from the other subject groups, and several items exhibit an absolutely consistent developmental trend from a lower to a higher score (e.g. *lawyer – law, doggie – dog, birdhouse – bird, shepherd – sheep, handle – hand,*

Table 2. *Mean scale ratings for the 'comes from' test*

Word pairs	Subject groups				
	ELEM	JHS	SHS	UNIV	Total
1 quietly – quiet	3·67	3·81	3·75	3·97	3·82
2 eraser – erase	3·62	3·47	3·47	3·94	3·68
3 teacher – teach	3·52	3·47	3·44	3·97	3·65
4 lawyer – law	3·27	3·50	3·81	3·91	3·64
5 wilderness – wild	3·48	3·47	3·69	3·80	3·63
6 dirty – dirt	3·40	3·56	3·39	3·95	3·62
7 hungry – hunger	3·65	3·44	3·44	3·80	3·62
8 doggie – dog	3·27	3·50	3·67	3·88	3·61
9 wonderful – wonder	3·10	2·69	3·36	3·88	3·35
10 messenger – message	2·85	3·27	3·25	3·72	3·32
11 birdhouse – bird	2·85	2·89	3·19	3·85	3·28
12 shepherd – sheep	2·83	3·00	3·11	3·69	3·22
13 handle – hand	2·77	2·92	3·28	3·45	3·14
14 kitty – cat	3·06	3·50	3·08	2·54	2·97
15 numerous – number	2·42	2·44	2·97	3·43	2·89
16 strawberry – berry	2·87	2·61	2·44	3·20	2·85
17 breakfast – break	2·27	1·89	2·64	3·26	2·62
18 cupboard – cup	1·84	2·22	2·72	3·35	2·62
19 month – moon	1·33	1·72	2·92	3·54	2·49
20 skinny – skin	2·33	2·00	2·91	2·97	2·46
21 holiday – holy	1·50	1·47	2·78	3·48	2·44
22 cookie – cook	2·23	1·83	1·75	2·91	2·30
23 slipper – slip	2·02	1·44	2·44	2·86	2·29
24 awful – awe	1·83	1·39	2·11	3·15	2·26
25 lousy – louse	1·65	1·06	2·28	3·34	2·25
26 handkerchief – hand	1·27	1·72	2·19	3·18	2·21
27 necklace – lace	2·04	1·69	2·11	2·58	2·18
28 heavy – heave	1·92	1·83	1·75	2·48	2·06
29 sweater – sweat	1·96	1·50	2·14	2·26	2·01
30 precious – price	1·10	1·44	2·28	1·69	1·96
31 Halloween – holy	1·00	1·31	2·06	2·72	1·87
32 hideous – hide	1·35	1·31	1·86	2·45	1·83
33 barber – beard	1·21	1·56	1·56	2·37	1·75
34 fabulous – fable	1·29	1·14	1·53	2·51	1·74
35 buggy – bug	2·46	1·47	0·88	1·77	1·72
36 timid – tame	1·10	1·08	1·75	2·45	1·70
37 rubber – rub	2·15	1·72	1·17	1·63	1·69
38 puppy – dog	2·21	2·64	1·25	0·92	1·65
39 weather – wind	1·96	2·19	1·22	1·35	1·65
40 muggy – mist	1·44	2·39	0·92	1·63	1·59
41 spider – spin	1·08	1·39	1·44	2·06	1·56

Table 2—cont. *Mean scale ratings for the 'comes from' test*

Word pairs	Subject groups				
	ELEM	JHS	SHS	UNIV	Total
42 gypsy – Egyptian	1·60	1·22	1·08	1·66	1·45
43 feather – fly	1·02	1·56	1·28	1·23	1·25
44 ladder – lean	1·02	1·31	1·06	1·26	1·17
45 eerie – ear	1·67	0·75	0·97	0·85	1·06
46 liver – live	0·90	0·50	0·61	1·55	0·99
47 Friday – fry	1·42	0·75	0·75	0·95	0·99
48 bashful – bash	1·31	0·69	0·53	0·76	0·84
49 cranberry – crane	0·81	0·56	0·53	0·78	0·70
50 carpenter – wagon	0·21	0·22	0·39	0·39	0·31

numerous — number, etc.), each coupled with a significant chi square (p <
0·05). These results reflect a generally increased capacity for morpheme
recognition in the more mature subjects, who tend to give higher ratings to
more and more items. Thus, for example, items 9–12 all receive average 'No
doubt' ratings from the UNIV subjects, but only average 'Probable' ratings
from the younger subject groups. (Even more dramatic are the differences in
the group means for the items *month – moon* and *holiday – holy,* whose
means ratings jump as much as two categories between the ELEM and
UNIV groups. It is quite likely that such changes are the result of specific
etymological knowledge acquired in school. Admittedly, our UNIV group
represents a selected sample and the results for this group may well provide a
somewhat inflated estimate of a more representative population.)

There are also, however, some notable exceptions to this general
developmental trend, with the items *kitty – cat, puppy – dog, eerie – ear,* and
bashful – bash serving as prime examples. For these items the trend is in
precisely the opposite direction: higher 'comes from' scores for the younger
subjects and lower scores for the older ones. Notably, all four of these items
rate very highly on one of the two independent measures of similarity: the
first two pairs rate over 3·7 on the semantic scale, while the second two rate
about 3·5 or above on the phonetic scale. This attests to a relatively strong
tendency among young children to (from the adult's point of view) identify
falsely, potential morphological relationships on the basis of only one of
these dimensions alone, provided that the 'transparency' of the relationship
along that one dimension is sufficiently high (cf. the large literature which
deals with the child's recognition of 'false analogies'; for some recent discussions of this phenomenon, see Hockett, 1968: pp. 89–99; Householder,

1971: pp. 61–80). More mature subjects (excluding some of the more imaginative of the modern-day linguists), on the other hand, require a reasonably high rating along *both* dimensions in order to be willing to accept a judgment of morphological relatedness.

A multiple regression analysis shows this changing role of the two independent variables in predicting the set of 'comes from' scores for the four different subject groups. For the ELEM subjects, for example, the phonetic similarity ratings are half again as important in predicting these scores as in the case of the UNIV (or adult) subjects, while, strangely, the contribution of this variable almost disappears (to only about a third of the UNIV coefficient) for the JHS group. The HS and UNIV subjects differ only minimally in this regard, while the semantic variable retains a very high rating throughout.

Finally, both the ELEM and UNIV (i.e. both the youngest and the oldest) subjects show a distinct tendency to accept historically false (or 'folk') etymologies, but evidently for rather different reasons. For the young children, items like *eerie – ear, Friday – fry,* and *bashful – bash* all receive uncommonly high 'comes from' ratings (the first is fully in the 'Can't decide' category and the others nearly so) for pairs which are so far removed from the generally acceptable similarity range for morphologically relatable pairs (see items 45, 47 and 48 in figure 1). This, though, seems to be a consequence of the phenomenon just described, namely, the tendency for the younger subjects to set excessive store by purely formal or 'phonetic' similarities. The adult anomalies lie in a rather different direction: alongside such etymologically correct (but psychologically borderline) 'comes from' relationships involving such word pairs as *necklace – lace, heavy – heave, Halloween – holy* and *fabulous – fable* (all rated in the 'Can't decide' range, despite their somewhat remote positioning in figure 1; see items 27, 28, 31 and 34), the UNIV subjects are also about equally attracted to such historically false pairings as *hideous – hide* and *timid – tame* (items 32 and 36). While it is true that all six of these items are located in the same rough 'central' area of figure 1, it is also notable that for five of these pairs their formal similarity is more apparent from their *spelling* than from their sound.[5] (The exception, *Halloween – holy,* is, of course, another excellent candidate for learning via special instruction in school.) The same is also true for several other of the more 'clearly' related pairs, such as *handkerchief – hand, holiday – holy, cupboard – cup, breakfast – break, numerous – number, messenger – message, shepherd – sheep,* and even *lawyer – law,* among others. And, indeed, for all of these items there is a very sharp jump in the

---

[5] That is, in the more strictly quantified terms of Derwing (1976), the 'grapheme indices' for these words all exceed their 'phoneme indices'.

'comes from' rating between the ELEM and UNIV subjects. Thus 'morpheme recognition', at least as measured in this study, may well be a skill which is acquired as much through formal education (as by learning to read) as through the ordinary process of learning to speak and to understand one's language. It will be no easy task to sort out the contributions of these rather two different sources of linguistic knowledge.

Again, as in the case of the previous section, work has scarcely begun on the problem of the 'psychological reality of the morpheme', and a great deal of thoughtful analysis is still required even on the data already available. But it's a start, and the results so far do anything but fly in the face of the fundamentals of formal descriptive linguistics. There can be no doubt that linguistics has much to offer to experimental psychology generally and to language acquisition research in particular. The main problem is largely one of sorting out the psychologically relevant concepts and formalisms from the purely descriptive artefacts and fables. The prudent psychologist will do well to recognize that the linguist undoubtedly offers a substantial amount of both kinds of commodity.

12. Learning how and when to use pronouns and determiners

Michael P. Maratsos

Learning how and when to say *a, the, this, that, he, she, it, they*, and other pronouns and determiners is a useful thing for a child, because he will have frequent occasion to use them in his speech. Though mostly 'small' terms, their use, like most things in language properly analysed, requires extensive and subtle analysis by the child.

Determiners include terms as diverse as *any, those, more, no, the, his, each, which,* and probably any possessive phrase – *Harry's, the boy's,* and so on. Pronouns include a large set of terms modulated by case, person, number, specificity, and under some referential conditions may expand as a set to include nearly all of the determiners as well. The use of both classes figures in many systems – negation, questions, relativization and many others. Despite this dispersion, however, there are some central semantic and grammatical processes which characterize large segments of the full set, such as modulation of conversational reference, arbitrary grammatical classificatory systems (gender), and noun phrase constituency. It is easy to show that in language, even what seem to be relatively simple things turn out to be hard, and the careful study of these uses of the terms shows this truism to apply no less than does the study of more clearly grand and complex systems.

1. Description of the classes

The classes of pronouns and determiners are bound together by overlapping semantic determinants of their use such as specificity of reference and contextual dependency. They are divided, yet partly bound together as well, by differences and similarities of grammatical privilege. There is some artificiality in separating from one another the grammatical and semantic characteristics, but such a separation conversely benefits the clarity of exposition.

1.1. Grammatical privileges

In English, determiner terms or phrases can appear before a noun in a noun phrase, and also in front of one or more prenominal adjectives. Terms we call determiners cannot, however, appear before or after other determiners. Using *big* as a typical adjective, we find that terms which are determiners, as gauged by their ability to appear in front of *big* but not each other, include *this, that, the, a, some, more, any, no, each,* and possessive terms and phrases such as *your, his, Harry's, the little boy's.* None of these may be placed after another determiner, as shown by the ungrammaticality of the following: **a no dog, *the Harry's dog, *the each dog,* and so on; all may appear before an adjective–noun sequence: *a big dog, no big dog, Harry's big dog, each big dog.* These constraints are not purely semantic: we cannot say **a Harry's big dog,* but we can say, in a related phrase, *a big dog of Harry's.* There is no simple unifying semantic property that groups determiners together. To say that terms are determiners is a shorthand for saying they combine in these ways with other terms.

Pronouns may contrastively substitute or appear in the same grammatical positions as full noun phrases: *I see the big dog – I see it; the old man left – he left.* Pronouns are not, with one possible exception, *nouns*: they cannot take modifiers and determiners as most nouns can. One cannot say **big he* or **the big he* or **the little it,* even though one can say *the big male* or *the little thing.* The problematic term is the indefinite pronoun *one,* which can act like a full noun phrase (*I ate one today*) or like a noun, taking prenominal determiners and adjectives (*I ate a big one today*). For the purposes of this chapter it is simplest to treat *one* as a bi-grammatical term, both a true noun and a pronoun (actually tri-grammatical, since it may be a determiner as well – *I'd like to see one big dog and one small one*).

In fact, however, many terms and phrases have both determiner and pronominal privileges. Many determiners may appear in the role of a pronoun when the reference of what would be the head noun in a full noun phrase is somehow understood. The following pairs illustrate this: *I see this thing – I see this; I took more cereal – I took more; I saw his dog – I saw his.* Sometimes a related term is the pronoun: *I want no mush – I want none; I want my mush – I want mine.* Thus the classes are not completely separated. Only the articles *a* and *the* apparently fail to show some aspect of this double use as determiner and pronoun. There is no **I see the* to correspond to *I see the dog,* nor **I see a* for *I see a man.* Rather, where *I want the* should be possible, there is instead the large set of definite pronouns: *I want {it, him, her, them ...}.* Similarly, instead of **I want a,* there is *I see one.* This distributional behaviour marks off the articles from the other determiners.

1.2. Context and reference

The most appropriate definition of determiners and pronouns is one made by grammatical privilege. A characteristic of most of them, nevertheless, that serves somewhat to bind together the two classes, is that their use is tied in diverse ways to a relation between the speaker, his knowledge, his listener's knowledge, and the physical and verbal conversational context of their references. This is clearly so of the demonstrative pronouns and determiners *this, that, these* and *those,* which refer to either physical or more abstract closeness. While these terms refer to relative nearness, the reference is to no absolute. *This dog* may be as close as 2 inches or 5 feet away, depending, for example, on whether another dog (*that dog*) is 1 foot or 10 feet away. The relevant distance is always determined in relation to the speaker, not the listener.

More subtle forms of contextual dependency and attention to the relative knowledge of speaker and listener are to be found in the systems of indefinite versus definite pronouns and full noun phrases. The contextual dependency of the personal pronouns may be contrasted to terms more stable in reference, such as personal names (e.g. *Mr Harold Wilson*) or class names (e.g. *male*). Mr Wilson remains Mr Wilson and a male through a variety of circumstances, regardless of who is speaking and who is spoken to or about. But whether the proper pronominal reference for him is *you, I, he,* or some other pronoun depends on his role in the conversational context. Speaking and referring to himself, he should use *I* (or *me,* or *mine,* or *my*). Spoken to, the reference is *you* (or *yours,* or *your*). Spoken about, he is *he, him,* or *his.*

There is furthermore something different about *he,* however, from *I* and *you. I* and *you* generally have at least some fixity of reference for a given speaker–listener pair, in a given conversation. The complexities of the use of *he* are far greater. *He* may be used of any male, but does not mean 'any male' or 'a male'. Walking into the house having been accosted by someone, one could not begin out of the blue by saying, 'He approached me on the street.' The use of *he* implies that there is a specific male such that in the conversational context, both speaker and listener will know which member of the class of males is the intended reference.

He may thus be said to make *specific* reference. It refers to a specific member of the class of males, one marked out in the physical or conversational context in some way. *She* similarly makes reference to a specific singular female, *it* to an object, and *they* to a specific set of any kind.

There are cases in which pronominal reference cannot be adequate or clear because one wishes to mention more than maleness, femaleness, objecthood, or set. For example, having said, 'I brought a vase and a glass', saying 'it broke' leaves the reference of *it* unclear, because there are two possible objects that might be referred to. One should say 'the vase', or 'the glass'; the definite article *the* helps to make specific reference to any specific class member. *The vase* refers to a particular vase so marked out, *the man* to a particular man, and so on.

All of these expressions – *he, she, it, they, the X* – are said to be definite expressions. They all denote reference to class members or sets already picked out in the conversational context.[1]

In the full range of usage, such definite reference is not restricted to actually existent referents. References may be hypothetical, as in 'I wish I had a car; I'd use {*the car, it*} right now.' *The car* takes on specific reference within the hypothetical context. Nor need the referent first be overtly mentioned, or physically present. Having said *I saw a car,* one automatically implies the existence of a particular hood belonging to the car, as well as an engine, windshield, and so on, all of which should then be referred to as *the hood, the engine,* or *the windshield.* And of course in the end reference is not restricted to objects. One can talk about *the conversation, the race, the idea,* and other nonobjects, all of which may also be referred to by *it* as well.

Finally, without saying very much about this, it is clear that 'conversational context' is too broad a term. Suppose someone says, 'John saw his coat slide off a table onto the floor, and picked *it* up.' *It,* in its meaning as referring to an already established singular unsexed referent, could mean either the coat, the table, or the floor. But because of the context provided by *picked— up, it* refers unambiguously to the coat. The context for interpretation of a definite reference may be very small; what matters is whether reference can be unambiguously assigned.

What, however, if one wishes to make reference to no particular member of a class at all? When we ask for *a drink,* or say we have never seen *a dinosaur,* we do not mean to refer to an already particular drink, or to say that there is some particular dinosaur we have never seen. The reference is to some unspecified drink, or to any dinosaur. Similarly, often no particular referent is intended in expressions such as 'I wish I had *a car*', or 'I don't have *a car.*'

Such nonspecific references to a class or class member are made by indefinite pronouns or determiners. The determiners include *a* for singular count nouns, or *some* for singular mass nouns ('Give me *some* mush') and plural count nouns ('*Some* men might come'). There are also indefinite pronouns. For a person, *someone*; for a thing, *something.* When the class is

---

[1] As throughout this brief paper, I ignore various special cases or subtleties. For example, generic expressions such as in *The llama lives in South America* do not refer to a particular llama.

established, *some* may be used by itself as a mass pronoun ('I saw *some*'). Or if the class is properly referred to with a singular count noun, the pronoun is *one* ('Speaking of drinks, I wish I had *one*').

Thus, when a reference is specific for both listener and speaker, a definite expression is mandatory. When a reference is completely nonspecific, an indefinite is to be used. But what of the case in which the reference is specific for the speaker, but not for his listener? For example, suppose the speaker has been accosted by someone on the way home, and wants to tell someone else. He cannot begin the conversation saying, 'I was walking home and *the man* accosted me.' That implies his listener knows from prior context what particular man is meant, which his listener does not. The problem is, a reference to *man* in the context *accosted me* relates to no referent already specific for the listener, though it does to one for the speaker. Similarly for *he* or *she* and other definite pronouns.

It is thus often the case that we have a particular referent in mind in a given context, but our listener as yet does not. If the specific reference is not contextually obvious or implied, an appropriate introductory reference is an indefinite expression: 'I was walking home and a man accosted me.' After this initial establishment of a specific man in the conversational context, reference to him when appropriate can (and should) be definite: *he,* or *him,* or *the man*. Reference to *a man* or *one* ('Then a man laughed at me') implies still another, new man.

Thus, in learning to use pronouns and determiners, the child must learn to refer and comprehend properly according to conversational role, distal–proximal relations around the speaker, and the specificity of references for both himself and his listener. The conditions of usage are obviously complex, and further analysis would uncover many more complications.

2. The acquisition of pronouns and determiners

2.1. Grammatical acquisition

2.1.1. The early use of pronouns and determiners. Possessives and demonstratives (*this, that*) appear in front of nouns even in the child's first two-word combinations (Brown, 1973). So, however, do verbs, other nouns, adjectives, occasional prepositions and other parts of speech. There is no basis at this time for speaking of the noun phrase as a linguistic unit with internal structure (i.e. NP = Determiner + Noun, NP = Adjective + Noun) at this point. Children also show frequent early use of a few of the pronouns. Brown (1973) has pointed out that in children's nonpronominal speech, prominent categories of referents include their listener, objects they act on, themselves and things they possess. Early pronouns accordingly include *you, it* (*get it, push it*), *I* and the determiner *my*.

Despite these similarities, Bloom *et al.* (1975), in a careful longitudinal investigation, found initial differences among individual children in the style and degree of pronoun use. Pronouns, viewed a certain way, are extremely useful general category names, though less explicit than most nouns. Some children they studied consistently (though not always) preferred the use of pronouns to refer to agents, objects of activity, possessives (determiner *my*); they also preferred prolocative terms such as *here* and *there* to full noun references for places. Thus some children would more often say *I go* or *you go* or *put there*, where others would say *Kathryn* (the speaker) *go, Lois* (listener) *go, put chair* (putting something on a chair). With time, the different children's relative proportional use of pronominal and nominal references became highly similar. By an MLU of around 2·5, for example, pronominal expressions comprised 80 per cent of initial NP position references for all five subjects, a generally common proportion in children's speech. The frequent use of pronouns seems to indicate an initial preference for learning the grammatical–semantic privileges of a few words (e.g. *it* in postverbal position) rather than the privileges of broad categories of many words. Why individual children should choose different beginnings is not known.

2.1.2. *Hierarchical structure acquired.* As three-word and longer utterances begin to appear in children's speech, two-word combinations such as Possessive + Noun (*my dog*) or Quantifier + Noun (*more cereal*) now begin to appear in the same positions as simple nouns or pronouns. The child may now say things such as *want it, want cereal, want more cereal, want my cereal,* in which *more cereal* and *my cereal* and *the cereal* have the same distributional privileges as *it* or *cereal*; i.e. they act as units, as NPs.

The first determiners to appear in such phrases are quantifiers such as *more* and possessives[2] such as *mommy('s)* or *my* (Brown, 1973). With time, adjectives, demonstratives and articles also appear prenominally (Brown and Bellugi, 1964). At this later time, all these terms form a single distributional class in terms of their prenominal appearance. There are no noun phrases, e.g. in which two terms, a determiner and an adjective, appear before the noun, such as *the big dog,* or *my big dog.* Brown and Bellugi (1964) do not discuss whether or not any of the determiners show the

---

[2] It may seem puzzling to put full noun possessives such as *mommy('s)* into the determiner class. Yet these appear in this position, and Poss + Noun phrases are used like NPs. The fact that nouns are used in other positions cannot be decisively cited against this, for in some children's speech (e.g. Adam, one of Brown's subjects) so are adjectives.

characteristic behaviour of appearing alone in pronoun-like usage (*want more, here daddy's*) though other discussions in Brown (1973) imply that such uses are not too late in appearing.

There is occasional evidence that the possibility of some determiners also being pronouns causes some children a little difficulty. Braine (1971) reports on his daughter's determined use of *another one* as a determiner in sentences like *want another one spoon*. The generalization appears to be one backwards from pronominal usage to determiner, i.e. *I want more*: *I want more cereal* : : *I want another one*: *I want another one spoon*.

After this, the picture is much less clear. Brown and Bellugi (1964) give a brief sketch of the differentiation of the single determiner class into sub-classes eventually comprising possessive pronouns, demonstratives, articles, descriptive adjectives and other modifiers (presumably such as *more, some,* and others). But the citation of data is slight, and later comments (e.g. Brown, 1973; Brown *et al.,* 1969) show some error or possibility of rein-terpretation in the earlier analyses. Nor has the co-occurring development of the use of some terms both as determiners and pronouns been studied. We thus know that eventually the child differentiates out complex privileges such as the following: a singular count noun (e.g. *dog, game*) *must* take in front of it one of a diverse list of terms, such as *a, the, every, more,* or any possessive, but no more than one of these. One cannot say **dog is barking,* nor can one say **a more dog* or **that Harry's dog.* Nor is the rule simply that every such singular count noun reference must have one term in front: adjectives will not do – e.g. **big dog is barking.* The case is similar for count nouns in the plural unless they are certain kinds of indefinites (*dogs are barking*). Similarly complex contingencies apply for mass nouns – definite references must have some kind of determiner, while indefinite references may or may not. We do not know how the child formulates that, under certain circumstances, the choice of one and no more than one of the heterogeneous set of prenominal determiners is necessary. It is surprising that children do not say more things such as **Here's that Harry's dog* (under the interpretation where *that* refers to *dog*). Essentially, from published reports, children's acquisition seems to occur without drastic error, except for the difficulty of learning the obligatory placement of at least one deter-miner under the requisite referential conditions; it may be a matter of months to years before a child always uses a determiner when obligatory. Other difficulties may arise in the differentiation of mass from count nouns (Brown and Bellugi, 1964; Slobin, 1973), and the use of determiners in negatives (Bellugi, 1967). But it is perhaps most surprising that the general system can be acquired at all. We are not much further along towards giving an account of this than when Brown and Bellugi (1964) first remarked upon the difficulty of the problem.

2.1.3. Gender and case systems. An English speaker referring to a particular fork, spoon, or knife, may refer to each of them impartially as *it;* or if using the definite article, he may always say *the.* But the child learning German must learn to refer to the fork as *die Gabel,* to the spoon as *der Loffel,* and to the knife as *das Masser* (*die, der,* and *das* all meaning 'the'). The respective pronouns are *sie* for the fork, *er* for the spoon, and *es* for the knife. And these facts apply only to the nominative case. Other articles and pronouns must be chosen for the other grammatical cases: genitive, accusative and dative respectively.

German is one of the languages of the world which employ a system of arbitrary classification of nouns for the determination of case endings on surrounding morphemes – in the case of German, determiners, pronouns and adjectives. The three gender classes of German are called feminine, masculine and neuter. It is true that the pronouns and determiners for the nouns for 'boy' and 'man' are the same, which is why this set of pronouns and determiners is said to go with the 'masculine' class of nouns. But this same set of pronouns and determiners is also applied to the words for 'spoon', 'trivet', and 'truck'. The feminine set, used for 'woman', is also used for 'tureen', 'fork', and 'anxiety'. The neuter set (*es, das*) is used for 'knife', 'utensil', and 'secret', and even for 'girl'.

The classification is arbitrary. No underlying rationale can be guessed at. It is not even possible to learn that particular *objects* have one of the three sets associated with them. Translated literally, a speaker would say, referring to the fork as a fork (*die Gabel*), 'Here is a (eine) fork; you may have her', but referring to it as a utensil (*das Gerat*), 'Here is a (ein) utensil; you may have it.'

The presence of such systems in a human cognitive system constitutes by itself an excellent testimony to the occasional nonsensibleness of the species. Not only was this system devised by humans, but generation after generation of children peaceably relearns it. The child (and adult) must memorize for each noun the appropriate set of determiners and pronouns. Presumably after some time the task becomes a less arduous one since there are only three sets, and often just one usage signals the whole set. Hearing *Der X ist hier* ('the X is here') one knows *X* is masculine – i.e. it takes the corresponding sets of pronouns, determiners and adjectival endings as do other nouns of the same classification. But the classification associated with the noun remains arbitrary.

Clearly the child's learning of such an organization of syntactically, abstractly organized classes offers an interesting problem for investigation, especially since the grammatical cases of nominative, accusative, genitive and dative are not themselves directly tied to underlying semantic or grammatical function. This may be shown with the almost vestigial case system of English, which has nominative pronouns (*he, she, it, they*), genitive pronouns and determiners (*my, mine, your(s), his, her(s), their(s), its*) and objective pronouns (*him, her, them*). Consider the logical subject of *sing*, in *he is singing*. In simple sentences and some complements, it is indeed *he*. But in infinitives it is *him* (*I want him to sing*) and in gerunds *his* (*I dislike his singing so loudly*). Similarly, possession is sometimes signalled by genitives (*this is his*) but sometimes by nominatives or objectives (*he owns this – it belongs to him*), all depending on the surrounding grammatical environment.

Little is known at present about the acquisition of determiners and pronouns in German, but more than for any other language with a gender system for pronouns and determiners. There are a few diary reports having to do with the acquisition of articles. The German articles seem to enter productively in the third year, roughly like the English. When they do enter, the usage of gender, surprisingly, is generally correct (Stern and Stern, 1928; Park, 1971). What are reasonably common are case errors. Park reports a case in which the nominative case was often used when others should have been, in one child's early acquisition. Leopold (1939) reports a later time at which the accusative masculine *den* was overgeneralized to nominative masculine uses. Case confusions occur sometimes in English as well, commonly in the substitution of the objective case *me* for nominative *I* (e.g. *me has it; why me spilled it* – Bellugi, 1971; Brown, 1973).

That there are case errors is not surprising, given the clear possible difficulties in figuring out the rules of use. The absence of gender errors is more surprising. Apparently the child does well at memorizing individual determiner–noun usages until such time as he can abstract the general co-occurrence patterns. This impressive feat must take place in long-term memory, since the child presumably only hears and memorizes one or two determiner–noun co-occurrences in a given utterance. What we call gender must arise from the fact that the same sets of determiners (e.g. *der Loffel, dem Loffel, den Loffel, des Loffel*) are stored over and over with diverse individual nouns, a regularity that is somehow noticed and analysed. As interesting as the ramifications of this system of storage are, however, the acquisition of pronouns provides an even more difficult problem. The determiners at least occur in close grammatical conjunction with their respective nouns. Pronouns do not. The child does not hear **es Messer* ('it knife') or **sie Gabel* ('she fork'). Rather, he hears, perhaps, someone pointing to a fork and saying *Gib mir sie* ('Give me her') or pointing to a spoon and saying *Der Loffel – gib mir ihn* ('The spoon – give me him'). The child may begin to associate the appropriate pronouns to the appropriate determiner sets by hearing the pronouns used of the same *object* as referred to by the noun in front of which the determiners appear. In the end, however, complete determination must come from inference from linguistic context. As pointed out earlier, the association of pronouns is with class name, not with the objects or other referents. A fork as a 'fork' is *sie* (*die Gabel*), but as a 'utensil' it is *es* (*das Gerat*). The child must hear utterances such as 'Hier ist eine Gabel, nimmst du sie' ('Here is a fork, you take her') and through interpreting *sie* as referring to the referent of *die Gabel,* learn to associate the appropriate choice of pronoun with the set of determiners appropriate to the noun. It is a remarkable achievement.

As remarkable as this knowledge is, the child may acquire much of it quite early. McWhinney (1978) has written of results with the following procedure, a generalization of a Berko nonsense morpheme task. The child is shown an object for which he has no name, and told, for example, 'Gann. Ich nehme {es, ihn, sie} in die hand' (i.e. 'Gann. I hold {it, him, her} in the hand'). (*Gann* is a nonsense term.) The child is then asked, 'Wie fragst du, "wo ist . . .?" ' ('How do you ask, "where is . . .?" '). By saying how to ask the question, the child shows what he thinks the appropriate choice of determiners is. For example, having heard, 'Gann, Ich nehme *ihn* in der hand', the child should say, 'Wo ist der Gann?' Or hearing the pronoun *sie,* he should say *die Gann.* Even some 3 year olds were capable of carrying out this and related procedures correctly.

Thus children must store data about highly abstract, partly purely formal systems at an early age, and cull from the data generalizations about related arbitrary pronominal and determiner uses. McWhinney (1978) writes that in order to do this the child must form an abstract featural system to assign to the determiners and pronouns, features such as +Neuter, +Masculine and +Feminine. These may be, however, just labels we use to rename the problem, a summary of the system of related uses. The positing of an ability to form symbolic markings of this completely abstract type constitutes a powerful addition to what we have to analyse as part of the language formulation equipment of the child, and thus requires strong justification. Such an addition may, however, turn out to be necessary.

The above findings offer some contrast to those reported by Slobin (1973). He cited data from gender errors in children learning Slavic languages (in which gender determiner systems are not used, but gender is expressed in other parts of speech), which indicated that gender errors were frequent, and case errors few. This result was taken as showing that children greatly prefer semantically based grammatical distinctions. As we have seen, grammatical case itself is often not transparently semantically based. Thus neither the general presence or absence of case errors automatically entails a general conclusion. The so-far reported absence of gender errors in the learning of German determiners and pronouns, however, shows children's ability to learn purely formal distinctions with unexpected ease. What the differences are between German and Slavic structures that leads to this difference of outcome cannot be guessed at easily. It must lie in either the differences in how and where gender is marked, or the method of report in the various studies, or possibly some combination of these.

2.2. The acquisition of conversational reference

2.2.1. *Early use of pronouns.* Children's early speech generally takes place within small contextual bounds – most, though not all, speech revolves about the present physical context. Nevertheless difficulties might easily arise. In the use of *you* and *I*, for example, the child hears himself addressed as *you*, and the person talking to him is *I*. If the child believed these were names, his name would be *you*, and his listener's *I*. Name-like reference to the self as *you* and the listener as *I* is in fact common in autistic children (Rimland, 1964), in accordance with their tendency to literal and sometimes mechanical interpretations of speech events; so the problem is in fact not so easy to solve. Normal children's early acquisition nevertheless does not show much difficulty of this kind, for poorly understood reasons. The child may figure out the code by hearing others talk to each other, such that he hears the reference shift; or other natural interpretive inclinations may operate.

Investigators have not carried out longitudinal studies of the acquisition of the entire system of pronouns and determiners. Most investigations have been concentrated on particular aspects of the acquisition of the terms. I shall concentrate my account here on various findings about the conversational use of pronouns and articles (cf. chapter 13 below for studies of deictic terms).

2.2.2. *Specificity for the self.* Whether or not a reference is to a particular class member, or to any class member, marks the dimension of specificity of reference. Piaget (1962) in early observations of his own children proclaimed young preschool children's lack of differentiation between same and different class members, and between individual particular class members and the notion of any member, particularly in conceptual thought, and thus implicitly in linguistic usage. Later naturalistic and experimental studies, however, suggest a contrary result. Brown (1973) studied the use of the indefinite articles *a* and *the* in three children observed longitudinally. He found that when the child and listener shared the same viewpoint, the child's observation of the specific–nonspecific dimension appeared very good.

Nonexistent or nonparticular referents were apparently referred to with *a* correctly, as in utterances like *I don't have a spoon* or *I want a spoon.* The article *the* was complementarily used appropriately for specific references.

Later experimental study has confirmed this early sophistication. Maratsos (1976) devised a number of procedures to test children's competence in comprehending and producing the articles. In one of these, for example, the child was shown a boy talking to one of three dogs in cars. The child was then told either, 'Then suddenly *the dog* drove away', or 'Then suddenly *a dog* drove away.' If told '*The dog* drove away', the child should have picked the dog being talked to, who had been made contextually specific. Conversely, '*a dog*' should lead to choice of another dog, one not already conspicuous in the context. Three- and 4 year old subjects were equally accurate and well above chance (about 0·85) in correctly choosing referents, showing that even this somewhat unnatural differential use of the articles could carry great referential weight. Through a range of procedures in which children completed brief stories or asked for hidden toys, Maratsos showed that their knowledge of specific and nonspecific reference also applied to invisible or fictional referents.

Again this relatively early competence is surprising. The problem for the child is not simply one of having the appropriate conceptual apparatus of particular versus nonparticular class members. As in all cases in semantic learning, the child does not begin the task *knowing* the most likely candidates for meanings to attach to these small linguistic terms, and here it is quite unlikely that dramatic aspects of the situation point up the connection. Somehow he must guess that the slight phonological distinction *a–the* should be correlated to the underlying conceptual and conversational differences. How the child should come to hypothesize the appropriate connection of this difference to these small segments of the linguistic stream is at present very difficult to understand.

2.2.3. Specificity for the self and others. Knowledge for the self, however, as noted earlier, comprises only half of the picture. The child must also learn that definite reference requires that one's listener, either from the context, prior interaction with the speaker, or general knowledge, also be able to retrieve a specific reference as well. The child appears to have far more trouble with this aspect of definite–indefinite semantics.

Once again the first to complain, at least systematically, was Piaget. In a well-known study (1955b), he had children hear a fairy tale and learn how to work an apparatus. After it was ascertained that they truly understood for themselves the content of the story and the workings of the apparatus, they told the story and explained the apparatus to another child. Piaget expected that young children, used to having others around who shared or understood their viewpoint, would not have learned to modulate their speech in a manner appropriate to explaining to someone who did not share their knowledge. The results agreed with his expectations. Most pertinent to the discussion here, he noted that: 'Pronouns, personal and demonstrative [determiners] etc., "he, she" or "that, the, him" etc. are used right and left, without indication of what they refer to. The other person is supposed to understand' (Piaget, 1955b: p. 166).

It is easy to show that even in the case of the examples Piaget selected as showing real incompetence, usage was not as bad as it could have been, and some competence was shown. Even adults often make elliptical or unclear pronominal references. But the errors he found were nevertheless substantial.

The question of egocentrism has not been further studied in the case of the pronouns, but the definite and indefinite articles have received recent attention. Brown (1973) noted from naturalistic studies that children's use of *a* and *the* was accurate in observing the specific–nonspecific for self dimension, but found many errors when the children's viewpoints diverged from those of their listeners. Frequently the listener showed resulting signs of referential incomprehension. One such exchange: 'Sarah: *The cat's dead.* Mother: *What cat?'*

A variety of studies have confirmed preschool children's difficulties in introducing referents to their listeners properly with indefinite expressions. Maratsos (1976) found such difficulties evident in a story-completion task and in a procedure in which children asked for one toy which could not be easily specified out of a group of similar toys, such that they should have said 'a boy', and so on. Some 4 year olds, not necessarily the same ones in both tasks, made very good use of indefinite references, but errors were common in the other children. Warden (1976) had children describe pictures in which characters performed various actions to someone who could not see the pictures and did not know the characters. Preschool children sometimes used indefinite expressions to introduce referents, and nearly always used definite expressions to refer to referents already mentioned. But overuse of definite expressions was endemic, and errors remained common even in 7 year olds; they became few only in the 9 year old group.

Peterson (1974) made perhaps the most naturalistically convincing test. An adult told a child stories in a room. They contained a series of interesting 'accidents' such as finding someone's lost coat, cleaning up spilled Kool-aid, or retrieving a lost hamster. A week or so later, the child talked to either the same adult in the same room, with whom he thus shared much knowledge, or to another adult, with whom he thus shared no previous experience. Both 3 year olds and 4 year olds talked very differently to the adult with whom they had shared the experiences, and appropriately so. Talking to the unknowledgeable adult, the children of both ages gave fuller descriptions, required less prompting to describe what had happened, and so on. Three year olds, however, made no significant discrimination in their use of definite and indefinite references to particular referents. Four year olds were far better, though still making many errors. This study shows that there is no point in appealing to a generalized lack of conversational ability to take the other's viewpoint in explaining children's errors with definite reference. Peterson's 3 year olds showed many manifestations of understanding conversational requirements, but had not been able to sort out the nonegocentric use of definite references according to past experience with their listener or the lack of it.

The growth of formulation and application of the nonegocentric use of definite and indefinite reference is thus a slow process. That this understanding grows slowly and may never become perfect is not surprising. Establishing the proper use of definite and indefinite expressions requires, first of all, a realization that the listener's knowledge regarding the specificity of the reference is actually relevant to the use of the particular linguistic terms. Earlier it was discussed how difficult it was to imagine how the child makes the relevant hypotheses about specificity–nonspecificity for himself. It is far more difficult to imagine how the steps are taken towards understanding that *mutual* specific reference is important, nor is it easy to imagine how this information is represented in the mind. The problem is complicated by the fact that there are so many ways in which such knowledge may come about, and thus in which children may hear definite reference used by adults. Sometimes referents are introduced and established in the particular conversational context. But as shown earlier, overt mention is not necessary when the referent is implied (*the hood* of a car). Some particular references are understood by all without previous interaction, such as references to *the sky*. Or general knowledge and conversational context may interact to make references to *the war* or *the president* comprehensible and appropriate. Sometimes referents are mutually specific in a given context through prior mutual experience a long time before, as in Peterson's study. It is therefore quite difficult to imagine how the child begins to determine the connecting thread among all these circumstances to discover the particular conditions of referential use, and how he encodes this knowledge.

Second, even once some apprehension of the correct ideal use has begun, there is the problem of seeing when the problem arises in particular referential situations, and computing the appropriate indefinite introductions or the appropriately detailed definite expressions, or knowing when no introduction is necessary or appropriate. It is not always easy to estimate or remember when one's listener's viewpoint diverges with regard to referential specificity; the variety of ways in which knowledge may be shared or not makes this clear.

The child may be aided in discerning these conditions of usage by the reactions of others to incorrect uses. But the child must still come to guess that the problem is the choice of determiner or pronoun, the poorly introduced referent, and so on. At present we do not really have evidence of whether his initial partial competence, when it appears, is largely correct in formulation but lacking in application, or whether initial formulations are useful but qualitatively incorrect or incomplete.

Finally, in both theoretical and empirical terms, as noted above, it is useless to appeal to some general notion of children being 'egocentric' or not to 'explain' acquisition. As many have pointed out (de Villiers and de Villiers, 1974; Flavell, 1977; Maratsos, 1976), egocentrism is not a measles-like disease which a child either has or does not have. Egocentrism is a cover term for a wide variety of failures, stemming probably from a wide variety of causes, to take into account the point of view of the other person. It is easy to imagine a child who understands much about the requisites of communication with others (as it is becoming increasingly apparent that preschool children do; cf. Flavell, 1977 for a summary), but who fails to attach to the use of *the* and *a,* or the other definite and indefinite terms the more subtle required understanding of referential specificity for the 'other', a dimension often not determined by physically present information. It has been clearly established that children have difficulties learning how to use definite and indefinite reference in conversations, which is not surprising. What is surprising, and at present no account can clearly elucidate this, is that they ever begin to get it right.

3. Conclusion

This chapter has obviously not been an attempt to present a unified account of the structure and meaning of determiners and pronouns. This results from the heterogeneity of the terms. Despite their usually being small and inconspicuous they are obviously terms that present the child with a variety of problems. Adults have an implicit knowledge of the system, and consequently their thinking about it may be too simplistic and general. The child does not. He is only presented with individual instances of use in particular linguistic and nonlinguistic environments, and from these he must draw out the complexities of nonegocentric references, distributional classes and classes such as gender, along with much else not specified here. In all the cases I have discussed, it is clear that both empirical and theoretical understanding of the problems and data are not very advanced, but enough is known to point up the complexity of what is acquired. It is almost a tribute to the self-confidence of the species that it sets its young such difficult problems of analysis in the use of such inconspicuous words.

13. Deixis*

Roger Wales

Deixis is the Greek word for indicating or pointing. It has been taken over as a technical term in linguistics to refer to those terms or expressions which serve this linguistic function. Thus the category of deictic expressions includes, typically, pronouns, demonstratives, some verbs of motion like *come* and *go*, adverbs of place, definite articles, etc. That is, they are all expressions which serve to direct the hearer's attention to spatial or temporal aspects of the situation of utterance which are often critical for its appropriate interpretation. They do this in a way which is particularly interesting, since they serve as a meeting point for syntactic, semantic and pragmatic aspects of language. This is because they are, to use Stern's (1964) term, contingent expressions. By this is meant that, to interpret them, the interpreter not only needs context independent semantic information, but also information which is contingent on an actual (or construed) context. The aspect which is most critical in this regard is, typically, information about the speaker, but anyway this information must be such as to enable decisions to be made about person and/or place in relation to the utterance. What these expressions do when grouped as 'deictic', is to introduce an explicitly subjective orientation into linguistic classification. Some useful recent discussions of deixis from a linguistic point of view are E. V. Clark (1974b), Fillmore (1966, 1970, 1971b), Kuryłowicz (1972) and Lyons (1968, 1975, 1977a: vol. ii). There has been, of late, a flurry of studies of children's language incorporating some reference to deixis, some more enthusiastic than others. A typical sample of such are Bates (1976), Bowerman (1973a), Bruner (1974), H. Clark (1973a), Macrae (1976a, 1976b), Richards (1976), Wales (1971, 1974) and Wills (1977). To date the only serious attempt to make systematic sense of the area of deixis from a developmental viewpoint has been Clark (1977b).

* I am grateful to the following who have had a direct hand in some part or other of the contents of this chapter: Caroline Bingham, Beatrice Clayre, Patrick Griffiths, Libby Robin, and especially Jane Breekveldt and Michael Garman. Also to John Lyons for first introducing me to the excitements of deixis.

In this chapter, we will attempt to pull out some of the key issues raised by deixis. To that end we will present some of the empirical cum methodological issues that we must grapple with in order to try and give a profile of this area of the child's linguistic development. Before dealing briefly with some topics covered in other chapters in this book (e.g. pronouns, chapter 12), we shall concentrate in more detail on studies of the acquisition of demonstratives and locative adverbs. This is because these terms are in many ways central to any discussion of deixis.

1. *This* and *that*, and *here* and *there*

There are two deictic aspects of these terms which we will look at in particular:

(i) their attention-directing function – roughly, 'look', 'see'
(ii) their contrastive spatial functions – *this* and *here* usually referring to objects and locations proximal to the speaker, *that* and *there* to objects and locations not proximal to the speaker

Given the latter, speaker-oriented semantic contrast, it is clearly possible that the process of acquisition might be constrained by the child's cognitive egocentricity (as generally proposed by Piaget (1926 =1955b), Piaget and Inhelder (1956) and explicitly argued in this context by Webb and Abramson (1976) and argued against by de Villiers and de Villiers (1973b)). It is striking that diarists of early language development have found that at least some of these terms occur in the earliest utterances of young children – sometimes in the first ten words, always (where the data are available) in the first fifty (Nelson, 1973b). Perhaps even more striking is that they are used extensively in two-word utterances. Such observations already exist for at least the following languages: Chinese, Danish, English, Finnish, French, German, Japanese, Korean, Modern Hebrew, Italian, Quechua, Samoan and Swedish. It seems reasonable to suppose the phenomenon to be universal; particularly in the light of Lyons' (1975) extensive arguments, centred on these terms, that deixis is the source of linguistic reference. For some indication of the relevance of this to development, note that Cross (1977) has observed that 73 per cent of all mother–child utterances involve immediate reference (i.e. reference to objects and events in the immediate environment).

First, let us look at how the young child, and his mother, use these expressions. A detailed analysis was done of some of the mother–child interactions videoed and studied by Toni Cross. The occasion of the use of each of these terms was noted (plus the contrast between definite and indefinite article, and pronouns). Where a term was used, a note was also made of the kind of gesture (or lack of gesture) accompanying it. Ten mother–child pairs in a total of fifteen recording sessions (of about half an hour each) were thus categorized. Because of differences in the total amount of speech used, all scores were transformed into percentages. The results of the coded categories are summarized in table 1. It is clear that the terms are used very frequently by both mothers and children and, for both, the dominant strategy for the use of these linguistic 'pointing' expressions is associated with some explicit pointing or handling gesture. Among the more striking details, note the mothers' concentration on the use of *that, there* and *the*, whereas a more even spread of terms was used by the children. Also, the dominant mode of gestural support for these expressions is some form of explicit handling. The pattern of gestural response is clearly geared to attracting and holding the listener's attention to the relevant referential domain. These results are from children aged 19 months upwards. The basic pattern of use seems fairly constant across all the mothers and children irrespective of the linguistic level of the children. What does change, as a function of the linguistic sophistication of the child, is what the mother puts into the referring expression, not how it is introduced.

Table 1. *Mean percentage scores of mothers' and children's use of demonstratives and locative adverbs with associated gestures (standard deviations in parentheses)*

Utterance type	Mothers	Children
this	4·6 (3·2)	7·0 (5·1)
that	25·5 (5·6)	19·3 (8·4)
here	5·0 (3·3)	16·8 (6·6)
there	14·0 (5·4)	18·3 (11·4)
the	31·9 (6·5)	15·3 (10·4)
a	19·6 (5·1)	21·3 (14·0)
Total number of these utterances	6026	3123
Mean (½ hour) session	402 (166)	208 (165)

Category of associated gesture	Mothers	Children
1. Pointing	7·4 (2·9)	8·7 (6·5)
2. Handling – speaker, throughout	19·5 (8·4)	41·2 (12·1)
3. – speaker, putting down	2·9 (1·6)	4·7 (3·7)
4. – listener, throughout	15·2 (6·1)	4·2 (3·3)
5. – listener, putting down	1·7 (1·6)	0·5 (0·7)
6. – picking up	8·2 (3·4)	9·8 (2·8)
7. After putting down (speaker)	0·7 (0·8)	1·0 (1·0)
8. No handling	21·9 (4·4)	18·1 (7·7)
9. No concrete reference present	22·6 (8·9)	12·3 (10·2)

While it is difficult at this point to quantify, what seems clear is that the mothers of the linguistically less advanced children (on the measures of Cross (1977)) tend to relate only one or two items together semantically – almost as if they impart semantic information by a process of casual chaining. The mothers of the more advanced children, however, are using the same deictic devices to introduce referring expressions which relate to a wider network of semantic relations (e.g. while they placed toy furniture in various rooms of a house, an account of the functions of those rooms was given). It is almost as if the mothers are using the same introductory devices, but tuning their 'tutelage' to the competence of the child. Of course, it is an open question on this evidence as to which is the chicken and which the egg – the children's competence or the mother's communicative strategy. However that question may ultimately be resolved, it is evident that children have early mastered the general attention-directing function of these deictic terms, typically with accompanying gesture. There is a real question, however, as to whether they have yet mastered the contrastive aspects of these terms. Many of the utterances used by both mothers and children are difficult to categorize reliably from the videotapes, as either proximal or nonproximal to speaker. In the clear cases (approximately one third of the utterances), it is obvious that the proximal/nonproximal distinction is not usually utilized by the children. But then neither is it by the mothers! The dominant use is simply introducing the referring expression and directing attention to the appropriate spatial domain of the conversational environment by means of the gesture. The children do, however, make use of *this* and *here* when an object is introduced into the environment of discourse (say, a toy being brought out of a box) and *that* and *there* are used when such objects 'disappear'. This is a similar result to that reported by Macrae (1976b) for children's use of *come* and *go*. This result was also anticipated by Griffiths (1974b).

What hypotheses and strategies do children use in order to develop the contrastive use of these expressions? The results of a few simple studies will now be reported; these start to explore differences in linguistic inferential performance, by children using these expressions without the aid of gesture, in different situations and at different ages. All these studies were of eighty children equally divided into four age groups of 4, 5, 6, and 7 year olds (thirty-eight boys participated).

Each task consisted of four trials, one each on the deictic words *this, that, here* and *there*. The order of trials and tasks was randomized. Pairs of identical toys were used (varying for each task), and instructions were of the form: 'Make this pig jump', 'Make the monkey there run', etc. The verb of motion was varied and was always one the children were familiar with.

Otherwise, the syntactic structure of each sentence was identical. The tasks are laid out schematically in figure 1 and were as follows:

I. The child's perspective was the same as the experimenter's i.e. they sat side by side at the table.

II. The child and the experimenter sat opposite each other, so their perspectives differed. (If the problem of the shifting boundaries associated with deictic reference is what makes for the child's difficulty in interpreting these terms, then making clear, by demarcation, the areas denoted by each word should facilitate performance. Tasks I and II were therefore repeated with a 15 centimetre high screen across the middle of the table as used by de Villiers and de Villiers (1973b) (Screen Condition).)

III. The toys were placed on the floor under two different distance conditions – the 'short distance' being similar to Webb and Abramson's (1976) study of *this* and *that*. (This was a different perspective task, as in task II.)

IV. The same as task II, except that the locations for each animal were established before the test itself, and the locations marked with contrasting coloured paper.

V. A further test of the child's ability to shift perspective with the two experimenters seated opposite each other, and each presenting the four instructions.

ANOVAs were used for the analysis. These were for fixed effects since the interest was specifically in these words (cf. H. Clark, 1973b). Analyses were typically four-way designs with repeated measures on all factors, except age and sex. For the sake of brevity, only statistically significant results will be reported here.

A comparison of task I with task II (cf. table 2) revealed no overall differences. In fact there was a tendency for performance to be better on the opposite perspective task (II), the effect reaching significance for the youngest group ($F = 7.8$, df $(1,19)$, $p < 0.05$). So much for egocentricity! (The anomaly of arguing for a global application of egocentricity was argued some time ago by Vygotsky (1962), and many of the contradictions in the use of the term are brought out by Hughes (1975).)

Performance on *here* and *there* (locatives) was better than on *this* and *that* (demonstratives) ($F = 14.7$, df $(1,76)$, $p < 0.01$), an effect found in most of these tasks (cf. table 3).

The younger children did not perform better on the two types of words. Near perspective words (*this, here*) were significantly higher than far perspectives (*that, there*) ($F = 6.3$, df $(1,19)$, $p < 0.05$). Because of a position effect (to take the toy nearest the child), there was a significant task by word effect (F = 55·3, df (1,76), p < 0·01) which diminished with age as the children learned to use the words more reliably.

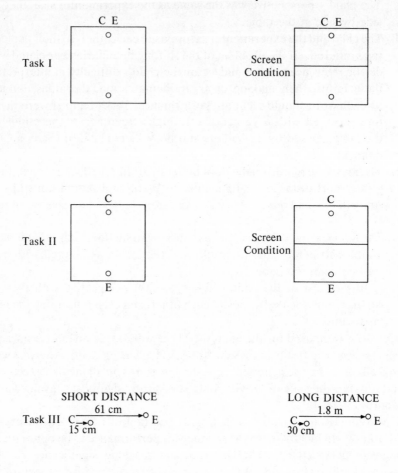

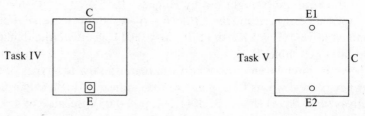

Figure 1.

Table 2. *Performance on tasks I and II*

Age	Task I (same perspective)		Task II (different perspective)	
	Mean score	Per cent correct	Mean score	Per cent correct
4 years	1·1500	57·5	1·4750	73·7
5 years	1·2500	62·5	1·4250	71·25
6 years	1·3750	68·75	1·4750	73·7
7 years	1·4250	71·25	1·4500	72·5
Total	1·3000	65	1·4563	72·8

Table 3. *Performance on demonstratives and locatives (tasks I and II)*

Age	Demonstratives		Locatives	
	Mean score	Per cent correct	Mean score	Per cent correct
4 years	1·2750	63·75	1·3500	67·5
5 years	1·2750	63·75	1·4000	70
6 years	1·2500	62·5	1·6000	80
7 years	1·2750	63·75	1·6000	80
Total	1·2688	63·4	1·4875	74·4

Comparing the Screen/No Screen tasks, there was no overall effect for screen, but this factor was involved in a significant word × task × screen interaction ($F = 8.52$, df $(1,36)$, $p < 0.01$). The screen aided performance in the near perspective task but not the opposite one. This occurred specifically for the demonstratives. (The locatives were understood better.) Thus when the child and speaker share the same perspective, the presence of a distinguishing feature such as a screen aids performance. When the speaker is opposite the child, the speaker provides a sufficient spatial cue.

Task III (the distance effect) yielded somewhat similar results, although not achieving significance. In task V, performance on locatives was again better than on demonstratives ($F = 20.8$, df $(1,36)$, $p < 0.01$). An interesting result is that the responses to the experimenter who sat in the position vacated by the child were significantly less correct than those to the other experimenter ($F = 5.1$, df $(1,36)$, $p < 0.05$), suggesting some perseveration from the preceding tasks. (This was confirmed by repeating the task with an independent group who had not had any preceding tasks, where the effect went away.) Comparing tasks IV and II showed no differences.

A further task (VI) was similar to II except that children were given both a demonstrative and a locative term in the instruction: e.g. 'Make this dog run there', etc. When the terms were contrasted in the instructions (proximal versus nonproximal), the children performed better than when the polarity was noncontrasted. To give just the total scores by items for when the children correctly followed both parts of the instruction:

this/here 19, *this/there* 25, *that/here* 29, *that/there* 17.

This trend was maintained when pooling across individual subcomponents of the instructions. Having two terms in the instructions results in better overall performance presumably because having two terms helps to highlight the relevant spatial contrast.

One odd result here is that unlike all the earlier results, whether reported above, or by Clark (1977b), the demonstratives are significantly better than the locatives (F = 6·9, df (1,36), p < 0·05). Presumably this is a function of the task. In Clark's studies and those reported above, the locatives were evaluated by *initial* location. In studies such as Wales (1974), the locatives were evaluated in terms of *final* location, but in a context where it may make more intuitive sense to change the locations of the objects. Thus this result may be one more instance of children giving silly answers to silly questions! The answers themselves are not so silly in that there is a nearly significant age by word effect, which stems from clear improvement of the demonstratives by age.

It seems clear from these results that the children have some notion of how to sort out the relevant deictic contrasts, but that the way in which this limited competence is expressed is situation-specific, often in quite predictable ways.

Another way of looking at these kinds of data is to look at each individual subject and try to work out the strategies being used across the various tasks. As Clark and Sengul (1978) have also suggested, the children fall into three main categories: *no contrast, partial contrast* and *full contrast.* Clark and Sengul subcategorized the crucial partial contrast set into two: speaker-, or self-orientated, this based on two studies – essentially equivalent to tasks I and II here. Taking as a rule 70 per cent of responses as being necessary for inclusion in any given category, only six of the children in our studies were at all difficult to classify.

I *No contrast stage.* 20 per cent of all subjects showed no evidence of the contrast between proximal and nonproximal. They scored 50 per cent, almost invariably having a bias for the object nearest them. There existed an almost perfect correlation between inability to distinguish between contrastive terms, and inability to shift perspective as speaker roles were exchanged in task V.

II *Partial contrast.* 56·25 per cent of the children showed some sign that a contrast existed. Unlike the suggestions of Clark and Sengul, at least four subcategories were established here:

(a) *Random shifting of focus between the toys* (20 per cent of the children)
(b) *Alternating strategy*: each toy manipulated alternately, although not always correctly (17·5 per cent)
(c) *Egocentric*: either used themselves as the reference point in task II, or performed better on task I than II (11·5 per cent)
(d) *Speaker centred*: these children could only make the contrast successfully when the speaker sat opposite them

III *Full contrast.* 23·75 per cent had mastered the deictic contrast. The distribution of the various strategies is shown in figure 2 and shows a definite improvement in understanding with age. The observation that less than 50 per cent of the 7 year olds had mastered the deictic contrast suggests a tentative link between its acquisition and concrete operations, but our evidence shows that cognitive egocentrism is not involved in this relationship. (The apparent rise in egocentrism by age is simply a function of the rise in number of those using a spatial contrast, and is an effect specific to language.) This is not at all surprising, given the centrality of deixis to

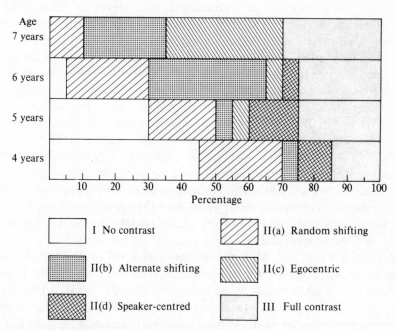

Figure 2. Strategies used by children of different ages

reference, reference to communication, and communication to social interaction.

Other studies we have conducted have included variation on these types of tasks: e.g. a 'gedanken' type of experiment (where 'I am thinking about one of the animals and will tell you something about it. You then try to work out which one I am thinking about'), giving such information as *this* versus *that* (without of course revealing the actual animal). When conducted in the same perspective situation, the children performed almost identically to the task II (opposite perspective) results reported earlier. This is presumably because in this task the children are explicitly being required to take the experimenter's viewpoint.

In another version of the 'gedanken' task, the objects were in pairs on each side of the table and were manipulated so as to 'appear' or 'disappear'. In one study just one item was made to 'appear' or 'disappear' – i.e. move into or out of sight (and be placed on the appropriate place on the table). In another condition one item was made to 'appear' and another 'disappear' on each trial. The location of the items being manipulated in relation to the instruction was randomized. The children focused most of their response choices for the deictic terms on the manipulated object, though this effect diminished with increasing age. This is because as greater mastery is achieved of the relevant spatial contrast so more choices of a nonmanipulated object come to be made, if this is a more appropriate candidate for the term – 'appropriate' here being determined not only by the spatial contrast, but also, in keeping with the observations reported on the spontaneous language use, as a function of how the spatial contrast relates to the object's 'appearance' or 'disappearance'. What was interesting here was that a significantly greater number of 'appearance' choices were for 'that' and 'there' ($F = 9.5$, df $(1,79)$, $p < 0.003$); and conversely for 'disappearance', there were a greater number of choices for 'this' and 'here' ($F = 4.1$, df $(1,79)$, $p < 0.05$). No, this is not an error in reporting, it does appear to be the converse of the observations on the spontaneous use of these expressions. But note, the task was for the child to indicate which toy the person doing the manipulating was thinking about when using the expression. Thus the children were in fact reversing roles appropriately to take the speaker's point of view, and increasingly doing so by age.

A version of task VI, with both a demonstrative and locative term in each instruction, was conducted some years ago on children aged 3 and 4 years (ten each) in each of three language groups: English, Tamil (a Dravidian language) and Lun Bawang (a Malayo-Polynesian language). The English instructions were of the form, 'Move this (or that) block here (or there)'. The arrangements for testing are shown in figure 3, where 'this block' is labelled

CHILD

Adult
Observer

Speaker

Figure 3. Arrangements for testing

B and 'that block' A (versions of the results have been reported in Wales
(1974) and Garman (1977)). Fully appropriate responses are presented in
table 4. Performance seems rather low, though looking at individual components obviously improves the picture. The English (i.e. Scottish) group
contained spuriously high scores on *this/here,* due to a general strategy of
many of the children to take the block nearest to the speaker and move it
toward the speaker. If we ignore the results of these strategists for a moment,
then it can be said that, overall, for each group *that/there* is hardest and
that/here is easiest. Furthermore, mixed polarity instructions (relative to
the speaker) are easier than nonmixed. The sequential response patterns –
'How many of those subjects who chose the wrong block placed it in the right
location?' etc. – are shown in figure 4. (This ignores the responses of the
English 'behavioural strategists'.) It is clear by inspection that the groups are
very similar. Subjects are more than three times more likely to select the
right block than the wrong one and, regardless of which block is selected, are
two to three times more likely to place it in the right location. Thus there
seems to be much better incipient comprehension of deictic terms than 'fully
appropriate' responses reveal. Complicating factors in the various groups
and conditions seem to stem from the application of one or other of the
following 'naïve' assumptions:

(i) that proximity of block to speaker implies that speaker will be the agent
of any block shifting
(ii) that a deictic instruction is going to require a change in the deictic
specification of the relevant object (it is presumably this principle which
makes instructions with terms of similar polarity 'difficult')

Table 4. *Fully appropriate responses (both demonstrative and
locative components simultaneously) in terms of an adult model*

	that/there	*this/there*	*this/here*	*that/here*
Tamil	3	8	6	12
Lun Bawang	0	8	12	19
English	0	3	15	6

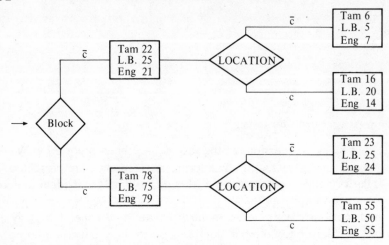

Figure 4. Per cent responses to all instructions
  Tamil (Tam) Σ = 78
  Lun Bawang (L.B.) Σ = 77
  English (Eng) Σ = 29

c = correct; c̄ = not correct

It is possible that especially the English group could have been influenced by block B (in figure 3) being in the direction of gaze of the speaker to child. One way to control for this is to have both objects in the same gaze path, thus:

SPEAKER   A   B   CHILD

This study has been done with both English and Tamil 3 and 4 year old children, who in this situation behave very similarly. The dominant strategy is to move one block from one location (on a stool) to the other, i.e. A to B or B to A. With *this/here* most move B to A; with *that/there* most move A to B; with *this/there* most move A to B; and with *that/here* most move B to A. That is, whenever the choice is between the correct block or the correct final location, the latter tends to win out. This of course fits in well with the general finding that the children are using the locative expressions more easily than the demonstratives.

Yet other studies, one of which will be presented later, have shown that in more overt game playing situations with a wider set of response options, their overall performance can be made to 'improve'. This is neither surprising nor itself relevant. It should be clear that with a wide set of experimental manipulations and a variety of methods of analysis what is of interest is not some absolute level of performance – 'the child's got it', or 'not', as the case may be. Rather they serve to indicate that the acquisition of these terms is a gradual process of putting a system of contrasts together and learning when and how it is appropriate to apply them. The system acquired seems to be roughly as follows:

(i)   A simple 'pointing function' (consistent incidentally with the mother's dominant use of *that* and *there* and consistent with the priority Lyons (1975) gives these as terms of primitive deixis)

(ii) A recognition that sometimes a contrast of some sort is relevant. This is hooked into initial 'existence' assumptions like 'appearance' and 'disappearance' relative to the domain of discourse

(iii) The realization that the contrast of (ii) is related to the spatial location of the speaker, and that some spatial cues are helpful in different ways in different situations in determining this. The problem is in general, to work out what the appropriate frame of reference relative to the speaker is

(iv) A 'typical' adult system is developed, though is perhaps still prone to what may be more sociolinguistic assumptions, like 'proximity of object to speaker implies that the agent of any object shifting will be the speaker'

In all, the process of acquisition seems orderly. It is consistent with the assumptions made about these terms, namely that they have a semantic as well as a syntactic and pragmatic function, which starts off being organized as a general *linguistic* attention-directing device which subsequently comes to include a more specialized spatial contrastive component. Now let us turn more briefly to consider studies of the acquisition of some other deictic expressions.

2. Pronouns

Until recently, pronouns have not figured largely in studies of children's language. One rationale for this is given by Brown (1973) in his excellent overview of his own and related work. He indicates that while some pronouns occur early and are used often, they are sufficiently restricted in type that it would require more features than there are pronouns to describe them. On the other hand statistical studies of Suppes and his colleagues have indicated that pronouns are always in the young child's three most frequently used noun phrase types. Recent work by, for example, Chomsky (1969), Huxley (1970), Maratsos (1973) and Tanz (1974, 1977) shows that children not only use pronouns early on – typically *I, you, it,* and *mine* – but also observe many of the crucial constraints in their use and comprehension, e.g. the distinction between definite and indefinite reference, which the adult use of such pronouns requires.

To give a picture of pronominal usage that fits in with the earlier studies and results, table 5 presents the results of percentage pronoun use by mothers and children in the same format as table 1 (from the same population of subjects). A few points are worthy of note: the pronouns used reasonably often are *I, you* (in subject position); *we, he, (him, she* and *her* not as often), *it* (in both subject and object position); *they; mine* (by the

Table 5. *Mean percentage scores for spontaneous use of pronouns by mothers and children (standard deviations in parentheses)*

Utterance Type	Mothers	Children
I	7·99 (2·97)	18·70 (8·19)
me	21·16 (0·57)	8·57 (4·05)
you (subject)	27·28 (6·83)	11·34 (6·33)
you (object)	0·74 (0·50)	1·11 (2·05)
we	8·70 (5·25)	0·44 (0·70)
us	0·53 (0·57)	0·54 (1·42)
he	7·08 (4·68)	5·88 (6·77)
him	2·27 (1·69)	0·73 (1·02)
she	3·12 (2·70)	1·06 (1·22)
her	1·77 (1·47)	0·93 (1·15)
it (subject)	16·92 (6·21)	11·71 (11·53)
it (object)	8·96 (3·76)	17·57 (17·69)
they	5·21 (3·57)	2·19 (3·82)
them	1·91 (1·99)	0·78 (1·33)
my/mine	0·28 (0·43)	15·27 (16·95)
your/yours	2·21 (1·28)	1·50 (2·14)
his	2·27 (1·31)	1·16 (1·36)
her/hers	0·51 (0·17)	0·24 (0·43)
its	0·34 (0·91)	0·00 (0·00)
their/theirs	0·55 (0·68)	0·09 (0·24)

Category of associated gesture	Mothers	Children
1. Pointing	2·01 (2·48)	3·96 (3·26)
2. Handling – speaker, throughout	15·90 (4·96)	30·56 (9·14)
3. – speaker, putting down	1·30 (0·70)	2·15 (1·41)
4. – listener, throughout	16·15 (3·86)	7·03 (5·55)
5. – listener, putting down	0·32 (0·36)	0·59 (1·02)
6. – picking up	1·85 (1·23)	2·47 (1·88)
7. After putting down (speaker)	0·56 (0·38)	0·29 (0·49)
8. No handling	53·47 (7·46)	46·53 (14·19)
9. No concrete referent present	8·44 (2·64)	6·42 (7·63)

children); *your* (and *yours*); and *his* (by the mothers). What is most obvious about the associated gesture table, is the much larger incidence of 'no handling' behaviour (as compared to the demonstratives and locatives of table 1). This rise in 'no handling' is directly a product of 'no gesture' being associated with the use of the first and second person pronouns. Thus the picture for third person usage, of whatever type, is very similar to that, say, for demonstratives. Thus it seems reasonable to hypothesize that the children learn person deixis, i.e. the use of pronouns to 'point to' persons, initially through the medium of the 'real' personal pronouns *I* and *you*. Indicating persons in the third person (implied by gender distinctions) has gestural support as a typical concomitant as found with the demonstratives. This suggests that experimental studies of children's use of the third person pronouns might run into similar problems in the children's ability accurately to infer what the reference was when there was no gestural support.

This result was found in a study with two groups of English-speaking children, twenty in each and with mean ages 4;6 and 6;0 years. Each child was given in various orders situations where there were four dolls, two of each 'gender', plus associated proper names, each doll possessing (by introduction) some object. The experimenter would say something which the child then had to act out 'for the dolls' thus: 'Mary says to John, "Give me your hat" ', etc. The personal pronouns used were *I, me, my, you, your, yours, she, her, hers, him, his, it, its*. Although the older group did better, none of the age differences was statistically reliable. Overall, all the first and second person references were much better handled than the third person ones. For half the children, it seems likely, considering the strategies implied by the results, that only the announced interlocutors were considered. The hardest sentences were those involving *him, her, his* or *hers*. This latter result is particularly interesting given that the children observed the relevant gender distinction correctly 85 per cent of the time. Thus it seems that with pronouns also, the 'pointing function' comes first. Gender distinctions are observed in an appropriate fashion, but contrastive use of the relevant person/gender distinctions is a later development. On the egocentricity front, it is also worth noting that a reversal of (a) 'Give him my . . .' to (b) 'Give me his . . .', is much less likely than the converse. This would seem to argue more for Vygotsky's (1962) view of egocentrism than Piaget's.

3. *Front*, *back* **and** *sides*

There is an ambiguity about expressions like *in front of* and *behind* which has some interesting consequences for considering the development of deixis. Essentially the ambiguity is a result of the fact that many objects have an intrinsic front. That is, they have a part of them which is characteristically interpretable as 'the front' (H. Clark (1973a) argues that it is from knowing this that one can work out 'the back'). On the other hand, something may be said to be 'in front of' the speaker. So, in making a judgment as to whether something is, say, 'in front of an aeroplane', the person may have to decide between two conflicting judgments: the one involving the interpretation which uses the intrinsic front of the plane, and the other using the 'egocentric' front of the speaker (note again that this speaker orientation is not necessarily the same as Piagetian 'egocentrism'). Of course, this conflict will only arise as a function of the orientation of the plane and speaker to each other and to the object. Following Fillmore (1971b) there has been an interesting study of this issue by Kuczaj and Maratsos (1975), who found several interesting results with children between the ages of 3 and 4 years.

The children apparently acquire the notion that *front* and *back* are opposites before they have a general understanding of either term – and they subsequently acquire both correctly simultaneously. *Sides* is a later acquisition. Further, correct use of the terms seems to begin with reference to the self and spreads to objects with fronts. This latter result is in line with results obtained by Hall (1975). The relevant two studies were part of a thesis looking at scanning strategies used by children when evaluating the truth or falsity of particular perceptual arrays. Three groups of children were studied, aged 5, 7 and 9 years, and one group of adults; in each case subjects were required to evaluate the truth of statements regarding 'in front of' and 'behind' two-dimensional representations of intrinsically fronted objects as seen in profile. The most striking result was that most of the subjects in the younger two age groups judged both true and false sentences as 'false' because the relevant object was not placed between the subject and the array! To follow this up, Hall had subjects place the pictures of objects 'in front of' or 'behind' a specified picture (SP) of a faced (fronted) object, either in a two-dimensional or three-dimensional frame. When the SP extended along a horizontal axis there was a tendency for all subjects from all groups to make 'egocentric' responses, especially on the three-dimensional array. Thus the 'faced' aspect of the SPs tended to be ignored when the SP was placed along a horizontal axis. However, when it came to placing a picture relative to a SP whose front/back corresponded to the vertical axis, even the youngest subjects were able to take note of the front/back cues. In yet other studies looking at the scanning eye movements evaluating various instructions relating to faced as opposed to unfaced object pictures, the results indicate that even though the relationships between the pictures were not specified by the instructions, the subjects tended to look in the faced direction of the faced object. Presumably because of this the visual search performance of young subjects was superior to chance when required to verify sentences requiring faced responses, but not so when handling sentences involving unfaced ones. Taken together these studies help to add substance to our growing knowledge of how subtle differences in linguistic and spatial information may influence children's (and our) view of the world. It is also relevant to refer to the studies of Hall since they highlight the utility and need to study the relevant parameters of visual search with adequate precision – adequate in the sense that we can be sure that the observations have been accurately made. This minimal level of adequacy is not met by many studies currently making claims about where the mother and child look.

4. *Come* and *go*

The typical interpretation of these verbs involves deixis in that the motion described is conditioned by the relative positons of the speaker and addressee. Thus the addressee moves toward the speaker for *come* and away from the speaker for *go*. Similarly *bring* may be distinguished from *take*. Although temporal expectations may complicate the picture – e.g. on meeting a guest at the garden gate, a host may say 'Come into the house and bring your bottle with you' – it is clear that deictic considerations are critical and are as stated. The question is how and under what conditions do children come to make the relevant spatial distinction? Clark and Garnica (1974) studied children's comprehension of these terms in simple experimental situations where there were limited options and the child, on being given a sentence using one of the verbs, had to select either speaker or addressee. Their findings with four groups of children aged 6, 7, 8 and 9 years were that *come* seemed to be handled better than *go* and *bring* better than *take,* and that only in the oldest group was performance on both pairs of verbs clearly similar. Somewhat similar results have been obtained by Macrae (1976a), although she shows that the children's performance is sensitive to small changes in the experimental situation which do not obviously fit into a typical adult framework of interpretation. What Macrae argues is that *come* is easier in some of her studies, and in those of Clark and Garnica's, because its adult interpretation more often matches the strategies the children use in experiments, but that others of her studies suggest that this does not have to be the case. Both Clark and Garnica, and Macrae, argue that the basic strategy used by the children to identify the speaker or the addressee on a particular occasion depends on identifying the goal of the movement rather than its source. Given a pronounced tendency for young children to handle directional terms in an allative manner (directions towards; cf. Garman, Griffiths and

Wales, 1970; Macrae, 1976a; Wales, 1974), it seems clear that *come* is likely to be given an adult-like response by the children for reasons which do not strictly follow from a grasp of the relevant deictic parameters.

Another complicating factor in these studies is suggested by an observation by Macrae (1976b). Seven 2 year old children in their spontaneous speech would use either *come* or *go* when an action was carried out in full vision of the child, but they would use *go* to describe the movement of an object or person which disappeared from sight, and *come* for one where something or someone came into view. Note that the experimental studies referred to were all carried out in full view of the child.

Another interpretation of the source of difficulty in these kinds of study (specifically citing Clark and Garnica) has been proposed by Richards (1976). He argues that these kinds of simple experimental task place too heavy a load on the child's inferential processes and that a more naturalistic game which 'involved' the children more directly would result in superior performance on the part of the children. He constructed games where the children had to phone information relevant to the occurrence of fires, or communicate about visiting other houses whose occupants and location were known to the children. These games certainly seemed to elicit better performance with these verbs than the earlier studies suggested. Interesting as this is however, the usefulness of the comparison is only marginal. Not only do the children have many more response options – a factor Macrae (1976a) in particular has shown to be crucial – but Richards' task is a *production* one. The obvious interest therefore may more properly be that as far as these deictic terms are concerned, it may be the case that production is easier to elicit than comprehension. If other results support this, it could be because actions guide this domain of language rather than the converse.

One attempt has been made by us to check whether a simple variant of one of Richards' games, taken as a comprehension task, produced analogous results. There were three chairs in a room: one assigned to the child as his/her 'house', another to the experimenter as his, and another as yet a third 'house'. The child was given a toy 'fireman's hose' and told to follow instructions as to which house needed to have a fire extinguished. Eighty children (equally divided into four age groups of 4, 5, 6 and 7 year olds) participated with relish. Expressions were of the form: 'Go to the house', 'Come to this house', 'That house is on fire', etc. Expressions varied were *this, that, here, there, come, go, go there, come here, go . . . that, come . . . this, my, your, come . . . my* and *go . . . your.* Unlike the earlier comprehension studies reported, there was often more than one option available to the child as a possible 'correct' response. Not surprisingly therefore the impression was of overall better performance. Certainly performance on the demonstrative and locative deictics was 10–15 per cent higher than the norm reported earlier.

Although these were the expected trends, there was no age effect for any ANOVA. The demonstratives and locatives yielded no significant differences on comparison, nor was there a significant effect for proximity versus nonproximity to the speaker. With both the pronouns, performance was virtually perfect. With *come* and *go, go* was significantly better than *come* ($F = 72.9$, df $(1,4)$, $p < 0.005$); *go* being already sufficiently well handled, there were no significant increases due to further deictic specification of the instruction using *that* or *there*. (The superiority of *go* in this task is obviously at least partially attributable to the greater number of options available as 'correct' responses.) However, with *come* as compared to *come . . . this,* there was a dramatic improvement ($F = 247$, df $(1,4)$, $p < 0.001$), as also with *come here* ($F = 226$, df $(1,4)$, $p < 0.001$). This result most dramatically illustrates two points:

(i)   that the relative priority in performance with *come* and *go* is task dependent, and that the children are again sorting out the relevant deictic contrasts on the basis of a preceding semantic interpretation – in this case, directional movement

(ii) when the opportunity is available, the children have enough knowledge of the deictic system to enable them to buttress their interpretations interactively, by pooling information appropriately from more than one linguistic source

5. Temporal deixis

We will not make any extended comment on temporal deixis despite H. Clark's (1973a) interesting arguments that linguistic expressions regarding time are effectively an extended spatial metaphor. This is simply because the acquisition of time by children is poorly understood, understudied, and such studies as have been made make little or no attempt to relate the child's understanding of temporal expressions to the speaker's own location in space and time – the basis of temporal deixis. One suggestive result is that of Clark (1969, 1971), who has shown that children's understanding of *before* and *after* is critically related to the way in which the order of the events described matches the order of the events in the description. When the orders are the same, the result is much more likely to be used spontaneously, and understood by the children. This result may well be a consequence of the child's understanding of his/her own position relative to the temporal order of events, but that has not actually been shown. The details of the basic result have been challenged by, for example, Cromer (1971a), Amidon and Carey

(1972), and Harner (1976), but these challenges have either to do with the cognitive assumptions behind Clark's interpretation, or to do with whether verbal tense antecedes the acquisition of these expressions. Bronckart and Sinclair (1973) have come closest to a directly relevant study in their attempt to show that in the acquisition of temporal expressions children use aspectual distinctions before they make tense distinctions. It may be that aspectual distinctions provide the framework for the sharpening of contrasts relevant to temporal deixis in the way we have observed elsewhere – the general preceding the contrastive particular. However, our knowledge of the development of temporal deixis is minimal at present.

6. Concluding observations

There are a number of methodological issues we have skipped over. The most obvious is the relevance to much of the work on the development of deixis of direction of gaze – although note the comment on need for accuracy made earlier. It is chiefly because of uncertainty on this point that no discussion has been attempted of claims made by some regarding the antecedents of deixis in so-called prespeech. The potential importance of studies of the latter sort is underlined by the apparent lack of any evidence regarding the joint shared attention to other objects by nonhuman mothers and children. However, even without the support of such claims, it seems clear, at least as far as spatial deixis is concerned, that development is orderly and explicable. Furthermore, as Keenan and Schieffelin (1976) demonstrate in their data, the devices which articulate the child's use of deictic expressions enter, often crucially, into the processes of conversational discourse. The most striking phenomenon is the precedence of the general 'indicating' function – specialized by person or spatial location. Specific contrasts are only acquired later. This precedence is consistent with work in historical and comparative linguistics, and at variance with emphases in the interpretations of these expressions of some modern grammarians. The children seem to agree with Shakespeare in their emphasis: 'That, that is, is', with the possible rider 'That which moves has direction towards.'[1]

[1] Aspects of the research reported here were funded in part by the Social Science Research Council, London, and in part by the Australian Research Grants Commission.

14. The development of the verb phrase

Paul Fletcher

The focus of this chapter is a discussion and synthesis of available research on the development of the verb phrase (from now on VP) in children acquiring English (with occasional reference to other languages). The term verb phrase is used here to summarize the range of auxiliaries, modals and inflections which signal temporal, aspectual or modal meanings[1] (and thus differs in its extension from the same term in transformational grammars, where it covers the whole predicate phrase – see, for example, Chomsky, 1965: p. 106). The syntactic and morphological features of VP in the sense used here are best summarized by a slightly amended version of Chomsky's (1957) phrase structure rule for the expansion of AUX:[2]

AUX→Tns (M) (have + en) (be + ing)

Very briefly, this rule makes certain *syntactic* claims about English VPs: that any VP will be marked for tense (either present or past); that a VP may contain one of the modal auxiliaries; that it may contain a perfect form, consisting of the appropriate form of *have* + past participle; that it may

---

[1] I am leaving out of consideration here the passive, considered as a type of VP by, for example, Quirk *et al*. (1972: p. 73). This is partly because the syntactic changes associated with passive are not confined to the verb phrase and partly because it is a rather later development in children than the period I am considering here (see Bates (1969) for a general discussion, and chapters 15 and 16 below).

[2] To adopt this analysis of the VP is to follow a respectable tradition in the analysis of Modern English, but it should be pointed out that it is not uncontroversial, particularly among some transformational grammarians, who have put forward proposals for analysing auxiliaries (and even verb inflections) as themselves main verbs (see Huddleston, 1976: ch. 14, McCawley, 1971; Pullum and Wilson, 1978; Ross, 1969). There are reasons however for preferring the traditional analysis in considering VP acquisition; a) it is not clear what empirical consequences for child language studies follow from the auxiliaries-as-main verbs analysis to distinguish it from the traditional analysis; b) one of the analytical consequences of an analysis which treats auxiliaries as main verbs is that many simple sentences (in the sense of Quirk *et al*., 1972: p. 342) are treated as complex sentences at a deep structure level. To the extent that 'auxiliaries' appear in the child's speech before any surface complex sentences, such an analysis would be misleading.

261

contain a progressive form, consisting of the appropriate form of *be* + *ing*; or that it may contain any two or all three of these (modal, perfect, progressive) in the appropriate order.[3]

As a framework within which to consider the child's spontaneous productions over time, and his errors and omissions at particular points in development, this formulation has obvious advantages. Using syntax (or more specifically, syntactic generalizations from the adult grammar) as a heuristic in acquisition research has its dangers, however, particularly in the case of the VP where the meanings of grammatical features need to be carefully considered. Clearly the child has to learn the forms that make up the English verbal paradigm, the orders in which they occur in declarative and interrogative sentences,[4] and the co-occurrence restrictions that hold among them. But equally the functions of the VP systems have to be mastered. In the first place there are three quite distinct areas of meaning represented in the VP – time, aspect and mood; also it is the case that while the 'basic' meaning of, say, past tense forms may be said to be deictic, in that they relate the time of action to the time of utterance, the forms are also widely used to refer to 'unreal' events, particularly in conditionals – *if he came, I'd leave*. Most of the forms which fall within the VP are plurifunctional in this way (see the account of present tense, or of various modals, in Palmer (1974)).

A consideration of function within the VP raises the question of functionally similar non-VP forms: for some semantic notions within the verb phrase there are alternative means of coding. The modal notion of possibility, for example, often expressed in English by *might* (e.g. *John might be sleeping*), can be expressed by other modals (with slight meaning differences) – *John may be sleeping, John could be sleeping*; by adverbs, without a modal – *maybe/possibly John's sleeping*; or by an alternative syntactic structure – *it's possible that John is sleeping*. Futurity can also be coded in a number of different ways (e.g. *John is coming (tomorrow), John will come (tomorrow), John is going to come (tomorrow), John comes (tomorrow)*). The study of the development of the VP cannot restrict itself to syntactic forms, and once a functional analysis (however rudimentary) is undertaken, the investigator has to be prepared to include in the set of forms that are of interest not only those which fall under the syntactic definition of VP which we have used, but also those forms which, while falling outside the definition, perform similar

---

[3] The full range of forms generated by this rule (in association with the appropriate set of PS rules and T rules) is listed in Huddleston (1976: pp. 58–9).

[4] Though this is an important feature of the child's syntactic development generally, it is exhaustively dealt with elsewhere, and I will have little to say about it (see especially Hurford, 1975; Klima and Bellugi, 1966; Kuczaj, 1976; Labov and Labov, 1978; Prideaux, 1976).

functions. A further complication for our account of the development of VP forms is that it is quite possible, given what is known of semantic development generally (see chapter 8 above), that the forms which we find the child using have, in comparison with the adult, a restricted range of functions, or an overextended range or, in some cases, have functions which the comparable adult form never has.

To ask how the VP develops, within a purely syntactic framework, is then to ask a potentially misleading question; to ask how it develops, taking function into account, is to ask a very complex one. What is required, to answer the question fully, is not simply a catalogue of forms used over time (problematical enough – see below) but also a detailed account of how the forms are used (and misused) by the child, and, where possible, relevant experimental studies comparing children's use of VP (and other relevant) forms with those of adults in the same situation. The rest of this chapter is concerned with what is known about this development: the account begins with a 'catalogue of forms' and then considers some features of the three main VP systems, tense, aspect and mood, in separate sections.

1. The course of development: Hildegard's VP forms

The purpose of this section is to illustrate, mainly from one set of diary data, but with reference to other published studies and unpublished data, the differentiation of early VP forms. The diary data are those of Leopold (1949b), an account of the development of his daughter Hildegard (H.). The detail of the account is concentrated on the third year of her development, and this is outlined in table 1 below.[5] It is of course impossible to generalize from this one child. Nevertheless it is possible to see parallels between her development and that of other children reported in the literature, and with my own diary data. There are also some links between the course of development that emerges for H., and the data on auxiliary development from the Bristol survey (Wells, 1979a).

1.1. Some remarks on methodology

Any interpretation of diary data, or other records of spontaneous speech, runs up against a central analytical problem: it is not possible to say with any

---

[5] Obviously the account given here reflects the Leopold selectivity, and the interpretation of the developing 'systems' must be in the light of this selectivity *and* the variability in the use of particular forms. As far as one can tell from the diary, none of the forms mentioned here was 'acquired' according to the criteria used by Brown (1973: p. 258).

degree of conviction when a form has been acquired, or when development has stopped. One can note the first appearance of a form, or talk about its frequency in samples, or in some cases it might be feasible to determine when it has been omitted from an utterance. This is a general problem for syntax acquisition research, but it has a particular relevance for the VP, if form and function are considered. One of the features of early VP development is said to be the variability in use of inflections like -*ing* and -*ed* (see Brown, 1973: p. 256). There are, it is generally claimed, certain syntactic contexts in which it is possible to recognize when an item like this has been omitted. The gradual elimination of omissions leads eventually to error-free usage, and the form in question is 'acquired'. This is the basis for the ordering which Brown imposes on the grammatical morphemes which characterize his Stage II. But is it always easy to determine when a form has been left out by the child? In certain contexts most observers would agree that it is. If the child says *Daddy work yesterday* (provided the use of *yesterday* is appropriate), then it is reasonable to talk of an omitted past inflection; similarly in a sentence like *Daddy is swim,* the absence of -*ing* is obvious. And it is sensible to talk of a missing *is* or *'s* in *Daddy laughing.* But other VP forms present difficulties for this kind of analysis. With the homonymy between past and past participle, for the vast majority of English verbs, it is not often a straightforward matter to decide if in a sentence like *Daniel picked his story,* said by a child who is using perfect forms in some cases, *picked* is a correct past tense or a perfect with *have* omitted. Part of the reason for this, of course, is the difficulty we face in stating the conditions for use of the perfect. The analytical problem that we can see developing approaches an impossibility when we consider other VP forms like modals, where there are no co-occurring adverbials or other forms to spotlight an omission. We are not in a position to establish any criterion of acquisition for such forms, and hence their inclusion in a list of forms developing over time is largely a matter of an intuition of 'reasonable productivity', on the part of the investigator. The occasion of the first occurrence (or the first noted) assumes importance for some analysts (see Wells, 1979a). It may be, however, that a first occurrence of a form is in a stereotyped utterance (cf. H.'s *Rita was here,* in (iv) below), which suggests restricted or no productivity, and the use of first occurrence as criterial for including an item in a developmental course may be distorting. Even for the clear cases of omission, for some forms the achievement of error-free usage, and hence 'acquisition', may be disturbed by developments in general syntactic or lexical ability. So the development of more complex structures in which sequence of tense rules needs to be maintained may affect one's estimate of the acquisition of past tense, for example; since a child whose usage was error-free when assessed on simple sentences might now omit past tense in the second or third clause of complex structures.

This leads us into even more hazardous analytical terrain, where we try to consider the child's ability in terms of whether he uses a form appropriately, or with the full range of functions. Does the child use a past tense where a perfect would seem called for? Does the child use past tense in its 'unreal' sense? Is *will* used volitionally and also to refer to future events? The question of function will be addressed more directly in the separate sections on tense, aspect and mood, but taking functional problems in conjunction with the methodological difficulties associated with form, it is apparent that any acquisition order set up for VP forms has to be examined most carefully, and considered in the light of our discussion.

1.2. H.'s 'steps' in VP development, 2;0 to 2;6

(i) Leopold reports for H. (at 2;0 to 2;1) that on his return after a six week absence one of the most important changes he noted in her language was the number of verbs used – there had previously been very few. Some are unmarked, and the unmarked verb forms (UVFs) are used not just as imperatives, but within sentences as well, contracting subject and object relations: *My fix my dress, My eat too much, I got my clothes.* In addition the *-ing* form is said to be frequent 'although not prevailing'. While the early appearance of the *-ing* form is generally attested (see Brown 1973: p. 271), as is its variable use, little is known about an increase in the number of lexical verbs, and its relevance for syntax, at or before this point. Little is known either about which of the verbs that the child has in his lexicon is first marked for *-ing*, or in what contexts the *-ing* marking is used. Nor is it known what conditions, if any, govern the increased application of *-ing* over time.[6]

The *Other Relevant Forms* section (ORF) includes *got,* which turns up in examples like *My got my clothes.* Although *got* can be used with either present or past meaning, it is used here, as Leopold says, with present meaning; there is no *get* in the child's language with which *got* contrasts. The other form included here, *don't,* has one example cited, *don't sleep*; Leopold also says that it occurs on its own as an imperative.

(ii) As with the children from whom Brown derives his data, and as with the diary data from Daniel (see below), the first auxiliaries to appear from H. at 2;2 are *won't* and *can't* (cf. Klima and Bellugi, 1966). Examples are given of *won't* on its own, as a 'compliant answer to a negative command', or

---

[6] By increased application here I mean *both* the overall increase in frequency of use (independently of the verbs to which it is applied) *and* the increase in the range of verbs to which it is attached.

Table 1. *Hildegard's VP forms, 2;0 to 2;6*

	Modal	Verb	Pres	Past	Perf	Prog	Other Relevant Forms
(i)		UVF				ing	got don't
(ii)	won't – can't		PRES	PAST IRREG	PAST PART		be
(iii)	will – can						have to
(iv)	may			PAST REG			was
(v)	must						is
(vi)	will (fut.)					be + ing	going to TEMPORAL ADVERBIALS

as part of a VP, *I won't eat that.* The diary entry suggests that *can't* only appears on its own. Since there are no positive forms for these items to contrast with, they are normally interpreted at this stage of the child's development as monomorphemic. The child's pronunciation of the items at this point lends support to this view: both forms are produced without a nasal consonant or any vowel nasality, as [wot] and [daːt] respectively.[7] While H. has learned, at this point, that these items have distinct performative functions, that they can be used as responses to questions, and that *won't* has a preverbal syntactic position, it would be inappropriate to analyse these items as modals plus a negative particle within the child's 'grammar'. The other new VP form, entered in the ORF column, is *be.* The diary entry suggests that this occurs only in the sentence *I be Nackedei,* though this sentence is used repeatedly. No other copula forms appear.

(iii) Within a very short time (by 2;3) H. begins to add to the list of items the adult modal class. *Will* turns up frequently in questions, and as a response to questions, in its full form: *Shall I put your watch on? – No, I will.* There is no mention of a contracted form of *will.* The early appearance of *will* and *can* in the correct position in *yes/no* questions accord with Klima and Bellugi (1966) and Miller (1973: p. 382). Indeed Miller finds for his data that *will* and *can* were rarely found in noninverted position, which also seems to fit the Leopold data.

Other forms which now appear are some irregular pasts (cf. Brown, 1973: p. 260; Ervin, 1964), the first present tense singular marking, and a past participle in *Where you been.* The *did* form occurs, like *be* earlier, in a particular sentence often repeated, *What did you buy?* In the ORF column a form with modal meaning, *have to,* which is not an auxiliary, occurs in *You have to wash.* The child's range of forms is expanding though there is little evidence of systematicity.

(iv) Here, at 2;4, we find one more form being added to the set of modals used, though again most often in a restricted context: *I may,* after permission has been granted her to do something. Irregular past tenses are being used more frequently, but still not in all possible cases: we find *My balloon went way up,* but *I fall down again.* The first regular past tenses are noted; the present tense singular marking appears more frequently. The past tense copula *was* is used 'repeatedly'. To underline the development of tense forms in the verbs, the first temporal clause is cited: *When you want more, I give you more.* To return to modals, *will* now appears in a sentence where it is not dependent on a question, *Mama will help me.*

---

[7] Apparently *want* and *won't* were at times homophones ([wɔt]), leading one to wonder whether Leopold always interpreted them correctly, and also what H. made of the similarity.

(v) The occurrence of the auxiliary *be* with *-ing* is noted here, and the inference is that it is used variably. A steady increase in 'strong and weak past tenses' is remarked. The present tense form of the copula turns up, and we have the first notice of a temporal adverbial to specify a tense form: *You did not see me long long time.*

(vi) The entries for the month half-way through H.'s third year refer almost exclusively, as far as the VP is concerned, to temporal relations. We are told that H. can form correct temporal clauses with *when,* and that *when* now appears as an interrogative (cf. Tyack and Ingram, 1977). H. now uses *will* to refer to the future, and also *going to: Now I am going to put on my new stockings.* For both the forms which refer to future, and the past tense forms, the support of a time adverbial 'seems to be felt as necessary'. These time adverbials are often vague: *last summer* is used to refer to *any* past time. For future reference, we find *pretty soon, some day, after a while.* It is of course the case that tenses in the adult language are generally specified by adverbials (see Crystal, 1966), and sometimes it is only by means of the adverbial that the time reference of a sentence can be understood (compare *John runs regularly* with *John runs tomorrow*). To achieve adult competence with the tense and aspect systems within the VP the child must also learn to cope with temporal adverbial specifiers, and hence any account of development cannot leave these out.

Following this point in H.'s development, the diary becomes more sporadic. Notable omissions up to now have been modal forms like *should, would, could,* and the perfect. The first full perfect form (in a question) is cited at 3;10, though a form with *have* after *should* occurs at 3;6 – *You should have been sleeping.* This occurrence suggests that the perfect may well have occurred earlier (though for Brown's children the perfect was a rather late acquisition: Cromer (1974b: p. 222) claims that Adam and Sarah were both over four when it was acquired).

This account, it has to be emphasized again, is merely an illustration, with all the imperfections of its data base, of how the VP forms differentiate during the third year. While there do seem to be parallels with other reported studies,[8] any picture that emerges from this survey must stand to be

[8] A paper by Wells (1979a), which is a welcome addition to our knowledge of the VP, gives some preliminary results of the Bristol survey, and incidentally provides some comparison with this account of H.'s development. In a 'tentative' acquisition order based on frequency of occurrence, the proportion of the sample using the form at least once, and the age at which the first use of the form was noted, this order obtains: *do, have + en, can, be + ing* and *will.* Frequency of occurrence can of course be misleading as an index of acquisition – in particular *do* probably owes its pre-eminence to its frequency in questions, negatives, and responses to questions from towards the end of the third year on. Once *do* is excluded, the major anomaly

modified in the light of more complete evidence. With this qualification, what does emerge?

1. The development of forms is a relatively unsystematic piecemeal development at first, with forms often apparently learned individually and separately (e.g. negative and positive *will*); their first appearances are often restricted to repetitions of the same sentence.
2. The syntactic environments in which forms can appear tend to be heavily restricted at first, particularly the modal forms, which are dependent on question–response sequences, and tied to immediate action (or inaction).
3. Progressive and past tense forms are applied variably, and used with increasing frequency over the period considered.
4. There appears to be some connection between the differentiation of past and 'future' tense forms, at the middle-point of the year, and the development of temporal adverbials and interrogatives.

With this perspective, we can now go on to consider features of each of the VP systems in some more detail, and complement the formal account with some discussion of the uses to which the forms are put.

2. Tense

This section will be chiefly concerned with the development of past tense, the VP form that has been of most interest to investigators because of the apparent tendency of many English children to overgeneralize the regular past tense suffixes to nonregular cases (see Berko, 1958; Brown, 1973; Derwing, 1977). This one instance of (morphological) rule learning by the child has played a disproportionate role in theoretical discussion of rule learning in acquisition studies.

It is worth emphasizing that English tense forms are marked for regular verbs by the presence or absence of a past suffix (variously /-t/, /-d/, /-ɪd/). For irregular verbs there are a variety of ways of marking past tense: by vowel change (e.g. *ring – rang*), by vowel change and suffix (e.g. *sleep – slept*), by suppletion (e.g. *go – went*); while in some cases there is no marking (*hit – hit*, *put – put*). The primary function of past tense as marked in English is deictic: 'it grammaticalises the relationship which holds between the time of the situation that is being described, and the temporal zero-point of the deictic context' (Lyons, 1977a: p. 678). In being used primarily to locate an action or state in the past with respect to the moment of speaking, tense as a grammatical category is to be distinguished from aspect, which is not deictic

between Wells' sample and H.'s development (excluding past tense, which he does not mention in this paper) is *have* + *en*. This is both frequent and early (by his criterion) in his sample, and is discussed in more detail below.

(Lyons, 1977a: p. 687), but, rather, concerned with 'the temporal contours of actions' (Hockett, 1958: p. 231), with distinctions like continuous/noncontinuous in English. Unfortunately the two categories are not always kept separate by researchers. Harner (1976), for example, refers to the present perfect form as 'past tense', and *will* as 'future tense' in experimental materials. The fact that English does not grammatically oppose a future tense to the past/nonpast distinction is also often not recognized: Herriott (1969), in a comprehension study of 3 to 6 year olds uses *going to* as 'future tense'. Both these investigators are primarily interested in the child's developing frame of temporal reference, and it might be argued that, as long as some appropriate linguistic form is used, it does not really matter what it is called. However, if we are investigating temporal deixis generally then aspectual or modal categories are *not* appropriate, and their effect could be distorting.

Apart from the primary deictic function of past tense, the child has to learn its place in tense sequences, and also a function that is not deictic, but modal, when the form is used in counterfactual conditionals: *If he came, I'd leave* (see Lyons (1977a: pp. 818ff.) for a discussion of tense as modality). A similar use of past tense is seen after verbs like *wish*: *I wish I went to nursery all day*. It has been suggested (Lodge, 1979) that this function of past tense is extended to simple declaratives by children aged 6 to 8 in certain circumstances: Lodge cites children giving stage directions in the course of a play acting game: the actors use appropriate tenses, but the scene is set always with past tense:

Speaker A   Where are you going? (aside: you said you were going to the ball)
Speaker B   I'm going to the ball

We can now examine one child's development of past tense in a little more detail. Table 2 lists some past tense uses by Daniel, which can be used, like H.'s form, as a framework for discussion. In relation to any form for the child, these questions can be posed: when does it appear, when is it acquired, and how is it used? To these might also be added a fourth, the most difficult to answer – what can we say of the determinants of its acquisition and use? As we have suggested earlier, however, even the first question is not straightforward. The first 'pasts' to appear are one or two irregular verbs: these are sporadic, and may well be learned by rote: it is possible that the child will hear *spilt*, for instance, as the only form of the verb *spill*. If this generally is the case then it is probably not reasonable to see these items as past tenses at all. Let us say however, for the sake of argument, that some irregular pasts are the first past items to occur in the Daniel data – a parallel finding to Brown,[9] Ervin and Leopold. Is it possible now to approach the other questions, concerning the development, use and determinants of past tense?

The step after the irregular pasts is the use of some regular pasts, and then there is a gradual increase of these and overregularized strong verbs between 2;2 and 2;5. Occasionally a temporal adverbial occurs without a past tense, as in the example *I blow them out once time* (in reference to candles). In the adult language, many past tense forms are temporally specified with adverbials (Crystal, 1966). This is one way of making past tense reference definite, as recent grammatical accounts assert that it always is (Allen, 1966; Huddleston, 1975; Quirk *et al.*, 1972: p. 86). If the point or period of time referred to is not adverbially specified then it should be recoverable from context, or presumed by the speaker to be part of the information shared with the hearer. For Daniel, and, as we have seen, for Hildegard, adverbial specifiers turn up quite early, either as supports for past tenses or on their own. They are generally semantically vague (see also Ames, 1946; Harner, 1976; Weber and Weber, 1976) in the early days, and often inappropriate (e.g. *yesterday* for future time). In terms of overall frequency in relation to past tenses adverbials remain relatively rare in the period being considered – the child is able to assume that the past tense he uses will be, or is, made definite by the speaker or the context. But it is clear that in some cases which refer to remote events he is aware of the need to supply a specification even though his ability to 'point' appropriately within the temporal frame of reference is still minimal. Fixed phrases are common – cf. Daniel's *when I was a baby* in (1) where it is appropriate, and (2) where it is obviously not:

(1) I didn't have much hair when I was a baby (looking at photographs of himself) 3;0
(2) I have seen it somewhere . . . a long time ago when I was a little baby (in response to the question *Has anyone seen my book?*) 3;3

This is perhaps the point at which to consider the claim made by Antinucci and Miller (1976) that early past tense is used aspectually, rather than temporal-deictically. Antinucci and Miller, arguing mainly from Italian, but extending the claim to English, maintain that the child's early uses of past tense occur only when the past events that they refer to result in present end-states of objects. The reason they adduce is a cognitive one: children this young (around 2;0), if they are to be able to refer to past events, must be able to build a *representation* of them, in the Piagetian sense of this term. To re-present past states of affairs will be easier for the child (or may only be possible for the child) if the past event or process is related to some present

---

[9] This is true for Brown only for his averaged acquisition order for morphemes. See Matthews (1975) for some criticism of Brown's practice here.

Table 2. *The development of past tense in one English child*

2;0	Some irregular pasts	I spilt my juice I found my juice
2;2	Some regular pasts	Mummy painted the wall
2;3	Some temporal adverbials Use of *did* in declarative	I blow them out once time I did some time
2;4	*Did* in *yes/no* questions	Did you write?
2;5 to 3;0	Increase in past tense forms More temporal adverbials as specifier Occasional *when* clauses	Did that thing used to be up against the wall last time? It was high when I throwed it up I didn't have much hair when I was a baby
3;1	*Was* + *-ing* *Did* + unmarked verbs	I was doing a chalking You did hurt me Lisa did hit me
3;3	*Did* + regular verbs	My balloon did pop
3;5	*Did* +(*did*) + irregular verbs	Why did Peter did sleep here? Why did Rachel left one of her domino cards behind?
(a) 3;3	D. What are you eating? F. I've finished D. What were you eating?	(b) And he throwed it high and I couldn't catch it
(c) 3;1	I show you what I do	(d) We went to Jo's house/but not Douglas/and Rachel came back/and she makes some cakes

observable state. Those verbs which are change-of-state verbs, which describe a situation in which some end-state comes into existence as the result of a process, Antinucci and Miller say, will be marked for past, whereas other verbs will not. 'The past event and the present moment are related not simply by an abstract temporal relation but by a more concrete effectual relation.'

The linguistic evidence for this hypothesis in the English data Antinucci and Miller examine depends on a semantic classification of verbs: change-of-state verbs are marked for past; state verbs are not, and nor are activity verbs without any result. Now an argument of this kind based entirely on spontaneous speech data and the analyst's semantic classification runs a risk of circularity. In addition, there do seem to be occasional past tense uses early on in the Daniel data where it seems difficult to rule out deixis. The example in table 2, *Mummy painted the wall,* at 2;2, was said to his father of an event that had taken place two months before. Certainly there is an 'effectual relationship' between the action referred to and the present moment (just as there would be for an adult using a similar sentence), but there also seems to be an 'abstract temporal' link as well. So although Antinucci and Miller have produced an intriguing hypothesis about the cognitive factors that determine the child's use of past tense, it needs testing on a wider data base for English.[10] Indeed, even from the diary data for Daniel and Hildegard it would seem that specification by adverbials of past tenses, and suggesting a deictic function, comes quite early, and that if the form is used only aspectually it is for a relatively brief period.

To return to table 2: over the period of 3;0 past tense usage becomes more frequent (at least on main verbs), but then a change in strategy was noted. Daniel began to use *do*-support to mark positive past tense, as he extended the use of *do* in questions and negatives. The *did* was unstressed, like any other auxiliary. It was first used to mark irregular verbs which have zero past tense marking, then with some regular verbs, and finally with some strong verbs. (See Fay (1978) for some similar data.) This became his dominant (but not exclusive) strategy for about six months, before he appeared to revert to the kind of overgeneralization he had been using before. Over this period he also began to mark past tense *be* forms (see (a) on table 2), past tense of modals (see (b)), but did not always maintain a sequence of past tenses in complex sentences ((c) and (d)). At 4;0 he was still overgeneralizing and very rarely using counterfactual conditionals appropriately, though he could use *wish* followed by a complement including a past tense.

In summary, then, it cannot be said that Daniel has 'acquired' past tense: there are still uses to be learnt, and a proper differentiation of forms to be achieved. In charting the course of development it is appropriate to correlate form and use, and to try to explain why a form is used variably. Some of the factors affecting use are morphophonological: Derwing (1977), in a systematic replication of Berko (1958), establishes that children up to 9 years of age have difficulty with certain stems in past tense formation, particularly those that end in alveolar consonants. Other factors are syntactic, as we have seen: tense is not marked on auxiliaries and modals until after it is used on main verbs, and in addition the syntactic complexity of sentences may affect

[10] The Bronckart and Sinclair (1973) study, based on French children aged 3 to 8, also asserts the primacy of aspect over deictic tense uses. In this study, forms were elicited from children who described actions which were structured along dimensions like durative/nondurative, perfective/unperfective. Up to 6 years of age the children tended to concentrate on the character of the action rather than its place in time. One reason for this may be the nature of the experimental task, in which children were always faced with toys which performed in front of them, in the relatively immediate past. The study remains, however (as Wales notes, p. 260 above), still the only serious experimental study of temporal deixis, in any language.

past tense marking. Other factors still may be semantic, if Antinucci and Miller are correct. And if their interpretation of the semantic factors governing early past tense use is soundly based, then it is possible that early tense is used not for its primary adult function of deixis at all. Their hypothesis, however, awaits further study, and the balance of the evidence here is that quite early in his use of past tense the child is aware of the requirement to make his time reference definite, to the extent that he can, leading us to the conclusion that at least some of the uses are deictic.[11]

3. Aspect

Partly because of the confusion of aspect with tense, and partly because of the general lack of interest in VP systems by child language researchers, there is a dearth of data on this area of the VP in either English or other languages; and in English what interest there has been has concentrated on the progressive. While it is not possible here to consider aspect as a grammatical category in any detail, a brief account will serve as background to a survey of what is known and what remains to be established about the development of progressive and perfect in English.

The term aspect is used to refer to a variety of semantic notions (Jespersen, 1924: p. 287; Lyons, 1977a: p. 707) such as stativity, progressivity, duration, habituality, completion and momentariness. Lyons points out that these are all temporal notions, but are nondeictic. A specific language will not of course grammaticalize all these notions; English has progressive and perfect forms within the VP: these are related to progressivity and (less obviously) to stativity (Lyons, 1977a: p. 715). There are however nonauxiliary forms used in conjunction with other verbs which can refer to other aspects: he *used to* run (habituality); he *began to* walk (inception); he *kept* singing (duration). A full account of the development of aspect in English would consider these forms; here we will confine our attention to the progressive and perfect.

3.1. Progressive

The progressive suffix -*ing* is generally agreed to be the first, or at least a very early, verb marking to appear in the child's speech. There are some obvious

---

[11] Studies in the psychology of time (e.g. Fraisse, 1964; Piaget, 1946) are of little help on this issue. First, experimental studies are with older children and are concerned with complex notions such as the estimation of duration, and the child's gradual freeing of himself from wholly subjective bases for the estimation (see Fraisse, 1964: ch. 8). Second, it seems to be agreed that young children do have at least some kind of temporal horizon based on past experience (Fraisse, 1964: pp. 158ff.), and so we cannot rule out deictic time reference on cognitive grounds.

reasons for this: its salience – it is a suffix coded as a separate syllable; and its regularity: there are no irregular progressive forms or conditioned variants of the regular form. The suffix appears some time before the auxiliary *be* forms which co-occur with it, and Brown states that it is never overgeneralized (1973: p. 324): it never occurs with stative verbs, i.e. any of the (relatively small) number of verbs in English which have as part of their meaning the notion of a stable and unchanging condition. For 'verbs of inert perception and cognition' (Quirk *et al.*, 1972: p. 96) like these, use of the progressive is inappropriate, since an essential part of its meaning is non-stativity: to attach the progressive inflection to a verb is to emphasize the dynamic nature of the action named by the verb, over a particular period of time. Thus it is usually not the case that we say **I am hating George*, or **I am understanding*, unless we want to emphasize the dynamic nature of the action referred to for a particular reason (e.g. *I am understanding him better now*).

The children in Brown's study all used a small number of stative verbs (*want, like, need, know, see* and *hear*), and never used the progressive with them. They applied the suffix however to some of the large number of dynamic verbs in their vocabularies. Brown considers as possible reasons for the different treatment of the verbs (a) that the child has learned the semantic distinction stative/nonstative, and (b) that the child has learned individually, for each verb in his lexicon, whether it can take the *-ing* or not. If we consider that the child has only to learn that there are a very few verbs in his vocabulary that cannot take the *-ing* suffix, then the second explanation might seem more plausible. But since we are still relatively ignorant of the details of the course of development of the early progressive, there is perhaps nothing conclusive to be said. Kuczaj (1978) gives details of some 'creative' applications of the progressive, however, by children applying it to stems which are not verbs, e.g. *Why is it weathering?* While examples like this do suggest that there may be a 'rule' for progressive formation (and Kuczaj agrees with Brown that *-ing* application is restricted to nonstatives), the examples all come from children aged 3;6 and above, while Brown's arguments relate to children under 3;0. The data from H., and that from Daniel, also attest to the central feature of early progressive use, that it is restricted to nonstative verbs.[12]

---

[12] The questions raised here are not the only ones of interest concerning progressive: its combination with tense, both within the VP (*He was coming* vs. *He is coming*), and in complex sentences (*When John came in Lisa was sleeping*) would be obvious areas of inquiry.

3.2 Perfect

The temporal relevance of the perfect in English is its indication (for present tense) of a period of time that 'stretches backwards into earlier time' (Quirk *et al.*, 1972: p. 91). The straightforward examples are those where the activity of the verb begins before, and continues right up to, the present: *I've waited for an hour, She's loved him for years.* However, the perfect is also used in cases where the activity plainly does not extend over the whole period: *I've broken my arm, I've phoned the doctor, Griffiths has written another good play.* The use of the perfect in these cases is usually explained by the term 'current relevance': the activity, while not necessarily extending over the period of time to the present, is nevertheless relevant to the speaker (or judged by him to be relevant to the hearer) at the present time. It is this link between past and present which is used to explain why a perfect is selected instead of a past when they both refer to the same event: *I've broken my arm* versus *I broke my arm.* In this case the perfect is likely to be used where the event is recent enough for its result to be apparent, or if the speaker wants to excuse himself from further activity; in either case there are features of the present to which the past event is linked, or relevant. The past tense locates the event relative to the present, but does not provide any link. The difficulty, for analysts and presumably the child, is in defining the conditions under which this apparently subjective notion of relevance applies.[13]

As well as the potential functional difficulty, the range of realizations of the auxiliary *have* in various syntactic and phonological environments could be assumed to be a factor in the late development of the present perfect. These are outlined in table 3. It will be apparent that the child, to achieve mastery, has to group at least six forms which are in complementary distribution, though the complementarity depends on both phonological and syntactic factors. This, it might be argued, is no different from the problems encountered elsewhere with other auxiliaries – modals have different stressed and unstressed forms and contracted forms in some cases, or more directly the auxiliary *be,* where there is the added problem of suppletion. If, however, we add to the total range of forms the homonymy between *have* and *be* for the third person singular form, and the homonymy of the past tense and past participles of most English verbs, then it seems probable that syntactic generalizations for this VP form will not be easy.

Studies of the perfect are rare, and studies of its development which

---

[13] There are also said to be variations in use between British and North American usage, with the North American usage of current relevance being 'stricter' (Palmer, 1974: p. 53). This could affect the way in which the present perfect is acquired in the two varieties.

Table 3. *Forms of auxiliary* have

Form	Context
[haev]	(1) Stressed, all persons except third singular
	(2) Elliptical responses, emphatic affirmation, negatives
[haez]	(1) Stressed, third person singular
	(2) As above
[həv]/[əv]	(1) Unstressed, all persons except third singular
	(2) *Yes/no*-questions, *wh*-questions, after modals. In declaratives as auxiliary after preceding consonant (first and third persons plural)
[həz]/[əz]	(1) Unstressed, third person singular
	(2) *Yes/no*-questions, *wh*-questions. In declaratives as auxiliary after consonant
[v]	(1) Unstressed, all persons except third singular
	(2) As auxiliary, declaratives, following a vowel
[z]	(1) Unstressed, third person singular
	(2) As auxiliary, declaratives, following a vowel

supply a sufficiently detailed formal and functional perspective are nonexistent. What work there has been mostly emphasizes the relative lateness of the development. The information so far published on Brown's data (see Cromer, 1974b: p. 222) makes this clear: 'in Adam's record the first meaningful use of the perfect occurred at four years six months, but Sarah never once used the perfect tense through five years six months in the protocols examined'. Nussbaum and Naremore (1975), using a variety of elicitation tasks with children aged 4;0 to 6;0, found that even though they were successful in eliciting some forms from the youngest children, the use of the present perfect was not stabilized for the 6 year olds. Haber (1977) also provides support for late acquisition of the perfect. Data which apparently contradict the general finding are however supplied by Wells (1979a), and since his is a large-sample study (see chapter 19 below for more details), it is worth examining in a little more detail. Wells finds that *have + en* is, for children up to 3;6, the second form after *do* in his frequency distribution; it is also the second most frequent form used by parents to children. Further, all of his sample used the form at least once, and half the sample had used the form at least once by the time they were 2;3. While we would not want to interpret a frequency distribution of forms as an acquisition order, Wells' large-sample study provides clear evidence that children under 3;6 use present perfects in some numbers. To evaluate his findings properly, however, we need further information. First, it is important to know which forms have been analysed as present perfects. As Lenneberg (1976: p. 25) points out, we cannot assume without further evidence that a form used by a child has its adult systemic value, or that the child has made the same syntactic generalizations as the adult. For the present perfect, for example, analytical problems are presented by third person singular contracted forms of *have,* particularly with regular past participles of intransitive verbs: *He's jumped, She's finished, It's died.* A contracted *'s* appears for the child in a bewildering range of environments: *What's that, When's he coming, It's broken, She's singing, He's tired, She's happy.* It seems at least possible that in the early stages the child makes no distinction between, for example, *'s* as copula (in *He's tired*) and as a form of *have* (in *He's jumped*). Recognition of this possibility, among others, should lead to considerable care in identifying early perfect forms to avoid over-analysing the child's output.

The second piece of information required concerns individual variation. Is the overall frequency of present perfects due to only some of the children in the sample? If this is so, it could explain the apparent conflict between the Bristol data and that of Brown, since the two children who remained through to the later stages of Brown's study could simply be slow developers. A final question we might want to ask is whether certain tokens contributed dispro-portionately to the total of *have + -en* forms: it seems to be the case, for example, that some children use *have got* forms widely, but do not use forms of *have* so readily with other past participles. Data of this kind, if they turned up, would certainly influence our interpretation of Wells' findings.

The diary data are not particularly helpful here – we have already noted that there is little in Leopold on the present perfect. The data from Daniel, however, show him using the occasional present perfect as early as 2;3: *Mummy hasn't gone school has she?* Immediately before this, however, he had said *Mummy been school already,* and two weeks earlier had produced *Mummy's gone to school.* Another example of an early 'present perfect' is *and you haven't got shoes* (2;5), said during the same session as *You got new shoes, haven't you.* What the orthography obscures here is that *haven't* is pronounced in both cases as [hã?]; this and the absence of an auxiliary before the *got* might suggest that once again this form is unanalysed, and that its analysis and the inclusion of part of it in the *have* paradigm is a later development. Over a year later Daniel is using present perfect more fre-quently but there are still some identifiable occasions when it is omitted, as this exchange shows:

F. Has anyone seen my book?
D. I have seen it somewhere . . . a long time ago when I was a little baby
   . . . I seen it somewhere.

From the data we have, it is not easy to get a full picture of the develop-ment of the present perfect, but what emerges is not seriously at odds with the other forms we have considered. The first appearances of the form are likely to be heavily constrained by factors which in some cases we can define as syntactic, in others as lexical, in still others as semantic. Even though a form may increase in frequency, this will be largely token frequency to begin with. Gradually constraints will be lifted, and more variants of the form will appear in more syntactic environments or under more semantic conditions. Eventually the paradigm will be filled out, or at least enough of it will be filled out for the child to make the appropriate generalization (which must concern both form and function). The generalization or rule is now seen as a reanalysis and restructuring of information already available in a relatively unorganized fashion. The language learning process for syntactico-semantic variables in the early stages thus parallels the pattern of early phonological development (see chapter 3 above).

4. Mood

Modal auxiliaries play an important part in VPs for the child. We have already seen that negative modals are one of the earliest VP modifications, and available data suggest that modals, considered as a category, are the most frequent VP forms used by young children. The frequency data in Wells (1979a) indicate that a third of all VP forms used by children up to 3;6 contained modals; the vast majority of these were *can* and *will*.[14] Although learning of modals is not complete by 5 (see Fletcher, 1975; Major, 1974), members of the category play a central role in the VP from around the second birthday.

The modals comprise a grammatical category which behaves syntactically like other auxiliaries, but covers a wide range of meanings: possibility and necessity, permission and obligation, ability and volition (see Palmer (1979) for a comprehensive account). Some of these meanings can be carried by alternative syntactic categories: some modals are closely related in meaning to catenatives (e.g. *must* – *have to*; see Palmer, 1974: p. 16), and we have already discussed some of the alternative ways of coding possibility. Once again, a full account of this part of the VP is impossible here and now. Indeed, we will look in detail at a very small part of the total development – Daniel's modals between 2;0 and 2;2 – in order to illustrate some analytical points as well as the child's early achievements.

Table 4 gives a representative set of forms used by Daniel during the two months after his second birthday, together with relevant details of the linguistic and extralinguistic context in which his uses were embedded. The

[14] Wells appears to count *can't* and *won't* under the *can* and *will* headings.

Table 4. *Modals between 2;0 and 2;2*

Previous utterance (PU)	Daniel	Context
1.	Can't	Child stuck in large pot, unable to get out
2. Can daddy go and get his tea?	You can	PU spoken by father
3a.	Can't	Trying to zip up bag
3b. Can't what, Daniel?	Can't do my zip up	
4. Eat your toast	I willn't	In kitchen having breakfast
5.	Can you do that Daddy?	Perching on edge of chair
6. Can I shut the door?	You can	PU by father
7.	Can I see that?	Wants to be lifted up to see birthday cake, which is on a shelf
8.	Can I blow candles out, can I?	Still re birthday cake
9.	Shall I do that	Father is kicking balloon around living-room
10. Shall I take that?	You can	Father asking for marble
11. Will you carry Bu up, Paul?	You can't	Mother is preparing him for bed, and asks father to carry him upstairs
12.	I can come in your bed	On his way to bed he goes in parents' room and clambers in their bed
13. Can I wind it up?	I can	Father is asking if he can wind up a tortoise from which the child has taken winder. Child takes toy back saying this
14. Do you want it?	I can. I can	Child going to sleep. Father points at tortoise on bedside table and asks him if he wants it. Stretches arm through bars of cot, and picks it up himself, saying this
15. You go and tell Mummy	I will	PU by father
16. Mummy have it then	You willn't. You willn't	He has been offered juice and refused it

Table 4—*cont. Modals between 2;0 and 2;2*

Previous utterance (PU)	Daniel	Context
17.	Will you do that again for me	Father had built up some Lego. D. wants additional building
18.	I can see my cake	Cake is on top of cupboard, and he climbs on to a toybox to look at it
19.	I can't open my bag	D. having problems with a zip
20.	You can't fix my bag	Said to mother as she tries to help him

forms found during this period are *can, can't, will, willn't* and *shall.* The bare statement of forms however tells us little. A careful look at the distribution of the forms indicates first of all that the syntactic distribution of these forms is limited, and that their distribution is inextricably linked with their meaning. It is analytically uninformative at this point in the child's development to consider form and function separately. To underline this, the examples from Daniel at this point (and it is necessary to remember that these are diary data, with all their limitations) are all either with first or second person pronouns. That is, he is either using the modal for himself (to indicate willingness, inability, or request for permission), or to allow or prohibit an action by his addressee. He does not use modals to refer to the willingness or ability of third persons. Two-thirds of his modal utterances are either questions, or responses to questions, and many of the responses occur without main verbs. There are two relevant comments here: first, the question–response framework is a useful one within which the child can learn appropriate forms (though it is not always the form of the question which dictates the form of the response – see 10). Second, the questions are not requests for information but preliminaries to activity. If the adult asks the question, it is to request permission from the child (2, 6, 10). If the child asks a question, it is to request permission himself (8), to get the adult to act for him or on his behalf (7), or simply to get the adult to act. The modals are not used to give or request information about intentions or ability independently or the actions to which they refer. Table 5 shows the syntactic distribution of the five modal forms relative to Questions (Q), Responses (R) and Declaratives (D). D indicates either modal only or pronoun plus modal, and D+ indicates that a full sentence is used including a modal. The subscripts 1 and 2 indicate first and second person.

Table 5. *Syntactic distribution of Daniel's modals*

	Q_1	Q_2	R_1	R_2	D_1	D_2	$D+_1$	$D+_2$
can	X	X	X	X	X		X	X
can't					X	X	X	X
will		X	X		X			
willn't					X	X		
shall	X							

Can, as the most frequent and widely distributed form at this stage, is worth further comment. For adults, *can* has a variety of uses. Palmer (1979), in his detailed account of English modals and modality, makes a three-way classification of modality into epistemic, deontic (or discourse-oriented) and dynamic (which subdivides into subject-oriented, and neutral). Uses of the modals are labelled and included under one of these headings. Most of the set of modal verbs are seen to be plurifunctional, and *can* has a particularly complex set of uses. Sometimes when negative it can be interpreted as epistemic (meaning 'it is not possible that', as in, for example, *It can't have been a meteor*). More usually *can* is either deontic – it is used to give (or request) permission, or to command; or it is dynamic – *can* is used to indicate that an event is possible (neutral dynamic), or to refer to the ability of the subject (subject-oriented dynamic). This summary of a highly detailed taxonomy will serve to illustrate the place which *can* contracts in an adult system with a complex network of functions. How do Daniel's uses of *can*, at the outset of his VP learning, relate to the adult system?

It is quite possible, for some of the forms in table 4, to attribute uses to the child's *can* which are like those of the adult. In particular, permission (either granting or requesting) is involved in 2, 6, 7, 8 and 10. And one might discern reference to ability in 5, and also in 13. And 12 might even be considered implicative *can* – the *can* of possibility used to suggest that the possible action will be, or is being taken (Palmer, 1979). For a 2 year old to have developed this range of uses would of course be remarkable, and a consideration of the contexts in which Daniel uses *can* shows that the imposition of the full complexity of the adult framework has no basis, and that the form is, for him, only performative: it relates to action which is possible, within the social limits which he perceives.

We have already noted that the modals used at this stage are without exception interpersonal and action-oriented. The most common use of *can* is in requests for permission, followed by the appropriate action. Even second person questions like 5, which seems to be about ability, are interpreted as requests for action: 5 is followed by the father copying the action referred to by the child. There is an interesting sequence not fully illustrated in table 4 which underlines neatly the connection between *can* and 'possible action'. The first sentence in the sequence is 18 (repeated here for convenience as (a)):

(a) I can sèe my cake
(b) I càn see it
(c) I can sée it if I wànt to
(d) I càn see my Humpty-Dumpty cake

The cake in question is on top of a cupboard. The first sentence in the sequence is spoken as he catches sight of the cake. Daniel could just be referring to his ability to see the cake. But as he says (b), which now receives the nuclear tone, he moves towards the cake, and (c) and (d) are said as he clambers on to an adjacent toybox in an attempt to reach it. This assertion of 'possible for me' is seen again in 13 and 14 in table 4. Here Daniel is asserting his right and acting at the same time; he is saying that the action is possible (permitted) for him and at the same time performing it.

The child has at this point in development learned to use more than one member of the modal category, and has learned something about their syntactic behaviour. Intimately linked with the syntax of the modals, however, are the uses to which they are put. These uses have certain inevitable syntactic consequences, reflected in the distribution in table 5. There is a wide distribution of *can* which, with its sense of possible action within limits, can apply to child or adult, in question or declarative; *willn't* on the other hand, which for reasons which may have to do with egocentricity refers only to child's volition, is accordingly restricted in syntactic scope.

The further development of modals will therefore depend in part on the separation from immediate action, and their use to refer to the possibility and probability of propositions and events, and the abilities and wishes of other people. The child must develop (as he must for the successful differentiation of other areas of the VP) an objectivity and a cognitive perspective which allow him to use linguistic devices 'displaced' from the events to which they refer.

5. Conclusion

The scope of the problem and the selectiveness of research so far into the development of VP systems make any useful generalizations premature. There do seem, however, to be guidelines for future research. First, any work on the VP must concern function as well as form. We saw with past tense, for example, how it has been argued that its early use is aspectual, and that this in part explains its early variability. This claim can only be evaluated by considering function in detail. Whatever the eventual fate of the hypothesis, it and others like it have the merit of forcing us to look for potential explanations of syntactic behaviour in semantics or cognitive development, areas which the syntactically based research of the 1960s was unable to consider. Second, forms cannot necessarily be taken at their face value. If a form like *Lisa's hided* turns up in our data from a 3 year old, we cannot simply call it a present perfect and leave it at that. We need to know if there are putative perfect forms other than this contracted form, if they occur with transitive verbs, if any forms occur with irregular past participles, if forms of *have* occur in questions, negatives, or tags. This list does not exhaust the questions to be asked, but it is an improvement on the assumption that this form is a present perfect, simply because it would be analysed as such in an adult grammar.

The use of data from experimental investigations, and a perspective on VP forms used to the child which is similar to that applied to his forms, would provide further assistance towards a clearer view of what is a central and relatively ignored area of the child's language development.[15]

[15] My thanks to David Crystal, Gordon Hart, Arthur Hughes, and Peter Trudgill for their helpful comments on an earlier draft of this chapter.

15. The acquisition of complex sentences*

Melissa Bowerman

Complex sentences are structures that are built up of simpler sentences through the recursive operations of *co-ordination* and *embedding*. In the early period of syntactic development, children are working on the structure of simple sentences and do not yet have knowledge of these operations (Brown *et al.*, 1969). The onset of ability with complex sentences greatly increases the child's generative capacity and thus is an important step forward in language acquisition. This chapter reviews recent evidence on how this step takes place.

A brief overview of the major types of complex sentences is first in order.[1] In co-ordination, the constituent sentences (termed 'clauses' when they become part of a larger sentence) are linked together by a co-ordinating conjunction (e.g. *and, but, or, either . . . or, both . . . and, and then, or else*), with neither sentence being syntactically dependent on the other. In embedding, in contrast, one sentence (the 'embedded sentence') is subordinated to – i.e. serves as a constituent in – the other (the 'matrix sentence'). There are two major types of embedding. In one, the embedded sentence fills in an empty slot in the matrix sentence and functions in a syntactic role such as subject, object, or indirect object (THE FACT THAT JOHN LEFT/JOHN'S LEAVING/ FOR JOHN TO LEAVE *surprised me; Mary wanted* JOHN TO LEAVE; *I'll give this cookie to* WHOEVER WANTS IT). This is called *complementation*. In the second type of embedding, the embedded sentence modifies a constituent of the matrix sentence, e.g. a noun phrase (resulting in a relative clause: *The man*

* This research was supported in part by Grant HD00870 from the National Institute of Child Health and Human Development.
[1] This overview, which is drawn from Quirk *et al.* (1972) and Langacker (1973), deals only with sentences that are complex at the level of surface structure – i.e. that contain more than one clause. However, Langacker suggests that 'all sentences are probably complex at the level of conceptual structure, being decomposable into component propositions' (p. 112). There is discussion in a later section of this chapter of some sentence structures that superficially appear to be simple but that many linguists have argued should be assigned complex underlying representations.

WHO CAME TO SEE YOU *was tall*), an adjective (*Harry is ready* TO LEAVE), or the main verb (resulting in an adverbial clause introduced by a subordinating conjunction of time, causality, conditionality, etc.: *Mary left* BEFORE/AFTER/ WHEN/BECAUSE YOU CAME, *You can come* IF YOU ARE READY).[2]

1. The development of complex sentences in spontaneous speech

Most research on the acquisition of complex sentences has consisted of experimental studies of comprehension in children of 3 years or older. There are surprisingly few studies detailing the development of complex sentences in spontaneous speech. The following discussion draws primarily on Limber (1973) and Brown (1973), supplemented by other sources where possible.

Investigators differ somewhat in the age at which they place the onset of the ability to produce complex sentences.[3] Most studies indicate that the major types of complex sentences emerge between the ages of about 2 and 4. On the basis of data collected from his three subjects during this age period, Brown proposed that learning about sentence embedding is a major task of Stage IV (Mean Length of Utterance (MLU) from 3·0–3·50 morphemes), while productive ability with co-ordination comes a bit later, at Stage V (MLU 3·50–4·0).

The first complex sentences appear after simple sentences about four words long become common. These involve *object complementation*: embedded sentences functioning as nominals in the role of direct object of the verb of the matrix clause. Explicit grammatical subjects are initially lacking from the embedded sentences (e.g. *I wanna read book*), but these appear before long (e.g. *I don't want you read that book, Watch me draw circles, I see you sit down, Lookit a boy play ball;* these examples are from Limber, 1973). In addition to *want, watch, see,* and *lookit,* other complement-taking verbs that appear early include *like, need, make*[4], *ask,*

---

[2] Alternatively, adverbial clauses can be interpreted as attached directly to S_1 rather than as a constituent of the verb phrase; see Williams (1975).

[3] These differences stem from individual variation among the children studied, from differences in the kinds of sentences defined as 'complex', and from differences in the kind of knowledge attributed to a child on the basis of the sentences he produces (cf. Limber, 1973). With regard to this last factor, Ingram (1975a) and R. Clark (1974) argue that early 'complex' sentences probably do not involve recursive operations at all, but are produced by the simple juxtaposition of sentence fragments. Arguments in the extreme opposite direction are presented by Antinucci and Parisi, who conclude on the basis of evidence from Italian-speaking children that 'aside from nominalizations, all the basic structural mechanisms of human language [including embedding] appear to have . . . been acquired by the 2-year-old child' (1975: p. 199).

[4] See Baron (1972) on the development of complex causative constructions with *make, get,* and *have* in spontaneous speech.

let, and – to express direct speech – *say* and *go.* Somewhat later in the third year come *think, know, hope, show, help, forgot,* and a number of others. Complement-taking verbs first appear with simple NP direct objects if syntax allows this (e.g. *want book, make train, help me*); clausal direct objects follow within a few weeks.

After sentences involving object complements, the next complex sentences to appear (at about age 2;6 in Limber's data) are a variety of constructions involving embedded clauses introduced by *wh*-words: *Do it how I do it, Can I do it when we go home?, I show you how to do it, I don't know who it is.* These *wh*-clauses function either as direct object in the matrix sentence or as place, manner and time adverbials. Soon after this, explicit relative clauses modifying abstract nouns of place and manner (although not yet time) come in: e.g. *I show you the place I went, This is the way I did it.* Still later come relative clauses attached to 'empty' head nouns functioning as direct object in the matrix sentence (. . . *thing I got,* . . . *ones mommy got*), and even later (still rare before age 3) come relative clauses on common nouns in object position (e.g. . . . *ball that I got*). The first relative clauses involve no relative pronouns; later, *that* is used in this role (Limber, 1973). Errors in relative pronoun selection at later stages of development include the frequent substitution of *what* for *who, which,* or *that,* e.g. *I get everything what you got* (Menyuk, 1969).

Co-ordinating and subordinating conjunctions begin to appear in about the second half of the third year (Hood, 1977; Jacobsen, 1974; Limber, 1973). Before this, sentences that in adult speech would ordinarily be linked by a conjunction are simply temporally juxtaposed, as in *You lookit that book, I lookit this book* (Clancy *et al.,* 1976; Hood, 1977; Limber, 1973). The conjunction that appears first and is used most frequently is *and,* followed shortly by *and then*; later, apparently in somewhat variable order, come *because, so, when, if, or, but, while, before* and *after* (the last two are still very infrequent at age 5 (Cromer, 1968)). The order in which these conjunctions emerge seems to be related in part to the relative difficulty of the concepts they encode. Clancy *et al.* (1976), who studied the order in which English-, German-, Turkish- and Italian-speaking children began to juxtapose propositions, with or without conjunctions, found the following shared sequence of development: first, notions of symmetric co-ordination, antithesis, sequence and causality; next, conditional notions; then conditional and temporal statements with *when*; then simultaneity with *when*; and finally *before* and *after.* These authors observe that their findings support Slobin's hypothesis that 'The rate and order of development of the semantic notions expressed by language are fairly constant across languages, regardless of the formal means of expression employed' (1973: p. 187).

Still missing at the end of the third year are *participial* object complements (e.g. *I like eating lollipops*) and operations on sentence subjects, including subject complementation and relative clauses modifying subjects (Limber, 1973). Object complementation at this stage nearly always involves infinitival forms (e.g. *I like to eat lollipops*), juxtaposition of simple sentences with optional *that* missing (*I hope I don't hurt it*), or *wh*-clauses (*I show you how to do it*) (Brown, 1973; Limber, 1973). Limber (1976) proposes that the delay in subject operations may be due to pragmatic factors rather than to deficits in linguistic knowledge or information processing capacity. According to Limber's analyses, most subject noun phrases in children's simple sentences are pronouns, demonstratives, or proper names, which do not lend themselves well to sentential expansion or modification; in contrast, many object noun phrases are common nouns or 'empty' nouns like *one*, which do.

2. Strategies for parsing complex sentences

Complex sentences present formidable challenges to a listener's ability to break a sentence down into its components and match the parts up with each other in the right way to arrive at an accurate interpretation (cf. Bever (1970a) for relevant discussion). Problems may arise because one clause interrupts another, because major constituents such as subject or object are replaced by pronouns or missing entirely in embedded and conjoined clauses, because the normal word orders of free-standing sentences are rearranged, and for a variety of other reasons. Much of the research on children's acquisition of complex sentences has consisted of experimental studies designed to explore how children of different ages resolve these problems of parsing and of inferring the referents for missing or underspecified elements. These studies have revealed interesting regularities in the way children approach the problem of interpreting sentences whose structures they do not yet fully understand.

2.1. The Minimal Distance Principle

An important early investigation of how children interpret complex sentences was carried out by Carol Chomsky (1969). Among other things, Chomsky was interested in how children understand object complement sentences that do or do not conform to a very general principle of English termed the Minimal Distance Principle (MDP) (Rosenbaum, 1967). According to the MDP, the implicit subject of a verb in a complement clause that is missing a subject is the first matrix clause NP preceding it. Thus, in *John wanted to leave, John wanted Bill to come* and *John told Harry what to do,* it is *John, Bill,* and *Harry* who are to *leave, come,* and *do* something, respectively. Most verbs that take object complements adhere consistently to the MDP but a few, such as *promise,* consistently violate it and a few others, such as *ask* and *beg,* follow the MDP in some sentences, allow a choice of subject in other sentences, and violate the MDP in still others. For example, in *John promised Bill to leave* it is *John,* not *Bill* who is to leave. In *Mary asked to leave,* it is *Mary* who will leave. In *Mary asked Laura to leave* it is normally *Laura* who is to leave but a reading such as *Mary asked Laura (for permission for Mary) to leave* is possible, and in *Mary asked Laura what to feed the doll* it is *Mary,* not *Laura,* who will be doing the feeding.

Chomsky explored how children from 5 to 10 interpret such sentences by asking them to follow instructions like these (using toys where called for):

> Donald tells Bozo to lie down. Make him do it
> Donald promises Bozo to lie down. Make him do it
> Ask Laura what to feed the doll

Her results indicated that children start out applying the MDP everywhere. Thus, they consistently get sentences with *tell* right (Bozo is made to lie down) and they misinterpret those with *promise* and *ask.* Gaining control over verbs that violate the MDP appears to be a very late acquisition. *Promise* is mastered before *ask,* which Chomsky attributes to the fact that *promise* at least consistently violates the MDP while *ask* does not. An additional finding was that children at first interpret *ask* as if it means *tell.* Thus, when presented with a sentence like *Ask Laura what to feed the doll* they promptly *tell* Laura what to feed the doll. Learning to interpret *ask* correctly is a drawn-out process that is accomplished at different times for sentences with different kinds of object complements introduced by *ask.*

Kessel (1970) and Kramer *et al.* (1972) have replicated aspects of Chomsky's study with similar results, although Kessel found earlier mastery of *ask* than did Chomsky. Aller *et al.* (1977) found that the MDP is over-generalized by Arabic-speaking children just as by English-speaking children. Interestingly, though, they found that *tell* is misinterpreted as *ask* rather than the other way around; they account for this by reference to language-specific factors. Additionally, they note that although their subjects, like Chomsky's, mastered *ask* later than *promise,* this cannot be attributed to differences in the consistency with which the two verbs violate the MDP, since both verbs are consistent violators in Arabic.

Aspects of Chomsky's study have been challenged by researchers who have delved further into the problem of how children retrieve 'missing subjects' in complement clauses. For example, Maratsos (1974b) notes that Chomsky's test sentences do not allow one to select between two possible interpretations of why children choose the NP nearest to the complement verb as subject: the MDP strategy – i.e. simply computing the surface structure distance between the complement verb and candidate NPs in the matrix clause – versus the semantic knowledge that the missing subject of complement clauses after verbs of speaking (*tell*, etc.) is usually the *goal* to whom speech is directed. Maratsos pitted these interpretations against each other by asking 4 and 5 year olds to act out passive sentences like *The bear is told by the elephant to get in*. The semantic role principle (choose *goal*) was clearly supported: as long as children could understand passives in simple sentences, they consistently selected the bear as the missing subject, not the elephant as the MDP principle would predict.

It has generally been assumed that selection of the nearest preceding NP as complement subject in active sentences is children's first strategy, whether it is interpreted in terms of the MDP or in terms of knowledge of semantic roles. But Tavakolian (1977) reports data indicating that there is an earlier stage of development (roughly ages 3 to 4) in which children pick the *subject* of the matrix clause, rather than the indirect object, as the subject of the complement verb. Thus, they interpret sentences with *promise* and *ask* correctly and those with *tell* incorrectly. This pattern is exactly opposite to the one Chomsky obtained with children of 5 years and older. Tavakolian argues that this earlier strategy results from children's attempt to parse multiple-clause sentences as if they were conjoined sentences, for which it is appropriate to pick the first NP as the subject of both verbs: e.g. *The lion jumps over the pig and stands on the horse*.

2.2. 'John is easy/eager to see'

A second type of complex sentence that poses a challenge to children's powers of sentence analysis is illustrated by the following pair:
(1) John is eager to see
(2) John is easy to see
Who is going to be doing the seeing? In (1), interpretation is fairly straightforward, since standard word order is preserved. *John* is the subject of the sentence and also the subject of the complement verb *see*. But in (2), John is only a surface structure subject. In underlying structure, *John* is the *object* of *see*; that is, it is someone else who will be seeing *John*. Surface word order is thus misleading as to the underlying relationships that hold between the sentence constituents.

Children's acquisition of the structures illustrated by this pair has been extensively studied, starting with Chomsky's (1969) pioneering work on later problems of syntactic acquisition. Chomsky presented children with a blindfolded doll and asked them 'Is this doll easy to see or hard to see?', following this up with further questioning. She found that almost all 5 year olds answered incorrectly ('hard to see'), taking *doll* to be the logical subject of the verb *to see,* presumably on the model of sentences like (1) above. Answers by 6 to 8 year olds were mixed and by 9 all children answered correctly.

Several subsequent studies have confirmed that there is an initial stage at which children interpret *John* as the logical subject of the infinitive in sentences like *John is easy to see* (Cambon and Sinclair, 1974; Cromer, 1970, 1972, 1974c; Kessel, 1970; Morsbach and Steel, 1976); Cromer (1970) has termed this the use of the 'primitive rule'. However, these investigations (plus that of Fabian, 1977) have shown that the lateness with which the children in Chomsky's study demonstrated understanding of the structure is attributable to her use of a stimulus (the blindfolded doll) that seems to bias towards incorrect answers. When this bias is eliminated by the use of more neutral stimulus objects or other techniques, children show an understanding of this sentence structure sometime between the ages of about 4 and 7.

Interestingly, the 'primitive rule' is not simply part of a more general strategy of taking the first-mentioned noun to be subject, since it is used even by children who are correctly able to assign an object role to the first noun in passives such as *The wolf is bitten* (Cromer, 1970). Progress from the end of the 'primitive rule' stage to adultlike knowledge is slow, with children vacillating in their responses from day to day (Cromer, 1970) or as a function of the particular verbs the test sentences contain (Fabian, 1977). Sentences like *John is easy to see* are apparently mastered earlier than closely related sentences like *Mary is pretty to look at* (Solan, 1978).

2.3. Relative clauses

Two variables are of major importance in describing the structure of relative clause containing sentences in English (de Villiers, Tager Flusberg, Hakuta and Cohen, 1976). One is the position of the relative clause in the sentence, termed its *embeddedness.* This is a function of the syntactic role of the matrix clause NP (called the 'head' NP) that the relative clause modifies. If the clause modifies the subject it is called 'centre-embedded', while if it modifies the object it is termed 'right-branching'. The other variable is the way the head NP functions syntactically within the relative clause, called its *focus.* These two variables jointly specify four major kinds of relative clause containing sentences on which most research has centred.[5]

[5] The examples are taken from de Villiers *et al.* (1976).

Embeddedness (Role of complex NP)	Focus		
Subject	Subject	(SS)	The cat that bit the dog ate the rat
Subject	Object	(SO)	The cat that the dog bit chased the rat
Object	Subject	(OS)	The cat bit the dog that chased the rat
Object	Object	(OO)	The cat bit the dog that the rat chased

Many investigators have explored how children process different kinds of sentences containing relative clauses (e.g. Brown, 1971; Cook, 1973; de Villiers, Tager Flusberg, Hakuta and Cohen 1976; Gaer, 1969; Gordon, 1972; Lahey, 1974; Sheldon, 1974; Smith, 1974; Solan and Roeper, 1978; Tavakolian, 1977). This literature presents a tangled web of conflicting findings and alternative interpretations. Some of the discrepancies can probably best be attributed to the fact that some studies concentrated only on the role of embeddedness and failed to control adequately for focus. Task differences may also be a factor (see de Villiers, Tager Flusberg, Hakuta and Cohen, 1976 for an excellent critical review). However, even when we consider only well-controlled studies using comparable tasks, certain differences in obtained response patterns and interpretation remain.

Three major types of hypothesis have emerged from these recent studies. The first was Sheldon's (1974) 'parallel function hypothesis'. In a study of children aged 3;8 to 5;5 involving an acting-out comprehension task, Sheldon found that neither embeddedness nor focus alone could account for the obtained pattern of relative difficulty of the four sentence types outlined above. Rather, these variables interacted such that SS sentences were responded to the most accurately, followed by OO, OS and SO, in order of increasing difficulty. Sheldon proposed that the ease of SS and OO sentences, relative to OS and SO sentences, is due to the fact that the head NP of the relative clause plays the *same grammatical role* in both the matrix clause and the relative clause – either subject or object. In OS and SO sentences, in contrast, the head NP plays one role in the matrix clause and another in the relative clause. Sheldon hypothesized that double grammatical function was difficult for children (cf. also Bever, 1970a: pp. 336–7).

The parallel function hypothesis has been challenged on at least two grounds. Tavakolian (1977), studying 3 to 5 year olds with an acting-out task, obtained the same basic pattern of outcomes as Sheldon did (SS < OO < OS < SO). However, after performing detailed analyses of her subjects' errors, she concluded that the parallel function hypothesis does not account for this pattern as well as the hypothesis that children initially attempt to impose a *conjoined clause analysis* on sentences containing relative clauses. That is, children try to process the sentence as if it consisted of two conjoined clauses, and, in accordance with this analysis, they select the first NP as subject of both the first verb and the second verb. This strategy leads to correct acting out responses for SS sentences (e.g. *The cat that bit the dog ate the rat*), and systematically incorrect ones for OS sentences (*The cat bit the dog that chased the rat*), since these latter require that the *second* NP be taken as the subject of the second verb. Tavakolian's subjects responded to OO and SO sentences much more variably than to SS and SO sentences. Tavakolian hypothesizes that this is because these sentences are difficult to process by means of the conjoined clause analysis, since, unlike conjoined sentences, they involve rearrangements of normal word order (e.g. *the cat* THAT THE DOG BIT *(O-S-V) chased the rat*).

Other researchers have rejected the parallel function hypothesis on the ground that their subjects did not respond to SS and OO sentences more accurately than to OS and SO sentences (de Villiers, Tager Flusberg, Hakuta and Cohen, 1976; Smith, 1974 (English-speaking children); Hakuta, 1976 (Japanese); Aller, 1977 (Arabic)). For example, Smith (1974), using a sentence-imitation task (a technique thought to tap comprehension, cf. Slobin and Welsh, 1973; Smith, 1970) with 29 to 36 month olds, found OS to be less difficult than SS, followed by OO and SO, in order of increasing difficulty. De Villiers, Tager Flusberg, Hakuta and Cohen (1976), who used an acting-out task similar to Sheldon's and Tavakolian's with 3 to 5 year olds, obtained results very similar to Smith's, except that they found OS and SS to be of approximately equal difficulty.

These data challenge the parallel function hypothesis, since sentences involving parallel function nouns were not consistently easier than those involving double function nouns. They also conflict with the conjoined clause analysis hypothesis. The most serious disagreement in this respect concerns children's handling of OS sentences. Recall that Tavakolian found that children systematically misinterpreted these, acting them out such that the subject of the first (matrix) verb was taken to be the subject of the second (embedded) verb as well. De Villiers, Tager Flusberg, Hakuta and Cohen (1976), in contrast, found this analysis to be somewhat less popular among their subjects than the analysis whereby the direct object of the matrix verb is chosen to be the subject of the embedded verb.

On the basis of their outcomes, Smith (1974) and de Villiers, Tager Flusberg, Hakuta and Cohen (1976) conclude that children's early interpretations of sentences containing relative clauses reflect their efforts to parse received strings into N-V-N sequences that can be construed as representing agent–action–object relations.[6] The N-V-N strategy, which de Villiers,

[6] See Bever (1970a), de Villiers and de Villiers (1973b), Roeper (in press) and Sinclair *et al.* (1971) for discussion of this strategy, which appears to be used widely

Tager Flusberg, Hakuta and Cohen (1976) term a type of 'processing heuristic', gives accurate results on OS strings like *The cat bit the dog that chased the rat* (N_1-V_1-N_2-V_2-N_3), where N_2 can be the object of V_1 and the subject of V_2.

At this point it is unclear why different researchers have obtained different patterns of results, which in turn point towards conflicting interpretations of how children process sentences containing relative clauses. It is possible that children have at their disposal more than one strategy for handling multiple-clause sentences; which strategy appears dominant in a given study may be a function of the exact nature of the task, the scoring procedures adopted, etc. (Tavakolian, personal communication).

3. Sentences with adverbial clauses

Unlike the sentence structures discussed in the section above, sentences containing adverbial clauses introduced by subordinating conjunctions like *before, after, when, until, if, because,* etc., need not present serious parsing problems for children. All the basic constituents may be present and normal word order is preserved in the two clauses: e.g. *John went downtown after he ate dinner.* Nevertheless, many studies have shown that children as old as 6 or 7 have trouble interpreting such sentences. What accounts for this difficulty?

Clark (1971) proposed an explanation focusing on knowledge of word meaning. On the basis of the results of an acting-out task she conducted with 3 to 5 year olds, she hypothesized that children pass through the following sequence in their approach to sentences with adverbial clauses introduced by *before* or *after*. At first children do not know the meanings of either *before* or *after*. They act out the first clause first and the second clause second, apparently assuming that the order in which the clauses are mentioned mirrors the order in which the events should occur.[7] This strategy results in correct responses for sentences like (3) and (4) below, but incorrect responses for those like (5) and (6).

(3) The boy jumped the fence before he patted the dog
(4) After the boy jumped the fence he patted the dog
(5) Before the boy patted the dog, he jumped the fence
(6) The boy patted the dog after he jumped the fence

in the early stage of development, but is not applied indiscriminately to all sentence patterns.

[7] See Bever (1970c) for further evidence for this strategy in comprehension tasks, and Ferreiro and Sinclair (1971) and Clark (1970) for discussion of children's tendency to order clauses in spontaneous or elicited sentences on the basis of order-of-event occurrence.

Later children learn the meaning of *before* and act out sentences with this word correctly, but they either treat sentences with *after* as if they contained *before* or they interpret them according to the order-of-mention strategy. Finally, children learn the meaning of *after* and interpret all the sentences correctly.

Several researchers have questioned whether children's initial problems interpreting sentences with adverbial clauses are due to ignorance of the meanings of the conjunctions. They suggest that even when the meanings are known, children may have trouble processing the syntax of the sentences. Amidon and Carey (1972), using an acting-out task with 5 to 6 year olds, found no evidence for an order-of-mention response strategy. Most errors by their subjects involved omission of the event mentioned in the subordinate clause, suggesting that the event described in the main clause was more accessible to them, regardless of whether it came first or last. Children who received feedback on their performance improved rapidly, which Amidon and Carey took as evidence that initially poor performance was due to the main clause response strategy rather than to failure to understand *before* and *after*.[8]

Related evidence that children's interpretive difficulties may stem from syntactic rather than semantic problems has been presented by Coker (1978). Coker, also studying 5 and 6 year olds with an acting-out task, found that even children who, by their correct responses to questions like *What did I show you before/after the X?*, showed that they knew the meanings of the words in one syntactic context, made many errors when acting out sentences in which *before* and *after* functioned as subordinating conjunctions. Coker's findings are consistent with those of a number of other recent studies of children's knowledge of word meaning (e.g. Grieve, Hoogenraad and Murray, 1977; Richards, 1976) in indicating that factors irrelevant to word meaning can affect children's performance under some conditions, thereby obscuring knowledge that they are able to demonstrate under different conditions.

Regardless of whether children's difficulties with sentences containing adverbial clauses are due to semantic or syntactic problems, information about how children proceed in attempting to interpret such sentences is valuable for the light it can shed on their 'operating principles' (Slobin, 1973) for language acquisition. At present, however, findings on children's

---

[8] After performing a second study, Amidon (1976) concluded that children's difficulties in interpreting sentences with adverbial clauses do in some cases reflect ignorance of word meaning. She found that even after her subjects became capable of retaining the information in both clauses they continued to make errors with *unless* and *unless – not*.

response patterns are mixed (see Flores d'Arcais (1978) for a recent review). Some investigators hypothesize that children's 'choice' of strategy is strongly influenced by task factors. For example, Amidon (1976), Hood (1977) and Johnson (1975) suggest that tasks that call for an acting out of two events tend to elicit an order-of-mention response organizing strategy, whereas tasks not making this demand do not (see Johnson (1975) for positive experimental evidence). Factors in the child as well as in the task may also be at work. For example, Bever (1970c) proposes that the two strategies are developmentally ordered, with 2 year olds tending to omit subordinate clauses in their acting out and 4 year olds relying heavily on order of mention. In a similar vein, Amidon and Carey (1972) and Coker (1978) propose that the main-clause-first approach is a '5 year old strategy'.

Finally, however, a recent study by French and Brown (1977) casts doubt on the whole concept of strategies for interpreting sentences with *before* and *after*. Although these investigators found weak group trends for their $3\frac{1}{2}$ to 5 year old subjects, their inspection of individual response patterns indicated that half the children used no consistent strategies at all and that there was no apparent developmental ordering among the strategies used by the other half.

Clark's claim that the meaning of *before* is mastered earlier than the meaning of *after* has, like her proposals about the order-of-mention strategy, been a source of controversy. For example, Barrie-Blackley (1973), who studied 6 year olds, found performance better on *after* than on *before*; Amidon (1976), Amidon and Carey (1972), Coker (1978) and French and Brown (1977) found no differences; Harner (1976) found that *before* is understood better than *after* when these words introduce subordinate clauses but *after* is understood better than *before* in adverbial contexts (e.g. *a toy for* AFTER *this day*); and Coker and Legum (1975) found that some children learned *after* first while others learned *before* first.

What is lacking from all these studies, as from most investigations of children's comprehension of word meaning, is information about how the words in question are used in spontaneous speech. Does failure to understand sentences with temporal subordinating conjunctions imply inability to produce them? Or might accurate production precede (the demonstration of) comprehension in this domain, as has been shown in other domains (e.g. Chapman and Miller, 1975; see Bloom (1974) for general discussion)? If the latter is true, then we must view these various comprehension studies not as investigations of how children pass from not knowing to knowing something, but rather as studies of how children come to extend information that they already draw upon in one performance modality to meet the demands of another performance modality.

Unfortunately, little is known about the development of sentences with *before* and *after* in spontaneous speech (although see Clark, 1970; Cromer, 1968; Jacobsen, 1974). However, Hood (1977), in a recent longitudinal study of the acquisition of two-clause sentences expressing causal relations, presents findings that may well have parallels in the acquisition of other kinds of sentences with adverbial clauses. Hood's eight subjects began to produce causal sentences containing *because* and *so* between the ages of 2 and 3. The clauses in these sentences were ordered appropriately for the conjunction: S_1 (cause clause) *so* S_2 (effect clause) and S_2 *because* S_1. This early production with appropriate ordering stands in sharp contrast to experimental outcomes that have indicated that children's concept of causal relations is global and undifferentiated up to the age of 7 or 8, such that regardless of the causal connective involved, they interpret cause and effect propositions as either randomly juxtaposed (Piaget, 1955b, 1969) or as temporally ordered with cause preceding effect (Werner and Kaplan, 1963). Hood suggests that one important reason that past studies have placed the emergence of the ability to understand sentences with *because* so late is that they have focused primarily or exclusively on types of causal relations (physical, logical) that differ from those expressed in early spontaneous speech (motivational, psychological).

Hood's findings bear not only on the nature of the relationship between production and comprehension for sentences with adverbial clauses but also on the sequence in which the particular members of a conjunction pair are learned. She found that the order in which her subjects acquired *so* and *because* was related to clause ordering preferences that were established well before the conjunctions themselves were learned. Those children who tended to juxtapose causally related sentences in the order S_1-S_2 (cause, effect) acquired *so* first, while those who preferred the reverse order, S_2-S_1, acquired *because* first. Children who used both orders approximately equally acquired both words at about the same time and used them in sentences of the appropriate clause order. Interestingly, the causal clause order preferences of Hood's subjects were matched by those of their mothers, although, as Hood notes, the direction of causal relationship, if any, cannot be inferred from this information alone.

Before and *after,* like *because* and *so,* have opposite clause order requirements in the normal main clause-preceding-subordinate clause pattern: S_1 (first event) *before* S_2 (second event); S_2 *after* S_1. Therefore, differences in the order in which children acquire *before* and *after* in spontaneous speech (see Jacobsen, 1974) may also be related to patterns established earlier for juxtaposing temporally related clauses and perhaps to mother's speech.

4. Derivational complexity and patterns of acquisition

For many aspects of language structure, the sequence in which various forms appear is consistent across children. What determines this regular order of emergence? Regularities have been linked to both complexity of meaning and formal linguistic complexity (Brown, 1973; Slobin, 1973).[9]

Relatively little is yet known about the effects of meaning on the acquisition of complex sentence patterns, since this topic has been largely unexplored except for some studies investigating the emergence of the concepts underlying certain conjunctions (e.g. Clancy *et al*., 1976, see p. 287 above; Beilin, 1975). The complexity of the meaning encoded by a given linguistic form is presumably the ultimate constraint on time of acquisition, since no matter how simple the form is linguistically it will not be mastered unless the child has achieved at least a rough understanding of the meaning it expresses. However, Slobin (1973, 1975) has amply demonstrated that even when a meaning is potentially accessible to a child, he may be delayed in expressing it, at least in the conventional way, because of complexity in the formal linguistic mechanism used to encode it.

One way of approaching the concept of formal linguistic complexity for certain sentence structures is to define complexity in terms of *derivational history*: a sentence, Y, is considered more complex than another sentence, X, if the derivation of Y from the underlying structure assigned to it involves all the rules that the derivation of X involves, plus at least one more rule (Brown and Hanlon, 1970).[10] Derivational complexity, defined *cumulatively* in this way, is particularly relevant to the question of how complex sentences are acquired. This is because many sentences that superficially appear to be simple – i.e. do not contain more than one clause – may be complex at an underlying level (see p. 285, n. 1 above). A 'simple' sentence of this type would actually be derivationally more complex than its semantically equivalent multiclausal counterpart, since its derivation would require extra rule(s) to compress material into a single surface clause. We might

---

[9] Slobin uses the term 'linguistic complexity' in a very general sense to cover many sources of formal difficulty for the child. It should not be confused with the use of the term 'complex' to refer specifically to sentences composed of more than one underlying proposition. The relative linguistic complexity, in Slobin's sense, of various kinds of complex sentences is a matter for empirical investigation.

[10] It is now well understood that a psychologically meaningful measure of relative derivational complexity cannot be obtained simply by comparing the absolute number of rules involved in the derivation of sentences (see Brown and Hanlon (1970), Fodor and Garrett (1966) for discussion). This is why contemporary discussions of the role of relative derivational complexity are limited to the special case of relative *cumulative* complexity, as defined here.

therefore expect that the child would master it later. With this possibility in mind, let us look at some recent investigations of the acquisition of sentences involving co-ordination with *and* and sentences expressing causal relations.

4.1. Co-ordination

According to a widely accepted model of co-ordination (e.g. Chomsky, 1965), sentences containing phrases linked by *and* have deep structures that contain two (or more) full propositions. For example, *Mary sang and danced* would be derived from a structure such as *Mary sang and Mary danced*. The phrasal co-ordination is achieved by deletion of repeated constituents through an operation termed 'conjunction reduction'. Which redundant element is deleted? Several linguists (e.g. Harries, 1973) have argued that there is a universal constraint on direction of deletion such that it always takes place in a *forward* direction: *Mary sang and [Mary] danced→Mary sang and danced*. When the redundant elements are positioned in such a way that forward deletion would result in an ungrammatical sentence – e.g. *Mary sang and John [sang]→* Mary sang and John* – a further transformation such as a rule to group like constituents together is applied: **Mary sang and John→Mary and John sang.*

If the conjunction reduction model is correct and if cumulative derivational complexity plays an important role in the acquisition of complex sentences, then we should expect to find that children produce and understand sentential co-ordinations earlier than phrasal ones, since the latter require application of an extra rule (conjunction reduction) and therefore are cumulatively more complex. Additionally, if there is a universal constraint on direction of deletion such that sentences with apparent backward deletions are derived from structures with forward deletions, we can predict that children understand and produce sentences with forward deletion patterns earlier than those with backwards deletion patterns.

After reviewing the sparse available literature on co-ordination in child speech (e.g. Menyuk, 1969; Slobin and Welsh, 1973), Lust (1974, 1977) set these predictions out and tested them on 3 to 5 year olds, using elicited imitation tasks. She found support for both: the children performed more accurately on sentential than on phrasal co-ordinations, and a fine analysis of their errors (e.g. deletions or additions of elements) indicated that phrasal conjunctions with forward deletion were easier than those with backward deletion. Lust concluded that 'in the temporally extended acquisition process, sentential conjunction forms are available as structural referents in the language system for the emergence of phrasal conjunctions, as the grammatical model of conjunction reduction would require' (1977: pp. 283–4).

Lust's conclusions have been challenged by de Villiers, Tager Flusberg and Hakuta (1976, 1977). These researchers did two experiments with 3 to 5 year olds, one an elicited imitation task similar to Lust's and the other an act-out comprehension procedure. Contrary to Lust, they found that sentential co-ordinations and backward deletion patterns were no more difficult than phrasal co-ordinations and forward deletion patterns. They suggest that even when children do imitate sentential co-ordinations better than phrasal co-ordinations, this outcome may reflect not differences in derivational complexity, but rather the fact that the former sentences, but not the latter, contain repeated elements that could aid memory.

Noting that their negative findings in themselves give few clues to the development of co-ordination, de Villiers, Tager Flusberg and Hakuta (1976) turned to analysis of spontaneous speech samples from Brown's (1973) subjects, Adam, Eve and Sarah. They found that phrasal co-ordination emerged long before sentential co-ordination. They conclude from this that the conjunction-reduction model does not provide a valid account of the structure of phrasal co-ordination for children. They propose instead that 'the roots of coordination are found in the conjunction of similar elements. The elements increase in complexity and length until the ability to coordinate complete propositions develops' (1976: p. 9).

Interestingly, almost all the phrasal co-ordinations of Adam, Eve and Sarah involved *forward* deletions. Put structurally, this means that almost all constituents linked by *and* were elements of the predicate rather than subjects. De Villiers, Tager Flusberg and Hakuta (1976) propose that this preference in production for predicate conjunction can be accounted for without invoking a universal constraint on deletion direction by reference to the difficulty of *planning* for compound subjects, given the characteristic right-branching structure of English (i.e. recursive operations typically take place in a forward, or rightward, direction). A recent study by Lust and Wakayama (1977) lends support to this proposal. They found that children learning Japanese, a left-branching language with subject-object-verb word order, imitated *backwards* phrasal co-ordination patterns better than forward ones, even though these often involved compound subjects.

4.2. Reorganization of linguistic knowledge: causative sentences

Predictions about order of acquisition that are based on relative derivational complexity may fail for several reasons. For example, in some cases the derivational history that linguists have assigned to a given structure may be faulty: the form that is putatively more complex should in fact not be derived from the same underlying structure as the form that is putatively less complex. Alternatively, even if the assigned derivational history is optimal, other factors may be more important as determinants of order of acquisition (see Smith (1970) for some suggestions along these lines). A third possibility is that the derivational history assigned to a sentence pattern correctly captures adult knowledge, but that children initially produce such sentences *without* the full adult knowledge. In this case, a child at some point would have to analyse the construction pattern more deeply and restructure it.

De Villiers *et al.* (1977) raise the possibility that a reorganization takes place in children's knowledge of co-ordinated structures at around the age of 4, although they leave open the question of whether this means that phrasals become derived from sentential forms at this time. The primary evidence for restructuring was a significant increase among their 4 year old subjects in errors of imitation involving the *addition* of redundant elements to phrasal co-ordinations and the *deletion* of redundant elements from sentential co-ordinations: 'Children at this age are evidently confused about whether the model sentence was presented in phrasal or sentential form' (1977: p. 6). Additional evidence was that in the spontaneous speech data at about age 4, 'sentential forms with and without potentially deletable elements appear at approximately the same time, thus allowing for the possibility that one serves as a model for the other' (1977: p. 6).

Some related evidence for linguistic reorganization is presented by Bowerman (1974, 1977), who studied the acquisition of sentences expressing causal relations. The proper representation of the underlying structure of superficially simple causative constructions like *Mommy opens the door* and *Daddy cut the tree down* has been hotly debated in the recent linguistic literature. Some linguists argue that sentences like these are complex at an underlying level, having structures such as are suggested by the paraphrases *Mommy makes the door (become) open* and *Daddy cut the tree, which made it fall down* (e.g. Fillmore, 1971b; Kastovsky, 1973; Lakoff, 1970; McCawley, 1968; Talmy, 1976). Other linguists maintain that these sentences are simple in underlying as well as in surface structure (e.g. Fodor, 1970; see Shibatani (1976) for a review of the controversy).

A cursory analysis of spontaneous speech development would appear to favour the latter interpretation, since surface structurally simple causative sentences (e.g. *Mommy open door, Daddy cut tree down*) emerge well before their surface structurally complex counterparts (e.g. *Mommy make door open, Daddy cut tree, and that made it fall down*, etc.). However, Bowerman argued that children's knowledge of the structure of the simple sentences is initially superficial. The evidence lies in the existence of errors of over-regularization involving these sentence patterns, and in the timing of their onset. In Bowerman's longitudinally collected spontaneous speech data from two children, acceptable simple sentences with transitive causative verbs like *open* and *break* emerged several months before the appearance of structurally analogous but overregularized sentences involving 'novel' causative verbs, such as *I'm just gonna fall this on her* (= make fall/drop), *She came it over there* (= made come/brought) and *How would you flat it?* (= make flat/flatten). Similarly but at a later stage of development, acceptable sentences like *Daddy cut tree down* and *I eat cereal allgone* appeared many months before structurally analogous but ungrammatical sentences like *Untie it off* (= untie it, thereby causing it to come off), *I pulled it unstapled* (= I pulled on it, which caused it to become unstapled) and *I'm patting her wet* (= I'm patting her, which is causing her to become wet).

This sequence of development is very similar to that involved in the better known phenomenon of morphological overgeneralization, in which the acceptable production of particular inflected forms (*shoes, walked,* etc.) considerably predates the extension of the inflectional pattern to irregular lexical items to produce novel forms such as *foots* and *comed.* In the morphological case, correct forms used prior to the onset of overregularization are generally interpreted as 'unanalysed': it is assumed that the child has not yet grasped the regular patterning that underlies them (e.g. Ervin, 1964). Bowerman argues that the initial correct use of causative verbs can be interpreted similarly. More specifically, she hypothesizes that in order to acquire rules for creating truly original causative sentences, both grammatical and overregularized, the child must break down 'received' causative sentence patterns such as *open X, break X, cut X down, pull X up,* and *eat X all gone* into components corresponding to a cause proposition and an effect proposition. With this knowledge the child can manipulate the components independently to create novel structures cut to the same linguistic pattern. Thus, at some point the child comes to recognize implicitly that a conceptual structure such as *Mommy* CAUSE *door open* underlies a sentence like *Mommy open door.* At this point (and not before), when she entertains a novel but analogous structure like *She* CAUSE *it came over there,* she assumes that an analogous surface realization such as *She came it over there* is possible. Similarly, but at a later time, the following type of analysis and generalization takes place: the child recognizes (again implicitly) that underlying a sentence like *Daddy cut tree down* is a conceptual structure like *Daddy cut tree* CAUSE *tree (come) down.* Now when she wants to express the semantic content suggested by the structure *(you) untie it* CAUSE *it (comes) off,* she assumes that a surface realization analogous to *'Cut X down'* is possible, i.e. *Untie it off.*

Intriguingly, the onset of errors of overgeneralization, which provide the evidence that Bowerman's subjects had performed implicit analyses such as these, was just slightly preceded by the onset in their spontaneous speech of complex sentences encoding equivalent semantic content. For example, the first errors of the *how would you flat it* (= make it flat) type came just after the appearance of embedded sentences with *make*, e.g. *This make me sneeze.* Similarly, the first errors like *I pulled it unstapled* (= I caused it to come unstapled by pulling on it; I pulled on it and that made it come unstapled, etc.) came right after the emergence of complex multi-clause sentences that explicitly relate two events causally, e.g. *You made me cry with (= by) putting those up there, Don't put my blanket on because that makes me too hot, The boy pushed the witch in the oven and that made her dead.* This coincidence of timing suggests that – just as the hypothesis that derivational complexity plays a role in order of acquisition specifies – the structure of superficially simply causative sentences is not fully grasped until after the structure of their 'less derived', surface structurally complex counterparts is understood.

5. Conclusions

How children acquire complex sentence structures has been the subject of extensive investigation over the last decade. As a result of this research we have gained a rough picture of the sequence in which complex sentences of various types enter spontaneous speech and quite a bit of information about how children tend to interpret sentences whose structures are hard for them to process. A great deal remains to be done, however.

The first and most critical need is for more, and more detailed, studies on how and when children begin to *produce* complex sentences of various kinds. Particularly valuable would be investigations that analyse the emergence of a broad range of structures in the same children, so as to reveal possible links in acquisition across structural domains. Identifying such links and determining their nature (e.g. a function of shared conceptual content? transfer across similar structural patterns? development of a cognitive skill prerequisite to more than one sentence structure?) would lead to a much deeper understanding than we currently have of the processes underlying the acquisition of complex sentences.

A second important need is for studies that explore the role played by 'interpretive strategies' in the acquisition of complex sentence structure. In a discussion of the currently widespread interest in developmental strategies for language, Cromer makes the following well-taken point:

> 'The emphasis on "strategy" has had, overall, a beneficial effect. It has made us aware of some of the ways by which the child may possibly "get

into" the linguistic system. It has shown us the importance of perceptual mechanisms for interpreting utterances, and how as adult speakers with full linguistic competence we nevertheless rely on a number of short-cuts to understanding . . . The concept of language acquisition strategies has told us much – except how the child acquires language' (1976: p. 353).

The problem, as Cromer points out, is that children seem to apply strategies to sentences that they cannot process fully. Once they *can* process these sentences, they no longer need the strategies and begin instead to interpret them on the basis of structural knowledge. But how is the necessary knowledge acquired? This is the critical question, and it is one for which we as yet have few answers. In particular, it is unclear whether the response patterns detected in children's performance on psycholinguists' tests of comprehension actually play any role at all in acquisition. Different children appear to use different strategies for the same sentence structures, and some children seem to use no consistent strategies at all. Yet, as Cromer notes, they all end up learning the constructions.

A first step in efforts to come to a better understanding of the function of strategies in the acquisition of complex sentences will be to find out more about the relationship between the comprehension and production of these structures. Are strategies often applied as processing shortcuts for sentences of a type the child already knows something about, as demonstrated in his spontaneous speech? Or are they more typically used in connection with structures about which the child is truly ignorant? What conclusions we draw about the role of interpretive strategies in learning about complex sentences will depend in part on the outcomes of studies addressing these questions.

Finally, it should be noted that our knowledge of how complex sentences develop is still limited because only a rather narrow range of topics has been investigated. As coverage in this paper indicates, most attention has been paid to questions of how children acquire knowledge of object complementation, relative clause formation and *easy to please* structures, how they handle sentences with adverbial clauses, and what the develop-mental relationship is between sentential and phrasal co-ordination.[11] But

[11] Two other important questions that have been experimentally investigated, but have not been dealt with in this chapter due to space limitations, are (a) how do children learn to identify the referents for pronouns in two-clause sentences like *After he got the candy, Mickey left* and *Susie jumped over the old woman, and then she jumped over Harry* and (b) when do children begin to understand presupposed information in sentences like *John thought/knew/pretended/forgot/was glad (etc.) that Mary came* (did Mary come?) and *It isn't surprising/true/nice that the fish pushed the tree* (did the fish push the tree?)? For studies on the former topic see

we still know nothing about many other important topics. For example, when and how do children learn to distinguish between *restrictive* and *nonrestrictive* relative clauses (those that single out the intended referent versus those that simply add more information about it)? When children start to co-ordinate sentences, do they just string any two sentences together with *and* or do they respect, from the beginning, certain restrictions on what propositions can be meaningfully co-ordinated? When do children begin to produce and understand sentences with verbless clauses like *With John away at school, the house is quiet*? In summary, there is much virgin territory left to explore in the study of how complex sentences are acquired.

Chomsky (1969), Maratsos (1974b) and Tavakolian (1976). For information on the latter, consult Harris (1975), Hopmann and Maratsos (1975) and Macnamara *et al.* (1976).

16. Language development after five

Annette Karmiloff-Smith

Browsing through the literature on child language acquisition, one is struck by the fact that many studies either cover the period from 2 to 5 years of age, or from 5 to 10. Far less frequent are those which investigate the age span between 3 and 7, for instance. What is so crucial about the frontier age of 5? Of course, many children start their formal schooling around 5, partly due to a long-established assumption that language, considered essential for the learning process, is fully acquired by that age. Many investigators have either not extended their research beyond the age of 5 because they have been studying simple linguistic categories which they considered were mastered early, or else have concentrated on over 5 year olds and probed complex constructions such as the passive voice, the relative clause and so forth.

The first part of this chapter deals with the over 5 year old's acquisition of complex linguistic categories. Consideration will be given in the second part to hypotheses about more general aspects of the older child's language. I shall endeavour to show that certain rather fundamental changes are still to take place in the over 5 year old's organization, or rather reorganization, of his language. These involve not only complex constructions but also the seemingly simple categories, such as determiners. Particular emphasis will be placed on the hypothesis that, outside the specific cognitive content of children's utterances and of their communicative intentions, language is for the child at all ages, and perhaps particularly between 5 and 8, a problem area within its own right. Clearly, language development cannot be explained by cognitive development alone. Children have to come to grips with the intricacies of the linguistic structures themselves and may spend a number of years organizing linguistic categories into systems of relevant options. But before pursuing this argument, let us first review some of the more specific aspects of language development after 5.

A common assumption held until the late 1960s was that the 5 year old had mastered the syntactic structures of his native tongue, and that later development mainly consisted of the addition of a sophisticated lexicon.
307

Two main psycholinguistic currents were to challenge such assumptions: one was cognition-oriented, the other linguistics-oriented. Whilst the theoretical bases for questioning early language mastery were substantially different, both of these currents led to the study of rather similar problem areas.

One of the cognition-oriented currents stemmed from Piagetian developmental psychology. Piaget's studies on various categories of knowledge showed that many crucial cognitive developments take place well beyond the age of 5. As is well known, Piaget stressed that language development is dependent on more general mechanisms governing the child's overall cognitive growth. The fact that many fundamental cognitive changes still take place between the ages of 5 and 14, led psycholinguistic interpreters of Piagetian theory to hypothesize that the child's linguistic competence must also reflect these changes beyond the age of 5.

Sinclair (1967), for example, maintained that despite the fact that certain terms (e.g. *more than, less than, thicker, longer,* etc.) were present in the young child's lexicon, these were not fully comprehended nor used as *relational* terms until the child's corresponding concepts in conservation and seriation were mastered. Consideration of the effects of cognitive growth on child language extended from lexical development to the over 5 year old's syntax. From a cognitive point of view, any linguistic structure which violates canonical order (e.g. agent of an action not in subject slot of the sentence, temporal order of events described in reverse order, and so forth) may be a candidate for acquisition after 5. Basic cognitive acquisitions which take place around 6 or 7, e.g. the first quantitative invariants with their reversible operations, were invoked to explain children's difficulties with semantic invariants across transformations in word order (Sinclair and Ferreiro, 1970).

The linguistics-oriented current to challenge early language mastery was exemplified by Carol Chomsky's work on the development of complex constructions (Chomsky, 1969). Chomsky hypothesized that children first use those linguistic rules which hold for a great number of constructions across a language. Rules such as the following were considered already to be part of the implicit competence of the under 5 year old: (a) grammatical subject is equivalent to logical subject, (b) word order necessarily reflects canonical order, (c) the implicit subject of a complement verb is the NP most closely preceding it (Minimal Distance Principle, MDP), and so forth. Any structures which violated such general principles (e.g. examples (1)–(4) below) would be candidates for acquisition after 5. It was expected to be a slow process before the child became able to refrain from overgeneralizing the principles which applied to superficially identical constructions (e.g. examples (1a)–(4a), (4b) below). Chomsky thus tested 5 to 10 year olds' understanding of complex adjectival, verbal and pronominal constructions governed by rules which are exceptions to general principles, as in the following:

(1)   Is the doll *easy to see*? (asked about a blindfolded doll)

(1a) . . . *eager to see*?

(2)   Donald promises Bozo to hop up and down. Make him do it.

(2a) Donald *tells* Bozo . . .

(3)   *Ask* Laura what colour this is.

(3a) *Tell* Laura what . . .

(4)   *He* found out that Mickey won the race. Who found out?

(4a) If *he* wins the race, Pluto will be happy. If . . . who . . . ?

(4b) Pluto thinks *he* is going to win the race. Who is . . . ?

The results of Chomsky's experiments indicated that acquisition of the structures illustrated by examples (1), (2) and (3) was a very gradual process extending over a number of years between 5 and 10. Children's errors mainly consisted of equating grammatical subject with agent and failing to understand that certain verbs are governed by special syntactic rules which require violating the MDP. The only exception to late acquisition was pronominalization which seemed to be fully mastered around 5. The earlier and more uniform acquisition of pronominal reference was explained by the fact that pronominalization does not pertain to any specific word or word class, but derives from general principles which cover the structural relationships obtaining for whole sentences. Chomsky thus drew a distinction between, on the one hand, 'basic tools of language' (e.g. pronominalization), which she maintained are acquired by 5, and, on the other hand, specialized syntactic rules for complex constructions, gradually mastered between 5 and 10.

Many critical replications from both the cognition- and linguistics-oriented currents were to follow in the 1970s, particularly with respect to structures such as *easy to see* (e.g. for English-speaking children: Cromer, 1970, 1972; Kessel, 1970; Morsbach and Steel, 1976; and for French-speaking children: Barblan, forthcoming; Cambon and Sinclair, 1974). Whilst some of these were rebuttals that stressed the younger age levels at which success could be obtained if misleading features were removed from the experimental design, others sought alternative or complementary explanations to Chomsky's concept of syntactic complexity. More general cognitive factors were found to be involved also. One difficulty seemed to stem from the broad semantics of the verb *to see*. Others arose from the need for the child to differentiate between his own perspective and that of others. The early success levels of 5 year olds, found in some of the later studies, could be explained by the tendency of small children to take themselves as the agent of all verbs (i.e. *easy to see* implies '*I* can see easily'). Successful 8 year olds, on the other hand, really understood the nonspecific agent function of the missing grammatical object (i.e. *easy to see* implies 'easy to see by someone'). Problems of decentration, a well-known cognitive phenomenon in spheres outside language, gave rise to some of the difficulties encountered by children. However, decentration could not alone account for the child's problems with this construction since, when investigators tested children with a different verb, e.g. 'the doll is easy to *draw*' (Cambon and Sinclair, 1974) which is clearly biased towards a correct answer, younger children nonetheless persisted in equating grammatical subject with agent and had the doll pretend to perform the action.

What is clear from the critical replications is that many *interacting* factors are involved. Whilst differing in their theoretical explanations and in situating the exact age of successful performance, most of the studies indicated, as did Chomsky's, that the over 5 year old does in some circumstances have difficulty in understanding that the grammatical subject of a sentence need not necessarily be identified with the agent of an action. The over 5 year old therefore continues to work from a very sound theory about language, a theory which is correct for many constructions but which he has not yet clearly tagged with standby procedures regarding exceptions (see Karmiloff-Smith (1978) for discussion of the cognitive processes involved in the interaction of theory construction and exceptions thereto).

Other complex categories investigated in over 5 year olds were: the passive voice (e.g. in English: Bever, 1970a; Hayhurst, 1967; Sinclair *et al.*, 1971; Turner and Rommetveit, 1967; in French: Sinclair and Ferreiro, 1970; in Swiss-German: Caprez *et al.*, 1971); constructions reversing temporal order of events (e.g. in English: Cromer, 1971b; Weil, 1971; Weil and Stenning, 1978; in French: Ferreiro, 1971); as well as relative clauses (e.g. in English: Brown, 1971; Gaer, 1969; Limber, 1973; Maratsos, 1973; Sheldon, 1972, 1974; in French: Kail, 1975a, b; in Spanish: Ferreiro, 1974).

These and similar studies confirmed that certain aspects of language are still being acquired by over 5 year olds, and that many interacting linguistic and general cognitive problems are involved. The passive voice studies, for instance, demonstrated that 5 year olds could correctly act out passives if they involved non-reversible actions (as in example (5a) below) because their interpretation could be based on pragmatic factors. The same children, however, encountered many difficulties in coping with reversible sentences such as in (5b):

(5a) The cup is washed by the girl
(5b) The boy is pushed by the girl

Just as with the *easy to see* construction, children interpreted examples such as (5b) by taking the first noun to be the agent of the action. Clues to the fact that children gradually become aware of the linguistic structure were apparent in the behaviour of children around 6, who opted for compromise, reciprocal solutions and had the boy and girl push one another. Here we witness something more general about the growing child's procedures, in that when two conflicting interpretations arise, the child may pass through a period of compromise between the two interpretations before adopting the more elaborate one.

Understanding that the grammatical subject is not necessarily the agent of the action is not the only difficulty inherent in structures such as the passive voice. Other problems stem from the cognitive implications of the semantics of the verbs and actions involved. Sinclair and Ferreiro (1970) showed that sentences such as (5e) were understood considerably later than (5d), whereas sentences like (5c) were the earliest to be acquired:

(5c) The car is knocked down by the lorry

(5d) The car is pushed by the lorry

(5e) The car is followed by the lorry

Thus reverse word order, the causal relations expressed by different verbs, whether actions are perfective or durative, etc., are all factors which interact in the development of the over 5 year old's understanding of complex structures.

Likewise, research on the relative clause indicated that the difficulties children encountered were not solely due to the complexity of that particular linguistic structure. Sheldon (1972, 1974) argued that children interpret relative clauses with a 'parallel function hypothesis' which explained why they could cope with the linguistically complex embedded relative, such as in example (6a), before they understood the seemingly simpler construction of example (6b):

(6a) The dog that jumps over the pig bumps into the lion

(6b) The pig bumps into the horse that jumps over the giraffe

In example (6b) the horse changes function from patient of the main clause to agent of the subordinate clause, whereas in (6a) there are no changes in function. However tempting it might be to generalize the 'parallel function hypothesis' to several spheres of the over 5 year old's language, Sheldon's subsequent experiment indicated that this only partially accounts for the child's behaviour. Indeed, contrary to their difficulties in interpreting relative clauses, children had none whatsoever with shifts of function when dealing with the co-ordinate structure counterparts to the relative sentences, such as in example (6c):

(6c) The pig bumps into the horse and the horse jumps over the giraffe

There are of course many nonlinguistic difficulties involved in handling three animals more or less simultaneously, and sentences like (6a)–(6c) above are most atypical of normal language usage. Nonetheless, the difference in the results for each sentence type does tend to suggest that co-ordination is an earlier linguistic achievement than subordination, that the parallel function hypothesis has some effect on children's behaviour and that the actual structure of the relative clause is also determinant in children's difficulties.

Many of these investigations were more recently replicated and extended to other linguistic categories (e.g. Baldie, 1976; Harris, 1976; Maratsos, 1974a; Richards, 1976; Scholnick and Adams, 1973). As with the replications of Chomsky's work (1969), investigators demonstrated that, contrary to earlier studies, either a structure is acquired before 5 or understanding temporarily decreases with age and that the structure is truly mastered rather late in development.

Whilst each new study adds a few more pieces to the total language puzzle, I should like to submit that talented investigators will always be able to devise novel techniques and contexts which make it possible to demonstrate that a particular structure is understood either much earlier or much later than previous work had indicated. But this tells us relatively little about the *general nature* of developmental changes or about the *function* a given category may have for the child. Should we continue to revisit specific, old structures with ingenious, new techniques? Will we not discover more about the 5 year old's language if emphasis is placed on *why* a change in experimental design elicits a change in procedure in the 5 year old, whereas by 8 or 9 years, children use the same procedure across a series of situations?

In his comprehensive review of developmental strategies for language, Cromer (1976) placed particular stress on the fact that around the age of 6, children appear to enter an intermediate stage of language development lasting for some three years. During this period, children may use, for example, the rule 'grammatical subject implies agent' in interpreting the *easy to see* structure, but do not follow the same rule for interpreting the passive. Moreover, Cromer showed that the intermediate child's behaviour was inconsistent from one day to the next, even across a number of items testing the same structure in identical experimental settings.

It can thus be argued that changes in procedure are not only elicited by changes in experimental design, but are actually characteristic of the over 5 year old's behaviour. As of roughly 5, the child can be said to have built up a series of juxtaposed procedures for language use and understanding, which now need to be organized into coherent systems of relevant options.

Why is it that over 5 year olds seem to have a wide repertory of linguistic procedures but are inconsistent in their use of them, whereas in spontaneous speech they appear to cope with language well? One of the reasons may be deeply interwoven with what I termed 'the experimental dilemma' in a discussion of the thorny issue of distinguishing between *ad hoc,* experiment-generated behaviour and normal language usage (Karmiloff-Smith, 1979). On the one hand, we are all aware that if we design an experiment with all the extralinguistic and discourse clues available normally in language, then the child's understanding may be due to the accumulation of interacting clues and not of the linguistic category under study. Yet if we remove all these clues, we cannot be sure that we are not dealing with *ad hoc*, experiment-generated procedures, atypical of the child's everyday behaviour.

Let us very briefly illustrate this from the field of determiners. Say an experimenter decides to study the 'article contrast'. The very use of the word 'contrast' carries theoretical assumptions that are not necessarily true of the child's behaviour. How do we know that the articles actually do function as contrastive terms for the small child? In order to set up as clean an experiment as possible, we narrow down our task to one linguistic contrast (e.g. *the/a*) and our situational context to one cognitive contrast (e.g. singletons/ groups of identical objects). But the child's problem in a comprehension task of this kind need not be specifically linguistic at all. Rather he may seek to discover each of two distinctions and then map one pair onto the other. A very small amount of knowledge about one of the terms will suffice to elicit, by exclusion, correct responses for the other term. In this way a child may show very consistent, and thus statistically significant, behaviour across the two-way mapping. However, it should be recalled that *we* have placed the articles in contrastive functions in an experimental setting. What the child *can* do is not necessarily equivalent to what the child *does* do. The articles may have quite distinct functions initially for the child. Even when they gradually become part of a common system, it is possible that the child does not let the articles carry such a heavy communicative burden if particular contrasts are to be encoded; instead of *the/a*, he may add relevant linguistic emphasizers such as *the only X/one of the Xs*. At all events, the behavioural patterns observed in an experiment may be generated on the spot by the child's general problem-solving procedures and do not necessarily allow us to draw conclusions about the child's normal language development.

Let us look at what this might imply in relation to some of the constructions violating canonical order which were singled out as candidates for acquisition after 5. It should be recalled that most investigators of these complex structures explicitly removed from their experimental design all extralinguistic, paralinguistic and discourse clues in order to attain the child's competence solely in respect of the structure under study. However, it is a truism to assert that we do not normally speak in monotonous, isolated sentences! Understanding is based on many interacting clues from syntax, semantics, pragmatics, intonation, presuppositions, dialogic rules, discourse and situational context. Moreover, linguistic categories have various specific *functions* within a language and children may also be sensitive to this fact. Certain structures which violate canonical order, for instance, have at least one function in common: a syntactic focusing device for highlighting constituents (or information) *intra*sententially, and simultaneously linking this information *inter*sententially to the overall discourse.

Take, for instance, the reversed temporal order. One good reason for violating the canonical order is that the hearer already knows about the second of two subsequent actions and is being informed by the speaker about the first event which preceded it. Are children really sensitive to this functional aspect of language? In a study of temporal relations in French-speaking children's language, Ferreiro (1971) demonstrated that young children have difficulty in coping with reversed temporal order, as in example (7a), yet spontaneously produce and find it much easier to understand longer, redundant strings also reversing temporal order, as in (7b):

(7a) Before the boy went upstairs, the girl washed the boy
(7b) The boy went upstairs, and before the boy went upstairs, the girl washed the boy

Ferreiro noted similar, spontaneous redundancy in her study of Spanish-speaking children's use of the relative clause. In my view, the redundancy children introduce in this way makes such isolated sentences 'functionally grammatical', i.e. the redundant clause makes it possible to insert a distinction between given and new information, and makes the violation of canonical order meaningful.

Changes in word order seem to be far more than stylistic variations and their functions carry implicit information of which both speaker and hearer make use (see Hupet and Costermans (1974) for relevant discussion of the passive voice). Now if the child is sensitive to information of this kind, and he indeed seems to be after 5, what happens in an experiment where functional, syntactic, semantic, pragmatic and other clues are purposely missing? I would suggest that it is here that we may find an explanation for the inconsistent behaviour often observed in the 5 to 8 year old, i.e. the child's behaviour is experiment-generated from his stock of varied procedures because the normal interplay of clues is not available. However, from the *consistent* experimental behaviour of the over 8 year old, we can deduce that by that age the child has attained a more abstract level of linguistic competence, a 'metaprocedural level', probably closely linked to his developing metalinguistic awareness. This does not imply that the over 8 year old always copes without the functional, semantic and pragmatic procedures symptomatic of his normal language usage, but that a more abstract level of linguistic analysis is now part of his competence. Even if atypical of normal language usage, the fact that by around 8 years children can, if need be, rely solely on a linguistic clue should not be underestimated. It may well be symptomatic of an internal reorganization of linguistic categories and a new phase in development.

Thus far our discussion has centred on the over 5 year old's behaviour vis-à-vis complex structures. Does this mean that simpler linguistic categories, e.g. noun determiners, verb inflections, etc., present no problems for the older child? A closer look at the *functions* that these markers have in the growing child's language indicates that this may be an erroneous assumption.

One of the basic aspects of many languages is the fact that verb and noun markers are plurifunctional. Take for instance the articles in French. *Une femme* marks both indefinite reference ('a woman') and the numeral function ('one woman'). The plural definite article *les* simultaneously marks pluralization (as opposed to the singular *le/la*) and totalization (as opposed to the partitive *des*). The plural possessive adjective *mes* marks possession, pluralization (as opposed to *mon/ma*), totalization of a subclass of possessed objects, and the partitive (as opposed to *les*). A modifier such as *red* may be used in its descriptor function, giving information about redness, or in its determiner function, picking out a referent which is red from similar objects of a different colour. Such markers are present early in child corpora, but do they have plurifunctional status from the outset and, if not, is this an important facet of language development after 5?

In a series of experiments aimed at analysing how French-speaking children cope with various elements of the noun phrase (Karmiloff-Smith, 1979), it was found that children pass through three phases.

The first phase stretches between the ages of 3 and approximately 5½ years. During this period, children's use of determiners appears on the surface to be rather efficient. However, a deeper analysis of the *functions* children attribute to each determiner during the first phase disclosed several facts. First, although children made frequent use of the plural definite article *les*, its main function in production was to mark pluralization. This was also apparent in comprehension tasks: *les X* did not necessarily imply 'all the Xs present' but any plural amount of Xs. Similar patterns were found in experiments devised to study the child's use of the possessive adjective. Under 5 year olds *used* the plural *mes* correctly in its various functions to mark plural possession. However, they *understood* neither its totalizer function for possessed objects nor its determiner function to distinguish a subordinate class of possessed objects from a superordinate class of similar ones. With regard to the indefinite article, the under 5 year olds did seem in many cases to use it correctly to indicate various functions. Developmental trends apparent in the second phase, however, raise questions about the actual functions of the indefinite article earlier. As far as the use of the singular definite article (*le/la*) was concerned, its function *for the child* was clearly deictic in the first phase, even if *for the observer* it sometimes appeared to be functioning anaphorically.

This brief description of the functions of determiners for the under 5 year old, in a chapter on later language development, is given to highlight the new behavioural patterns that occur after 5. The second phase lasts from roughly 5 to 8 years of age. Productions of children in the second phase were often agrammatical and full of redundant marking. This of course does not mean that the 5 to 8 year old normally speaks agrammatically, but rather that in an experimental setting where special contrasts had to be encoded linguistically, these children behaved very differently from younger subjects.

Each time a new function was understood cognitively (e.g. totalization, which is developed in part from class inclusion concepts), the over 5 year old first expressed the new function by a separate morpheme (e.g. *tous* in the case of totalization) and did not make use of a morpheme already serving another function (e.g. *les* which was already being used to mark pluralization). Thus, whereas smaller children used *les X* in a given situation but only meant to convey pluralization, children of the second phase added *tous* in the same situation (*tous les X*) in order to cover totalization also. It was not until the third phase that children used *les X* to mark pluralization and totalization *simultaneously*. Many of my results on the acquisition of determiners tend to indicate that initially treating a morpheme as if it were unifunctional is a characteristic feature of the language development of the under 8 year old. This does not mean that one word does not have more than one function in different contexts for the observer, but that from the *child's* point of view, when he wishes to mark several functions simultaneously in the same utterance, he will tend to mark each by a separate morpheme.

Further evidence of the gradual development of a plurifunctional system came from two patterns which had not been apparent in behaviour before 5: the tendency to make multiple overmarking and to create agrammatical forms to distinguish between the dual functions of one marker. First let us look at an example of overmarking, which was particularly clear in children's attempts to make anaphoric reference in a potentially ambiguous situation. Whereas over 8 year olds in the third phase made anaphoric reference such as in (8a) below, children in the second phase tended to use multiple overmarking (see (8b)) in the same situation:

(8a) La fille a poussé un chien et puis le garçon a poussé le chien (The girl pushed a dog and then the boy pushed the dog)

(8b) La fille a poussé un chien et puis aussi le garçon il a repoussé encore le mefie chien

(The girl pushed a dog and then also the boy he re-pushed once more the same dog)

In their endeavour to make *intra*linguistic co-reference clear, these children behaved as if they did not yet fully understand which of the sentence elements should be marked anaphorically and they therefore opted for multiple marking. Again, it should be stressed that this does not imply that such an exaggerated form is typical of the child's everyday speech where such potential ambiguity rarely exists. However, it does represent a clue to subtle problems the older child endeavours to cope with and which are not apparent in the behaviour of the under 5 year old. In general, small children tended to clarify potential ambiguity by making reference to details of the extralinguistic setting, e.g. colour of objects, temporary spatial location and so forth. It was not until after 5 that in such cases children endeavoured to make use of intralinguistic means such as anaphora, first by overmarking and finally as in adult language.

Other evidence pointing to the gradual construction by over 5 year olds of a plurifunctional system came from children's tendency to create agrammatical forms. As they gradually became aware of new functions, e.g. the numeral function of the French indefinite article (which they already knew as a counting term when used without a noun), they created a surface distinction which exists in some languages but not in French. Thus, *un mouchoir* was used to imply 'a handkerchief' and the same children of phase two used the slightly agrammatical *un de mouchoir* to imply 'one handkerchief'. Similar behaviour could be gleaned from children's distinctions between the descriptor and determiner functions of modifiers and possessive adjectives. *La voiture jaune* was used to convey the descriptor function and the same children created the agrammatical *la jaune de voiture* to convey the determiner function; likewise, children made a distinction between *mes voitures* and *les miennes de voitures*.

The fact that children between 5 and 8 add redundant markers and create agrammatical strings for contrastive purposes, suggests that when younger children of the first phase use these morphemes correctly in various situations, they in fact represent a series of *unifunctional homonyms*. The same may hold true for lexical development in the language of the under 5 year old.

Further evidence came from the spontaneous corrections which occur towards the end of the second phase. Typical corrections from 8 year olds are illustrated by examples (9a) and (9b):

(9a) Tu as caché toutes les voitures rouges . . . enfin, *les* voitures rouges
   (You hid all the red cars . . . well, *the* red cars)
(9b) Tous les camions de mon côté . . . *mes* camions, quoi
   (All the lorries on my side . . . *my* lorries, I mean)

It is interesting to note in contrast that children of the third phase did not accentuate morphemes to convey plurifunctionality, whereas this was particularly apparent at the end of the second phase.

Whilst such spontaneous corrections occur around 7 or 8 years of age, metalinguistic awareness of the plurifunctional status of determiners develops considerably later in the third phase. Prior to this, typical comments from 7 to 8 year olds who were interviewed (and who correctly use the plural definite article alone to convey totalization for experimental items) are exemplified in (10):

(10) Il faut dire '*toutes* les voitures rouges', si tu dis seulement '*les* voitures rouges', on ne saurait pas combien prendre
   (You must say '*all* the red cars', if you just say '*the* red cars', you wouldn't know how many to take)

Clearly such children are not yet aware of the implicit rule that they had been using in an earlier part of the experimental session.

The third phase covered the period between roughly 8 and 12. Almost all redundant marking and agrammatical forms disappeared; markers had by then acquired plurifunctional status. Wherever possible, children were economical in their utterances and had one marker carry simultaneously several functions. It also seemed that when children had reached the third phase, they had organized various determiners into a coherent system, in which a hierarchy had been established concerning their presuppositional force. The following is an example from an advanced 9 year old:

(11) My yellow cars must . . . euh, *the* yellow cars must go to the petrol station. [Experimenter asks the child why he changed from *mes* to *les* . . .] It's because 'les' is shorter . . . well it's not true for the number of letters, but it's just as if . . . I can't quite explain . . . well, you can say both, 'les' or 'mes', but if there [points to another parking lot] there were some yellow cars then I would have to say 'mes'; but there aren't any there, so it's better to say 'les voitures jaunes . . .' even if they belong to me

This, and other similar examples, are a clear indication that there is a tendency by the third phase to avoid overdetermining, i.e. to prefer 'weaker' determiners wherever this is feasible. Has not the over 8 year old finally come to terms with an important Gricean principle?

Examples (12a) and (12b) from 11 year olds illustrate the most elaborate form of metalinguistic awareness regarding the presuppositions that the use of one determiner in preference to another conveys:

(12a) I say *'my* watch' because it's mine, but *'the* watch' because it's the only one present, otherwise you'll think there's another one

(12b) [Experimenter asks the child why he changed from an initial indefinite reference to definite reference.]Because if you continue to say 'a', then it could be any old ring, a small one, a big one . . . but here it's not just any ring. *'A* ring', well that belongs to anyone, so you must say *'your* ring'. I have to say *'my* ring' if yours is here, but *'the* ring' if I compare it to all that [pile of objects containing no rings]

Such examples bear eloquent witness to the fact that determiners are finally organized into a system of relevant options.

All my experiments on the plurifunctionality of determiners concluded with an exploratory, metalinguistic interview. The results highlighted an important linguistic development that takes place around 9 years of age. In a variety of different situations, under 9 year olds tended to make reference to characteristics of the *extralinguistic* context when asked to reflect metalinguistically upon their responses, as can be seen in examples (13a) and (13b) below. It was not until after 9 in most cases that children *explicitly* referred to the *linguistic* clue they had used (see (13c) and 13d)):

(13a) I knew you were talking to the boy because he's got only one book

(13b) There are no apples left because there was only one in the basket in the beginning

(13c) I know you're talking to the boy, because you said 'lend me *the* book', and if you'd been talking to the girl, you would have said 'lend me *a* book'

(13d) In the story there was only one, because you were precise, you said *'the* apple', and if there had been several of them you could have said 'one of the apples'

The capacity to refer to the presuppositions implied by the *absence* of a contrastive marker was only present in the oldest children's explanations.

Whilst most of the illustrative data given thus far has been from French-speaking children's utterances, much of the discussion regarding the passage from unifunctionality to plurifunctionality could equally hold for various aspects of acquisition of English after 5 (e.g. use of determiners, verb inflections, etc.). But what about linguistic categories which are specific to certain languages only? How, for instance, do French-speaking children come to grips with problems of grammatical gender? Is this something entirely settled by 5, or is gender yet another sphere in which the over 5 year old still has some ground to break? It is important to recall that in French, grammatical gender has relatively little to do with natural gender.

In a study of the child's acquisition of gender, another of the functions which French determiners mark, it was shown that well before 5, i.e. as soon as the articles were used consistently, the child had constructed a very powerful, implicit system of phonological rules based on the consistency, but not necessarily the frequency, of phonological changes to word endings (Karmiloff-Smith, 1975, 1979). This phonological procedure was so strong that neither syntactic clues (i.e. gender of indefinite article furnished by the experimenter) nor semantic clues (i.e. sex of imaginary persons depicted in drawings) were determinant in eliciting gender agreement. Attribution of gender was predominantly based on a phonological procedure from word endings. It was argued that whilst the phonological procedure remained dominant even in the over 8 year old's behaviour, the *function* of gender for the child changed considerably between the ages of 4 and 8 years. For the under 7 year old, gender served primarily to mark local lexical concord, initially between determiner and noun, and subsequently between determiner, noun and modifier. For over 7 year olds, on the contrary, the morphological function of gender seemed to become relevant; these children used gender to mark extended syntagmatic cohesion across noun and verb phrases.

Let us look briefly at the contrast between the younger and older child's behavioural patterns (see (14a) and (14b) below). Given, for instance, two pictures of females called 'deux bicrons' (nonsense word), children of all ages referred to either one of them spontaneously as *le bicron vert*, i.e. they used masculine gender despite the fact that they were referring to a picture of a female. Children were clearly basing themselves on the typically masculine ending *-on* of the nonsense word (as opposed to the feminine ending *-onne*) and not on natural gender. However, developmental differences became apparent in the use of gender in more extended discourse. In telling a story, small children based the gender of pronoun reference on extralinguistic factors and not on the gender of the noun. Typical stories from under 7 year olds about the female 'bicron' ran as follows:

(14a) . . . alors *le* bicron vert est sorti . . . et ensuite *elle* est allée . . . et puis c'est *elle* qui a . . . [Experimenter intervenes and asks: 'Elle, c'est qui?'] *celle-là, le* bicron vert

The gender examples are not translated since they are of course not relevant to English, but gender markers have been italicized. From the above, it can be clearly seen that local lexical concord is phonologically based, whereas pronoun reference and demonstratives are semantically based. Small children thus seem to juxtapose a series of different procedures within the same situation.

Over 7 year olds also use a phonological procedure for lexical concord, but extend the *same* procedure to pronoun reference which is clearly intralinguistic. The gender of the pronoun is based on the gender of the noun previously referred to linguistically, and not on the extralinguistic referent. These older children's stories about the female 'bicron' ran typically as follows:

(14b) C'est *le* bicron ve*rt* qui est parti . . . ensuite *il* est allé chez . . . c'est *lui* qui a trouvé . . . [Experimenter intervenes and asks: 'Lui, c'est qui?' Child points to picture] ben, c'est *lui* . . . non, non, *elle,* je veux dire, *la* bicr*onne* . . . *celle* qui est ve*rte* . . .

Thus the older child uses a phonological procedure throughout; when faced with the conflict between grammatical and natural gender, he makes revealing changes to the noun suffix, leaving the phonological procedure intact. (See Karmiloff-Smith (1975, 1979) for further details of gender acquisition between 3 and 12.) For the purposes of the more general discussion on language after 5, it is important to note from the above examples that *intralinguistic* reference, i.e. truly nondeictic reference, appears to be an achievement that takes place well after 5 years.

The gender study particularly highlighted the fact that the child develops a variety of *different* procedures in language development. Apart from the obvious semantico-syntactic ones, it seems clear that phonological procedures are also an active facet of early language acquisition processes, and remain so after 5 years. Another procedure used very early in language acquisition is the pragmatic one. It was mentioned in the first part of this chapter that under 5 year olds used pragmatic procedures in their correct interpretation of nonreversible passive constructions. Does this mean that later, when the child becomes capable of attending to intralinguistic factors, he completely drops pragmatic procedures for understanding language? In a story-telling task (Karmiloff-Smith, 1979), it was shown that children as old as 8 years continue in some circumstances to use pragmatic interpretation procedures.

The stories told by the experimenter related counterpragmatic situations and purposely placed a heavy communicative burden on the singular definite article. Children had to deduce from a story (e.g. one involving a garden and a little dog who crushed *the* flower . . .) that the garden contained only one flower. The vast majority of children under 8 did not pick up the clue from the definite article; they interpreted the story based on their general knowledge of gardens. Indeed, children justified their responses by stating that 'Gardens *usually* have lots of flowers, so there must have been several.' Only after 8 years did children correctly respond that the garden contained only one flower. However, it was particularly revealing that only the over 10 year olds repeated exactly what the experimenter had said, e.g. 'He crushed the flower.' Between 8 and 10, although children picked up the clue from the definite article, they repeated the experimenter's story and insisted that the experimenter had actually stated: 'He crushed the *only* flower' or, for instance, 'He crushed the flower which was growing *alone* . . . ' In other words, between 8 and 10, children inserted into their repetition the linguistic emphasizers which would normally be present in a counterpragmatic message. It is not the function of the definite article to carry alone such a heavy communicative burden, and children are sensitive to this fact. In the gender study also, children did not let an article carry alone the communicative burden of indicating natural gender, but made corresponding changes to suffixes also.

Finally, a topic not yet touched upon is that of intonation. Whilst intonation is an essential aspect of the structure of normal discourse, it has long been assumed that the intonational patterns of a language are acquired very early in development. Indeed, there have been some excellent studies on infant acquisition in this sphere (e.g. Ryan, 1978). Cruttenden (1974) seems to be one of the few investigators to have looked at the development of the over 5 year old's understanding of the function of intonation to mark presuppositions. Although his study is somewhat restrictive because of the very specific content (i.e. commentaries on football results), I nonetheless feel he is quite justified in drawing certain generalizations about the function of intonational nuclei to mark for the hearer the distinction in discourse between presupposed and new information. Cruttenden's study suggests that such intonation functions are still in the process of being mastered between 7 and 10 years of age, and perhaps even later. Here we have a very important area of study on the over 5 year old which, to my knowledge, is almost entirely uncharted.

In general, experimental work on the over 5 year old needs to be rooted in the normal functions and constraints of extended discourse. Whilst the over 5 year old's language is often superficially correct, important clues to ongoing development can be gleaned from children's hesitations and spontaneous corrections. Learning studies in language acquisition may also provide indicators to developmental problems (e.g. Barblan, forthcoming; Cromer, 1972). Above all, naturalistic data on the over 5 year old's everyday language could usefully complement the by now plentiful naturalistic data on the under 5 year old.

The purpose of this chapter was to suggest some general implications about language development, particularly between 5 and 8 years of age. In my view, the gradual passage from juxtaposed, unifunctional homonyms, to plurifunctional systems of relevant options for modulating meaning, may be a general feature of development of the noun and verb phrase after 5 years.

Related aspects of later language development were shown to include the tagging of general principles with rules for exceptions, the progressive passage from co-ordination to subordination, the gradual capacity to be economical in utterances, to avoid redundant marking, to gauge the communicative burden a morpheme can carry, to understand the presuppositional constraints of discourse conveyed by the use of various linguistic means such as intonation. A further characteristic of language development after 5 appears to be the gradual passage from extralinguistic to intralinguistic reference, both in spontaneous utterances and, later, in metalinguistic awareness. Five years does indeed seem to be a frontier age, representing the beginning of a new phase in language development. Another new phase appears to begin around the age of 8; parallel to the development of metalinguistic skills, the over 8 year old seems to attain the capacity for a more abstract level of comprehension and can cope, if need be, without the interplay of functional, syntactic, semantic and pragmatic clues used in normal discourse.

At the outset of this chapter, reference was made to the emphasis placed by Piagetian theory on children's interaction with their physical environment and the effects of cognitive growth on language growth. Obviously many of the linguistic developments described in the preceding pages are affected by ongoing cognitive developments. In this chapter, however, particular stress has been placed on the child's constructive interaction with linguistic 'objects', i.e. on the importance of children's processing procedures on their linguistic environment, which may in turn affect cognitive growth. Clearly language does not only have essential representative and communicative functions; it is for a number of years a problem space *per se* for children. Only after 8 years does language seem to become *solely* the important instrument for representing and communicating thought. But who knows, perhaps it remains a problem space. It could be that the rich and complex process of language development never ceases entirely, particularly for the developmental psycholinguist who continuously learns about his language from children.

Note. This chapter was completed in March 1977. The author now uses the term 'metaprocedural behaviour' (see p. 314 above) to refer to more general processes that take place throughout development and in adult problem-solving behaviour. See, for example, Karmiloff-Smith (in press).

Part III

CONTEXTS AND DETERMINANTS

Introduction

1.0. The first two Parts of this book have sought to present a fairly comprehensive and detailed account of the way that language develops in the normal child, with special reference to English. As far as possible, the contributions have been organized so as to allow the reader to appreciate the developmental ordering of particular phenomena. It is now the task of Part III to consider the course of language acquisition as a whole: (a) looking at whatever general principles can be discovered (i.e. not confined to one period, or area of language acquisition), (b) looking at language acquisition in the context of the general development of the child, and (c) setting language acquisition in the more basic context of the biology of the species. In addition, it is quite usual in a book of this sort to include a discussion of methodological issues, since these are indeed formidable in child language research. Accordingly, this Part was originally conceived with a title such as 'Methodological and general issues' in mind. In an ideal world, of course, the distinction between Parts I and II on the one hand and Part III on the other would correspond to 'Facts' versus 'Explanations'; but the day which will bring such a concise organization of our knowledge is still far off. The present Part, which we have actually entitled 'Contexts and determinants' falls somewhere between this ideal and our original conception. Nothing is included which explicitly and exclusively bears on methodological issues, and this reflects the fact that a number of these issues are addressed, in their proper contexts, in the chapters of Parts I and II; this leaves more space here for views on the acquisition process as a whole, and we feel that the contributors have, from many different points of view, managed to clarify many issues. Any future 'Explanations' will rely on much that is referred to here, by way of (as Marshall puts it in chapter 22) identifying areas where 'hypotheses are desperately needed'.

2.0. All the following chapters are in one way or another linked to the important and wide-ranging notion of *contextual support for language acquisition*.

327

2.1. Dore (chapter 17) notes the existence of linguistic as well as nonlinguistic contexts of utterances, and stresses the primacy of conversation in language acquisition. Conversational acts are linguistic, but as 'units of mutual display' they have roots far back in prelinguistic behaviour (as noted in the Introduction to Part I). Conversation therefore involves elements of behaviour which the child can bring to a significant part of the language acquisition process, and within which immediate feedback is possible. Within this contextual framework we have to classify the large number of conversation act types, in ways which reflect not just their 'function' (in terms of their illocutionary function, their place in conversational procedure and in the larger social setting) but also their 'form' (including propositional content and grammatical structure).

Snow (chapter 18) is concerned with the more specific topic of the nature of the language that is addressed to children (concentrating particularly on the language of mothers). The importance of 'motherese' research lies partly in calling attention to the nature of the 'primary linguistic data' (PLD) of language acquisition: to the extent that this is distinct from regular adult language, the potential role of a specific 'language acquisition device' is correspondingly modified. Such modification has been a noticeable trend of research in the 1970s, and the logic of the argument is quite clear; but it has taken a good deal of work to clarify the much-used concept of 'simplicity' in the PLD. On the basis of what information do mothers modify the speech they address to their children? What is the precise nature of these modifications? How far do adults generally – and older children – employ such modifications? Is there an observable progression in modifying speech addressed to the child as the child develops? Is there any formal and/or functional correlation between the level of PLD and the child's linguistic level? Snow stresses the point (consistent with Dore's view of the importance of conversation acts) that feedback from the child plays an important role in the way speech is modified in addressing the child. Further, the primary goal of mother–child interaction is not teaching–learning but communication, and this in turn suggests that considerations of syntactic form are subordinate to what is talked about: Snow suggests that it is semantic (not syntactic) complexity which is importantly under control in simplified PLD, and that it is at this level that correlations can be found between the PLD and the child's developing system.

Such considerations take us a good deal further forward in our understanding, but, as Snow points out, there is as yet only a little evidence as to how far simplified PLD facilitates language acquisition. We can all too easily swing from the view that language acquisition is inexplicable in terms of input (the 'essential deep structures' are simply not available to the child in its linguistic environment – e.g. Bever *et al.*, 1965) to the view that a theory of simplified PLD constitutes an explanation of development.

Wells (chapter 19) points to the complexity of the situation in which the child acquires language, and explicitly warns against such dichotomizing tendencies. A great many of the methodological difficulties in child language acquisition studies are illustrated in Wells' discussion of the many variables involved – inherent factors (relating to the child), social factors, features of the immediate situation of utterance, and the style of interaction. All these have to be considered when describing the context of acquisition; and they then have to be related in a systematic way to the formal characteristics of the developing linguistic system – in itself a problematic object of description. Beyond the methodological difficulties involved (in collecting representative data and appropriately quantifying it), however, Wells is able to draw a number of conclusions which are consistent with those of other contributors in this Part. Most importantly, the data from the Bristol Project provide preliminary support for the view that a facilitating linguistic environment for child language acquisition characteristically seems to involve paying attention to the meaning-intention of the child; by contrast, variations in feedback from parents relating to grammatical form of child utterances do not seem to account for individual differences in rate of development. Concerning social factors, it is particularly important that Wells finds no support for claims that have been made by, for example, Bernstein (1971) and Tough (1977) concerning the effect of social class on linguistic competence; here is a clear example of what Wells describes as 'the disturbing effect that is produced when social variation is reduced to an opposition between two monolithic classes'.

2.2. Thus far, we have been considering aspects of the 'external' situation, or contextual setting, of language acquisition. In many instances, these lead naturally to less obvious 'internal' or personal factors, such as 'cognitive process' (chapter 17), communicative function in mother–child interaction (chapter 18), and intelligence and personality as inherent variables (chapter 19). We shall now turn to the nature of the child's resources – what might be called the 'internal contexts' of linguistic functioning. In this area we have chapters 21 (Campbell) and 22 (Marshall); both are broadly speculative and rightly emphasize the deficiencies in our present understanding. In terms of the distinction that Marshall refers to, between linguistic, psychological and neurological levels of description, Campbell deals mainly with the psychological, considering what it might be that we refer to by 'cognitive' development in relation to language. Marshall himself concentrates more on the neurological level, attending particularly to certain aspects of the neuroanatomical basis of the species-specific language capacity.

Chapter 21 begins, appropriately, with a warning concerning the dispro-portion between the enormous amount of research in cognitive develop-ment and the limited nature of our understanding; this is certainly true insofar as the relationship between cognitive and linguistic development is concerned. Accordingly, Campbell addresses the really basic issues which are still not settled, and outlines a challenging position involving a particular sort of dualism, between 'cryptic' and 'phenic' functions. This position is illustrated in relation to more conventional recent attitudes, and also to a much older tradition of research. Finally, he turns to the implications of his view for language acquisition studies, and makes contact with the main issue, the relationship between language structure and the overall communicative system. He is concerned particularly with ontogenetic and microgenetic considerations (i.e. the relationship between cognition and language both in the development of the individual and in the individual's use of his com-municative system), and it will be convenient here, by way of background, to introduce some wider issues which have had a bearing on the way that child language acquisition studies have come to terms with the ontogenesis of the child's communicative abilities. We shall then return to consider Campbell's account.

There are basically three viewpoints to consider, although each has been elaborated in various ways. The first, in recent history, was that of learning theory, which attempted to account for the growth of language in behaviour-ist terms, relating linguistic elements and structures to much simpler, more primitive, and not specifically human behaviour patterns of stimulus and response. The second position, consistent with Chomskyan linguistics and largely stemming from Chomsky's (1959) attack on Skinner's (1957) learn-ing theory of language, laid emphasis on the necessity for postulating innate linguistic abilities. By calling attention to formal properties of language, Chomsky argued that learning theory was in principle insufficient to account for the (then) known facts of language development. The task that he outlined was, in effect, an exploration of the nature of innate linguistic abilities by examining the discrepancy between what the child achieves (in formal terms) and what are the apparent bases for that achievement. The attraction of this view lay in its emphasis on the ability of the child to create his own formal linguistic system, as evidenced in examples of overgeneral-ized incorrect forms (such as *sitted* for *sat*, and the occurrence of *me* in subject position: it is clearly impossible to explain utterances such as *Me sitted there* on the basis solely of imitation of adult models). But, of course, it has been very difficult to be precise about the 'apparent bases' of language development (as we have seen, in considering chapters 17, 18 and 19 by Dore, Snow and Wells). And, as research went on in the Chomskyan tradition, evidence was gathered which was increasingly problematic for the view that formal properties of language were the basic determinants of child language acquisition. The dilemma is neatly illustrated in Brown and Hanlon's (1970) interpretation of the order of emergence of linguistic structures in terms of an *Aspects*-type grammar, and in Bever's (1970b) reinterpretation of their findings in much more general terms. And Bever (1970a) suggested that, far from there being specifically linguistic abilities, independent of other aspects of cognition, language development should be considered as an ontogenetic recruitment of general cognitive abilities to linguistic ends (the phylogenetic implications of this view are also clear).

This way of looking at the relationship between linguistic and other cognitive abilities (cf. also Macnamara (1972) for a similar and influential statement) brought a good deal of child language acquisition research within reach of the third position, perhaps most influentially represented in the work of Piaget (Piaget, 1970; Piaget and Inhelder, 1969; and numerous other works; cf. Flavell (1963) for a useful survey and the appendix to Donaldson (1978) for a brief summary). Piaget has proposed no theory of language acquisition, but he has a well-documented and sophisticated theory of cognitive development, in terms of which language has been argued to be a product of intellectual growth, with its roots far back in the simplest reflex behaviour patterns of the neonate. Like the learning theory account, Piaget's view sees language as an outgrowth of simpler patterns of behaviour; unlike the learning theory account, however, it has been interpreted as being compatible with linguistic form and with the nature of the child's errors.

One very great stumbling block, however, apparently lies in the way of a wholesale shift from the innate linguistic abilities position to the Piagetian cognitive-source position: this is that, according to Piaget's account, the cognitive abilities of young children are very limited, particularly during the period when (as research in the Chomskyan tradition has made clear) considerable linguistic developments take place. In this respect, many child language acquisition researchers have had the experience of finding themselves working in a difficult no man's land between specific cognitivist and linguistic theories. The question that must be asked in relation to Piaget's theory is 'How does such a theory of intellectual growth account for language acquisition?' From a strict Piagetian viewpoint, the answer is simple: it describes the ontogenetic origins of linguistic elements and structures. Language, according to this view, is a product of intellectual development. The sudden spurt in the child's vocabulary around 1;6 to 2;0 is explained as the result of an intellectual transition to mental representations; over-generalizations in the use of early words result from the dominance of certain perceptual attributes (all creatures with four legs are dogs); the emergence of certain syntactic operations (e.g. active–passive) must wait upon the development of certain intellectual grouping abilities; and so on.

There are many difficulties with such a view. It is first necessary to establish correlations between intellectual and linguistic orders of development; it is then necessary to find evidence for the direction of causality, intelligence→language. A good deal of work has, quite properly, attempted to fill these needs, e.g. Sinclair (1967), but this way of looking at language development has not gone unchallenged, and researchers today are much more inclined towards an 'interactionist' view of the relation between cognitive and linguistic development. This represents a fourth position in addition to the others mentioned above.

Notice, in this connection, that it is by no means the case that theories of cognitive development necessarily treat language as derivative; Vygotsky (1962), working with a somewhat similar system to Piaget's, stresses the role of language in directing cognitive development. And Bruner (1964, 1975; Bruner et al., 1966) has consistently laid emphasis on linguistic (and social) influences on cognitive development; he argues that the language system matures earlier than abstract cognitive representations, and that it antici-pates and extends subsequent intellectual capacities. We can therefore recognize many possible positions between the two extremes of 'thought yields language' and 'language moulds thought'.

Moreover, as our knowledge of the developing linguistic system has advanced, particularly in the last two decades, many child language re-searchers have found it increasingly difficult to justify linguistic develop-ment in purely cognitive terms: we have already referred (Part II, Introduc-tion) to the significance of Karmiloff-Smith's suggestion, from within the Genevan tradition, that the developing language system eventually comes to represent an object of cognitive attention in its own right. If Piaget's view were simply correct, then one would expect more detailed examination of language development to supply increasingly corroborative data; experi-ence has been largely otherwise. A major concern, from the mid-1960s, of Margaret Donaldson and Roger Wales in The Edinburgh Cognition Project was to examine Piaget's claims relating to language development in a linguis-tically sophisticated manner; and their work has called a number of these claims into question. Now, Donaldson (1978) has presented compelling evidence that Piaget's account of cognitive development is itself in certain respects inaccurate. It is (perhaps ironically) significant that the evidence comes largely from the field of language development. It is most important to be quite clear about Donaldson's conclusions:

(i)   children can be shown to have certain concepts considerably earlier than Piaget's theory allows for

(ii) language skills are not isolated from the rest of cognitive development

It might, from this account, be thought that (i) is not particularly serious, simply requiring a chronological readjustment of Piaget's stages. All developmental theories must welcome such adjustment on the basis of fresh evidence. But Donaldson's conclusion is more far-reaching than this, calling certain fundamental concepts into question: e.g. 'Children are not at any stage as egocentric as Piaget has claimed' (1978: p. 58). (In this connection, we should recall the negative evidence relating to egocentricity noted by Maratsos, Wales and Karmiloff-Smith, in chapters 12, 13 and 16.)

The second point proceeds crucially from the first, since evidence of early intellectual abilities equally attacks the basis for the view that language is a special product (of some 'language acquisition device'), independent of the rest of cognitive development, and calls into question the interpretation of language as derivative with respect to cognitive development. What children are doing, rather, is attending to both linguistic form and the perceptible properties of the situation of utterance, in order to grasp the 'meaning' (what is required, in the interview situation, in order for them to respond appropriately). Donaldson's discussion of McGarrigle's experiments with Piaget's 'class-inclusion' task (1978: pp. 43–50) provides an excellent illustration: first, class-inclusion abilities are demonstrated to occur considerably earlier than Piaget allows for, and secondly, it is possible to show that not just perceptual contrasts and not just the form of the linguistic instruction contribute to the result, but the two operating together.

The picture that emerges is one of two delicate balances, one resulting from the interaction of *linguistic form* and *context*, the other between *linguistic* and *cognitive development*. It is quite clear that the context of an utterance is regularly determined by linguistic form; the speaker signals those features of the situation that the hearer is to attend to by a variety of linguistic (as well as nonlinguistic) means – cf. Wales' comments on the 'directing function' of deictic elements, for example. But it is also the case that elements in the situation help to determine the value of linguistic forms, and Donaldson shows the effect of this in, for example, the way children interpreted the description 'All the cars are in the garage' in relation to a particular array: they seem to have taken it to refer to 'all the cars which ought to be there' (1978: p. 66). This balance between mutually defining linguistic forms and context can, of course, be upset, in either direction. Donaldson notes evidence of children attending to 'sheer linguistic form' in a bizarre fashion (pp. 71–2); and Clark (chapter 8) notes instances where linguistic form is overridden by the features of the context (it is more 'natural' to place a cup *on* a saucer than under it). Such strong influence of context is found not just in early stages of language acquisition, of course: for an adult hearer, the instruction 'Run up the flag' will (probably) represent two quite different linguistic forms, depending on whether the context is that of a 'jeux sans frontières' competition (between teams of different nationalities, with huge flags enticingly strung between wall and ground), or that of an independence day celebration (with a nearby flagpole, and flag all ready to be hoisted). Concerning the other balance, between developing linguistic and cognitive abilities, there is evidence for an 'interactionist' view in the earlier stages (Bruner, 1975; Cromer, 1974b; Macnamara, 1972; Ryan, 1974), which has increasingly found favour among researchers in this decade. Heber (1977) presents findings which are consistent with such a view, for the 5;0 to 6;0 period, from a study of seriation; and Wells (chapter 19) similarly suggests that level of intelligence is not independent of language level.

It is in this respect that Campbell's chapter makes a particular contribution: the distinction between inner or 'phenic' processes and outer or 'cryptic' processes parallels that between function and form, respectively. His picture is one of complementary (rather than competing) levels of activity, with a flexible boundary layer between them, subject to ontogenetic development and microgenetic fluctuation. Correspondingly, messages or intentions are not 'linguistic objects', though they *are* open to awareness and rational operation; but their linguistic forms are not available to our awareness, and are not part of what Campbell wishes to recognize as 'cognitive' psychology. In this respect, we may recall the findings of Snow and Wells (chapters 18 and 19), that it is at the semantic level that modification and feedback most commonly occur in interaction with the child, rather than at the level of syntactic form.

Chapter 22 (Marshall) opens in an anti-reductionist spirit, and certainly a great deal of what follows serves to warn those who search for explanations for psycholinguistic data and processes in the assumed neurological substratum. Instead, of course, what is found is a set of problems couched in neurological terms. But the warning is for those who approach this level of description for the wrong purpose; for those who wish to characterize development at this level there is an important and a rich field of research. Surely students encountering this field for the first time (or at least after limited acquaintance) in Marshall's account will find his '(almost) entirely negative' approach a stimulating one (much as a judicious catalogue of early maps for a largely uncharted territory). It is important to have a realistic assessment of the limits of our knowledge concerning such relationships as between genotype and phenotype, between neurological abnormalities and language abilities, between localization of brain function and development, and between neurological maturation and level of linguistic ability. Indeed, it is perhaps too easy for linguists (or others) to think that matters are really much clearer than this at the linguistic level of description. At no level of description is there a device 'that "drives" language acquisition through its "stages" or along its continuous function'.

2.3. Chapter 20 deals with a different sort of context again; Suppes, Léveillé and Smith consider the formal properties of the language development process, for what evidence can be found to throw light on the relationship between different developmental levels. Child language acquisition studies in general have not been sufficiently concerned with this problem, and reference to 'different developmental levels' has often been made (as immediately above) in quite a vague way, to refer to widely divergent conceptions of what language development actually might be: for example, whether it be a smooth continuum, or a stagewise progression. The term 'stage', similarly, is used in a variety of ways. As Suppes *et al.* point out, much of what they say is of a preliminary, exemplificatory nature. But it is noteworthy that they find some evidence to support an incremental model as opposed to a strict stages model. This conclusion is tempered by two considerations: first, that the superiority is demonstrated for what are, in their terms, the highest level groups of rules: and secondly, that the stages model being compared here is a strict one characterized by complete discontinuity of each stage with others. The conclusion nonetheless seems to justify both the notion of an overall probabilistic 'context' (within which each incremental level is related to preceding development), and the concept of 'conducive occasion' for the operation of rules of grammar. Such work is all the more important for laying emphasis on the continuing need for a better understanding of the formal, as well as the functional, aspects of the language acquisition process.

17. Conversation and preschool language development

John Dore

It is not surprising that, after almost two decades of intense research on children's linguistic competence, several investigators have begun to focus upon the conversations that children engage in. What is surprising is that so much progress could have been made without taking into account more explicitly the crucial role of conversation in learning language. This shift of interest has been stimulated by concern for at least the following three factors: the character of the input to the process of acquiring grammar, the functions of utterances and the nature of the contexts in which children's talk occurs. The purpose of the present chapter is to demonstrate how the structure of the speech the child hears, the functions of his own and others' utterances and the relevant aspects of context are all reflected, in varying ways, in his conversations. The central argument will be that conversation itself is the immediate and primary context for acquisition; that conversation is the most significant environment for learning language.

One specific aim of this chapter is to suggest the form of a sociolinguistic schema that a child must have in order to participate effectively in conversation. As is amply documented in the literature, by the age of 3, children engage in coherent and extensive conversations with their parents and peers. In a nursery school setting they can co-operate in the accomplishment of goal-directed activities which involve many kinds of institutional rules and procedures and which are achieved in large part through conversation. Any model attempting to explain this kind of 'communicative competence' must take into account not only the child's knowledge of grammar, but also his ability to say the appropriate thing at the appropriate time and place to the appropriate listeners and in relation to the appropriate topics.

In order to characterize what exactly constitutes a conversation for children, one must deal with at least the following four major issues. First, what is to be the *unit of analysis*; is it the sentence, the utterance or the turn at speaking; and how is the unit to be theoretically justified and operationally defined? Second, how do speakers arrive at the appropriate *interpretation* of each other's utterances; are meanings recognized on the basis of grammar, or by rules of their use in contexts, or by some kind of general rational procedures? Third, what are the principles for determining an effective *taxonomy* of such units; what level of utterance function should a taxonomy be formulated at and how can one limit the inclusion of appropriate functions to this level? And fourth, what *contextual constraints* operate so that speakers understand each other, so that they share the same presuppositions about the topics and purposes of their conversations, so that they can eliminate the inherent ambiguity of linguistic meanings and the equivocality of utterance functions? Each of these four issues has received attention in recent work on child discourse and each is treated as a major aspect of the model of conversation proposed below.

In addressing the issues, the discussion will be organized in the following way. First I will indicate the need for an approach to language learning in terms of conversation and point out some of the theoretical and methodological advantages of such an approach. I will then review some of the recent work on children's conversations. This highly selective review will focus on studies which have influenced the proposed model and it will emphasize the talk of children at nursery school rather than that of younger children. The third section will provide an overview of our model, with a detailed illustration of how the model handles our data. And some implications of the model will be taken up in the concluding section.

1. The need for a conversational model

Brown (1973) summarized much of the significant progress during the 1960s concerning children's initial knowledge of grammatical structures. Based upon one or another version of the transformational generative theory of language, it is now possible to write at least partial grammars (that is, structural descriptions of phonological, syntactic and semantic knowledge) for children at various stages of development. Earlier work by Brown and his colleagues (1964), as well as by others, focused on the formal distribution of words in syntactic patterns; and later work, such as that by Bloom (1970), described how underlying semantic relations were expressed by surface patterns. Despite differences in their approaches, these investigators agreed that the child's early multiple-word utterances were highly structured and that the child was inducing grammatical rules from the speech he heard. But more recent work, which focuses upon psychological processes rather than grammatical knowledge, has indicated the limitations of earlier research. Bruner (1978), for example, points out that

'the early language for which a grammar is written is the end result of psychological processes leading to its acquisition, and to write a grammar of that language at any point in its development is in no sense to explicate the nature of its acquisition [p. 2] . . . to master a language a child must acquire a complex set of broadly transferable or generative skills – perceptual, motor, conceptual, social, *and* linguistic – which when appropriately coordinated yield linguistic performances that can be described (though only in a limited sense) by the linguist's rules of grammar.' (p. 3)

Bruner makes it quite clear that a more comprehensive approach to language learning is necessary, and below I will point out how a conversational model can handle at least the conceptual, social and linguistic skills he refers to.

Another reason for the need for a conversational approach concerns the functions of utterances. Just as the prelinguistic child's pointing is multiply ambiguous (as to whether he is referring to the object, event or some property), during the early stages of speech what a child says is often difficult to interpret. The difficulty arises not only because his meanings for words are different from adult meanings, but also because it is often unclear how he intends his utterance to be taken. For example, as adults we know what a child *means* by, say, the word *apple*, but we may not be sure about what he *intends* to convey by the use of the word. *Apple* could be a description (equivalent to 'That is an apple') or a question ('Is that an apple?') or a command ('Give me the apple!') and so on. Most often, as will be shown below, it is the function of such an utterance relative to the ongoing conversation that allows the adult to interpret the child's intention.

Moreover, it is necessary to be aware of the utterance's conversational function in assessing the complexity of a child's speech. One influential measure for calibrating children's grammatical competence has been the mean length of utterance (MLU) in morphemes. But although they are a useful index of development, MLUs do not reflect the functions of an utterance nor the semantic relations it expresses. Nor have MLU counts been correlated with the role of utterances in conversations. Yet these indices are more revealing when used with reference to the kinds of functional acts children can perform in actual conversation. The length of utterances varies with the purpose they serve. Among young children, for example, responses to questions are shorter than the spontaneous descriptions and statements they produce when initiating the topic of conversation. Some utterance types are only a few words, such as calls, greetings, requests for attention, acknowledgments of another's utterance, etc. Furthermore, MLU counts for the same child using the same utterance types vary according to the setting, the participants and the task to which his speech is related (see Cole *et al.*, 1978). Thus, the correlation of MLU count with the conversational status of the utterance provides both a structural and functional index that offers a more complete measure of the development of the child's communicative competence.

The need for a conversational view of language data can be further demonstrated by two additional examples, one from a child's one-word stage and the other from the later period called 'telegraphic' speech. The far-reaching effect of having prior conversation, and of the co-participant structure of conversation, can be seen in the following example (from Snow, 1978); an experimenter (E) is talking to an 18 month old child (C) before the child's mother (M) walks in:

    C: Bandaid.
    E: Where's your bandaid?
    C: Bandaid.
    E: Do you have a bandaid?
    C: Bandaid.
    E: Did you fall down and hurt yourself?
        [Mother enters]
    C: Bandaid.
    M: Who gave you the bandaid?
    C: Nurse.
    M: Where did she put it?
    C: Arm.

Snow points out that the mother and child continue an extensive conversation about their visit to a doctor's office. Not only did they share the visit but they shared the experience of discussing the visit; and the mother knew what questions the child could answer and the child knew what questions the mother was likely to ask. The example is especially revealing when we consider that experimental studies, in which an experimenter probes a child with various questions, may not be getting at an adequate representation of the child's linguistic capability. For our purposes it is important to note the social roles of the child's interlocutors. That it was the child's mother who elicited the appropriate answers, while the experimenter did not, is understandable. And to us it suggests that any model of children's conversations must take into account the roles of participants and must try to explain those aspects of the conversation that depend upon different participant structures.

We can take our second example of early syntax from Bloom (1970). One of her (by now famous) examples is the utterance of *Mommy sock* by the same child on two different occasions; once while her mother picked up her own sock and once while her mother was putting on the child's sock. Bloom pointed out the ambiguity of the surface form: the first occurrence meant something like 'This is mommy's sock' and the second something like 'Mommy is putting on my sock'; the first involving the semantic category of possession, and the second the category of predication with possession by a different agent. Bloom concludes that the analysis of semantic structure requires information about the extralinguistic context.

However, an examination of the conversations in which these two utterances occurred also reveals the role that 'conversation-as-context' plays in the child's production and adult's comprehension of such utterances. Bloom gives the first as follows:

> [Mother (M) holding M's sock]
> M: Here's mommy's dirty socks. Wash. We'll do a laundry and we'll wash 'em. We do the laundry on Thursday too. You help me do the laundry?
> [Kathryn (K) pointing to M's socks]
> K: Mommy sock. [də]-dirty.
> M: Yes. They're all dirty. I know.

Apart from the extralinguistic context, the information relevant to understanding the meaning of the child's utterance is given in the preceding conversation. Her utterance is an imitation, with reduction of several morphemes, of her mother's *Mommy's dirty socks*. After her imitation her mother expands it by acknowledging it affirmatively, and this provides yet a third version of the same phrase. Thus the child is given in the course of the conversation several examples of the linguistic coding of the semantic information.

The other instance of *Mommy sock* in Bloom's data reveals still other contributions from the conversational context to the child's language development:

> [M putting K's sock on K]
> K: Mommy sock.
> M: There.
> K: Mommy sock.
> M: That's not mommy's sock. That's your sock. There.
> K: Kathryn sock.

In this instance the child's utterance is evaluated by the mother as an inadequate description of the current state of affairs. As a consequence the child changes her description both to fit her mother's reading of her own initial utterance and to fit the current state of affairs. Thus we see two notions of context in effect here: the context-of-ongoing-activity (involving people, objects and events) and the context-of-conversation (involving utterances as descriptions, evaluations, acknowledgments and repetitions). Both operate to provide the child with feedback as to how his utterances are taken by others.

1.1. The advantages of conversational units

The above examples illustrate the advantages of taking conversational units as the elements of communicative competence. If we construe an utterance as a functional act which conveys both a proposition and the speaker's attitude toward that proposition, and if we identify particular acts partly on the basis of their relation to others in the conversation, several advantages follow. First, we can use the same unit to describe all the stages of language development; in the case of a single-word production the child typically has an 'illocutionary' intention as to how he wants it taken; and even in prelinguistic communication the infant conducts 'proto-conversations' with others without linguistic content. Second, the 'double-contextedness' of utterance acts, as described above, provides the child with two sources in terms of which he can interpret the utterances of others; the ongoing task they are involved in and their talk both constrain how utterances will be heard. The child may even learn much about the meaning of words and about the syntactic patterns expressing structural meanings on the basis of (a) how adult expressions relate to the objects and events in the ongoing activity, (b) how adults order their words to describe activities and (c) how they evaluate his descriptions of the activities. A third advantage is that the child language theorist can use the 'double-contextedness' of talk as contextual constraints in postulating particular functional acts for children's utterance forms. Contextedness of this sort allows the investigator to have a firmer basis for assuming that his act categories converge with the child's own categories of utterance function. This is so because (a) act categories are derived from the interaction itself, from the relations between forms and contexts, (b) the child constantly displays his understanding of these contexts in his talk, and (c) others in the conversation constantly ratify the child's understandings.

Insofar as utterances function as acts in conversation, we may call these 'conversational acts' or C-acts. As a unit the C-act offers methodological advantages over the sentence, or related units of linguistic structure, in describing development. In addition to choosing forms, participants in conversation must also display (a) their orientation to the topics of discourse, (b) the purposes of their talk, and (c) their attitudes toward topics, purposes and other participants. It is not merely the case that utterances happen to occur in a setting and in relation to an activity; participants must *actualize* for each other how settings and activities are relevant to their mutual concern of the moment. And since any concern of social interaction must be shared by participating members, each must display not only his own understanding of their concerted activity, but also his understanding of other participants' understandings of such activity.

C-acts are the units of mutual display, and as such they are always subject to *immediate feedback*. This is the central methodological value of the unit. Since participants must make clear their orientations, this process of making things clear becomes available for observation by the investigator. There are several levels of feedback. Most obviously, when a participant has not adequately heard or understood another, he can seek clarification. Or when one participant states a position, another may corroborate, contest, evaluate, ignore it, etc. More pervasively, ethnomethodological analyses of conversation reveal how participants regularly open, close, maintain, monitor, repair, formulate, conclude and otherwise structure their conversational interactions (Sacks *et al.*, 1974).

Consider one of these conversational devices. Formulations occur when participants

'treat some part of the conversation as an occasion to describe that conversation, to explain it, or characterize it, or explicate, or translate, or summarize, or furnish the gist of it, or take notice of its accordance with rules, or remark on its departure from rules.' (Garfinkel and Sacks, 1970: p. 350)

As an example they offer the following remark by a policeman to a motorist: 'You asked me where Sparks Street is, didn't you? *Well, I just told you.*' Here the italicized segment formulates their conversational activity. The value of this precise form of feedback is that, in making explicit their view of what is going on, participants provide their own glosses as to how they understand their conversations and events. This in turn provides the investigator with the participant's own categories for his theoretical description, assuming that he has some independent grounds for describing events (for such grounds see McDermott and Dore, 1977).

Two other methodological advantages of focusing upon conversational episodes and acts concern adult attributions of intentionality to infants and the fact that C-acts occur in sequences. Ryan (1974) has shown how 'during extensive verbal interchanges . . . the mother actively picks up, interprets, comments on, extends, repeats and sometimes misinterprets what the child has said' (p. 199). And several studies have pointed out that from the earliest vocalizations of infants most mothers respond as though these were somehow meaningful. Adult imputations of intention thus provide the child with a crucially important model of the *conventional* interpretation of their intentions as signalled by vocalizations. It is rather obvious that adults introduce children to the community's shared meanings for words, but somewhat less obvious that they also display for the infant how others interpret the intention motivating the choice of words on any particular occasion. Yet interpreting whether an utterance is to be taken as, say, a command, a comment, a protest, etc., must contribute to the child's learning of how to use utterances appropriately in context.

Finally, C-acts must occur in sequences. That is, apart from the overall social episode, talk must accomplish its purposes on a local utterance-to-utterance basis. Dore (1978) defined a sequence as a series of utterances across speaking turns that share a topic and an 'illocutionary domain'. Topic sharing requires that constituents of contiguous C-acts have a specifiable semantic relation; sharing an illocutionary domain requires that the utterances be related in terms of phenomena such as intentions, expectations and beliefs relative to information being exchanged. For instance, in a sequence such as

(1) What is that?
(2) A ball

the first utterance solicits information about a noun phrase constituent signalled by *what* and the speaker expects the listener to provide that information. The second satisfies the conceptual, grammatical and illocutionary conditions raised by the question: it supplies the solicited label for an object in the form of a noun phrase constituent, and it satisfies the speaker's expectation.

The fact that C-acts must occur in sequences provides a basis for describing the relations between utterance forms and social contexts. A participant's C-act must be taken up by another in order to become operative in the conversation. If it is not taken up, the C-act may have no effect on subsequent conversation: if a listener does not hear a question, he is not responsible for answering it; if a listener acknowledges a speaker's assertion of a rule, he is responsible for abiding by it, and so on. In a sense, a C-act provides the raw material for creating social facts, and responses to it ratify that material as fact. Thus, ongoing verification of C-act phenomena is necessary for them to become operative as shared understandings.

2. Some recent studies of children's conversations

Some assumptions have already been made above concerning the units of conversation, and these will be treated explicitly below. I will mention here some of the work that has influenced our model, and I will focus on the issues raised in the introduction. I will not be able to refer to all those whose work contributed to the issues, but will refer to summaries of relevant work where possible. I am particularly interested in nursery school conversation.

Bruner (1978) has summarized much of the research on prespeech development relative to vocal communicative behaviour. Before producing words infants can secure the attention of another participant. They can sustain joint attention with another on an object or event in 'joint action formats'. They can convey intentions and expectations relative to the joint activity, which can be consistent with a role they take relative to another's role in the activity. They can take turns at participating in an orderly manner and they can perform actions which contribute to the success of joint concerns. Bruner gives as an example a description of an infant playing 'peekaboo' with his mother, where he displays most of the above features. These behaviours can be construed as 'proto-conversational acts' in that the properties of attention getting, intentionality, role playing, turn taking and goal-directed action are all necessary components of the verbally constituted C-acts which appear later in development. Notice, however, that all of these early behaviours concern the pragmatics of interaction as distinct from the representation of linguistic knowledge.

The talk of older children will only be mentioned here, but some recent work analysing dialogues between younger (grade-school) children and their teachers is of interest. Mishler (1975) focused on some of the social power relations realized by talk in classrooms. He identified questioning strategies used by teachers to control the flow of talk during lessons. Mehan (1978), using ethnographic methods and a restricted set of global utterance-act types, showed how lessons actually get accomplished on an utterance-by-utterance basis in school. In particular, he described how children 'get the floor' during a lesson and how they construct their speaking turn relative to lesson topics; and he suggested how such skills may relate to academic performance and evaluation. In a study closely resembling ours, Sinclair and Coulthard (1975) provided a model of classroom discourse, employing units ranging from linguistic acts to the structure of lessons. Although theirs was a ground-breaking study and we sympathized with their emphasis on linguistic structure, their scheme could not be applied successfully to our data. Apparently, a great deal of curriculum structure and socially determined presuppositions operate as shared knowledge between teachers and students which highly constrains their interactions. Nor did we find empirical support in our data for the hierarchical relations Sinclair and Coulthard claim to be operating among the levels of nonlinguistic organization, discourse and grammar.

The period during which children produce only one word at a time has been the focus of much controversy, primarily concerning whether or not to view the word as equivalent to a sentence (or 'holophrase'). Dore (1975) reviewed the arguments both for and against the holophrase position and concluded that the question of whether or not the word is a sentence is itself misleading. I proposed rather that the single word does involve a relation, but not a structural linguistic one. The single concept relates to the intention motivating its choice. The word partakes of the linguistic category of reference, but not of 'unsurfaced' sentence relations like subject or verb. The intention motivating the word manifests its relation to a context or participants or other aspects of the conversation in which it occurs.

Consider an utterance by a 13 month old girl who was just beginning to produce words (from Dore, 1973):

Child: Pot. pot.
     [She is looking at the research nursery supervisor, Cathy, who is at
     the coffee stand which does not yet have the coffee pot on it]
Cathy: What?
Child: Pot.
Cathy: Yes, I'm gonna bring the pot out.

Notice first that the child cannot merely be labelling a perceived object since it is not present. She must be referring to the entire action of the supervisor's preparing coffee, an action pattern which the child has often observed and which always concludes with the pot on the table. A conversational analysis of this sequence would yield the following. The child initiates the sequence with the C-act of description. Cathy acknowledges the description affirmatively and states her intention of bringing out the pot. Thus, as early on in development as this, conversation operates as an environment for learning. The adult both grammatically expands the child's utterance and provides feedback as to how she perceived the child's intention.

To turn now to the age range of from 2 to 4 years, Bloom *et al.* (1976) found that, while 2 year olds did not sustain the topic of interchanges initiated by adults, these same children at age 3 did sustain topics across turns by adding new and relevant information to the adult's. Yet at this age, of their utterances that occurred after an adult's, less than half were linguistically contingent on it, and less than 20 per cent of these were also contingent on the child's prior utterance if one preceded the adult's in such cases. In other words, children's topically related exchanges were seldom sustained for more than two turns. Bloom *et al.* (1976) suggest that the children found it easier to produce spontaneous, topically unrelated speech than contingent speech. Yet this need not mean that children of this age cannot sustain longer sequences. Garvey (1977), for example, found that children only slightly older could sustain extensive turn taking for certain kinds of interactions. Dyads as young as 34 months produced many (as many as 21 in one case) turns in trying to reach a mutual understanding.

The problem of constructing relevant speaking turns, turns with 'recipient design' orienting to the listener, is complicated by several factors. Participant structure (who is involved and in what status) and setting (including the situation at hand) are obviously paramount. Differences in these alone could account for different findings: data from the Bloom *et al.* (1976) study involved interaction between a single child and an adult visiting the child's home; Garvey's data were of peer interaction gathered in the 'quasi-experimental' setting of a 'nurseryschool-like' room. The task of the interaction, the topics of conversation and the kinds of conversational acts involved influence not only turn taking procedures but also the variety, length and structure of children's speech. In studies by Cole *et al.* (1978), 3 and 4 year old children attending a Head Start program in New York were taken to a supermarket; their talk there was compared to their talk when they returned to the classroom where they were questioned about their experience in the market. Among our findings were: (a) when two children were together, instead of one with the adult, their turns were more frequent, longer and more consequential for the course of conversation; (b) most of the children's talk in the market was more varied in C-act type, longer and more complex grammatically; but (c) answers to *wh*-questions were more frequent, longer and complex in the classroom. Apart from participant and setting differences, then, the task from the children's point of view made a difference in their talk. In the market the task was the informal one of talking about products, possibly shopping and of having fun, while in the classroom the task was conceived as more formal and test-like.

An increasing number of studies have been focusing on a variety of conversational skills and on the functions of utterances in speech events. Keenan (1974) found in the speech of twin boys, at 2;9, not only questions and commands, but also comments, acknowledgments and repetitions; moreover, they were also sensitive to overlap in turns, the audibility of a turn's content, interruptions, the lack of an expected response, even to nonrequestives, and other organizational features of their conversations. McTear (1978) has distinguished imitations from repetitions in children's speech and has pointed out several functions of the latter relative to participant relationships, roles, obligations, prior discourse and context. Gearhart (1977) suggests how 3 year olds in a nursery school setting negotiate the 'beginnings' of conversational episodes. And many interdisciplinary and cross-cultural perspectives on child sociolinguistics are represented in Ervin-Tripp and Mitchell-Kernan (1977).

2.1. Utterances as acts and their interpretation

Here we will consider particular kinds of C-acts and the rules for interpreting them. Garvey (1975) identified all the utterances which functioned as Requests for Action by her $3\frac{1}{2}$ to $5\frac{1}{2}$ year olds in dyadic peer interaction; utterances included not only imperatives but also indirect requests of many kinds where listeners could infer requestive intent. Garvey analysed all the utterances related to the requests and found that the children shared eight 'interpersonal meaning factors' (IMFs) relevant to the *domain* of requesting:

1. The request and response are reasonable
2. S (speaker) wants H (hearer) to do A (the future action)
3. H is willing to do A
4. H is able to do A
5. H is obligated to do A
6. H is an appropriate recipient of the request
7. H has rights which may conflict with the performance of A
8. Before the request, H did not intend to do A

In other words, the method was to interpret the children's own utterances as evidence of their understandings relative to requests. If a child, for example, responded with *I don't want to*, *I can't* or *I don't have to*, these were taken as evidence that factors 3, 4 and 5 were operative for the children.

Using the same method, Dore (1977a) characterized all the response types to questions (from both peers and the teacher) by the 3 year olds in the study described in the present chapter. Less than half of their responses matched the grammatical constituent solicited by the question (e.g. locative adverbials in the case of *where*-questions), but almost all their responses were 'pragmatically appropriate'. For example, there were response clarifications (*What did you say?*), internal reports (*I don't know*), answering the question with another question, qualified responses (to *What kind of number are you making?* a child replied *I'm not making a number*) and verbal compliances (such as *Okay* to *Why don't you do it?* question-directives).

Taking their responses to be evidence for the conditions they understand to underlie question–answer sequences, the following rule was formulated: the child will provide a canonical response if he:

1. Comprehends the presupposed proposition underlying the question
2. Believes this proposition to be true (or accurate)
3. Recognizes the addresser's expected illocutionary effect
4. Believes the addresser wants the requested information

5. Believes the addresser does not know the answer (or, as in examination questions, believes he is to display his knowledge)
6. Is able to (knows the answer)
7. Is willing to answer, that is, has no more pressing desire

These conditions for providing canonical information, like Garvey's Interpersonal Meaning Factors for requests, can be taken as operating in the domain of *wh*-questions for our children.

Apart from Garvey's and Dore's, a third kind of formulation for an illocutionary rule was provided by Ervin-Tripp (1977). She analysed the utterances of children of various ages and in a variety of situations relative to directives (the entire class of utterances whose intent is to get a listener to do something). She notes that the array of forms which children actually hear is quite large, and that many of these forms do not explicitly refer to conditions on requesting nor do they even mention the act to be performed (these latter being only 'hints'). In a nursery school setting, for example, children regularly interpret as directives such utterances as *It's clean-up time!* and *Twelve o'clock!* and *What's that on the table?* She proposes the following rule to account for the interpretation of indirect directives:

> 'Those utterances will be interpreted as directives which break topical continuity in discourse, refer to acts prohibited to or obligatory for addressees, mention referents central to such acts, or give exemplars of the core arguments of understood social rules. Examples would be "Somebody's talking", "I see chewing gum" and "Where does your dish go?"'

Notice that her 'talking' and 'gum' examples can be taken as directives only if talking and chewing gum are understood by all participants to be prohibited in those contexts.

Two theoretical points must be made about the factors for requesting, conditions on responding, and interpretations of directive intent; the first concerns differences in the phenomena they appeal to and the relations among the phenomena, the second concerns the problem of degrees of indirectness of form. Notice first that the conditions specified by Dore (1977a) for responding to questions refer both to propositional content (conditions 1 and 2) and also to illocutionary attitudes such as expectations, beliefs and desires relative to propositions. Garvey's eight factors, in addition, refer to social constructs such as rights, obligations and the appropriateness of the recipient. Ervin-Tripp's interpretive rule, furthermore, refers to what is obligated or prohibited in a given situation and to general rules for interacting in that situation.

How exactly illocutionary rules are to be written, and whether they should refer to social constructs or be tied to particular situations, are complex problems whose solution is beyond the scope of this chapter. But it seems clear that grammatical, illocutionary and social phenomena are distinct and partly independent, and that the conventional illocutionary force of propositional types can operate across social contexts. We might say that the relations among the phenomena are 'stratal', i.e. speakers can recognize the grammaticality of utterances independent of contexts, and they use this grammatical competence to parse surface structures they hear. For actual utterances, hearers also attribute illocutionary attitudes to speakers, and the conventional force of grammatical forms holds, unless otherwise indicated. However, for any particular context, different social factors will influence the interpretation of both propositional content and illocutionary intent.

These issues become clearest when participants (and investigators) must interpret acts of indirect forms. Beyond the canonical forms (i.e. imperatives for requests, interrogatives for questions, etc.) there are several kinds of indirectness. For requests, for example, there are *idiomatic* forms such as *Why don't you do X?* (Sadock, 1973). There are the forms, referred to above, which make *explicit conditions* on requesting. And there are the *hints* which require social rules for interpretation. We can phrase the relations among grammatical, illocutionary and social phenomena, with respect to the indirectness problem, in terms of the degree of inference a hearer must make in order to interpret a speaker's intent correctly. In canonical cases, the speaker's illocutionary intent and expected perlocutionary effect are conventionally paired; if he produces an imperative (or its idiomatic equivalent), for example, the hearer need infer nothing beyond what is given by the form. In the explicit-conditions cases, the hearer infers that, although the speaker produced an interrogative or declaration of desire, his expected perlocutionary effect is to get the hearer to perform the act referred to in the question or statement. In the hint cases, the degree of inference is greatest since the act is not mentioned in the non-canonical form – the gap between conventional force and expected effect is widest. Without mutually known rules, hints are not likely to be effective, and where rules are shared, any reference to them could suffice to convey a directive. The point is that in the above cases the basis for inference is shifted from the grammatical to the illocutionary to the social–interactional–contextual factors at hand.

There is a growing body of evidence that children both recognize and produce indirect forms of requests. To the question-directive *Can you take the baby?* from Garvey's (1977) data, the addressee reached for the doll. Examples of children from 3 to 5 responding to all the degrees of indirectness correctly have been reported in each of the Dore, Ervin-Tripp and Garvey works cited above. Shatz (1974), in fact, found that in experimental situations children as young as 2;0 responded as expected to their mother's indirect directives such as *Is the door shut?* It has been suggested, on the basis of reaction time experiments, that adults process the literal meaning of such forms first and the 'conveyed meaning' second (Clark and Lucy, 1975), but Shatz provides evidence that 2 year olds do not do this. She argues that the children do not have to process all the linguistic information, but can simply identify the act referred to in the adult utterance and perform it. This suggests that young children have sources other than the grammar to guide their appropriate conversational behaviour. Such sources may be in the form of interactional routines repeatedly engaged in with their mothers.

2.2. Taxonomies of acts and contextual constraints

Two issues remain to be reviewed: the basis for constructing taxonomies and the constraints on comprehending utterance functions. Many investigators have taken the 'lowest level of utterance function' to be those sentence moods explicitly marked by surface grammatical forms. In English this includes the declarative, interrogative, imperative and 'moodless' forms like the conditional; these moods have been conventionally paired with the functions of assertions, questions, commands and so on, respectively. The functions of children's utterances have been formulated at several different levels. Three fundamental prototypes were distinguished by Bühler (1934) as the 'expressive' (expressing emotions and attitudes), the 'evocative' or 'appeal' (affecting the behaviour of others) and the 'representational' or 'propositional' (representing and conveying information). This kind of typology originated in response to the need to distinguish the development of the infant's vocalizations, the latter function being the last to become manifested vocally. Most recently, arguing from the perspective of clause functions, Halliday (1975) proposed a similar trichotomy: the 'ideational', the 'interpersonal' and the 'textual' functions. This last concerns how utterances are linked to each other formally and to the situation in which they are used. His work is important in that it makes explicit relations between social context and grammatical structure. In discussing the development of what he calls the 'textual function' of language, he argues that 'textual' meanings are expressed

> 'through the medium of the lexicogrammatical system, and hence there
> is a systematic, though indirect, link between grammatical structure and
> the social context. This is the central feature of the environment in
> which the child learns language. Since everything that he hears is text –
> language that is operational in a context of situation – the fact that it is

systematically related to this context is the guarantee of its significance for the learning process. It is this that makes language learnable.' (p. 134)

Halliday expanded his set of functions in describing his child's earliest utterances. The functions, with his glosses for them, are: instrumental (the 'I want' function), regulatory ('do as I tell you'), interactional ('me and you'), personal ('here I come'), heuristic ('tell me why'), imaginative ('let's pretend') and informative ('I've got something to tell you'). These are quite useful categories, descriptively adequate on a general level and motivated on sociolinguistic, but nonstructural, grounds. But the list has problems. In applying it to other data, it is not always clear which function an utterance serves (no decision procedure for classification is provided). Contrary to Halliday's claim, a single vocalization during the earliest period can serve more than one function, or is at best equivocal. Halliday's own glosses for his data often strike some readers as bizarre, the basis for them being unclear. Despite his theoretical insights into the relations between structure and function, Halliday leaves unanswered (a) how the forms of utterances constrain the functions they perform and (b) how to constrain theoretically the list itself (see Dore, 1977b for details). At any rate, his functions are not based on the conversational status of utterances, nor are they directly constrained by the context in a principled way.

Inspired by the earlier work of Halliday's, a manual by Wells (1973) proposed an exhaustive coding scheme for scoring the interpersonal function, cognitive content and discourse structure of preschool children's talk. Most relevant to our concern, he posited approximately 140 act functions subcategorized by 'sub-sequence mode'. Each mode and some of the acts within it are given here (mode type is italicized): *Control*: wanting, offer, formulation, command, command to verbalize, command not to verbalize . . . ; *Expressive*: query state or attitude, approval, disapproval, command to apologize . . . ; *Representational*: statement, content question, response, justification of a universal moral sort . . . ; *Social*: talk routine, correction of form, demand for required form . . . ; *Procedural*: call, new topic marker, silence filler, persist in demanding response . . . ; *Tutorial*: correction of form, evasion, demand for required form . . . ; and the *Imaginative* subsequence was a tag-code for any of the above act functions.

Notice that the same act type is often repeated under different sequence modes, which partly accounts for the large number of act types. But, more importantly, the acts are formulated to cover a wide array of phenomena, ranging from the purely linguistic (question) to the social (silence filler, evasion). As a consequence of these facts, a generality crucial to act types may be lost (e.g. the last one or two acts listed for each sequence mode, except representational, above are all Action Requests); and the acts are formulated at different functional levels. Further, these codes can be applied only given several other kinds of distinctions, such as between 'social' and 'egocentric' speech, between 'role playing' and 'nonrole playing' and between 'appropriate' and 'inappropriate' responses. And the function of a given utterance is also affected by the content and structure of clauses on the one hand and the 'situational context' on the other. These important distinctions are discussed and assigned category codes in Wells and Ferrier (1976), but they provide no model explaining how these numerous 'levels' affect one another in the interpretation of utterances. Thus, the central problems for all such coding schemes remain; that is, we must find principled criteria for (a) motivating the level of linguistic act identified, (b) constraining the kinds of acts to be included and (c) defining a decision procedure for classifying utterances into acts. It should be pointed out, however, that several of the categories described by Wells, such as 'modes' of sequences, could function as the contexts constraining utterance interpretation.

3. The 'task' model of nursery school conversation

Dore *et al.* (1978) proposed a smaller set of acts which conflates many of those in Wells' scheme. Our taxonomy is based upon four criteria: grammatical form, illocutionary force, conversational status and contextual relevance. We assume that surface structures manifest underlying propositions and their presuppositions (Chomsky, 1965, 1975), some of the primary illocutionary forces of utterances (Searle, 1969) and the coherence of utterances in relation to discourse and social contexts (Halliday and Hasan, 1976). The central goal of our task model is to identify how children understand the illocutionary functions of utterances; but such functions are mitigated by the conversational positions of the utterances and the tasks in which they occur. For example, if a child says *That is a ball* in response to *What is that?*, his utterance functions primarily as a response, apart from its formal status as a description. Similarly, in a nursery school setting if a child says *That's my toy* during a play session, he is *claiming* possession, as distinct from merely describing the toy as his. Moreover, on a still 'wider' level of social context *That's my toy* could also function as a complaint (Sacks *et al.*, 1974), but our C-act scheme does not capture this level because its formulation requires more than specifying an attitude toward a proposition. Figure 1 is a network representation of the distinctions we do capture in our C-act scheme, and table 1 is a list of the C-act types we identified.

Primary conversational
function

General conversational
class

Particular conversational
act

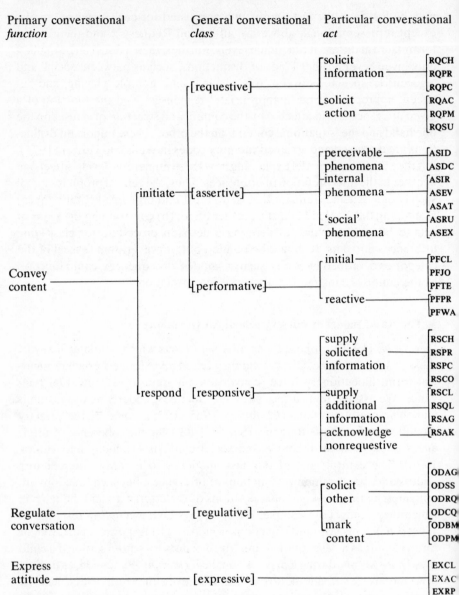

Figure 1. A network representation of the primary conversational functions, general classes and particular conversational acts in the coding schema

Table 1. *Codes, definitions and examples of conversational acts*

CODE DEFINITION AND EXAMPLE

Requestives: solicit information or actions

RQCH   CHOICE QUESTIONS seek either/or judgments relative to propositions: *Is this an apple?, Is it red or green?, Okay?, Right?*

RQPR   PRODUCT QUESTIONS seek information relative to most *wh*-interrogative pronouns: *Where's John?, What happened?, Who?*, When?

RQPC   PROCESS QUESTIONS seek extended descriptions or explanations: *Why did he go?, How did it happen?, What about him?*

RQAC   ACTION REQUESTS seek the performance of an action by hearer: *Give me it!, Put the toy down!*

RQPM   PERMISSION REQUESTS seek permission to perform an action: *May I go?*

RQSU   SUGGESTIONS recommend the performance of an action by hearer or speaker both: *Let's do it!, Why don't you do it?, You should do it.*

Assertives: report facts, state rules, convey attitudes, etc.

ASID   IDENTIFICATIONS label objects, events, people, etc.: *That's a car, I'm Robin, We have a boat.*

ASDC   DESCRIPTIONS predicate events, properties, locations, etc., of objects or people: *The car is red, It fell on the floor, We did it.*

ASIR   INTERNAL REPORTS express emotions, sensations, intents and other mental events: *I like it, It hurts, I'll do it, I know.*

ASEV   EVALUATIONS express personal judgments or attitudes: *That's good.*

ASAT   ATTRIBUTIONS report beliefs about another's internal state: *He does not know the answer, He wants to, He can't do it.*

ASRU   RULES state procedures, definitions, 'social rules', etc.: *It goes in here, We don't fight in school, That happens later.*

ASEX   EXPLANATIONS state reasons, causes, justifications and predictions: *I did it because it's fun, It won't stay up there.*

Performatives: accomplish acts (and establish facts) by being said

PFCL   CLAIMS establish rights for speaker: *That's mine, I'm first.*

PFJO   JOKES cause humorous effect by stating incongruous information, usually patently false: *We throwed the soup in the ceiling.*

PFTE   TEASES annoy, taunt or playfully provoke a hearer: *You can't get me.*

PFPR   PROTESTS express objections to hearer's behaviour: *Stop!, No!*

PFWA   WARNINGS alert hearer of impending harm: *Watch out!, Be careful!*

Responsives: supply solicited information or acknowledge remarks

RSCH   CHOICE ANSWERS provide solicited judgments of propositions: *Yes.*

RSPR   PRODUCT ANSWERS provide *wh*-information: *John's here, It fell.*

RSPC   PROCESS ANSWERS provide solicited explanations, etc.: *I wanted to.*

RSCO   COMPLIANCES express acceptance, denial or acknowledgment of requests: *Okay, Yes, I'll do it.*

RSCL   CLARIFICATION RESPONSES provide solicited confirmations: *I said 'no.'*

RSQL   QUALIFICATIONS provide unsolicited information to requestive: *But I didn't do it, This is not an apple.*

RSAG   AGREEMENTS agree or disagree with prior nonrequestive act: *No, it is not, I don't think you're right.*

RSAK   ACKNOWLEDGMENTS recognize prior nonrequestives: *Oh, Yeah.*

Regulatives: control personal contact and conversational flow

ODAG	ATTENTION-GETTERS solicit attention: *Hey!, John!, Look!*
ODSS	SPEAKER SELECTIONS label speaker of next turn: *John, You.*
ODRQ	RHETORICAL QUESTIONS seek acknowledgment to continue: *Know what?*
ODCQ	CLARIFICATION QUESTIONS seek clarification of prior remark: *What?*
ODBM	BOUNDARY MARKERS indicate openings, closings and shifts in the conversation: *Hi!, Bye!, Okay, Alright, By the way.*
ODPM	POLITENESS MARKERS indicate ostensible politeness: *Please, Thank you.*

Expressives: nonpropositionally convey attitudes or repeat others

EXCL	EXCLAMATIONS express surprise, delight or other attitudes: *Oh!, Wow!*
EXAC	ACCOMPANIMENTS maintain contact by supplying information redundant with respect to some contextual feature: *Here you are, There you go.*
EXRP	REPETITIONS repeat prior utterances.

Miscellaneous codes

UNTP	UNINTERPRETABLES for uncodable utterances.
NOAN	NO ANSWERS to questions, after 2 seconds of silence by addressee.
NVRS	NONVERBAL RESPONSES for silent compliances and other gestures.

We recognize that many levels of contextual frames affect the interpretation of illocutionary intent, where 'frames' may refer to phenomena as diverse as the sentence frame for a word, the sequence frame for an utterance, the topic, ongoing event, social episode, mode of interaction, plans of the participants and so on. Our model is intended to try to explain how utterances were understood by the participants in our study in terms of the 'tasks' they were performing at the time of utterance. The participants in the study were seven 3 year old middle-class children and their teacher who met four days a week, two hours per day over a seven-month period at a research nursery at the Rockefeller University. We videotaped and transcribed their talk for one consecutive hour of each of the last four months of the study. Their tasks included lessons, painting, drawing, block-building, having snacks, cleaning up the room and so on. Our model is cast in the form of a global 'sociolinguistic schema' which the participants use in conducting their goal-directed, task-oriented conversations. In terms of cognitive processing we assume that the task operates as a 'top-down' constraint on how propositions and intentions are understood, while grammatical form operates as a 'bottom-up' constraint on meanings.

By displaying for each other in successive turns at talking what they are actually orienting to, participants together accomplish the task, but on varying levels of completeness and complexity. The children, on the basis of their knowledge of grammar and illocutionary functions, are able to control local sequences which often accomplish task-related transactions. But the teacher must structure, on the basis of her curriculum goals, the higher order aspects of planning the tasks. She must supervise, for example, the temporal sequencing of the tasks in phases (making sure that materials are available and that things are properly done before concluding); and she must control the hierarchical requirements of task accomplishments such as regulating the step-wise requirements of cooking for instance. Figure 2 is a display of the elements of text and task in our model, and it indicates some of the relations between them.

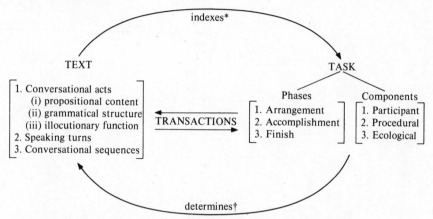

Figure 2. Schema of text and task elements and their relationships

Indexing factors include:
1. Display
2. Announce
3. Formulate
4. Repair
5. Hold accountable

Determining factors include:
1. Choice and recognition of
   (i) propositional content
   (ii) grammatical structure
   (iii) C-act
2. Interpretation of sequence

In this model tasks are organized sequentially in terms of 'arrangement', 'accomplishment' and 'finish' phases; and hierarchically, C-acts (or more often sequences of C-acts) constitute 'transactions' which realize 'components' of tasks. Components include the 'ecological' (concerning locations and materials for the task), the 'procedural' (how it is to be done), and the 'participant' (who is involved) components. Among the relations between talk and task are that, on the one hand, in their talk participants announce, formulate, repair and otherwise hold each other accountable to doing the task; on the other hand, the ongoing task strongly influences participant talk on the propositional, grammatical and pragmatic levels. All of these notions are exemplified in table 2 which contains excerpts from a coded transcript of a 'clean-up' task.

In the opening sequence E, the teacher, announces the task that is to come and solicits volunteers to wash the table. K and D then compete for first turn

Table 2. *Excerpts from a coded transcript of a clean-up task* (T is the teacher and other initials represent the children: from Dore et al., in press)

Sequence	Turn	Speakers	Utterances (and context)	C-act	Transactions/comments
			Arrangement phase of clean-up task		
E		T–?	Alright,	ODBM	Announcement
			Let's clean the table so we can eat!	RQSU	
			[D, K & R talk and play with markers while		
			T washes sponges at sink]		
		T–all	Who'd like to wash the table?	RQPR	Participation
			[K and then D run toward sink]		
	7	K–T	ME.	RSPR/PFCL	
	8	D–T	ME.	RSPR/PFCL	
F	9	K–D	NO, ME.	PFPR	
	9′	D–T	ME too.	RSQL	
G	10	T–K/D	Well,	ODBM	
			Wait a minute!	RQAC	
			Don't fight!	RQAC	
			There's three sponges.	ASID	
H	11	D–T	The BIG sponge!	PFCL	
E	11′	R–T	No, ME. [R walking to sink]	?RSPR	
G	10c	T–?	Where's the blue sponge?	EXAC	
I	12	D–T	I have the *big* sponge.	PFCL	
J	12′	R–T	Ca . . . Can I clean up the table too?	RQPM	
I	13	T–D	What?	ODCQ	
	14	D–T	I have the *big* sponge.	PFCL	
			I have the *big* sponge	EXRP	
J	15	R–T	Ca . . . Can I have a big sponge?	RQPM	Allocation
	16	D–R	No,	RSCO	
			I have a big sponge.	PFCL	
I	17	T–D	Big or beige?	ODCQ	
			What are you saying?	ODCQ	
	17′	D–T	Big. [D points to sponge]	RSCH	
			[D takes big beige sponge; T gives K		
			sponge; they run to table to wipe]		
J	18	R–T	Can I have one?	RQPM	Participation
	19	T–R	Yes.	RSCO	
K	19′	J–T	I want to *wash* the table. [walks to sink]	RQPM	
	20	R–T	Can I have one?	RQPM	

	Turn	Speaker	Utterance	Code	Note
M			[R begins wiping but sponge falls to floor]		
	28	K–?	Where's my sp....		?
	29	R–K	Not on the table.		?
	30	D–K/R	[R gets sponge; others pat the table with sponges; S watches them; 12 seconds pass]		
	31	T–all	It's done. [K looks at his sponge]	ASDC	premature closing
	32	R–T	It's done. [R looks at her sponge]	RSRP	Hold-accountable
	33	K–?	It's not. It's...	RSAG	
			What's done?	ODCQ	
			It's done.	RSPR	
			The table, the table . . . [chanting]		
N	34	T–R/K	Turn it around. [K and R chant 'the table'; T puts cleanser on the table]	RQAC	
O		–all	Can you get this off, all that where the brown is?	RQCH/RQAC	
	35	D–T	[D and R try to wipe it off] We can't	RSCH/RSCO	
	36	R–T	We can't.	RSCH/RSCO	
P	37	T–all	You have to push hard. Scrub!	RQSU	
				RQAC	
...			Finish phase of clean-up task		
Z	51	T–all	Let's put the sponges in the sink! [D walks away, leaving sponge on table] If you think the table's clean, put your sponge in the sink!	RQSU	Instruction
			[T, holding cups, wipes table with D's sponge; R tries to take cups from T's hand]	RQAC	
		–D	D,	ODAG	
			Can you put your sponge in the sink? [K, J and D run off with sponges]	RQCH/RQAC	

Procedural

at washing. (Braces on the left in the utterance column indicate overlap in speaking turns; the longer brackets to the far right indicate the components actualized by the corresponding utterances which, in turn, are coded in the C-act column.) In turn 11, D claims the biggest sponge (thereby initiating an ecological component of allocating the washing materials). And then other children negotiate participation with the teacher. The accomplishment phase begins when R starts to wipe the table. When the children encounter difficulty, the teacher issues procedural instructions to help them. The task ends with the teacher trying to get the sponges returned to the sink. It is hoped that this brief sketch will adequately demonstrate how conversation can constitute the accomplishment of nursery school tasks.

4. Conclusion

The model outlined here provides a framework for further research. In fact, we are now in the process of (a) refining the theoretical constraints on the level of C-act formulation, (b) constructing an adequate decision procedure for classifying utterances exhaustively into C-act categories, (c) specifying the properties of shared social plans which seem to determine much of the talk, (d) of inferring some of the cognitive processes (especially inferences among utterances and between them and tasks) that underlie verbal interaction, and (e) identifying the 'social frames', intermediate between C-act sequences and tasks, which affect utterance interpretation. The items listed above as kinds of 'frames', from the linguistic to the 'macro-social', in particular must be understood in order for us to make claims about what controls interpretation.

If it is possible to construct a theory of utterance interpretation, we believe that the natural conversation occurring in school settings is a convenient place to begin because it is constrained by the purposes of educational interaction. If our model is on the right track, then it appears that work on several clearly delimited domains should continue. At the very least, a model of conversation must deal with the levels of propositional *content*, grammatical *form*, illocutionary *function*, cognitive *process*, conversational *procedure* and social *frame*. Hints as to how each of these domains operate are available in the literature, across several disciplines. However ambitious (not to say naïve) it seems, we believe it is time to try to integrate the insights into these domains and to bring this integration to bear on actual conversations in order to test models for observational adequacy if possible. Whether or not there can now exist a theory of utterance interpretation seems to depend upon how well the findings of linguistics, psychology and the other social sciences can be integrated. After this attempt we might then be able to focus upon what most needs doing first. We are betting that some version of a transformational grammar is a necessary foundation for such an enterprise, but that it will only provide a very limited account of what is actually understood in interpreting an utterance. It will have to be supplemented by the levels mentioned above. And, it is hoped, we will not have to know each participant's encyclopedic knowledge in order to discover how conversations are organized.

18. Conversations with children

Catherine E. Snow

Only ten years ago it was thought possible to study language acquisition without studying the language addressed to children. All the research done before the late 1960s on the nature of linguistic input to children was carried out by linguists and anthropologists studying 'baby talk'; i.e. they collected data on the special lexicon used with babies, and several noted that the baby talk words could be analysed as simplified forms of adult words (reviewed in Ferguson, 1977). Other features of baby talk noted fairly generally were prosodic – high pitch and exaggerated intonation contours (see, e.g. Blount and Padgug, 1977). This research on baby talk was done primarily with the purpose of describing a certain speech register, not with any specific interest in the relevance of baby talk to language acquisition (though several papers noted that the informants justified using baby talk with a didactic motive, 'to make the language easier to learn'). Much more recently, psychologists and linguists interested in language acquisition have started studying the nature of the speech addressed to children. They have concentrated on syntactic and semantic rather than lexical or phonological aspects of that speech, and have tended not to use the term 'baby talk' to refer to their object of study. Other terms have been coined, such as 'motherese', which gives the misleading impression that only mothers talk in a special way to children. In this chapter, I will avoid both such neologisms and the term baby talk, and will use clumsy descriptions like 'the speech addressed to children' instead.

This chapter will be primarily concerned with the nature of speech addressed to children as a factor in acquisition. Until very recently, children's acquisition of language was studied without considering the speech addressed to children because it was assumed that the nature of that speech made very little difference to the course of language acquisition. It was thought that there was a large innate component in linguistic ability which buffered language acquisition against sparseness, complexity and confusion in the primary linguistic data. Two positions on the nature of this innate linguistic component can roughly be identified: the notion that the innate component supplied knowledge of linguistic universals such as the existence of word

363

classes and the importance of order of elements (McNeill, 1966b), and the position that the innate component supplied procedures for discovering the grammar of the language to be learned (Fodor, 1966). Under the assumption of either innate grammatical knowledge or innate grammar discovery procedures, it could be argued that only a minimum of linguistic input was adequate to enable the child to learn language, and that both a high level of complexity and a large amount of misinformation (e.g. ungrammatical utterances, slips of the tongue) in this linguistic input could easily be tolerated.

In this chapter I will attempt to present the current position regarding the relationship between the linguistic environment of the language learning child and language acquisition. Since the present position is the result of several major shifts of emphasis within a relatively short time, it is perhaps useful to review the research which has been done on this topic historically.

1. Stage I: Simple, well-formed, redundant

The first analyses of speech addressed to children were undertaken in response to the view that such input was ill-formed (characterized by mistakes, garbles, ungrammaticalities, false starts, mispronunciations and stutters; see, for example, Miller and Chomsky, 1963, and McNeill, 1966b) and that it was very complex. This description assumed that the 'primary linguistic data' available to the child did not differ in any important way from the language used among adults (Fodor, 1966). It was a fairly simple matter to disconfirm that view. Various investigators collected and analysed samples of speech addressed to children in the age range 18 to 36 months by their mothers (Broen, 1972; Drach, 1969; Kobashigawa, 1969; Phillips, 1973; Remick, 1976; Sachs et al., 1976; Snow, 1972a). Every measure used in these studies for grammatical complexity (mean length of utterance, incidence of subordinate clauses, mean preverb length, incidence of conjunction, etc.) or for well-formedness (incidence of hesitations, disfluencies, within constituent pauses, false starts, etc.) revealed that the speech addressed to children aged 18 to 36 months was much simpler and much more grammatical than the speech addressed to adults. Not only was speech to children found to be simple and well-formed, but it was also found to be highly redundant. Mothers repeated phrases and whole sentences and paraphrased their own utterances frequently (Snow, 1972a). Individual mothers used certain 'sentence frames' (e.g. That's NP; Where's NP; See NP) quite frequently (Broen, 1972).

The general conclusion drawn from the Stage I studies of mothers' speech was that the speech addressed to children of language learning age was well adapted to the children's own linguistic level. In view of the nature of this speech, it could also be concluded that the innate component to language ability might be considerably smaller than proposed by Chomsky (1965), McNeill (1966b) or Lenneberg (1967), and that it need not contain a great deal of specific linguistic structure. Information about linguistic structure was available from the input; the innate component need only ensure that children attended to linguistic input, distinguished it from irrelevant input, and expected it to be structured.

Two additional bits of information which became available at about the same time as the results of the early mothers' speech studies supported this conclusion. First, it was found that not only mothers, but also all adults and even children aged 4 to 5, produced simplified, redundant speech when addressing 16 to 36 month olds (Andersen and Johnson, 1973; Sachs and Devin, 1976; Shatz and Gelman, 1973). This finding meant that such speech could be assumed to be universally available to language learning children; not just children growing up in middle-class North America and cared for by their mothers, but also children living in extended families and cared for by older siblings or cousins have access to a modified speech register. Second, it was found that children can play an active role in selecting which sentences they hear. Adult sentences which were far more complex than the child's own utterances, and those begun with an unfamiliar word, were less likely to be attended to than simple sentences begun with familiar words (Shipley *et al.*, 1969; Snow, 1972b). This finding helped explain why children did not become confused and misled by the complex utterances overheard from adult–adult conversation or from radio and television. Not only was most of the speech available to young children adapted to their linguistic level, but speech not adapted to their level could simply be filtered out.

The findings of the first set of mothers' speech studies were purely descriptive. No one had undertaken to sort out what it was about talking to children that caused speakers to speak simply, grammatically and redundantly – whether their age, their inability to speak correctly, their low status, their size, their cuteness, or their unwillingness to do as they were told was the relevant variable. An indication that feedback from the child played some role in influencing the mother to talk simply and redundantly came from a study in which mothers were asked to make tapes which would later be played to their children (Snow, 1972a). Although the mothers in this situation did speak more slowly, simply and redundantly than they would have to an adult, they did not speak as simply or redundantly as when the child was present with them. This finding suggested that the characteristics of maternal speech could be explained primarily as adjustments made in response to cues from the child. If maternal speech was too complex, the children would tend to become inattentive and would fail to comply with requests or respond to questions. These cues would cause the mother to simplify her speech until it reached a level of complexity at which the child was optimally compliant and attentive. An implication of this suggestion was that mothers' speech would be quite well adapted to the child's linguistic level. The characteristics of maternal speech would thus be expected to change abruptly in the direction of simplicity, well-formedness and redundancy at 12 to 14 months, when the child first showed signs of understanding, and then gradually over the next three to four years to reapproach the normal adult values.

Oversimplification 1: Mothers' language lessons. One possible interpretation of the findings discussed above is that the mothers were providing their children with ideal 'language lessons' – a carefully graded curriculum of information about the structure of their mother tongue (Levelt, 1975). Such an interpretation is, of course, an unwarranted extrapolation from the findings. Although mothers do often teach their children about language, about the meanings of words, about how to form plurals, past tenses, etc., what mothers are doing most of the time is simply trying to communicate with their children. A side effect of their attempts to communicate is the set of modifications described. These modifications are not the result of attempts by the mothers to teach their children to talk: rather, they are the result of attempts to communicate effectively with them. See Garnica (1977) for comments from mothers about why they talk to young children as they do.

Oversimplification 2: No innate component. Another misinterpretation of these early findings was the conclusion that there was no innate component to language ability. It is, of course, absurd to argue that any complex behaviour is entirely innate or entirely learned. Innate and environmental factors always interact in the development of complex abilities, and both are of crucial importance. It is not, however, absurd to ask what proportion of the developmental variation in some complex ability like language is attributable to innate as opposed to environmental factors, for it is certainly the case that environmental factors can be relatively more important in determining an individual's achievements for one type of ability (e.g. solving arithmetic problems) than for another type (e.g. singing on key). Chomsky's position regarding language was that it was more like singing on key than like arithmetic; anyone with an innately good ear can learn to sing on key, with only minimal practice and exposure to music, and any human being (i.e. any possessor of the species-specific innate linguistic structure) can learn language on the basis of minimal exposure to even complex and ill-formed utterances. The correct conclusion to be drawn from the Stage I studies was that Chomsky's position regarding the unimportance of the linguistic input was unproven, since all children, in addition to possessing an innate linguistic ability, also receive a simplified, well-formed, and redundant corpus. Thus, the relative importance of the innate and the social factors could not be determined. The prediction was made that children without access to such a simplified, redundant corpus would be unsuccessful or retarded in learning language. If such could be proven to be the case, then it could indeed be concluded that an innate, species-specific, linguistic component was relatively less important than Chomsky had hypothesized. But the conclusion could be drawn that the innate component was of no importance only if the provision of a simplified, well-formed and redundant corpus enabled nonhumans with human-like cognitive capacities, e.g. young chimpanzees, as well as human children, to learn language.

It has been suggested that the results of the mothers' speech studies actually support Chomsky's position, by demonstrating that the speech addressed to children is really syntactically quite complex (Newport, 1976; Newport et al., 1977). The basis for saying that such speech is complex, despite the short utterance length and absence of complex sentences, is that questions and imperatives are used very frequently in addition to declaratives. Newport et al. argue that a well-designed curriculum for second language learners starts with the 'basic sentence type', the sentence type in which the order of elements in surface structure shows the least deviation from deep structure. In English, this is the declarative, which maintains the underlying order of elements Subject NP–Aux–V–Object NP, and in which none of these elements is deleted. In questions, the order of the Aux and the subject NP is inverted, and in the imperative the subject NP is deleted. How could a child learn the underlying order, argue Newport et al., from a corpus which has about 40–60 per cent of such deformed sentence types? It is clear that English-speaking children do operate with a general S-V-O rule, since not only their declaratives but also their early questions show this order of elements.

The fact that children hear a mixture of surface orders would indeed be confusing, if there were no basis for distinguishing among those orders or for noting that they are used for different functions. In such a case, one would expect that the child might pick the most frequently offered order, and use that as his basic order of elements. Evidence from children learning Italian and Finnish suggests that this does indeed happen. In Finnish, declarative sentences have a free order for subject, verb and object, although the S-V-O order is most frequent. One child studied chose the order her mother used most often, S-V-O, and used it almost exclusively (Bowerman, 1973a). Italian mothers most often use the emphatic V-O-S order, rather than the normal S-V-O, to their children, and Italian children are relatively late in acquiring correct word order (Bates, 1976). Why, then, do English-speaking children not start using verb-first orders in their declarative sentences, since imperatives and questions, which show a verb-first order, are more frequent than subject-first declaratives? One reason is certainly that the three sentence types are well distinguished in English by intonation contour. Imperatives and questions addressed to children have a final rise in intonation, whereas declaratives show a falling intonation. There is evidence that mothers use, and even very young children interpret, sentences which end in a rise as signals that some response is required (Ryan, 1978). Thus, children do have a salient acoustic basis for separating out declaratives, imperatives and questions, rather than treating them as one class of utterances. But then why do they choose the less frequent declarative rather than the more frequent question to model their word order on? Perhaps they don't in the beginning, since in fact both declaratives and almost all questions show the same order of subject and main verb. It is the auxiliary which is preposed in questions in English. If no auxiliary is present, one is introduced by the rule of *do*-support. There are various sources of evidence suggesting that children may not attend to such auxiliaries, since they are unstressed (Van der Geest, 1975) and unfamiliar (Shipley *et al.*, 1969). Thus, the child presented with the questions:

> Is daddy going?
> What's the doggie doing?
> Who is eating the cookie?

may in fact be hearing

> Daddy going + rising intonation
> What doggie doing + rising intonation
> Who eating cookie + rising intonation

In every case, the S-V order is maintained. This specific explanation only holds, of course, for languages like English in which questions are formed by S-Aux inversion. A much more common pattern is S-V inversion, which would present the problem envisaged by Newport *et al.* More study of languages which form questions by S-V inversion is needed in order to determine whether children learning such languages start forming utterances using an order of elements not frequently modelled in the input language. In French, for example, it may be the case that mothers more often use questions of the form

> Est-ce qu'il va?

which maintain the declarative S-V order, rather than forms like

Va-t-il?

There is evidence that Dutch-speaking mothers very often use modal or other auxiliaries in their utterances, which cause the lexical verb to be placed in the final position in questions and imperatives as well as in declaratives (Klein, 1974). Thus, Dutch children hear utterances which almost all show the surface order S-Aux-O-V (declaratives), Aux-O-V (imperatives), or Aux-S-O-V (questions), corresponding to the generally accepted underlying order S-O-V.

The general conclusion from the available evidence must be that the basic order of elements is modelled for children more frequently than the distribution of utterances across sentence types might suggest.

2. Stage II: The here and the now

The Stage I descriptions of speech addressed to children showed a curious oversight: no description was given of what the mothers were talking about. This oversight becomes more comprehensible if one realizes that the Stage I studies were done in the late 1960s, at a time when analyses of child speech were primarily concerned with children's acquisition of syntactic knowledge. It seemed, thus, most relevant to analyse maternal speech so as to determine how it could provide information about syntactic structure. The child's task was seen as one of testing many different innately supplied hypotheses about the syntax of the language being acquired against the patterns observed in the input, and thus eventually eliminating the incorrect hypotheses. Under this view, the acquisition of semantics was seen as a separate task facing the child.

In 1972, Macnamara argued that this view of language acquisition was incorrect, that the acquisition of syntax could be explained only if it is recognized that children collect information about the relationship between syntactic forms and semantic structures. (Similar views were expressed by Schlesinger (1971a).) In other words, children figure out the rules underlying syntactic structure by using the cues provided by the meaning of an adult's utterance. This implies that children must be able to determine what an utterance means on the basis of nonsyntactic information – since the syntax is precisely what must be learned. Macnamara suggested that knowledge of the meaning of the important lexical items plus knowledge of what is likely to be said about those entities or actions given the situation must enable the child to guess correctly what the utterance means. This implies, of course, not only that the child must be a good guesser, but also that the adult must say the kinds of things the child expects to hear, that adult and child share a way of looking at the world. Greenfield and Smith (1976) have argued that such a shared view of the world does exist, and that this is what enables adults to interpret children's early, presyntactic utterances. Macnamara's argument goes the other way around – that adult utterances have no syntactic structure as far as young children are concerned, and that children in the early stages of language acquisition must, therefore, interpret adult utterances in the same way as adults interpret children's utterances, by relating the words used to aspects of the situation being described. After many thousands of chances to observe that the word referring to the agent precedes the word referring to the action in adult sentences, the child can start to induce a rule about the order of those semantic elements. Much later, after the child starts to hear sentences in which words which obviously do not refer to the agent stand in the first position (e.g. passives like *The cake got eaten*) he will be forced to abandon this simple semantic rule for a syntactic rule incorporating the notion of sentence subject.

This model of how language acquisition proceeds rests on the presumption of *semantic* limitations on adult utterances – that they describe those aspects of the situation at hand which are most obvious to the child, and that the adult utterances are limited to those topics about which the child has extralinguistic information.

If one reanalyses maternal speech keeping this model of semantic matching in mind, then it becomes clear that the semantic content of speech addressed to young children is indeed severely restricted. Mothers limit their utterances to the present tense, to concrete nouns, to comments on what the child is doing and on what is happening around the child (Phillips, 1973; Snow *et al.*, 1976). Mothers make statements and ask questions about what things are called, what noises they make, what colour they are, what actions they are engaging in, who they belong to, where they are located, and very little else (Snow, 1977b). This is a very restricted set of semantic contents, when one considers that older children and adults also discuss past and future events, necessity, possibility, probability, consequence, implication, comparison and many other semantic subtleties. This limitation on the semantic content of maternal speech can to a large extent explain the syntactic simplicity commented on above. Propositions of name, place, state and action can be expressed in short utterances without subordination or other syntactic complexities. The syntactic simplicity can thus to a large extent be seen as an artefact of semantic simplicity.

The conclusion drawn from the Stage I studies was that because of the constant 'steering' function of the child's attention and signs of comprehension, the syntactic complexity of the maternal speech would be quite well matched to the child's linguistic level. It has since been demonstrated that no high correlation exists between the child's linguistic level and most measures of the syntactic complexity of maternal input (Cross, 1977; Newport, 1976; Newport *et al.*, 1977). It is of course true that mothers speak more simply to 2 year olds than to 4 year olds or to 8 year olds, but there is no strong evidence that there are precise gradations of complexity in maternal speech, i.e. that mothers adjust their speech complexity one notch upwards every time their children learn one new construction or expand their mean length of utterance by one morpheme. This is, of course, unsurprising, since speakers possess no mechanism for very precisely adjusting the syntactic complexity of their speech. Speakers do, however, have semantic complexity under control – their choice of lexical items (cf. Brown, 1958), of topics to discuss and of comments on those topics. So it is not surprising that the syntactic complexity of maternal speech only grows by fairly large jumps as children get older. One would expect, however, that semantic complexity would be more finely tuned to the child's linguistic level – that the topics discussed and the sorts of comments made would indeed grow slowly with the child's comprehension and production abilities. Although no one has ever performed quite the correct analysis, there is indirect evidence that such is the case. Mothers limit the kinds of semantic relations used in their own speech to those used by their children (Snow, 1977b). Furthermore, mothers start using semantic categories frequently in their speech to children only after the children have introduced these categories in their own speech (Van der Geest, 1977). Children may also introduce empty forms (cf. Van der Geest's example of his son's use of the passive with active meaning: *I am being jumped off it* for *I am jumping off it*), or unifunctional forms, thus leading their mothers to think that they control these forms fully and that they can be used in speech addressed to the child. Children almost always introduce a semantic category with no explicit marking (e.g. *Go circus* referring to a past event; *Mama do it* meaning 'Mama will do it'). After such a category is introduced by the child, the mother starts to use it frequently, thereby providing information about how these new semantic notions should be realized. Thus, although a mother's speech is morphologically and syntactically much more complex than her child's speech, semantically it is less in advance.

3. Stage III: Talking to one another

Assuming that the semantic component of maternal speech is finely adjusted to the child's linguistic ability, how does this happen? By what mechanism do mothers keep their speech content pitched at the right level?

The answer to this question is quite simple, as soon as one attains the seemingly obvious (but for researchers in this field, long awaited) insight that mothers do not talk at children, but with them. A large proportion of maternal utterances are responses to child utterances, and almost all maternal utterances are directly preceded and followed by child utterances. In other words, mothers and children carry on conversations with one another. These are, in fact, very special kinds of conversations, in that the partners are very unequal. The mother can speak the language much better, but the child nonetheless can dominate the conversation, because the mother follows the child's lead in deciding what to talk about. A very common pattern is for the child to introduce a topic, and for the mother to make a comment on that topic, or for the child to introduce a topic and make a comment, and for the mother to then expand that comment. Thus, at a semantic level, the mother's speech is very much shaped by the child's linguistic abilities, his cognitive abilities, his ideas and interests.

Interestingly, the above description of child-directed discourse accounts for the occurrence of expansions, the characteristic of maternal speech which was first commented upon by Brown and Bellugi (1964). Expansions are full, correct expressions of the meanings encapsulated in children's telegraphic utterances. They are, thus, the ultimate example of a maternal utterance which is semantically related to the preceding child utterance. It was hypothesized that provision of expansions might greatly aid the acquisition of syntax, since the expansion gives information about the full, correct realization of the child's intended meaning at the time the child wishes to communicate that meaning. Evidence for positive effect of expansions has been found (Nelson et al., 1973), though provision of extra conversation with the child even without including expansions seems to have an equally beneficial effect (Cazden, 1965; Nelson et al., 1973). It may well be that expansions can provide crucial bits of information about syntax or morphology, but that this information if not available from expansions will be picked up from other sources. Greenfield and Smith (1976), for example, note a number of cases in which early two-word utterances were modelled on sequences in the immediately preceding dialogue.

Too few conversationally based analyses of maternal speech have been performed to say anything about how general the description of maternal speech as adding comments to conversational topics introduced by the child is. Various researchers have described mother–child interaction in ways which correspond to the above model. Shugar (1978), for example, refers to mothers and children interacting dyadically to 'create text'. She has described how mothers produce utterances which create context within which very simple child utterances become meaningful parts of the rather complex whole. For example, if the mother says

Who's just coming in?

and the child answers

Dada

then the child utterance can be interpreted semantically as referring to an agent of a presently occurring action, whereas the same utterance without the linguistic context might be uninterpretable. Cross (1978) has found that the percentage of maternal utterances which are semantically related to preceding child utterances is the best predictor of the child's linguistic ability. This implies that children who learn to talk quickly and well have constant access to such semantically related maternal utterances. Bates (1975) has suggested that second children, twins and institutionalized children may learn language more slowly than children whose input comes mainly from adults because egocentric peers do not provide enough interpretable, semantically relevant messages. But Lieven (1978a, b) has described one mother–child pair where well-constructed dyadic texts were extremely rare. A high proportion of child utterances were not responded to by the mother at all, and the responses which did occur were very often semantically unrelated to the child utterance. They were very likely to be comments like 'Oh, really?' Despite receiving very little semantically relevant speech from her mother, the child in question did eventually learn to talk normally, though her speech at the time Lieven was studying her was highly repetitive, uninformative and difficult to interpret. Thus, though it seems clear that the provision of much semantically relevant speech is advantageous for language acquisition, it has not been proven that access to such speech is crucial to normal language acquisition. Although the amount of semantically relevant and interpretable speech available to children may vary greatly, as suggested by Lieven's findings, it seems unlikely that any but the most socially deprived children have no access at all to such speech.

Mothers are able to provide semantically relevant and interpretable speech because they follow up on topics introduced by the child. It seems clear that some mothers will be better at doing this than others but also that some children will be better at eliciting semantically relevant and interpretable speech than others. Children with poor articulation, for example, will produce fewer interpretable utterances for the mother to expand upon. Children whose speech is highly repetitive, such as the little girl studied by Lieven (1978a), are less interesting to converse with than children who frequently introduce new topics. It is also possible for mother and child to be focused on different aspects of the world, in which case the kinds of comments made by the mother do not match the child's intentions or interests. In such cases, the child's language acquisition can be slowed down (Nelson, 1973b).

Interestingly, the kind of semantically relevant and interpretable speech described above begins long before the children themselves begin to talk. This indicates that it is not produced purely in response to utterances from the child. Mothers talking to babies as young as 3 months show many of the same characteristics of 'mothers' speech style' as are present in speech to 2 year olds. Some of the characteristics, such as questions, occur with even greater frequency in speech to younger children. The most striking similarity between speech to very young babies and speech to children aged 18 to 35 months is the extent to which the mother's speech is directed by the child's activities. Infant behaviours such as reaching for something, changing gaze direction, laughing, smiling, vocalizing, even burping, coughing and sneezing, can always evoke specific relevant responses from the mother. At 3 months of age, the majority of maternal utterances refer only to the child. By the time the baby is 6 to 8 months of age, and is showing many clear signs of interest in objects and activities about him, the maternal utterances also refer to those objects and activities (Snow, 1977a). Thus, the semantic steering of maternal speech by the child begins very early, and may be the basis for the child's discovery of some predictable relationship between utterances and events.

Another aspect of early mother–baby interaction which may contribute to the child's acquisition of language is the opportunity provided to the baby to communicate effectively by using some minimal signal. An example of this, described by Bruner (1975), comes in the course of bouncing games like 'Ride a cock horse'. The mother bounces the baby with a regular rhythm while reciting the first lines of the verse, but gives a 'big bounce' on the last line. After a number of repetitions, the mother often pauses before the 'big bounce' until the baby jiggles expectantly. The mother interprets the jiggle as a message to go on. This interpretation probably has two effects: (a) the mother receives the satisfaction of feeling that her baby is communicating with her, and (b) the baby learns that his own behaviours function as communicative signals. Mothers' use of questions to small babies creates a very similar situation: in response to a question like 'Have you had enough to eat?', almost any behaviour, from fussing to remaining perfectly still, can be interpreted as either, 'yes' or 'no'. By posing the question, the mother creates the possibility of interpreting her baby's behaviour. It seems very likely that much experience during the prelinguistic period with interactions within which the baby can communicate effectively, despite his limited communicative skills, contribute to the acquisition of language.

4. Conclusion

Two basic questions have motivated research into the nature of the speech addressed to children:
1. Why do people use a special speech style when addressing children?
2. Does the special speech style used with children have any effect on the course of language acquisition?

It has been hypothesized that people talk as they do to children because they are trying to teach them to talk, because they are trying to get them to understand, because they are tying to hold their attention and because they are trying to carry on conversations with them. No doubt each of these motives plays some role in producing the modifications of speech style described above. The most important factor seems to be the desire to communicate with children – to respond to their utterances and to elicit responses from them. The desire to communicate implies talking so as to hold their attention and be understood. It may also involve some explicit teaching of language, especially of vocabulary. Aside from fulfilling the communicative function, some aspects of the modified speech style used with small children undoubtedly serve an affective function. Soft tones of voice, diminutives and special baby talk words may be used with babies just because they seem appropriate for cute and cuddly addressees (Brown, 1977; Garnica, 1977). Finally, many of the features of speech addressed to children, such as the high frequency of questions, the provision of syntactic and semantic expansions on child utterances, result from the process of carrying on conversations with immature conversational partners.

Does the use of special speech styles with children facilitate language acquisition and, if so, which features of the modified speech style have an effect? All the evidence suggests that every child growing up in any culture has access to simplified, redundant, well-formed and semantically concrete speech, so it is impossible to say whether children without such input acquire language normally. There is only a small amount of evidence relevant to the question whether language acquisition can be facilitated by access to certain features of modified speech style. This evidence suggests that semantic interpretability and relevance are the crucial features in facilitating language acquisition. It seems likely that the speech must also observe certain limits on syntactic complexity and ill-formedness, but that these limitations are introduced automatically as a result of the semantic simplicity. If one were asked right now to advise an anxious mother how to teach her child to talk, the best answer would be 'Watch what he's doing, listen to what he's saying, and then respond.'

19. Variation in child language

Gordon Wells

It is entirely appropriate that the chapter on variation in child language should be found in the Part entitled 'Contexts and determinants'. In spite of the fact that overviews of the subject contain a number of confident assertions about variation in child language development (e.g. sex and class differences), most of the work on variation has been extremely naïve – mainly because researchers have only just begun to understand the theoretical and methodological problems that have to be resolved before any worthwhile results can be obtained.

1. Types of variation

Let us imagine that we pick a group of children and attempt to describe them – their personalities, the sort of homes they come from, their favourite activities, who they spend their time with, and so on. We shall quickly find that they are all different – different, probably, with respect to each of the headings that we consider, and certainly different in the combined profiles that we might attempt to construct. Let us now imagine that we also record some samples of speech from each of these children in the course of their everyday activities, and without anyone being aware that we are making the recordings. When we come to describe these speech samples, we shall even more quickly realize that each one is different, and that a large part of this difference is directly related to the differences that we have already observed in the activities, preferences, etc., of the children, and in the situations in which the speech samples were recorded.

The researcher into child language is thus faced with a dilemma: he must decide either to reduce the problem to manageable proportions by strictly limiting the number of variables that are taken into account, or to take account of as many as possible, at the risk of being overwhelmed by the complexity of the task. In practice, most researchers have attended to only one or two sources of variation, usually those that are most amenable to description, making the simplifying assumption that the remaining variation is arbitrary or coincidental. Such a strategy has had the effect of leaving completely unexplored such pervasive parameters as the situation in which speech occurs (Cazden, 1970), and of reducing to polarized dichotomies such parameters as social background (e.g. Bernstein, 1971), which are, in reality, made up of a cluster of interacting parameters, each varying continuously over the total population. As a result, there is as yet no overall theory of variation, merely a number of relatively unrelated findings that still await integration. Given this situation, it may be helpful to start by making a number of broad distinctions between different types of variation, and by considering the ways in which they may be related.

Firstly, there is the child's actual language behaviour. The most frequently used general measure is Mean Length of Utterance (MLU), originally measured in words, but in more recent studies in morphemes, following Roger Brown's procedures (Brown et al., 1969; Slobin, 1967). The validity of this measure has been the subject of a considerable amount of critical discussion,[1] but because of its global nature and the ease with which it can be calculated, it probably remains the most satisfactory, although crude, general indicator of stage of development, at least in the first few years (Brown, 1973: pp. 53–4). Other measures that have been used include vocabulary size (Nelson, 1973b); vocabulary comprehension (Brimer and Dunn, 1963; Huttenlocher, 1974); sentence comprehension (Lee, 1969; Reynell, 1969) and a variety of measures based on samples of spontaneous speech, including syntactic complexity (Menyuk, 1969), semantic modification, semantic range and pragmatic range (Wells, 1978). A further possibility involves the construction of a profile from several of these measures, but this raises difficult problems of quantifying what are essentially qualitative differences.

Variation on these linguistic measures is of little interest in itself, however; what is of interest is the co-variation between linguistic behaviour and other child attributes with respect to which variation is found in the population. Since language changes and develops over time, age is obviously the first such attribute to consider. A typical strategy here is to assume the existence, over the population as a whole, of a linear correlation between age and linguistic development, and to examine rate of development (defined as score at a given age on one of the measures discussed above) in relation to other nonlinguistic attributes. A second strategy is to look at changes in linguistic behaviour over time in particular individuals in an attempt to identify styles of development (Nelson, 1973b; Ramer, 1976), which are then related to other child attributes.

---

[1] Crystal et al. (1976) contains a summary of these criticisms and Brown (1973) and Wells (1978) offer a qualified defence.

It is possible to divide the other attributes that have been the subject of investigation into four main groups, as shown in figure 1. Only one group is, strictly speaking, concerned with attributes of the children themselves, those that might be called *inherent* attributes: sex, intelligence, personality, etc. The remaining three cover different aspects of the children's environment: long-term characteristics of children's *social background;* factors in the social and physical *situation* in which the children's linguistic behaviour occurs; and the style of *linguistic interaction* which provides the context for their acquisition and use of language. Of course, variation, whether in children's overt linguistic behaviour, or in rate or style of development, is not caused uniquely by any one of these groups of attributes, but is the outcome of an interaction between all of them, as figure 1 attempts to indicate.

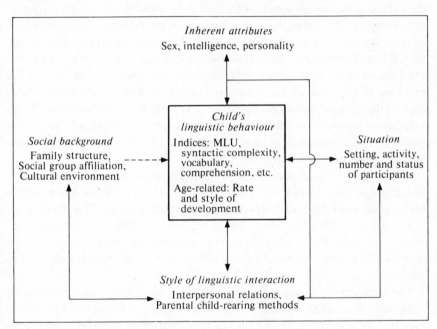

Figure 1. Types of variation

2. Methodological problems of data collection and analysis

The systematic study of linguistic variation is a comparatively recent development, and has so far been largely restricted to investigation of the linguistic correlates of social differentiation in the population of mature speakers of varieties of American English (e.g. Labov, 1972, 1977).

Although his work is not of direct relevance to the subject of variation in early child language, there are many important lessons to be learned from the methodology that he has developed, and in particular from his discussion of the problems that have to be faced in any text-based study of language. Three of these will be briefly considered.

2.1. Obtaining reliable data

Labov refers to this problem as the 'observer paradox', as in the absence of an observer it is difficult to obtain interpretable data, but the very presence of an observer may so alter the situation that the speech that is observed lacks the qualities of spontaneity and naturalness which are essential for the investigation. Child language researchers, rightly convinced of the need for the richest possible contextual information to assist in the interpretation of the children's utterances, have usually convinced themselves that the effect of their presence is minimal; but we should remain sceptical. I have suggested elsewhere (Wells, 1977a) on the basis of our own recorded data, that the frequency of 'expansions', for example, may owe a great deal to the presence of an adult who is relatively unfamiliar with the child, for whose benefit the mother, quite unconsciously, expands or interprets all the child's utterances that may be difficult for the visitor to understand. There are probably other systematic changes in parents', if not in children's, behaviour when an observer is present.

A second problem associated with reliability concerns the child's physical and emotional state when the speech sample is obtained. Even when there is no bias introduced by an observer, it is important to ensure that the data are not distorted by the child being ill or upset or in any other way not 'on form'. Whilst it is probably not possible to measure this in any very precise way, the mother will usually be able to say whether or not her child is behaving as usual.

The same problems arise, but in an even stronger form, when the data for study are obtained in experimental or test-like situations. Labov (1970) has vividly described the way in which many children respond to the questioning of unknown adult research workers by a stubborn refusal to utter anything more than monosyllables, and Rose and Blank (1974) have shown how children may be led to produce apparently illogical or inappropriate responses as a result of their misperception of the artificial testing context in which the questions or instructions are presented.

2.2. Obtaining representative data

This issue needs to be considered on two levels. Firstly there is the need to sample from the child population in such a way that variation within that population is adequately represented. Where there are *a priori* theoretical grounds for distinguishing particular subgroups, this is relatively straightforward; but in the absence of theoretically motivated distinctions, it is necessary to draw a sample of randomly selected individuals which is large enough for significant groupings within the population to be empirically determined from a *post hoc* analysis of the data. Although this issue is well understood in the field of experimental psychology, it has frequently been ignored in child language research, presumably because of the dominating interest in the universal characteristics of language development.

Secondly there is the need to sample from the population of situations in which speech occurs. Since what people say is usually relevant to the communication situation as they perceive it, we can expect the characteristics of a speech sample to be influenced by the nature of the situation in which it is recorded. This may be most apparent with respect to the lexical selections that are made, but it will also be true of functional categories, and to a certain extent of syntactic structures also. For example, requests for permission are more probable in the presence of an adult than amongst children, and clauses linked by causal conjunction more probable when playing with construction toys, for example, than when playing a rough and tumble game.

Even if it were possible to control the kaleidoscopic shifting from one context to another that makes up a typical child's day, we do not yet know enough about the significant parameters of situations to sample from them in such a way as to maximize the chances of obtaining a speech sample that represents a child's range of control over all aspects of language. For example, in a study of the emergence of early semantic relations within the sentence, I found that the expression of possession was likely to emerge earlier in children with older siblings (Wells, 1974). Of course it is possible to control this particular source of variation by studying only first-born children (although this would make the study unrepresentative in other important ways), but the example is indicative of the enormous range of differences in the patterns of organization of family life which subtly influence the range of experiences, and through them the specific structures, meanings and functions of language, which provide the context for the child's acquisition of language as a means of communication and reflection.

2.3. The quantification of linguistic data

Even when the researcher has satisfactorily resolved the problems of obtaining reliable and representative data, he is still faced with the problem of quantifying them in some appropriate way. Labov (1977) notes that 'even the simplest type of counting raises a number of subtle and difficult problems. The final decision as to what to count is actually the solution to the problem in hand; this decision is approached only through a long series of exploratory maneuvers'(p. 82). It is just such a series of exploratory manoeuvres that are necessary when analysing children's speech. Firstly, there are problems in the allocation of tokens to types. For example, in the relatively unstructured speech of an 18 month old, is the *'s* in *What's that?* to be counted as a token of the contracted copula, or is it to be treated as an inseparable part of an unanalysed question-asking utterance type? If it is recognized as a copula, is the contracted copula to be treated as a separate type from the uncontracted copula, as in *What is that?*, or are instances of contracted and uncontracted equally tokens of the same type – the copula? Similarly, with somewhat older children, it has been observed that relative clauses occur almost exclusively in relation to verb complements (Limber, 1973). Is it necessary, therefore, to set up more than one relative clause type, one for verb complements, another for subject relative clauses, and so on; or should it be argued that there is only one type, with the imbalance in position of occurrence being attributed to pragmatic factors, such as the tendency for the subject of a sentence to express 'given' information, with a consequent lack of necessity for it to be fully specified linguistically?

Having resolved such problems, a decision still has to be made as to whether it is the occurrence of types that will be treated as significant or whether some frequency of tokens will be treated as the measure of control. When a particular element is well established, it may well be that it is variation in frequency that is of interest, but where the focus is on the point at which a particular element is acquired, one single token of the type may have to be taken as the appropriate evidence, because a criterion set in terms of a greater token frequency would seriously underestimate the number of children having control of the type in question. For example, in a sample of approximately 18,000 utterances that we have obtained from 60 children, each recorded three times between 36 and 42 months, 12 children used a passive verb a total of 19 times, no child producing more than 3 tokens, and several children producing 1 token on the first occasion but none on the two subsequent occasions. Here, there is no obligatory context (Brown, 1973) in which to look for proportional occurrence, and given so low an absolute frequency there can be no certainty that children who are not observed to use a passive do in fact lack control of this type. A possible solution here is to use cumulative frequency over a number of observations.

2.4. Problems of size

As will be apparent by now, the biggest problem facing research on child language that tries to take systematic account of even one or two of the multiple sources of variation, whilst at the same time obtaining data amenable to detailed linguistic analysis, is the sheer size of the sample required. Early research, such as the normative studies reviewed by McCarthy (1954) and the later study by Templin (1957), was based on a substantial number of children (480 in Templin's case), but the corpora obtained were neither reliable nor representative as samples of naturalistic speech,[2] and the linguistic analysis was extremely crude. More recent research, in the tradition inaugurated by Brown et al. (1969), and Miller and Ervin (1964), has succeeded in obtaining corpora of data large enough to allow a detailed linguistic analysis, but at the price of restricting the number of children to a handful and by ignoring most of the social and situational causes of variation.

The Bristol study, with a sample of 128 children, representative of the urban child population in terms of sex, month of birth and class of family background, and with recordings made of each child once every three months at frequent intervals over a normal day at home without an observer present, has attempted to overcome the problems of reliability and representativeness, but the quantity of child speech obtained at each recording (120 utterances on average) and the intervals between recordings still pose problems for certain types of quantitative analysis, as suggested above.[3]

3. Inherent attributes

3.1. Sex

References to the superiority of girls with respect to almost all aspects of language development abound in the literature, although it is extremely rare to find such extreme differences as those reported by Ramer (1976), in

[2] Templin's method of obtaining her speech data, which she claims was as nearly as possible a replication of that used by McCarthy, is described as follows: 'Children were taken into a room with an adult examiner and, after rapport was established, fifty remarks of the child, usually consecutive, were taken down' (1957: p. 15). It is worth remembering, also, that 'taken down' means taken down in writing on the spot.

[3] For a fuller account of this study, cf. *Journal of Child Language* 1 (1974): 158–62.

whose sample all the girls but none of the boys were characterized by a style of acquisition associated with rapid development. Reviewing the literature in 1954, McCarthy wrote:

> 'The vast accumulation of evidence in the same direction from a variety of investigators working in different parts of the country [USA] employing different situations and methods of observation, and employing different analyses and linguistic indices, certainly is convincing proof that a real sex difference in language development exists in favor of girls . . .' (1954: p. 580)

However only a few years later, Templin, summarizing her own findings, had this to say:

> 'When the performance of boys and girls is compared over the entire age range, girls tend to receive higher scores more frequently than the boys, but the differences are not consistent and are only infrequently statistically significant . . . It may be that the differences which have appeared in the literature have been overemphasised in the past. It may also be that over the years differences in language ability of the two sexes have actually become less pronounced in keeping with the shift towards a single standard in child care and training in the last few decades.' (Templin, 1957: pp. 145–7)

A similar conclusion is reached in a more recent review by Cherry (1975), and our own research strongly supports the view that what differences there are between the sexes are in rate rather than style of acquisition, and that they are rarely significant.

However it is the last sentence of the quotation from Templin that is most interesting, for it heralds a new trend in studies of sex differences, towards an investigation of the differential treatment of the two sexes as an explanation of what had previously been taken to be a genetic superiority. Under this hypothesis, the relatively greater loquacity and fluency of girls (Smith and Connolly, 1972) would be attributed to differential expectations of, and communication with, the two sexes by their parents. There is some evidence for this in the responses in our maternal interview when the children were aged $3\frac{1}{2}$ years.

In this context another finding from the Bristol research is of particular interest. Using the corpus of speech collected at $3\frac{1}{2}$ years, sequences of conversation were distinguished according to whether they were initiated by the child or by another person. All sequences were also categorized according to the context in which they occurred and the dominant purpose of the conversation. Seventy per cent of all sequences whose initiator could be determined were initiated by the child, and for these sequences there were only small and mainly insignificant differences between boys and girls with respect to context or purpose. In the remaining 30 per cent of sequences, the vast majority of which were initiated by the mother (and a few cases by the father), there were highly significant differences in the contexts in which adults chose to initiate conversations with boys and girls (table 1). The most striking contrasts are in the contexts of Play with Adult Participation, Helping and nonplay activities. Adults initiate a far greater proportion of sequences with boys in contexts of play (a ratio of 3·5:1); in contrast, over half the sequences with girls were in Helping and Non-play contexts (a ratio of 2:1 compared with boys). This suggests that adults emphasize more 'useful' and domestic activities in their interaction with girls, whilst the emphasis with boys is towards a more free-ranging, exploratory manipulation of the physical environment.

Table 1. *Percentage proportion of conversations initiated by adults with boys and girls in different contexts*

	Toileting, dressing & meals	Playing alone	Play with other child	Helping & nonplay activities	Play with adult	Talking & reading	Watching TV	Total
Boys	14·4	8·1	2·7	28·8	18·1	22·5	5·4	100%
Girls	12·1	3·4	2·6	56·8	5·2	19·0	0·9	100%

$\chi^2 = 25·037$ p<0·001

3.2. Intelligence and personality

Interpretation of the undoubted correlations between intelligence and linguistic development reviewed by McCarthy (1954) is made more difficult by the fact that most tests of intelligence, even those purporting to test nonverbal intelligence, require certain minimal skills in communication, usually through language, for their administration, if only so that the subject can be made aware that a response is required and that it should take a particular form. Furthermore, neither intelligence nor language is a unitary phenomenon and developments in the two domains interpenetrate each other in an interactive way which suggests that any effort to establish a global, unidirectional, causal relationship – in whichever direction – is almost certainly misguided. It seems much more plausible, instead, to hypothesize a continuum of causality extending in both directions, on which observed correlations between particular tests and linguistic subskills might be located. The relationship between size of vocabulary and a test of intelligence such as the English Picture Vocabulary Test (EPVT) (Brimer and Dunn, 1963), which depends on the comprehension of pictured objects and events, for example, would probably fall at the language → measured intelligence end, whilst the relationship between the ability to recognize spatial or temporal sequences or configurations, as measured by Raven's Progressive Matrices, and rate of acquisition of the hierarchical structure of syntax, particularly subordination and embedding, would probably fall towards the intelligence → language end.

Attention has recently also been focused on the problems of cultural bias in tests of intelligence and in many of the instruments that have been used to assess linguistic skills and maturity (Labov, 1970). It is clear, therefore, that the co-variation between intelligence and language must also be firmly related to environmental variation, and particularly to social and cultural differences in the valuation that is put upon different types of intellectual and linguistic performance.

Finally in this section, brief mention should be made of the variation associated with what I called earlier 'personality'. Here again the relationship is difficult to untangle, since communication style is one of the bases on which judgments of personality are made (Argyle and Kendon, 1967; Crystal, 1975). To the extent also that personality is learned through interaction with the social environment, the directionality of causation is likely to be complex. In practice, this aspect of variation has so far received little attention at any level, although some of the work in literary stylistics bears on this issue. In the field of child language, Nelson's (1973b) investigation of the effect of interaction strategies takes account of certain variables in both mother and child that could be included under the heading of personality, and finds that degree of match or mismatch between mother and child on these variables is 'most potent in accounting for the child's progress during the second year' (p. 113). It seems likely that the differences between the active, outgoing child and the placid, retiring child will influence many aspects of the linguistic interactions that they experience, and that this in turn may have an effect on both rate and style of language learning, just as it has already been shown to affect some aspects of social learning.

4. Social background

This is probably the most controversial of all the dimensions of variation in child language and more has certainly been written on this subject and its supposed implications for educability than on all the other dimensions of variation added together. For this reason, only selected aspects will be considered here; for a comprehensive and critical review of the literature, the reader is referred to two recent books: Dittmar (1976) and Edwards (1976a).

Since the formal organization of language and the meanings and purposes it serves to communicate are learned chiefly through social interaction, it seems self-evident that insofar as this varies from one social group to another there will be variation in child language which can be related to group membership. And on this point there is very little disagreement. Where the disagreement is to be found is on (a) the nature and size of the variation, (b) the parameters that should be used to distinguish significant social groupings and (c) the mechanisms responsible for the relationship between social group membership and linguistic variation.

The greater part of the debate has taken socio-economic status (SES), or social class, as the point of departure (they are usually treated as if they were equivalent), thus pre-empting a serious consideration of possible alternative parameters. Research findings were initially presented in terms of rate of development, with children from lower SES groups showing a developmental lag, frequently at a statistically significant level (McCarthy, 1954; Templin, 1957). An evaluative element was soon added, and the developmental lag became a linguistic deficit (Deutsch, 1967; Loban, 1963); then, under the influence of Bernstein's formulation of the class–code relationship, a difference in style of acquisition was introduced, the middle class being said to develop an exploratory and explicit use of language in contrast to the expressive and implicit use of the lower class (Bernstein, 1960, 1965; Bereiter and Engelman, 1966).

At about this point, in reaction to the extreme 'deficit' claims, two new strands entered the debate. On the one hand, Labov used evidence from his studies of nonstandard English to point out that many of the characteristics of lower-class speech that were being treated as indices of deficit were in fact systematic differences of dialect. On the other hand, and at about the same time, Bernstein reformulated his theory in terms which made it clear that the codes regulated habitual 'performance' and were not to be taken as a description of underlying 'competence', or if so, only of 'communicative competence' (Bernstein, 1971: p. 146). However, this reformulation is less radical than might appear, for restriction to a restricted code is still seen as the probable cause of cognitive deficit.

These two new developments have been seen by many to be in direct opposition to each other. But this is not the case. Labov's argument, that nonstandard dialects are as adequate for the development of logical thought as any other dialect of English, is surely compatible, in principle, with Bernstein's thesis concerning underlying code orientations to different orders of meaning, particularistic and universalistic, in whatever dialect, standard or nonstandard. The main reasons for the assumed incompatibility of the two arguments are, firstly, the fact that the majority of the nonstandard dialect speakers considered by Labov are working-class and, secondly, that Bernstein has persistently argued that the restricted and elaborated codes have social origins in orientation to the means of production: the restricted code both springs from, and transmits, the social structure experienced by the working class. The working class are, almost by definition, restricted code speakers.

There appear to be two main hypotheses concerning the relationship between social class and language development:

(i)   that lower-class children are relatively retarded in acquiring control of the dialect of their community
(ii) that lower-class children are more likely to use restricted speech variants and to have restricted code orientation towards context-dependent, particularistic meanings

The evidence for and against both hypotheses is, as might be expected, difficult to disentangle.

Hypothesis (i). In the Bristol project we have tried to make a start by (a) stratifying an original random sample to give equal representation to four divisions on a continuum of social class, (b) sampling from a wide range of the naturally occurring contexts in which speech occurs in the children's daily lives, with no researcher present during the recording and (c) treating local dialect forms, where they occur, in the same way as the equivalent standard forms. The results of the analyses carried out so far do not lend strong support to the hypothesis of a developmental lag.

No significant class differences have been found with respect to the amount of speech produced in the time-based samples, in the contexts in which child speech occurs, or in the range of pragmatic functions realized. It seems, therefore, that in very general terms, language plays the same sort of role for children of all social classes. Only one clear test of the hypothesis has been carried out so far with respect to rate of acquisition of syntax: age at reaching the criterion for control of the auxiliary verb system. On this there was no significant difference in rate, neither was there any class difference in style. However there was a significant correlation between class of family background and number of different auxiliary verbs, both forms ($r = 0.331$, $p < 0.01$) and meanings ($r = 0.363$, $p < 0.01$) that had been used by the age of $3\frac{1}{2}$ years (Wells, 1979a).

With respect to MLU, the results are equally indeterminate: at some ages, and with respect to some measures of MLU only, there are significant correlations between class and MLU. But even when statistically significant, such correlations are only of the order of r = 0·3, showing that class alone accounts for only a minor part of the variance in MLU. The one index on which there is a clear-cut relationship with class is score on the test of oral comprehension (r = 0·589, p < 0·001).

However, before accepting these latter results as supporting evidence for the hypothesis, it is necessary to distinguish carefully between what children can do and what they actually do. As far as MLU is concerned, there are two important qualifications to be made to the results as they stand. Firstly, although it is possible to treat different dialect forms as equivalent when considering the acquisition of grammatical rules, it is less easy to make adjustments for the same forms when measuring utterance length. Some of the class difference in MLU is therefore probably caused by certain features of the local Bristol dialect, which is most marked in the speech of some of the lower-class children. In this dialect a number of grammatical morphemes are frequently omitted, such as -s on third person singular nonpast verbs, be and have in affirmative, declarative sentences containing be going to, have got, have got to, and perfective aspect. Secondly, measures of MLU are derived from spontaneous behaviour and are thus an index of what the speaker chooses to do rather than of what he can do. Beyond a certain level of development, a speaker selects the forms through which he realizes his meaning intention according to what he considers appropriate in the context. It may be the case that in a variety of contexts lower-class children select grammatical forms which have the effect of depressing their MLU; but this by itself cannot be taken as an indication of less mature language development, unless there is also evidence that they cannot use the full range of grammatical options in contexts in which they judge them to be appropriate. Insofar as this question has been properly investigated, the evidence does not support the hypothesis that lower-class children show a general developmental delay in grammatical development, although there is considerable evidence that they do not habitually exploit their grammatical resources to as full an extent as their middle-class peers (Edwards, 1976a).

Hypothesis (ii). On the second hypothesis, the evidence is less conclusive. Much of the relevant research has been carried out by Bernstein and his colleagues, and many of their results lend support to the hypothesis of a relationship between class and code. However, the contexts from which the speech data were obtained were both nonspontaneous and highly specific, so it is difficult to assess how far the results were distorted by the differential responses of the two groups to the task situations and by their differential perception of the task demands, as Adlam (1977) admits in her discussion of these investigations. Hawkins (1969), in a study of the different uses of the nominal group in telling a story from pictures, found that the restricted code stories, with their high proportion of exophoric reference, were typical of the working-class group. But they could be taken as entirely appropriate in the situation, since child and researcher were both able to see the pictures.

Furthermore, the relationship between the hypothesized underlying code, with its somewhat speculative cognitive implications, and the speech variants actually observed in specific situational contexts has continued to elude really satisfactory description. The fact that, under what they consider to be appropriate circumstances, working-class children can be lexically explicit, producing utterances of appropriate grammatical complexity and lexical specificity to achieve their communication goals (Edwards, 1976b; Francis, 1974) makes it inappropriate to continue to characterize the differences in terms of a binary distinction of either class or code, and must cast doubt on the usefulness of the construct 'code' itself. Or, if the concept is to be retained, we should allow for a plurality of codes, in the same way as we do with registers. Certainly, much greater attention must be paid to aspects of context than has typically been the case in such studies (but cf. Adlam (1977) for an attempt to relate code and context).

It is in relation to education that the putative relationship between class and restriction in the uses of language has assumed the greatest importance, for large-scale policy decisions (e.g. Halsey, 1972; Plowden, 1967) have been based on evidence such as that produced by Bernstein's Sociological Research Unit, and by similar research in the United States (e.g. Deutsch, 1967; Hess and Shipman, 1965, 1968). In her research in this tradition into class differences in the uses of language, Tough (1977) even labels her two contrasted groups of 3 year olds in terms of predicted educational 'advantage' and 'disadvantage', although the chief criterion for selection was parental status: professional as opposed to unskilled or semi-skilled occupation. In this research it is not code as such which is the focus of investigation, but the relative frequency with which children from the two groups make use of different functions of language. The major functions distinguished are Self-maintaining, Directive, Interpretative and Projective, with distinctions of uses within these categories being arranged in a notional order of complexity. Comparing samples of speech recorded in a play situation, Tough found marked differences between the two groups, to the point that only one child in the disadvantaged group 'had scores on some measures that are better than the scores of one or two children in the advantaged group' (1977: p. 85). Although the meaning of 'better' is not defined, these results lead her to conclude that 'these children, coming from differing home environments, had established different priorities for expressing meaning, and different orientations towards the use of language' (p. 87).

However, these conclusions were reached on the basis of data that failed to meet the criteria discussed in the opening section of this chapter. The speech samples were obtained from only one situation, with the observer present and taking notes, and the frequency data were not submitted to statistical analysis. In an attempt to carry out a partial replication of Tough's research, I undertook a similar analysis of samples of spontaneous speech at home for a subsample of the Bristol project children, who were drawn from the full spectrum of family background (Wells, 1977b). Statistical tests on both sets of data revealed that the Bristol sample showed a much less clear-cut picture. In the first place, the frequency of uses considered to be most complex by Tough was so low for the samples as a whole that no statistical significance could be attached to differences between groups. In the second place, although there were still some significant differences between classes with respect to the more frequently occurring categories, there were few of the linear trends indicative of simple correlation, and some of those that did occur were in the opposite direction from that predicted by Tough. As with the first hypothesis, therefore, the evidence is conflicting and certainly does not allow firm conclusions to be drawn on the relationship between class and language use.

Nevertheless one point of very general significance does emerge from the comparison of these two studies and that is the distorting effect that is produced when social variation is reduced to an opposition between two monolithic classes, and claims made that ignore the very large degree of variation that certainly exists within these classes. There is a persistent tendency to reduce variation to dichotomy, and nowhere is this tendency more prevalent than in discussion of class and code differences.

5. Experience of linguistic interaction

Given this emphasis on the social context of language acquisition, it is natural that attention should have come to focus more and more on characteristics of caretakers' conversation with their children. The qualitative modifications of mother's speech to young children are now well documented (Snow and Ferguson, 1977; chapters 17 and 18 above). Naturally, most of this research has been searching for the universal characteristics of the linguistic input to the child. In the remainder of this chapter, however, I shall examine the evidence for variation in input.

5.1. Context

In an earlier pilot study (Wells, 1975), a qualitative distinction was made between three groups of contexts in which conversation occurred: *Mother-*

ing (which included such contexts as bathing, dressing, feeding and cuddling), *Independent* (all contexts where the child was alone, with other children only, or receiving no more than sporadic and divided attention from an adult) and *Joint Enterprise* (contexts of shared activity, such as doing the housework together, play with adult participation, looking at books together or just talking). Comparing the proportion that occurred in each of the three groups of contexts, a significant relationship was found between rate of development at $2\frac{1}{2}$ years and proportion of speech addressed to the child in contexts of Joint Enterprise. There was also a suggestion that it was the greater opportunity that the mothers of first-born children had to engage in talk in the context of shared activities, compared with the mothers of the children with one or more siblings, that accounted in large part for the first-born children's more rapid development. This finding still has to be confirmed with respect to the larger sample, but in analyses to date, effect of birth order alone has not been found to relate to variation in rate of acquisition.

5.2. Linguistic features

The systematic modification of caretaker speech to young children has been investigated in a number of experimental studies, and has been found to vary with the age of the child: caretaker speech increasing in MLU, grammatical complexity, proportion of disfluency and vocabulary type–token ratio with increasing age of the child (Brown, 1973; Fraser and Roberts, 1975; Snow, 1972a). Fraser and Roberts (1973) also found similar trends in analyses of naturalistic speech data from the Bristol project. Whether or not variation in the extent of such modification for children at a given age or stage of development affects rate or style of development is a topic that still has to be investigated, although Cross' (1977) study of mothers' speech to accelerated language developers suggests that the effect of such modifications will be greatest when they are finely tailored to the child's linguistic level and the maturity of his communication strategies.

Cross makes the important point that effective communication is interactive, and that, in the case of these accelerated children, the mothers' communication strategies were in part determined by those of the child. Nelson (1973b) also stresses the importance of matching between the strategies of caretaker and child at different stages of development. Taking the three dichotomous variables, *match/mismatch* between the child's cognitive structure and the semantic structure of the adult lexicon, selection by the child of a *referential/expressive* hypothesis concerning the central functioning of language, and *acceptance/rejection* as the mother's dominant feedback to the child's utterances, she identified eight interaction patterns and examined the relationship between these and rate of vocabulary acquisition. 'Match–referential–acceptance' was found to be most strongly associated with rapid acquisition and, as might be expected, 'Mismatch–expressive–rejection' with slowest acquisition. Of the three variables, cognitive–linguistic match or mismatch appeared to be most powerful in accounting for progress during the second year, but the parental feedback variable was considered to have the greatest long-term effects. It seems, therefore, that the child's initial strategies may be important in getting him off to a good start, but that in the longer term it is the quality of caretaker feedback in interaction with the child that contributes more to rate of development.

The characteristics of caretaker feedback was one of the topics investigated by Brown and his colleagues in their study of Adam, Eve and Sarah (Brown et al., 1969). In one of their investigations they examined the effect of what they called 'training variables', and found no conclusive evidence for a relation between linguistic development and either frequency with which particular constructions were modelled in parental speech or with parental approval or disapproval of the syntactic form of children's utterances. Parents, it seems, are more concerned with the truth value than the syntactic well-formedness of their children's speech – which, they conclude, 'renders mildly paradoxical the fact that the usual product of such a training schedule is an adult whose speech is highly grammatical but not notably truthful' (Brown et al., 1969: p. 330). In their earlier work (Brown and Bellugi, 1964), they had been struck by the frequency with which parents expanded their children's grammatically incomplete utterances, and the effect of a systematic regime of expansions was investigated by Cazden (1965) in a controlled comparison with a regime of language modelling through semantically appropriate responses. Two groups of black children, aged 28 to 38 months, received one or other treatment for forty minutes each day for three months, whilst a third, control, group received no specific treatment. Contrary to expectation, the expansion treatment was not found to aid in the acquisition of grammar, whilst those children who had received the modelling treatment made greater progress. A re-examination of the spontaneous data from the Harvard children confirmed these results. Reviewing all these studies in the conclusion to A First Language, Brown wrote:

> 'In sum, then, we do not presently have evidence that there are selection pressures of any kind operating on children to impel them to bring their speech into line with adult models. It is, however, entirely possible that such pressures do operate in situations unlike the situations we have sampled, for instance away from home or with strangers. It is also

possible that one should look more closely at the small number of child utterances which turn up in most samples where the adult just does not seem able to make out what the child means. Perhaps these are the leading edge where the pressures operate.' (Brown, 1973: p. 312)

If parental feedback to the grammatical form of children's utterances does not seem to be the explanation of variation in rate of development, what else might be? Perhaps the answer lies in the direction indicated by the relatively greater success of the modelling condition in Cazden's experiment. One of the explanations suggested to account for that result was that 'richness of verbal stimulation might be more important than the grammatical contingency of the adult response' (Brown et al., 1969: p. 324). This is surely the case, but might not an even more important quality of parental speech be its relevance to the meaning intention of the child, and the extent to which conversation is jointly constructed by parent and child together? This seems to be implied by the findings of Cross and Nelson referred to above, and perhaps also by the quotation from Brown. Our own longitudinal records provide ample evidence of variation of this kind, and in a comparison of typical speech samples from two girls, from otherwise similar bacgrounds, I have shown how the reciprocal negotiation of meaning which characterizes the conversational experience of one, but not the other, of these children also provides an opportunity for extending control over the formal features of language (Wells, 1979b).

We have not as yet been able to test this hypothesis with respect to our whole sample, but Evans (1977) has made some progress in this direction by investigating, for twenty of the children, the effect on a number of indices of linguistic development at the beginning of schooling of the level of communicative relevance in mothers' responses to children's utterances at earlier stages of development. Using the recordings made at $3\frac{1}{4}$ and $3\frac{1}{2}$ years, she classified and scored each maternal response to a child utterance in child-initiated sequences according to the following scale: *Inappropriate*: 0; *Procedural* (check/expansion, correction, request for repetition or clarification, etc.): 1; *Plateau* (confirmation, yes/no response, command, evaluation, etc.): 2; *Developing* (instruction/suggestion): 2; *Yes/no question*: 3; *Statement/explanation*: 4; *Content question*: 5. Two overall scores were calculated for each mother: the mean level of response and a 'richness of interaction' score (mean response × mean number of exchanges per sequence), and these were correlated with MLU, syntactic complexity and oral comprehension (EPVT) at age 4;9, and with reading attainment at ages 6 and 7 years. With the exception of MLU, all correlations were positive and significant, thus lending support to the hypothesis that the quality of response that a mother gives to a child's speech in the early years has a significant influence on his subsequent linguistic development.

However, before we conclude that experience of this kind is crucial for satisfactory development, we should pause to consider whether such emphasis on the mother does not reflect a cultural bias resulting from the predominance of studies carried out in western societies. Blount (1977) points out that older children are the primary socializers of younger children in nonwestern societies, and even in western societies there is considerable variation in the age at which children are allowed to roam outside the home in peer groups, and the amount of time that they spend in such activities. From this it would appear that conversation with an *adult* caretaker is not essential for the acquisition of language, although it may still be the case that some systematic modification of the input to young children such as has been found in parental speech is essential, but that it is a characteristic of caretaker speech, whatever the age or status of the caretaker. However, in those societies where parental caretaking is the norm, the evidence does seem to suggest that differences between children in the quality of their conversational experience are related to their rate of language development. It seems likely that the same will be true for differences between children in the uses to which they habitually put their linguistic resources, but this has not yet been investigated in any detail.

20. Probabilistic modelling of the child's productions

Patrick Suppes, Madeleine Léveillé and Robert Smith

1. Introduction

The purpose of this chapter is to show how probabilistic methods may be used in the analysis of children's speech. To do this, we decided that it would be best to concentrate on one corpus as an example rather than to give a superficial survey, in the space available, of our prior work on several different corpora in English, French and Chinese.

This is the second paper we have written concerned with the analysis of the spoken French of a young Parisian child, Philippe. The first (Suppes *et al.*, 1973) was concerned only with the grammar of noun phrases occurring in Philippe's speech. The details of the collection of the corpus, the recording conditions and the procedures for transcribing and editing are all described there. We recall here only the fact that the corpus consists of 56,982 tokens recorded in thirty-three one-hour sessions of spontaneous speech occurring approximately once a week and ranging from the time that Philippe was 25 months old to 38 months old.

The present account of Philippe's speech represents a drastic condensation of a much longer technical report (Suppes *et al.*, 1974). Unfortunately, in this kind of work it is not possible to give all the details within the compass of a chapter of reasonable length. We have tried to extract those features that are most important for understanding the analysis that was undertaken and have provided detail adequate for the reader to make some judgment of his own about what we have done. However, we fully realize that the reader interested in the technical details of the grammar and of the probabilistic developments that follow may well want to consult the longer technical report and the related publications cited later.

The present chapter is organized along the following lines. First, in the following section we extend the dictionary developed earlier for noun phrases alone to cover the other parts of speech. The account given here does not depend on the earlier one. As much as possible we have used classical grammatical categories in constructing the dictionary, and we have followed when possible the kinds of categories used or suggested in Dubois (1970).

397

Section 3 is concerned with the grammar. This section particularly is drastically simplified. We give mainly the groups of rules and some illustrative examples, which are all drawn from Philippe's speech. At the end of this section we present summary results of the extent to which the grammar satisfactorily parses the corpus of Philippe's speech. We emphasize the complexity of the grammar we have written for this medium-sized corpus. The number of rules in the grammar is 317, and even though this number is large we have not taken into account the many inflectional patterns, including plurality of pronouns, verbs, etc. In constructing the grammar we have used Dubois (1970), as mentioned above, and also such classical sources as Grévisse (1969), but we have found that the completely systematic approach we have adopted has required us to make emendations and changes on a number of minor matters that only turn up in a full-scale attempt to fit a grammar to a corpus.

We turn in section 4 to a brief presentation of the probabilistic grammar, which means that we move from the grammar itself to the introduction of probabilistic parameters for the use of the individual rules. The techniques of analysis used here follow earlier work in the Institute for Mathematical Studies in the Social Sciences (IMSSS) at Stanford University. We show how the probabilistic grammar can be used to provide a method of probabilistic disambiguation that we think has interesting applications beyond simply the instances analysed in detail here.

In section 5 we turn to some probabilistic developmental models of Philippe's speech. Because there is such a natural tendency to speak in terms of stages of development, we have systematically tried to test a stage model against an alternative incremental model. As might be expected from complex data of the kind collected in a corpus arising from unstructured conversations between Philippe and his parents or other persons, neither model fits the data exactly, but we believe that the methodology is itself of interest and there is sufficient evidence in favour of the incremental model in comparison to the stage model to challenge the continual use of stage models in conceptual discussions of the linguistic development of children. As far as we know, the present attempt, preliminary though it may be, is among the very first to make a systematic comparison of the two basic kinds of models of developmental trends in the acquisition of grammatical rules. We would be happier if we were able to present developmental trends for a variety of children, but it will be evident from the details in the present chapter that the task of testing developmental models in a systematic way for any substantial number of children is an almost overwhelming one at the present level of our technology of data collection and reduction. Our tentative conclusion that the incremental model fits better than a stage model is of course applicable only to Philippe's speech behaviour. We hope that the kind of models we have begun to test in the present chapter will be of interest to other workers concerned with developmental psycholinguistics and that more systematic comparisons of different types of models of development will be tested on other corpora.

To avoid misunderstanding about our use of probabilistic notions, we emphasize the following point. In no sense do we consider the probabilistic account of the use of production rules or the use of probabilistic developmental models an ultimate account of Philippe's spoken utterances. It is apparent enough in a multitude of cases that the probabilities assigned are overruled by the semantics or context of a particular utterance. The probabilities assigned represent the results of averaging over a number of utterances and do not provide a fully detailed analysis of a particular utterance occurring on a particular occasion. The enormous complexity of the spoken speech of any child, including Philippe, strongly argues for the use of probabilistic methods for an understanding of the central features of the speech, particularly of the central features of development. The present corpus is quite large but the total amount of speech, either spoken or heard, by a young child during the crucial ages from 24 months to 36 months or 42 months is overwhelming in its quantity and variety. During this critical period we would estimate that Philippe heard on the order of a million words and responded with approximately half as many. It is our belief that it will be a long time before we have developmental models of children's speech sufficiently deep and detailed to avoid the use of probabilistic averaging methods, at least insofar as the objective is to account systematically for a corpus of any size.

2. Dictionary

Our previous article (Suppes *et al.*, 1973) presents in a detailed way the principles which guided the construction of the dictionary. Here we briefly characterize the lexical categories and some of the additional sub-categories.

Articles. The indefinite articles are *un* and *une*. The definite articles are *le*, *la*, *l'*, and *les*. Following Dubois' suggestion (1970: p. 152), the words *du*, *de*, *des*, *d'*, *au*, and *aux* (traditionally thought of as articles) have been coded as prepositions. Such a simplification has the advantage of reducing the lexical ambiguity: had we followed classical grammarians, several of these words should have been multiply classified. Furthermore, this simplification lets us avoid the delicate question of partitive articles.

Nouns. Nouns are divided into the two classical categories of common nouns and proper nouns. Common nouns are coded as to gender and number.

Pronouns. The five main categories of pronouns are: personal, demonstrative, possessive, interrogative and relative, and indefinite. Personal pronouns are coded by taking into account their position within a subject–object sentence, since it is their position that determines their syntactic form and semantic role.

Adjectives. The six main subcategories of adjectives are: qualitative, numerical, demonstrative, interrogative, possessive and indefinite.

Verbs. In written French most verbs have a different ending for each form. These variations of inflectional patterns are not reflected in the spoken language. For example, *(j')aime, (tu) aimes, (ils) aiment* do not differ phonetically. Our coding, which agrees to a large extent with Martinet (1958), is based on the phonetic pattern of verb endings.

The main distinction is between transitive, intransitive, auxiliary, impersonal, pronominal and semiauxiliary verbs, and verbs which may be either intransitive or transitive.

Several aspects of the coding of verbs need to be emphasized. In the first place, we have coded with the smallest number phonetically possible for a given form. Thus, the past participle *allé* and the imperative *allez* are coded the same. The exception to this rule is in those verbs for which the past participle has the same phonetic form as the simple past. Example: *je pris, pris.* The other point is that the individual words of the vocabulary are coded independently of their context and, consequently, composed forms, such as *j'aurai reçu* are not coded as a single verb form but rather the individual words *aurai* and *reçu* are coded separately.

Adverbs. We distinguish seven subcategories of adverbs: adverbs of time, location, quantity, quality, affirmation, negation and interrogation, plus undetermined ones.

Prepositions are divided into eight subcategories whose description we omit. All *conjunctions of subordination*, such as *puisque, parce que*, are coded without any elaboration of subcategories. *Conjunctions of coordination* are similarly coded. Philippe used *et*; in a few cases, he used *ou* and *ni*.

Interjections and onomatopeias. In the broad category of interjections and onomatopeias are classified such words as *ah, oh, eh, ben.* Many of these words are onomatopeias that French-speaking children frequently use.

Locutions. There are four subcategories: undetermined, adverbial locution, prepositive locution and interrogative locution.

Concluding remarks. A given word may function in different ways, depending upon its context. Words of this kind have been assigned to two or more categories. For instance, *cours* may be the plural form of a substantive, or the first person singular of the verb *courir*. When this occurs, we say that the word is *multiply classified*. We have not included all multiple classifications that are in all likelihood present in Philippe's speech. When it was highly unlikely that Philippe would have used a certain word in more than one context, we did not multiply classify that word. For example, the word *mets* has been coded as a verb but not as a noun, since it is our belief that the latter usage ('something related to food') was unlikely to occur.

3. Grammar

Using the coding scheme outlined in section 2, the next step was to write a context-free grammar at the level of abstraction already mentioned; for example, inflections were ignored. The grammar, consisting of 317 rules, is too long to describe in detail here. What we have done is to list the various groups of rules, giving their function and the number of rules in each group. In the headings introducing the various groups we have indicated the number of rules in that group; for example, in group 1 we have used the indication 'Highest level rules – 3' to indicate there are three rules in this group.

Group 1. Highest level rules – 3. Three main kinds of utterances are generated: (a) utterances of length 1 and 2 consisting of adverbs, locutions, interjections and numerals; (b) noun phrases and adjective phrases that stand alone, that is, without a verb; (c) utterances in which a verb is present, and questions (with or without a verb).

Group 2. Incomplete utterances – 17. Most of the rules in this group generate terminals directly. The rules have only one or two branches; they parse the following grammatical categories introduced in the dictionary: adverbs, locutions, onomatopeias and interjections, and several combinations of these categories.

Group 3. Noun phrase and adjective phrase utterances – 20. This group recognizes noun phrases and adjective phrases that are not combined with a verb. We had two motivations for generating with separate rules noun phrases that occur as the complete sentence without a verb: first, we wanted to improve the probabilistic fit of the grammar; second, we wanted to reveal a developmental trend in the usage of noun phrases.

Group 4. Utterance combination – 17. The rules in this group generate more complex utterances from simple utterances. For example, one of the rules introduces an adverb of negation at the beginning of the sentence; another rule parses sentences that begin with the conjunction of subordination *parce que,* where the *que* has been omitted.

Group 5. Utterances with a verb – 8. This group presents the rewrite rules for utterances that have a verb. One rule recognizes sentences in which the subject is missing: *Mettre dans le bol le sucre, A des sous dans mon porte-monnaie.* Another rule is the basic rule for sentences that have a subject: *Je sais pas.*

Before presenting the production rules of groups 6, 7 and 8, we explain the reason for introducing the three nonterminal symbols SN, SNS and SNP, which have similar production rules. These nonterminals have been intro-duced to differentiate the three main functions of the noun phrase: subject, object, nominative predicate. We wanted to formulate correctly the seman-tics associated with each rule and also see if there was a developmental trend in the usage of noun phrases depending on their function. In the first grammars we wrote, the noun phrase was derived using only one rule, S → N, and it was impossible to separate the noun phrases by their function. Fur-thermore, the same derivations were obtained for a noun phrase object of a transitive verb, as in *Il fume une cigarette,* as for a noun phrase subject of an intransitive, when the subject was repeated at the end of the sentence, as in *Il marche l'hélicoptère.* In order to have different derivations depending upon the nature of the verb, we introduced the nonterminals SN, SNS and SNP.

Group 6. Nominative predicate noun phrases – 4. The rules of this group involve the nonterminal symbol SN, discussed immediately above.

Group 7. Subject noun phrases – 9. The rules of this group involve the nonterminal symbol SNS.

Group 8. Object noun phrases – 4. The main difference between SNS (group 7) and SNP (group 8) is that the latter parses prepositional noun phrases while the former does not. A second difference is that SNP is used for parsing noun phrases that occur with verbs other than the copula.

Group 9. Basic noun phrases – 7. The rules of this group are the basic rules for recognizing noun phrases that are subjects, objects, or nominative predi-cates. Rules for noun phrases that end with an adverb or a vocative are also included.

Group 10. Prepositional noun phrases – 7. As we have already mentioned, this group of rules recognizes noun phrases beginning with a preposition.

Group 11. Determiner introduction – 25. This group of rules contains the detailed structure of the noun phrases. They determine the way in which determiners, numerical adjectives, and adjectives in pre- and post-position can be generated. They are comparable to the rules used in the analysis of noun phrases in Suppes *et al.* (1973).

Group 12. Noun phrase utterances – 19. The rules of this group use many but not all of the rules of groups 9 and 10 to generate noun phrase utter-ances.

Group 13. Some pronouns and common and proper nouns – 5. This group mainly governs possessive and indefinite pronouns and nouns.

Group 14. Adjective phrases – 2. This group governs adjectives in pre-position, that is, adjectives that precede the noun modified.

Group 15. Post-position adjectives – 1.

Group 16. Determiners – 5. This group permits rewriting the nonterminal symbol DET as any of the five terminal symbols standing for a grammatical category of determiner.

Group 17. Numerical expressions – 2. This group governs cardinal and ordinal adjectives.

Before presenting the rewrite rules of the verb phrase, we shall note again that the present analysis does not take into account the mood, the tense, or the person of the verb, since subscripts that convey this sort of information are disregarded by the grammar. As a result, our grammar recognizes sentences in which the verb has a correct form as well as sentences in which the mode, the tense, or the person is not appropriate.

On the basis of this general scheme, we have introduced several groups of rules that allow the parsing of different forms of verb phrases.

Originally, following Dubois' suggestion (1970: p. 93), AUX was rewritten as an auxiliary (*être* and *avoir*) and as a modal. With the intended semantic interpretation in mind, AUX has been divided into two categories: AUX 1 for the auxiliary verbs *être* and *avoir* and AUX 2 for modals.

Group 18. Verb phrase structures – 15. The many rules of this group provide the productions for the basic verb phrase structures. The rules have too heterogeneous a character to describe in simple terms. For example, the fourth rule allows the insertion of an adverb between the auxiliary and the verb; the sixth rule introduces modals; the tenth rule produces utterances in which the negation applies to the modal; the thirteenth rule produces utterances in which the personal pronoun is the direct object of the verb that follows the modal.

Group 19. Auxiliaries – 2. The two rules in this group produce particular auxiliary structures, the first governing *être* and *avoir,* when they are used as auxiliaries, and the second governing utterances in which the modal has a compound form: *a pu sortir.*

Group 20. Modals – 3. The rules of this group govern modals, including the recognition of utterances in which there are two modals in succession used to express the notion of future: *Je vais aller galoper.*

Group 21. Verbal groups – 80. The number of production rules in this group is the largest of any. They are used to produce the wide diversity of verb phrase forms encountered in Philippe's speech. We give only a few examples. The second rule governs utterances in which an adverbial locution follows the verb *être: Il est là-bas.* The ninth rule generates negative utterances with an adjective predicate: *C'est pas vrai.* The eleventh rule generates utterances in which the verb *être* is followed by an adverb: *Je suis là.* Rule 24 governs verb phrases formed with transitive verbs and verbs that can be transitive or intransitive when there is no direct object or prepositional noun phrase. Rule 40 governs utterances in which the second personal pronoun is the indirect object of the verb: *Montre-la moi.*

We summarize at this point the remaining groups 22–9, the rules of most of which are intuitively understandable from the titles of the groups. Group 22, with twenty-five rules, governs verb phrases with prepositions or personal pronouns. Group 23, with two rules, governs intransitive and impersonal verbs. Group 24, with one rule, governs the copula. Group 25, with three rules, governs transitive and pronominal verbs. Group 26, with two rules, governs predicate adjectives. Group 27, with three rules, governs adjectives. Group 28, with twenty-four rules, governs questions, and group 29, with two rules, governs adverbs of quantity.

Summary results of the grammatical analysis. There are 15,057 token utterances (6539 types) in the corpus; 11,294 tokens (4000 types) have been recognized by the grammar, which corresponds to about 75 per cent of the tokens and to 61 per cent of the types. We should mention that a large number of types, 571 accounting for 1480 tokens, include one or more occurrences of uncoded sounds. Since the grammar makes no effort to account for such sounds, we note that 67 per cent of the types and 83 per cent of the tokens were recognized when utterances involving these sounds were discarded.

4. Probabilistic grammar and probabilistic disambiguation

The relatively detailed and complex grammar described in section 3 parses about 75 per cent of the utterances in Philippe's corpus. This criterion alone is not sufficient to judge the grammar, for it would be easy enough to write a grammar that would parse 100 per cent of the utterances, namely, the universal grammar. There are different ways of thinking about how additional criteria may be imposed on a grammar in order to determine its appropriateness for a given corpus. For a number of reasons, we consider a probabilistic criterion of goodness of fit one of the better ways to evaluate a grammar. This probabilistic viewpoint has been developed extensively in previous publications originating in IMSSS (Gammon, 1973; Smith, 1972; Suppes, 1970; Suppes *et al.,* 1973).

The basic strategy of the probabilistic approach to grammars is to attach a parameter to each rule of a group with the requirement that the parameters be interpreted as probabilities, that is, each parameter is nonnegative and the sum of the parameters for a given group of rules is equal to 1. The parameter is meant to correspond to the relative frequency of use of the given production rule of the grammar in generating the utterances of the corpus. Once such parameters are assigned, we can estimate them by standard methods, for example, in many straightforward cases by maximum-likelihood methods. Having estimated the parameters we are then able to move on to consider a standard goodness-of-fit criterion for evaluating the adequacy of the grammar to the corpus. We should say at once that in the present stage of investigation the goodness-of-fit criterion is not well satisfied; i.e. if we take a large corpus, for instance that of Philippe's speech, we do not anticipate obtaining a reasonable level of significance for the fit of the probabilistic grammar to the corpus. We can, as was done in the case of our earlier article (Suppes *et al.*, 1973), use the goodness-of-fit criterion to distinguish between two grammars. In the present case we want to use the probabilistic apparatus to disambiguate grammatically ambiguous utterances. As we describe below, we believe that this represents a useful application of probabilistic grammars and one that has some theoretical interest.

In table 1 we show the observed and predicted frequencies of utterance types for those that have a frequency of at least 30 in the corpus. It will be seen immediately from a perusal of this table that the fit of the probabilistically computed predictions is not perfect and, in fact, is not as good as one would like in a completely satisfactory theory. On the other hand, it is our judgment that, without increasing the number of rules extravagantly, it would be hard to improve substantially the fit as indicated in this table.

We turn now to discussion of probabilistic disambiguation. When an utterance has more than one dictionary representation, the utterance is *lexically ambiguous*. If only one of those dictionary representations is parsed by the grammar, we say that the ambiguity is only *apparent*. However, if more than one representation is recognized, then we have to account for that ambiguity.

One tenable view is that the several lexical ambiguities are all intuitively reasonable. While this is possible, it is nevertheless plausible that Philippe only acts upon one interpretation – he makes some decision about which interpretation to accept.

We have proposed in Smith (1972) and Suppes *et al.* (1973) that lexical ambiguity be treated syntactically and probabilistically. Of the several lexical interpretations for a sentence, we accept the most likely interpretation according to the probabilistic grammar that we have offered. In doing so, we are not claiming that disambiguation does not involve semantic considerations in a crucial way. Rather, we are claiming that syntactic features (of

Table 1. *Observed and predicted frequencies of utterances in Philippe*

Observed	Predicted	Utterance type
1494	1494·00	Adverb
705	705·00	Negation
295	156·36	Indef. article + common noun
253	328·51	Def. article + common noun
246	242·43	Common noun
198	198·00	Interjection or onomatopeia
154	91·20	Preposition + common noun
137	136·39	Proper noun
132	123·58	Preposition + def. article + common noun
109	91·52	Trans. verb
100	24·62	Personal pronoun + trans. verb + negation
87	122·45	Demon. pronoun
76	27·21	Trans. verb + def. article + common noun
73	73·00	Interrog. pronoun
57	13·39	Demon. pronoun + copula + qual. adjective
56	51·31	Preposition + proper noun
48	34·99	Verb (can be trans. or intrans.)
44	4·48	Demon. pronoun + copula + indef. article + common noun
43	19·61	Qual. adjective + common noun
42	52·96	Qual. adjective
42	42·00	Interjection + adverb
40	15·54	Indef. article + qual. adjective + common noun
40	3·90	Demon. pronoun + copula + proper noun
40	0·59	Interrog. pronoun + demon. pronoun + copula + proper noun
38	2·93	Adverb + personal pronoun + copula + def. article + common noun
38	32·01	Personal pronoun + copula + qual. adjective
36	10·40	Verb (trans. or intrans.) + def. article + common noun
35	35·00	Locution
33	4·58	Personal pronoun + auxiliary verb + verb (trans. or intrans.)
31	8·35	Indef. article + common noun + adverb
30	58·82	Preposition + indef. article + common noun
30	9·40	Demon. pronoun + copula + def. article + common noun
30	31·21	Personal pronoun + trans. verb + def. article + common noun

which the probabilistic grammar is a key example) may well play a role in disambiguation. This could happen in several ways, but the way we consider to be the most reasonable would involve interaction between probabilistic analysis and semantic and contextual analysis, where the initial decision on what to consider semantically is made by the probabilistic grammar. We should remark that this interpretation is, of course, a listener-oriented view.

We have also been concerned to analyse the intuitively incorrect decisions made by probabilistic lexical disambiguation. These apparent errors fall into several simple categories. Two criteria have guided us in deciding whether or not the ambiguity is solved correctly by the method described: a reference to the context in which the utterance has been emitted, and the grammatical analysis of the elements of the utterance. Two examples will illustrate the point.

The utterance *la tienne* is recognized as a personal pronoun followed by a verb and as a possessive pronoun. Reference to the context shows that Philippe was using the personal pronoun. Consequently, our conclusion is that the ambiguity is incorrectly solved, since the structure personal pronoun + verb has a higher probability than the personal pronoun.

As a second example, the structure of the utterance *il est vide le pot* is ambiguous because *vide* can be either a verb or an adjective, with the choice of its being a verb having higher probability. We then judge the grammatical analysis as incorrect because in this utterance *vide* is an adjective, not a verb.

The surprising feature about probabilistic lexical disambiguation is the degree to which it appears to work in a plausible way. There were 660 grammatically ambiguous types (938 tokens) of utterances. Of these, only 88 types (133 tokens) were resolved in an unsatisfactory way. This corresponds to 13 per cent of the types and 14 per cent of the tokens.

5. Developmental models

One of the most significant and important topics in developmental psychology is that of the language development of the child. There exists a large literature on the subject, and many interesting examples of the acquisition of particular language skills, either of comprehension or of production, have been given. On the other hand, because of what appears to be the bewildering complexity of the language usage taken as a whole, even of a fairly young child, there have been few if any attempts to test systematic models of language development. It should be apparent that the kind of probabilistic grammar that we have constructed for Philippe's speech provides the sort of quantitative framework within which it is possible to conceive and test specific mathematical or formal models of language development.

Because of the conceptual interest in deciding whether language development occurs in discrete stages or continuously, we have chosen to test alternative models that represent in a global manner these two ways of thinking about development. Before entering into any details, it is important to recognize that in either a discrete-stage or a continuous, incremental approach we must take account of the obvious fact that all normal children develop new language capacities and new skills as they get older, in an especially striking way in the period running from approximately 24 to 48 months. The intellectually interesting task is not to affirm this obvious fact, but rather to distinguish whether the concept of stages or the equally intuitive concept of continuous development provides a better account of the kind of detailed data we have collected in the case of Philippe.

Although the data analysis we present is in some respects rather massive, we regard our own efforts as very much preliminary in character. Perhaps the most important reason for saying this is that the data do not show the kind of smoothness properties we would need to test decisively the choice between the two models. The fit to the corpus of more than 15,000 utterances of either class of models we consider is rather bad. The real point of our analysis is to show how one can look at the entire systematic grammar of a child's speech, and not merely at examples of individual utterances. On this point we do not want to be misunderstood. We think that it will continue to be of value to look at individual utterances and to extract from them insights into particular changes in the child's speech. At the same time, it is our thesis that it is valuable to analyse in a more global fashion the character of linguistic development.

In considering the overall development of Philippe's grammar during the period under study in this chapter, it is perhaps natural to begin by asking what sort of curve we get for the introduction of the large number of rules in the grammar. An easy way to look at these data is to graph the cumulative curve, with the abscissa being Philippe's age, and the ordinate being the number of rules used in our sample up to a given age. An analysis of this kind is shown in figure 1.

The kind of analysis exemplified in figure 1, however, is quite restricted in character. In the first place, we have to be careful in making inferences of a strong character about the time at which rules are introduced, because our sample based on one hour per week is less than 1 per cent of Philippe's speech per week, and in view of the fact that in the later periods the spacing is even more sparse an even smaller percentage of his total speech is being sampled in a given period. Also, it is reasonable to view the introduction of a particular rule as being only of minor importance. Of greater importance is the central tendency of his development and the extent to which he continues to use a rule once it has appeared. For the purpose of catching such central tendencies, the probabilistic kind of grammar we have considered earlier seems appropriate and natural.

To pursue this analysis, what we have done is to divide the thirty-three sessions into six sessions of about an equal number of utterances, with a break being imposed during the long summer vacation in 1971. Even when

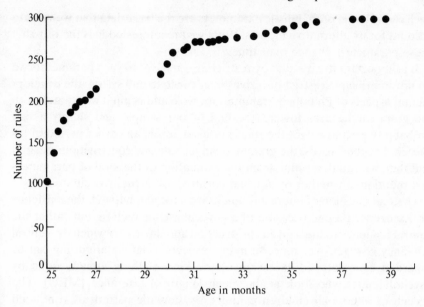

Figure 1. Cumulative curve of first use of grammatical rules

individual sessions are consolidated into blocks, some of the individual rules have a low probability of being used and consequently the behaviour of the probabilistic parameters over time can scarcely be studied systematically because of the expected sampling fluctuation being too large relative to the frequency of occurrence of a rule itself.

To meet this problem of small probabilities being assigned to certain rules, as necessarily must be the case when the number of rules in a given group is large, we have merged within each group of rules individual rules into small numbers of classes, these classes themselves being based upon what seem to be relatively intuitive linguistic considerations.

Merging of the data. Three main principles have guided us in grouping the grammatical rules:

(i)   Rules which have a low frequency of usage and analyse similar types of utterances should be in the same subgroup
(ii) rules of high frequency of usage should be in separate subgroups
(iii) rules which are likely to reveal different developmental trends should be in separate subgroups

Reduction of the data. For each of the six time sections, and each of the subclasses of rules in each group of rules, we have estimated, in the same statistical fashion as before, the probabilistic parameters to be attached to each class. These probabilistic parameters are the basic data that we want to account for by alternative models. What we are interested in is the way that these parameters change over time.

It is important to note that by restricting ourselves to such parameters we do not in principle restrict ourselves in advance to any systematic developmental aspects of Philippe's grammar, for we could begin if we wanted with the grammar he uses toward the end of our sample and simply assign probability zero to any of the rules not used during an earlier period of his speech. In other words, the grammar can include any constructions desired and then we can determine from the estimation of the kind of parameters just mentioned whether or not that construction actually occurs.

The real question of interest is not, as we have emphasized, the existence or occurrence on one occasion of a particular construction, but rather the central tendency to use a given construction and the way in which the central tendency changes over time. In many respects, what we are doing can be regarded as a detailed extension of the kind of thing already done by psycholinguists who look at the mean length of utterance (MLU). The speech of almost all children exhibits a systematic pattern of continued increase in the MLU over the period of development covered by the Philippe corpus. Our problem is to determine whether similar systematic tendencies can be determined for the use of various grammatical rules.

The all-or-none stage model. The basic assumptions of the all-or-none stage model are two. First, development is discontinuous and may be represented by a relatively small number of stages. Second, within each stage, there is a constant probability p_r of rule r being used. The technical assumption is that these probabilities within a given stage for a given group of rules constitute a multinomial distribution, and thus satisfy assumption of independence and stationarity. Because the intuitive idea of stages is widely accepted and used, it does not seem necessary to formulate the model in a more general context and derive it by imposing special restrictions on more general models of learning. It should also be emphasized that we shall not test the assumption of a multinomial distribution with fixed parameters for each rule during a given stage of testing, for example, for independence or stationarity. The only detailed test we shall consider is the identification of stages and the comparison of the fit of the stage model to the incremental model described below.

It also should be clear that, if we do not limit the number of stages, then for each group of rules the data can be fitted exactly by a six-stage model, namely, we just assign a stage for each of the time sections and fit each probability without error. Such a model is not interesting and does not give us any insight into the comparison between stage and incremental models.

What we have done is impose the requirement that for each group of rules only two stages of development are to be looked for within the period covered by our data. Thus, for example, if a given group of rules is n in number, then we want to fit $2n - 2$ parameters. If we have n rules or n subgroups of rules and six stages we have in general $6n - n$ degrees of freedom and with $2n - n$ parameters we have left a net of $4n - (n+2)$ degrees of freedom that provide a test for the two-stage model. We shall not really make use, from a statistical standpoint, of this number of degrees of freedom; that is, we shall not really be interested in assigning a significance level to the goodness of fit of the models, because the data are in too crude a form and the fit of the models not sufficiently good to warrant a detailed statistical assessment.

Incremental model. A qualitative formulation of the discrete stage model is relatively straightforward and has been outlined above. Matters are more complicated in the case of the incremental model. The most desirable approach is to derive a stochastic differential equation from qualitative considerations, and then to solve this differential equation to obtain the predicted developmental curve for a given group of grammatical rules.

Without claiming that we are yet in a position to give a definitive qualitative theory of the incremental model, we can offer postulates that are intuitively sensible at a relatively gross level of approximation. As in the case of many attempts to model a highly complex situation, we introduce probabilistic assumptions that we test only in the mean without any claim to being able to extend the theory to examine individual sample paths.

In the five assumptions that follow, a central concept is that of a *conducive occasion* for a given group of rules to be used. Some such notion is needed because the developmental probabilities for use of a rule are conditional probabilities – conditional on the use of some one rule of the group to which it belongs. It is apparent from the formulation of the five assumptions that this concept of conducive occasion is taken as primitive, and the fifth assumption makes explicit our probabilistic postulate about the occurrence of such occasions. In our judgment it is a central task of a deeper developmental theory that includes the semantics of context to account for the specific character and occurrence of such occasions. It is not within the power of a purely syntactic developmental theory.

Assumption 1. On the occasion of an utterance the probability is one that the child will try a grammatical rule from a group that is conducive to the occasion.

Assumption 2. Immediately after a rule r is used, from his more developed model of comprehension the child will judge the appropriateness of the best choice of a rule from the given group. This appropriateness is represented in the mean by a constant probability π_r.

Assumption 3. For each rule r of a group there is a linear incremental change in the probability of use on a conducive occasion as a function of the constant probability π_r of its appropriateness. Thus on conducive occasions

$$p(t + h,r) = (1 - \theta)p(t,r) + \theta\pi_r.$$

Assumption 4. The probability of using a rule r is changed only on occasions conducive to use of the group of grammatical rules to which r belongs.

Assumption 5. The occurrence of occasions that are conducive to the child's use of any given group of grammatical rules follows a Poisson law, i.e. the intervals between occurrence of these conducive occasions are independently and identically distributed.

From these five assumptions, we can derive a simple mean stochastic equation. We omit the derivation. Let μ be the parameter of the Poisson process for the occurrence of occasions conducive to the use of a given group of rules. Then for the boundary condition $p(t,r) = p_r$ for $t = t_1$ the incremental model is characterized in the mean by:

$$p(t,r) = \pi_r - (\pi_r - p_r)e^{-\alpha(t-t_1)}$$

where $\alpha = \theta\mu$.

Test of the two-stage model. Using the six temporal sections made up from the thirty-three sessions as described earlier, we tested the two-stage model individually for each of the twenty-nine groups of rules. Second, for each class of rules within a given group, we estimated two parameters, the probability of use in the first stage and the probability of use in the second stage.

To give the two-stage model the optimal chance of fitting the data, we determined on the basis of the data the best breakpoint between the stages for each class of rules. We determine the best breakpoint by computing the sum of squares (of the difference of observed and predicted frequencies) for each possible breakpoint for the two-stage model. The fit of the two-stage model to the data is rather poor. The sum of squares for the best break, break 2, is $4 \cdot 4 \times 10^8$.

Test of the incremental model. The equation for the incremental model requires that for a given group of rules we estimate the parameter α and that for each rule r of a group we estimate its initial probability p_r and its asymptotic probability π_r of appropriateness. We estimated p_1 by using the probability of use of a rule in the first time section. In the case of π_r and α we used a more complicated procedure that we do not have the space to describe here, but is related to statistical methods of estimation used in learning theory.

The sum of squares for the incremental model is $1 \cdot 4 \times 10^5$, which is considerably less than the sum of squares for the two-stage model and is indicative of a definitely better fit.

We illustrate the fit of the incremental model to various groups of rules. The figures displaying the fit of the incremental model all have the following format: the abscissa shows Philippe's age (in months), and the ordinate shows the probability of use. For each rule subgroup of the rule class, the encircled numbers show the 'observed' probabilistic data points as described above. The curves, labelled with corresponding numbers in square boxes, show the theoretical curves predicted by the incremental model. Data for group 1 are shown in figure 2. The three very general production rules of

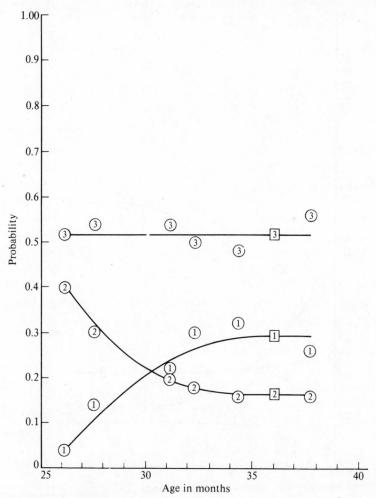

Figure 2. Fit of incremental model for rules of group 1, highest level rules

group 1 are used at a high level in any syntactic tree that generates an utterance. Rule 1 is the production rule for one- and two-word utterances, and this production rule shows a marked increase over the developmental period, whereas the second rule, which is the rewrite rule for utterances that consist of noun phrases and adjectival phrases that are not combined with verbs, would as expected show a definite decrease in usage. The third rule, which is the rewrite rule for whole sentences as well as verb phrases, has a fairly constant use over the developmental period. These basic facts in the observable data are nicely expressed in the theoretical curves, as may be seen from figure 2.

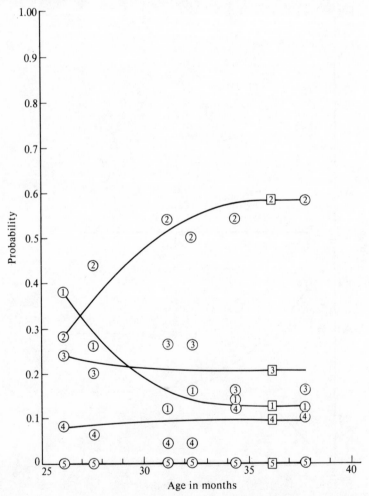

Figure 3. Fit of incremental model for rules of group 7, subject noun phrases

Group 7 produces noun phrases as the subject of a verb, and what we get is increasing complexity of these subjects over the developmental period as reflected in the relative usage of the production rules – see figure 3. For example, the simple first rule has a sharply decreasing usage and the second rule, which introduces personal pronouns as subject of the verb, has a sharply increasing use. Philippe, as is also the case for English-speaking children, does not have a frequent use of personal-pronoun subjects of utterances in his early speech but uses them increasingly over the period covered by our data.

The rules in group 16 introduce the determiners – see figure 4. There is a

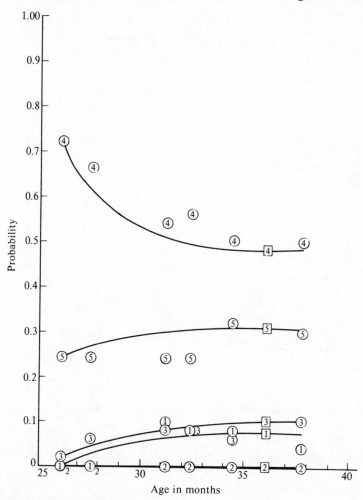

Figure 4. Fit of incremental model for rules of group 16, determiners

mild increase in the use of demonstrative adjectives (rule 1), possessive adjectives (rule 3), and indefinite articles (rule 5). The definite article shows a marked decrease over the period, as shown in the observed data and theoretical curve for rule 4.

In contrast, the two low-level rules governing predicate adjectives that constitute group 26 do not show any marked developmental trends – see figure 5.

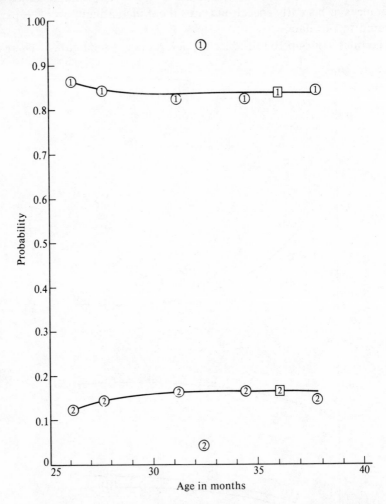

Figure 5. Fit of incremental model for rules of group 26, predicate adjectives

An overall observation about the accuracy of the fits of the incremental model is that it fits best the data for the highest level groups of rules. One reason for this could be that there are more data to support the predictions. Another reason may be that it was clearer what linguistic considerations were relevant to the top level rules.

21. Cognitive development and child language*

Robin N. Campbell

1. Introduction

To explore the relationships between cognitive development and language development is to enter a very dark forest indeed! It is not so much a question of not being able to see the wood for the trees: one cannot even see the trees! Accordingly, the best advice one might offer to, say, a graduate student would be 'Danger, keep off!' For those with more leisure and securer positions it is perhaps possible to make an occasional foray without becoming entirely lost, but it should be emphasized that what is both desirable and possible in the study of language development at the present time is more facts, more flower-picking natural history. However, it is sometimes useful to make the attempt at a larger enterprise, if only as a source of ideas about where to look for new flowers.

The large mass of research with a bearing on this relationship has been recently reviewed by Bowerman (1976b) and in a number of publications by Cromer (e.g. 1974a, b, 1976).[1] It would be absurd for me to attempt a similar job here. I think it can fairly be said that one thing missing from these reviews is any sign that a coherent theoretical framework informs current work on the relationship. Indeed, the same might be said of psycholinguistics in general. So, what I will try to do here, and to do briefly, is to justify a rough sketch of the links between these two domains of developmental speculation (theory is much too grand a word) – which brings me to the first great difficulty, namely, that when we wish to explore relationships between two psychological aspects of an organism we can do so only within the framework of general psychological theory, which is (some would say rightly) a currently uninhabited field of study. Since the collapse of behaviourist theory in the 1950s, few psychologists have been anxious to get

* I am grateful to the Max Planck Gesellschaft for providing me with facilities and resources for the period in which this paper was written and to my erstwhile colleagues at the Projektgruppe für Psycholinguistik for stimulation and support.
[1] I would like to acknowledge an especial debt to Bowerman's 1976 review. In addition, Bloom (1973) and Brown (1973) contain many useful sections.

involved. Instead, we have become problem-orientated: we study this or that and develop theories of how the organism does this or that, instead of theories of the organism. Thus, except for a few enclaves where theoretical optimism persists, we discover that the organism is a collection of *ad hoc* mechanisms and structures (the brain as tool-bag), rather than a system capable of constructing such mechanisms. The reason that this approach doesn't and can't work towards theory construction is plain enough: it simplifies and in the end ignores the problem of boundary conditions, of the nexus between theory and reality, by fixing the meaning of all measured variables through instruction or special training in the context of a fixed task. Chomsky used this point to dispose of Skinner's systematic aspirations. It can with equal validity be used to dispose of a good deal of what has taken Skinner's place. For compelling arguments, see Joynson (1974).

What then are our theoretical alternatives? Undoubtedly there are viable aspects of Freudian and, to a far greater extent, Piagetian theory but they have too much of the character of religious movements to be adapted to truly general purposes. The same might be said of Chomsky's position. Ecumenism is best left to the faithful. The theory I shall explore here owes something to Boole (1854) and to Wundt (1902) and is rooted in the thought of Brunswik (especially 1952, 1956) as developed by Smedslund (1969) and Heider (1958). Similar proposals have been sketched by Polanyi (e.g. 1968). As Smedslund (1969) has made clear, this is essentially a dualist theory: there is an inner domain of the organism, the contents of which are constantly changing and available to awareness and whose dynamic is rational; there is an outer domain, the contents of which change only slowly, are not available to awareness, and whose dynamic is causal.[2] For convenience, in what follows I shall use the term *phenic* to describe structures and processes of the *inner* domain and the term *cryptic* to describe structures and processes of the *outer* domain.[3] The boundary between these two domains is

---

[2] The appeal to the opposition between rational and causal dynamics is no more than a wave of the hand in the direction of an area of intense debate and dissension in recent philosophy. Moreover, even if a distinction between reasons and causes can be sustained in theory it does not follow that reasons and causes will be distinguishable empirically. Similarly airy gestures have been made by Smedslund (1969) and by Piaget (*cf.* e.g. Fraisse and Piaget, 1968).

[3] The motivation for this terminology is twofold. Firstly, it has a clear interpretation *from the point of view of the experiencing subject:* what is evident to the subject is *phenic*, what is hidden is *cryptic*. Of course I do not intend a perfect correspondence between the theoretical distinction (phenic/cryptic) and the phenomenal one (aware/unaware): only that the latter is the usual empirical mark of the former. Secondly, the terminology avoids the unfortunate anatomical distinctions suggested by the usual spatial metaphors – i.e. higher/lower, central/peripheral, inner/outer.

extremely flexible, being subject to change (a) phylogenetically, (b) ontogenetically and (c) microgenetically. Thus, contrasting man with ape, (a) the inner domain cannot include representations of experientally remote objects, but the outer domain must do, since recognition is excellent (Köhler, 1925); likewise, contrasting adult with child, (b) infants less than 9 to 10 months old exhibit a similar disparity (Piaget, 1955a); thus, again, (c) in the microgenesis of speech as in other skilled acts adults are capable of editing their performance at a preparatory stage and in listening can shift attention 'downstream' to lower levels if the normal process of understanding encounters a difficulty (common observation). For a particularly clear and insightful account of this process, see Laszlo (1966). In such a theory there are thus two main external functions (i.e. involving interaction with the external world): *perception*[4] (which includes sensation as a special, usually arduously acquired case involving stretching of the inner domain to the periphery (Gibson, 1966)) and *action* (likewise including individual muscle control as a special case), both of which are complicated integrative functions relating cryptic structures to phenic structures. These functions 'reflect' similarly complex physical functions relating peripheral events to configurations of reality. Thus the model is represented as a 'double lens' (Brunswik, 1952: p. 20; Smedslund, 1969). In addition to these two external functions the organism has two main internal functions – *information* and *direction* – which introduce structures to the inner domain, structures which invest the functions of perception and action with, respectively, meaning and purpose and which maintain continuity of awareness. A great deal is known about the external functions; Piaget has explored the growth of the inner domain, the nature of its dynamic and of the structures which are formed within it; recently Minsky (1975), following the insights of Bartlett (1935) and Craik (1943), has made some progress in describing the informative function; about the directive function we know least of all. I shall not attempt a lengthy justification of this theoretical sketch. Instead I will follow a more devious course. To begin with, I shall discuss cognitive development, what it is and how it is studied. Next I shall indicate how the study of language development has led to a certain reformulation of subject matter in such a way as to involve us in linking our accounts of linguistic and cognitive development. In the succeeding section I shall try to shed some light on some traditional puzzles in this grey area of investigation.

[4] It may be objected that perception is now correctly regarded as an *active* process and thus cannot be separated from the function of action. However, from my point of view the various active accommodations of the perceptual organ, though certainly *movements,* do not count as actions unless they are deliberately (phenically) initiated.

2. Cognitive development

What is cognitive development and how should it be studied? There is widespread disagreement about this. One can discern two clear positions, one represented in mainstream American psychology, the other in the genetic epistemology of Jean Piaget. In the former case, cognitive structures and processes are identified with symbolic structures and processes (often called information structures and processes), which mediate the connection of outputs from sensory mechanisms with inputs to motor mechanisms. Thus every action of the organism beyond the simplest reflex is said to involve cognitive processes. In the latter case, cognitive structures and processes are identified with representations and operations upon representations that are tied in an intimate way to explicit knowledge and awareness. Thus only certain functions in certain organisms are said to involve cognitive processes. The use of the qualifier 'explicit' in the penultimate sentence will seem strange to those who are not accustomed to the sophistries of the information processing idiom. In that idiom it is commonplace to speak of 'tacit' knowledge in circumstances where the justification for calling something a cognitive event is noticeably lacking. Thus, Chomsky often speaks of tacit knowledge of rules of language. What is meant by this is of course that the rules in question are *not* known but merely observed. Falling apples ignorant of the laws of motion are generally not accused of possessing 'tacit' knowledge of them, but then apples (whether falling or not) know nothing 'explicitly' either. More to the point, apples are not capable of independent action; they contribute nothing to their fall beyond certain physical properties. Put another way, it is not *necessary* for them to know anything, tacit or not, about the laws of motion, in order to fall in the way that they do: they merely have to *be*. Most organisms, on the other hand, *are* capable of independent action. They are driven by motives the origins of which are remote and complex. The ape's controlled descent of a tree is mediated by something more than its physical properties. It seems to be necessary that the ape should *know* something about the shape of the tree, the disposition of its branches, the shape of its own body and the pull of the earth in order to descend in the way that it does. However, it is conceivable that we could, by considering possible trees, possible apes and actual dynamics, devise an extrinsic theory of tree-descents amounting to a set of rules, which rules are *observed* by our ape in the course of his descent. Since common experience and the study of language tells us that (a) there are rules of language and (b) in using language we observe them but are not aware of them, it is possible that the ape is similarly unaware of the structures and rules that guide his progress down the tree and hence knows them only tacitly. It is, however, more likely that just as we know *something* about the rules of our language and exercise this knowledge on *some* occasions, the ape, too, has as a back-up some knowledge of the rules for descending trees and sometimes employs it (e.g. when in fog, in unusual trees, broken limbs (ape) or broken limbs (tree)).

We have arrived at a point where it is possible to frame what, for me at any rate, is the fundamental question of cognitive psychology (some would say of psychology *simpliciter*). The question is 'What criteria determine the attribution of explicit knowledge?' Or, in the terms of my introduction, 'How can we know that we are dealing with a phenic process or structure?' For adherents of the first approach to cognitive psychology this question is *not* fundamental: an answer will be provided, if at all, only when a theory is completed. For what an organism knows explicitly is regarded as epiphenomenal (i.e. devoid of causal significance). On the other hand, for Piagetians and their like, the question *is* fundamental since it affects *description* of psychological events. Theory cannot *begin* until a way is found of deciding when to attribute explicit knowledge and what knowledge to attribute. It should be evident that there are no easy answers to this fundamental question. There is available neither a convincing refutation of epiphenomenalism nor a general method for selecting criteria; on the other hand, information processing analyses are bedevilled by paradoxes and absurdities. For example, perceptual and inferential processes often receive identical treatments and manipulate structures with identical descriptions.[5] Again, no formal distinction (there is often some lip-service paid) is or can be made between an automatic routine process which carries out a certain function and a deliberate conscious process which is 'called in' to carry out the *same* function when the routine process fails. The experimental/statistical requirements of reliability, replicability and low mean variance have led to widespread adoption of techniques which involve either lengthy periods of practice or many experimental trials per subject, with the result that the functions which are studied, though normally functions carried out – if at all – by phenic processes, are in fact observed only as cryptic routines.

This has had several disastrous consequences: (a) 'cognitive psychology' – which once had a clear meaning, denoting the psychology of phenic structures and processes – has slid through a period of ambivalence into its present appalling state, being now almost exclusively concerned with cryptic

[5] Escape from this paradox is not easy. The suggestion is sometimes offered (cf., e.g., Brunswik, 1956) that whereas errors of perception – illusions – are incorrigible, mistakes of reasoning can be corrected. But this is fallacious, since mistakes of reasoning are corrected only by further reasoning.

processes; (b) success in modelling these cryptic processes has given rise to the illusion that we have achieved some understanding of the (normally phenic) functions that they carry out; (c) valid work carried out within older or more peripheral traditions has been mistakenly called in question by robust mountains of data which in fact pertain to quite different processes – the most striking and unfortunate case of this is the persistent and breathtakingly insensitive impeachment of Genevan results in the field of cognitive development by American psychologists; (d) onlookers from neighbouring disciplines encounter insurmountable difficulties in evaluating psychological research. Philosophers of mind, for example, who – to my mind correctly – often tend to discount the usefulness of 'images', 'concepts' and 'meanings' in epistemological contexts are repelled and bewildered by the welter of such notions employed in *soi-disant* cognitive psychology: in fact, of course, these notions (sometimes just the labels) have usually been misappropriated and applied to cryptic structures which have none of the properties of the phenic structures to which these terms were originally applied.

In the case of models of the adult we are constantly reminded by our own nature of the need to be clear about which domain we are describing and can often determine independently of any empirical criteria what sort of process or structure is being described. Thus, for example, in Forster's (1976) analysis of the lexical decision task as a massive search process we are sure that any such search occurs within the outer, fixed domain of information and that the role of the inner domain in such a task (once initial orientation has been achieved) is simply to hold constant the *ad hoc* links established between perception, information and action. Hence we learn nothing from such work about *cognitive* structures and processes (if the term cognitive is restricted to its traditional referential domain, as I am urging that it should).[6] However, in studying cognitive development we lack such empathetic guidance and are often at a loss. We thus encounter difficulties and paradoxes which, I believe, can only be resolved by adopting assumptions of the kind that I am advocating and, ultimately, by discovering methods of investigation and descriptions which are sensitive to these assumptions. I will describe in detail only one such troublesome phenomenon – space perception in infancy – but similar difficulties arise in many disparate aspects of cognitive development, for example in perception of weight (Mounoud and Bower, 1974) and classification (Campbell *et al.*, 1976): for relevant reviews see Donaldson (1971) and Bower (1974b).

Brunswik (1956) elucidated a crucial distinction, originally due to Koffka (1935) and later elaborated by Heider (1939), between *distal* and *proximal*

---

[6] Henceforth, unless otherwise indicated, the term 'cognitive' will be used in this restricted sense.

stimulus variables. To illustrate, the distance of an object from the eye (a distal variable – i.e. a goal of description) is partially specified by the values – strictly speaking, simple functions of these values – of various *proximal* variables: retinal expansion, motion parallax, ocular convergence, lenticular accommodation, etc. Successful discrimination of variation in distance is thus achievable on the basis of sensitivity to variation of these proximal variables. *Which* proximal variable will vary in the appropriate way will depend upon the circumstances. However, successful discrimination does not tell us *anything* about how such proximal variation is interpreted by the infant, still less does it tell us that it is interpreted as variation in the distal variable, in this example – distance. Various remedies have been proposed (see Bower, 1974b: pp. 79ff.; Yonas and Pick, 1975: *passim*). Bower makes two suggestions. First of all, it is known that infants habituate to any constant and regular stimulation. If their discriminations are based upon variation in distance rather than on proximal variation, then a slight change in the task which shifts the basis of discrimination from one proximal variable to another should not interrupt habituation. Otherwise, it should. Bower claims that methodological difficulties get in the way of attempting this ingenious experiment. His second suggestion is not accompanied by any argument: he states baldly (1974b: p. 80) that 'faced with problems of this sort, one feels that natural response methods are a refuge. If an infant reaches out for an object intentionally . . . there can be no doubt that the infant sees the object in the third dimension. This kind of simple certainty we just cannot get from discrimination experiments.' While one might well agree with this, the problem of determining whether or not a reaching movement is *intentional* (i.e. distally aimed) is not conceptually different from the problem (to be solved) of whether a spatial discrimination is distally based. Yonas and Pick likewise offer two suggestions, that on the one hand distally invariant stimulus presentations which have variable proximal outcomes and which elicit a common reaction (stimulus convergence, in their terms) and, on the other hand, proximally diverse response movements with an invariant distal outcome and a common eliciting stimulus (response convergence, in their terms) each indicate that perception is distally oriented, since other explanations of such convergence are grossly unparsimonious.

There are many things that remain unclear here. Is distal orientation a necessary or a sufficient condition for a claim about explicit knowledge? Do all or any of the suggested remedies constitute sufficient conditions for a distal claim? It seems to me that there is still room for doubt. Is there not in the behaviour of a butterfly landing on a flower a co-ordination and integration of sensory information and a flexibility of motor response that equally invites the inference that the butterfly has constructed a representation of space and objects in space by means of which the sensory data and motor commands are interpreted? However, despite these uncertainties *some* things are clear. Able practitioners like Bower, Pick and Yonas evidently recognize the need to distinguish at least two qualitatively distinct levels of function of the organism, one which involves direct sensorimotor connections and another which requires an intermediate interpretative structure which gives *meaning* to the sensory data and *purpose* to the motor commands. Moreover, there is a laudable reluctance in the field as a whole to fudge the issue by means of either of the two well-worn stratagems, (a) 'It's a complicated internal process; that's cognitive enough for me' or (b) 'Any criterion will do, so long as we stick to it!' To return to the first point, a common reaction to the claim that levels or domains of function must be distinguished is simply to deny the possibility of doing so in an empirically principled way. My retort to this is that for sixty years or so we have tried to create a valid psychology without making such distinctions and in most important human functions we have failed. Likewise, philosophers of mind have attempted for centuries to found epistemology on analyses of different sorts of judgments and varieties of reasoning – all functions of the inner, conscious domain – and have also failed. It is time to have a look at the foundations of this building which is always falling down. If we had some clear idea of the special value of this higher level of functioning then we would be in better shape to attempt empirical determinations. Not altogether surprisingly, we have to dig fairly deep to find suggestions about its value. One of the more illuminating discussions is by Claparède (1917, 1918),[7] who argued that in microgenesis the higher level – which he identified with awareness – functioned as a catch-all default. Low-level processes which ran smoothly did not involve awareness, but if some breakdown or exceptional input occurred, the data were 'handed up' to the higher level and the process continued there. But this is surely just one role for 'awareness': it suggests a normally dormant organism which occasionally 'lights up' when things go wrong. Surely our intuitions tend in exactly the opposite direction – we are normally switched-on organisms which, when things go easily, switch off! So Claparède's 'law of awareness' explains only the movements of what Polanyi calls 'focal' awareness. For example, it does not explain, except by means of trivializing extensions, why we are on the one hand constantly aware of our physical surroundings when we move around and on the other hand aware of the muscular adjustments involved in thus moving around only rarely. The few recent attempts to describe the function of awareness

---

[7] See also Kirkpatrick (1908), which is acknowledged by Claparède as a source.

(e.g. Shallice, 1972) seem to suffer from the same limitation. Alternatively, we might examine the empirical procedures of say, Piagetians, to see what criteria are actually used in practice, when phenic structures or processes are under investigation. If there *is* a single characteristic procedure, it is surely the employment of an interview method which has as its goal the discovery of the rational basis for judgments and actions and as its principal technique the elicitation of verbal justifications. Thus, this research tradition (and I seriously doubt whether other viable ones presently exist in cognitive development) has one great limitation from the present point of view, namely that crucial evidence for the nature and course of phenic development consists of what children *say*, so, as Smedslund (1970) has pointed out, facts about the nature of the child's language are assumed in order to derive facts about phenic structure. Without some independent method, it would evidently be ludicrous *then* to use facts about phenic development to explain language development. And yet this is a commonly held view that language development is explicable in terms of cognitive development. In fact, I do not believe that Piagetians have yet discovered a valid method for investigating cognitive development in the age range $1\frac{1}{2}$ to 4 years. Their investigations of sensorimotor intelligence provide a basis for speculation about the phenic framework governing very early language (cf. D. Edwards, 1974)[8] and, of course, by 4 years child language is sufficiently adult-like to make it a plausible tool for exploring cognitive development. But in the intervening age range there has been little convincing progress. Indeed, Piagetian claims about what are supposedly vital characteristics of child thought during this period (e.g. inability to reason deductively, egocentricity) seem at best to be dubious now (cf. Donaldson, 1978) and are very probably false. So, even if we can justify causative links between cognitive and linguistic development, this is no panacea, since information about cognitive development in the important growth period of $1\frac{1}{2}$ to 4 years is either completely lacking or unreliable and there is no obvious methodology available for securing such information.

3. Early language: the problem of perspicuous description

About ten years ago, or thereabouts, a new approach to the study of early language development emerged in which attempts were made to investigate the properties of child language considered as a *system for communication*. To begin with (in accordance with the Wernerian developmental principle –

[8] Even here the needed basis lacks an immediate empirical justification. Some preliminary work has been carried out by Golinkoff (1975, Golinkoff and Kerr, 1978).

that new forms (of investigation) first serve old purposes (of theory)) this shift was largely a shift of method, the goal being as formerly a specification of the set of sentences the child could produce or understand (in some limited sense of this word, e.g. 'assign a structural description to'). The most remarkable effort of this sort was Lois Bloom's (1970) thesis. The point of investigating the system for communication rather than the language *per se* was that it seemed plain that syntactic description was an impossibly arbitrary exercise unless some additional constraining data could be found. A natural step was then to examine not just the child's utterances but also the messages which were transmitted by these utterances. Assumptions about correspondences between message forms (i.e. meanings) and utterance forms (i.e. sentences) invoking bi-uniqueness could then be used to constrain grammatical description of the child's language. In fact, Bloom made much less use of these putative correspondences than did other workers like Schlesinger (1971b) and, later, Brown (1973) and Halliday (1975), preferring instead to follow the line urged by Chomsky (1965, 1968) and supported by McNeill (1970) in which arguments about adult English yield a ready-made apparatus for the description of child language. This may be regarded as an aberration from which Bloom (cf. 1973, 1974; Bloom *et al.*, 1976) has made an admirable recovery.[9]

However little use Bloom may have made of the child's messages (as determined by adult interpreters), she established the fundamental methodological point, namely that this sort of analysis is possible. This method became known as the 'method of rich interpretation', a misnomer – since it is simply the 'method of interpretation', and its use has been a common feature of most subsequent work on early language. Its use has not gone unquestioned (e.g. Brown, 1973; Campbell, 1976; Edwards, 1978b), but the questions have been concerned with details rather than general principles. A little reflection and some data show that the method must be sound. The data come from many sources (e.g. Clark, in press; Käsermann, 1978; Schaerlaekens, 1973: pp. 50–1) and show that very young children know perfectly well when they have been misunderstood, and make that

---

[9] It seems quite remarkable that Chomsky (cf. 1975; and the wholly bizarre Chomsky and Lasnik, 1977: pp. 434–8) persists with the notion that linguistic research can reveal innate constraints governing language acquisition, in the face of (a) profound and growing disagreement about how the most-studied language – English – should be described, (b) gross differentiation of the concept 'human language' (cf. the recent clarifications of the nature of pidgins, creoles and dying languages), with consequent weakening of the notion 'empirical linguistic universal', (c) cogent and very early criticisms of his hypothesis by, for example, Lyons (1966) and Putnam (1967) and (d) a stubborn concern amongst students of child language for independent empirical justification of descriptive categories.

knowledge evident in obvious ways. Accordingly it is not possible, in stable and constant dyads, for the adult's interpretations to be badly amiss. In a well-designed study where the investigator is either the mother or has spent sufficient time with the child to establish communication with him, these interpretations should be of clear value in describing the child's system for communication and, consequently, his language. However, there remains a difficulty. To me, at any rate, it remains an open question whether at any intermediate point in development these two constructions, the system for communication and the language, are to be given identical descriptions or not. Certainly it seems clear that in the adult they are not: attempts to describe the former construct (Grice, 1967; Lewis, 1969; Stalnaker, 1972) have so far failed to make significant contact with attempts to describe the latter (*Linguistic Inquiry: passim*) as has been forcefully pointed out by Chomsky (1975) and Katz (1977a). Equally certainly, the two constructs have distinct ontogenies (Vygotsky, 1962). In the case of the adult a good case can be made for pursuing investigation of each system independently and it may even be the case (as Chomsky (1975) and Katz (1977a) have argued) that it is better (easier) to begin with description of language. For the case of the child, this possibility does not exist. Gold (1967) has shown that languages of nonfinite cardinality cannot be identified on the basis of a text presentation, i.e. sequence of sentences belonging to them. Since this is exactly (no more, no less) what is available to the child linguist who eschews study of the system of communication, it is clear that we cannot proceed with child language in the same way as we have with the language of the adult.[10] But here now is our difficulty: we have not so far found a way of integrating knowledge about human communication with knowledge about human language. Indeed, in a way they seem to pass each other by. On the one hand, efforts have been made to extend structural linguistic analysis to larger and larger structures – from sound to word to sentences to complete texts – and on the other hand the rational analysis of communication lately initiated by Grice, Lewis and other philosophers has encouraged a downward extension into grammatical processes by functionally minded linguists such as Garcia (1975) and Dik (1978). From the point of view of this chapter, this is a clear absurdity: complementary explanations are being presented as if they were in competition! They are complementary, of course, because the rational processes at the heart of communication belong to the inner domain – to strictly cognitive activity – while the grammatical processes at the heart of

---

[10] This seems to me to be the most effective use for results like Gold's, namely to apply them to the activities of linguists rather than to the activities of children (Campbell, 1978), since these formal results cannot readily be interpreted in the context of language acquisition (see Levelt (1975) for discussion).

language belong to the outer domain – 'grammar is an underground process' (Seuren, 1978). Naturally, each kind of process functions as a default for the other so that (a) in contexts that are familiar and habitual, communication can proceed in a routine manner and (b) in contexts where deviant or unusual utterances are received, grammatical analysis can proceed under rational control. Thus, as I see it, the case for autonomy of grammar stands or falls with the case for psychological dualism! Further, Chomsky – though perhaps correct in claiming autonomy for grammar – errs massively in his view that linguistics is a branch of cognitive psychology; on the contrary, it has nothing to do with cognitive psychology (strictly conceived) but deals exclusively with cryptic structures and processes. On the other hand, communicative processes, such as understanding, involve not just the autonomous language function but the whole being (cf. Ziff, 1972 – easily the best and clearest presentation of this point of view; amongst psychologists, Herbert Clark's is perhaps the most congenial treatment – see Clark and Clark, 1977).

The way in which grammatical and rational processes interlock in deriving a message from a text (i.e utterance or inscription) is a matter of current speculation (see Campbell and Bowe, 1978; Clark and Clark, 1977: chs. 2 and 3, for some suggestions) and need not be explored here. It is sufficient to note that, from this point of view, messages *qua* products of understanding are *not* linguistic objects. Thus, somewhat longwindedly, our difficulty is now clear: certainly it is possible to make defensible guesses about what messages are associated with which utterances in the speech of young children, but without knowledge of the structure of their message representations and the rational processes available to them we still have not radically improved our position as far as linguistic description is concerned. The point may be clearly illustrated with respect to the description of one-word utterances where at least three distinct positions can be discerned. According to one common view (now less popular – for cogent criticism see Miller (1976)) such utterances transmit propositional messages which are initially encoded as a (cryptic) isomorphic structure which is converted via grammatical processes of reduction into a single morph. A second extreme

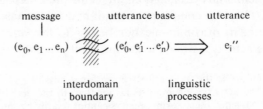

$$\begin{matrix} \text{message} & & \text{utterance base} & & \text{utterance} \\ | & & & & \\ (e_0, e_1 \ldots e_n) & & (e'_0, e'_1 \ldots e'_n) & \Longrightarrow & e_i'' \end{matrix}$$

interdomain   linguistic
boundary   processes

Model 1

view, still uncommon but perfectly viable (Campbell, 1976; Klein, 1977), is that such utterances transmit nonpropositional structureless messages which are encoded directly as single morphs. A third intermediate view (Bloom, 1973) is that such utterances transmit propositional messages by first selecting (by a rational process) a single message element and then proceeding as in model 2. A converse version of this third scheme is explicitly suggested by Sachs and Truswell (1978) as a means of accounting for comprehension of multi-word utterances by children whose own utterances are limited to single words. It seems to me that the evidence favours a sequence of model 2 followed by model 3 (see Bowerman (1976b) for a thorough review).

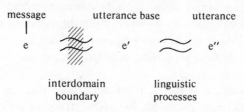

Model 2

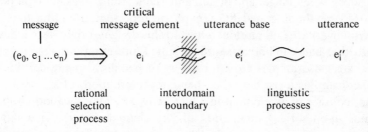

Model 3

As may be seen by inspecting the models, how the language of a child at this stage is to be described depends on (a) the complexity of the phenic structures that we think are involved and (b) whether we think that the child can learn that a single message element (suitably encoded) will convey a complex message. Thus analysis of a corpus consisting of pairings of messages and utterances must proceed on two fronts – cognitive and linguistic.[11] The discussion of cognitive development in section 2 should make it clear

---

[11] Braine (1976a) has made a valiant attempt to do just this. However, the requirement of independent analysis of message and utterance corpora calls for new techniques on both fronts. While Braine has certainly improved on older ones, there still seems a long way to go. Long (1976) has made many interesting suggestions about how syntactic analysis may be improved.

that there are few grounds for optimism amongst students of early child language. An adequate methodology seems more distant than ever.

4. Puzzles and prospects

What I have outlined in the previous sections is plainly little more than a thumbnail sketch of what *may* be a viable framework for relating work in cognitive and linguistic development. I have not sufficient confidence to take this further at the moment. To do so, would require the development of a richer terminology and I am unsure how best to proceed, since nothing hinders communication so much as injudicious terminology. Accordingly, in this last section I will discuss a number of puzzling phenomena that seem to me to be susceptible of resolution by means of a dualist approach, but in each case I shall stop short of proposing detailed accounts of how this might be achieved.

One obvious degree of freedom introduced by such an approach is the possibility of dual representation, for every structure may be represented *differently* at different levels. Thus, for example, in the case of the famous dialogue between Piaget and his daughter concerning slugs, it might be said that for Piaget the slugs had different phenic representations (due to reasoning involving space and motion) whilst for his daughter they were identical; on the other hand, in both cases the cryptic representations were identical. More extreme examples are afforded by such skills as plant identification and medical diagnosis: here the phenic representation (of species or syndrome) consists of an element in a hierarchy, and identification ultimately depends upon serial examination of key characters and the making of inferences based on this hierarchy. However, the skilled botanist or clinician soon acquires a cryptic representation of these plants and diseases which permits rapid and reliable (although unjustified) identification. The representations are obviously quite different in character, since different information is employed at cryptic and phenic levels. This example also shows that we must be careful not to confuse the method of acquisition of a skill with its eventual representation. For someone may learn to identify, e.g. mushrooms, with the aid of a phenic representation and a sequence of diagnostic tests. At the conclusion of this learning, however, he will have acquired an independent method of identifying mushrooms – 'by eye'. Of course, the phenic method is still potentially available as a back-up (and in medical cases one would hope rather more than just a potential back-up) technique, but if the cryptic method is more efficient, then knowledge of the phenic technique may lapse through disuse. Again there are surely skills, e.g. swimming, bicycle-riding, which do *not* have a phenic origin. Consequently, although grammar in the adult is an 'underground process', we need not suppose either that (a) all grammatical structures and processes have cryptic *origins* or that (b) those which *do* have phenic origins are isomorphic to the phenic structures/processes from which they derive. For example, syntactic categorization of early vocabulary may reflect simple early phenic distinctions of object, action, etc., although, of course, such distinctions cannot be noncircularly applied to later vocabulary, by which time related but different cryptic distinctions have taken their place. Again, if objects are initially distinguished phenically in terms of what actions can be carried out with them (as Piaget has maintained) then this need not deter us from supposing that a cryptic distinction is simultaneously developing on the basis of low-level sensory variables. This seems to be the implicit basis of Nelson's (1973b, 1974) suggestion that cognitive categories have a functional origin despite the fact that identification of instances depends upon registering perceptual similarities.

Questions concerning the origins of categories are indeed those which have proved most difficult to answer for epistemologists and psychologists alike. Successful resolution of the long-standing problems in this area would therefore add greatly to the credibility of a dualist approach. An old guess about how categories are acquired is the following: a series of denotata of the word in question, say *dog*, are ostensively presented to the child, who notices what features these denotata have in common. This set of common features, so abstracted, then functions as a dog-identifying-criterion and constitutes the meaning of the word *dog* and the child's concept of doghood. This is often regarded as an absurd story because in order to 'notice what is common' to the various denotata the child would have to have available a means for identifying each of the relevant criterial attributes, i.e. a categorial framework. According to this model of category formation, all that the child learns in acquiring a new word is what particular logical function of existing primitive categories is to be associated with that word. There are two, related, difficulties with this theory of category formation. Firstly, where do the elements of the framework come from? Evidently they cannot be acquired in the manner just described. One answer (Fodor, 1975) is that they are innate. How happy one is likely to feel about this rather depends on how rich the primitive framework is required to be. Fodor's notion is that it must indeed be quite rich – in which case there is an obvious objection, namely that an ontogenetic mystery has been dispelled by postulating a phylogenetic one! But if the prior conceptual framework consists of a small set of very general attributes, then the second difficulty arises. As was noted long ago by Brown (1958) and recently confirmed by Nelson (1973a) and Ninio and Bruner (1978), the earliest predicates are words of *moderate* generality –

denoting kinds of objects (attribute-clusters) rather than properties – and even as adults it is concepts of this 'weight' that we naturally employ (Rosch *et al.*, 1976).

To some degree these difficulties are avoided by the currently popular notion of stereotype or prototype.[12] Instead of the story given above, we would now say that natural kinds are identified by comparing each exemplar to a stored stereotypical individual (or, possibly, by comparison with a small set of such individuals). Words are then linked to their denotata via these stereotypes and similarity relations. This theory has many advantages. It relates early vocabulary acquisition in a natural way to the objects that have functional importance for the young child and the obviously spontaneous quality of these acquisitions (laboriously demonstrated by Nelson and Bonvillian (1973)) is easily explained. The fact that such natural categories have a nuclear member or members, coupled with a global metric of similarity, allows for the possibility that two individuals, sharing *no* salient properties, can belong to the same category – a frequently noted finding (Bowerman, 1978; Vygotsky, 1962). Finally, overgeneralization – such a characteristic feature of early use of language – can be accounted for either by supposing that *relative* similarity is what is involved (i.e. the 'nearest' stereotype determines what word is used) or that new individuals get added to a pool of stereotypes, each such addition stretching the boundaries of the category.

This theory has numerous merits. However, the notion of similarity must be unpacked. What does it mean for an individual to be similar to some other individual? Surely, only that they share certain properties. So *this* theory of category formation and semantic development, like the older one, makes an appeal to the notion of a primitive categorial system, albeit in a less immediate and forthright manner![13] It does not seem likely that there is any escape from such a notion. Even Quine, not noted for ontological generosity, now talks of 'innate similarity standards' (1975: pp. 69ff.) as a basis of language learning.

Now what is problematic about this theory? A line of argument leads inescapably to the view that at the onset of language acquisition the child is armed with a primitive categorial system which groups objects together on the basis of fixed attributes with elementary perceptual consequences. But there is a mass of evidence (Inhelder and Piaget, 1964; Vygotsky, 1962),

---

[12] The earliest formulation of this notion appears in Vygotsky (1962). While the discussion of 'family resemblance' in Wittgenstein (1953) poses the problem (which stereotypes solve) it is not until Putnam (1970) and Ziff (1972) that the notion is once more clearly expressed. It is now, of course, pervasive.

[13] There is an excellent and conclusive demonstration of this point in Bowerman (1978).

derived from children's behaviour in matching and sorting tasks, which shows that young children have very great difficulty in grouping objects together on the basis of an elementary fixed attribute. Certainly, Ricciuti (1965) and Nelson (1973a) have shown that young children can perform well with such tasks when it is members of a natural kind (i.e. a complex cluster of attributes) that are to be grouped, but use of an elementary attribute as a basis for sorting or matching is a much later acquisition. Moreover, it is also clear (Nelson, 1976) that the first attributive adjectives acquired by young children denote attributes which are *transitory* (e.g. *wet, hot, broken*) or *context-dependent* (e.g. *big*) rather than fixed and intrinsic.

So, on the one hand, we have evidence for the existence of a certain kind of category and, on the other hand, evidence for its absence. The way to a resolution, it seems to me, is clear. The elements of the primitive categorial system, Quine's 'innate similarity standards', are represented only cryptically and participate solely in cryptic processes: such categories have no phenic representation initially and their establishment at that level is a lengthy developmental process.

A second difficult area where a dualist framework should prove helpful is the development of linguistic awareness. Experiments of my own (Campbell and Bowe, 1978), and of Braun-Lamesch (1972) show that 3 to 4 year olds have enormous difficulty in making inferences about the meaning of nonsense words occurring in otherwise straightforward utterances which, *qua* utterances, have been accurately understood by them. An obvious guess about why this should be so, is that individual words lack phenic representations at this stage of development (and so cannot participate in inferences). Likewise Karmiloff-Smith (1978) found that children of much the same age 'explained' gender assignment in French in terms of rules that they were plainly *not* following. Her explanation for this contradictory result was that gender concord was at this stage a matter of cryptic phonological processes except for a small number of exceptional cases which were defaulted to a phenic process involving determination of sex. Their explanations reflected this phenic process entirely and the cryptic process not at all. Other examples could be cited but the point is already clear enough. However, there is a residual puzzle here. While it seems obviously correct that 3 to 4 year olds lack phenic representations of words in particular and indeed of linguistic objects generally, this is odd in a way since language learning *begins* with single words. Indeed, in section 3 I argued that there was a reasonable case for supposing that at certain early stages of acquisition (following Bloom and Sachs) inferences involving words were employed in the production of single-word utterances and in the comprehension of multi-word utterances. It seems possible that it is wrong to think of the development of linguistic awareness as a one-way process (from cryptic to phenic).[14] What is most shaming about this example and my discussion of it, is that it exposes brutally how little we know about human learning. We still lack a method of determining when an adjustment of the organism is phenically mediated (involving inference) and when it is not (cf. the early chapters of Weimer and Palermo, 1974).

In conclusion, I would like to emphasize the unoriginality of these proposals: they are to my mind (at least) latent in the recent writings of Bloom, Bowerman, Brown and Nelson.[15] It is, of course, difficult for psychologists trained in Britain or America to feel comfortable with psychological dualism because of the strong empiricist/determinist traditions in these countries. However, in French and German literature (e.g. Claparède, Wundt) from the early part of this century there is the basis for an alternative approach. Because of the unsolved methodological problems associated with it, such an approach can hardly be said to challenge current scientific practice seriously. However, it seems to me that its considerable theoretical advantages recommend us to reconsider these methodological problems and seek solutions to them. At any rate, no one need be afraid of psychological dualism. Certainly, we may acknowledge, with Eliot, that 'Between the motion/And the act/Falls the Shadow' but nevertheless insist, with Kety (1969), 'I cannot conceive any more than Leibniz was able to do, how a vortex of events in one world can effect a change in the other, yet it is our common experience that they do. Nor for that matter, can I conceive of how one body of matter attracts another body across empty space, and yet it does.'

[14] That is, *loss* of awareness may be as important for acquisition as growth. People who wear inverting spectacles manage to stay on their bicycles just so long as no one asks them whether they see the world the right way up or not!

[15] What I have in mind here is the tendency, common to these writers, to resist the easy identification of the conceptual basis of an utterance with its semantic basis (in their terms). Of course, in my terms the former is a phenic structure and the latter is cryptic so that such an identification becomes impossible.

22. Language acquisition in a biological frame of reference

John C. Marshall

1. Introduction

George Henry Lewes (1879) has remarked that, 'Just as birds have wings, man has language. The wings give the bird its peculiar aptitude for aerial locomotion. Language enables man's intelligence and passions to acquire their peculiar characters of Intellect and Sentiment.' Just so . . . but the important questions concern our ability to spell out in detailed theory the exact nature of this biological aptitude and its manifestations in anatomy and behaviour.

The (human) language acquisition device (LAD) begins its life as a proper subpart of a fertilized egg containing (in the normal case) twenty-two pairs of autosomes and a twenty-third pair of sex chromosomes (either xx or xy); LAD ends its major developmental progression some five, ten, or twenty years later when we see it in the form of a fully programmed central nervous system plus a peripheral nervous system which is in turn connected up to various input or output terminals (that is, ears, eyes, hands and vocal tract).

During the course of this development the unfolding of the structures and associated functions of LAD are controlled and regulated by (at least) a genetic programme (represented within the chromosomes) for growth, cell division and protein synthesis; numerous principles of embryological growth, specialization and neural connectivity; and various properties of the external environment in which the post-partum LAD finds itself.

The most beautiful image for the general case of such development has been provided by Waddington (1969). Waddington writes:

> 'we can imagine a multidimensional space with one dimension for each
> type of gene, so that a particular genotype can be represented as a single
> point within it . . . Now from any particular genotype there eventually
> develops a corresponding phenotype, which again we could locate as a
> point within a multidimensional phenotype space. However, between
> the genotype space and the phenotype space . . . there is a whole series
> of processes in which the various genetic instructions interact with one

another and interact also with the conditions of the environment in which the organism is developing. The system therefore moves from the genetic space into the phenotype space through what we may call an "epigenetic space", i.e. a space of developmental processes, which we may represent by vectors, or diagrammatically by arrows, which are tending to push the developing processes in one direction or another.'

There is, I think, little doubt that Waddington's metaphor of the organism (a structure–function complex) moving through an epigenetic landscape is an apt and sensible way of stating the problem. But this is a somewhat unfortunate fact: the mere expression of the problem now shows in only too obvious a fashion how far we are from being able to solve it, or give substance to the parameters. Relevant (one hopes) data have been accumulated in alarming bulk, but biological theories within which language data can be interpreted have not been forthcoming. Furthermore, as is so often the case in the human sciences, it is unclear how the few principles that have been formulated really relate to the phenomena they purportedly 'explain'. Ludwig's lament – 'problem and method pass one another by' – although dulled a little by frequent repetition is no less true now than when originally formulated (Wittgenstein, 1953). Nonetheless, we can begin to flesh out Waddington's somewhat abstract 'vectors' by considering the primary types or levels of data that bear upon the description of language acquisition.

2. Three levels of description

I shall assume that no one currently believes in reductionism and the unity of the sciences (Marshall, 1977), and that consequently a theory of language will be formulated on a variety of levels with 'bridge laws' linking the postulated levels. It seems that we will need three *primary* levels; first, a level that characterizes the 'objects' that are acquired (that is, the sentences of French, Japanese, Turkish, and so on, for the approximately 3000 extant 'official' languages); second, a level that represents the properties of the functional system employed when the above 'objects' are expressed and comprehended; third, a level that specifies the physical structures that constitute the instantiation of the functional model. These levels obviously correspond with the traditional disciplines of 'linguistics', 'psychology' and 'neurology' respectively, in the sense that level one will presumably make reference to such theoretical entities as *noun phrases* and *distinctive features,* level two to such theoretical entities as *working memory* and *parallel processing,* and level three to such theoretical entities as *synaptic knobs* and *nerve impulses.* Although it is difficult to see how one could proceed without distinguishing these levels, it is salutary to bear in mind Chomsky's warning that some ways of separating disciplines are more conducive to administrative convenience than scientific understanding (Chomsky, 1976). I shall accordingly digress, briefly, in order to show the point of the separation.

The first distinction – between linguistic and psychological descriptions – is simply Chomsky's distinction between competence and performance. It reflects the fact that from the existence of two (or more) algorithms for multiplication we do *not* wish to infer the existence of two (or more) sets of laws of arithmetic. Katz (1977b) has recently advanced the following version of this argument: Suppose that there were creatures, say Martians or porpoises, with whom we could communicate in English as easily as we could with any human English speaker. Suppose that these creatures had radically different speech production and perception mechanisms from our own. Would we wish to claim that these hypothesized differences in processing mechanisms force us into concluding that the creatures do *not* speak English? Surely not, for to do so would render our ability to understand them (without further learning) totally inexplicable. Katz brings the argument slightly closer to home by remarking that 'it could turn out that human beings whom we presently suppose to speak English, say Australians, have processing mechanisms as different from ours as these creatures we have been imagining. Would we want to say then that Australians are not speakers of English?'

Since little is known about the comparative psycholinguistics of Australians and Martians it might be thought that Katz's line of reasoning is merely fanciful. However, since we already know that there are extensive individual and group differences among many sets of cognitive skills (Chiang and Atkinson, 1976; Sternberg, 1976), it would hardly be surprising to discover related differences in linguistic strategies and mechanisms. And indeed there are well-known examples of such processing differences for both visual and acoustic language skills. For example, Baron and Strawson (1976) have shown clear differences between (adult) readers who rely primarily upon grapheme–phoneme conversion and those who rely upon holistic visual recognition with immediate access to lexical information. Both subject groups (the 'phoenecians' and the 'chinese') are, however, reading *English*. In the acoustic modality, Marslen-Wilson (1973; 1975) has convincingly demonstrated the existence of a small group of highly atypical 'close shadowers'. Typical response latencies for the accurate shadowing of continuous prose range between 500 and 1500 ms. Some of Marslen-Wilson's subjects could shadow accurately, making full use of syntactic and semantic information, and with good (incidental not intentional) recall at latencies of circa 250 ms. At normal speaking rates this is a mere syllable or two behind the message. Let us conjecture that 'normal' (i.e. distant) shadowers are basically 'stimulus-driven'; they accumulate stretches of speech in an acoustic memory store that is periodically wiped clean when enough information is available to permit phrasal or clausal analysis. By contrast, let us hypothesize that 'atypical' (i.e. close) shadowers are 'prediction-driven'; they run an internal model of possible sentence continuations at a faster rate than the input speed; periodically they sample the speech signal to check that their hypotheses are borne out, or to reduce the set from n to 1. Such speculations (if elaborated and made more precise) could turn out to be empirically false, but I see no reason to believe that they must necessarily be conceptually incoherent. Yet it is undoubtedly the case that both distant and close shadowers speak English. That the respective optimal grammars for the two groups would differ is, of course, possible but hardly likely.

These arguments suggest, then, that attempts to conflate linguistics and psychology (or to 'reduce' formal grammars to processing strategies) are likely to be ill-founded and unrevealing. Nonetheless, it is pleasing to be able to observe that, after twenty or so years of effort, a relationship of compatibility is coming to be established between syntactic theories and processing models. On the psychological side, this has been due to the extensive development of augmented transition network parsers (Thorne, 1968); from the linguistic side, convergence has resulted from attempts to restrict the power (Chomsky and Lasnik, 1977) and number (Bresnan, 1978) of transformations, and from attempts to develop 'enriched' surface structure representations (Chomsky, 1977). There is, at last, some hope that psychologically plausible parsing might fit with the structural descriptions of grammatical theory (J. D. Fodor, 1978; Marcus, 1977).

What now of the relationships between levels two and three – psychological and neurological description? Much the same argument for (partial) autonomy holds in this case too. Once again, it does not seem logically incoherent to claim that there could be two (or more) quite distinct 'engineering' (or hardware) solutions to the problems of instantiating an abstract machine that meets certain constraints (input–output relations, timing and memory requirements, etc.) derived from empirical (psychological) inquiry. That some variations in wiring-diagrams result in different behaviours does not imply that all variations do so. Or to repeat the best-known example: There is a functional level at which one would want to represent valves and transistors as the same mechanism despite the fact that their 'physiologies' are quite different from each other. The finest discussion of these issues is to be found in Lashley (1937), where he remarks upon the significance of (spatial) localization of function in the central nervous system: 'The fundamental problem for the student of localization is to discover what functions are served by this grouping and arrangement? What functions does it permit that could not be carried out if the cells were uniformly distributed throughout the system?' For present purposes, the important point to bear in mind is that Lashley does not assume that structural differences *must* have functional significance. Thus he writes:

'Some part of the structural diversity of the nervous system may well be an accidental product of the mechanism of embryonic development. By the general principles of neurobiotaxis, neuroblasts developing simultaneously in a given region are subject to the same developmental forces and will send their axons to a common field. Thus local groups of cells having similar functional connections will arise; yet the fact of their aggregation and the consequent 'localization of function' may be entirely without significance for the integrative processes in which they participate.'

Lashley then contrasts the above situation with one in which structural factors do impose strong constraints upon the functioning of the system. In this latter case

'separate localization of functions is determined by the existence of diverse kinds of integrative mechanisms which cannot function in the same nerve field without interference. If temporal order is determined by space factors in the nervous system, the fields in which this type of organization is dominant cannot also serve other space systems. There is thus some reason to believe that the utilization of the spatial arrangement of excitations in the timing functions determines an additional group of isolated cerebal areas.'

For Lashley, then, the issue of whether structural considerations affect function is an empirical problem, to be solved for each individual case on the basis of functional evidence. Such a situation is by no means rare in engineering contexts. Thus a recent advertisement (*Sunday Telegraph* Magazine, 1978) posed the question 'Why doesn't the Renault 14 have a wheel at each corner?' The back wheels are further apart than the front, and one of the back wheels is further forward than the other. With respect to some aspects of performance this strange arrangement does have functional consequences – the distance that the back wheels are apart gives more room for passengers and luggage; placing the back wheels out of line creates enough space to install transverse torsion bars and hence gives a smoother ride. On the other hand these modifications in wheel positioning do not affect the road holding and general handling of the car. (I assume for purposes of the argument that advertisements may be believed.)

To return to more directly psychological examples, there is now reasonably convincing physiological and neuropsychological evidence that structural brain organization in women and left-handers (or at least in some subsets of these populations) differs from that which is characteristic of right-handed men (Davidson *et al*., 1976; McGlone, 1977; Marshall, 1973; Subirana, 1952). Informed speculation seems to suggest that the neurological substrate for language skills in these 'deviant' groups extends across both cerebral hemispheres (the 'bilateral representation' hypothesis) or that it extends more widely within a single hemisphere (the 'diffuse representation' hypothesis). Whilst it has been proposed that these variations in structure are correlated with particular patterns of (relative) superiority and deficit in performance (Kocel, 1977), it is by no means clear that normal women and left-handers are anything other than normal with respect to either language or other cognitive skills (Fairweather, 1976; Hardyck *et al*., 1976). It is, however, only fair to point out that our current formulations of what might constitute different mechanisms are in a fairly pitiful state.

When we turn to the bridge between psychological mechanism and neurological realization matters become even worse. It may be possible (now) to individuate a nerve cell or axon anatomically and histologically and link that description to an input–output function that has some behavioural significance. But it certainly is not possible (yet) to individuate a cell assembly physically and link that description to a component in a psycholinguistic process. We continue to confuse localization of symptoms with localization of functions (Caplan and Marshall, 1975). Worse still, we continue to conflate levels of description, despite Freud's warning:

> 'Is it justified to immerse a nerve fibre, which over the whole length of its course has been only a physiological structure subject to physiological modifications, with its end in the psyche and furnish this end with an idea or memory?' (Freud, 1891)

That the temptation to do precisely this is still with us can be seen from Colby's recently updated version of Freud's warning:

> 'To mix hardware and program descriptions ("that transistor has a missing right parenthesis") is to make a category mistake. The conceptual distance between symbolic rules and neurons is so great that it is difficult to propose how knowledge about one might contribute to knowledge of the other.' (Colby, 1978)

3. Characterizing development at three levels

Developmental phenomena (i.e. changes over time) can obviously be characterized at all the levels of description (linguistic, psychological and neurological) that we have discussed. At the linguistic level, the issue is (in principle) quite simple. We characterize the development of the language learning child by postulating that he adds, deletes and reorders rules, and that he restricts and extends the domain of operation of rules within his internalized grammatical system. Language acquisition is thus described by an ordered series of grammars (Cohen, 1925). Within this overall framework some very elegant descriptions have been produced for syntactic (Klima and Bellugi, 1966; Mayer *et al.*, 1978), phonological (Berman, 1977; Smith, 1973) and semantic (Carey, 1978; Clark, 1977c) development.

When we turn to studies of the development of psychological mechanisms implicated in language production and comprehension, there is a relative paucity of information. Nonetheless, a number of first steps have been taken. Morton and Smith (1974), for example, have tried to show how the child's systematic mispronunciations could be accounted for within the framework of Morton's logogen theory. Tyler and Marslen-Wilson (1978) have demonstrated how limitations of immediate memory capacity in young children force them into a different trade-off relationship between syntactic and semantic strategies from that characteristic of older children. Tingley and Allen (1975) have studied the development of speech timing control in children, showing that the influence of peripheral feedback is minimal, and that a model which postulates a memoryless neural 'clock' can give a reasonable account of the data.

There is, however, a very general problem with practically all studies of language development, whether investigated from the standpoint of rule acquisition, strategy change, or elaboration of mechanism. The problem arises both for accounts that postulate 'stages' of development (i.e. a finite number of qualitatively distinct levels of organization through which the organism passes en route from molecule to maturity), and for accounts that view development as a continuous function or simple accumulation. The difficulty is this: No one has seriously attempted to specify a mechanism that 'drives' language acquisition through its 'stages' or along its continuous function. Or more succinctly: There is no known learning theory for language (or in all probability for anything else either).

Paul (1891) notes that 'In the process of naturally mastering one's mother-tongue no rule as such is given but only a number of examples . . . it thus comes about that the rule is unconsciously abstracted from examples.'

Perhaps so . . . , but why have we so conspicuously failed to provide any sensible accounts of how this 'comes about' ? In the first place, I suspect that the terminological change whereby 'language learning' became 'language acquisition' was not helpful (as no doubt Whorf could have predicted). In the second place, it is just very difficult to formulate learning theories in the absence of the conceptual tools that would allow us to think about the forms of interaction between 'innate' and 'environmental' variables. How, then, has the interaction been seen?

It is fairly clear to us, even if it was not so to Psammetichos, that exposure to a linguistic environment is a necessary precondition for a child to learn his first language. Children brought up outside such an environment do not 'spontaneously' talk Phrygian or even Hebrew; parental and other utterances must accordingly play a role in the 'acquisition' process – but what role? The literature contains two basic ways of looking at this problem. According to one proposal, the role of the environment is to provide *models*; the infant attempts to copy ('imitate') these models. He is rewarded for making good ('accurate') copies, punished for making poor copies. Under this interpretation, the child plays the game of *forger*. The game is over when all of the child's utterances are indistinguishable from the real thing. Since this theory rather conspicuously fails to address itself to the issue of generalization, no one believes in it (although behaviourists sometimes pretend that they do). A second proposal therefore arises. The role of the environment is to provide *data*; the child attempts to check out various hypotheses against these data. Some hypotheses are seen to be falsified and are thus dropped (or revised in order to save the appearances). Under this interpretation, the child plays the game of *scientist,* deriving and testing predictions from a general theory of language. The game is over when the child decides that his current set of hypotheses have passed a sufficient number of tests and that he will not bother to attempt any further falsification. Everyone believes this theory (in some form or other), although, in order to confuse one, some people who do so call themselves 'empiricists' and others call themselves 'rationalists' (Marshall, 1970).

Unfortunately, however, Fodor (1975) has recently produced a very convincing set of arguments to the effect that one cannot 'learn a language whose expressive power is greater than that of a language that one already knows', or, slightly more precisely, that one cannot learn a language 'whose predicates express extensions not expressible by those of a previously available representational system'. This effectively disposes of the hypothesis testing account of language 'learning' by demonstrating that everything (i.e. all the hypotheses that are tested) must be innate.

Everyone, Fodor included, agrees that this conclusion is untenable, but, to my knowledge, no one has yet brought forth a convincing counter-argument. At this point a wholesale retreat into 'biologism' takes place. Fodor concedes that the notion 'maturation' may be logically sound (and may increase the computational power of a developing system); and Chomsky (1976) remarks that 'The idea of regarding the growth of a language as analogous to the development of a bodily organ is thus quite natural and plausible.' He elaborates the point of view by noting that 'No one would take seriously a proposal that the human organism learns through experience to have arms rather than wings, or that the basic structure of particular organs results from accidental experience.'

It seems, then, that we must follow this retreat and inquire into the neurological characterization of developmental changes and their structural and functional consequences.

From first cell division to the appearance of six-layered isocortex some seven or so months later, the gross architecture of the human nervous system develops according to a predetermined structural plan and a (fairly) rigid timetable. Throughout (and beyond) the second half of this schedule, macroneurones grow long axons which develop patterns of invariant connectivity that constitute the basic 'hard wiring' of the brain. There is little doubt that this system unfolds under strong genetic and epigenetic constraints (Jacobson, 1970).

It might seem beyond dispute that acquisition of a native language is dependent upon a normal, intact (and peculiarly human) central nervous system. That is, the gross architecture and hard wiring mentioned above must stay within very narrow limits if even approximately normal language behaviour is to emerge. A moment's thought will, however, show that – stated thus baldly – the position is simply false.

Human kind are all too susceptible to a wide variety of genetic, transcriptional and exogenous ills that result in severe anomalies of cerebral morphogenesis or final structure. But it is emphatically not the case that *all* such anomalies *always* result in strikingly impaired linguistic functioning. To casual observation (and in some cases to more rigorous testing) the following malformations of the central nervous system are compatible with language acquisition and fair (or better) linguistic performance: Nathan and Smith (1950) have described a man of 34 (who died of visceral carcinoma) with arrhinencephaly (nondivision of the cerebral hemispheres) but normal intellect, language and temperament; Dennis (1977) has reported a case (JT, male, 14 years of age) of non-communicating hydrocephalus with dilated ventricles and EEG abnormalities in the left postcentral region who nonetheless obtained a verbal IQ of 121; Sperry (1968) has studied a 20 year old girl with the entire corpus callosum missing. The girl had been obtaining average grades in a Junior City College whilst working twenty hours a week as an office clerk.

It is no part of my claim that these (and related) conditions are *typically* asymptomatic with respect to language functioning; but even solitary examples suffice to show that, in principle, a variety of brain types (characterized in terms of gross anatomy) may mediate linguistic skills. Of course when discussing such instances as the above one talks of 'developmental compensation' and the remarkable 'plasticity' and capacity for 'reorganization' of the immature brain; but such phrases are not explanations. They refer to phenomena in search of explanation. What is lacking is any set of principles which show why some anomalies and insults can be compensated for whilst others apparently cannot (Hebb, 1949).

Notions concerned with the supposed 'equipotentiality' and 'plasticity' of the young brain have had a stormy career in neurolinguistics ever since Paul Broca (1865) claimed that although the left hemisphere was 'innately' pre-eminent in language skills, its dominance could be strengthened, modified or reversed by experience or injury during certain critical periods. There is thus a long-standing tradition in the study of the neurological substrate for language acquisition that runs something like this: At birth the two cerebral hemispheres (or the relevant subparts thereof) are equally capable of supporting the acquisition of language. They remain 'equipotential' in this sense for, perhaps, two years or so. There then begins a slow process of cerebral specialization which culminates in the left hemisphere acquiring command over the major (if not the entire) set of language processes. Progressive lateralization of language functions to the left hemisphere is supposed to be characteristic of the vast majority of right-handed people, and of a substantial proportion of left-handers. The development of lateralization is purportedly complete (in normal individuals) by puberty, or, in the opinion of some workers, by age 5. Among the reasons advanced in 'explanation' of this lateralization are the following: The left hemisphere matures faster than the right; the right hemisphere's linguistic abilities atrophy; the development of right-handedness (either genetically preprogrammed or taught) 'induces' greater skill in left hemisphere control of speech; the left hemisphere inhibits the right hemisphere's capacities for language via cortico–cortico and cortico–subcortical pathways. The implication drawn from calling this the 'normal' progression was, of course, that left lateralization of language is *good*. It therefore became popular to interpret various pathologies of language in terms of 'developmental lag' in rate (and extent) of lateralization, or in terms of atypical patterns of lateralization. This in turn led to such phenomena as 'diagnosing' the left handed or ambidextrous child as 'at risk' for this, that and the other, and it likewise led to such 'therapies' as tying the left arm behind the back. Whilst a grain of truth can be found in the above tradition, such ideas are dangerous if applied overenthusiastically in practical contexts, and they lack a compelling theoretical motivation.

In the last ten years or so we have therefore seen the rapid construction and proliferation of a counter-tradition. This new tradition starts from the observation – now widely reported – that there are numerous right–left asymmetries in the human brain associated with the classical speech areas. These structural differences, favouring the left side (on the assumption that bigger equals better), are present at birth (Wada *et al.*, 1975), and indeed some of them can be observed as early as 31 weeks of gestation (Chi *et al.*, 1977). There has recently been much speculation that these anatomical differences may be related to individual differences in aptitude and correlated with various types of learning disability (Galaburda *et al.*, 1978).

That morphological asymmetries are present at birth does not, in itself, prove that functional asymmetries are in operation from an early age. Independent evidence, however, suggests that – in some sense – they are. Electrophysiological techniques (Molfese *et al.*, 1975), cardiac conditioning (Glanville *et al.*, 1977) and the nonnutritive sucking paradigm (Entus, 1977) combined with dichotic stimulation, all seem to produce data consistent with the notion that some of the patterns of adult cerebral laterality are already present at 3 months of age (and in some cases at 3 weeks!). Such evidence, combined with the fact that the very young infant is capable of making highly sophisticated perceptual discriminations in the speech mode has conspired to suggest that cerebral dominance does *not develop*. It is nonetheless necessary to point out that we are far from a full understanding of exactly *what* is lateralized in the 3 week old (Wada, 1977). Whatever it is, it is clearly not language. We should likewise bear in mind that to say that the biological matrix for phoneme perception is 'innate' is not to deny that the child must, for instance, learn the particular values of voice onset time (VOT) and the nature of the first-formant transitions that are distinctive for the language community to which he is exposed (Simon and Fourcin, 1978).

Further evidence for the new dogma is found in the fact that – contrary to earlier belief – it is *not* the case that injury to either side of the brain is equally likely to result in developmental delay in language acquisition or in traumatic aphasia for the child who has already embarked upon his linguistic career. Left hemisphere injuries have a more deleterious effect upon the child's language just as they do upon the adult's (Annett, 1973; Dennis and Whitaker, 1977). It does appear, however, that right hemisphere injuries in the child are more likely to lead to aphasic impairment than right hemisphere lesions in the adult. Exactly how much more likely is open to question (Kinsbourne and Hiscock, 1977), for there are, of course, enormous difficulties in attempting to compare either the nature and extent of the lesion or the associated behavioural disturbance in child and adult (Jacobs, 1977). Nonetheless, the available data from brain trauma, and from dichotic listening studies of the normal child (Geffen, 1976), do suggest that provisional acceptance of the null hypothesis – cerebral dominance for language does not develop – is rational. One would, however, feel happier with this claim if we had some ideas about the mechanism whereby environmental factors serve to change structural capacity into functional skill. To assert that the left hemisphere is 'innately pre-eminent' as a neurological substrate for language still leaves open the possibility that the young brain is more 'plastic' than the mature brain. This is to claim that the prognosis for recovery from acquired aphasia becomes worse with increasing age. To the extent that this is true, it could be the case that either the left hemisphere speech areas of the child are better able to recover than the adult's, or that other left hemisphere areas can 'take over' language functions, or that the right hemisphere can subserve language skills if the left is inactivated at a sufficiently early age.

Prognosis for recovery probably is better in child than adult, although the picture is complicated by etiological considerations (van Dongen and Loonen, 1977). Some evidence has been presented for right hemisphere 'take over' (Hécaen, 1976), but the precise conditions under which this takes place are not well-understood. An excellent discussion of this issue can be found in Rasmussen and Milner (1977), who suggest that 'the continuing dominance of the left hemisphere for speech is largely contingent upon the integrity of the frontal and parietal speech zones'. It must, however, be emphasized that there is a paucity of research literature concerning recovery from aphasia in children. No detailed, longitudinal studies have been published; until such basic data are available, it is difficult to see how one could devise and evaluate really effective training programmes which attempt to speed the course of recovery and reduce the level of residual impairment (Oelschlaeger and Scarborough, 1976).

The extent to which language skills may be mediated by the right hemisphere in cases where, following hemispherectomy, the subject only possesses a right hemisphere has always occasioned controversy. There is little doubt that if the left hemisphere is removed early in life, then the right can acquire and sustain good comprehension of language, good expressive skills, and an adequate verbal IQ. Indeed, Smith and Sugar (1975) have reported one such case in which the right hemisphere has sustained language skills which are well above average. However, Dennis and Whitaker (1977), whilst agreeing that a solitary right hemisphere can acquire excellent phonological and semantic abilities, have presented data which show that the syntactic competence of the right hemisphere is quite restricted; it would appear that the right hemisphere compensates for lack of truly syntactic abilities by reliance upon semantically based strategies. Deficits of auditory comprehension show up in situations where specific syntactic structures must be analysed and integrated. This conclusion is consistent with that reached by Curtiss *et al.* (1978) on the basis of studies of a child ('Genie') in whom right hemisphere language was consequent (probably) upon severe environmental deprivation from an early age.

Whilst definite answers about the equipotentiality and plasticity of the infant and child brain are hard to find, it is at least clear what questions should be asked in cases where brain damage is directly demonstrable. The issues are, however, considerably less clear in cases where language acquisition difficulties are purportedly associated with 'minimal brain damage' diagnosed on the basis of 'soft' neurological signs and, circularly, on the basis of the observed *behavioural* deficit. It is far from obvious which patterns of 'atypical' laterality should be regarded as pathological and which should be seen as falling within the range of perfectly normal individual differences. Let us repeat the most frequently cited example: despite strident claims to the contrary, there seems to be no evidence that left-handedness or motoric ambilaterality is intrinsically pathological – it is not associated with 'high-risk' births (Hicks *et al.*, 1978), nor is it associated, in unselected populations, with either verbal or visuo-spatial difficulties (Hardyck, 1977a). The difficulties of inferring neuropsychological integrity (or otherwise) from lateral preferences are well brought out in Crinella *et al.* (1971).

When we turn to other – purportedly more direct – measures of hemispheric specialization, a similar situation obtains. It is, for example, totally unclear whether or not there is any truly reliable relationship between cerebral lateralization as indexed by dichotic listening or split visual field scores, and the acquisition of effective speech or effective reading. If there is a relationship, it is similarly unclear whether (and at what ages) large or small right ear (or visual field) advantages are associated with good or poor performance (Sadick and Ginsburg, 1978; Springer and Eisenson, 1977; Vellutino *et al.*, 1978). Although some very careful studies have been reported which lay the foundations for inferring cause–effect relationships (e.g. Bouma and Legein, 1977), routine interpretation of dichotic listening or visual fields scores is a practice that should be firmly discouraged. Unless the strictest attention is paid to experimental methodology and control, such measures are of doubtful reliability and validity. Practical applications for diagnosis, prognosis and therapy in clinical practice remain to be worked out and will be crucially dependent upon the construction of models of *normal* individual differences in hemispheric functioning (Hardyck, 1977b). Studies of structural damage have placed great emphasis upon the left hemisphere's contribution to language abilities; whether or not we should give equal weight to the left in theories of normal functioning is a matter of debate (Day, 1977). Likewise, the extent to which disorders of language, in the absence of gross, observable trauma or demonstrable EEG abnormalities, should be attributed to malfunction of a single hemisphere rather than to failures of co-operation between hemispheres is not known. Where there is clear pathology, our best generalization so far is that, on average, malfunctioning nervous tissue has more deleterious effects upon language acquisition and performance than *no* nervous tissue (although some minimal volume is presumably necessary!). But whatever conclusion one comes to about the importance (or otherwise) of hemispheric specialization, it seems highly unlikely that the crude dichotomies characteristic of the lateralization literature will be of much help in understanding the acquisition of language.

4. Language and learning

Let us return then to basics. It is not unreasonable to assume that the nervous system must have attained some degree of structural maturity before it can support a process as complex as language acquisition. But exactly what degree? Consider two primary parameters of neuronal growth – axonal myelination and dendritic arborization. Modern histological methods allow the chronology of myelination in different brain regions and fibre systems to be estimated with some accuracy. This permits Lecours (1975) to postulate the notion of a *myelogenetic cycle* for a particular area. The cycle is defined as 'the period extending from the time of the first appearance of stainable myelin sheaths in that system or region to the age when the tinctorial intensity shows no further visually discernible gain when compared with the same system or region in the (normal) brain of a 28-year-old adult . . .'. Lecours then claims that these cycles of myelination 'reflect the functional maturation of the brain and therefore can be related to the emergence and gradual differentiation in man of behavioural patterns such as locomotion, manipulation of instruments, articulated speech and language'. Now, the structural and functional data can indeed be put into correspondence in this fashion, but one should note that correlations permit one to infer neither causes nor necessary preconditions. For example, Lecours shows that the post-thalamic pathways to the auditory cortex show a relatively late onset of myelination and a long, slow progress to their 'mature' values. Do we infer from this that the auditory capacities of the infant are minimal? Clearly not, for we know – to pick an example at random – that 'two-month-olds are sensitive to place-of-articulation differences occurring in either the initial or medial positions of multisyllabic stimuli' (Jusczyk and Thompson, 1978). What is demonstrated then is either that myelination is (relatively) unimportant for effective conduction of impulses to the auditory cortex or that thalamic nuclei can mediate subtle perceptual differences. But there is no way in which straightforward inferences can be made from the physiological to the psychological domain. As Lipsitt (1969) has remarked in a related context, it was for many decades assumed that 'myelination was insufficiently advanced to permit learning in the newborn, and this premature conclusion inhibited functional studies of learning processes'. Similar conclusions apply to the study of dendritic arborization and the formation of axodendritic synapses. One cannot deduce that such-and-such a density of cortical synapses is required before such-and-such a behaviour may emerge. One can only see if the behaviour can be elicited at a certain age; we then *interpret* (or infer) structure in the light of our knowledge of functions. As our experimental techniques have improved (i.e. as we have put more sensible questions to nature) we have pushed further and further back the ages at which we believe the child or infant can display components or elements of the emerging language system. Whatever theoretical constraints we do succeed in setting up are more likely to be constraints that functional models can bring to bear upon the physiology rather than vice versa.

We can see this fact in operation when we notice that the only learning theories currently available in a (quasi) physiological notation are *associative* theories of the most classical kind; neuronal networks become programmed by principles no more sophisticated than contiguity in time or space. Whatever importance one attaches to the role of the linguistic, social and physical environment in which language learning takes place, it is unlikely that these principles (plus the minimal 'stimulus generalization' that simple conditioning theories make available) will suffice to project the examples to which the child is exposed to the language that constitutes his final steady state. It is a fair guess that modifiable synapses do indeed exist in the central nervous system, and it may well be that environmental influences can lead to hypertrophy, branching and atrophy of these dendritic synapses. Biochemical models for the selective stabilization of developing synapses (e.g. Changeux and Danchin, 1976) look quite elegant, but the concepts that would allow us to individuate any principles of linguistic interest at this level of micro-structure do not immediately spring to mind.

One might also note at this point that current theories of the 'multiplex' neuron (Waxman, 1972) seem to indicate that the computing power of individual elements of the nervous system is of quite breathtaking magnitude. It is more than likely that in physiology (as in linguistics) the real problems are concerned with restriction not augmenting the generative capacity of formal models.

From the standpoint of acquisition theory the most successful (I am tempted to say the only) attempts at providing linguistic constraints of sufficient power to ensure that (interesting) languages are, in principle, learnable from a finite corpus of examples are to be found in the work of Kenneth Wexler and his colleagues (see Wexler, 1978). It would be a useful, albeit far from easy, exercise to consider how, for a limited domain, one might recast Wexler's results in the form of a neuronal machine (i.e. a system of synaptic connectivities) that actually did project corpus to language.

It is perhaps unfortunate that we now have a large body of data which show that the speech addressed to young children is typically very different from that addressed to older children and to adults. For psychologists have misinterpreted the undoubted existence of 'motherese' to mean that 'innate constraints' upon the acquisition process can be partially relaxed. It is important to note that there is no evidence that even vaguely suggests that this is so. The progress of linguistic theory and identifiability theory (Hamburger and Wexler, 1975) has, if anything, suggested that Chomsky's early formulations of universal grammar were over optimistic about the nature, range and constraining power of the devices that one could 'get away with' in ensuring that a language is learnable.

Linguistic theory attempts to specify the 'abstract conditions that unknown mechanisms must meet' (Chomsky, 1976). It is not likely that these mechanisms will become any less unknown if we continue to assume that patterns of neuronal connectivity simply reflect the 'glueing together' of cell assemblies as a consequence of pre- and postsynaptic activity in the shared cells.

5. Coda

I note with some embarrassment that this chapter has been (almost) entirely negative, and thus feel obliged to attempt an answer to the criticism 'why then bother to write it?' In the first place the response must be that to delude ourselves into believing that we already know something about the biology of language acquisition is not the best way of preparing for the future. In the second place, I think we can now see a little more clearly the areas in which hypotheses are desperately needed.

Ramón y Cajal (1892) remarks that

'intellectual activity, since it cannot lead to the production of new cells (nerve cells, unlike muscle cells, do not proliferate), promotes the further development of protoplasmic expansions and nerve collaterals, fostering the establishment of new and more extensive intercortical connections'.

Children are existence proofs for the truth of Cajal's conjecture; let us hope that adult brains have not lost so much of this intellectual capacity that language learning will be for ever beyond our powers of comprehension.

Bibliography (and citation index)

Adams, N. 1972. Unpublished phonological diary of son Philip from 1;7 to 2;3. p. 136

Adlam, D. S. 1977. *Code in Context*. London: Routledge & Kegan Paul. pp. 389, 390

Allen, R. L. 1966. *The Verb-System of Present-day American English*. The Hague: Mouton. p. 271

Aller, S. K. 1977. The acquisition of relative constructions in Arabic. Paper presented at the 6th Annual University of Wisconsin-Milwaukee Linguistics Symposium, Milwaukee, March. pp. 289, 293

Aller, W. K., Aller, S. K. and Saad, L. M. 1977. The acquisition of Ask, Tell, Promise, and Show structures by Arabic Children. Paper presented at the 6th Annual University of Wisconsin-Milwaukee Linguistics Symposium, Milwaukee, March. p. 289

Ames, L. B. 1946. The development of the sense of time in the young child. *Journal of Genetic Psychology* 68: 97–125. p. 271

Amidon, A. 1976. Children's understanding of sentences with contingent relations: Why are temporal and conditional connectives so difficult? *Journal of Experimental Child Psychology* 22: 423–37. pp. 295, 296

and Carey, P. 1972. Why five-year-olds cannot understand *before* and *after*. *Journal of Verbal Learning and Verbal Behavior* 11: 417–23. pp. 259–60, 295, 296

Andersen, E. S., 1978. Lexical universals of body-part terminology. In J. H. Greenberg (ed.) *Universals of Human Language*, vol. III. Stanford, Calif.: Stanford University Press. p. 150

and Johnson, C. E. 1973. Modifications in the speech of an eight-year-old to younger children. *Stanford Occasional Papers in Linguistics* 3: 149–60. p. 365

Anglin, J. M. 1975. On the extension of the child's first terms of reference. Paper presented at the Biennial Meeting of the Society for Research in Child Development, Denver, Colorado. (Also in S. Erlich and E. Tulving (eds.) Special issue of *Bulletin de Psychologie* on semantic memory, 1976.) pp. 9, 155

Annett, M. 1973. Laterality of childhood hemiplegia and the growth of speech and intelligence. *Cortex* 9: 4–33. p. 447

Antinucci, F. and Miller, R. 1976. How children talk about what happened. *Journal of Child Language* 3: 167–89. pp. 10, 271, 272, 273, 274

Antinucci, F. and Parisi, D. 1973. Early language acquisition: a model and some data. In C. Ferguson and D. Slobin (eds.) *Studies of Child Language Development*. New York: Holt, Rinehart & Winston. p. 10
1975. Early semantic development in child language. In E. H. Lenneberg and E. Lenneberg (eds.) *Foundations of Child Language Development*, vol. I. New York: Academic Press. p. 286
Argyle, M. 1975. *Bodily Communication*. London: Methuen. p. 33
and Kendon, A. 1967. The experimental analysis of social performance. In L. Berkowitz (ed.) *Advances in Experimental Social Psychology*. New York: Academic Press. p. 386
Arlman-Rupp, A. J. L., van Niekerk-de Haan, D. and van de Sandt-Koenderman, M. 1976. Brown's early stages: some evidence from Dutch. *Journal of Child Language* 3: 267–74. pp. 164, 180
Atkinson, M. 1974. Prerequisites for reference. Paper presented to BAAL seminar, Newcastle. To appear in E. Ochs (ed.) *Studies in Developmental Pragmatics*. New York: Academic Press. pp. 112, 114, 115, 116
Atkinson-King, K. 1973. *Children's Acquisition of Phonological Stress Contrasts*. UCLA Working Papers in Phonetics 25. pp. 42, 45
Austin, J. 1962. *How to Do Things With Words*. New York: Oxford University Press. p. 73
Baldie, B. J. 1976. The acquisition of the passive voice. *Journal of Child Language* 3: 331–48. p. 312
Barblan, L. Forthcoming. Facile à voir? Vers l'analyse des conditions de réalisation de l'apprentissage d'une structure syntaxique complexe par l'enfant. PhD thesis, University of Geneva. pp. 309, 322
Baron, J. and Strawson, C. 1976. Use of orthographic and word-specific knowledge in reading words aloud. *Journal of Experimental Psychology, Human Perception and Performance* 2: 386–93. p. 439
Baron, N. A. 1972. The evolution of English periphrastic causatives. Unpublished doctoral dissertation, Stanford University. p. 286
Barrie-Blackley, S. 1973. Six-year-old children's understanding of sentences adjoined with time adverbs. *Journal of Psycholinguistic Research* 2: 153–65. p. 296.
Bartlett, F. C. 1935. *Remembering: a study of experimental and social psychology*. Cambridge: Cambridge University Press. p. 421
Barton, D. P. 1976. The role of perception in the acquisition of speech. PhD thesis, University of London. pp. 51, 56, 124
Bates, E. 1975. Peer relations and the acquisition of language. In M. Lewis and L. A. Rosenblum (eds.) *Friendship and Peer Relations: the origins of behavior*, vol. III. Chichester: Wiley. p. 373
1976. *Language and Context: the acquisition of pragmatics*. New York: Academic Press. pp. 90, 241, 368
Bates, E., Camaioni, L. and Volterra, V. 1975. The acquisition of performatives prior to speech. *Merrill-Palmer Quarterly* 21 (3): 205–26. pp. 73, 74, 92
Bates, R. R. 1969. A study in the acquisition of language. Unpublished dissertation, University of Texas at Austin. p. 261
Beilin, H. 1975. *Studies in the Cognitive Basis of Language Development*. New York: Academic Press. p. 298

Bellugi, U. 1967. The acquisition of the system of negation in children's speech. Unpublished doctoral dissertation, Harvard University. p. 231
  1971. Simplification in children's language. In R. Huxley and E. Ingram (eds.) *Language Acquisition: models and methods*. New York: Academic Press. p. 233
  and Brown, R. (eds.) 1964. *The Acquisition of Language*. Chicago and London: Chicago University Press. p. 123
Benedict, H. 1979. Early lexical development: comprehension and production. *Journal of Child Language* 6: 183–200. pp. 6, 7, 8, 9, 179, 183, 188, 207
Bereiter, C. and Engelman, S. 1966. *Teaching Disadvantaged Children in the Pre-School*. Engelwood Cliffs, NJ: Prentice-Hall. p. 387
Berko, J. 1958. The child's learning of English morphology. *Word* 14: 150–77. pp. 126, 210, 211, 212, 217, 269, 273
Berlin, B., Breedlove, D. E. and Raven, P. H. 1973. General principles of classification and nomenclature in folk biology. *American Anthropologist* 75: 214–42. p. 155
Berman, R. A. 1977. Natural phonological processes at the one-word stage. *Lingua* 43: 1–21. p. 443
Bernstein, B. 1960. Language and social class. *British Journal of Sociology* 11: 261–76. p. 387
  1965. A sociolinguistic approach to social learning. In J. Gould (ed.) *Penguin Survey of the Social Sciences*. Harmondsworth, Middx: Penguin Books. p. 387
  1971. *Class, Codes and Control*, vol. I. London: Routledge & Kegan Paul. pp. 329, 387
Bever, T. G. 1961. Prelinguistic behaviour: a systematic analysis and comparison of early vocal and general development. Honors thesis, Harvard University. p. 16
  1970a. The cognitive basis for linguistic structures. In J. R. Hayes (ed.) *Cognition and the Development of Language*. New York: Wiley. pp. 288, 292, 293, 310, 331
  1970b. Comments on R. Brown and C. Hanlon paper. In J. R. Hayes (ed.) *Cognition and the Development of Language*. New York: Wiley. p. 331
  1970c. The comprehension and memory of sentences with temporal relations. In G. B. Flores d'Arcais and W. J. M. Levelt (eds.) *Advances in Psycholinguistics*. Amsterdam: North-Holland. pp. 294, 296
Bever, T. G., Fodor, J. and Weksel, W. 1965. On the acquisition of syntax: a critique of 'contextual generalisation'. *Psychological Review* 72: 467–82. p. 329
Bierwisch, M. 1967. Some semantic universals of German adjectivals. *Foundations of Language* 3: 1–36. p. 157
Blank, M. 1974. Cognitive functions of language in the preschool years. *Developmental Psychology* 10: 229–45. p. 6
Bloch, O. 1913. Notes sur le langage d'un enfant. *Mémoires de la Société Linguistique de Paris* 18: 37–59. pp. 137, 138, 142
Bloom, L. 1970. *Language Development: form and function in emerging grammars*. Cambridge, Mass.: MIT Press. pp. 119, 120, 161, 162, 163, 169, 192, 196, 206, 207, 338, 340, 341, 428

1973. *One Word at a Time: the use of single word utterances before syntax.*
The Hague: Mouton. pp. 3, 6, 10, 41, 44, 45, 95, 108, 110, 111, 112, 113,
115, 117, 118, 183, 184, 419, 428, 431

1974. Talking, understanding and thinking. In R. L. Schiefelbusch and L. L.
Lloyd (eds.) *Language Perspectives: acquisition, retardation and
intervention.* London and Basingstoke: Macmillan; Baltimore, Md:
University Park Press. pp. 6, 93, 296, 428

Bloom, L., Lightbown, P. and Hood, L. 1975. *Structure and Variation in Child
Language.* Society for Research in Child Development Monographs 40.
pp. 180, 183, 191, 192, 196, 200, 201, 203, 230

Bloom, L., Rocissano, L. and Hood, L. 1976. Adult-child discourse:
developmental interaction between information processing and linguistic
knowledge. *Cognitive Psychology* 8: 521–52. pp. 346, 347, 428

Bloomfield, L. 1926. Approaches to the study of language. *Language* 2: 153–64.
p. 73

1933. *Language.* New York: Holt, Rinehart & Winston. p. 210

Blount, B. G. 1977. Ethnography and caretaker–child interaction. In C. E. Snow
and C. A. Ferguson (eds.) *Talking to Children: language input and
acquisition.* Cambridge: Cambridge University Press. p. 395

and Padgug, E. J. 1977. Prosodic, paralinguistic, and interactional features in
parent–child speech: English and Spanish. *Journal of Child Language* 4:
67–86. pp. 47, 363

Bohn, W. E. 1914. First steps in verbal expression. *Pedagogical Seminary* 21:
578–95. p. 150

Bolinger, D. L. 1950. Rime, assonance, and morpheme analysis. *Word* 6:
117–36. p. 217

1964. Intonation as a universal. In *Proceedings of the IXth International
Congress of Linguists, Boston, 1962.* The Hague: Mouton. p. 36

1965. The atomisation of meaning. *Language* 41: 555–73. p. 131

1972. Accent is predictable (if you're a mind-reader). *Language* 48: 633–44.
pp. 35, 36

Boole, G. 1854. *An Investigation of the Laws of Thought.* London: Walton &
Maberly. p. 420

Bosma, J. F. 1972. Form and function in the infant's mouth and pharynx. In
J. F. Bosma (ed.) *Third Symposium on Oral Sensation and Perception: the
mouth of the infant.* Springfield, Ill.: Thomas. pp. 22, 23

1975. Anatomic and physiologic development of the speech apparatus. In
D. B. Tower (ed.) *Human Communication and Its Disorders*, vol. III. New
York: Raven Press. pp. 22, 27

Bosma, J. F., Truby, H. M. and Lind, J. 1965. Cry motions of the newborn
infant. In J. Lind (ed.) *Newborn Infant Cry.* Acta Paed. Scan. Supplement.
Uppsala: Almquist and Wiksells. p. 22

Bouma, H. and Legein, C. P. 1977. Foveal and parafoveal recognition of letters
and words by dyslectics and by average readers. *Neuropsychologia* 15:
69–80. p. 449

Bower, T. G. R. 1974a. *Development in Infancy.* San Francisco: Freeman. p. 74

1974b. Repetition in human development. *Merrill-Palmer Quarterly* 20:
303–19. pp. 424, 425

Bowerman, M. 1973a. *Early Syntactic Development: a cross-linguistic study with special reference to Finnish*. Cambridge: Cambridge University Press. pp. 119, 120, 161, 163, 168, 170, 184, 192, 193, 196, 241, 367

1973b. Structural relationships in children's utterances: syntactic or semantic? In T. E. Moore (ed.) *Cognitive Development and the Acquisition of Language*. New York: Academic Press. pp. 165, 184

1974. Learning the structure of causative verbs: a study in the relationship of cognitive, semantic, and syntactic development. *Stanford Papers and Reports on Child Language Development* 8: 142–78. pp. 301, 302

1975. Commentary on *Structure and Variation in Child Language* by L. Bloom, P. Lightbown and L. Hood. In Society for Research in Child Development Monographs 40. p. 191

1976a. Commentary on *Children's First Word Combinations* by M. D. S. Braine. In Society for Research in Child Development Monographs 41. p. 191

1976b. Semantic factors in the acquisition of rules for word use and sentence construction. In D. M. Morehead and A. E. Morehead (eds.) *Normal and Deficient Child Language*. Baltimore, Md: University Park Press. pp. 7, 9, 10, 152, 191, 195, 419, 431

1977. The acquisition of rules governing 'possible lexical items': evidence from spontaneous speech errors. *Stanford Papers and Reports on Child Language Development* 13: 148–56. pp. 301, 302

1978. The acquisition of word meaning: an investigation of some current conflicts. In N. Waterson and C. E. Snow (eds.) *The Development of Communication*. Chichester: Wiley. p. 434

Boyd, W. 1914. The development of a child's vocabulary. *Pedagogical Seminary* 21: 95–124. p. 150

Brackbill, Y. 1967. The use of social reinforcement in conditioning smiling. In Y. Brackbill and G. C. Thompson (eds.) *Behavior in Infancy and Early Childhood*. New York: Free Press. p. 12

Braine, M. D. S. 1963. The ontogeny of English phrase structure: the first phase. *Language* 39: 1–14. pp. 177, 186, 188, 189, 192, 195, 200

1971. The acquisition of language in infant and child. In C. Reed (ed.) *The Learning of Language*. New York: Appleton-Century-Crofts. p. 231

1976a. *Children's First Word Combinations*. Society for Research in Child Development Monographs 41. pp. 184, 189, 190, 191, 192, 193, 194, 196, 205, 207, 431

1976b. Review of N. V. Smith, *The Acquisition of Phonology*. *Language* 52: 489–98. p. 124

Branigan, G. 1976. Sequences of single words as structured units. *Stanford Papers and Reports in Child Language Development* 11: 60–70. pp. 183, 184, 185, 186, 187, 189

1977. Some early constraints on word combinations. Doctoral dissertation, Applied Psycholinguistics Program, Boston University. pp. 54, 56, 61

Braun-Lamesch, M. M. 1972. *La comprehension du langage par l'enfant: la role des contextes*. Paris: Presses Universitaires de France. p. 435

Bresnan, J. W. 1971. Sentence stress and syntactic transformations. *Language* 47: 257–81. p. 35

1978. A realistic transformational grammar. In M. Halle, J. Bresnan and
G. A. Miller (eds.) *Linguistic Theory and Psychological Reality*. Cambridge,
Mass.: MIT Press. p. 440

Brewer, W. F. and Stone, J. B. 1975. Acquisition of spatial antonym pairs.
Journal of Experimental Child Psychology 19: 299–307. p. 157

Brimer, M. A. and Dunn, L. 1963. *English Picture Vocabulary Test*. Slough,
England: National Foundation for Educational Research. pp. 378, 386

Broca, P. 1865. Sur le siège de la faculté du langage articulé. *Bulletin de la
Société d'Anthropologie de Paris* 6: 377–93. p. 446

Broen, P. A. 1972. *The Verbal Environment of the Language-learning Child*.
Monograph of American Speech and Hearing Association 17, December.
p. 364

Bronckart, J. and Sinclair, H. 1973. Time, tense and aspect. *Cognition* 2:
107–30. pp. 260, 273

Brown, H. D. 1971. Children's comprehension of relativized English sentences.
Child Development 42: 1923–6. pp. 292, 310

Brown, R. 1958. How shall a thing be called? *Psychological Review* 65: 14–21.
pp. 150, 154, 371

1973. *A First Language: the early stages*. Cambridge, Mass.: Harvard
University Press; London: Allen & Unwin. (Also published 1976 by Penguin
Books, Harmondsworth, Middx.) pp. 45, 102, 106, 119, 120, 126, 127,
128, 161, 164, 165, 171, 173, 179, 183, 184, 205, 206, 212, 229, 253, 263,
264, 265, 267, 269, 271, 275, 286, 288, 298, 300, 338, 378, 382, 392,
393–4, 419, 428

1977. Introduction. In C. E. Snow and C. A. Ferguson (eds.) *Talking to
Children: language input and acquisition*. Cambridge: Cambridge University
Press. p. 375

and Bellugi, U. 1964. Three processes in the child's acquisition of syntax.
Language and Learning (special issue of *Harvard Educational Review*) 34:
133–51. pp. 230, 231, 232, 372, 393

and Hanlon, C. 1970. Derivational complexity and order of acquisition in
child speech. In J. R. Hayes (ed.) *Cognition and the Development of
Language*. New York: Wiley. pp. 298, 331

and Hildum, D. O. 1956. Expectancy and the perception of syllables.
Language 32: 411–19. p. 56

Brown, R., Cazden, C. B. and Bellugi, U. 1969. The child's grammar from I to
III. In J. P. Hill (ed.) *Minnesota Symposium on Child Psychology*, vol. II.
Minneapolis: University of Minnesota Press. pp. 231, 285, 378, 383, 393,
394

Brown, R., Fraser C. and Bellugi, U. 1964. Explorations in grammar evaluation.
In U. Bellugi and R. Brown (eds.) *The Acquisition of Language*. Chicago
and London: Chicago University Press. p. 338

Bruner, J. S. 1964. The course of cognitive development. *American Psychologist*
19: 1–15. p. 332.

1974. From communication to language – a psychological perspective. *Cognition*
3: 255–87. pp. 95, 96, 241

1975. The ontogenesis of speech acts. *Journal of Child Language* 2: 1–19.
pp. 3, 12, 39, 40, 41, 166, 167, 332, 334, 374

1977. On prelinguistic prerequisites of speech. Mimeo, Oxford University. p. 73
1978. From communication to language: a psychological perspective. In I.
  Markova (ed.) *The Social Context of Language*. Chichester: Wiley.
  pp. 338–9, 345
Bruner, J. S., Olver, R. R. and Greenfield, P. S. 1966. *Studies in Cognitive
  Growth*. New York: Wiley. p. 332
Brunswik, E. 1952. *The Conceptual Framework of Psychology*. Chicago:
  Chicago University Press. pp. 420, 421
1956. *Perception and the Representative Design of Psychological Experiments*.
  Berkeley, Calif.: California University Press. pp. 420, 423, 424
Bühler, C. 1930. *The First Year of Life*, trans. P. Greenberg and R. Ripin. New
  York: John Day. pp. 108, 109
Bühler, K. 1922. Von Wesen der Syntax. Reprinted in A. Bar-Adon and W. F.
  Leopold (eds.) *Child Language: a book of readings*. Englewood Cliffs, NJ:
  Prentice-Hall, 1971. p. 183
1934. *Sprachtheorie: die Darstellungsfunktion der Sprache*. Jena: Gustav
  Fischer. p. 351
Bushnell, E. W. and Aslin, R. N. 1977. Inappropriate expansion: a
  demonstration of a methodology for child language research. *Journal of
  Child Language* 4: 115–22. p. 175
Cambon, J. and Sinclair, H. 1974. Relations between syntax and semantics: are
  they 'easy to see'? *British Journal of Psychology* 65: 133–40. pp. 291, 309,
  310
Campbell, R. N. 1976. Propositions and early utterances. In G. Drachman (ed.)
  Akten des 1. Salzburger Kolloquiums über Kindersprache. Tübingen: Gunter
  Narr. pp. 119, 428, 431
1978. Explanation and language acquisition. Max-Planck-Gesellschaft,
  Projektgruppe für Psycholinguistik Working Paper. (Copies obtainable from
  the author.) p. 429
and Bowe, T. 1978. Functional asymmetry in early child language. In
  G. Drachman (ed.) *Salzburger Beiträge sur Linguistik* 4. Salzburg: Wolfgang
  Neugebauer. pp. 430, 435
and Grieve, R. In press. Royal investigations of the origins of language.
  Historiographia Linguistica. p. 95
Campbell, R. N. and Wales, R. J. 1970. The study of language acquisition. In
  J. Lyons (ed.) *New Horizons in Linguisitcs*. Harmondsworth, Middx.:
  Penguin Books. p. 128
Campbell, R. N., Donaldson, M. C. and Young, B. M. 1976. Constraints on
  classificatory skills in young children. *British Journal of Psychology* 67:
  89–100. p. 424
Caplan, D. and Marshall, J. C. 1975. Review article. Generative grammar and
  aphasic disorders: a theory of language representation in the human brain.
  Foundations of Language 12: 583–96. p. 442
Caprez, G., Sinclair, H. and Studer, B. 1971. Entwicklung der passiveform im
  schweizerdeutschen. *Archives de Psychologie* 41: 23–52. p. 310
Carey, S. 1978. The child as word learner. In M. Halle, J. Bresman and G. A.
  Miller (eds.) *Linguistic Theory and Psychological Reality*. Cambridge, Mass.:
  MIT Press. p. 443

Carlson, P. and Anisfeld, M. 1969. Some observations on the linguistic competence of a two-year-old child. *Child Development* 40: 569–75. pp. 43, 45

Carroll, J. B., Davies, P. and Richman, B. 1971. *The American Heritage Word Frequency Book*. Boston: Houghton Mifflin. p. 212

Carter, A. 1974, The development of communication in the sensorimotor period: a case study. Doctoral dissertation, University of California, Berkeley. pp. 74, 75, 76, 77, 78, 82, 83, 84, 108, 109, 110, 111, 114, 116, 117, 118

  1975a. The transformation of sensorimotor morphemes into words: a case study of the development of 'here' and 'there'. *Stanford Papers and Reports on Child Language Development* 10: 31–47. pp. 84, 86

  1975b. The transformation of sensorimotor morphemes into words: a case study of the development of 'more' and 'mine'. *Journal of Child Language* 2: 233–50. pp. 3, 6, 9, 12, 17, 29, 84

  1978a. The development of systematic vocalizations prior to words: a case study. In N. Waterson and C. E. Snow (eds.) *Development of Communication*. Chichester: Wiley. pp. 85, 90, 99, 102

  1978b. From sensorimotor vocalisations to words: a case study of the evolution of attention-directing communication in the second year. In A. Lock (ed.) *Action, Gesture and Symbol: the emergence of language*. London: Academic Press. pp. 74, 80, 84, 85, 89

  1979. The disappearance schema. In E. Keenan (ed.) *Studies in Developmental Pragmatics*. New York: Academic Press. p. 84

  In press. Speech acts in the second year of life. In R. L. Schiefelbusch (ed.) *Communicative Competence: acquisition and intervention*. Baltimore, Md: University Park Press. p. 81

Cazden, C. 1965. Environmental assistance to the child's acquisition of grammar. Doctoral dissertation, Harvard University. pp. 312, 393, 394

  1970. The neglected situation in child language research and education. *Journal of Social Issues* 25: 35–60. p. 378

Chamberlain, A. F. and Chamberlain, J. C. 1904. Studies of a child. *Pedagogical Seminary* 11: 264–91. p. 152

Chaney, C. 1978. Production and identification of /j,w,r,l/ in normal and articulation impaired children. Doctoral dissertation, Applied Psycholinguistics Program, Boston University. p. 65

Changeux, J. P. and Danchin, A. 1976. The selective stabilization of developing synapses: a plausible mechanism for the specification of neuronal networks. *Nature* 264: 705–12. p. 451

Chapin, P. 1967. On the syntax of word-derivation in English. PhD dissertation, MIT; and *Information Systems Language Studies* 16. Bedford, Mass.: Mitre Corporation. p. 126

Chapman, R. S. T. and Miller, J. F. 1975. Word order in early two and three word utterances: Does production precede comprehension? *Journal of Speech and Hearing Research* 18: 355–71. p. 296

Cherry, L. 1975. Teacher–child verbal interaction: an approach to the study of sex differences. In B. Thorne and N. Henley (eds.) *Language and Sex: difference and dominance*. Rowley, Mass.: Newbury House. p. 384

Chi, J. G., Dooling, E. C. and Gilles, F. H. 1977. Left–right asymmetries of the temporal speech areas of the human fetus. *Archives of Neurology* 34: 346–8. p. 447

Chiang, A. and Atkinson, R. C. 1976. Individual differences and relationships among a select set of cognitive skills. *Memory and Cognition* 4: 661–72. p. 439

Chomsky, C. S. 1969. *The Acquisition of Syntax in Children from 5 to 10*. Cambridge, Mass.: MIT Press. pp. 47, 131, 253, 288, 289, 290, 305, 308, 309, 310, 312

Chomsky, N. 1957. *Syntactic Structures*. The Hague: Mouton. p. 261
  1959. Review of B. F. Skinner, *Verbal Behavior*. *Language* 35: 26–58. p. 330
  1964a. Current issues in linguistic theory. In J. A. Fodor and J. J. Katz (eds.) *The Structure of Language: readings in the philosophy of language*. Englewood Cliffs, NJ: Prentice-Hall. p. 210
  1964b. Formal discussion. In U. Bellugi and R. Brown (eds.) *The Acquisition of Language*. Society for Research in Child Development Monographs 29. p. 104
  1965. *Aspects of the Theory of Syntax*. Cambridge, Mass.: MIT Press. pp. 163, 261, 299, 353, 365, 428
  1968. *Language and Mind*. New York: Harcourt Brace Jovanovich. p. 428
  1975. *Reflections on Language*. Glasgow: Fontana/Collins. pp. 353, 428, 429
  1976. On the biological basis of language capacities. In R. W. Rieber (ed.) *The Neuropsychology of Language*. New York: Plenum Press. pp. 439, 445, 452
  1977. On *wh*-movement. In A. Akmajian, P. Culicover and T. Wascow (eds.) *Formal Syntax*. New York: Academic Press. p. 440
  and Halle, M. 1968. *The Sound Pattern of English*. New York: Harper & Row. pp. 46, 218
  and Lasnik, H. 1977. Filters and control. *Linguistic Inquiry* 8: 425–504. pp. 428, 440

Clancy, P., Jacobsen, T. and Silva, M. 1976. The acquisition of conjunction: a cross-linguistic study. *Stanford Papers and Reports on Child Language Development* 12: 71–80. p. 287, 298

Claparède, E. 1917. La psychologie de l'intelligence. *Scientia*, pp. 361–3. p. 426
  1918. La conscience de la resemblance. *Archives de Psychologie* 17: 77ff. p. 426

Clark, E. V. 1969. Language acquisition: the child's spontaneous description of events in time. PhD thesis, University of Edinburgh. p. 259
  1970. How young children describe events in time. In G. B. Flores D'Arcais and W. J. M. Levelt (eds.) *Advances in Psycholinguistics*. Amsterdam: North-Holland. pp. 294, 297
  1971. On the acquisition of the meaning of *before* and *after*. *Journal of Verbal Learning and Verbal Behavior* 10: 266–75. pp. 259, 294, 296
  1972. On the child's acquisition of antonyms in two semantic fields. *Journal of Verbal Learning and Verbal Behavior* 11: 750–8. pp. 155, 157
  1973a. What's in a word? On the child's acquisition of semantics in his first language. In T. E. Moore (ed.) *Cognitive Development and the Acquisition of Language*. New York: Academic Press. pp. 93, 130, 152, 212

464   Bibliography (and citation index)

1973b. Non-linguistic strategies and the acquisition of word meanings.
    Cognition 2: 161–82. pp. 131, 157, 159
1974. Normal states and evaluative viewpoints. *Language* 50: 316–32. p. 241
1975. Knowledge, context, and strategy in the acquisition of meaning. In
    D. P. Dato (ed.) *Georgetown University Round Table on Languages and
    Linguistics 1975*. Washington, DC: Georgetown University Press. p. 152
1977a. Strategies and the mapping problem in first language acquisition. In
    J. Macnamara (ed.) *Language Learning and Thought*. New York: Academic
    Press. pp. 149, 157, 159
1977b. Universal categories: on the semantics of classifiers and children's
    early word meanings. In A. Juilland (ed.) *Linguistic Studies offered to
    Joseph Greenberg on his Sixtieth Birthday*. Saratoga; Calif.: Anima Libri.
    p. 10
1977c. First language acquisition. In J. Morton and J. C. Marshall (eds.)
    Psycholinguistics Series, vol. I. London: Elek Science. p. 443
1978a. From gesture to word: on the natural history of deixis in language
    acquisition. In J. S. Bruner and A. Garton (eds.) *Human Growth and
    Development: Wolfson College lectures 1976*. Oxford: Oxford University
    Press. pp. 157, 241, 248
1978b. Awareness of language: some evidence from what children say and do.
    In A. Sinclair, R. Jarvella and W. J. M. Levelt (eds.) *The Child's
    Conception of Language*. Berlin and New York: Springer Verlag. p. 428
1978c. Strategies for communicating. Paper presented at the Biennial Meeting
    of the Society for Research in Child Development, New Orleans. pp. 152,
    154
and Garnica, O. K. 1974. Is he coming or going? On the acquisition of deictic
    verbs. *Journal of Verbal Learning and Verbal Behavior* 13: 559–72.
    pp. 157, 257, 258
and Sengul, C. J. 1978. Strategies in the acquisition of deixis. *Journal of Child
    Language* 5: 457–75. pp. 248, 249
Clark, H. H. 1973a. Space, time, semantics and the child. In T. E. Moore (ed.)
    Cognitive Development and the Acquisition of Language. New York:
    Academic Press. pp. 241, 256, 259
1973b. The language-as-fixed-effect fallacy: a critique of language statistics in
    psychological research. *Journal of Verbal Learning and Verbal Behavior* 12:
    335–59. p. 245
and Clark, E. V. 1977. *Psychology and Language*. New York: Harcourt Brace
    Jovanovich. pp. 149, 151, 159, 212, 430
and Lucy, P. 1975. Understanding what is meant from what is said: a study in
    conversationally conveyed requests. *Journal of Verbal Learning and Verbal
    Behavior* 14: 56–72. p. 351
Clark, R. 1974. Performing without competence. *Journal of Child Language* 1:
    1–10. pp. 100, 286
1977. What's the use of imitation? *Journal of Child Language* 4: 341–58.
    pp. 41, 189
Clark, R., Hutcheson, S. and Van Buren, P. 1974. Comprehension and
    production in language acquisition. *Journal of Linguistics* 10: 39–54. pp. 45,
    178, 184

Clements, G. N. 1976. Vowel harmony in nonlinear generative phenology. MS, Harvard University. p. 62

Clumeck, H. 1977. Studies in the acquisition of Mandarin. Doctoral dissertation, University of California, Berkeley, p. 62

Cohen, M. 1925. Sur les langages successifs de l'enfant. *Melanges Vendryes*. Paris: Michel. p. 443

Coker, P. L. 1978. Semantic and syntactic factors in the acquisition of *before* and *after*. *Journal of Child Language* 5: 261–77. pp. 295, 296

and Legum, S. 1975. An empirical test of semantic hypotheses relevant to the language of young children. In *Working Papers on the Kindergarten Program: quality assurance*. Los Alamitos, Calif.: South Western Research Laboratory for Educational Research and Development. p. 296

Colby, K. M. 1978. Mind models: an overview of current work. *Mathematical Biosciences* 39: 159–85. p. 442

Cole, M., Dore, J., Hall, W. and Dowley, G. 1978. Situation and task in young children's talk. *Discourse Processes* 1: 119–76. pp. 340, 347

Collis, G. and Schaffer, H. 1975. Synchronization of visual attention in mother–infant pairs. *Journal of Child Psychology and Psychiatry* 16: 315–20. p. 74

Cook, V. 1973. The comparison of language development in native children and foreign adults. *International Review of Applied Linguistics* 11: 13–28. p. 292

Corrigan, R. 1978. Language development as related to stage 6 object permanence development. *Journal of Child Language* 5: 173–89. pp. 11, 179, 183, 207.

Craik, K. J. W. 1943. *The Nature of Explanation*. Cambridge: Cambridge University Press. p. 421

Crinella, F. M., Beck, F. W. and Robinson, J. W. 1971. Unilateral dominance is not related to neuropsychological integrity. *Child Development* 42: 2033–54. p. 449

Cromer, R. F. 1968. The development of temporal reference during the acquisition of language. Doctoral dissertation, Harvard University. pp. 287, 297, 310

1970. 'Children are nice to understand': surface structure clues for the recovery of a deep structure. *British Journal of Psychology* 61 (3): 397–408. pp. 291, 309

1971a. The development of the ability to decenter in time. *British Journal of Psychology* 62: 353–65. p. 259

1971b. The development of temporal reference during acquisition of language. Prepared for T. G. Bever and W. Weksel (eds.) *The Structure and Psychology of Language*. New York: Holt, Rinehart & Winston. p. 310

1972. The learning of surface structure clues to deep structure by a puppet show technique. *Quarterly Journal of Experimental Psychology* 24: 66–76. pp. 291, 309, 322

1974a. The cognitive hypothesis of language acquisition and its implications for child language deficiency. In D. M. Morehead and A. E. Morehead (eds.) *Normal and Deficient Child Language*. Baltimore, Md: University Park Press. p. 419

1974b. The development of language and cognition: the cognition hypothesis. In B. Foss (ed.) *New Perspectives in Child Development*. Harmondsworth, Middx: Penguin Books. pp. 268, 277, 334, 419

1974c. Child and adult learning of surface structure clues to deep structure using a picture technique. *Journal of Psycholinguistic Research* 3: 1–14. p. 291

1976. Developmental strategies for learning. In V. Hamilton and M. D. Vernon (eds.) *The Development of Cognitive Processes*. London and New York: Academic Press. pp. 303–4, 312, 419

Cross, T. G. Mothers' speech adjustment: the contribution of selected child listener variables. In C. E. Snow and C. A. Ferguson (eds.) *Talking to Children: language input and acquisition*. Cambridge: Cambridge University Press. pp. 242, 244, 371, 392, 394

1978. Motherese: its association with rate of syntactic acquisition in young children. In N. Waterson and C. E. Snow (eds.) *The Development of Communication*. Chichester: Wiley. pp. 169, 373

Cruttenden, A. 1970. A phonetic study of babbling. *British Journal of Disorders of Communication* 5: 110–17. p. 31

1974. An experiment involving comprehension of intonation in children from 7 to 10. *Journal of Child Language* 1: 221–31. pp. 47, 322

Crystal, D. 1966. Specification and English tenses. *Journal of Linguistics* 2: 1–34. pp. 268, 271

1969. *Prosodic Systems and Intonation in English*. Cambridge: Cambridge University Press. pp. 33, 37, 46, 102

1975. *The English Tone of Voice*. London: Edward Arnold. pp. 33, 34, 35, 37, 38, 386

and Fletcher, P. 1979. Profile analysis of language disability. In C. J. Fillmore *et al.* (eds.) *Individual Differences in Language Ability and Language Behavior*. New York: Academic Press. p. 191

Crystal, D., Fletcher, P. and Garman, M. 1976. *The Grammatical Analysis of Language Disability: a procedure for assessment and remediation*. London: Edward Arnold. pp. 123, 181, 182, 191, 193, 194, 202, 203, 204, 205, 208, 378

Curtiss, S., Fromkin, V. A. and Krashen, S. D. 1978. Language development in the mature (minor) right hemisphere. *ITL: Review of Applied Linguistics* 39/40: 23–37. p. 449

Cutler, A. 1976. Phoneme-monitoring reaction time as a function of preceding intonation contour. *Perception and Psychophysics* 20: 55–60. p. 48

Davidson, R. J., Schwartz, G. E., Pugash, E. and Bromfield, E. 1976. Sex differences in patterns of EEG asymmetry. *Biological Psychology* 4: 119–38. p. 442

Davis, E. A. 1937. *The Development of Linguistic Skill in Twins, Singletons with Siblings, and Only Children from Age Five to Ten Years*. Institute of Child Welfare Monographs Series 14. Minneapolis: University of Minnesota Press. pp. 180, 181

Day, E. J. 1932. The development of language in twins: a comparison of twins and single children. *Child Language Development* 3: 179–99. p. 180

Day, J. 1977. Right-hemisphere language processing in normal right-handers. *Journal of Experimental Psychology: human perception and performance* 3: 518–28. p. 450

de Laguna, G. 1927. *Speech: its function and development*. New Haven, Conn.: Yale University Press. p. 10

Dennis, M. 1977. Cerebral dominance in three forms of early brain disorder. In
M. E. Blaw, I. Rapin and M. Kinsbourne (eds.) *Child Neurology*. New
York: Spectrum Publications. p. 445
and Whitaker, H. A. 1977. Hemispheric equipotentiality and language
acquisition. In S. Segalowitz and F. Gruber (eds.) *Language Development
and Neurological Theory*. New York: Academic Press. pp. 447, 448
Derwing, B. L. 1974. English pluralization: a testing ground for rule evaluation.
Paper presented at the Annual Meeting of the Canadian Linguistic
Association, Toronto. To appear in G. D. Prideaux, B. L. Derwing and
W. J. Baker (eds.) *Experimental Linguistics: integration of theories and
applications*. Ghent: E. Story-Scientia. pp. 210, 211
1976. Morpheme recognition and the learning of rules for derivational
morphology. *The Canadian Journal of Linguistics* 21: 38–66. pp. 214, 217,
222
1977. Is the child really a 'little linguist'? In J. Macnamara (ed.) *Language
Learning and Thought*. New York: Academic Press. pp. 210, 269, 273
In press. Against autonomous linguistics. In T. A. Perry (ed.) *Evidence and
Argumentation in Linguistics*. Berlin and New York: de Gruyter. p. 209
and Baker, W. J. 1976. On the learning of English morphological rules. Final
report to the Canada Council (File no. S73-0387). p. 212
and Baker, W. J. 1977. The psychological basis for morphological rules. In J.
Macnamara (ed.) *Language Learning and Thought*. New York: Academic
Press. pp. 210, 211
Deutsch, M. (ed.) 1967. *The Disadvantaged Child*. New York: Basic Books.
pp. 387, 390
Deutsch, W. 1977. The conceptual impact of linguistic input: a comparison of
German family-children's and orphan's acquisition of kinship terms. Paper
presented at the XIIth International Congress of Linguists, Vienna. p. 157
Dever, R. 1978. *T.A.L.K.: teaching the American language to kids*. Baltimore,
Md: University Park Press. p. 123
and Bauman, P. 1971. Scale of children's clausal development. Mimeo.
Reprinted in T. M. Longhurst (ed.) *Linguistic Analysis of Children's Speech:
readings*. New York: MSS information Corporation. p. 191
Deville, G. 1890–1. Notes sur le développement du langage. *Revue de
Linguistique et de Philologie Comparée* 23: 330–43; 24: 10–42, 128–43,
242–57, 300–20. p. 135
de Villiers, J. G. and de Villiers, P. A. 1973a. A cross-sectional study of the
development of grammatical morphemes in child speech. *Journal of
Psycholinguistic Research* 2: 267–78. p. 126
1973b. Development of the use of word order in comprehension. *Journal of
Psycholinguistic Research* 2: 331–41. pp. 242, 245, 293
de Villiers, J. G., Tager Flusberg, H. and Hakuta, K. 1976. The roots of
coordination in child speech. Paper presented at the First Annual Boston
University Conference on Language Development, October. p. 300
de Villiers, J. G., Tager Flusberg, H. and Hakuta, K. 1977. Deciding among
theories of the development of coordination in child speech. *Stanford
Papers and Reports on Child Language Development* 13: 118–25. pp. 300,
301

468   Bibliography (and citation index)

de Villiers, J. G., Tager Flusberg, H., Hakuta, K. and Cohen, M. 1976. Children's comprehension of relative clauses. Unpublished paper, Department of Psychology and Social Relations, Harvard University. pp. 291, 292, 293–4

de Villiers, P. A. and de Villiers, J. G. 1974. On this, that, and the other: nonegocentrism in very young children. *Journal of Experimental Child Psychology* 18: 438–47. p. 239

Dik, S. C. 1978. *Functional Grammar*. Amsterdam: North-Holland. p. 429

Dingwall, W. O. and Tuniks, G. 1973. Government and concord in Russian: a study in developmental psycholinguistics. In B. B. Kachru *et al.* (eds.) *Issues in Linguistics: papers in honor of Henry and Renee Kahane*. Urbana: University of Illinois Press. p. 211

Dittmar, N. 1976. *Sociolinguistics*. London: Edward Arnold. p. 387

Donaldson, M. C. 1971. Preconditions of inference. In J. K. Cole (ed.) *Nebraska Symposium in Motivation*. Lincoln, Neb.: University of Nebraska Press. p. 424

1978. *Children's Minds*. Glasgow: Fontana/Collins. pp. 331, 332, 333, 427

and Balfour, G. 1968. Less is more: a study of language comprehension in children. *British Journal of Psychology* 59: 461–72. p. 130

and Wales, R. J. 1970. On the acquisition of some relational terms. In J. R. Hayes (ed.) *Cognition and the Development of Language*. New York: Wiley. p. 157

Dongen, H. van and Loonen, M. 1977. Factors related to prognosis of acquired aphasia in children. *Cortex* 13: 131–6. p. 448

Dore, J. 1973. The development of speech acts. Doctoral dissertation, City University of New York. pp. 30, 74, 346

1974. A pragmatic description of early language development. *Journal of Psycholinguistic Research* 3: 343–50. pp. 107, 110, 111, 114, 115, 117, 346

1975. Holophrases, speech acts and language universals. *Journal of Child Language* 2: 21–40. pp. 11, 39, 40, 41, 107, 110, 111, 114, 115, 117, 346

1977a. 'Oh them sheriff': a pragmatic analysis of children's responses to questions. In S. Ervin-Tripp and C. Mitchell-Kernan (eds.) *Child Discourse*. New York: Academic Press. pp. 348, 349, 350

1977b. Review of M. A. K. Halliday's *Learning How to Mean*. In *Language and Society* 6: 190–5. p. 352

1978. Requestive systems in nursery school conversations: analysis of talk in its social context. In R. N. Campbell and P. T. Smith (eds.) *Recent Advances in the Psychology of Language: language development and mother–child interaction*. New York and London: Plenum Press. p. 344

Dore, J., Franklin, M. B., Miller, R. T. and Ramer, A. L. H. 1976. Transitional phenomena in early language acquisition. *Journal of Child Language* 3: 13–28. pp. 3, 5, 6, 17, 30, 41, 74, 75, 76, 90, 184, 185, 186, 187, 188, 189, 353

Dore, J., Gearhart, M. and Newman, D. 1978. The structure of nursery school conversation. In K. Nelson (ed.) *Children's Language*. New York: Gardner Press. pp. 353, 358

Drach, K. 1969. The language of the parent: a pilot study. Working Paper no. 14, University of California, Berkeley. p. 364

Dubois, J. 1970. *Grammaire structurale du Français: nom et pronom*. Paris:
    Larousse. pp. 397, 398, 399, 403
Du Preez, P. 1974. Units of information in the acquisition of language.
    Language and Speech 17: 369–76. pp. 46, 48
Edwards, A. D. 1976a. *Language in Culture and Class*. London: Heinemann.
    pp. 387, 389
    1976b. Speech codes and speech variants: social class and task differences in
    children's speech. *Journal of Child Language* 3: 247–66. p. 390
Edwards, D. 1974. Sensory-motor intelligence and semantic relations in early
    child grammar. *Cognition* 2: 395–434. p. 427
    1978a. Social relations and early language. In A. J. Lock (ed.) *Action, Gesture
    and Symbol: the emergence of language*. London: Academic Press. p. 170
    1978b. The three sources of children's early meanings. In I. Markova (ed.)
    The Social Context of Language. Chichester: Wiley. pp. 103, 428
Edwards, M. L. 1974. Perception and production in child phonology: the testing
    of four hypotheses. *Journal of Child Language* 1: 205–19. p. 124
Eilers, R. E. 1975. Suprasegmental and grammatical control over telegraphic
    speech in young children. *Journal of Psycholinguistic Research* 4: 227–39.
    p. 46
    1976. Discrimination of synthetic prevoiced labial stops by infants and adults.
    Paper presented at the 92nd Meeting of the Acoustical Society of America,
    San Diego. p. 32
    and Oller, D. 1976. The role of speech discrimination in developmental sound
    substitutions. *Journal of Child Language* 3: 319–30. p. 57
Eimas, P. 1974. Linguistic processing of speech by young infants. In R. L.
    Schiefelbusch and L. L. Lloyd (eds.) *Language Perspectives: acquisition,
    retardation and intervention*. London and Basingstoke: Macmillan;
    Baltimore, Md: University Park Press. p. 50
Enstrom, D. H. and Stoll, F. 1976. Babbling sounds of Swiss-German infants: a
    phonetic and spectrographic analysis. Paper presented at the American
    Speech and Hearing Association Convention, Houston. p. 29
Entus, A. K. 1977. Hemispheric asymmetry in processing of dichotically
    presented speech and nonspeech stimuli by infants. In S. Segalowitz and F.
    Gruber (eds.) *Language Development and Neurological Theory*. New York:
    Academic Press. p. 447
Ervin, S. 1964. Imitation and structural change in children's language. In E. H.
    Lenneberg (ed.) *New Directions in the Study of Language*. Cambridge,
    Mass.: MIT Press. pp. 267, 271, 302
Ervin-Tripp, S. 1977. 'Wait for me, Rollerskate!' In S. Ervin-Tripp and
    C. Mitchell-Kernan (eds.) *Child Discourse*. New York: Academic Press.
    pp. 349, 350
    and Mitchell-Kernan, C. (eds.) 1977. *Child Discourse*. New York: Academic
    Press. p. 347
Escalona, S. 1973. Basic modes of social interaction: their emergence and
    patterning during the first two years of life. *Merrill-Palmer Quarterly* 19:
    205–32. p. 74
Evans, J. 1977. The significance of adult feedback on child language development.
    M.Ed. dissertation, University of Bristol School of Education. p. 394.

470   Bibliography (and citation index)

Fabian, V. 1977. When are children hard to understand? Paper presented at the Second Annual Boston University Conference on Language Development, October. p. 291

Fairweather, H. 1976. Sex differences in cognition. *Cognition* 4: 231–80. p. 442

Farwell, C. B. 1976. Some strategies in the early production of fricatives. In *Stanford Papers and Reports on Child Language Development* 12. p. 67

1977. The primacy of *goal* in the child's description of motion and location. In *Stanford Papers and Reports on Child Language Development* 13: 126–33. pp. 151, 153

Fay, D. 1978. Transformations as mental operations: a reply to Kuczaj. *Journal of Child Language* 5: 143–50. pp. 129, 273

Ferguson, C. A. 1964. Baby talk in six languages. *American Anthropologist* 66 (6, part 2): 103–14. p. 150

1976. Learning to pronounce: the earliest stages of phonological development in the child. *Stanford Papers and Reports on Child Language Development* 11. Also in F. Minifie and L. L. Lloyd (eds.) *Communicative and Cognitive Abilities – early behavioral assessment*. Baltimore: University Park Press, 1977. pp. 3, 4, 5, 8, 49, 71, 72, 185

1977. Baby talk as a simplified register. In C. E. Snow and C. A. Ferguson (eds.) *Talking to Children: language input and acquisition*. Cambridge: Cambridge University Press. pp. 47, 150, 363

and Farwell, C. B. 1975. Words and sounds in early language acquisition. *Language* 51: 419–39. pp. 54, 67, 142

Ferreiro, E. 1971. *Les relations temporelles dans le langage de l'enfant*. Paris: Droz. pp. 310, 314

1974. Producción, comprensión y repetición de la proposición relativa. MS. p. 310

and Sinclair, H. 1971. Temporal relations in language. *International Journal of Psychology* 6: 39–47. p. 294

Ferrier, L. J. 1978. Some observations of error in context. In N. Waterson and C. E. Snow (eds.) *The Development of Communication*. Chichester: Wiley. p. 100

Fillmore, C. J. 1966. Deictic categories in the semantics of 'come'. *Foundations of Language* 2: 219–27. p. 241

1968. The case for case. In E. Bach and R. T. Harms (eds.) *Universals in Linguistic Theory*. New York: Holt, Rinehart & Winston. p. 163

1970. Subjects, speakers and roles. *Synthese* 21: 251–74. p. 241

1971a. Santa Cruz Lectures on Deixis. MS. Summer program in linguistics, University of California at Santa Cruz. (Reproduced by the Indiana University Linguistics Club, November 1975.) p. 301

1971b. Some problems for case grammar. In R. J. O'Brien (ed.) *Monograph Series on Language and Linguistics*. 22nd Annual Georgetown University Roundtable. Washington, DC: Georgetown University Press. pp. 241, 256

Fisher, M. S. 1934. *Language Patterns of Preschool Children*. Child Development Monograph 15. Chicago: University of Chicago Press. p. 180

Fisichelli, R. M. 1950. A study of prelinguistic speech development of institutionalized infants. Unpublished doctoral dissertation, Fordham University. p. 15

Flavell, J. H. 1963. *The Developmental Psychology of Jean Piaget*. Princeton, NJ: Van Nostrand Reinhold. p. 331

1977. *Cognitive Development*. Englewood Cliffs, NJ: Prentice Hall. p. 239

Fletcher, P. 1975. Review of D. Major, *The Acquisition of Modal Auxiliaries in the Language of Children*. *Journal of Child Language* 2: 318–22. p. 279

and Garman, M. 1978. Child language development. In V. Kinsella (ed.) *Language Teaching and Linguistics: surveys*. Centre for Information on Language Teaching. Cambridge: Cambridge University Press. p. 123

Flores D'Arcais, G. B. 1978. The acquisition of the subordinating constructions in children's language. In R. N. Campbell and P. T. Smith (eds.) *Recent Advances in the Psychology of Language: language development and mother–child interaction*. New York and London: Plenum Press. p. 296

Fodor, J. A. 1966. How to learn to talk: some simple ways. In F. Smith and G. A. Miller (eds.) *The Genesis of Language*. Cambridge, Mass.: MIT Press. p. 364

1970. Three reasons for not deriving 'kill' from 'cause to die'. *Linguistic Inquiry* 4: 429–38. p. 301

1975. *The Language of Thought*. Hassocks, Sussex: Harvester Press; New York: Thomas Y. Crowell. p. 433, 444, 445

and Garrett, M. 1966. Some reflections on competence and performance. In J. Lyons and R. J. Wales (eds.) *Psycholinguistics Papers*. Edinburgh: University of Edinburgh Press. p. 298

Fodor, J. A., Bever, T. and Garrett, M. 1974. *Psychology of Language*. New York: McGraw-Hill. p. 56

Fodor, J. D. 1978. Parsing strategies and constraints on transformations. *Linguistic Inquiry* 9: 427–73. p. 440

Forster, K. I. 1976. Accessing the mental lexicon. In R. J. Wales and E. Walker (eds.) *New Approaches to Language Mechanisms*. Amsterdam: North-Holland. p. 424

Fox, A. 1973. Tone-sequences in English. *Archivum Linguisticum* (new series) 4: 17–26. p. 35

Fraisse, P. 1964. *The Psychology of Time*. London: Eyre & Spottiswoode. p. 274

and Piaget, J. 1968. *Experimental Psychology: its scope and method*, vol. I. New York: Basic Books. p. 420

Francis, H. 1974. Social class, reference and context. *Language and Speech* 17: 193–8. p. 390

Fraser, C. and Roberts, N. 1973. How adults talk to children. Final Report to the Nuffield Foundation. p. 392

1975. Mothers' speech to children of four different ages. *Journal of Psycholinguistic Research* 4: 9–16. p. 392

French, L. A. and Brown, A. L. 1977. Comprehension of *before* and *after* in logical and arbitrary sequences. *Journal of Child Language* 4: 247–56. p. 296

Freud, S. 1891. *Zur Auffassung der Aphasien*. Vienna: Deuticke. p. 442

Fujimura, O. and Lovins, J. 1978. Syllables as concatenative phonetic units. In A. Bell and J. B. Hooper (eds.) *Syllables and Segments*. Amsterdam: North-Holland. p. 54

Gaer, E. P. 1969. Children's understanding and production of sentences. *Journal of Verbal Learning and Verbal Behavior* 8: 289–94. p. 292, 310

Galaburda, A. M., Le May, M., Kemper, T. L. and Geschwind, N. 1978. Right–left asymmetries in the brain. *Science* 199: 852–6. p. 447

Gammon, E. M. 1973. A syntactical analysis of some first-grade readers. In K. J. J. Hintikka, J. M. E. Moravcsik and P. Suppes (eds.) *Approaches to Natural Language*. Dordrecht: Reidel. p. 404

Garcia, E. C. 1975. *The Role of Theory in Linguistic Analysis: the Spanish pronoun system*. Amsterdam: North-Holland. p. 429

Garfinkel, H. and Sacks, H. 1970. The formal properties of practical actions. In J. C. McKinney and E. A. Tiryakian (eds.) *Theoretical Sociology*. NewYork: Appleton-Century-Crofts. p. 343

Garman, M. A. 1977. Crosslinguistic study of deixis. Paper presented at the IVth Salzburg Psycholinguistics Conference, August. p. 251

Garman, M. A., Griffiths, P. D. and Wales, R. J. 1970. Murut (Lun Buwang) prepositions and noun particles in children's speech. *Sarawak Museum Journal* 18: 214–25. pp. 159, 257–8

Garnica, O. 1973. The development of phonemic speech perception. In T. Moore (ed.) *Cognitive Development and the Acquisition of Language*. New York: Academic Press. pp. 50, 51

   1977. Some prosodic and paralinguistic features of speech to young children. In C. E. Snow and C. A. Ferguson (eds.) *Talking to Children: language input and acquisition*. Cambridge: Cambridge University Press. pp. 251, 366, 375

   1978. Nonverbal concomitants of language input to children: clues to meaning. In N. Waterson and C. E. Snow (eds.) *The Development of Communication*. Chichester: Wiley. p. 158

Garvey, C. 1975. Requests and responses in children's speech. *Journal of Child Language* 2: 41–59. pp. 348, 349, 350

   1977. Contingent queries. In M. Lewis and L. Rosenblum (eds.) *Interaction, Conversation and the Development of Language*. New York: Wiley. pp. 346, 347, 350

Gearhart, M. 1977. How children accomplish beginnings. Unpublished MS, City University of New York. p. 347

Geffen, G. 1976. Development of hemispheric specialization for speech perception. *Cortex* 12: 337–46. p. 448

Gentner, D. 1975. Evidence for the psychological reality of semantic components: the verbs of possession. In D. A. Norman, D. E. Rumelhart and the LNR Research Group (eds.) *Explorations in Cognition*. San Francisco, Calif.: Freeman. p. 157

Gesell, A. and Thompson, H. 1934. *Infant Behavior: its genesis and growth*. New York: McGraw-Hill. pp. 27, 30

Gibson, J. J. 1966. *The Senses Considered as Perceptual Systems*. Boston: Houghton Mifflin. p. 421

Gilbert, J. H. V. 1977. A voice onset time analysis of apical stop production in 3-year-olds. *Journal of Child Language* 4: 103–10. p. 138

Glanville, B., Best, C. and Levenson, R. 1977. A cardiac measure of cerebral asymmetries in infant auditory perception. *Developmental Psychology* 13: 54–9. p. 447

Gleitman, L. R., Gleitman H. and Shipley. E. 1972. The emergence of the child as grammarian. *Cognition* 1: 137–64. p. 6

Gold, E. M. 1967. Language identification in the limit. *Information and Control* 10: 447–74. p. 429

Goldin-Meadow, S., Seligman, M. E. P. and Gelman, R. 1976. Language in the two-year-old. *Cognition* 4: 189–202. pp. 6, 8, 179, 188, 200, 207

Goldsmith, J. 1976. An overview of autosegmental phonology. *Linguistic Analysis* 2: 23–68. p. 62

Golinkoff, R. M. 1975. Semantic development in infants: the concepts of agent and recipient. *Merrill-Palmer Quarterly* 21: 181–95. p. 427

and Kerr, J. L. 1978. Infants' perception of semantically defined action role changes in filmed events. *Merrill-Palmer Quarterly* 24: 53–62. p. 427

Goodglass, H., Fodor, I. G. and Schulhoff, C. 1967. Prosodic factors in Grammar – evidence from aphasia. *Journal of Speech and Hearing Research* 10: 5–20. p. 48

Gopnik, A. 1977. *No, there, more* and *allgone*: why the first words aren't about things. Paper presented at Nottingham Child Language Seminar. pp. 110, 111, 113, 116

Gordon, A. 1972. Psychological and linguistic complexity in child language. Doctoral dissertation, Stanford University. p. 292

Gordon, D. and Lakoff, G. 1971. Conversational postulates. *Chicago Linguistic Society Regional Meeting Papers* 7: 63–84. p. 109

Grant, J. R. 1915. A child's vocabulary and its growth. *Pedagogical Seminary* 22: 183–203. p. 150

Greenfield, P. 1968. Development of the holophrase: observation on Lauren Greenfield. Unpublished paper, Harvard University Center for Cognitive Studies. p. 10

and Smith, J. H. 1976. *The Structure of Communication in Early Language Development.* New York: Academic Press. pp. 90, 95, 150, 151, 153–4, 166, 184, 370, 372

Greenfield, P., Nelson, K. and Saltzman, E. 1972. The development of rulebound strategies for manipulating seriated cups: a parallel between action and grammar. *Cognitive Psychology* 3: 291–310. p. 90

Gregoire, A. 1939. L'apprentissage du langage: les deux premières années. Bibliotheque de la Faculté de Philosophie et Lettres de l'Université de Liege. p. 90

Grévisse, M. 1969. *Le bon usage: grammaire française avec des remarques sur la langue française d'aujourd'hui.* Gemblouz, France: Duculot. p. 398

Grice, H. P. 1967. William James Lectures. Harvard University. Published in part as Grice (1975). p. 429

1975. Logic and conversation. In P. Cole and J. L. Morgan (eds.) *Syntax and Semantics*, vol. III, *Speech Acts*. New York: Academic Press. p. 109

Grieve, R., Hoogenraad, R. Murray, D. 1977. On the young child's use of lexis and syntax in understanding locative instructions. *Cognition* 5: 235–50. p. 295

Griffiths, P. D. 1974a. Review of M. Bowerman, *Early Syntactic Development*. *Journal of Child Language* 1: 111–23. pp. 170, 180

1974b. That there deixis I: that. MS, University of York. p. 244

and Atkinson, M. 1978. A *'door'* to verbs. In N. Waterson and C. E. Snow (eds.) *The Development of Communication*. Chichester: Wiley. pp. 112, 153

Griffiths, P. D., Atkinson, R. M. and Huxley, R. 1974. Project report. *Journal of Child Language* 1: 157–8. p. 113

Gruber, J. S. 1967. Topicalization in child language. *Foundations of Language* 3: 37–65. p. 47

Guillaume, P. 1927. Les débuts de la phrase dans le langage de l'enfant. *Journal de Psychologie* 24: 1–25. pp. 150, 152, 153

Haber, L. 1977. A linguistic definition of language delay: evidence from the acquisition of AUX. Paper presented at the Linguistic Society of America Summer Meeting. p. 277

Hakuta, K. 1976. The role of word order in children's acquisition of Japanese. Paper presented to the New England Child Language Association, Brown University, December. p. 293

Hall, L. C. 1975. Linguistic and perceptual constraints on scanning strategies: some developmental studies. PhD thesis, University of Edinburgh. pp. 256, 257

Halle, M. 1973. Prolegomena to a theory of word-formation. *Linguistic Inquiry* 4: 3–16. p. 127

Halliday, M. A. K. 1970. Language and language function. In J. Lyons (ed.) *New Horizons in Linguistics*. Harmondsworth, Middx: Penguin Books. pp. 74, 95

1973. Early language learning: a sociolinguistic approach. Paper presented at IXth International Congress of Anthropological and Ethnological Science, Chicago. pp. 74, 90

1975. *Learning How to Mean: explorations in the development of language*. London: Edward Arnold. pp. 42, 43, 44, 61, 62, 74, 75, 76, 95, 96, 97, 98, 99, 100, 101, 102, 105, 109, 110, 112, 114, 115, 116, 117, 118, 351–2, 428

and Hasan, R. 1976. *Cohesion in English*. London: Longman. p 353

Halsey, A. H. 1972. *Educational Priority*, vol. I. London: HMSO. p. 390

Hamburger, H. and Wexler, K. 1975. A mathematical theory of learning transformation grammar. *Journal of Mathematical Psychology* 12: 137–77. p. 452

Hardyck, C. 1977a. Laterality and intellectual ability: a just not noticeable difference? *British Journal of Educational Psychology* 47: 305–11. p. 449

1977b. A model of individual differences in hemispheric functioning. In H. A. and H. Whitaker (eds.) *Studies in Neurolinguistics*, vol. III. New York: Academic Press. p. 449

Hardyck, C., Petrinovich, L. F. and Goldman, R. D. 1976. Left-handedness and cognitive deficit. *Cortex* 12: 266–79. p. 442

Harner, L. 1976. Children's understanding of linguistic reference to past and future. *Journal of Psycholinguistic Research* 5: 65–84. pp. 260, 270, 271, 296

Harries, H. 1973. Coordination reduction. *Stanford Working Papers on Language Universals* 2: 139–209. p. 299

Harris, M. 1976. The influence of reversibility and truncation on the interpretation of the passive voice by young children. *British Journal of Psychology* 67: 419–27. p. 312

Harris, P. 1975. Children's comprehension of complex sentences. *Journal of Experimental Child Psychology* 19: 420–33. p. 305

Haviland, S. E. and Clark, E. V. 1974. 'This man's father is my father's son': a study of the acquisition of English kin terms. *Journal of Child Language* 1: 23–47. p. 157

Hawkins, P. R. 1969. Social class, the nominal group and reference. *Language and Speech* 12: 125–35. p. 389

Hayhurst, H. 1967. Some errors of young children in producing passive sentences. *Journal of Verbal Learning and Verbal Behavior* 6: 634–9. p. 310

Hebb, D. O. 1949. *The Organization of Behavior*. New York: Wiley. p. 446

Heber, M. 1977. The influence of language training on seriation of 5–6 year old children initially at different levels of descriptive competence. *British Journal of Psychology* 68: 85–95. p. 334

Hécaen, H. 1976. Acquired aphasia in children and the ontogenesis of hemispheric functional specialization. *Brain and Language* 3: 114–34. p. 448

Heider, F. 1939. Environmental determinants of psychological theories. *Psychological Review* 46: 383–410. p. 424

1958. *The Psychology of Interpersonal Relations*. Chichester: Wiley. p. 420

Herriott, P. 1969. The comprehension of tense by young children. *Child Development* 40: 103–10. p. 270

Hess, R. and Shipman, V. 1965. Early experience and the socialisation of cognitive modes in children. *Child Development* 36: 869–86. p. 390

1968. Maternal influences upon early learning. In R. Hess and R. Beer (eds.) *Early Education*. London: Aldine. p. 390

Hicks, R., Evans, E. and Pellegrini, R. 1978. Correlation between handedness and birth order: compilation of five studies. *Perceptual and Motor Skills* 46: 53–4. p. 449

Hockett, C. F. 1958. *A Course in Modern Linguistics*. London: Macmillan. p. 270

1968. *The State of the Art*. The Hague and Paris: Mouton. p. 221

Hood, L. H. 1977. A longitudinal study of the development of the expression of causal relations in complex sentences. Doctoral dissertation, Columbia University. pp. 287, 296, 297

Hopmann, M. and Maratsos, M. P. 1975. Some facts about learning factives. Paper presented at the meeting of the Society for Research in Child Development, Denver, April. p. 305

Householder, F. W. 1971. *Linguistic Speculations*. Cambridge: Cambridge University Press. pp. 221–2

Howe, C. J. 1976. The meanings of two-word utterances in the speech of young children. *Journal of Child Language* 3: 29–47. pp. 44, 168, 170

Hsieh, Hsin-I. 1972. Lexical diffusion: evidence from child language acquisition. *Glossa* 6: 89–104. p. 125

Huddleston, R. 1976. Homonymy in the English verb paradigm. *Lingua* 37: 151–76. p. 271

476   Bibliography (and citation index)

1976. *An Introduction to English Transformational Syntax*. London: Longman.
pp. 261, 262

Hughes, M. 1975. Egocentrism in preschool children. PhD thesis, University of
Edinburgh. p. 245

Hupet, M. and Costermans, J. 1974. Des fonctions sémantiques du passif.
Cahiers de l'Institut de Linguistique 2. University of Louvain. p. 314

Hurford, J. 1975. A child and the English question-formation rule. *Journal of
Child Language* 2: 299–301. pp. 129, 205, 206, 262

Huttenlocher, J. 1974. The origins of language comprehension. In R. L. Solso
(ed.) *Theories in Cognitive Psychology*. Potomac, Md: Erlbaum. pp. 3, 6, 9,
10, 74, 103, 109, 114, 131, 153, 378

Huxley, R. 1970. The development of the correct use of subject personal
pronouns in two children. In G. B. Flores D'Arcais and W. J. M. Levelt
(eds.) *Advances in Psycholinguistics*. Amsterdam: North-Holland. p. 253

Hyman, L. and Schuh, R. 1974. Universals of tone rules: evidence from West
Africa. *Linguistic Inquiry* 5: 81–115. p. 43

Hymes, D. and Fought, J. 1975. American Structuralism. In T. A. Sebeok (ed.)
Current Trends in Linguistics, vol. XIII, *Historiography of Linguistics*. The
Hague and Paris: Mouton. p. 209

Ingram, D. 1974a. Phonological rules in young children. *Journal of Child
Language* 1: 49–64. pp. 51, 66, 138, 143

1974b. The relationship between comprehension and production. In R. L.
Schiefelbusch and L. L. Lloyd (eds.) *Language Perspectives: acquisition,
retardation and intervention*. London and Basingstoke: Macmillan;
Baltimore, Md: University Park Press. p. 100

1974c. Fronting in child phonology. *Journal of Child Language* 1: 233–42.
p. 124

1975a. If and when transformations are acquired by children. In D. P. Dato
(ed.) *Developmental Psycholinguistics: theory and applications*. 26th Annual
Georgetown University Roundtable. Washington, DC: Georgetown
University Press. p. 286

1975b. Surface contrast in phonology: evidence from children's speech.
Journal of Child Language 2: 287–92. p. 143

1976a. *Phonological Disability in Children*. London: Edward Arnold; New
York: Elsevier. pp. 66, 133, 134

1976b. Phonological analysis of a child. *Glossa* 10: 3–27. p. 143

1976c. Current issues in child phonology. In D. Morehead and A. Morehead
(eds.) *Normal and Deficient Child Language*. Baltimore, Md: University
Park Press. p. 143

1977. The acquisition of fricatives and affricates in normal and linguistically
deviant children. In A. Carmazza and E. Zuriff (eds.) *The Acquisition and
Breakdown of Language*. Baltimore, Md: John Hopkins University Press.
p. 136

Inhelder, B. and Piaget, J. 1964. *The Early Growth of Logic in the Child:
classification and seriation*. London: Routledge & Kegan Paul. p. 434

Innes, S. J. 1974. Developmental aspects of plural formation in English. MSc.
thesis, University of Alberta. pp. 211, 213

Irwin, O. C. and Chen, H. P. 1946. Development of speech during infancy:

curve of phonemic types. *Journal of Experimental Psychology* 36: 431–6.
p. 15

1947. A reliability study of speech sounds observed in the crying of newborn
infants. *Child Development* 12: 351–68. p. 15

Jacobs, J. 1977. An external view of neuropsychology and its working milieu. In
S. Segalowitz and F. Gruber (eds.) *Language Development and Neurological
Theory*. New York: Academic Press. p. 448

Jacobsen, T. 1974. On the order of emergence of conjunctions and notions
of conjunctions in English-speaking children. Unpublished paper,
Department of Psychology, University of California at Berkeley. pp. 287,
297

Jacobson, M. 1970. Development, specification and diversification of neuronal
connections. In F. O. Schmitt (ed.) *The Neurosciences: second study
program*. New York: The Rockefeller University Press. p. 445

Jaffe, J., Stern, D. and Peery, J. 1973. 'Conversational' coupling of gaze
behavior in prelinguistic human development. *Journal of Psycholinguistic
Research* 2: 321–9. p. 12

Jakobson, R. 1968. *Child Language, Aphasia and Phonological Universals*, trans.
A. R. Keiler. The Hague: Mouton. First published 1941 as *Kindersprache,
Aphasie und allgemeine Lautgesetze*. Uppsala: Almqvist and Wiksell.
pp. 16, 49, 124

Jespersen, O. 1922. *Language, Its Nature, Development and Origin*. London:
Allen & Unwin. pp. 90, 133, 183

1924. *The Philosophy of Grammar*. London: Allen & Unwin. pp. 210,
274

Johnson, H. L. 1975. The meaning of *before* and *after* for preschool children.
Journal of Experimental Child Psychology 19: 88–99. p. 296

Johnston, J. R. and Slobin, D. I. 1977. The development of locative expressions
in English, Italian, Serbo-croation and Turkish. *Stanford Papers and Reports
on Child Language Development* 13: 134–45. p. 157

Jones, L. G. 1967. English phonotactic structure and first-language acquisition.
Lingua 19: 1–59. p. 61

Joynson, R. B. 1974. *Psychology and Common Sense*. London: Routledge &
Kegan Paul. p. 420

Jusczyk, P. W. and Thomson, E. 1978. Perception of a phonetic contrast in
multisyllabic utterances by 2-month-old infants. *Perception and
Psychophysics* 23: 105–9. p. 451

Kahn, D. 1976. Syllable-based generalizations in English phonology. Doctoral
dissertation, Linguistics Department, MIT. p. 54

Kail, M. 1975a. Etude génétique de la réproduction de phrases relatives: I.
Réproduction immédiate. *Année Psychologique* 75: 109–26. p. 310

1975b. Etude génétique de la réproduction de phrases relatives: II.
Réproduction différée. *Année Psychologique* 75: 427–43. p. 310

Kaplan, E. L. 1970. Intonation and language acquisition. *Stanford Papers and
Reports on Child Language Development* 1: 1–21. p. 38

Karmiloff-Smith, A. 1975. Can developmental psycholinguistics provide clues to
the historical origins of gender? MS, University of Geneva. pp. 320, 321,
435

1978. The interplay between syntax, semantics and phonology in language acquisition processes. In R. N. Campbell and P. Smith (eds.) *Recent Advances in the Psychology of Language: language development and mother–child interaction*. New York and London: Plenum Press. p. 300

1979. *A Functional Approach to Child Language: a study of determiners and reference*. Cambridge: Cambridge University Press. pp. 313, 315, 320, 321

In press. Micro- and macro-developmental changes in language acquisition and other representational systems. *Cognitive Science* 3. p. 323

Käsermann, M.-L. 1978. Spracherwerb und Interaktion. Doctoral dissertation, University of Berne. p. 428

Kastovsky, D. 1973. Causatives. *Foundations of Language* 10: 255–315. p. 301

Katz, J. J. 1977a. *Propositional Structure and Illocutionary Force*. Hassocks, Sussex: Harvester Press. p. 429

1977b. The real status of semantic representations. *Linguistic Inquiry* 8: 559–84. p. 439

and Fodor, J. A. 1963. The structure of a semantic theory. *Language* 390: 170–210. p. 130

Keenan, E. O. 1974. Conversational competence in children. *Journal of Child Language* 1: 163–83. pp. 40, 41, 42, 43, 117, 347

and Schieffelin, B. B. 1976. Topic as a discourse notion: a study of topic in the conversations of children and adults. In C. N. Li (ed.) *Subject and Topic*. New York: Academic Press. p. 260

Keynereš, E. 1926. Les premiers mots de l'enfant. *Archives de Psychologie* 20: 191–218. p. 151

Kerek, A. 1975. Phonological rules in the language of Hungarian children. Paper presented to Mid-America Linguistics Conference. p. 135

Kessel, F. S. 1970. *The Role of Syntax in Children's Comprehension from Ages Six to Twelve*. Society for Research in Child Development Monographs 35 (6). pp. 289, 291, 309

Kety, S. S. 1969. New perspectives in psychopharmacology. In A. Koestler and J. R. Smythies (eds.) *Beyond Reductionism*. London: Hutchinson. p. 436

Kewley-Port, D. and Preston, M. S. 1974. Early apical stop production: a voice onset time analysis. *Journal of Phonetics* 2: 195–210. pp. 17, 29

Kinsbourne, M. and Hiscock, M. 1977. Does cerebral dominance develop? In S. Segalowitz and F. Gruber (eds.) *Language Development and Neurological Theory*. New York: Academic Press. p. 447

Kiparsky, P. and Menn, L. 1977. On the acquisition of phonology. In J. Macnamara (ed.) *Language Learning and Thought*. New York: Academic Press. p. 66

Kirkpatrick, P. 1908. The part played by consciousness in mental operations. *Journal of Philosophy* 5: 421ff. p. 426

Klein, E. 1977. Some remarks on the semantics of children's two word utterances. *Semantikos* 2: 37–46. p. 431

Klein, R. 1974. *Word Order: Dutch children and their mothers*. Publication 9, Institute for General Linguistics, University of Amsterdam. p. 369

Klima, E. and Bellugi, U. 1966. Syntactic regularities in the speech of children. In J. Lyons and R. J. Wales (eds.) *Psycholinguistics Papers*. Edinburgh: Edinburgh University Press. pp. 206, 262, 265, 267, 443

Kobashigawa, B. 1969. Repetitions in a mother's speech to her child. Working Paper no. 14, University of California, Berkeley. p. 364

Kocel, K. M. 1977. Cognitive abilities, handedness, familial sinistrality, and sex. *Annals of the New York Academy of Sciences* 299: 233–43. p. 442

Koffka, K. 1935. *Principles of Gestalt Psychology*. New York: Harcourt Brace. p. 424

Köhler, W. 1925. *The Mentality of Apes*. London: Routledge & Kegan Paul. p. 421

Konopczynski, G. 1975. Etude experimentale de quelques structures prosodiques employées par les enfants français entre 7 et 22 mois. *Travaux de l'Institut de Phonétique de Strasbourg* 7: 171–205. p. 42

Kornfeld, J. and Goehl, H. 1974. A new twist to an old observation: kids know more than they say. In A. Bruck, R. Fox and M. W. La Galy (eds.) *Papers from the Parasession on Natural Phonology*. Chicago Linguistic Society. p. 125

Koziol, S. M. 1970. The development of noun plural rules during the primary grades. *Stanford Papers and Reports on Child Language Development* 2: 76–96. p. 211

Kramer, P. E., Koff, E. and Luria, Z. 1972. The development of competence in an exceptional structure in older children and young adults. *Child Development* 43: 121–30. p. 289

Kress, G. (ed.) 1976. *Halliday: system and function in language*. Oxford: Oxford University Press. p. 95

Kuczaj, S. 1976. Arguments against Hurford's 'AUX Copying Rule'. *Journal of Child Language* 3: 423–7. pp. 206, 262

  1978. Why do children fail to over-generalise the progressive inflection? *Journal of Child Language* 5: 167–71. p. 275

  and Maratsos, M. 1975. On the acquisition of Front, Back and Side. *Child Development* 46: 202–10. p. 256

Kuhl, P. K. 1976. Speech perception in early infancy: perceptual constancy for vowel categories. Paper presented at the 92nd Meeting of the Acoustical Society of America, San Diego. p. 32

Kuryłowicz, J. 1972. The role of deictic elements in linguistic evolution. *Semiotica* 5: 174–83. p. 241

Labov, W. 1970. The logic of non-standard English. In F. Williams (ed.) *Language and Poverty*. Chicago: Markham Publishing Co. pp. 380, 386

  1972. *Sociolinguistic Patterns*. Philadelphia: University of Pennsylvania Press. p. 379

  1977. *Language in the Inner City*. Oxford: Blackwell. First published 1972, University of Pennsylvania Press. p. 379

  and Labov, T. 1978. Learning the syntax of questions. In R. N. Campbell and P. T. Smith (eds.) *Recent Advances in the Psychology of Language: language development and mother–child interaction*. New York and London: Plenum Press. pp. 128, 262

Lahey, M. 1974. Use of prosody and syntactic markers in children's comprehension of spoken sentences. *Journal of Speech and Hearing Research* 17: 656–68. p. 292

Lakoff, G. 1970. *Irregularity in Syntax*. New York: Holt, Rinehart & Winston. p. 301

480 Bibliography (and citation index)

Langacker, R. W. 1973. *Language and its Structure: some fundamental linguistic concepts*. 2nd ed. New York: Harcourt Brace Jovanovich. p. 285
Lashley, K. S. 1937. Functional determinants of cerebral localization. *Archives of Neurology and Psychiatry* (Chicago) 38: 371–87. pp. 440, 441
Laszlo, E. 1966. Piano performance memory. *British Journal of Aesthetics* 6: 172–92. p. 421
Lecours, A. R. 1975. Myelogenetic correlates of the development of speech and language. In E. H. and E. Lenneberg (eds.) *Foundations of Language Development*, vol. I. New York: Academic Press. p. 450
Lee, L. 1969. *The Northwestern Syntax Screening Test*. Evanston, Ill.: Northwestern University Press. p. 378
  1974. *Developmental Sentence Analysis: a grammatical assessment procedure for speech and language disorders*. Evanston, Ill.: Northwestern University Press. pp. 191, 378
Lenneberg, E. H. 1962. Understanding language without ability to speak: a case report. *Journal of Abnormal and Social Psychology* 65: 419–25. p. 16
  1967. *Biological Foundations of Language*. New York: Wiley. pp. 39, 365
  1976. The concept of language differentiation. In E. H. Lenneberg and E. Lenneberg (eds.) *Foundations of Language Development*, vol. I. New York: Academic Press. pp. 44, 277
Leonard, L. B. 1973. The role of intonation in recall of various linguistic stimuli. *Language and Speech* 16: 327–35. p. 37
Leopold, W. 1939. *Speech Development of a Bilingual Child: a linguist's record*, vol. I, *Vocabulary Growth in the First Two Years*. Evanston, Ill.: Northwestern University Press. pp. 110, 111, 115, 118, 151, 152, 233
  1947. *Speech Development of a Bilingual Child: a linguist's record*, vol. II, *Sound-Learning in the First Two Years*. Evanston, Ill.: Northwestern University Press. p. 15
  1949a. *Speech Development in a Bilingual Child: a linguist's record*, vol. III, *Grammar and General Problems in the First Two Years*. Evanston, Ill.: Northwestern University Press. pp. 10, 90, 111, 113, 114, 116, 118, 119
  1949b. *Speech Development of a Bilingual Child*, vol. IV, *Diary from Age 2*. Evanston, Ill.: Northwestern University Press. pp. 152, 205, 263, 265, 267, 271
Levelt, W. J. M. 1975. What became of LAD? In *Ut Videam: contributions to an understanding of linguistics, for Pieter Verburg on the occasion of his 70th birthday*. Lisse: Peter de Ridder Press. pp. 129, 366, 429
Lewes, G. H. 1879. *The Study of Psychology*. Cambridge: Riverside Press. p. 437
Lewis, D. K. 1969. *Convention*. Cambridge, Mass.: Harvard University Press. p. 429
Lewis, M. M. 1951. *Infant Speech: a study of the beginnings of language*, 2nd ed. London: Routledge & Kegan Paul; New York: Harcourt Brace. 1st ed. 1936. pp. 15, 24, 38
  1963. *Language, Thought and Personality*. New York: Basic Books. p. 51
Li, C. N. and Thompson, S. A. 1977. The acquisition of tone in Mandarin-speaking children. *Journal of Child Language* 4: 185–99. p. 43
Lieberman, P., Harris, K. S., Wolff, P. and Russell, L. H. 1971. Newborn infant

cry and nonhuman primate vocalization. *Journal of Speech and Hearing Research* 14: 718–27. p. 19

Lieberman, P., Buhr, R., Keating, P., Hamby, S. V. and Landahl, K. H. 1976. Speech development in infants – vowel production. Paper presented at the 92nd Meeting of the Acoustical Society of America, San Diego. p. 26

Lieven, E. 1978a. Conversations between mothers and young children: individual differences and their possible implications for the study of language learning. In N. Waterson and C. E. Snow (eds.) *The Development of Communication*. Chichester: Wiley. p. 373

1978b. Turn-taking and pragmatics: two issues in early child language. In R. N. Campbell and P. Smith (eds.) *Recent Advances in the Psychology of Language: language development and mother–child interaction*. New York and London: Plenum Press. p. 373

Limber, J. 1973. The genesis of complex sentences. In T. E. Moore (ed.) *Cognitive Development and the Acquisition of Language*. New York: Academic Press. pp. 202, 203, 208, 286, 287, 288, 310, 382

1976. Unravelling competence, performance and pragmatics in the speech of young children. *Journal of Child Language* 3: 309–18. pp. 128, 201, 202, 203, 204, 288

Lipsitt, L. P. 1969. Discussion. In R. J. Robinson (ed.) *Brain and Early Behavior*. New York: Academic Press. p. 451

Loban, W. 1963. *The Language of Elementary School Children*. US National Council of Teachers of English. Report no. 1. p. 387

Lock, A. 1975. On being picked up. Paper read at ASAB symposium, Mother–Child Interaction in Man and the Higher Mammals, London. p. 74

1977. Towards a theory of language development. PhD dissertion, University of Hull. p. 166

(ed.) 1978. *Action, Gesture and Symbol: the emergence of language*. London: Academic Press. p. 74

Lodge, K. 1979. The use of the past tense in games of pretend. *Journal of Child Language* 6: 365–9. p. 270

Long, C. 1976. A dynamic theory of language. MS. (Copies obtainable from the author, Department of English, Strathclyde University, Glasgow, Scotland.) p. 431

Lust, B. 1974. Conjunction reduction in the language of young children: studied with particular concern for the directionality of the deletion component. Doctoral dissertation, City University of New York. p. 299

1977. Conjunction reduction in child language. *Journal of Child Language* 4: 257–87. p. 299

and Wakayama, T. K. 1977. The structure of coordination in children's first language acquisition of Japanese. Unpublished paper, Cornell University. p. 300

Lynip, A. W. 1951. The use of magnetic devices in the collection and analysis of the pre-verbal utterances of an infant. *Genetic Psychology Monographs* 44: 221–62. p. 16

Lyons, J. 1963. *Structural Semantics*. Publications of the Philological Society 20. Oxford: Blackwell. p. 130

482   Bibliography (and citation index)

1966. In J. Lyons and R. J. Wales (eds.) *Psycholinguistic Papers*, pp. 129–32. Edinburgh: Edinburgh University Press. pp. 207, 428

1968. *Introduction to Theoretical Linguistics*. Cambridge: Cambridge University Press. p. 241

1975. Deixis as a source of reference. In E. Keenan (ed.) *Formal Semantics and Natural Language*. Cambridge: Cambridge University Press. pp. 241, 242, 253

1977a. *Semantics*, 2 vols. Cambridge: Cambridge University Press. pp. 107, 110, 131, 241, 269, 270, 274

1977b. Deixis and anaphora. In T. Myers (ed.) *Development of Conversation and Discourse*. Edinburgh: Edinburgh University Press. p. 114

McCarthy, D. 1930. *The Language Development of the Preschool Child*. Institute of Child Welfare Monograph Series 4. Minneapolis: University of Minnesota Press. pp. 130, 180, 181, 182, 183, 189, 201

1954. Language development in children. In L. Carmichael (ed.) *Manual of Child Psychology*, 2nd ed. New York: Wiley. pp. 10, 94, 178, 179, 180, 383, 384, 385, 387

McCawley, J. D. 1968. Lexical insertion in a transformational grammar without deep structure. Papers from the Fourth Regional Meeting of the Chicago Linguistic Society. p. 301

1971. Tense and time reference in English. In C. J. Fillmore and D. T. Langendoen (eds.) *Studies in Linguistic Semantics*. New York: Holt, Rinehart & Winston. p. 261

McDermott, R. and Dore, J. 1977. The social organization of talk in a first grade reading lesson. Paper delivered at the annual meeting of the American Anthropological Association. p. 343

McGlone, J. 1977. Sex differences in the cerebral organization of verbal functions in patients with unilateral brain lesions. *Brain* 100: 775–93. p. 442

Macken, M. A. and Barton, D. P. 1980. The acquisition of the voicing contrast in English: a study of voice-onset time in word-initial stop consonants. *Journal of Child Language* 7. pp. 65, 66, 125

Macnamara, J. 1972. Cognitive basis of language learning in infants. *Psychological Review* 79: 1–13. pp. 331, 334, 369

Macnamara, J., Baker, E. and Olson, C. L. 1976. Four-year-olds' understanding of *pretend*, *forget*, and *know*: evidence for propositional operations. *Child Development* 47: 62–70. p. 305

McNeil, D. A. 1966a. Developmental linguistics. In F. Smith and G. A. Miller (eds.) *The Genesis of Language*. Cambridge, Mass.: MIT Press. p. 192

1966b. The creation of language by children. In J. Lyons and R. J. Wales (eds.) *Psycholinguistics Papers*. Edinburgh. Edinburgh University Press. pp. 364, 365

1970. *The Acquisition of Language*. New York: Harper & Row. pp. 10, 428

1974. Semiotic extension. Paper presented to the Loyola Symposium on Cognition. pp. 184, 189

Macrae, A. J. 1976a. Meaning relations in language development: a study of some converse pairs and directional opposites. PhD thesis, University of Edinburgh. pp. 159, 241, 257, 258

1976b. Movement and location in the acquisition of deictic verbs. *Journal of Child Language* 3: 191–204. pp. 241, 244, 258

McTear, M. 1978. Repetition in child language. In R. N. Campbell and P. Smith (eds.) *Recent Advances in the Psychology of Language: language development and mother–child interaction*. New York and London: Plenum Press. p. 347

McWhinney, B. 1978. *Processing a First Language: the acquisition of morphophonology*. Society of Research in Child Development Monographs 43. p. 234

Major, D. 1974. *The Acquisition of Modal Auxiliaries in the Language of Children*. The Hague: Mouton. p. 279

Maratos, O. 1973. Development of imitation. Paper presented at the British Psychological Society Conference. p. 12

Maratsos, M. P. 1973. The effects of stress on the understanding of pronominal co-reference in children. *Journal of Psycholinguistic Research* 2: 1–8. pp. 47, 253, 310

1974a. Children who get worse at understanding the passive: a replication of Bever. *Journal of Psycholinguistic Research* 3: 65–74. p. 312

1974b. How preschool children understand missing complement sentences. *Child Development* 45: 700–6. pp. 289, 290, 305

1976. *The Use of Definite and Indefinite Reference in Young Children*. Cambridge: Cambridge University Press. pp. 236, 237, 239

and Kuczaj, S. A. 1978. Against the transformationalist account: a simpler analysis of auxiliary overmarkings. *Journal of Child Language* 5: 337–45. p. 206

Marckworth, M. L. 1977. Knowledge of English derivational processes in a sample of normal monolingual, normal bilingual, and language-delayed children. Unpublished paper. p. 214

Marcus, M. P. 1977. A theory of syntactic recognition for natural language. PhD thesis, MIT. p. 440

Marshall, J. C. 1970. The adequacy of grammars. *Proceedings of the Aristotelian Society*, Supplementary Volume XLIV, 157–73. p. 444

1973. Some problems and paradoxes associated with recent accounts of hemispheric specialization. *Neuropsychologia* 11: 463–70. p. 442

1977. Minds, machines and metaphors. *Social Studies of Science* 7: 475–88. p. 438

Marslen-Wilson, W. 1973. Linguistic structure and speech shadowing at very short latencies. *Nature* 244: 522–3. p. 439

1975. Speech perception as an interactive parallel process. *Science* 189: 226–8. p. 439

Martinet, M. A. 1958. *De l'économie des formes du verbe en français parlé*. In A. G. Hatcher and K. L. Selid (eds.) *Studia Philologica et Litteraria in Honorem L. Spitzer*. Bern Switzerland: Francke. p. 400

Matthews, P. H. 1974. *Morphology: an introduction to the theory of word-structure*. Cambridge: Cambridge University Press. pp. 209, 217

1975. Review of R. Brown, *A First Language*. *Journal of Linguistics* 11: 322–43. pp. 128, 169, 179, 192, 271

Mattingly, I. G. 1973. Phonetic prerequisites for first-language acquisition.

484   Bibliography (and citation index)

Status Report on Speech Research. SR 341–5 Haskins Laboratories. p. 28
Mayer, J. W., Erreich, A. and Valian, V. 1978. Transformations, basic
    operations and language acquisition. *Cognition* 6: 1–13. pp. 129, 443
Mehan, H. 1978. *Learning Lessons.* Cambridge, Mass.: Harvard University
    Press. p. 345
Menn, L. 1971. Phonotactic rules in beginning speech. *Lingua* 26: 225–51. p. 67
    1973. On the origin and growth of phonological and syntactic rules. *Chicago
    Linguistic Society Regional Meeting Papers* 9: 378–85. p. 118
    1975. Counter example to 'fronting' as a universal of child language. *Journal
    of Child Language* 2: 293–6. pp. 137, 138
    1976a. Pattern, control and contrast in beginning speech: a case study in the
    development of word form and word function. PhD thesis, University of
    Illinois at Urbana-Champaign. Univ. Micro. 76–24, 139. pp. 39, 40, 41, 42, 43,
    44, 52, 61
    1976b. Evidence for an interactionist discovery theory of child phonology. In
    Stanford Papers and Reports on Child Language Development 12: 169–77.
    p. 67
    1978. Phonological units in beginning speech. In A. Bell and J. B. Hooper
    (eds.) *Syllables and Segments.* Amsterdam: North-Holland. pp. 62, 66
    and Haselkorn, S. 1977. Now you see it, now you don't; tracing the
    development of communicative competence. In J. Kegl (ed.) *Proceedings
    of the Seventh Annual Meeting of the Northeast Linguistic Society.* pp. 61,
    62
Menyuk, P. 1968. The role of distinctive features in children's acquisition of
    phonology. *Journal of Speech and Hearing Research* 11: 138–46. p. 16
    1969. *Sentences Children Use.* Cambridge, Mass.: MIT Press. pp. 47, 126,
    287, 299, 378
    1971. *The Acquisition and Development of Language.* Englewood Cliffs, NJ:
    Prentice-Hall. pp. 49, 54, 67
    1972. *Speech Development.* Indianapolis, Indiana: Bobbs Merrill. p. 54
    1976. Relations between acquisition of phonology and reading. In J. Guthrie
    (ed.) *Aspects of Reading.* Baltimore, Md: Johns Hopkins University Press.
    p. 54
    1977. *Language and Maturation.* Cambridge, Mass.: MIT Press. p. 56
    and Bernholtz, N. 1969. Prosodic features and children's language production.
    MIT *Quarterly Progress Report* 93: 216–19. p. 44
Miller, G. and Chomsky, N. 1963. Finitary models of language users. In
    R. Bush, E. Galanter and R. Luce (eds.) *Handbook of Mathematical
    Psychology,* vol. II. New York: Wiley. p. 364
Miller, G. and Nicely, P. 1955. Analysis of perceptual confusions among some
    English consonants. *Journal of the Acoustical Society of America* 27:
    338–52. p. 54
Miller, M. 1976. *Zur Logik der frühkindlichen Sprachentwicklung.* Stuttgart:
    Ernst Klett. p. 430
Miller, W. R. 1973. The acquisition of grammatical rules by children. In C. A.
    Ferguson and D. I. Slobin (eds.) *Studies of Child Language Development.*
    New York: Holt, Rinehart & Winston. p. 267
    and Ervin, S. M. 1964. The development of grammar in child language. In

U. Bellugi and R. Brown (eds.) *The Acquisition of Language*. Society for Research in Child Development Monographs 29 (1). p. 383

Minsky, M. 1975. A framework for representing knowledge. In P. H. Winston (ed.) *The Psychology of Computer Vision*. New York: McGraw-Hill. p. 421

Mishler, E. 1975. Studies in dialogue and discourse: II. Types of discourse initiated by and sustained through questioning. *Journal of Psycholinguistic Research* 4: 99–121. p. 345

Molfese, D., Freeman, R. and Palermo, D. 1975. The ontogeny of brain lateralization for speech and nonspeech stimuli. *Brain and Language* 2: 356–68. p. 447

Moore, K. C. 1896. The mental development of a child. *Psychological Review, Monograph Supplements* 1 (3). pp. 152, 153

Morehead, D. M. and Morehead, A. E. (eds.) 1976. *Normal and Deficient Child Language*. Baltimore, Md: University Park Press. pp. 7, 9, 10, 152, 191, 195, 419, 431

Morgan, G. A. and Ricciuti, H. N. 1969. Infants' responses to strangers during the first year. In B. M. Foss (ed.) *Determinants of Infants' Behaviour*, vol. IV. London: Methuen. p. 97

Morris, C. 1946. *Signs, Language and Behavior*. Englewood Cliffs, NJ: Prentice-Hall. p. 79

Morsbach, G. and Steel, P. M. 1976. 'John is easy to see' re-investigated. *Journal of Child Language* 3: 443–7. pp. 291, 309

Morse, P. 1974. Infant speech perception: a preliminary model and review of the literature. In R. L. Schiefelbusch and L. L. Lloyd (eds.) *Language Perspectives: acquisition, retardation and intervention*. London and Basingstoke: Macmillan; Baltimore, Md: University Park Press. p. 50

Morton, J. and Smith, N. 1974. Some ideas concerning the acquisition of phonology. In F. Bresson and J. Mehler (eds.) *Problèmes actuels en psycholinguistique*. Paris: Editions du CNRS. p. 443

Moskowitz, A. 1970. The acquisition of phonology. Working paper no. 34, Language-Behavior Research Laboratory, University of California, Berkeley. p. 63

Mounoud, P. and Bower, T. G. R. 1974. Conservation of weight in infants. *Cognition* 3: 29–40. p. 424

Murai, J. 1960. Speech development of infants: analysis of speech by sonograph. *Psychologia* 3: 27–35. p. 24

Nakazima, S. A. 1962. A comparative study of the speech development of Japanese and American English in childhood (1): A comparison of the developments of voices at the prelinguistic period. *Studia Phonologica* 2: 27–46. pp. 17, 24

   1966. A comparative study of the speech development of Japanese and American English in childhood (2): The acquisition of speech. *Studia Phonologica* 4: 38–55. p. 17

   1970. A comparative study of the speech developments of Japanese and American English in childhood (3): The reorganization process of babbling articulation mechanisms. *Studia Phonologica* 5: 20–35. pp. 17, 51

Nakazima, S. A., Okamoto, N., Murai, J., Tanaka, M., Okuno, S., Meda, T. and

Shimizu, M. 1962. The phoneme systemization and the verbalization process of voices in childhood. *Shinrigan-Hyoron* 6: 1–48. p. 16

Natalicio, D. S. 1969. Formation of the plural in English: a study of native speakers of English and native speakers of Spanish. PhD thesis, University of Texas, Austin. p. 211

Nathan, P. W. and Smith, M. C. 1950. Normal mentality associated with maldeveloped 'rhinencephalon'. *Journal of Neurology, Neurosurgery and Psychiatry* 13: 191–7. p. 445

Nelson, K. 1973a. Some evidence for the cognitive primacy of categorisation and its functional basis. *Merril-Palmer Quarterly* 19: 21–39. pp. 433, 435

   1973b. *Structure and Strategy in Learning to Talk*. Society for Research in Child Development Monographs 38 (1–2). pp. 3, 6, 7, 30, 55, 66, 95, 150, 169, 172, 179, 183, 207, 242, 374, 378, 386, 392, 394, 433

   1974. Concept, word and sentence: interrelations in acquisition and development. *Psychological Review* 81: 267–85. pp. 10, 131, 433

   1976. Some attributes of adjectives used by young children. *Cognition* 4: 13–30. pp. 200, 207, 435

Nelson, K. E. and Bonvillian, J. D. 1973. Concepts and words in the 18-month-old: acquiring concept names under controlled conditions. *Cognition* 2: 435–50. p. 434

Nelson, K. E., Carskaddon, G. and Bonvillian, J. D. 1973. Syntax acquisitions: impact of experimental variation in adult verbal interaction with the child. *Child Development* 44: 497–504. p. 372

Newport, E. 1976. Motherese: the speech of mothers to young children. In N. Castellan, D. Pisoni and G. Potts (eds.) *Cognitive Theory*, vol. II. Hillsdale, NJ: Erlbaum. pp. 367, 371

Newport, E., Gleitman, L. and Gleitman, H. 1977. Mother, I'd rather do it myself: some effects and noneffects of maternal speech style. In C. E. Snow and C. A. Ferguson (eds.) *Talking to Children: language input and acquisition*. Cambridge: Cambridge University Press. pp. 367, 368, 371

Newson, J. 1974. Towards a theory of infant understanding. *Bulletin of the British Psychological Society* 27: 251–7. p. 74

Nice, M. M. 1915. The development of a child's vocabulary in relation to environment. *Pedagogical Seminary* 22: 35–64. pp. 150, 155, 156

   1917. The speech development of children from eighteen months to six years. *Pedagogical Seminary* 24: 204–43. p. 150

   1925. Length of sentences as a criterion of a child's progress in speech. *Journal of Education Psychology* 16: 370–9. pp. 177, 180, 188

Nida, E. A. 1949. *Morphology: the descriptive analysis of words*, 2nd ed. Ann Arbor: University of Michigan Press. pp. 209, 216

Ninio, A. and Bruner, J. 1978. The achievement and antecedents of labelling. *Journal of Child Language* 5: 1–16. pp. 74, 433

Nussbaum, N. and Naremore, R. 1975. On the acquisition of present perfect 'have' in normal children. *Language and Speech* 18: 219–26. p. 277

Oelschlaeger, M. and Scarborough, J. 1976. Traumatic aphasia in children: a case study. *Journal of Communication Disorders* 9: 281–8. p. 448

Oller, D. K. 1976. Analysis of infant vocalizations: a linguistic and speech scientific perspective. Invited miniseminar given at the American Speech and Hearing Association Convention, Houston, pp. 24, 28, 30, 31

and Smith, B. L. 1977. Effect of final syllable position on vowel duration in infant babbling. *Journal of the Acoustical Society of America* 62 (4): 994–7. p. 29

Oller, D. K., Wieman, L. A., Doyle, W. J. and Ross, C. 1976. Infant babbling and speech. *Journal of Child Language* 3: 1–11. pp. 17, 24, 30

Olmsted, D. 1966. A theory of the child's learning of phonology. *Language* 42: 531–5. p. 49

1971. *Out of the Mouth of Babes*. The Hague: Mouton. pp. 59, 125

Olney, R. L. and Scholnick, E. K. 1976. Adult judgments of age and linguistic differences in infant vocalization. *Journal of Child Language* 3: 145–55. p. 39

Osgood, E. C. 1953. *Method and Theory in Experimental Psychology*. New York: Oxford University Press. p. 16

Palmer, F. R. 1974. *The English Verb*. London: Longman. pp. 262, 276, 279

1979. *Modality and the English Modals*. London: Longman. pp. 279, 282

Park, T.-Z. 1971. The acquisition of German morphology. MS, Psychological Institute, Bern. p. 233

1979. Some facts on negation: Wode's four-stage development theory of negation revisited. *Journal of Child Language* 6: 147–51. p. 207

Paul, H. 1891. *Principles of the History of Language*, trans. H. A. Strong. London: Longmans, Green. p. 443

Pavlovitch, M. 1920. *Le langage enfantin: acquisition du serbe et du français par un enfant serbe*. Paris: Champion. p. 152

Peirce, C. 1932. *Collected Papers*, ed. C. Hartshorne and P. Weiss. Cambridge, Mass.: Harvard University Press. p. 79

Peterson, C. L. 1974. Communicative and narrative behavior of preschool-aged children. Doctoral dissertation, University of Minnesota. pp. 237, 238

Phillips, J. 1973. Syntax and vocabulary of mothers' speech to young children: age and sex comparisons. *Child Development* 44: 182–5. pp. 364, 370

Piaget, J. 1946. *La développement de la notion de temps chez l'enfant*. Paris: Presses Universitaires de France. p. 274

1952. *The Origins of Intelligence in Children*. New York: Norton. pp. 28, 80

1955a. *The Child's Construction of Reality*. London: Routledge & Kegan Paul. p. 421

1955b. *The Language and Thought of the Child*. Cleveland: Meridian Books, The World Publishing Company. First published 1926. pp. 236, 237, 242, 297

1962. *Play, Dreams, and Imitations*, trans. C. Gattegno and F. M. Hodgson. New York: Norton. pp. 6, 235

1969. *Judgment and Reasoning in the Child*. New Jersey: Littlefield, Adams & Co. First published 1928. p. 297

1970. Piaget's theory. In P. H. Mussen (ed.) *Carmichael's Manual of Child Psychology*, vol. I. New York: Wiley. p. 331

and Inhelder, B. 1956. *The Child's Conception of Space*. London: Routledge & Kegan Paul. p. 242

1969. *The Psychology of the Child*. London: Routledge & Kegan Paul. p. 331

488   Bibliography (and citation index)

Plowden, Lady. 1967. *Children and their Primary Schools*. London: HMSO.
  p. 390
Polanyi, M. 1968. Logic and psychology. *The American Psychologist* 23: 34–42.
  p. 420
Preston, M. S., Yeni-Komshian, G. H., Stark, R. E. and Port, D. K. 1969.
  Certain aspects of the development of speech production and speech
  perception in children. *Journal of the Acoustical Society of America* 46:
  A102. pp. 17, 29
Preyer, W. 1889. *The Mind of the Child*. New York: Appleton. p. 152
Prideaux, G. 1976. A functional analysis of English question acquisition: a
  response to Hurford. *Journal of Child Language* 3: 417–22. pp. 206, 262
Priestly, T. M. S. 1977. One idiosyncratic strategy in the acquisition of
  phonology. *Journal of Child Language* 4: 45–66. pp. 144, 147
Pullum, G. and Wilson, D. 1978. Autonomous syntax and the analysis of
  auxiliaries. *Language* 53: 741–88. p. 261
Putnam, H. 1967. The innateness hypothesis and explanatory models in
  linguistics. *Synthese* 17: 12–22. p. 428
  1970. Is semantics possible? *Metaphilosophy* 1: 187–201. p. 434
Quine, W. v. O. 1975. The nature of natural knowledge. In S. Guttenplan (ed.)
  Mind and Language. Oxford: Oxford University Press. p. 434
Quirk, R., Greenbaum, S., Leech, G. N. and Svartvik, J. 1972. *A Grammar of
  Contemporary English*. London: Longman. pp. 47, 123, 181, 190, 191, 193,
  194, 261, 271, 275, 276, 285
Raffler Engel, W. von. 1964. *Il Prelinguaggio Infantile*. Brescia: Paideia. pp. 71, 75
  1972. The relationship of intonation to the first vowel articulation in infants.
  Acta Universitis Carolinae, Philological 1, Phonetica Progensia IV: 197–202.
  p. 75
Ramer, A. L. H. 1976. Syntactic styles in emerging language. *Journal of Child
  Language* 3: 49–62. pp. 185, 189, 202, 378, 383
Ramón y Cajal, S. 1892. El nuevo concepto de la histología de los centros
  nerviosos. *Revista de Ciencias Médicas de Barcelona* 18: 457–76. pp. 452–3
Rasmussen, T. and Milner, B. 1977. The role of early left-brain injury in
  determining lateralization of cerebral speech functions. *Annals of the New
  York Academy of Sciences* 299: 355–69. p. 448
Rees, N. 1972. The role of babbling in the child's acquisition of language.
  British Journal of Communication Disorders 7: 17–23. p. 16
Reich, P. A. 1976. The early acquisition of word meaning. *Journal of Child
  Language* 3: 117–23. p. 9
Remick, H. 1976. Maternal speech to children during language acquisition. In
  W. von Raffler Engel and Y. Lebrun (eds.) *Baby Talk and Infant Speech*.
  Lisse: Peter de Ridder Press. p. 364
Renfrew, C. E. 1966. Persistence of the open syllable in defective articulation.
  Journal of Speech and Hearing Research 38: 304–15. p. 141
Reynell, J. 1969. *The Reynell Developmental Language Scales*. Slough, England:
  National Foundation for Educational Research. p. 378
Rheingold, H. L., Gewirtz, J. L. and Ross, H. W. 1959. Social conditioning of
  vocalizations in the infant. *Journal of Comparative and Physiological
  Psychology* 52: 68–73. p. 17

Ricciuti, H. 1965. Object grouping and selective ordering behavior in infants 12–24 months old. *Merril-Palmer Quarterly* 11: 129–48. p. 435

Richards, M. M. 1976. *Come* and *go* reconsidered: children's use of deictic verbs in contrived situations. *Journal of Verbal Learning and Verbal Behavior* 15: 655–65. pp. 241, 258, 295, 312

Richards, M. P. M. 1974. *The Integration of a Child into a Social World.* Cambridge: Cambridge University Press. p. 74

Rimland, B. 1964. *Infantile Autism.* New York: Appleton-Century-Crofts. p. 235

Ringel, R. L. and Kluppel, D. D. 1964. Neonatal crying: a normative study. *Folia Phoniatrica* 16: 1–9. p. 19

Rinsland, H. D. 1945. *A Basic Vocabulary of Elementary School Children.* New York: Macmillan. p. 212

Robson, K. S. 1967. The role of eye-to-eye contact in maternal–infant attachment. Child Research Branch, NIMH, Bethesda, Md. p. 12

Rodgon, M. M. 1976. *Single-word Usage, Cognitive Development and the Beginnings of Combinatorial Speech: a study of ten English-speaking children.* Cambridge: Cambridge University Press. pp. 3, 11, 165, 184

Roeper, T. In press. Children's syntax. In T. Shopen (ed.) *Variation in the Structure and Use of English.* Cambridge, Mass.: Winthrop. p. 293

Rogers, D. 1978. Information about word-meanings in the speech of parents to young children. In R. N. Campbell and P. T. Smith (eds.) *Recent Advances in the Psychology of Language: language development and mother–child interaction.* New York and London: Plenum Press. p. 154

Rosch, E., Mervis, C. B., Gray, W., Johnson, D. and Boyes-Braem, P. 1976. Basic objects in natural categories. *Cognitive Psychology* 8: 382–439. pp. 131, 156, 434

Rose, J., Rose, S. N. and Stark, R. E. 1975. A new approach to the classification problem: an algorithm and application. Unpublished paper, Johns Hopkins University. p. 18

Rose, S. A. and Blank, M. 1974. The potency of context in children's cognition: an illustration through conservation. *Child Development* 45: 499–502. p. 380

Rosenbaum, P. 1967. *The Grammar of English Predicate Constructions.* Cambridge, Mass.: MIT Press. p. 288

Ross, A. S. C. 1937. An example of vowel-harmony in a young child. *Modern Language Notes* 52: 508–9. pp. 141, 147

Ross, J. 1969. Auxiliaries as main verbs. In W. Todd (ed.) *Studies in Philosophical Linguistics,* series 1. Evanston, Ill.: Great Expectations Press. p. 261

Roussey, C. 1899–1900. Notes sur l'apprentissage de la parole chez un enfant. *La Parole* 1: 870–80; 2: 23–40. pp. 137, 142

Routh, D. K. 1969. Conditioning of vocal responses in infants. *Developmental Psychology* 1: 219–26. p. 17

Ryan, J. 1974. Early language development. In M. P. M. Richards (ed.) *The Integration of a Child into a Social World.* Cambridge: Cambridge University Press. pp. 104, 334, 343

Ryan, M. L. 1978. Contour in context. In R. N. Campbell and P. T. Smith (eds.) *Recent Advances in the Psychology of Language: language development and mother–child interaction*. New York and London: Plenum Press. pp. 322, 368

Sachs, J. and Devin, J. 1976. Young children's use of age-appropriate speech styles in social interaction and role-playing. *Journal of Child Language* 3: 81–98. pp. 48, 365

Sachs, J. and Truswell, L. 1978. Comprehension of 2-word instructions by children in the 1-word stage. *Journal of Child Language* 5: 17–24. p. 431

Sachs, J., Brown, R. and Salerno, R. 1976. Adults' speech to children. In W. von Raffler Engel and Y. Lebrun (eds.) *Baby Talk and Infant Speech*. Lisse: Peter de Ridder Press. p. 364

Sacks, H., Schegloff, E. and Jefferson, G. 1974. A simplest systematics for the analysis of turn-taking in conversation. *Language* 50: 696–735. pp. 343, 353

Sadick, T. and Ginsburg, B. 1978. The development of the lateral functions and reading ability. *Cortex* 14: 3–11. p. 449

Sadock, J. 1973. Speech act idioms. Papers from the Eighth Regional Meeting of the Chicago Linguistic Society. p. 350

Saussure, F. de. 1916. *Cours de linguistique générale*. Paris: Payot. p. 210

Savic, S. 1975. Aspects of adult–child communication: the problem of question-acquisition. *Journal of Child Language* 2: 251–60. p. 206.

Scaife. B. K. and Bruner, J. S. 1975. The capacity for joint visual attention in the infant. *Nature* 253 (5489): 265–6. p. 12

Schaerlaekens, A. M. 1973. *The Two-Word Stage in Child Language Development: a study based on evidence provided by Dutch-speaking triplets*. The Hague: Mouton. pp. 119, 120, 161, 163, 164, 165, 169, 173, 428

Schlesinger, I. M. 1971a. Learning grammar: from pivot to realisation rule. In R. Huxley and E. Ingram (eds.) *Language Acquisition: models and methods*. London: Academic Press. p. 369

  1971b. The production of utterances and language acquisition. In D. I. Slobin (ed.) *The Ontogenesis of Grammar*. New York: Academic Press. pp. 10, 161, 162, 164, 196, 428

  1974. Relational concepts underlying language. In R. L. Schiefelbusch and L. L. Lloyd (eds.) *Language Perspectives: acquisition, retardation and intervention*. London and Basingstoke: Macmillan; Baltimore, Md: University Park Press. pp. 161, 196

Scholnick, E. K. and Adams, M. J. 1973. Relationships between language and cognitive skills: passive voice comprehension, backward repetition and matrix permutation. *Child Development* 44: 741–6. p. 312

Scollon, R. T. 1974. One child's language from one to two: the origins of construction. *University of Hawaii Working Papers in Linguistics* 6 (5). pp. 118, 119, 184

Searle, J. R. 1969. *Speech Acts*. Cambridge: Cambridge University Press. pp. 106, 109, 353

Sebeok, T. A., Hayes, A. S. and Bateson, M. C. (eds.) 1964. *Approaches to Semiotics*. The Hague: Mouton. p. 33

Seuren, P. 1978. Grammar as an underground process. In A. Sinclair, R. Jarvella and W. J. M. Levelt (eds.) *The Child's Conception of Language*. Berlin: Springer Verlag. p. 430

Shallice, T. 1972. Dual functions of consciousness. *Psychological Review* 79: 383–93. p. 427

Shatz, M. 1974. The comprehension of indirect directives: can two-year-olds shut the door? Paper delivered at the Linguistic Society of America meeting, Summer. p. 350

and Gelman, R. 1973. *The Development of Communication Skills: modifications in the speech of young children as a function of listener.*. Society for Research in Child Development Monographs 38 (5). p. 365

Sheldon, A. 1972. The acquisition of relative clauses in English. PhD thesis, University of Texas, Austin. pp. 310, 311

1974. The role of parallel function in the acquisition of relative clauses in English. *Journal of Verbal Learning and Verbal Behavior* 13: 272–81. pp. 129, 292, 293, 310, 311

Sheppard, W. C. 1969. Operant control of infant vocal and motor behavior. *Journal of Experimental Child Psychology* 7: 36–51. p. 17

Shibatani, M. 1976. The grammar of causative constructions: a conspectus. In M. Shibatani (ed.) *Syntax and Semantics*, vol. VI, *The Grammar of Causative Constructions*. New York: Academic Press. p. 301

Shipley, E., Gleitman, L. and Smith, C. 1969. A study in the acquisition of language: free responses to commands. *Language* 45: 322–42. pp. 365, 368

Shirley, M. M. 1933. *The First Two Years: a study of twenty-five babies*, vols. II and III. Institute of Child Welfare Monographs Series 7 and 8. Minneapolis: University of Minnesota Press. pp. 180, 188

Shugar, G. W. 1978. Text analysis as an approach to the study of early linguistic operations. In N. Waterson and C. E. Snow (eds.) *The Development of Communication*. Chichester: Wiley. pp. 117, 372

Shvachkin, N. 1973. The development of phonemic speech perception in early childhood. In C. A. Ferguson and D. I. Slobin (eds.) *Studies of Child Language Development*. New York: Holt, Rinehart & Winston. p. 50

Siegel, G. M. 1971. Vocal conditioning in infants. *Journal of Speech and Hearing Disorders* 34: 3–19. p. 17

Simon, C. and Fourcin, A. J. 1978. Cross-language study of speech pattern learning. *Journal of the Acoustical Society of America* 63: 925–35. p. 447

Sinclair, A., Sinclair, H. and de Marcelus, O. 1971. Young children's comprehension and production of passive sentences. *Archives de Psychologie* 161: 1–22. pp. 293, 310

Sinclair, H. 1967. *Langage et opérations: sous-systèmes linguistiques et opérations concrètes*. Paris: Dunod. pp. 308, 332

1972. Sensorimotor action patterns as a condition for the acquisition of syntax. In R. Huxley and E. Ingram (eds.) *Language Acquisition: models and methods*. New York: Academic Press. p. 92

and Ferreiro, E. 1970. Etude génétique de la compréhension, production et répétition des phrases au mode passif. *Archives de Psychologie* 40: 1–42. pp. 308, 310, 311

Sinclair, J. and Coulthard, R. 1975. *Towards an Analysis of Discourse: the English used by teachers and pupils*. London: Oxford University Press. p. 345

Skinner, B. F. 1957. *Verbal Behavior*. New York: Appleton-Century-Crofts. p. 330

Slobin, D. I. (ed.) 1967. *A Field-Manual for Cross-Cultural Study of the Acquisition of Communicative Competence*. University of California, Berkeley. p. 378

    1973. Cognitive prerequisites for the acquisition of grammar. In C. A. Ferguson and D. I. Slobin (eds.) *Studies of Child Language Development*. New York: Holt, Rinehart & Winston. pp. 10, 158, 231, 234, 287, 295, 298

    1975. The more it changes . . .: on understanding language by watching it move through time. In *Stanford Papers and Reports on Child Language Development* 10: 1–30. (Revised version, 'Language change in childhood and in history', in J. Macnamara (ed.) *Language Learning and Thought*. New York: Academic Press, 1977.) p. 298

    and Welsh, C. A. 1973. Elicited imitation as a research tool in developmental psycholinguistics. In C. A. Ferguson and D. I. Slobin (eds.) *Studies of Child Language Development*. New York: Holt, Rinehart & Winston. pp. 293, 299

Smedslund, J. 1969. Meanings, implications and universals: towards a psychology of man. *Scandanavian Journal of Psychology* 10: 1–15. pp. 420, 421

    1970. Circular relation between understanding and logic. *Scandinavian Journal of Psychology* 11: 217–19. p. 427

Smith, A. and Sugar, O. 1975. Development of above normal language and intelligence 21 years after left hemispherectomy. *Neurology* 25: 813–18. p. 448

Smith, C. 1970. An experimental approach to children's linguistic competence. In J. Hayes (ed.) *Cognition and the Development of Language*. New York: Wiley. pp. 293, 300

Smith, M. D. 1974. Relative clause formation between 29–36 months: a preliminary report. *Stanford Papers and Reports on Child Language Development* 8: 104–10. pp. 292, 293

Smith, M. E. 1926. *An Investigation of the Development of the Sentence and the Extent of Vocabulary in Young Children*. University of Iowa Studies in Child Welfare 3. pp. 178, 179, 180, 183, 188, 196, 204

    1935. A study of some factors influencing the development of the sentence in preschool children. *Journal of Genetic Psychology* 46: 182–212. pp. 180, 183

Smith, N. V. 1973. *The Acquisition of Phonology: a case study*. Cambridge: Cambridge University Press. pp. 51, 124, 125, 135, 138, 443

Smith, P. and Connolly, K. 1972. Patterns of play and social interaction in pre-school children. In N. B. Jones (ed.) *Ethological Studies of Child Behaviour*. Cambridge: Cambridge University Press. p. 384

Smith, R. L. Jr. 1972. *The Syntax and Semantics of ERICA*. Technical Report 185, Psychology and Education Series. Stanford, Calif: Stanford University, Institute for Mathematical Studies in the Social Sciences. pp. 404, 405

Smoczyńska, M. 1978. Semantic intention and interpersonal function: semantic analysis of noun + noun constructions. In N. Waterson and C. Snow (eds.) *The Development of Communication*. Chichester: Wiley. p. 119

Snow, C. E. 1972a. Mothers' speech to children learning language. *Child Development* 43: 549–65. pp. 364, 365, 392

    1972b. Young children's responses to adult sentences of varying complexity. Paper presented at IVth International Congress of Applied Linguistics, Copenhagen. p. 365

    1977a. The development of conversation between mothers and babies. *Journal of Child Language* 4: 1–22. pp. 3, 12, 13, 40, 117, 374

    1977b. Mothers' speech research: from input to interaction. In C. E. Snow and C. A. Ferguson (eds.) *Talking to Children: language input and acquisition*. Cambridge: Cambridge University Press. pp. 370, 371

    1978. The conversational context of language learning. In R. N. Campbell and P. Smith (eds.) *Recent Advances in the Psychology of Language: language development and mother–child interaction*. New York and London: Plenum Press. p. 340

Snow, C. E. and Ferguson, C. A. 1977 (eds.) *Talking to Children: language input and acquisition*. Cambridge: Cambridge University Press. p. 391

Snow, C. E., Arlman-Rupp, A., Hassing, Y., Jobse, J., Joosten, J. and Vorster, J. 1976. Mothers' speech in three social classes. *Journal of Psycholinguistic Research* 5: 1–20. p. 370

Solan, L. 1978. The acquisition of tough movement. In H. Goodluck and L. Solan (eds.) *Papers in the Structure and Development of Child Language*. University of Massachusetts Occasional Papers in Linguistics, vol. IV. p. 291

    and Roeper, T. 1978. Children's use of syntactic structure in interpreting relative clauses. In H. Goodluck and L. Solan (eds.) *Papers in the Structure and Development of Child Language*. University of Massachusetts Occasional Papers in Linguistics, vol. IV. p. 292

Sperry, R. W. 1968. Plasticity of neural maturation. *Developmental Biology Supplement* 2: 306–27. p. 445

Springer, S. and Eisenson, J. 1977. Hemispheric specialization for speech in language-disordered children. *Neuropsychologia* 15: 287–93. p. 449

Staats, A. W. 1967. Emotions and images in language: a learning analysis of their acquisition and function. In K. Salzinger and S. Salzinger (eds.) *Research in Verbal Behavior and Some Neurophysiological Implications*. New York: Academic Press. p. 49

Stalnaker, R. 1972. Pragmatics. In D. Davidson and G. Harman (eds.) *Semantics of Natural Language*. Dordrecht: Reidel. p. 429

Stampe, D. 1969. The acquisition of phonetic representation. In R. Binnick, A. Davison, G. Green and J. L. Morgan (eds.) *Papers from the Fifth Regional Meeting, Chicago Linguistic Society*. pp. 126, 133

Stark, J., Poppen, R. and May, M. Z. 1967. Effects of alterations of prosodic features on the sequencing performance of aphasic children. *Journal of Speech and Hearing Research* 10: 844–8. p. 48

Stark, R. E. 1978. Features of infant sounds: the emergence of cooing. *Journal of Child Language* 5: 379–90. p. 25

    and Nathanson, S. N. 1974. Spontaneous cry in the newborn infant: sounds and facial gestures. In J. F. Bosma (ed.) *Fourth Symposium on Oral*

Sensation and Perception: development in the fetus and infant. Bethesda, Md: US Government Printing Press. pp. 18, 19, 22.

Stark, R. E., Rose, S. N. and McLagen, M. 1975. Features of infant sounds: the first eight weeks of life. *Journal of Child Language* 2: 205–21. pp. 3, 18, 20–1, 22, 38

Stark, R. E., Heinz, J. and Wright-Wilson, C. 1976. Vowel utterances of young infants. Paper presented at the 92nd Meeting of the Acoustical Society of America, San Diego. pp. 24, 26

Stern, C. and Stern, W. 1928. *Die Kindersprache: eine psychologische und sprachtheoretische Untersuchung*, 4th ed. Leipzig: Barth. 1st ed. 1907. pp. 10, 147, 153, 177, 233

Stern, D. 1974. Mother and infant at play: the dyadic interaction involving facial, vocal and gaze behaviors. In M. Lewis and L. A. Rosenblum (eds.) *The Effect of the Infant on its Caregiver*. New York: Wiley. p. 12

Stern, G. 1964. *Meaning and Change of Meaning*. Bloomington, Ind.: Indiana University Press. p. 241

Stern, W. 1924. *Psychology of Early Childhood up to the Sixth Year of Age*. New York: Holt. pp. 183–4

Sternberg, R. 1976. *Intelligence, Information Processing and Individual Differences*. Hillsdale, NJ: Erlbaum. p. 439

Stevens, K. 1972. The quantal nature of speech: evidence from articulatory–acoustic data. In P. Denes and E. David (eds.) *Human Communication: a unified view*. New York: McGraw-Hill. p. 54

Subirana, A. 1952. La droiterie. *Archives Suisses de Neurologie et Psychiatrie* 69: 321–59. p. 442

Sugarman, S. 1973. A sequence for communicative development in the prelanguage child. Undergraduate honors thesis, Hampshire College. p. 74

Sully, J. 1896. *Studies of Childhood*. London: Longman; New York: Appleton. pp. 110, 152

Suppes, P. 1970. Probabilistic grammars for natural languages. *Synthese* 22: 95–116. p. 404

Suppes., Léveillé, M. and Smith, R. L. 1974. *Developmental Models of a Child's French Syntax*. Technical Report 243, Psychology and Education Series. Stanford, Calif.: Stanford University, Institute for Mathematical Studies in the Social Sciences. p. 397

Suppes, P., Smith, R. and Léveillé, M. 1973. The French syntax of a child's noun phrases. *Archives de Psychologie* 42: 207–69. pp. 397, 399, 402, 404, 405

Taine, H. 1877. Acquisition of language by children. *Mind* 2: 252–9. p. 152

Talmy, L, 1976. Semantic causative types. In M. Shibatani (ed.) *Syntax and Semantics*, vol. VI, *The Grammar of Causative Constructions*. New York: Academic Press. p. 301

Tanz, C. 1974. Cognitive principles underlying children's errors in case-marking. *Journal of Child Language* 1: 271–7. p. 253

1977. Learning how 'it' works. *Journal of Child Language* 4: 225–36. p. 253

Tavakolian, S. L. 1976. Children's understanding of pronominal subjects and missing subjects in complicated sentences. Paper presented at the Winter Meetings of the Linguistic Society of America. p. 303

1977. Structure and function in child language. Doctoral dissertation, University of Massachusetts. pp. 290, 292, 293

Templin, M. C. 1957. *Certain Language Skills in Children.*. Minneapolis: University of Minnesota Press. pp. 179, 180, 181, 204, 205, 383, 384, 387

1966. The study of articulation and development in early school years. In F. Smith and G. A. Miller (eds.) *The Genesis of Language*. Cambridge, Mass.: MIT Press. p. 59

and Darley, F. L. 1960. The Templin–Darley tests of articulation. Iowa City: Iowa Bureau of Educational Research and Service. pp. 16–17

Thompson, J. R. and Chapman, R. S. 1977. Who is 'Daddy'? The status of two–year–olds' over-extended words in use and comprehension. *Journal of Child Language* 4: 359–75. p. 153

Thorne, J. P. 1968. A computer model for the perception of syntactic structure. *Proceedings of the Royal Society B* 171: 377–86. p. 440

Tingley, B. M. and Allen, G. D. 1975. Development of speech timing control in children. *Child Development* 46: 186–94. p. 443

Tough, J. 1977. *The Development of Meaning*. London: Unwin Education Books. pp. 329, 390

Trevarthen, C. 1974a. Conversations with a two month old. *New Scientist* 62: 230–3. pp. 74, 95, 96

1974b. Infant responses to objects and persons. Paper presented at the Spring meeting of the British Psychological Society, Bangor. pp. 12, 74

and Murray, L. 1975. The nature of an infant's ecology. In *The Proceedings from the International Society for the Study of Behavioural Development, Third Biennial Conference*, June. p. 101

Truby, H. M. and Lind, J. 1965. Cry sounds of the newborn infant. In J. Lind (ed.) *Newborn Infant Cry*. Acta Paed. Scan. Supplement. Uppsala: Almquist & Wiksells. pp. 18, 19, 20

Tse, J. K.-P. 1978. Tone acquisition in Cantonese: a longitudinal case study. *Journal of Child Language* 5: 191–204. p. 43

Turner, E. A. and Rommetveit, R. 1967. The acquisition of sentence voice and reversibility. *Child Development* 38: 649–60. p. 310

Tyack, D. and Ingram, D. 1977. Children's production and comprehension of questions. *Journal of Child Language* 4: 211–24. pp. 205, 206, 268

Tyler, L. K. and Marslen-Wilson, W. 1978. Some developmental aspects of sentence processing and memory. *Journal of Child Language* 5: 113–29. p. 443

Van der Geest, T. 1975. *Some Aspects of Communicative Competence and their Implications for Language Acquisition*. Assen/Amsterdam: Royal van Gorcum. p. 368

1977. Some interactional aspects of language acquisition. In C. E. Snow and C. A. Ferguson (eds.) *Talking to Children: language input and acquisition*. Cambridge: Cambridge University Press. p. 371

Vellutino, F., Bentley, W. and Phillips, F. 1978. Inter- versus intra-hemispheric learning in dyslexic and normal readers. *Developmental Medicine and Child Neurology* 20: 71–80. p. 449

Velten, H. 1943. The growth of phonemic and lexical patterns in infant language. *Language* 19: 440–4. pp. 135, 136, 142

Vihman, M. M. 1971. On the acquisition of Estonian. *Stanford Papers and Reports on Child Language Development* 3: 51–94. p. 135
    1976. From prespeech to speech: on early phonology. *Stanford Papers and Reports on Child Language Development* 12: 230–44. p. 68
    1978. Consonant harmony: its scope and function in child language. In J. H. Greenberg (ed.) *Universals of Human Language,* vol. ii, *Phonology.* Stanford, Calif.: Stanford University Press. p. 59
Vinson, J. 1915. Observations sur le développement du langage chez l'enfant. *Revue de Linguistique* 49: 1–39. p. 135
Vogel, I. 1975. One system or two: an analysis of a two-year-old Romanian–English bilingual's phonology. *Stanford Papers and Reports on Child Language Development* 9: 43–62. p. 140
Vuorenkoski, V., Lind, J., Wasz-Höckert, O. and Partanen, T. J. 1971. Cry score: a method for evaluating the degree of abnormality in the pain cry response of the newborn and young infant. *Quarterly Progress Report on Speech Research.* Royal Speech Transmission Laboratory. pp. 18, 21
Vygotsky, L. S. 1962. *Thought and Language,* trans. E. Hanfmann and G. Vakan. Cambridge, Mass.: MIT Press. pp. 245, 255, 332, 429, 434
Wada, J. A. 1977. Pre-language and functional asymmetry of the infant brain. *Annals of the New York Academy of Sciences* 299: 370–9. p. 447
Wada, J. A., Clark, R. and Hamm, A. 1975. Cerebral hemispheric asymmetry in humans: cortical speech zones in 100 adults and 100 infant brains. *Archives of Neurology* 32: 239–46. p. 447
Waddington, C. H. 1969. The theory of evolution today. In A. Koestler and J. R. Smythies (eds.) *Beyond Reductionism.* London: Hutchinson. pp. 437–8
Wahler, R. G. 1969. Infant social development: some experimental analyses of an infant–mother interaction during the first year of life. *Journal of Experimental Child Psychology* 7: 101–13. p. 17
Wales, R. J. 1971. Comparing and contrasting. In J. Morton (ed.) *Biological and Social Factors in Psycholinguistics.* London: Elek. p. 241
    1974. The child's language makes sense of the world. In *Problèmes actuels en psycholinguistique.* Paris: Editions CNRS. pp. 241, 248, 251, 258
Warden, D. 1976. The influence of context on children's use of identifying expressions and references. *British Journal of Psychology* 67: 101–12. p. 237
Wasz-Höckert, O., Lind, J., Vuorenkoski, V., Partanen, T. J. and Valanne, L. 1968. *The Infant Cry: a spectrographic and auditory analysis.* New York: Heinemann Medical Books. pp. 18, 20–1, 22
Waxman, S. G. 1972. Regional differentiation of the axon: a review with special reference to the concept of the multiplex neuron. *Brain Research* 47: 269–88. p. 451
Webb, P. A. and Abramson, A. 1976. Stages of egocentrism in children's use of 'this' and 'that': a different point of view. *Journal of Child Language* 3: 349–67. pp. 242, 245
Weber, J. and Weber, S. 1976. Early acquisition of linguistic designations for time. *Language and Speech* 19: 276–84. p. 271
Webster, R. L. 1969. Selective suppression of infants' vocal responses by classes of phonemic stimulation. *Developmental Psychology* 1: 410–14. p. 17

Weeks, T. 1971. Speech registers in young children. *Child Development* 42: 1119–31. p. 48

Weil, J. 1971. The relationship between time conceptualization and time language in young children. PhD dissertation, City University of New York. p. 310

　and Stenning, K. 1978. A comparison of young children's comprehension and memory for statements of temporal relations. In R. N. Campbell and P. T. Smith (eds.) *Recent Advances in the Psychology of Language: language development and mother–child interaction*. New York and London: Plenum Press. p. 310

Weimer, W. B. and Palermo, D. S. 1974. *Cognition and the Symbolic Processes*. Hillsdale, NJ: Erlbaum. p. 436

Weir, R. H. 1962. *Language in the Crib*. The Hague: Mouton. pp. 39, 43

Weisberg, P. 1963. Social and non-social conditioning of infant vocalizations. *Child Development* 34: 377–88. p. 17

Weisenburger, J. L. 1976. A choice of words: two-year-old speech from a situational point of view. *Journal of Child Language* 3: 275–81.

Wells, C. G. 1963. *Coding Manual for the Descriptions of Child Speech*. University of Bristol School of Education. Revised ed. 1975. p. 352

　1974. Learning to code experience through language. *Journal of Child Language* 1: 243–69. pp. 10, 106, 119, 196, 201, 202, 381

　1975. The contexts of children's early language experience. *Educational Review* 27: 114–25. p. 391

　1977a. A naturalistic approach to the study of language development. *Research Intelligence* 3: 34–5. p. 380

　1977b. Language use and educational success: an empirical response to Joan Tough's *The Development of Meaning* (1977). *Research in Education* 18: 9–34. p. 391

　1978. What makes for successful language development? In R. N. Campbell and P. T. Smith (eds.) *Recent Advances in the Psychology of Language: language development and mother–child interaction*. New York and London: Plenum Press. p. 378

　1979a. Learning and using the auxiliary verb in English. In V. Lee (ed.) *Cognitive Development: language and thinking from birth to adolescence*. London: Croom Helm. pp. 263, 264, 268, 277, 278, 279, 388

　1979b. Describing children's language development at home and at school. *British Educational Research Journal* 5: 75–98. p. 394

　and Ferrier, L. 1976. A framework for the semantic description of child speech in its conversational context. In W. von Raffler Engel and Y. Lebrun (eds.) *Baby Talk and Infant Speech*. Amsterdam: Swets & Zeitlinger. p. 353

Werner, H. and Kaplan, B. 1963. *Symbol Formation*. New York: Wiley. pp. 10, 71, 72, 79, 297

Wexler, K. 1978. Empirical questions about developmental psycholinguistics raised by a theory of language acquisition. In R. N. Campbell and P. T. Smith (eds.) *Recent Advances in the Psychology of Language: language development and mother–child interaction*. New York and London: Plenum Press. p. 452

Wickelgren, W. A. 1966. Distinctive features and errors in short-term memory for English consonants. *Journal of the Acoustical Society of America* 39: 583–8. p. 54

Wieman, L. A. 1976. Stress patterns of early child language. *Journal of Child Language* 3: 283–6. p. 47

Wilbur, R. D. In press. Theoretical phonology and child phonology: argumentation and implication. In D. L. Goyvaerts (ed.) *Phonology in the 1970's*. Ghent: E. Story & Scientia. pp. 51, 52

Williams, E. 1975. Small clauses in English. In J. P. Kimball (ed.) *Syntax and Semantics*, vol. IV. New York: Academic Press. p. 286

Wills, D. D. 1977. Participant deixis in English and baby talk. In C. E. Snow and C. A. Ferguson (eds.) *Talking to Children: language input and acquisition*. Cambridge: Cambridge University Press. p. 241

Wittgenstein, L. 1953. *Philosophical Investigations*. Oxford: Blackwell. pp. 434, 438

Wode, H. 1975. Grammatical intonation in child language: a case from German and some complaints. To appear in L. Sangster and C. H. Van Schooneveld (eds.) *Intonation and Prosodic Analysis*. p. 47

    1977. Four early stages in the development of L1 negation. *Journal of Child Language* 4: 87–102. p. 206

Wolff, P. H. 1969. The natural history of crying and other vocalizations in early infancy. In B. M. Foss (ed.) *Determinants of Infant Behaviour*, vol. IV. London: Methuen. pp. 24, 37

Wundt, W. 1902. *Outlines of Psychology*, trans. C. H. Judd. Leipzig: Engelmann. p. 420

Yonas, A. and Pick, H. L. 1975. An approach to the study of infant perception. In L. Cohen and P. Salatapek (eds.) *Infant Perception: from sensation to cognition*. London: Academic Press. p. 425

Young, F. M. 1941. *An Analysis of Certain Variables in a Developmental Study of Language*. Genetical Psychology Monographs 23. p. 180

Zarębina, M. 1965. *Kształtowanie się systemu Językowego dziecka*. Wrocław: Ossolineum. p. 135

Zemlin, W. R. 1968. *Speech and Hearing Science: anatomy and physiology*. Englewood Cliffs, NJ: Prentice-Hall. p. 24

Ziff, P. 1972. *Understanding Understanding*. Ithaca: Cornell University Press. pp. 430, 434

Zlatin, M. 1975. Explorative mapping of the vocal tract and primitive syllabification in infancy: the first six months. Paper presented at the American Speech and Hearing Association Convention, Washington, DC. pp. 18, 20–1, 26.

General index

Certain entries include italicized headings in parentheses, which indicate a more general entry under which this item is subsumed. Child names are in each case followed by the principal investigator's name in parentheses.

acoustic (*phonetics*), 16–18, 20–1, 29, 38, 50–7, 368, 439, 440
action, 63; child's action, 101, 111; joint action, 13, 345, 392
action (*semantics*), 166, 230, 311; *see also* semantics: relations
acquisition criteria, 263n, 264, 273
acknowledgment (*utterance*), 347
Adam (Brown), 166, 230, 268, 275, 278, 286, 300
addressee, 111–13, 115–17, 227, 229, 257, 271, 276
adjective/adjectival (*grammar*), 162, 200, 226, 229, 230, 231, 232, 308, 315, 400, 401, 403, 404, 407, 414, 416, 435
adult norms, for interpretation of child's language, 15, 19, 24, 28–9, 31, 38, 46–7, 49, 51, 53–4, 57, 61–3, 66–8, 94, 98, 100, 102–3, 106, 109, 111, 114–15, 125, 127, 128, 130, 137, 143, 145, 147, 148, 150, 151, 153, 155, 156, 158, 163, 168, 170, 181, 204, 211, 214, 215, 216, 221, 253, 262, 263, 268, 271, 278, 284, 301, 304, 317, 342, 343, 363, 369, 393, 424, 427, 428
adverb/ial (*grammar*; *sentence*), 241, 242, 243, 245, 247, 248, 250, 252, 255, 259, 264, 266, 267, 268, 269, 271, 272, 273, 287, 294, 295, 297, 304, 400, 401, 404
affective, 98–9
affirmation (*semantics*), 164
age-level norms, 15, 19, 24, 27–8, 38, 46–8, 50, 55, 58, 70
agent (*semantics*), 161, 163–6, 169, 172–4, 230, 255–7, 261–3, 309–12; *see also* semantics: relations
alinguistic elements, 71–92; *see also* prelinguistic elements

Allison (Bloom), 110, 111, 112, 113, 116, 118, 184
allomorph, 212, 213
allophone (*phonetics*; *phonology*), 58–9, 64
ambiguity (*meaning*: *relations*), 127, 255, 317, 341, 405
analysis by synthesis, 56; *see also* processing
anaphora, 207, 315, 316, 317, 321
antonymy (*meaning*: *relations*), 130
apical (*consonant*): dental, 138, 146; alveolar, 134–7, 144, 273
Arabic, 289
archiphoneme (*phonology*), 62
article (*noun*), 255–40, 307, 313, 315, 316, 317, 318, 319, 320, 321, 322, 399, 403, 406, 416
articulatory (*phonetics*), 19–31; *see also* place of articulation
aspect: (*semantics*) aspectual meaning, 261–284; (*verb*) 204; *see also* perfective; progressive
assent (*utterance*), 115
assertion (*utterance*), 351
assimilation (*phonology*: *process*), 137–8
attention/al (*inherent*), 12, 98, 112, 114, 117, 260, 345, 370
attitude/attitudinal (*inherent*), 36–8, 46–7
attribution/attributive: (*semantics*) 170, 192; (*grammatical type*) 11, 162, 165, 200
auditory (*phonetics*), 16–18, 28–9, 31, 38, 45, 53, 59, 61, 64, 66, 68–70, 101, 145, 213, 373, 450
Austin, J. L., 106
autosegmental (*phonology*), 62
auxiliary (*verb*), 201–6, 261–84, 367, 368, 369, 388, 400, 403

babbling, 4, 16, 28–32, 38, 41, 49–50, 53–4, 60, 62, 69; *see also* word